# Italian Opera in
# Late Eighteenth-Century
# London

# Italian Opera in Late Eighteenth-Century London

## VOLUME I

*The King's Theatre, Haymarket*
1778–1791

Curtis Price, Judith Milhous
and Robert D. Hume

CLARENDON PRESS · OXFORD

1995

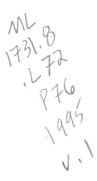

*Oxford University Press, Walton Street, Oxford* OX2 6DP

*Oxford New York*
*Athens Auckland Bangkok Bombay*
*Calcutta Cape Town Dar es Salaam Delhi*
*Florence Hong Kong Istanbul Karachi*
*Kuala Lumpur Madras Madrid Melbourne*
*Mexico City Nairobi Paris Singapore*
*Taipei Tokyo Toronto*
*and associated companies in*
*Berlin Ibadan*

*Oxford is a trade mark of Oxford University Press*

*Published in the United States by*
*Oxford University Press Inc., New York*

*British Library Cataloguing in Publication Data*
*Data available*

*Library of Congress Cataloging in Publication Data*
*Price, Curtis Alexander, 1945– .*
*Italian opera in late eighteenth-century London / Curtis Price,*
*Judith Milhous, and Robert D. Hume.*
*Includes bibliographical references and index.*
*Contents: v. 1. The King's Theatre, Haymarket, 1778–1791.*
*1. Opera—England—London—18th century. 2. Opera—Italy—18th*
*century. I. Milhous, Judith. II. Hume, Robert D.*
ML1731.8.L72P76   1995   791.5'09421—dc20   94–36462
*ISBN 0–19–816166–2*

1 3 5 7 9 10 8 6 4 2

*Printed in Great Britain*
*on acid-free paper by*
*Biddles Ltd*
*Guildford and King's Lynn*

For John M. Ward

# *Preface*

RELATIVELY little has been written about Italian opera in London during the second half of the eighteenth century. The reason is obvious: after Handel's withdrawal from opera in 1741 conditions were such that no composer of similar stature could be recruited to replace him. None the less Italian opera remained a prominent and controversial part of London's cultural life. The King's Theatre in the Haymarket (the principal venue for Italian opera) was the most glamorous and exclusive of London's theatres, a satellite of the English court and a magnet for the rich and powerful. It continued to attract the finest performers at the highest salaries paid anywhere in Europe, despite the lack of a state subsidy. At the end of the 1770s the company passed from a period of some artistic distinction and financial stability into one of its stormiest and most exciting phases.

A reader unfamiliar with the subject might wonder why we should want to write at length about the 1780s and early 1790s in London. The answer is simple: the King's Theatre housed an ambitious and interesting company in the 1780s. Under the management of Giovanni Andrea Gallini (1785–89), the theatre formed close links with Vienna, engaged promising composers such as Luigi Cherubini and Stephen Storace as well as leading singers such as Luigi Marchesi and Francesco Benucci, and offered a boldly innovative repertoire. After the fire of 1789 it was replaced by the Pantheon, set up along radically different lines. And when the Pantheon too burnt, opera in London inevitably reverted to the rebuilt King's Theatre—and its debts. The fearful mess the King's Theatre got into in the 1780s was to have profound and long-lasting effects. Not until the 1850s was Italian opera in London to escape the morass in which the upheavals of the 1780s and the failure of the Pantheon landed it.

The key event from which all these developments sprang was financial, not musical. In June 1778 Richard Brinsley Sheridan and Thomas Harris acquired the King's Theatre and its resident company. The purchase was effected on borrowed money: today it would be called a leveraged buyout. The result was to encumber the theatre with enormous and escalating debts. Bankruptcy ensued in 1783, and the company became mired in a series of protracted lawsuits. The destruction of the theatre by fire on 17 June 1789 precipitated violent controversy and confusion. Yet throughout the 1780s the company continued to hire performers of international distinction, and ballet (helped by Noverre's stints as ballet-master) positively flourished. The long reign of the pasticcio (dominant since Handel's time) was beginning to weaken; original works by major composers were again sought; and in 1790 there was a very real possibility that Haydn and Mozart would become rival house composers in London.

This study is in a sense an extended investigation of the circumstances that lay behind the invitation to Mozart in October 1790 to become house composer at the Pantheon and the reasons why Haydn's only London opera, *L'anima del filosofo* (*Orfeo ed Euridice*), was in effect banned the following spring. The fire at the King's Theatre in 1789 created the possibility of radical change: the Pantheon was founded to embody an alternative approach to opera. It was conceived as a kind of court opera, a small, exclusive, heavily subsidized venture in which artistic decisions would not be dictated by popular appeal and ticket sales. The quick demise of the Pantheon experiment returned Italian opera in London to the rebuilt King's Theatre, Haymarket, and to the long-standing form of impresario management under which opera in London had functioned since the collapse of the Opera of the Nobility in the 1730s.

To understand why the Pantheon came into existence and what its aspirations were, one must comprehend its predecessor, for the two are inextricably entwined. Volume I is therefore a full-dress account of the King's Theatre in the decade between Sheridan's take-over and the 1789 fire; volume II tells the story of the Pantheon. The two books take very different approaches, reflecting the radically different nature of the surviving primary source material. Both, however, reflect our belief that opera—as an alliance of the capital arts—demands a multi-disciplinary approach. At this time any Italian opera company was equally a ballet company, and we have tried to give full consideration to both forms. Our treatment covers every facet of these companies for which documentation survives: management, finances, artistic policy, music, librettos or scenarios, singers, dancers, composers, arrangers, copyists, costumes, theatre architecture, stage-craft, scene painting, choreography, lighting, and so forth. Together, these volumes have two main objects: to untangle one of the most bizarre and confusing periods in the history of the London stage, and to assess how the development of Italian opera in England was affected by the companies that mounted it—the King's Theatre, Haymarket, and the Pantheon. These books are written in the conviction that music and librettos cannot best be studied in isolation. Ownership, management, and finances powerfully affect what a company does and how it mounts its repertoire. This seems self-evident, but to date few efforts have been made to approach eighteenth-century opera from such a perspective.

Any study of opera in London in this period needs to anticipate a certain amount of scepticism and confront some preconceptions. We are, of course, conscious that many readers will view this material with disdain, believing that had the company been any good it would have been doing *Così fan tutte* and *Don Giovanni*. With the benefit of hindsight, this prejudice is difficult to avoid. Some of our friends have suggested (not always tactfully) that only fools work on Bertoni when they could be studying Mozart. If music were the only issue, this would be true. The present volume, however, is an account of a company and its repertoire, not just a survey of the best of the music. Our concern is with the 'opera system' in London towards the end of the century.

The Italian operas mounted in London in the last three decades of the eighteenth century have mostly been ignored. Contemporary opinion on the music was divided. Dr Burney considered this the golden age of opera in England, but Horace Walpole and Mount Edgcumbe found the last quarter of the century a period of decline. The King's Theatre's house composers included J. C. Bach, Sacchini, Cherubini, and Storace—but only Sacchini in the 1770s was given circumstances in which he could flourish. A large part of the reason for this was the degree to which the King's Theatre featured capital performers for whom the music was merely a vehicle for display. This was the age of the last great castrati: Tenducci, Pacchierotti, Rauzzini, Rubinelli, and Marchesi all appeared on the London stage. About 1780 the King's Theatre embraced the simple, pristine style of Sarti and Cimarosa, tightly shackled by four-bar phrases and all but devoid of the simple counterpoint and mild chromaticism of the music of Sacchini and the previous generation. Adventurous and difficult numbers were sometimes replaced by something more tuneful, with the result that Italian opera in London came uncomfortably close to resembling its social nemesis, English opera. The King's Theatre continued to employ great and fabulously expensive singers and then allowed them to sing what were little more than ballads with graffiti-like ornamentation. Protest began to develop: not since Addison attacked the bilingual pasticcio in the first decade of the eighteenth century had such serious questions been raised about the nature of opera in

London. Even more important, the artistic standards and aesthetic commitments of the Haymarket opera house were challenged within the organization itself. Copyright lawsuits were beginning to establish operatic music as intellectual property; cut-and-paste pasticcios were on the way out; there was a growing sense that London needed a great composer to save it from artistic mediocrity. For a time in the later 1780s Gallini seemed to be revivifying the company, and certainly the opera department thrived under him, but the disappointing result of this period of artistic crisis was failure to escape the trammels of the Old Opera System. As we shall try to demonstrate, this failure was a direct result of the King's Theatre's debts and poor management.

Though the King's Theatre was never quite a world leader in the development of Italian opera, it was more adventurous in its ballet. During the 1780s the *ballet d'action* came to London, and Noverre and Dauberval created ballets that remain (in much altered form) in the repertoire today. The principal dancers (notably Vestris jun., Madame Théodore, Didelot, and Mlle Hilligsberg) were even more popular than the castrati. Yet despite good composers and great singers and dancers, the King's Theatre's managerial woes got it into such a mess that it had to operate in receivership, and the audience twice rioted in the spring of 1789 to protest against what it considered inadequate dancers. The Pantheon came into existence at a time of vehement demands for change.

The failure of music historians to recognize the enormous effect of the 1780s on the later history of opera in London is easy to explain: no other period has seemed quite so difficult to understand. The repertoire and principal performers are known from newspaper advertisements, and some nuggets of information have been gleaned from the inflammatory and abusive pamphlets that proliferated at the time. Many basic things about the company, however, have been unknown or are still misunderstood. Who was managing the theatre from year to year, who put it into receivership and why, and whether the theatre had a patent have been subjects of considerable confusion. The best managerial history of the King's Theatre to date states dismissively (or perhaps despairingly) that the 1780s were a 'confused period' and hastens on to more comprehensible topics.[1]

To make sense of the artistically distinguished and financially catastrophic events of the 1780s we must start by posing some basic questions.

[1] *Survey of London,* xxix. 231.

Who owned the company? Who managed it? On what authority did it perform? What caused such spectacular losses following a period of relative stability and solvency? What is known about salaries and budgets? What were the company's artistic and recruitment policies, and how did managerial upheaval affect them? What can be determined about the company's repertoire, performance practices, and standard of performance?

If ownership, finances, and management have heretofore been 'dark' subjects, how can we hope to do better than our predecessors? Daniel Nalbach's *The King's Theatre 1704–1867* (1972) is a broad and superficial overview based almost entirely on obvious printed sources. The *Survey of London* volumes covering the King's Theatre are respectable as far as they go, but almost completely ignore the potentialities of the Public Record Office. We have found twenty lawsuits directly concerned with the King's Theatre in the 1780s, most of them previously unknown to scholars. They are scrappy, particular, and sometimes inconclusive, but cumulatively they provide a vast amount of new information about the opera. We have utilized not only Bills of Complaint and Answers (C12), but Town Depositions (C24), Affidavits (C31), Decrees and Orders (C33), Master's Reports (C38), and Masters' Exhibits (C107). Particular information is footnoted, but to help sort out a mass of sometimes confusing references we have supplied a PRO source list in Appendix I.

Plunging into the maelstrom of financial and managerial specifics, obscure librettos, spottily preserved music, and unfamiliar personnel, the reader may tend to lose track of a vital fact: the concept of opera dominant in England towards the end of the eighteenth century was disconcertingly remote from twentieth-century norms. Performers, not composers, were the kingpins of the venture, though this period sees the beginnings of a move towards the nineteenth-century attitudes from which our own have grown. The 1780s and 1790s are pivotal in the development from *opera seria* pasticcio towards romantic opera. To understand the larger patterns of opera development in Europe, of which London was merely one part, we need to try to comprehend opera as it was then conceived and produced. The present book is a reconstruction of a tortuous and little-understood period in the history of a major opera-house. It is also, however, an attempt to re-create and analyse an aesthetic outlook now remote from us.

# Acknowledgements

MANY friends, old and new, have given us invaluable assistance during the eight years we have been working on this project. To name them all would probably now be beyond our memories and space, but for advice, information, generous readings of our drafts, and many other sorts of help we wish to offer our special thanks to Irene Auerbach, Derek Beales, Judith Chazin-Bennahum, Jackson I. Cope, Rachel Cowgill, Pierre Danchin, Frank Ellis, Kathryn M. Grossman, Ivor Guest, John T. Harwood, Henry Horwitz, David Wyn Jones, Edward A. Langhans, Lowell Lindgren, Dorothea Link, Marita Petzoldt McClymonds, Richard Macnutt, Nancy Klein Maguire, C. A. Prettiman, John Rice, Michael F. Robinson, Betty Rizzo, John Roberts, Sybil Rosenfeld, Arthur H. Scouten, Lars E. Troide, Brian Trowell, John M. Ward, William Weber, Roland John Wiley, and Saskia Willaert. We should also like to acknowledge the work of those students involved in the 1991–2 King's College London post-graduate seminar in historical musicology: Gabriella Dideriksen, Juan Carlos Jaramillo, Emma Kempson, Agnes Kory, Anna McCready, and Rebecca Mooney. For expert and generous help with computer formatting and printing we are much indebted to Thomas Minsker of the Pennsylvania State University Center for Academic Computing.

This project had its start when Mrs M. P. G. Draper, then Archivist for the Bedford Settled Estates, showed us the Pantheon Papers and helped us obtain permission to use them. They figure centrally in volume II, and only peripherally in the present book, but we wish to express our gratitude for Marie Draper's continuing advice, assistance, and friendship. We should also like to thank Bruce Phillips of Oxford University Press for his warm encouragement and advice during the lengthy gestation of what has sometimes seemed to be an ever-expanding project, and Bonnie J. Blackburn, our copy-editor, for her patience and expert advice far beyond the call of duty.

We have visited many libraries and written queries to many more. The present book owes much to the staffs and unique resources of the Public Record Office and the British Library. James Fowler of the Theatre Museum (Victoria and Albert), Bruce Martin of the Library of Congress,

## Acknowledgements

Jeanne Newlin of the Harvard Theatre Collection, Stephen Parks of the Osborn Collection (Yale University), Charles W. Mann, Jr. and Sandra K. Stelts of the Pennsylvania State University, Laetitia Yeandle of the Folger, Christina Scull of Sir John Soane's Museum, and Kenneth Craven of the Humanities Research Center (University of Texas) have given us help on more occasions than we had any right to ask, and always done so with the greatest courtesy.

To Kit Hume and Rhian Samuel we owe heartfelt thanks for much patience and tough, acute, critical readings of our many drafts.

We have adapted and reworked material from the following articles: Price, Milhous, and Hume, 'The Rebuilding of the King's Theatre, Haymarket, 1789–1791', *Theatre Journal*, 43 (1991), 421–44; Milhous, 'Lighting at the King's Theatre, Haymarket, 1780–1782', *Theatre Research International*, 16 (1991), 215–35; Price, 'Unity, Originality, and the London Pasticcio', *Harvard Library Bulletin*, NS 2, no. 4 (1991), 17–30. We are grateful to the editors of these journals for permission to reuse material that first appeared in their pages.

We are indebted to the Controller of Her Majesty's Stationery Office for permission to quote Crown Copyright material in the Public Record Office.

Finally, and far from least, we are deeply obligated to the National Endowment for the Humanities (USA) for a generous grant under the 'Interpretive Research' programme. The willingness of the NEH to support this kind of multi-person, interdisciplinary work has greatly assisted us in both our research and our writing.

# Contents

## Contents

# List of Plates

# List of Tables

# A Note on Names, Titles, and Quotation Policy

A large number of persons, operas, and ballets are mentioned in this book. There is great inconsistency in the form in which names and titles appear in both primary and secondary sources. We have generally given names of persons as entered in the *Biographical Dictionary*, except where they are spelt otherwise in quotations. Some English and Italian Christian names were used interchangeably (Giovanni Andrea / John Andrew Gallini), while others are unknown or uncertain. French and Italian opera and ballet titles are normally regularized in the form adopted in *New Grove* (that is, lower case after the first word, save for proper names). Especially for ballets, however, there is the additional problem that the King's Theatre was inconsistent about anglicizing French titles. When referring to Continental ballet productions, we have used original titles, but for London premières or revivals we have generally followed the form advertised in newspapers and bills (which are often, but not always, English).

Quotations in Italian and French present special problems because of our sources. The language is sometimes archaic, and the English compositors who set the dual-language librettos were often manifestly ignorant of foreign languages. To make the language 'correct' according to current usage would sometimes be virtually to rewrite the originals. Likewise newspapers often contain foreign phrases, some of them odd or mangled by current standards. Wanting neither to misrepresent our sources nor to litter our text with *sic* after *sic*, we have attempted to correct what seems flagrantly wrong by eighteenth-century standards, but have otherwise quoted our sources as we have found them.

English quotations are normally exactly as they appear in the sources, but, to avoid cumbersome apparatus, blatant typographical errors (which are frequent in 1780s newspapers) have been silently corrected and the minimum of punctuation necessary for clarity in lawsuit testimony (which is often lacking any) has been interpolated. Newspaper quotations are also regularized to the extent of ignoring typographical quirks—for example, the arbitrary use of lower and upper case. Where large and small capitals appear to convey substantive emphasis, they have been silently transposed into italic type. Individual copies of librettos, scenarios, and other published sources are not identified unless unique or cited for a special reason. Almost all the opera librettos are listed in Sartori; other contemporaneous printed sources can usually be located using Arnott and Robinson or the *Eighteenth Century Short Title Catalogue*.

# Abbreviations and Works Frequently Cited

| | |
|---|---|
| Arnott and Robinson | James Fullarton Arnott and John William Robinson, *English Theatrical Literature 1559–1900: A Bibliography* (London: Society for Theatre Research, 1970). |
| Bedford Opera Papers | Six boxes of manuscripts comprising the contents of the Pantheon Opera business office (1790–92) and the solicitor's papers connected with the insurance claim (1792–1815). These manuscripts were preserved in the Office of the Bedford Settled Estates, London, until January 1993 and are now kept at the Duke of Bedford's seat, Woburn Abbey, where a full catalogue compiled by Curtis Price and Robert D. Hume and edited by Judith Milhous is available. |
| *Biographical Dictionary* | Philip H. Highfill, Jr., Kalman A. Burnim, and Edward A. Langhans, *A Biographical Dictionary of Actors, Actresses, Musicians, Dancers, Managers and Other Stage Personnel in London, 1660–1800*, 16 vols. (Carbondale: Southern Illinois University Press, 1973–93). |
| *BUCEM* | *The British Union-Catalogue of Early Music*, ed. Edith B. Schnapper, 2 vols. (London: Butterworths, 1957). |
| Burney, *General History* | Dr Charles Burney, *A General History of Music*, 4 vols. (1773–89), ed. Frank Mercer, 2 vols. (New York: Dover, 1957). |
| Fanny Burney, *Diary & Letters* | *Diary & Letters of Madame D'Arblay*, ed. Charlotte Barrett, with a preface and notes by Austin Dobson, 6 vols. (London: Macmillan, 1904–5). |
| Fanny Burney, *Early Journals and Letters* | *The Early Journals and Letters of Fanny Burney*. Volume II: 1774–1777, ed. Lars E. Troide (Oxford: Clarendon Press, 1990). |
| Susan Burney | The Letter-Journal of Susan Burney. British Library Egerton MS 3691. |

| | |
|---|---|
| C | Chancery lawsuit material in the Public Record Office (Chancery Lane). Bills of Complaint and Answers are filed under the class number C12 (followed by a bundle number and a piece number). C33 (followed by a volume number) indicates Decrees and Orders of the Court. C24 (followed by a box number) refers to 'Town Depositions'. C31 (followed by box and piece numbers) refers to Affidavits. C38 (followed by a volume number) refers to reports by Masters in Chancery (unpaginated). C107 (followed by a box number) refers to material preserved from Chancery Masters' Exhibits. |
| *The Case of the Opera-House Disputes* | Anon., *The Case of the Opera-House Disputes, Fairly Stated* (London: H. Reynell, 1784). |
| Lady Mary Coke | Letter-Journals of Lady Mary Coke, 1756–91 (negative photostat of original MSS at the Lewis Walpole Library, Farmington, Connecticut). |
| Da Ponte, *Memoirs* | *Memoirs of Lorenzo Da Ponte*, trans. L. A. Sheppard (London: Routledge, 1929). |
| *ESTC* | *Eighteenth Century Short Title Catalogue* (on-line version, as of December 1993). |
| Gibson, 'Earl Cowper' | Elizabeth Gibson, 'Earl Cowper in Florence and his Correspondence with the Italian Opera in London', *Music & Letters*, 68 (1987), 235–52. |
| *The Impresario's Ten Commandments* | Curtis Price, Judith Milhous, and Robert D. Hume, *The Impresario's Ten Commandments: Continental Recruitment for Italian Opera in London, 1763–64*, RMA Monographs, 6 (London: Royal Musical Association, 1992). |
| Kelly, *Reminiscences* | Michael Kelly, *Reminiscences of the King's Theatre, and Theatre Royal Drury Lane*, 2 vols. (London: Henry Colburn, 1826). |
| Larpent MSS | Larpent Manuscripts (submitted to the Examiner of Plays in the Lord Chamberlain's Office). Now in the Huntington Library. See Dougald MacMillan, *Catalogue of the Larpent Plays in the Huntington Library* (San Marino: Huntington Library, 1939). |
| LC 7/3 | Public Record Office, Lord Chamberlain's records. LC 7/3 is a massive two-volume collection of miscellaneous documents from the late seventeenth and eighteenth centuries. The documents are in no overall order and the foliation is modern. |

| | |
|---|---|
| Le Texier, *Ideas on the Opera* | Antoine Le Texier, *Ideas on the Opera* (London: J. Bell, 1790). |
| *The London Stage* | *The London Stage, 1660–1800*, Part 5: 1776–1800, 3 vols., ed. Charles Beecher Hogan (Carbondale: Southern Illinois University Press, 1968). |
| Lynham, *Chevalier Noverre* | Deryck Lynham, *The Chevalier Noverre: Father of Modern Ballet* (London: Sylvan Press, 1950). |
| Mount Edgcumbe, *Musical Reminiscences* | *Musical Reminiscences, containing an account of the Italian Opera in England, from 1773, by the Earl of Mount Edgcumbe* (4th edn., 1834; rpt. New York: Da Capo, 1973). |
| Nalbach | Daniel Nalbach, *The King's Theatre 1704–1867: London's First Italian Opera House* (London: Society for Theatre Research, 1972). |
| *New Grove* | *The New Grove Dictionary of Music and Musicians*, ed. Stanley Sadie, 20 vols. (London: Macmillan, 1980). |
| 'Opera and Arson' | Curtis Price, 'Opera and Arson in Late Eighteenth-Century London', *Journal of the American Musicological Society*, 42 (1989), 55–107. |
| *Opera Grove* | *The New Grove Dictionary of Opera*, ed. Stanley Sadie, 4 vols. (London: Macmillan, 1992). |
| 'Opera Salaries' | Judith Milhous and Robert D. Hume, 'Opera Salaries in Eighteenth-Century London', *Journal of the American Musicological Society*, 46 (1993), 26–83. |
| O'Reilly, *An Authentic Narrative* | Robert Bray O'Reilly, *An Authentic Narrative of the Principal Circumstances Relating to the Opera-House in the Hay-market; from its Origin to the Present Period; but more particularly including the transactions from the year 1778* (London: J. Desmond for J. and J. Taylor, and J. Southern, 1791). |
| Parke, *Musical Memoirs* | W. T. Parke, *Musical Memoirs; comprising an Account of the General State of Music in England, from the first commemoration of Handel in 1784, to the year 1830*, 2 vols. (London: Colburn and Bentley, 1830). |
| Petty | Frederick C. Petty, *Italian Opera in London 1760–1800* (Ann Arbor, MI: UMI Research Press, 1980). |
| PRO | The Public Record Office (London). Documents referred to in this book are in the original branch, Chancery Lane, London WC2A 1LR, as of 1994. |

Robinson, *Paisiello*   Michael F. Robinson, *Giovanni Paisiello: A Thematic Catalogue of his Works*, Volume I (Stuyvesant, NY: Pendragon, 1991).

'A Royal Opera House in Leicester Square'   Curtis Price, Judith Milhous, and Robert D. Hume, 'A Royal Opera House in Leicester Square (1790)', *Cambridge Opera Journal*, 2 (1990), 1–28.

Sartori   Claudio Sartori, *I libretti italiani a stampa dalle origini al 1800*, 7 vols. in progress (Milan: Bertola & Locatelli Editori, 1990–  ).

Smith, *Italian Opera*   William C. Smith, *The Italian Opera and Contemporary Ballet in London, 1789–1820* (London: Society for Theatre Research, 1955).

*Survey of London*   *Survey of London*, vols. xxix–xxx, The Parish of St. James Westminster, Part I: South of Piccadilly, ed. F. H. W. Sheppard (London: Athlone Press, 1960).

Taylor, *A Concise Statement*   William Taylor, *A Concise Statement of Transactions and Circumstances respecting the King's Theatre, in the Haymarket* (2nd edn.; London: J. Debrett *et al.*, 1791).

Theatre Cuts   Volumes of theatrical cuttings in the British Library, Theatre Cuts 41 and 42.

'Veritas', *Opera House*   'Veritas', *Opera House* (London: Printed for the Author, [1818?]).

Walpole, *Correspondence*   *The Yale Edition of Horace Walpole's Correspondence*, ed. W. S. Lewis *et al.*, 48 vols. (New Haven: Yale University Press, 1937–83).

CHAPTER I

# The Italian Opera Establishment in London

To attend the King's Theatre in the late eighteenth century was to encounter a small part of Italy transported on to the south-west side of the Haymarket. Management aimed to give well-travelled members of the nobility and gentry essentially the same operatic experience to be had at La Scala or La Fenice. The company offered *opera seria*, *opera buffa*, and ballet in roughly equal measures. The star system prevailed, with a roster of principal performers hired into London from a Continental circuit that included Milan, Bologna, Venice, Florence, Rome, Naples, Cremona, Lucca, Padua, Turin, Bergamo, Verona, Mantua, Pesaro, Ferrara, Treviso, Udine, Lisbon, Dresden, Paris, Vienna, St Petersburg, and a few other places.

London's position on this roundabout was paradoxical. The King's Theatre was for much of the century a premier Italian opera-house, paying the highest salaries to the finest performers, but it was also one of the most isolated from the mainstream and therefore had to rely heavily on imported scores and pasticcios. The result was that after the time of Handel composers were generally regarded as less important than singers and dancers. Nevertheless, the King's Theatre engaged a number of internationally famous house composers—Gluck, Galuppi, Sacchini, J. C. Bach, Bertoni, Anfossi, Cherubini, Gresnick, Tarchi, Storace, Federici, Haydn, and Martín y Soler. Yet one is hard-pressed to find London opera premières of historic importance between Handel's *Alcina* (1732) and Weber's *Oberon* (1826). The century is peppered with missed opportunities and operatic disasters. In 1745–46 Gluck made no great impression with either *La caduta de' giganti* or *Artamene*, and his later reforms had little influence in England, except in the guise of heavily adapted revivals of *Orfeo ed Euridice*. J. C. Bach fared better in the mid-1760s and 1770s and *La clemenza di Scipione* is a splendid achievement, but he never really penetrated the cabal of Italian expatriates who dominated the King's Theatre. Sacchini, after a string of successful and often worthy operas, left London in 1782 amid accusations of plagiarism. Cherubini's main effort for the London stage, *Giulio Sabino* (1786), closed after one performance. And Haydn's 1791 commission, *L'anima del filosofo*, was never performed. The ballet, though often brilliantly executed, tended to be heavily derivative.

Given the catalogue of missed chances and squandered resources, the genuine artistic achievement of the King's Theatre in the late eighteenth century can too easily be overlooked, especially during the financially disastrous 1780s. When Richard Brinsley Sheridan and Thomas Harris bought the company in 1778 they did so in the belief that more imaginative management would make it highly profitable—a delusion that quickly ran the company into debts that were to plague it for decades. But as we commence a close investigation of the King's Theatre from the take-over of 1778, we need to supply some background and some explanations. How did 'little Italy' take such firm root in the Haymarket?—or to put the question more precisely, how did an Italian opera company come to be established in London, and on what financial and legal bases did it operate? What sort of opera was produced there? What musical and critical sources are available to the historical scholar, and what are their limitations? What do we know about the opera-house itself? And finally, what might a knowledgeable onlooker have expected to happen when the company was bought by ambitious new owners in 1778?

## I. The Old Opera Establishment

The events of 1778–91 make little sense unless one knows some history. Three subjects require particular elucidation: the origins of an opera company performing in a language few Londoners understood; the private entrepreneur system under which opera in London functioned; and the legal basis on which the company performed—a vital issue in the events that follow.

### Origins

In the beginning there was Vanbrugh. This observation is less frivolous than it may seem: John Vanbrugh was instrumental in introducing Italian opera to London. Ancient history this may be, but highly relevant to the events this book is devoted to untangling.

In late seventeenth-century London 'opera' meant semi-opera of the sort John Dryden and Henry Purcell had created. Such works were staged by regular theatre companies as occasional treats: they were fabulously expensive, but the costs could be covered in the general operating budget of a company that was performing 180 times or more each season. The usual number of opera performances was probably well under twenty. In 1703 Vanbrugh had the bright idea of building a lavish new theatre and securing a theatrical monopoly for himself. He clearly intended to stage all-sung opera of the new Italian variety as well as semi-opera, but he never planned to run an opera company *per se*. He built the Queen's (later King's) Theatre in the Haymarket and opened it in 1705, only to discover that the patentees at the Drury Lane theatre had no intention of shutting up shop and handing their business over to him. Indeed, Drury Lane promptly scored major hits with Clayton's *Arsinoe* (1705) and Bononcini's *Camilla* (1706), a pair of Italian-style operas in English translation. Vanbrugh then engineered his own downfall by persuading the Lord Chamberlain to order a genre separation, giving Drury Lane a monopoly on spoken plays and himself a monopoly on musical entertainment at the Haymarket.[1] This forced Vanbrugh to rely solely on a repertoire of all-sung operas, depriving him even of the popular semi-operas. After four months of ruinously low receipts and high costs, he was glad to bail out, and management passed to Owen Swiney.[2]

Vanbrugh never thought of trying to perform opera in any language but English. The transition to Italian was gradual, but under the circumstances inevitable. To mount true Italian opera one needed a *musico*, that is, a male alto or soprano. Drury Lane had hired Valentini, and Vanbrugh inherited his contract. Owing to a shortage of British castrati, Italians were requisite, and their English tended to be execrable, necessitating dual-language performance. Swiney gambled on hiring a world-class castrato, importing Nicolini at 800 guineas per annum—and one thing led to another. By 1710 even British singers were expected to perform in Italian, a state of affairs roundly but ineffectively ridiculed by Addison in the *Spectator* in 1711.

A company subsidized by a king or a wealthy noble could afford to mount opera alone, and this was the obvious Continental model.[3] In

---

[1] The order is PRO LC 5/154, pp. 299–300 (31 Dec. 1707).

[2] On these events, see Curtis Price, 'The Critical Decade for English Music Drama, 1700–1710', *Harvard Library Bulletin*, 26 (1978), 38–76; *Vice Chamberlain Coke's Theatrical Papers, 1706–1715*, ed. Judith Milhous and Robert D. Hume (Carbondale: Southern Illinois University Press, 1982); and Robert D. Hume, 'The Sponsorship of Opera in London, 1704–1720', *Modern Philology*, 85 (1988), 420–32.

[3] See Lorenzo Bianconi and Thomas Walker, 'Production, Consumption and Political

London, however, there was no realistic possibility of subsidy, and the market for glamorous entertainment in a foreign language was manifestly small. Swiney went broke and decamped to the Continent in 1713; the company limped on under John Jacob Heidegger, producing several Handel operas, and then closed down in 1717. Musical entertainment in English was flourishing (with the Lord Chamberlain's genre division now forgotten) at the Drury Lane and Lincoln's Inn Fields theatres. What revived Italian opera (in the original language) was an extraordinary series of coincidences: the Elector of Hanover, whose *Kapellmeister* was Handel, had become George I of Great Britain in 1714; the King understood Italian considerably better than he did English; and he was a great opera lover who appears to have attended fully half the performances given in London while he was in residence.[1] In 1719 the Royal Academy of Music was established by well-heeled subscribers to restore Italian opera to London as a recreation for the nobility and gentry.

The Royal Academy of Music was not a genuine court opera. George I agreed to supply a subsidy of £1,000 per annum (entitling him to free admission), but the operation was set up as a joint-stock company with a 21-year royal charter.[2] The prospectus issued to attract investors projected enormous profits and only a small call on the subscribers' capital, which was a fallacious view of the future: despite £20,000 capital and the royal subsidy, the company went bankrupt and ceased operations in 1728. It had, however, firmly established both a taste for Italian opera among upper-class Londoners and a sense of glamour that made the opera-house the place for socialites to be seen. The regular top price in an English-language theatre was 4s.; a seat in the pit or boxes at the opera was 10s. 6d.; a mere gallery seat was 5s. This was not entertainment for *hoi polloi*.

## The Impresario System

The collapse of the Royal Academy left the future of Italian opera in London in doubt. George II was willing to continue the £1,000 subsidy but, like his predecessor, evinced no willingness to cover the sort of deficit the Royal Academy had run up every year. The financial basis of the 'Second

Function of Seventeenth-Century Opera', *Early Music History*, 4 (1984), 209–96.

[1] See Donald Burrows and Robert D. Hume, 'George I, the Haymarket Opera Company and Handel's *Water Music*', *Early Music*, 19 (1991), 323–41.

[2] PRO C66/3531, no. 3. For a transcription and analysis, see Judith Milhous and Robert D. Hume, 'The Charter for the Royal Academy of Music', *Music & Letters*, 67 (1986), 50–8.

Academy' is a mystery: Handel and Heidegger ran it, but financial responsibility for the company remains unknown.[1] In one of the more peculiar twists in the history of opera in London, a second company opened in competition against them in 1733—the so-called 'Opera of the Nobility', funded by a clique of noble patrons. Almost nothing is known of its finances save that it lost a lot of money and went out of business by 1738.

In the 1740s there was another attempt at opera subsidized by patrons— the last before the Pantheon in 1790. The principal backer was Lord Middlesex, and his company shared the fate of its predecessors.[2] After that, opera at the King's Theatre became the domain of individual impresarios. In the late 1740s G. F. Crosa introduced *opera buffa* to London with an imported troupe, and wound up in prison for debt.[3] During the 1750s there was a succession of shaky companies, with management often supplied by performers, notably the *prima donna* Regina Mingotti. The soprano Colomba Mattei and her husband Joseph Trombetta ran a company for a while in the late 1750s and early 1760s. They engaged Gioacchino Cocchi and later J. C. Bach, but lost money and abandoned the field to the violinist Felice Giardini, who had been orchestra leader and had spent a year as co-manager in the 1750s. Giardini's management proved a fiasco in its one season (1763–64) but is exceptionally well documented, especially as regards its recruitment of foreign singers.[4] Giardini escaped going to prison by a hair's breadth; his immediate successors fared a bit better.

From 1765 to 1778 the company was owned and operated by a shifting group of outside investors. Peter Crawford, Thomas Vincent, and John Gordon bought it for £14,000; James Brooke subsequently bought out Vincent and Gordon, acquiring a five-sixths interest by 1773. Financially, the opera company limped along from year to year. It managed to make its expenses, but little more. The proprietors appear to have covered losses with profits from the masquerades given each year at the King's Theatre. At the time of David Garrick's retirement in 1776, Richard Brinsley Sheridan headed a consortium that bought Drury Lane. Within two years he had

---

[1] See Robert D. Hume, 'Handel and Opera Management in London in the 1730s', *Music & Letters*, 67 (1986), 347–62.

[2] For specifics, see Carole Taylor, 'From Losses to Lawsuit: Patronage of the Italian Opera in London by Lord Middlesex, 1739–1745', *Music & Letters*, 68 (1987), 1–25.

[3] See Richard G. King and Saskia Willaert, 'Giovanni Francesco Crosa and the First Italian Comic Operas in London, Brussels, and Amsterdam, 1748–1750', *Journal of the Royal Musical Association*, 118 (1993), 246–75.

[4] See *The Impresario's Ten Commandments*.

persuaded Thomas Harris, his counterpart at Covent Garden, that they should acquire the King's Theatre as a joint investment.

Glamorous the Italian opera unquestionably was, but any 'proprietor' of the King's Theatre faced substantial difficulties. The theatre was getting old and tatty, and the group of season subscribers was small. The company normally performed twice a week from December to June, fifty performances making a full subscription season. The entire operating budget had to be covered by subscriptions plus daily ticket sales. The capacity of the theatre in the 1770s is not known, but may well have remained as low as 700–900.[1] Capacity may have been increased before the revamping of the auditorium in 1778, but there is no proof of this and no evidence that the theatre was so jammed with paying customers that the proprietors needed to increase the seating. A season subscription cost 20 guineas, and in the middle of the century an impresario was apparently lucky to get 200 people to sign up. A good castrato might cost 1,500 guineas (as Manzuoli did in 1764–65), and a first-rate dancer could be almost as expensive: Mlle Heinel reportedly got 1,200 guineas in 1771–72, though rumour says that 'the Macaronis' (a club of young men) chipped in half the cost in that case.[2] The annual gross (extrapolated on the optimistic basis of 200 subscribers and 300 cash customers every night for fifty nights) was probably no more than £9,000 or £10,000. The impresario might hire expensive attractions who would fill the theatre to overflowing, and might expand the auditorium to accommodate the additional customers—but he would do so out of his own pocket and at his own risk. The opera in London had become a purely private enterprise conducted along capitalistic lines, to be sold to any entrepreneur who could put up the cash. It was, however, subject to government regulation.

## Patents and Licences

By what right could a theatre (or an opera-house) operate in London? On this issue the future of the Pantheon enterprise was to turn in 1790 when rival pretenders to the Italian opera monopoly engaged in a vicious battle over a promised patent. Authority to perform in eighteenth-century London has been the subject of much misunderstanding.

When Charles II was restored to the throne in 1660 he established a theatrical monopoly, granting perpetual patents to two favoured courtiers. These patents were combined in the union of 1682, and when a second

---

[1] See below, sect. IV.    [2] See 'Opera Salaries', 42–3.

company reopened in 1695 its authority was a licence 'at pleasure' issued by the Lord Chamberlain. This licence was reissued in Vanbrugh's name in 1704 when he took over the Lincoln's Inn Fields acting company, which he then moved to his new theatre in the Haymarket. With the exception of the period 1719–40 (covered by the patent to the Royal Academy of Music), opera companies in eighteenth-century London operated on annual licences issued at the discretion of the Lord Chamberlain. Opera was virtually unaffected by the Licensing Act of 1737, which restricted English-language theatre to the two patent operations, but took indirect cognizance of Italian opera at the King's Theatre as a special case by allowing performance under 'Licence from the Lord Chamberlain of His Majestys Household'.[1] The distinction between a patent and a licence made no difference to any single season, but was none the less extremely important. A patent was a royal grant guaranteeing the right to perform for at least a specified term of years; a licence was merely a notice issued by the Lord Chamberlain that performances at a particular location would be tolerated 'at pleasure' for a relatively short span of time—until 1790, never more than one season. A licence could be renewed, but there was no guarantee of renewal. After the Licensing Act, investors did not care to put up the money to erect a new theatre or opera-house without the assurance of the right to perform that only a patent could confer.

There was no 'opera patent' and had been none since 1740. Not even the editors of *The London Stage* have understood this. In the introduction to the season of 1789–90 Charles Beecher Hogan says that 'With the disappearance of the old theatre the patent had disappeared as well.'[2] This is untrue: there was no patent, nor was any operating authority consumed in the fire. After 1740 the King's Theatre applied annually for a licence and normally received it as a matter of routine. The Lord Chamberlain's principal concern was whether the impresario making the request was sufficiently solvent to pay the performers—which had not always been true in the 1740s, 1750s, and 1760s. But if there was no patent and no licence, then there was no right to perform.

By the 1780s the King's Theatre's monopoly on Italian opera was so well established that hardly anyone realized that it was a matter of custom, not of

---

[1] See 10 George II, ch. 28. Printed in Vincent J. Liesenfeld, *The Licensing Act of 1737* (Madison: University of Wisconsin Press, 1984), 191–3. Covent Garden operated under the combined perpetual patent, Drury Lane under a series of 21-year patents.

[2] *The London Stage*, Part 5, ii. 1179; Gibson, 'Earl Cowper', 251, repeats this mistake.

legal right. Even modern scholars have sometimes failed to appreciate that the 'King's Theatre' was a private venture, not one that held any offical right to perform, or in any sense belonged to the King.[1] Vanbrugh had constructed the theatre as a private speculation. It was built on ground leased from the Crown, but this was its only connection to the monarchy, name notwithstanding. The theatre building was owned by Vanbrugh's descendants (in our period, Edward Vanbrugh, Sir John's nephew), but ownership of the company of performers and its stock of scenes, costumes, music, and so forth was an entirely different matter. Vanbrugh and his heirs rented the theatre to a succession of tenants (who sometimes let to sub-tenants)—in the 1780s for an annual rent of £1,260. What Sheridan and Harris bought in 1778 was the opera company and its goods and chattels, a lease on the building included. Edward Vanbrugh could refuse to renew the lease. Or the Lord Chamberlain could refuse to issue a licence. Legally, the King could issue a limited-term patent to the current proprietor of the company—or to anyone else, should he decide to do so. The King's Theatre's stranglehold on Italian opera stretched back fully seventy years from the time this study commences, but there was no firm basis in law for the monopoly—a point to become crucial in the struggle for control of opera after the fire of 1789.

## II. Views of Opera, 1750–1790

As many readers will be aware, 'opera' did not mean to the late eighteenth-century London audience precisely what it means to us. The term was increasingly used by Covent Garden and Drury Lane to signify musical dramas and burlettas. 'Opera' at the King's Theatre meant all-sung Italian operas, many of which were pasticcios designed to show off imported virtuoso singers. One went to the opera-house not so much to see or hear Gluck's *Orfeo* or Piccinni's *La buona figliuola* as to admire the singing of Manzuoli, Allegranti, Pacchierotti, or Marchesi—and to chat with one's friends. Before moving into the specifics of opera practice, we need briefly to investigate the phenomenon of opera as it was viewed before and during the period we are investigating.

---

[1] Reinhard Strohm, for example, states erroneously that the theatre 'was the property of the king'. See *Essays on Handel and Italian Opera* (Cambridge: Cambridge University Press, 1985), 105.

## *The Audience*

Italian opera was entertainment for the socially élite. This will be the presumption of most readers, and it is absolutely true for the period at issue, but there are complexities, corollaries, and implications that need to be explored. From the time of Addison critics scoffed at the notion of an entertainment in a language the audience could not understand. They had a point, though the problem was alleviated in various ways. A small minority of the audience knew some Italian, and others probably picked it up. Dual-language librettos and a lighted auditorium allowed one to follow along. The conventions of gesture (discussed briefly in Ch. 3) were designed to assist in understanding both emotion and action. Many librettos were used over and over. The fact remains that subscribers might easily attend half (and some might attend all) of the company's fifty or more performances, seeing five or ten or fifteen performances of a work they understood no more than hazily, if that.

The King's Theatre, Haymarket, was in essence an exclusive club. People went to see and be seen; sour comments about the popularity of the card and coffee-rooms suggest that some of the subscribers paid a minimum of attention to the performances. We grant that many members of the audience were fond of the entertainments, knowledgeable in judging them, and concerned with their quality. But the Italian opera survived in London for essentially social reasons. The increasing popularity of ballet as a vital part of each evening's entertainment reflects in part the introduction of *ballet d'action* but also the preferences of an audience that was never fully able to appreciate the finer dramatic and poetic features of opera in Italian.

The exact identity of the opera subscribers, let alone of the audience as a whole, is not known and is unlikely ever to be known before the 1780s, when subscriber lists began to be published, some of which survive. None the less, from a variety of records enough can be learnt of the subscribers between the foundation of the Royal Academy of Music in 1719 and the collapse of Lord Middlesex's company in 1745 to prove that they were a very élite group indeed. The names of 425 known subscribers of various types have been collected by Carole Taylor, who has made a detailed analysis of about 130 long-term ones. Of 101 men, 71 were titled; of 29 women, 22 were titled.[1] Granting that titled persons may have been more noticed and better

[1] Carole Taylor, 'Italian Operagoing in London, 1700–1745', Ph.D. diss. (Syracuse Uni-

recorded than others, these are none the less striking figures. Taylor has likewise shown the high proportion of MPs and government officials who were subscribers; interestingly, she finds no tidy pattern of political affiliation among these people.[1]

From the time of the Royal Academy to 1778 the opera was evidently lucky to get as many as 200 season subscribers. Handel had 170 in 1731–32 and 140 in 1732–33.[2] What did they want? To judge from an anonymous pamphlet of 1753, the principal desiderata were a good castrato; novelty in the singers; dance; and new scenery.[3] The author is highly critical of Vanneschi's plans for the season of 1753–54 and sarcastically proposes mounting a parallel series of burlesque operas at the Little Haymarket. But beneath the satire, serious opinions are evident. The author commences by examining the list of proposed singers, vigorously denouncing the *prima donna* (Caterina Visconti) and the 'Eunuch' (Seraphino). The second woman (Giulia Frasi) is found 'charming . . . but she wants the Graces of Novelty'. The tenor has not yet been announced, but hardly matters: 'The Merit of a *Tenour* could never yet hinder an *Opera* from sinking.' The author grumbles that 'The *Decorations* will not keep up the *Opera*', since the sponsors 'intend only to patch up *old Scenes*'. He denounces Passerini as leader of the orchestra, and complains that 'The rest of the Band are but common Players, except *Vincent* the Ho-boy.' He blasts Vanneschi as a bad poet and a poor manager. The last straw is that 'the *Opera* is to be without *Dances*. So we shall have three Hours tedious Music without any Entertainment intermingled to relieve the Audience.' Composers are nowhere mentioned: they were comparatively insignificant. The pamphleteer concludes that the 'two hundred *Subscribers*' will be indignant at being asked to pay 'the same Sum they formerly did for hearing *Farinelli, Senesino, Faustina, Cuzzoni,* and other Singers of the same Standard, who were supported by superb Decorations and magnificent Dances'. How, he asks, will the manager 'be able to fill the House, and gather nine or ten thousand Guineas to defray the necessary Expences?'

versity, 1991), ch. 2 and appendices I and II.

[1] For a comparison with the contemporary French audience, see William Weber, 'L'Institution et son public: L'Opéra à Paris et à Londres au XVIIIᵉ siècle', *Annales Économies Sociétés Civilisations*, 6 (1993), 1519–39.

[2] Judith Milhous and Robert D. Hume, 'Box Office Reports for Five Operas Mounted by Handel in London, 1732–1734', *Harvard Library Bulletin*, 26 (1978), 245–66.

[3] *A Scheme for having an Italian Opera in London, of a New Taste* (London: W. Owen and T. Snelling, 1753). Published with English and French text on facing pages.

Two hundred subscribers at 20 guineas each (supposing that number were actually willing to pay) would generate 4,000 guineas. Later records imply that subscription proceeds and daily box-office receipts tended to be roughly equal. If the annual budget was in the vicinity of £10,000, the implication is that the break-even point might be reached with 200 subscribers and an average of 150 walk-in buyers of pit and box tickets (10s. 6d. each), plus 150 gallery patrons (5s. each) every night. Extant figures from later in the century imply that the number of subscribers who attended varied wildly from night to night (see Ch. 2), but even assuming 75 per cent attendance by subscribers, we must suppose that total average attendance in many mid-century seasons was no more than about 450—and, in bad seasons, perhaps a lot fewer. The King's Theatre must often have been less than half full. The power of a relatively small body of subscribers (or potential subscribers) is obvious.

Celebrity-watching was an important part of the evening's entertainment, and eventually someone had the bright idea of publishing a field guide to opera-house audience fauna. When such a list of box subscribers first appeared is unknown. The earliest recorded was apparently published in the winter of 1782–83 after a major rebuilding of the auditorium the previous summer: *A Descriptive Plan of the New Opera House, with the Names of the Subscribers to each Box taken from the Theatre Itself by a Lady of Fashion*.[1] A less complete list in the *Morning Herald* of 5 February 1783 gives 317 names, fully half of them titled. The next that is preserved is a simpler six-page *List of the Subscribers to the Boxes, at the King's-Theatre*, dated 1788.[2] The following year *A Correct List of the Subscribers to the Boxes at the King's Theatre, 1789* was printed. (See Pl. 1.)[3] By the time the Pantheon opened in 1790–91 such a list appears to have become a regular feature of the opera season. Exemplars apparently do not survive for every season, but we have located detailed published lists for 1793–94, 1796–97, 1798–99, 1799–1800,

---

[1] London: T. Becket, n.d. (32 leaves). Copies are preserved at the British Library and Harvard. This pamphlet has sometimes been mistakenly associated with the rebuilt King's Theatre of 1791. See Arnott and Robinson, no. 1458. 'New Opera House' clearly refers to Taylor's rebuilt auditorium of 1782. The *Plan* preserves the social convention that women were the principal subscribers to most of the boxes, though men outnumber women two to one overall.

[2] Arnott and Robinson, no. 1462.

[3] British Library 163.g.66—bound at the end of Cimarosa's *La villana riconosciuta*, but apparently bibliographically unrelated.

1800–1801, 1801–02, 1803–04, 1804–05, 1805–06, and 1806–07.[1] Analysis of the people reported in these lists is beyond the scope of this book. We remark merely that the regular publication of such lists is evidence of the growing social cachet enjoyed by the opera in the 1780s and 1790s. The demand for boxes led managers to cram ever more of them into the auditorium, and even to rebuild the auditorium twice in quick succession. Soaring prices around the turn of the century are likewise evidence of escalating opera mania in London. In the 1760s and 1770s the opera company limped along with support from a relatively small band of regular subscribers. Their number appears to have quadrupled between 1778 and the time of the Pantheon, or so the figures analysed later in this study seem to show.

A glance down the pages of the extant 1780s box-subscriber lists reveals that the subscribers were the nobility and gentry. Newspaper commentary often includes mention of prominent members of the audience in attendance, and two of the pamphlet commentaries on operatical matters reveal the public's evident fascination with the behaviour of persons of quality at the opera. *A Mob in the Pit: or, Lines addressed to The D–ch–ss of A—ll* is a short burlesque poem describing and mocking an ill-considered attempt by the Duchess of Argyll to 'mob it in the Pit'.[2] Exactly what happened is not stated (the author probably assumed that readers would know), but she was forced to beat a hasty and inglorious retreat to her box, from which she summarily evicted the people to whom she had allowed it to be rented. The occasion was evidently Madame Heinel's benefit, and she herself had to intervene (for reasons not at all clear) in the dispute over the box. The point of the poem is to gloat over the Duchess of Argyll's discomfiture and public display of temper—but in the process it gives us a vivid picture of box-holder behaviour and the gulf between titled lady box-holders and the inhabitants of the pit.

Tempers occasionally rose to considerable heights over disputed rights to boxes, especially in the 1780s when demand for prime boxes sometimes exceeded supply. A twenty-page doggerel 'Serio-Comic-Operatic Burlesque Poem' called *The Opera Rumpus; or, The Ladies in the Wrong Box!* commemorates in Popean style a public fuss in which Mrs Broadhead had the Countess of Jersey publicly ejected from a box claimed by both of them: their fracas disrupted a performance; the proprietor William Taylor had to

---

[1] Four of these are reported by Arnott and Robinson (nos. 1467–70); the remainder are in the New York Public Library and are described in 'Opera Salaries'.
[2] London: S. Bladon, 1773.

be fetched; the box was broken into and the offending squatter ejected.[1] The scandal was delightful, and the author had a fine time taking off various parts of the audience—Miss Buckram, an adoring Pacchierotti fan, old Mrs Tabby who 'likes the ballet', and a host of others. The audience enters, dressed to the nines:

> Dear Lady Flutter and Sir Harry
> Yawning: Alas! why did I marry?
>  In sep'rate coaches ventur'd:
> Next, Lady Turtle from the city,
> Her daughter Ann (egad she's pretty)
>  With flowing sattins enter'd.
> Neuters, non-entities, and noodles;
> *Brookes', Weltje's, Betty's, White's,* and *Boodles'*
>  Afforded various speci-
> mens of our thrice-renown'd lawgivers,
> Such good, such virtuous, holy livers,
>  So dapper, smart, and dressy!
> . . . . . . . . . . . . . . . . . . .
> Here, some o'er streams of coffee pouring,
> There Johnny Brute in vulgar snoring
> Proclaims *his taste* for singing . . .
> Whilst vast applause is ringing!
> . . . . . . . . . . . . . . . . . . .
> Paul Prig in yonder upper gallery,
> With silken phrase hits off *Cit* rallery,
>  Criticizing sattins:
> Whilst Mrs. Prig, stiff as a doll,
> Admires the Prince and all the qual.
>  As she takes off her pattens!

To judge from the diary of Lady Mary Coke (quoted at length at the end of Ch. 3), the 'Quality' gossiped among themselves while lesser mortals indulged in celebrity-spotting. No doubt the supply of celebrities changed less than it might from night to night, but an endless stream of comments in the newspapers implies that the Prince of Wales was always value for money, regardless of the quality of the performance.

Opera was for the *bon ton*, and those who wished to belong cultivated a taste for it. The price was high and the company relatively exclusive—a lot

---

[1] London: R. Baldwin, 1783.

more so than at Covent Garden and Drury Lane.[1] Competition was offered by the major concert series, variously at Hanover Square and the Pantheon in the 1780s. George III appeared only occasionally at the King's Theatre, but almost everyone else who was anyone was to be seen there, many of them very regularly indeed. A sprinkling of names from the 1782–83 subscriber list gives the social and political flavour: the Hon. Mr Fox and the Hon. William Pitt; the Dukes and Duchesses of Bedford, Cumberland, Gloucester, Marlborough, and Richmond (among others); Lords and Ladies Salisbury, Carlisle, Cavendish, Jersey, Melbourne (*et al.*); Generals Burgoyne, Johnstone, Pattinson (*et al.*); Sir John Eliot (a society doctor); Mrs Robinson—that is, the scandalous actress 'Perdita' Robinson, a former lover of the Prince of Wales, now cohabiting with Col. Tarleton, the celebrated British cavalry commander in the American Revolutionary War, who shared her box as well as her bed.

## Theory versus Practice

What was an opera supposed to be? During the first years of the eighteenth century, when Italian opera was a new and controversial phenomenon, a number of treatises and commentaries on it were published, many of them sceptical to hostile.[2] By the time of the Royal Academy the subject had ceased to attract the attention of aesthetic theorists. Newspapers might grumble over the extravagance of paying fortunes to foreign performers (and especially to castrati), but for the next half-century and more there is a singular lack of serious generic analysis or critical commentary. English drama and acting gradually developed a considerable popular and quasi-scholarly literature, but opera did not. One is left to deduce the expectations and desires of the audience largely from practice. But before leading the reader into the close surveys of Chapters 4, 5, and 6, we wish to raise certain conceptual issues. This is most easily done by considering two of the most

---

[1] As at those theatres, however, whores were a problem. For a particularly bitter complaint about their effect on behaviour in the second gallery, see the *Morning Herald* of 8 May 1786. Pickpockets were another problem. *The Times* of 27 Feb. 1789 says sourly that there is 'an unmolested swarm of thieves, every night the doors are open', because the 'pick pockets . . . do not divide the whole booty among themselves', but pay weekly protection money to '——'.

[2] For a survey of such criticism, see Lowell Lindgren, 'Critiques of Opera in London, 1705–1719', forthcoming in the proceedings of the 1993 Antiquae Musicae Italicae Studiosi of Como conference on 'Il melodramma italiano in Italia e in Germania nell'età barocca'.

important treatises on opera to appear in English in the latter half of the eighteenth century—Algarotti in 1767 and Le Texier in 1790.[1]

*An Essay on the Opera Written in Italian by Count Algarotti F.R.S. F.S.A.* appeared in English translation in 1767.[2] Algarotti was a poet bent on establishing the centrality of the libretto and the right of its author to control the venture as a whole, and he grinds that axe unremittingly. He is appalled by the selfishness of performers: 'What frequent jealousies and wranglings arise among the singers, on account of one person's having more ariettas than another, a loftier plume, a longer and more flowing robe, &c.' The solution, in his view, is for 'the poet' to 'resume the reins of power, which have been so unjustly wrested from his hands; and that, being restored to his rightful authority, he may diffuse through every department good order and due subordination' (6–7).

Algarotti was simply following Metastasio and Goldoni in his belief that the poet should control the production, and he was very much a man of his time in his conviction that the libretto was the foundation on which the whole must be built. He likens an opera to a painting for which the poet draws the picture while the composer merely supplies 'its colouring' (10). An opera is a psychological drama (to use a modern term) in which the poet selects an appropriate subject (Algarotti finds classical mythology and 'the courts of sovereigns, and palaces of princes' far too confining); the composer provides appropriate music; and dancers, machinists, costumers, and others all work to carry out the concept of the poet, who is 'to carry in his mind a comprehensive view of the *whole* of the drama' (11, 15).

Algarotti's long and vehement protests against divided authority refer to practice in Italy in the 1750s and early 1760s. The situation he describes, however, with composer, choreographer, scene-designer, costumer, and singers carrying out their own functions with a sturdy independence that severely reduced the possibility of a unified production concept, is precisely the situation that we shall find characteristic of London in the 1780s. Algarotti deplores this departmental fragmentation. He is arguing for an artistic director, or at least for a director in the modern sense of the term. His

[1] For a compilation of comments about the nature and rise of opera, published as a companion piece to Algarotti, the reader may wish to consult *The Lyric Muse Revived in Europe or A Critical Display of the Opera in all its Revolutions* (London: L. Davis and C. Reymers, 1768). The text is lifted—with acknowledgements—from a variety of English and foreign sources.

[2] London: L. Davis and C. Reymers, 1767. It had been published in Italian five years earlier. The dedication to William Pitt is signed 'Francesco Algarotti' and dated Pisa, 18 Dec. 1762.

concept of opera was dramatic and psychological: he did not see it as a display of great music, or flashy scenery or glorious singing, but as *drama* in a multimedia setting. *Words* are vital. Algarotti laments the insistence of the composer upon acting 'like a despotic sovereign. . . . It is almost impossible to persuade him, that he ought to be in a subordinate station; that music derives its greatest merit from being no more than an auxiliary, the handmaid to poetry.' The 'chief business' of the composer ought to be 'to predispose the minds of the audience for receiving the impression to be excited by the poet's verse' (27–8). If this was an uphill battle in Italy, it was doubly so in London, where the audience was hardly able to attend with fervency to the niceties of verse in Italian.

One might have expected operas in London to become concerts in costume. In fact, we shall discover that contrary to such expectation opera was consistently treated as drama, albeit sometimes rather simplistic drama. Vocal display and scenery were important, and poets remained underpaid dogsbodies, but perhaps because audiences were accustomed to clear-cut dramatic structure in English plays, the Italian operas adapted or composed for London show considerably more attention to dramatic form and logic than one might anticipate.

Unity of concept was something else again. To the twentieth-century sensibility, Algarotti is often remarkably prescient. He denounces overtures written to a pattern ('two allegros with one grave . . . as noisy as possible') that fail to prepare the audience emotionally for the story to follow (30). He decries superfluous ornaments, thick instrumentation, failure to use lutes and harps for lighter, clearer accompaniment of voices (37–8). He regards dance as a mere interlude, and inorganic dances disgust him: 'As soon as an act is over, several dancers sally forth on the stage, who have no manner of affinity with the plan of the piece [the opera]. For, if the scene of action be in Rome, the dance is often made to be in Cusco, or in Pekin; and if the Opera be serious, the dance is sure to be comic' (65). He calls for costumes and scenery appropriate to the time and place of representation, be it Egypt, Greece, Troy, Mexico, the Elysian Fields, 'or even up to Olympus' (72–3). If opera was not like this in either Italy or London, it was not because no one had ever conceived the possibility.

Algarotti gives a striking picture of noisy and inattentive audiences in Italy:

It is not to be doubted, that whenever music shall be restored to her pristine dignity, Operas will be honoured with the attention of the public, and be heard with the greatest delight from the beginning to the end, because then a grateful silence will be imposed on all spectators; whereas, quite the contrary is now observable in our theatres; on entering one of which, so great a confusion and uproar is heard, as to resemble the bellowing of a wood in a storm, or the roaring of the sea to a tempestuous wind. Even the most attentive of our now Opera-frequenters can be silent only to hear some air of Bravura; but they are all desire at the dances, which can never begin too soon for their impatience, nor last too long for their enjoying them. . . . It seems indeed, as if our theatre had been intended rather for an academy of dancing, than the representation of an Opera; and one would be induced to think, that the Italians have adopted the Frenchman's advice, who said, not unpleasantly, that, in order to make the theatre flourish, the dances should be lengthened, and the women's petticoats made shorter. (63–4)

This depressing picture of Italian practice in the 1760s is vividly confirmed in Samuel Sharp's *Letters from Italy*.[1] Describing the opera-house at Naples, Sharp says

The singers might be very well heard [despite the size of the theatre], if the audience were more silent; but it is so much the fashion at *Naples*, and, indeed, through all *Italy*, to consider the Opera as a place of rendezvous and visiting, that they do not seem in the least to attend to the musick, but laugh and talk through the whole performance, without any restraint; and, it may be imagined, that an assembly of so many hundreds conversing together so loudly, must entirely cover the voices of the singers. . . . Notwithstanding the amazing noisiness of the audience, during the whole performance of the Opera, the moment the dances begin, there is a universal dead silence, which continues as long as the dances continue. Witty people, therefore, never fail to tell me, the *Neapolitans* go to *see*, not to *hear* an Opera. (78–9, 82)

We deduce that as of 1767 London audiences were not quite so inattentive to the opera, despite their greater difficulty in comprehending the words.

How many of the London audience members followed along in a bilingual text when one was available remains purely speculative. This was, for obvious reasons, much less standard in Italy. Sharp comments that

It is the custom in *Italy* to light the stage only. . . . Dark as the boxes are, they would be still darker, if those who sit in them did not, at their own expence, put up a couple of candles, without which it would be impossible to read the opera. . . . It is not the fashion . . . in any part of *Italy*, to take a small wax light to the house, and, therefore, hardly any man has eyes good enough to make use of a book in the pit. (89–90)

[1] Second edition (London: R. Cave *et al.*, 1767).

The lighting of the auditorium in the King's Theatre seems a strong argument that a significant number of the London audience wished to be able to read the text during performances.

The pertinence of Algarotti to London performances of the 1780s may certainly be called into question, but on the testimony of Le Texier, we suspect *plus ça change* . . . Twenty-three years after the publication of the English translation of Algarotti, Antoine Le Texier published his *Ideas on the Opera* (1790). In sixty-six pages he lays out what was clearly a campaign manifesto: he hoped to be drafted as the 'good administrator' he described, and made head of the new opera-house that would replace the old King's Theatre (36). His complaints echo Algarotti's virtually point for point, and so does his concept of opera as drama. Le Texier clearly put together his pamphlet with Algarotti open on his table: he borrows ideas and examples, and at times closely paraphrases his predecessor. Neither essay is exactly a monument of opera criticism, but Le Texier's complaints tell us beyond reasonable doubt a lot about what was wrong with opera performance in London in the 1780s.

Like Algarotti, Le Texier works from the premiss that the crucial point is the choice of story: all other elements are to conduce to effective communication. He too is a stickler for historical and national authenticity, providing long and entertaining catalogues of costume and scenery horrors. When the theatre employs 'a magnificent decoration of columns of lapis lazuli enriched with gold, which some days before had formed the temple of Venus in the ballet of Psyche' as 'the house of a merchant-woman of Leipsick' (29), Le Texier splutters with incredulity. Even more than Algarotti, he is committed to the principle that opera and dance should be integrated, or at least related—a practice yet more difficult after the advent of *ballet d'action*. Le Texier himself was a celebrated dramatic reader, so his emphasis on acting is no surprise. His conviction that the opera's 'manager' ought to supply what we should now think of as directorial functions was no doubt unusual in 1790; he believed that singers should be helped to represent characters plausibly while communicating emotion effectively (38). From the twentieth-century point of view, Le Texier is dead right in this.

Where Le Texier differs profoundly from us is in his views of the composer. Like Algarotti, he sees the composer as the supplier of declamative decoration for what amounts to a dramatic poem with multimedia trimmings.

I do not think very necessary to follow the ancient custom, and to bring over here one single composer, who is always very expensive to the administration, since we may have the work of many at a very reasonable price. . . . If a composer's first Opera does not please, the prejudice will act upon the next; and having but one composer is sufficient to excite the desire of having others. It is then much better to let the Signori compose in Rome or Naples than in Suffolk-Street, and by a good correspondent all the Operas composed in Italy will be had with much less expence than what is given to one composer.

Some will perhaps oppose that the best and most successful Opera in Italy may not be convenient to the voice of the singers here. I shall answer, that the composers in Italy do not always know who will be the singers to perform their Opera: it will farther be said that these composers have the power to alter, according to the singer's desire, the part which is not suitable to his voice; then it would be very easy to have here a good musician able to make those trifling alterations, and we should not be deprived of the most exquisite works, which are the glory and delight of all Italy; besides, we should be at liberty to chuse. (5–7)

Here Le Texier does not accurately represent the nature of the 1780s London Italian opera: the principal house composers—Sacchini, Anfossi, Cherubini, and Tarchi—were major figures on the opera circuit. But Le Texier is evidently very much aware of Gallini's recent practice of mounting Continental favourites, such as Paisiello's *Il re Teodoro in Venezia* and *Il barbiere di Siviglia*, with only minor alterations. *Opera seria* (which is what is really under discussion) presented a potent situation or a powerful tale that showed off the characters and emotions of the principals, and gave the singers an opportunity to display their talents. Music was essentially secondary. Dance was normally disjunct. Algarotti and Le Texier are highly critical of opera-house practice in their day—but not altogether for the reasons we might expect. They protest against sloppy production and undisciplined principal singers, but empowering the composer clearly never crossed their minds. In a system in which the *primo uomo* and the *prima donna* normally earned three to five times as much as a top composer (£1,000 to £1,500 versus £300), and the house poet was lucky to get £150, we can hardly be surprised that London operas were showcases for singers.[1] The wonder is that operas retained as much dramatic cohesion as they did.

## Practical Criticism

Much of what can be learnt about opera performance in the 1780s must be pieced together from a variety of less than satisfactory sources. Newspaper

[1] See 'Opera Salaries', 45–54.

commentators, diarists, memoirists, and the great Dr Burney all have important information to offer—and must all be treated with a certain degree of caution. For ballet, the situation is markedly worse.

Italian opera flourished in London for more than half a century before the newspapers began to publish anything that might be described as serious opera criticism. Scrappy and occasional beginnings can be found in the 1770s, but only during the 1780s did a significant body of informed commentary start to appear. Reviews are always anonymous, and they range from brief accounts of who sang (or who attended) to long, penetrating essays that display considerable technical knowledge. In general, the closer one moves towards 1800 the likelier one is to find substantial and substantive reviews of any opera or ballet.

These reviews are, unfortunately, treacherous stuff. Anyone reading several newspapers over the same few weeks in the 1780s will quickly realize that the opera-house had an active public relations department. The appointment of Parkyns MacMahon as secretary in 1783 (see Ch. 3) merely formalized what was already standard practice. At the start of the decade we find a mocking summary of the raves about new performers being supplied by 'Messrs. the Operatical Intelligencers' coupled with a blunt statement that though the 'new performers have a great share of merit' they are inferior to those of the previous season, and a snide suggestion that the public should be allowed to 'judge for itself without a *Prompter*'.[1] Papers did routinely pick up paragraphs from one another, but the simultaneous appearance of oleaginous rapture is far too frequent to be merely a matter of space-filling. A lot of newspaper notices (including what are ostensibly reviews) have the ring of the in-house publicist. Lorenzo Da Ponte implies that Badini worked regularly as a reviewer while serving as house poet.[2] Other 'paragraphs' may have been bought, or paid for under pressure. One report implies attempts to take advantage of nervous foreigners. 'On the first coming to England of Signor Trebbi . . . the editor of a newspaper paid him a morning visit, and informed him he was a public writer, and had characters of all prices. "I understand you, Sir", said Trebbi, "and have heard of you; I have no guineas to throw away so ill; but I am a writer too; *Et voila ma plume!*" "This is my pen", showing him a good English oaken towel [cudgel]'. This story is credited to Richard Yates, former co-owner of the opera-house (*Morning Herald*, 21 October 1783).

[1] *London Courant*, 15 Dec. 1781.    [2] Da Ponte, *Memoirs*, 212–13.

Newspapers occasionally snipe at attempts to garner free publicity. The *Morning Post* of 15 January 1785, for example, carries a special note 'To Correspondents':

In the Lines on Signor Crescentini we recognize the hand writing of the common panegyrist of all the Italian singers and French dancers imported into this metropolis. We shall dispose of his last favour in the same manner as we did last winter of his odes, sonnets, and impromptus, on Theodore, Rauzzini, and various other personages of the same profession.

Newspapers were no doubt more tolerant of paid publicity. From the Bedford Opera Papers we know the Pantheon regularly supplied puffs and 'reviews' to several papers, and paid for their insertion. The practice clearly did not originate in 1791. Occasionally a production gets a great deal of advance notice—for example, Le Picq's *Macbeth* ballet in March 1785. Perhaps some of it was legitimate, but in the case of Rauzzini's *Alina, o sia La regina di Golconda* in 1784, we are interested to find the *New Spectator* of 23 March saying of the music, 'no small sum has been spent in *puffing* it in the newspapers'.

Though sometimes supplied by the theatre itself, newspaper reviews nevertheless yield remarkable details of some aspects of the performance. When several reports of a production survive, the puff is usually easy to spot, and one can arrive at a balanced assessment of the relative success or failure of an opera from the other 'paragraphs'. And, perhaps surprisingly, several newspapers paid close attention to attribution and seemed to have detailed knowledge of earlier, Continental versions of London productions.

Granting the importance, utility, and slipperiness of newspaper reviews, one must find them before one can try to use them—not a simple matter. A helpful selection of extracts from the newspapers has been reprinted by Petty in his *Italian Opera in London 1760–1800*. Users should be aware, however, that Petty edits out what he is not interested in—including a lot of performance and production detail. And the more one looks at actual daily newspapers, the more one realizes that Petty prints only a tiny sample from a vast body of material that is in fact very difficult of access. By the 1780s London had many newspapers, and complete runs survive of rather few of them. Some papers publish fairly regular opera commentary for a few weeks or months, and then dry up for months or years. Broken runs leave the scholar trudging from library to library, mostly frustrated. We have made an effort to scan at least two newspapers for opera news and reviews throughout the period covered by this book, and when feasible four or five. We have found a great deal more newspaper material than we have any way of including or referring to in this study, but much remains to be found. Much of what we have discovered comes (at various dates) from the *Morning Herald*, the *Morning Chronicle*, the *Public Advertiser*, *The Times* (and its predecessor, the *Daily Universal Register*), and the *Oracle*. Lesser and less well-preserved papers are represented to the degree that we have found runs of them and discovered useful material in them. To what extent any particular item is to be trusted one hardly ever knows.

An almost equally immediate and contemporaneous source of commentary on opera, and one much easier to assess, is Dr Charles Burney.[1] In exactly the period covered by this book he was living in London, hard at work on the fourth volume of *A General History of Music* (published in 1789). His grand, panoramic chapter on Italian opera in London draws in its later phases very directly on his own observation and consequently constitutes testimony of great importance. Burney gives a first-hand account of most of the singers, composers, and works discussed in the present volume in a chapter entitled 'Origin of the Italian Opera in England, and its Progress there during the present Century', the longest in the entire *General History*. His aims are to provide a complete record of operas performed and the principal singers engaged at the King's Theatre and to give a far from dispassionate critical appraisal of everything. Burney was able to judge the operas under discussion here from actual performance—not merely from their imperfect preservation in the *Favourite Songs*, on which he had been forced to rely almost exclusively for his knowledge of earlier operas.

Burney is unquestionably an important commentator, especially because he rarely pulls his punches, even when swinging at composers and singers of his personal acquaintance.[2] Unfortunately, he had some major limitations even by eighteenth-century standards: for him, an opera was rarely more than a succession of individual numbers. Consequently his treatment of

[1] The standard study remains Roger Lonsdale's admirable *Dr. Charles Burney: A Literary Biography* (Oxford: Clarendon Press, 1965).

[2] In Fanny Burney, *Early Journals and Letters*, ii. 178 n., Lars E. Troide states that Burney 'was also careful not to be offensive about living composers whom he did not particularly like'. While he was perhaps never totally dismissive of his friends, his 'balanced' assessments can be damning, as of Bertoni: 'Though the invention of this master is not very fertile, his melody is graceful and interesting; and though he never had perhaps sufficient genius and fire to attain the sublime, yet he is constantly natural, correct, and judicious; often pleasing, and sometimes happy' (*General History*, ii. 890).

contemporaneous opera is indistinguishable from one that could have been written merely from study of the printed aria collections. Burney's analysis concentrates on melodic style, ornamentation, orchestration, and basic form; he had little interest in or lacked the capacity for discussing large ensembles or the dramatic plan of, say, action finales. Ballet left him cold; he never really appreciated the multimedia French opera; and the full significance of Gluckian reform passed him by. His forte was pithy, painfully honest summations of a composer's or a singer's entire career and worth. Given the vast scope of *A General History of Music*, one can forgive Burney for reducing every work to a concert in costume, for not going behind the scenes, for failing to answer questions central to the present study: did the King's Theatre have an artistic policy? and, if so, how did it affect the history of opera? Burney was a direct and honest observer, but for our purposes a rather limited source.

The best critic we have encountered, and by far the most important source on opera in the period at issue, is one almost totally unknown and unused by historians—Burney's daughter Susanna Elizabeth Burney, later Phillips (1755–1800). Susan Burney (as her family generally called her at the time) supplies in unique and abundant detail much of what her father omitted to say about the London Italian opera, at least for the 1779–80 season, during which she wrote a remarkable letter-journal.[1] This document reveals a witty and lucid writer, one with good Italian, a technical grasp of music, and an insatiable appetite for rehearsals and backstage gossip. She opens a window for us on the inside of the opera performance world unique for this period. Hers is a remarkably independent voice, sometimes out of tune with her father and her more famous sister Fanny, and always more articulate about the dramatic side of opera. She was an opera fanatic, but a highly critical one, and her obsessively detailed reportage of rehearsals, performances, and conversations with performers is like nothing else in the period. Her letter-journal is the foundation of Chapter 4. Had she been able to continue her account of opera in London throughout the 1780s, and if more of her letter-journals had survived, the rest of this book would have been much easier to write.

Susan Burney was, to be sure, an altogether extraordinary member of the audience. Valuable as her special insights are, one must try to remember that most of the audience saw with different eyes and heard with different

---

[1] British Library Egerton MS 3691.

ears. Two other sources of some importance are the letters and diaries of
Horace Walpole and Lady Mary Coke—both long-term subscribers to the
King's Theatre and about as different from Susan Burney in aesthetic and
outlook as one could imagine. In the 1780s the ageing and crotchety Walpole attended the opera much less frequently than when in his prime; he
disapproved of almost everything he heard, and claimed the company was
artistically bankrupt and was surviving only by virtue of the ballet and the
supper room.[1] By this time he was clearly a very jaded observer. Lady Mary
Coke, whose letter-diary extends for decades and has been only partly published, was an enthusiastic opera-goer who found the music pretty or not;
approved or disapproved of the singers and dancers (whose names she seems
rarely to have learnt); and devoted most of her time and attention to gossip
and observation of her society friends. She was an acute and opinionated
lady, but for her, operas and ballets were a peripheral part of the evening's
entertainment—something to be glanced at when nothing more interesting
or urgent claimed her attention. Her comments constitute an important
reminder of what was probably a very common outlook among subscribers.

Only gradually was an analytic vocabulary developed to discuss operatic
music. The first systematic attempt to lay out the principles and to explain
Italian terminology to the British public appears to have been *Letters upon
the Poetry and Music of the Italian Opera*, by the Scottish painter John
Brown, published posthumously in 1789.[2] This is a remarkably unpolemical
beginner's guide to *opera seria*, which breaks down the post-Metastasian
model into its constituent parts: *recitativo semplice, recitativo instrumentato,
aria cantabile, aria di portamento*, and so forth. Brown's definitions are clear
and precise; though always starting from the poetry (most of his examples
are drawn from the works of Metastasio), he does indeed go on to discuss
arias *qua* music, in so far as he describes what each type demands of composer and singer. Curiously, for so lively and scrupulous a writer, he names
no composer, except Handel, and then not in the context of opera. Brown's
discourse seems to relate mostly to his experience of opera in Italy, and the
only reference (albeit oblique) to the King's Theatre ('the unmerciful scra-
pers of our orchestra'—pp. 88–9) is to mention the instruments carelessly
being allowed to overpower the voice. Brown was no fool, but he was an
amateur and his otherwise sympathetic discussion of Italian opera as drama
is hampered by an inability or reluctance to tackle technical issues or to

[1] Walpole, *Correspondence*, xi. 14–15.
[2] Edinburgh: Bell and Bradfute; London: C. Elliot and T. Kay, 1789.

venture any genuine criticism. His *Letters* are thus no substitute for the Burneys' collective chronicle of the Italian opera in London.

Most of the book and pamphlet commentary on the opera was inspired by managerial rows, bankruptcy, and legal wrangles, the famous instances being *The Case of the Opera-House Disputes* (1784) and the bitter pamphlet exchange between William Taylor and Robert Bray O'Reilly in 1791. One of the few exceptions is a substantial book of nearly 150 pages called *The Remarkable Trial of the Queen of Quavers*.[1] We do not pretend to understand this elaborate, jokey, highly personal satire very well. The conceit is that certain persons connected with the opera are being tried for 'Sorcery, Witchcraft, and Enchantment' (there being no other explanation for the attractions of the opera). Some of the hits are obvious (Sack = Sacchini, Jar = Giardini, Signor Wrong-call-ye = Roncaglia), but many others are baffling. The satiric stance seems to range from hostile and scoffing to lightly teasing and even affectionate. Only a *very* well-informed insider would have been able to make sense of the full text, or anything close to it. This odd pamphlet does, however, reinforce an important point in its flagrantly *ad hominem* basis: for most spectators, the opera was its performers, not the music nor the libretto.

Unless one is prepared to comb scattered newspapers for occasional nuggets of operatic commentary, the obvious sources for opera in the 1780s beyond Burney's *General History* are three well-known memoirists: the Earl of Mount Edgcumbe, Michael Kelly, and W. T. Parke. All three are worthy of attention but have decided limitations. None published until the mid-1820s, more than a generation after the events at issue in this book. They were, after a fashion, first-hand observers, but their comments are attended with all the problems of recollection long after the fact.

The most useful is Mount Edgcumbe, whose *Musical Reminiscences* went through four editions between 1824 and 1834. The period 1778–92 receives sixty small pages, including accounts of Mount Edgcumbe's travels through Germany and Italy. He regarded the late eighteenth century as 'the *golden age* of the Opera' (xii) and was essentially a *cognoscente* of great singers. Consequently his book amounts to a series of portraits of those he had heard, and is at times bitterly nostalgic for the lost age of *opera seria* and the heroic castrato. He is factually accurate and often perceptive, but one should remember that he was only 14 years old in 1778.

---

[1] [London:] J. Bew, [early 1778?]. Arnott and Robinson, no. 2065.

Michael Kelly's two volumes of *Reminiscences* (1826), while meandering, anecdotal, self-serving, and increasingly ponderous in volume II, have the undoubted virtue of giving us the views of a performer who was directly involved with opera. The *Reminiscences* are more accurate than some scholars have realized, but they are useful for opera in London only after 1787, when Kelly returned to England from Vienna to work at Drury Lane. He sang briefly at the old King's Theatre, but his account of Italian opera in the late 1780s is that of an outsider looking confusedly in.

The least useful are the massive *Musical Memoirs* (1830) of William Thomas Parke, 'forty years principal oboist to the Theatre Royal Covent Garden'. His account begins in 1784 and reads plausibly enough to the uninitiated. The work is, however, actually a pastiche. No doubt parts of it are genuine reportage of events at which Parke was present, or at least of which he was told by his friends. However, anyone who has read extensively in the newspapers quickly realizes that Parke is often paraphrasing (or simply reprinting) published reports of performances at which he was not present. He was, after all, supposed to attend at Covent Garden six days a week, so when he gives details of performances on particular dates at other houses, one must presume that the material is usually second-hand. Parke's dates are a welcome change from Kelly's airy generalities, but in essence he is often just giving us fragments of newspaper reports that are even harder to assess than such reports are when encountered at first hand. He clearly borrowed from other sources as well—Burney, for instance. Thus Parke's opinion of Bertoni ('though he did not reach the sublime, was often pleasing and occasionally happy'—i. 31) is so close to Burney ('though he never had perhaps sufficient genius and fire to attain the sublime, yet he is . . . often pleasing and sometimes happy'—ii. 890) that we cannot allow it independent authority. Parke is much more sparing in his criticism than Burney or Mount Edgcumbe, and even when he states opinions we cannot be sure that they are his.

With the tantalizing exception of Susan Burney for the season of 1779–80 the critical sources available for the reconstruction and assessment of King's Theatre performances in this period are very limited indeed. This state of affairs leaves one heavily dependent on librettos themselves and the scrappily preserved music for them.

## III. London Style and Practice in the 1780s

How did opera at the King's Theatre differ from that produced at other major Italian opera-houses? Probably less than one might imagine, considering the remoteness of London from the Continental mainstream. The most obvious difference between the King's Theatre and those houses known for mounting new works by leading composers—notably Naples, Milan, Vienna, and St Petersburg—is that London had to rely much more heavily on imports. Nevertheless, at no time during the period under discussion was the King's Theatre without at least one highly respected house composer. In Sheridan's regime, Sacchini, who was regarded as a master of *opera seria*, received several important commissions, though he was past his prime, often unwell, and therefore tended to assemble scores from earlier works. In 1782 Taylor hired Anfossi, who was also immensely experienced and celebrated throughout Europe, though he too did not quite live up to his reputation. Cherubini, at the beginning of a remarkable stage career, produced important work for London in 1785–86 but was hampered by lack of first-rate singers during his stay. In most seasons the company featured two or three newly commissioned works, but the repertoire was dominated by revivals and first London performances of imports, often extensively altered except during the latter part of Gallini's regime (1785–9). Every King's Theatre house composer, even one of Sacchini's stature, was expected to contribute to pasticcios and make arrangements.

### Substitutions and Pasticcios

The *opera seria* repertoire was largely determined by the principal singers, especially the castrati Pacchierotti (1778–80; 1782–4), Rubinelli (1786–7), and Marchesi (1788–90), who were permitted, even encouraged, to bring out works in which they had already triumphed on the Continent. The King's Theatre was further distinguished from other Italian opera-houses by an extremely liberal interpretation of what was called the 'choice of the book', a privilege granted certain performers, usually the *primo uomo* and the *prima donna seria*, to insert whatever music they wished into any work. This practice was known in many opera-houses across Europe but, after Handel, who strongly disapproved, it was carried to extremes in London. Not until the late 1780s did anyone voice much complaint. For example, an article in the *Morning Post* of 9 December 1789 called the practice absurd, because it gave singers 'a preposterous power over the composer'. A wilful *prima donna* could insist on inserting such and such an aria 'without having studied, or without capacity of studying, the fable, characters, and sentiments of the piece'. This attack on the 'choice of the book' was launched at a time when Gallini had begun to offer certain celebrated operas, such as Martín y Soler's *Una cosa rara* and Paisiello's *Il barbiere di Siviglia*, in nearly unaltered form. But the practice of virtually unlimited aria substitution was deeply ingrained in the system. Even newly commissioned original works, such as Anfossi's *I viaggiatori felici* (1782, after Livigni) and Federici's *L'usurpator innocente* (1790, after Metastasio), were affected by the substitution privilege. The latter is an extreme yet by no means isolated example: the *prima donna seria*, Gertrud Mara, insisted that all her arias be replaced with music of her own choosing.

One should not think that aria substitution was always practised, as the *Morning Post* article charged, with complete disregard for composer, plot, or characterization. Pacchierotti was usually sensitive to the drama in making substitutions. Nor could a singer's 'choice of the book' overrule the wishes of the manager who, as is known from the detailed records of the Pantheon, had the final say on all matters artistic. Considerable light is shed on this feature of London production practice by a series of disputes between the King's Theatre manager Francesco Vanneschi and the *prima donna* Regina Mingotti. Though these centred on the singer's failure to perform because of alleged illness, the practices described in Signora Mingotti's *Appeal to the Publick* (London, [1755]) were still commonplace twenty-five years later.

In her *Appeal* Mingotti commented on several operas in which she sang during her first two seasons at the King's Theatre (1754–55 and 1755–56). Despite the presence of an experienced house composer, Giovanni Battista Lampugnani, both she and the manager exercised considerable power in determining the final shape of the librettos and scores. Each work presented a different set of problems. For Signora Mingotti's London début on 9 November 1754, Vanneschi chose Hasse's *Ipermestra*, 'not as *Metastasio* originally writ it, and as it is exhibited in *Vienna* and all other Places', she alleged, 'but curtailed and changed by himself in a most unskilful and absurd manner' (2). The manager cut a duet and transferred the aria 'Tu sai ch'io sono amante' from Ipermestra (Mingotti's role) to Linceo. She protested to the composer Lampugnani,[1] but Vanneschi refused to restore the opera and then had the gall (so Mingotti claimed) to blame her for refusing to sing the duet. This version of Hasse's *Ipermestra*, which might be called a 'revival with alterations', was typical of King's Theatre practice throughout the second half of the eighteenth century. For another production, Jommelli's *Demofoonte* (9 December 1755), which Vanneschi did not apparently like, he allowed the singer to 'put in four of the best Airs I had, though neither my Contract, nor his Usage, entitled him to such Civility' (11). This type of alteration, which we would call a 'revival with substitutions', constitutes the vast majority of London Italian operas during the period. Revivals and imports were not the only works subjected to such treatment. Lampugnani was commissioned to compose a new work, *Siroe* (première 14 January 1755), 'but when *Vanneschi* heard me privately sing the Songs that were allotted me in this Opera, he found them so little to his Taste, that he begged of me as a Favour, to substitute other Songs of other Masters, knowing that I had better Compositions in my Possession' (3–4). Mingotti was referring of course to 'suitcase' arias.

The distinction between an old or new work with a significant number of substitutions and a pasticcio or medley opera is blurred. A true pasticcio may be defined as a patchwork comprising arias of several different composers fitted to a new or existing libretto, serious or comic.[2] It was an accepted form of Italian opera in London, and no strong objections were raised against it until the late 1780s; even then certain critics were enthusiastic about the practice because the pasticcio could bring variety to a dull libretto and allow singers to introduce new music in the latest style. But every pasticcio raises the question: who was in charge? The singers, the manager, the librettist, or the musical arranger? Again, Signora Mingotti is illuminating. When Vanneschi proposed Salvi's libretto *Andromaca* (11 November 1755),[3] she 'made the reasonable Objection, that being a Piece I never sung or heard of before, I had no Air that could fit it. . . . Yet *Vanneschi* had got *Andromaca* in his Head, and jealous of his Judgement and Prerogative, reminded me that he was Manager and Master, and would have it absolutely performed, and take the Chance of the Consequence' (9). Even with a determined manager, co-ordination of the various elements of a pasticcio

---

[1] Thus confirming his presence in London this season; cf. Michael F. Robinson and Fabiola Maffei, 'Lampugnani', *Opera Grove*, ii. 1091.

[2] See Curtis Price, 'Pasticcio', *Opera Grove*, iii. 907–10.

[3] See Sartori, no. 1909; Jommelli's version formed the core of this pasticcio.

was difficult. Signora Mingotti further objected that Vanneschi sent her part in the pasticcio *L'Olimpiade* 'with a Message full of his usual Politeness, that he did not think fit to let me see the Opera-Book [that is, the libretto], and that I had nothing to do, but to learn my Part against the Time that the new Opera was to be exhibited' (11).

In these disputes one can detect the beginnings of the 'choice of the book', but the *prima donna* was held firmly in check by a manager who, as a former librettist, had definite ideas about the operas he produced. In the 1770s, 1780s, and 1790s, the King's Theatre managers were not, by and large, very knowledgeable about the poetry or music of the Italian operas they mounted; when Sheridan, for example, tried to intervene, he threw librettist, composer, and singer into complete confusion. In consequence, more and more authority was passed to the artists themselves, amongst whom the principal singers held the most power. Hence the practice of the 'choice of the book'.

The prerogative granted principal singers was manifested most clearly in the 'Metastasian medley', which lies somewhere between the deliberate patchwork and the revival with substitutions. Several admired and well-used librettos served time and time again as structures on which to hang music that was advertised as being 'newly composed' but was actually a combination of fresh numbers (usually the finales), popular arias, and substitutions, all arranged and co-ordinated by one of the principal house composers—a Sacchini or Cherubini rather than a more menial Mazzinghi or Giardini. The favourite librettos for Metastasian medleys were De Gamerra's *Armida* (or *Rinaldo*), Giovannini's *Giulio Sabino*, Zeno's *Quinto Fabio*, and, above all, those Metastasio classics that were adapted into two-act *opere serie* with longer aria texts and climactic action finales: *Demofoonte, Artaserse, Alessandro nell'Indie,* and *Didone abbandonata.* Since the plots of these works and even many of the aria texts were well known to London audiences, the composer's chief purpose was to provide archetypal arias and ensembles that fulfilled rather than challenged expectation. Whether the music was freshly composed, adapted, or borrowed *in toto* from previous productions mattered little, provided that Alexander's magnanimity, Arianna's despair, or Armida's rage was fully exploited and the right chords of emotion struck.

The pasticcio remains a bugbear to an objective assessment of the nature and quality of Italian opera in eighteenth-century London. It is antithetical to all modern notions of authorial control, structural integrity, and originality. No one would claim that any of the revivals, adaptations, or pasticcios discussed in Chapters 4, 5, and 6 is as musically significant as early Mozart or second-rate Gluck. None the less each pasticcio or revival imported from the Continent needs to be examined as a work in its own right rather than constantly measured against a later model or ancestors from which it is bound to differ, often radically. Adaptation, revision, and substitution were not forms of corruption, but rather unavoidable features of the production process of the time.

## Operas for London

Because of the theatre licensing laws and snobbery associated with the sub-scription system, Italian opera was never really in direct competition with English opera and plays, which appealed to an essentially different audience. But the close proximity of theatres offering everything from Shakespeare to Sheridan forced the managers of Italian opera to be sensitive to English atti-tudes towards dramatic coherence, sophistication, and rationality—the three main grounds on which the foreign opera was consistently attacked.

Until Gallini's regime as manager, few operas composed or first per-formed in Italy were mounted in London without considerable revision.[1] The reasons for the 'choice of the book' are complex, but at the most funda-mental level it was an acknowledgement that a work composed especially for one set of singers would need to be adjusted to accommodate the different vocal characteristics, figures, and bearings of another cast. Only a few operas had achieved the status of classics; they were revived across Europe and in London with some respect for their original texts. Piccinni's *La buona figliuola* is perhaps the best example; later, Paisiello's *Il barbiere di Siviglia* also came close to canonization. However, London was different from most other opera centres in the degree of indulgence it allowed certain singers to make substitutions. Thus even the old and comfortable fabric of Piccinni's minor masterpiece might be soiled by a tasteless or wilful King's Theatre *prima buffa*.

That Italian operas were felt to need adjustment before they could be performed in London points to an English style of production. Some critics defined this style in terms of artistic sabotage: brutal cuts and insensitive substitutions, made all the easier by the audience's incompetence in the Ital-ian language (and alleged loathing of *recitativo semplice*), degraded musical

---

[1] *Pace* Petty, 38, who mentions certain 'operas imported from Italy and performed more-or-less according to their original plan'; until about 1788, these were in fact very few.

taste, and ignorance of the operas in their original form.[1] If, however, we survey the King's Theatre repertoire of the 1780s as a whole, we shall find that the reality is quite different. True, operas receiving their London débuts were invariably cut; but almost all revivals were cut to reduce running time, whether in London or Naples. Nor were cuts necessarily related to the importance of ballet at the King's Theatre, as has been claimed;[2] dance was just as firmly established in those opera-houses (at Venice, Milan, Bologna, and Florence) which were the main suppliers of the King's Theatre repertoire. And what exactly was being cut? To know what model the King's Theatre was following is sometimes extremely difficult; the house composer/arranger often had no access to a copy of a full score of the original work; more commonly, a libretto or short score which had already been cut served as the basis of a production.

Another factor that necessitated revision of Continental operas for London was the protocol of the singers' pecking-order. For example, in serious opera the *primo uomo*'s first aria usually had to come more than half-way into the first act, well after his first appearance, to prevent his being upstaged by the tenor or some lower-ranking singer.[3] And in both *seria* and *buffa* practically the only place where the *ultima parte* was allowed to sing an aria was at the beginning of the second act—traditionally an operatic junkyard. Foreign operas not conforming to these protocols were usually adjusted accordingly, a fact well known to critics, some of whom exaggerated the effects of cuts and rearrangement.

In spite of often extreme revision, most London Italian operas, even pasticcios, offered a high degree of dramatic interest and sophistication. The myth that the alleged unpopularity of simple recitative demanded wholesale, plot-mutilating cuts is not borne out by systematic investigation of the London librettos. In the 1780s at least, simple recitative was treated no more severely than arias, ensembles, or *recitativo accompagnato*. In fact, an amazing amount of simple recitative remained in some comic operas—page after page, scene after scene of dialogue for whose understanding most of the audience had to rely on the translations printed in the librettos and the mimic abilities of the singers. For example, Rauzzini's version of Sarti's *Le*

---

[1] These views are summarized and assessed by Petty, ch. 5, 'English Views on Italian Opera'.

[2] Petty, 40.

[3] For example, the 1778 London production of Gassmann's *L'amore artigiano* was criticized for moving an aria at the request of a principal singer in order to present the piece 'in a stronger point of view'; see Petty, 156.

*gelosie villane* (1784) would appear to be particularly uncompromising, as its subtle plot of unresolved class warfare is told largely in recitative—perhaps the reason that it enjoyed only three performances. Serious opera was little different in this respect; Bertoni's arrangement of Piccinni's *Alessandro nell'Indie* (1780) retains a great deal of the simple recitative; and some of the scenes in Bertoni's *Quinto Fabio* (1780) even continue in recitative after big exit arias.

Of course, *recitativo semplice* depends crucially on good acting, and some King's Theatre singers were better at it than others. The most popular with London audiences—notably Pacchierotti, Nancy Storace, and Gertrud Mara—were also capable of participating in the Lenten oratorios; Storace and Mara could cross over to 'legitimate' English opera at Covent Garden or Drury Lane, for which good declamation, a ready wit, and deportment were as essential as a fine *bel canto*. House composers may occasionally have botched the joins or been forced to make absurd substitutions, but King's Theatre productions were never merely 'concerts in costume'; they were true *drammi per musica* which depended upon full knowledge of all the conventions, however alien to the native theatre.

This is not to say that the King's Theatre offered audiences no concessions at the language barrier. English words and expressions were occasionally thrown in, as were topical references. The 1784 production of Piccinni's *La schiava* included a nightmare scene about bankruptcy with none-too-subtle allusions to the King's Theatre itself. There is even an aria with an English text ('Dear girls, be quiet') in Anfossi's multilingual *I vecchi burlati* (1783). But while topicality is fairly common in *opera buffa* in Italy during the period, only in a few instances do London librettos openly acknowledge their immediate physical surroundings. For example, the popular *basso caricato* Andrea Morigi, after a long absence from England, stepped out of his character Patterio in Anfossi's *I viaggiatori felici* (1782) to greet the audience, partly in their own language. While salutations, oaths, and expressions in French and Spanish regularly find their way into Italian librettos, English interjections are extremely rare. Equally rare are librettos written or adapted specifically to appeal to an English audience. Indeed, some effort was made to suppress English local colour: Burney thought Cimarosa's *L'italiana in Londra* was damaged in its 1788 King's Theatre production (as *La locandiera*) by changing the scene from London to Amsterdam. And when Paisiello's *Le gare generose* was produced in 1787 (as *Gli schiavi per amore*), three 'English' characters were transformed into Frenchmen.

The only King's Theatre poet who showed much concern for English sensibility was Carlo Francesco Badini. His power and influence grew gradually during the 1770s, 1780s, and 1790s, culminating in his libretto for Haydn's abortive *L'anima del filosofo* and heated clashes with Da Ponte in later years. Several of Badini's librettos are experimental in their attempt to break the moulds of post-Metastasian three-act *opera seria* and Goldonian, finale-centred domestic farce. The work with the clearest English resonance is *La governante* (1779). Set by Bertoni, it is based on Sheridan's popular English opera *The Duenna* (1775); Sheridan just happened to be the new co-owner of the King's Theatre, and Badini was obviously trying to curry favour. *La governante* is highly unusual in trumpeting its English origins; the only other case from this period is another Badini libretto, *Il duca d'Atene* (1780), which partly draws on *The Taming of the Shrew*. A much better-known example of Shakespearean adaptation, Storace and Da Ponte's *Gli equivoci* (Vienna, 1786), based on *The Comedy of Errors*, was not produced in London, even though it is probably Storace's finest work.

*Translations*

To understand the plots of Italian operas, most members of the King's Theatre audience had to rely on the parallel English translations printed in all London librettos of the period. The auditorium was lighted specially for this purpose, and loud complaints were heard when it was too dark to read. Opera historians have paid little attention to these translations (except to comment on their general awfulness as poetry), but the dual librettos were vital to the reception and production of Italian opera in London. Whether literal, poetic, or simply inaccurate, the English translations helped shape attitudes towards the alien art form. Intended as texts to be studied outside the theatre and quite independently of the music, they were the chief means by which critics could judge the dramatic merit of the works in question.

There was no shortage of persons capable of translating Italian verse. London boasted a large immigrant Italian community living in and around the Haymarket itself: merchants, dancing- and fencing-masters, musicians, and language teachers. There were also many Englishmen, gentlemen and others, who had lived and travelled in Italy and were willing to lend the house poet a hand. In librettos of the 1770s and early 1780s translators' names appear frequently on title-pages: F[erdinando?] Bottarelli (*Vittorina*, 1777; *La clemenza di Scipione*, 1778; *Il re pastore*, 1778); Mrs Rigaud (*L'avaro deluso*, 1778); Povoleri (*Il soldano generoso*, 1779; *Quinto Fabio*, 1780). For a revival of Gluck's *Orfeo* (1785), the arranger, producer, and principal singer, Giusto Ferdinando Tenducci, also provided the English translation of what was left of Calzabigi's libretto. In 1786–87 Gallini hired a Mr Molini as house translator, an expense that William Taylor regarded as unnecessary (see Ch. 3). Badini, a long-term London resident with great pretensions to language and learning (he even put his academic credentials on the title-pages of his librettos),[1] presumably made his own translations.[2]

Libretto translations fall into three broad categories: the quasi-literal; the poetic; and plot-aiding or -altering. While there is some overlap, one needs to be aware of these different types to appreciate the extent to which the audience was being informed, manipulated, and sometimes misled. Quasi-literal translations are confined to the early years of the decade under discussion and even then are fairly uncommon. The anonymous prose translation of Metastasio's *Ezio* (1782), a pasticcio arranged by Bertoni, is a good example. It eschews versification and makes little attempt to invent poetic conceits. The three types may be concisely illustrated by the first verse of the following trio, which appeared in three different operas. The original Metastasio text reads:

> Tremate, empi, tremate
> Dell'ire mie severe,
> Su quelle fronti altere
> Il fulmine cadrà.

The translation in *Alessandro nell'Indie* (1779) is:

> Dread ye traitors! dread my power
> Loose is broke my wrath severe;
> Your doom is fix'd, this fatal hour
> Shall the vengeful bolts appear

which is both poetic and plot-altering, since the translator has introduced the idea of vengeance to make the trio more relevant to the drama. Compare *Mitridate* (1781):

> Tremble ye traitors!
> Wherefore in my revenge should I be slow?
> Now in my wrath, I'll dash you at a blow.
> Oh vengeance, vengeance!

---

[1] 'A.M. and L.L.B. From the Royal University of Turin'—on the title-page of *La governante* (1779), for instance.

[2] The Pantheon's house poet in 1791–92, Girolamo Tonioli, was expected to provide his own translations. For discussion, see 'Opera and Arson', 88–9.

which also injects the notion of revenge, but is more overtly dramatic, if still execrable poetry. Finally, *Medonte* (1783):

I'll make the wretches tremble, I shall inflict the severest punishments on them.

This is a prose paraphase meant to convey situation and emotion.

Like the first two examples quoted above, the large majority of translations aspire to poetry in their own right. At best, they capture the meaning and tone of the original with language and imagery which is both exotic (to preserve the foreign flavour) and expressed in the familiar metres of contemporaneous English verse. The translation of Badini's *Il duca d'Atene* is a good example, presumably provided by the poet himself. Perhaps the best instance of an extremely free translation that nevertheless conveys the essence of the original is the anonymous rendering of Bertati's otherwise limp pasticcio *La vendemmia* (1789). Agatina, in mock despair and pretending to be a shepherdess, wanders in a wood intoning 'Ove sono? ove m'inoltro', which is whimsically translated 'to be or not to be?' But poetic translations can easily froth up into tasteless verse. That of the anonymous *Il barone di Torreforte* (1781) is consistently overwrought and at times intentionally crude. For example, Armidoro's simple love song 'Siete una amabile', which merely reveals a flame in his heart, is rendered thus: 'I value you more than my nose.' Of course, the crudity may convey something of the nature of the London production. Certainly in the case of *La vendemmia*, the translation suggests that the rather stiff disguise plot was acted as a rollicking farce.

Poetic licence would seem justified in attempting to find suitable vernacular expression of proverbs, which often defy translation. Italian dialects also presented the King's Theatre poets with a challenge. *Napoletano* was sometimes conveyed simply as bad English grammar, while the *commedia dell'arte* scene in Palomba and Cimarosa's *Ninetta*, as adapted by Giardini in 1790, was left untranslated, as was the Turkish scene in Anfossi's version of *L'albergatrice vivace* (1784).

The third kind of translation, which has not been previously commented upon, is that which departs entirely from the Italian original. The most striking case is the anonymous rendition of Sacchini's *Mitridate* (1781), which is as pompous and verbose as the Italian is plain and telegraphic. In fact, the plot would be virtually incomprehensible in places without the English version. The plot-aiding translation could also help to smooth out inconsistencies and to paper over the breaks in continuity that are endemic to the pasticcio and revival with substitute arias. With the complicity of the translator, an all-purpose aria expressing anguish or joy could thus be made to seem apropos. The deception was by no means confined to *opera seria*. For example, in *La vendemmia*, the translation of Agatina's 'Batte, batte in petto il core' relates this vague and cliché-ridden verse directly to the action.

'Deceptive' is perhaps too strong a word to describe this method of translating librettos, but audience perception of dramatic integrity (which could obviously be reinforced by a performance 'in character') is as important to the definition of English-style Italian opera as any 'literary' coherence. In this respect, one should not underestimate the skill of the house poets and composers whose difficult task was to give musical and dramatic consistency to operas that were either deliberately assembled from diverse numbers or whose existing structural integrity was disrupted by the substitution process.

## Musical Sources

Relatively few full scores of Italian operas performed in London in the last third of the eighteenth century survive. Many perished in the fires that totally destroyed the King's Theatre on 17 June 1789 and then the Pantheon on 14 January 1792—though some music was saved from the library of the old King's Theatre. With librettos we are much better provided. Bilingual quartos were prepared for virtually every production except revivals of recent works, and at least one copy has survived for a large majority of the King's Theatre's productions during the period 1778–91.[1] Manuscript copies (in Italian only) were submitted to the Lord Chamberlain's office for censoring in accordance with the Licensing Act of 1737, almost all of which are preserved in the Larpent collection.[2] Because a copy had to be delivered to the Lord Chamberlain's office in advance of the first performance (the interval varies between one or two days and a fortnight) and before the libretto was printed by the opera-house, comparison of the two often reveals the final stages of assembly—alterations, substitutions, cuts, second and third thoughts.

The music of the London Italian operas survives mostly in three kinds of sources: (1) printed excerpts issued within a few weeks or months of the first performance, the so-called *Favourite Songs*; (2) various collections of arias in

[1] These are helpfully catalogued by Sartori.
[2] See Dougald MacMillan, *Catalogue of the Larpent Plays in the Huntington Library* (San Marino: Huntington Library, 1939).

manuscript, prepared for amateurs or collectors, usually long after the event; (3) complete full scores in manuscript. A very few full scores were also printed, but invariably without the simple, obbligato, and accompanied recitative and sometimes also omitting longer ensembles such as finales. *Favourite Songs*, more often in full score than in piano-vocal format, are abundant throughout the period, but are by definition incomplete and, in appealing mainly to the amateur market, grossly distort the works in question. Some of these publications, notably those issued in the late 1770s and early 1780s by Bremner and after 1785 by Longman and Broderip, faithfully reproduce certain numbers in full score, but are often sketchy with respect to orchestration and accompanied recitative.

Who owned rights to the music performed at the King's Theatre was to become the subject of dispute during the 1780s. Prior to 1787, when Stephen Storace sued Longman and Broderip (see Ch. 6, sect. III), the theatre operated on the assumption that the company owned the music and that it could be sold to a publisher or the rights to its sale could be given away as a perquisite. Responding to interrogatories in a lawsuit, Gallini stated that the theatre had not profited from the sale of music during his term as trustee because

he gave the benefit of the printing of it to Leopoldo De Micheli who as this examinant has been informed and believes sold the same to the said Messrs Longman and Broderip for the sum of £40 or thereabouts each season. And this examinant believes it may be true that it had before the year 1785/6 been usual for the managers of the said house to sell music for the sake of making a profit thereby but this examinant believes very little profit was ever made thereby. (C107/201, testimony of 21 July 1789)

Whether rights to full scores and ballet music were deemed separate matters is not known.

As will be explained in Chapters 4 and 5, Italian opera as produced in London underwent a fundamental style change away from the harmonic and contrapuntal sophistication of J. C. Bach and Sacchini to the elegant simplicity of Paisiello and Cimarosa.[1] Stripped of potentially the most interesting and important parts of the operas—the *accompagnato*, ensembles, and finales—the *Favourite Song* collections seem to render the 'new simplicity' into something close to folk music. The commercial market and standard

[1] See Friedrich Lippmann, '"Il mio ben quando verrà": Paisiello creatore di una nuova semplicità', *Studi musicali*, 19/2 (1990), 385–405.

printing formats ensured that only the most loudly applauded arias and duets were included. Since the collections were unabashedly intended for domestic use, difficult, 'scientific' (that is, contrapuntal or harmonically complex), or exceptionally long pieces were rarely printed. A typical issue might include four or five arias sung by Pacchierotti or Marchesi, with emphasis on simple, lyrical pieces—cavatinas and *rondeaux*—second-act 'show-stoppers', jolly duets, and the like. The overtures, whose curtain-raising banality is not improved by five-finger piano arrangements, were nearly always published separately. The manuscript aria collections, which survive in considerable numbers in the British Library and the library of the Royal College of Music, are likewise selections of mostly simple, popular numbers. With a few exceptions, they cannot be linked to specific productions, were probably assembled long after the fact, and are therefore of limited value to this study. Ballet music presents its own problems, which will be addressed in Chapter 7.

The most important collection of late eighteenth-century London Italian opera manuscripts—that owned by the double bass player Domenico Dragonetti and bequeathed by him to Vincent Novello and subsequently acquired by the British Museum—was unfortunately started after the opera-house fires. (Dragonetti came to London in 1794.) For whatever reason, only a handful of full scores of London productions of the 1780s survive. Discussed in detail in later chapters, these may be identified both by their close correlation with the printed librettos (and Larpent copies) and by the presence of the handwriting of Leopoldo De Michele, a former singer and from the late 1770s the main King's Theatre music-copyist. Examples include: Florence, Conservatorio di Musica Luigi Cherubini MS D.1153, a copy of Cherubini's *Giulio Sabino* (London, 30 March 1786); Royal College of Music MS 570, Sarti's *Giulio Sabino* (London, 5 April 1788); British Library RM 22.K.12–13, an adaptation of Paisiello's *Le gare generose* as *Gli schiavi per amore* (London, 24 April 1787); British Library Add. MS 16079, a copy of Paisiello's *Il barbiere di Siviglia* (London, 11 June 1789); and Royal College of Music MS 441, the first act of Paisiello's *La discordia conjugale* (Little Haymarket, 31 March 1792). Closely related to this group is Paisiello's autograph of *La locanda*, commissioned by the Pantheon for the 1790–91 season, but evidently not the direct source for the London première.[1] Beyond these meagre remains, which are nevertheless invaluable

[1] See Robinson, *Paisiello*, i. 488–98.

for the light they cast on the London production process, there are only a few published fragments, the most important being Longman and Broderip's piano-vocal version of Rauzzini's *La regina di Golconda* (*Alina*) of 1784.

From the remarkably complete London scores of Sarti's *Giulio Sabino* and Paisiello's *Gli schiavi per amore*, plus lawsuit testimony, the musical part of the production process in the 1780s can be reconstructed with some confidence. Newly commissioned operas, including pasticcios, were submitted to the manager or assistant manager in short score.[1] Once a piece was approved and scheduled for performance, the composer (or arranger) and his assistants began the orchestration, while a team of copyists, comprising those on regular salary from the opera-house and piece-workers, prepared the full score and orchestra parts, the singers having already begun to learn their roles from separate parts copied from the short score. Insertions and substitutions could be made at any time during the run-up to the première, but were not always copied into the conductor's score or the parts. For revivals and first London productions of important works, especially during Gallini's administration, the score was often assembled from ready-copied fascicles (usually the larger ensembles and finales) acquired from Vienna or Italy, and inserted arias from diverse sources adapted by the house composer or by the director of a particular production, such as Joseph Mazzinghi. The recitative was altered or even composed by the house copyist De Michele, who also undertook transpositions. Shorter cuts were indicated by crayon, longer ones by glueing or stitching deleted pages together. When the text was more or less agreed, a libretto was extracted from the full score and sent to the Lord Chamberlain's office. One will thus appreciate that De Michele was no mere copyist. Every Italian opera company needed someone like him to co-ordinate the musical side of production, but at times De Michele assumed virtually the role of composer. His efficient hack-work and high-handed treatment of genuine composers and lower-ranking singers probably did little to raise general artistic standards, but he did help keep the opera-house running smoothly through some very difficult seasons.

---

[1] See the discussion of Samuel Arnold's *Giulio Cesare* in Ch. 6.

## IV. The King's Theatre, Haymarket, 1705–1789

A key factor in the history of Italian opera in London is its venue. On a site now encompassed by Her Majesty's, Vanbrugh had designed and built a new theatre essentially as a commercial speculation, though he was assisted by some thirty contributions of £100 made by members of the gentry and nobility in return for free lifetime admission to the premises. The Queen's Theatre (as it was originally called) was conceived as a general-purpose home for both spoken English plays and musical entertainments.[1] By the time the Royal Academy of Music was established in 1719 Drury Lane and the 'third' Lincoln's Inn Fields had become the venues for spoken plays, and opera simply took the premises available—which happened to be relatively elegant and also acoustically suitable for music. The Licensing Act of 1737 essentially codified existing practice, and by the 1770s hardly anyone alive could remember a time when the King's Theatre had not been 'the opera-house'. This association was to give the theatre a powerful claim to the opera monopoly, as the Lord Chancellor was to declare in patent hearings for the proposed Leicester Square theatre after the 1789 fire.

Vanbrugh's original design was for a relatively small and decidedly radical theatre. The concept was based on 'emphatic circularity' (in Graham Barlow's phrase): the proportions and geometry of both stage and auditorium were dictated by the radii of circles in their respective centres. Seating in the pit and the arrangement of boxes was circular in pattern. Six 20-foot-high columns supported a gilded cornice, with a dome rising to 40 feet. A very plausible reconstruction has recently been published by Barlow.[2] As originally built, the house had no side boxes; worse, it reportedly suffered from a severe echo. A fairly drastic alteration was undertaken at an uncertain date, but evidently no later than the summer of 1709. Colley Cibber records that

---

[1] See Judith Milhous, 'New Light on Vanbrugh's Haymarket Theatre Project', *Theatre Survey*, 17 (1976), 143–61.

[2] Graham F. Barlow, 'Vanbrugh's Queen's Theatre in the Haymarket, 1703–9', *Early Music*, 17 (1989), 515–21. Barlow's work represents a decided advance on the 'tentative' reconstruction advanced by Richard Leacroft, *The Development of the English Playhouse* (London: Eyre Methuen, 1973), fig. 68.

They contracted its Wideness by three Ranges of Boxes on each side, and brought down its enormous high Ceiling within so proportionable a Compass that it effectually cur'd those hollow Undulations of the Voice formerly complained of.[1]

Analysing these changes, Barlow concludes that they 'deprived the theatre of any of its former individuality and grandeur. . . . The semicircular arrangement of columns supporting the domed arch that had been an architectural triumph was swept away. No longer was this theatre very different from any other playhouse. Vanbrugh's extravagant gesture had been suppressed, and the design was reduced to conformity.'

Evidence about changes in the theatre between 1709 and 1778 is in very short supply. Redecorations of various sorts occurred, particularly during the relatively palmy 1720s under the Royal Academy, but there is no evidence of significant structural alterations. Box-office figures for the years around 1710 suggest that the theatre held about 670 in comfort; 'normal' capacity was about 760; and perhaps as many as 940 could be packed in with extreme crowding.[2] Small as this seems, the budget figures available after 1750 imply that if there was greater capacity by then, it was not often needed.

Most of what we know about the King's Theatre in the middle of the century must be deduced from the floor plan and section published by Dumont.[3] (See Pl. 2.) The Dumont plan shows circular seating (presumably benches) in the pit, side boxes, two galleries, an orchestra pit some 11 feet in depth, an apparently shallow forestage, a very deep stage, and five wing positions. Shutter positions, unfortunately, are not indicated.[4] The proscenium itself is not clearly marked, nor are the proscenium doors that the theatre presumably possessed. The only independent evidence against which we can check Dumont is a sketch plan of Edward Vanbrugh's property, drawn in 1776.[5] The authors of the *Survey of London* note 'one small

[1] *An Apology for the Life of Mr. Colley Cibber*, ed. Robert W. Lowe, 2 vols. (1889; rpt. New York: AMS Press, 1966), ii. 86–7.

[2] See Judith Milhous, 'The Capacity of Vanbrugh's Theatre in the Haymarket', *Theatre History Studies*, 4 (1984), 38–46. Reports of 1,500 and 2,000 attendance in the 1730s are for oratorios and special occasions on which large numbers of people were accommodated on stage and behind.

[3] G. P. M. Dumont, *Parallèle de plans des plus belles salles de spectacles d'Italie et de France* (c.1774). In some copies of Dumont the right–left orientation of both plan and section is accidentally reversed. The origin and date of this plan are not known.

[4] The lines on the stage are probably just a conventional indication of wing-and-shutter scenery arrangements, not an attempt to show particulars.

[5] PRO CRES 6/70, p. 200 (the PRO class was formerly LRRO 63). It is reproduced in

but important addition' in the 1776 sketch, 'the proscenium doors or boxes on the stage'.[1] We interpret these markings as proscenium doors: otherwise Dumont and the 1776 sketch show substantively the same building. There seems a high probability that the Dumont plan shows a theatre that did not change significantly in layout or capacity between 1709 and 1778.

A major renovation of the auditorium was carried out in 1778. Considerable 'alterations repaires and Improvements' on which the proprietors claim to have 'expended several thousand pounds' are reported in PRO C12/947/18. Fired with optimism and grand resolutions, Sheridan and Harris wanted to mark their accession to management with striking changes in the building, at least so far as the public would see it. According to the *Morning Chronicle* of 25 November 1778 they had

at a considerable expence, almost entirely new built the audience part of the house, and made a great variety of alterations, part of which are calculated for the rendering the theatre more light, elegant, and pleasant, and part for the ease and convenience of the company. The sides of the frontispiece are decorated with two figures painted by Gainsborough, which are remarkably picturesque and beautiful; the heavy columns which gave the house so gloomy an aspect that it rather resembled a large mausoleum or a place for funeral dirges, than a theatre, are removed.

The *Morning Post* added on 30 November that Gainsborough's figures represented Music and Dancing, and were painted in white on the side wings before the curtain. Sheridan and Harris evidently spent their money on the public parts of the house. According to an anonymous reviser of the work of Thomas Pennant, these alterations and redecorations were carried out under the direction of 'Mr. *Adams*, who made so entire an alteration, that nothing remained of the original plan'.[2]

No plans of the theatre appear to survive for the years 1778–82. The alterations carried out in 1778 were clearly meant to brighten the auditorium; they were probably also intended to increase the box capacity and hence the potential gross. Lady Mary Coke observed grumpily on 2 January 1779: 'I went this evening to the Opera for the first time & shou'd not have known our Box & am sorry to say the change is not to its advantage. This so much less that if all the subscribers were in it the box wou'd be much crowded.' Whether the capacity of the theatre was increased, or merely the

the *Survey of London*, xxx, pl. 27a.

[1] *Survey of London*, xxix. 227.

[2] Thomas Pennant, *Some Account of London*, 4th edn. (London: Robert Faulder, 1805), 101. 'Adams' presumably means Robert Adam.

number of box seats, there is no way to determine on present evidence. An expenditure of £4,000 implies substantial rebuilding, not merely redecoration. If Pennant is correct, then one result was presumably a major alteration in the seating pattern.

More drastic alterations were apparently considered. A set of plans for an opera-house on the King's Theatre site were published by James Lewis, dated '1779'.[1] *Survey of London* devotes only a desultory paragraph to these plans at the end of its discussion of Adam's grand but unexecuted designs (*c.*1790?) for a new opera-house. By those standards, the Lewis plans are indeed 'on a much smaller scale' and they are undeniably architecturally 'undistinguished'.[2] The Lewis plans should, however, be assessed in the context of 1778, not 1790. We suspect that they represent a more drastic (and too costly) alternative that was abandoned in the summer of 1778 in favour of Adam's refurbishment of the auditorium. The grounds for wanting a completely new building are easy to understand. Vanbrugh had built his theatre on an awkwardly pieced-together site with corridor access to the theatre from the Haymarket on the east and Market Lane on the west, plus a special 'royal' entrance from the 'King's Yard'. Because the opera-house was thus erected behind other buildings facing the street, the Haymarket frontage was small and unimposing. In the two decades before 1778 the dominant French and Italian concepts of theatre design had evolved considerably. What had become *de rigueur* on the Continent was a small, elegant horseshoe auditorium with tiers of boxes embedded in the midst of a grand, free-standing civic temple, with a principal façade and public promenades as impressive as the theatre itself. At almost exactly this time Luigi Piermarini was designing his Teatro alla Scala and Victor Louis his Grand Théâtre de Bordeaux—huge edifices emphasizing architectural show and public space. By comparison, the old King's Theatre was cramped, utilitarian, practically invisible from the outside, and altogether lacking the grandeur and sweep of what was being built on the Continent.

The reasons that Lewis's design remained unexecuted are obvious. An enormous amount of capital would have been required for construction; another venue for the opera would have had to be found for at least a year;

---

[1] James Lewis, *Original Designs in Architecture*, i (London: Printed for the Author, 1780), 12–13 and pls. XIX–XXII. For an account of these plans, see Judith Milhous and Robert D. Hume, 'James Lewis's Plans for an Opera House in the Haymarket (1778)', *Theatre Research International*, forthcoming.

[2] *Survey of London*, xxix. 250.

and the proprietors would have had to acquire all the shops and houses facing the Haymarket to the east and Pall Mall to the south—itself a matter of considerable difficulty and expense. The Lewis plans do show, however, that someone (probably the over-ambitious Sheridan) was starting to think in the terms current in France and Italy. A decade later the proposal for a new opera-house in Leicester Square in 1790 and Novosielski's design for the new King's Theatre, Haymarket, of 1791 show how strongly this grandiosity had affected the audience's notions of what such a building should be. But in 1778 or 1779 the 'civic temple' theory of an opera-house was not yet within the realm of possibility in London.

## The Alterations of 1782

Over the summer of 1782 the new proprietor, William Taylor, gutted his building and constructed an entirely new stage and auditorium. The reconstruction was carried out under the direction of Michael Novosielski, who was also to be the architect of the new theatre of 1791. He stayed within the outer walls of the theatre proper, which imposed some significant limitations, but he drastically altered the balance between stage and auditorium. The purpose was manifestly to expand capacity, especially box capacity. Taylor had good reason to believe there would be demand: Vestris-mania had created public interest, and twelve boxes had been added as recently as the season of 1781–82 (*Public Advertiser*, 23 November 1781).[1]

Most of what is known about the theatre as it existed between 1782 and the fire of 1789 must be deduced from two surviving plans—which are unfortunately somewhat contradictory in a number of respects. Neither has been carefully considered by theatre historians, and no attempt has yet been made at an architectural reconstruction. The better-known plan was printed in the *Survey of London* (xxx, pl. 27*b*), labelled 'Plan probably made by Novosielski for the alterations of 1782'.[2] (See Pl. 3.) This Soane Museum plan shows the same general ground and wall plan as Dumont, but presents drastically revamped interior proportions and logic. The crux of the matter is the proportion of space devoted to stage versus the proportion devoted to the auditorium. Omitting the vista stage extension (the room labelled 'Chambre servant à alonger le Théatre' to the south of the stage in his plan), Dumont shows a ratio of approximately 2:1, calculating the auditorium

[1] For analysis of the financial implications, see Ch. 2.
[2] The plan is preserved in Sir John Soane's Museum, drawer 61, set 5, no. 9 (formerly drawer 38, set 3, no. 9).

from the outer edge of the orchestra pit. That all of the stage depth was used for many productions may be doubted, but the balance of the building is obviously tilted heavily towards the stage, with only about 33 per cent of the total depth devoted to the auditorium. In the Soane Museum plan the ratio is about 4:3.5, or much more nearly equal. We calculate that roughly 45 per cent of the total length was devoted to the auditorium (again omitting the vista stage, which remained available). Calculating precise dimensions from such plans (even supposing them to be meticulously accurate) is risky, but precise figures are not the point here. What the Soane Museum plan shows is an increase on the order of 35 per cent in the space devoted to audience seating—and of course a corresponding reduction in space available for the stage.

The authors of the *Survey of London* (xxix. 231) note that 'Novosielski's remodelling . . . must have removed all traces of Vanbrugh's interior except the stone gallery behind the pit' and that 'The depth of the working stage was reduced to add length' to the auditorium. One must question, however, their comment that the auditorium was 'planned on the conventional lines of an Italian opera-house, with a large pit and five shallow tiers of [boxes in] horseshoe form'. The Capon drawing of 1785 (*Survey*, xxx, pl. 25 b) shows only four tiers of boxes, and *A Descriptive Plan of the New Opera House* published during the season of 1782–83 proves that there were three tiers, with boxes on either side of the stage in a fourth partial tier at the level of the Crown Gallery. (See Pl. 4.) The Soane Museum plan shows the side boxes only very slightly out of parallel. As compared with the pronounced horseshoe of the Repton alteration of 1816–18 (*Survey*, xxx, pl. 32 b), this is only a beginning of a move towards the familiar nineteenth-century concept of an opera-house auditorium.

Whether the Soane Museum plan represents what was actually built is unknown. The second extant plan—one that does explicitly claim to show the King's Theatre as it was in the 1780s—was published by Saunders in 1790.[1] (See Pl. 5.) Saunders's plan agrees with the one in the Soane Museum in many respects, but also exhibits 'considerable differences' (in the words of the *Survey*). Saunders shows parallel side boxes, a smaller orchestra pit, a deep apron, and a shallow working stage. The proportion of stage to auditorium is 4.25:5, thus devoting a startling 54 per cent of the length of the whole to the auditorium. The proscenium (and its doors) are

---

[1] George Saunders, *A Treatise on Theatres* (London: Printed for the Author, 1790), pl. X.

not clearly indicated. Saunders shows the vista stage space precisely as other plans do. His accompanying description deserves to be given in full.

This theatre underwent several alterations, the principal of which was in 1782, when it was enlarged under the direction of Mr. Novosielski. The form was then made an oblong rounded off at the end opposite the stage. The length was, from the stage-front to the opposite boxes, about 58 feet, and 23 feet more to the scene; the breadth between the boxes 43 feet; and the height 44 feet from the centre of the pit to the ceiling. There were three ranges of boxes, 34 in each range, besides 18 in a line with the gallery; in all 116, allowing the space of two for entrances into the pit. Each box was from 5 to 6 feet wide, from 7 to 7 feet 6 inches high, and 6 feet deep. Those in the first range being on a level with the stage, had their fronts continued in one even line to the central box; but all the ranges above, as also the first gallery, pro-jected in curved lines over the pit.[1] A second gallery was managed in the cove of the ceiling, which was groined for that purpose. Five entrances led into the theatre; three from the Haymarket, and two from Market-lane.

Being confined to the original walls, Mr. Novosielski had not the opportunity of giving it a greater width; the form therefore remained extremely bad, and the stage and it's appendages wretchedly confined and inconvenient. But I will desist from particularising these defects which were unavoidable, and speak of such as in my opinion might have been avoided.

The only assistance sound can have to reach the end of a long, confined space, is plain and smooth surfaces to conduct it: instead of which, the line of the box-fronts in this theatre was continually broken by the projecting curves, and these covered with paper ornaments, which were liberally distributed in every part of the theatre. The first gallery was low and inconvenient, and very little could be either discerned or heard there by those who were situated behind. The second gallery by being next to the ceiling was the best situation in the house for hearing, but very prejudicial to every other part. And thus that which was of necessity bad was rendered still worse, by adopting almost every means in the finishings, that could oppose the progress of sound. (79–81)

Saunders's plan is crude in its details and gives virtually no idea of the actual arrangement of the stage. The authors of the *Survey* are dismissive of it, in part because it reports 116 boxes instead of the 100 shown in the list of box-subscribers for 1782–83. This discrepancy is actually testimony in Saunders's favour: newspaper and diary reports during the mid-1780s prove that addi-tional boxes had been squeezed into the auditorium.[2] We are, therefore,

---

[1] This may account for an apparent discrepancy between the Saunders and Soane Museum plans.

[2] See the *Morning Post*, 12 Jan. 1785, *Morning Chronicle*, 14 Jan. 1785, and Lady Mary Coke, 15 Jan. 1785, on the abrupt appearance of eight new boxes in the course of a week.

decidedly sceptical about the wisdom of dismissing Saunders on account of such 'inaccuracies' and concluding that the Soane Museum plan 'is in the main reliable' (*Survey*, xxix. 231). The relationship of that plan to what Novosielski actually built is not determinable (it could easily have been a discarded sketch), while Saunders at least purports to show the remodelled theatre itself. There is no doubt that the Soane Museum plan shows a more attractive and desirable theatre, and that it is the more detailed representation. Which plan best represents the reality of the mid-1780s may never be known. What really matters is that both show a major expansion of the auditorium at the expense of stage space.

The rebuilding of 1782 was unquestionably much more drastic than the renovation of 1778. The *Morning Herald* of 28 October 1782 reported that 'On Friday the workmen employed at the new Opera-House were discharged. . . . The number that have been at work there since June last, has been some times near 300, and never less than 200.' According to O'Reilly, Taylor variously claimed a total expense of between £8,000 and £10,000 for the project.[1] William Taylor's description in a 1785 lawsuit is terse but telling: 'in the Summer of the Year [1782, your Orator] caused the whole of the Inside of the said Theatre to be pulled down and rebuilt the same with an additional Thirty Six intirely New Boxes which Increased the Yearly Subscriptions for Boxes . . . from about £4700 . . . to £8800.' The expense (he says here) was more than £4,000 for labour and nearly as much for materials.[2]

The results were variously described in the newspapers—but more often gushingly and impressionistically than helpfully. The *Public Advertiser* of 4 November 1782 says that the theatre

is very striking in its Effect, and not unpleasing;—if it appears 'too full of Gauds', it is therefore adapted to the Genius of the Opera. . . . The *Boxes* are . . . three Rows in Front of the House, and four Stories on the Sides; in all, we believe, increased to the Number 99! The *Pit* is enlarged apparently a good deal; it contains now nineteen Rows of Benches. The *First Gallery* is somewhat increased, and is more open than before. The *Upper Gallery*, though the Slips be taken into the Account, appears a good deal diminished.—The *Lobbies and Staircases* are extremely improved:—They are now so spacious as to admit three or four Persons to pass a-breast. The *Frontispiece* is formed by two large Corinthian Pillars, which advance some Feet on the Stage, and in their *Base* contain the *Prompter*, who

---

[1] O'Reilly, *An Authentic Narrative*, 16–17.
[2] C12/2012/53, bill of complaint (22 Apr. 1785).

through a small Aperture in each Pillar, communicates with the Persons on the Stage.—A great Improvement this, from the old Trap-door in Front.

The best description of the 1782 theatre we have discovered is in an unidentified cutting in the New York Public Library, dated in manuscript '4 November 1782'.

On Saturday night this Theatre was opened for the first time this season. The splendid alterations which have been made in it, in the course of the Summer, have made it the general subject of conversation in the fashionable circles; high ideas of its brilliancy have been formed; and if we might judge from the impression that its appearance made on the audience of Saturday night, it was pronounced to be the most superb, if not the largest Theatre in the Universe. The alterations do great credit to the taste and talents of M. Novosielski, and to the munificence of the manager. The house presents, altogether, a new appearance. It forms a horseshoe—the galleries have an equal projection with the boxes, by which the rounding of the whole is regular and unique. The pit is considerably enlarged; we understand 16 feet by 14. The first order in the formation of the boxes is the Doric. The columns are covered with looking glass, with gold margins. The two first ranges of boxes form regular inter-columniums, there being four boxes in each. The ground range of boxes is ornamented with festoons of flowers in gold on a lace ground. The boxes in the second row, project and form the segment of a circle.—The centre is devised with emblematical figures of music in chiaro scuro ornamented in grotesco. The centre figure is gilt in mosaic on a green ground; and the sides are a laloc ground, also gilt in mosaic. The Doric finishes on top of this row with a frieze fluted, and gilt ornaments. The third row of boxes has a parapet; they also project in the circular form of the second row, and pilasters rise out of the entablature, as a continuation of the Doric columns, and terminate in cariatides. This change of the order gives a beautiful lightness and variety to the whole.—The boxes on this range have their peculiar decorations.—On a tablet in the centre, there are musical instruments, gilt in mosaic on a yellow ground, with ornaments in chiaro scuro. On the sides, there are festoons of natural flowers on a laloc ground.

The fourth row of boxes presents a ballustrade in chiaro scuro with gilt ornaments. This ballustrade is continued along the front of the crown gallery, which thereby gives an uniform appearance to the whole.

The cariatides support an Ionic capital, gilt; the entabliture crowns the whole of the space from the stage to the gallery; the architrave of which is painted in a marble colour with gilt mouldings; the frieze is gilt in mosaic, on a green ground, with white ornaments; the cornish is marble, and the mouldings heightened with gold.

The cove is done in lunettes, or half moons, which form the upper gallery; they are divided with small pannels, gilt in mosaic on a green ground. The pannels are triangular, with marble ornaments, and a figure in the centre border is done in the same style; and the whole is finished with a border and open sky.

The frontispiece is the Corinthian order; the columns white marble, fluted; and the listels [*sic*] in gold, as are the base and capitals. It is crowned with the King's Arms.

There are in the whole one hundred and ten boxes [evidently an error]. They are lined with paper, a light green, with a jessamin sprig; and the cushions are covered with crimson sattin.

The staircases and passages are commodious and elegant, and the staircase to the galleries in particular was very much admired. It has a double revolution, which gives it great curiosity; we understand the only one of the same construction in England is at the house of Earl Spencer at Wimbledon.[1]

Other descriptions (for example, in the *Morning Herald* of 4 November) are less detailed but likewise concentrate on decoration and alterations in seating. Lack of commentary on changes in staging implies that the theatre retained its customary technical capacities but did not expand them. One of the few comments devoted to practical matters appears in the *Morning Herald* of 6 November, where a correspondent praises 'the ventilators which are placed along the top of the second gallery; they not only answer the purpose better, in admitting a more free circulation of air' but also leave the painted decoration of the ceiling unfragmented. In sum, no great thought appears to have been devoted to the stage or the technical fittings of the theatre (or even its acoustics), but capacity was substantially expanded and immense pains were taken with the decoration of the auditorium.

## The Capacity of the 1782 Theatre

For the purposes of understanding the King's Theatre's finances during the *Sturm und Drang* years of the 1780s a knowledge of its auditorium capacity is crucial. Neither the *Survey of London* nor Nalbach offers even a speculation on this subject, before or after the 1782 reconstruction. Fortunately, evidence does exist that permits calculation of how large an audience the theatre could hold just before the 1789 fire.

The number of pit and gallery places may be deduced from daily account-books for the seasons of 1786–87 and 1787–88 preserved in the Beinecke Library at Yale. They concern only cash received for pit and gallery tickets, and ignore subscription income and attendance by box-holders. For each performance the box-office prepared a fixed number of tickets, and then added the total 'sold' to the total 'returned' by the ticket-sellers to verify that all the tickets were duly accounted for. As a rule, 500 tickets were

---

[1] New York Public Library MWEZ x n.c. 8684.

printed for the pit (100 for the 'King's Door' and 400 for the 'Haymarket Door'), plus 300 for the first gallery and 200 for the second gallery. Since attendance averaged no more than about 50 per cent of these totals, there were normally a lot of unsold tickets.

On extraordinary occasions, however, extra tickets had to be prepared. By far the largest pit total recorded in these two seasons was 644 on Saturday, 5 April 1788 at the London première of Sarti's *Giulio Sabino* when Marchesi made his eagerly anticipated English début. On that day 400 tickets were prepared for the first gallery and 236 for the second; sales were 285 and 204 respectively.[1] Thus for that performance the theatre offered 660 pit tickets and 636 gallery tickets for sale (a total of 1,296), of which 1,133 were actually sold. To this number must be added sales at 'the Office' (as opposed to the door): 47 pit tickets, 6 for the first gallery, and 2 for the second. The implied total capacity for pit and galleries would be about 1,350, probably including some people seated on stage and some standees (see below).[2] How close to full did this make the theatre? Mount Edgcumbe comments that on this night 'the theatre was not only crowded to the utmost in every part, but on the rising of the curtain, the stage was so full of spectators that it was some time before order and silence could be obtained, and with some difficulty that Marchesi, who was to open the opera, could make his way before the audience'.[3] Since the box-office figures do not specify sale of places on stage, one can deduce that some of the extra 'pit' tickets represent temporary seating on the stage.

To obtain a total capacity for the theatre one also needs to know how many people could be accommodated in the boxes. This is fairly easy to calculate from the 1788 and 1789 subscriber lists.[4] The theatre had 100 numbered boxes, plus sixteen irregular ones added between 1782 and 1788. They held varying numbers of people, and the list poses a few problems (for example, Boxes 14 and 15 belonged to the Duke and Duchess of Cumberland, and the list does not specify the names of other occupants, or how

---

[1] The highest total gallery sale recorded was 303 and 205 (a total of 508) on 5 Feb. 1788, when 325 and 212 had been prepared.

[2] The *Morning Chronicle* says on 1 Nov. 1782 that the 'first gallery at the Opera-house, in consequence of the present alterations in it, will contain between seven and eight hundred people'. In the light of the Yale account-book totals this appears to be an exaggeration, even for both galleries together.

[3] *Musical Reminiscences*, 61.

[4] *A List of the Subscribers to the Boxes at the King's-Theatre, 1788* (Harvard Theatre Collection, Thr 465.45.4) and British Library 163.g.66.

many others could be accommodated). However, by counting the names and allowing for such anomalies, we arrive at a total of about 480 places in the boxes in 1782, and roughly 540 at the end of the decade. Adding upwards of 500 box seats to *c.*660 places in the pit and *c.*640 in the two galleries yields a total capacity of some 1,800 for the theatre.

This must, of course, be regarded as an elastic figure. Theatres with benches do not have the precise capacities possessed by theatres with individual seats. If Mount Edgcumbe is to be believed, 1,800 represented a jampacked theatre. We may guess from the usual total of tickets printed that a more comfortable normal capacity was in the vicinity of 1,500.

## V. The Outlook in 1778

In the mid-1770s the Italian opera at the King's Theatre, Haymarket, had settled into a rut. The company was solvent, but unadventurous in either opera or ballet. The presence of Sacchini as the star house composer contributed to a sense of complacency, but his powers of invention were beginning to diminish; the Italian opera in London was forced to follow developments on the Continent, and rarely led them. Entrenched tradition opposed fundamental changes. Throughout the 1770s and 1780s singers continued to dominate the repertoire through the 'choice of the book' and by their sheer celebrity and virtuosity. Opera and ballet were kept almost entirely separate, with complete ballets put on between the acts of an unrelated opera.

All this was part of a long-established *modus operandi*. But to an observer knowledgeable about recent developments on the Continent, change was in the air. Tenors were beginning to replace the long-dominant castrati, and composers were starting to claim a more substantial share of power and attention in the operatic process. The recruitment of Haydn to London in 1790, and the Pantheon's attempt to hire Mozart at the same time, were no coincidence. The most explosive changes, however, were in the realm of ballet. In the early 1760s the great Jean Georges Noverre had publicized if not created the concept of *ballet d'action* at the Stuttgart opera, and the idea spread like wildfire from opera-house to opera-house. Noverre had started from the conventional treatment of ballets as 'spectacles for the eyes alone, pleasing by their pattern and their colouring'.[1] In his second Lyons period

---

[1] Lynham, *Chevalier Noverre*, 50.

in the late 1750s he began to incorporate techniques of vivid mime and to appeal to human emotions. In Stuttgart he put the pieces together and began to tell serious stories. Londoners had been increasingly fascinated by dance during the 1760s and 1770s: that the *ballet d'action* would be introduced and would prove immensely popular was a virtual certainty.

In 1778 the King's Theatre was well placed to capitalize on Continental developments. Opera retained tremendous social cachet; ballet was ripe for exploitation. With some shrewd hiring and good publicity, an immense increase in subscriptions and attendance ought to have been easy to attract—as indeed proved to be the case. In the course of five years, attendance and gross receipts approximately doubled. The difficulty was to be the debts incurred when the theatre was bought in 1778. The purchaser ought to have been Giovanni Andrea Gallini. According to O'Reilly, Antoine Le Texier offered James Brooke 20,000 guineas for his five-sixths interest ('as it is supposed for Mr. Gallini').[1] This was an extravagantly generous offer, and it ought to have left Gallini in control of the King's Theatre—and in charge of the destiny of opera in London—for the rest of the century. When Richard Brinsley Sheridan and Thomas Harris outbid him, the theatre fell into the hands of absentee owners who knew little about opera.

Sheridan and Harris bought the opera-house as part of a grand plan for a theatrical monopoly. By the terms of the Licensing Act of 1737, Covent Garden and Drury Lane held sole rights to performance of spoken drama (though a 'summer' patent had been granted to Samuel Foote for the Little Haymarket in 1766). Buying the King's Theatre gave them a virtual stranglehold on upper-class London entertainment from October through June, and the owner-managers had long since arrived at a comfortable cartel agreement (never written down, so far as we know) to minimize competition and control actor salaries. What they were doing was unpopular but legally unassailable, unless someone could persuade King and Parliament to license a third winter theatre.[2] The proprietors of Covent Garden and Drury Lane naturally resisted any such incursion on their monopoly, and

---

[1] *An Authentic Narrative*, 5.

[2] For a bitter complaint about this cartel and the misuse of public authority in support of keeping the theatre private property to be exploited for private profit, see anon., *Theatrical Monopoly, being an Address to the Public on the Present Alarming Coalition of the Managers of the Winter Theatres* (London: Fielding and Walker, 1779).

did so with success for many years.[1] The expensive and ill-advised purchase of the King's Theatre by Sheridan and Harris in 1778 was thus part of a grand scheme for profit-making by means of monopoly. The partnership quickly came apart, and the opera company was left with the debts they ran up, including the entire purchase price. Sheridan and Harris had some good ideas. They redecorated the opera-house; hired an innovative foreigner (Le Texier) to serve as artistic director; and encouraged prompt importation of *ballet d'action*. They were a bit unlucky: increased cash flow failed to cover debt service and increased costs; Le Texier proved cranky, irresponsible, and a poor administrator. None the less the years 1778–81 were artistically exciting: the company hired a great *primo uomo* (Pacchierotti), a major dancer (Vestris jun.), and started doing some things entirely new to London.

This book is a study of a theatre in artistic and financial crisis. One might easily jump to the conclusion that the financial and managerial upheavals of the 1780s were the direct cause of artistic difficulties and failures. This is, in fact, only partially true. The relationship was far more complex and long-term. Italian opera at the King's Theatre was a remarkably resilient institution, exotic and alien to English culture, but a well-oiled machine that could continue to function under highly adverse circumstances. As balkanized as the company was, it tended to resist broad artistic vision, but its component departments could do their jobs despite absentee ownership, ignorant management, bankruptcy, endless lawsuits, receivership, irresponsible trustees, and budget caps imposed by the Court of Chancery. Ballet suffered in the later 1780s, but the company actually produced its best operatic work under Gallini while he functioned as trustee under hostile supervision of the court, with the owner bankrupt. In the long haul, however, the immense debts contracted in the early 1780s proved unpayable, inescapable, and disastrous. We now turn, therefore, to an account of ownership and management—which is essentially a tale of how the King's Theatre got into a financial mess from which it was never able to recover.

---

[1] For discussion, see Joseph Donohue, 'The London Theatre at the End of the Eighteenth Century', in *The London Theatre World, 1660–1800*, ed. Robert D. Hume (Carbondale: Southern Illinois University Press, 1980), ch. 12.

# CHAPTER 2

# *Ownership, Management, and Finances*

THE most crucial event in the history of opera in late eighteenth-century London was the sale of the King's Theatre and its opera company to a partnership headed by Richard Brinsley Sheridan in 1778. The sale itself is well known, though its significance has never been recognized. Sheridan took little part in the management of the opera-house, and he sold out after just three seasons. But the catastrophic tangle of debt he left behind was to haunt Italian opera in London for nearly seventy years.

The last decade of the old King's Theatre before the fire of 1789 is in large part the story of a viciously fought battle for possession of the theatre. Sheridan bought it in 1778, could not make it pay, and passed it on to his friend William Taylor. When Sheridan engineered his ill-advised purchase, he outbid Gallini, who was fanatically determined to become proprietor of the opera-house. Gallini bought up Sheridan's mortgage and spent the next seven years trying to batter his way into legal possession of the premises. After Gallini became manager in 1785 he found himself under permanent legal siege by the deposed Taylor, who was at least equally fanatic in his determination to regain his lost kingdom. Many other players participated in this long-fought civil war, some of them important and some transitory performers of bit parts. The infighting is incredible and the financial tangles bewildering. The reader may wish, therefore, to cling to the most basic facts. Sheridan bankrupted the theatre in a reckless leveraged buyout, and the next decade was devoted to Gallini's attempt to dislodge Taylor and gain secure possession of the opera-house. The company went publicly bankrupt in 1783 and operated under trustees the rest of the decade. Yet in the midst of this chaos, it somehow managed to hire some of the foremost performers in Europe and mount artistically distinguished seasons.

## I. The Sheridan–Harris Administration, 1778–1781

*The Sale of 1778 and its Financing*

Our story begins with the sale of the opera-house to ambitious and theatrically experienced new owners. On 26 January 1778 Sheridan (principal owner and manager of Drury Lane) and Thomas Harris (his counterpart at Covent Garden) agreed to purchase a five-sixths interest in the King's Theatre from James Brooke, Richard and Mary Yates, and John and Frances Brooke.[1] (The remaining sixth was owned by Peter Crawford.) The sale was consummated on 24 June 1778 in a six-part indenture preserved in C107/64. By this agreement Sheridan and Harris agreed to pay £22,000 for their five-sixths interest—£10,000 down plus a mortgage of £12,000 to be paid off in four annual instalments due on 24 June 1779, 1780, 1781, and 1782. Pending payment of the mortgage, they assigned the entire property in trust to the banker Henry Hoare of Fleet Street and posted bond of £24,000 guaranteeing payment.

Why should competing managers with no background in opera combine to purchase the King's Theatre? Sheridan had bought Garrick's interest in Drury Lane in 1776, and with the première of *The School for Scandal* in 1777 he had become the golden boy of English drama. He was famous, handsome, articulate, and full of grand schemes and vaulting ambition. He was to be one of the great figures in the House of Commons in the next thirty years—a brilliant debater who was usually in the forefront of the opposition. But Sheridan was also financially incompetent. He made a shambles of Drury Lane and was kept out of debtors' prison only by his seat in Parliament. This description, however, relies on hindsight. In 1778 Sheridan was a dazzling success and a social lion. He made an odd partner for Thomas Harris: circumstances, not temperament, brought them together. Harris bought into Covent Garden in 1767 and became principal manager in 1774. He was testy, prickly, and grasping, but also an honest man. Harris was both financially prudent and a very skilful day-to-day theatre manager. Sheridan's glib tongue persuaded him into a venture he was soon to rue.

Their joint purchase of the opera-house was part of a grandiose but short-lived scheme for a theatrical monopoly. The 1778–79 season marks the beginning of what was known at the time as the 'coalition' between Covent

[1] C12/2012/53.

Garden and Drury Lane.[1] At £22,000 the opera-house must have seemed like a relative bargain: Covent Garden had been sold in 1767 for £60,000, and a half share in Drury Lane had brought £35,000 in 1776. So able a theatre manager as David Garrick reportedly believed that 'the Opera House would prove a mine of gold, if conducted with ability'.[2] As for their plans, Harris informs us that they paid the price they did ('many thousands more than the property had been at any time before sold for') 'in contemplation of occasionally performing English pieces [that is, plays], under the authority of a dormant Patent, in the possession of Mr. Harris'.[3] Nothing came of this scheme for adding English plays to the theatre's offerings.

The King's Theatre had been sold in 1765 for £14,000;[4] implicitly six-sixths were now worth £26,400. There is no hard evidence as to the profits it had made in the 1770s (if any). But the buyers seem to have thought they could produce £3,000 per annum (plus interest) from somewhere to pay off the mortgage. To compound the problem, the £10,000 actually paid in June 1778 was borrowed: Sheridan and Harris put up virtually no cash when they bought the concern.[5] They apparently believed that it would generate enough cash to pay their debt service, which was a gross miscalculation.

On or about 1 October 1778 Sheridan and Harris sold thirty-eight 'renters' shares' in the theatre. For £300 per share, an investor would receive £20 per annum for a period of twenty-one years (a total return of £420), plus the right of free 'personal admission' into the theatre for all entertainments.[6] Had the investors been paid, this would have created a £760 drain on the

---

[1] For discussion, see *The London Stage*, Part 5, i. 191–3, 273, and above, Ch. 1, sect. v.

[2] Quoted by O'Reilly, *An Authentic Narrative*, 5, as part of some advice given by Garrick to Edward Vanbrugh in 1777. Garrick bought four renters' shares in the opera-house in 1778, expressing himself 'a little thoughtful' about the investment, 'but not uneasy—my Security is tolerably good'. See *The Letters of David Garrick*, ed. David M. Little and George M. Kahrl, 3 vols. (Cambridge: Harvard University Press, 1963), nos. 1182 and 1184.

[3] *Morning Chronicle*, 24 May 1783. The original patents had been united in 1682 and descended through the Rich family to Harris as proprietor of Covent Garden. Whether the Killigrew patent could be split off and used to authorize another theatre was a subject of endless legal dispute extending into the nineteenth century. British Library Add. MS 12201 comprises copies of documents collected in connection with a legal opinion sought on this subject from Francis Hargrave in March 1793, together with a dozen pages of 'Hargrave's Observations' on the points at issue.

[4] The indenture of sale is preserved among the papers in C107/65, 25 Nov. 1765.

[5] They tried to obfuscate this fact in their testimony, but William Taylor's answer of 24 May 1782 in C12/947/18 candidly admits that the £10,000 down payment was borrowed, and that the renters' shares sold in Oct. 1778 were designed to cover that loan.

[6] Full terms are specified in the sales agreement executed by Henry Kendall with Sheridan and Harris on 1 Oct. 1778, preserved in the Theatre Museum, V&A (King's Theatre Box, 1778).

theatre's income every year until the end of the century. The point was to raise as much as possible of the £10,000 down payment that the new owners had borrowed. In theory the shares should have brought in £11,400 at face value, and some were actually sold for £300. A substantial number, however, were sold at a discount to Albany Wallis, who then sold them for whatever he could get.[1] As a result, the sum raised seems to have been only £7,000–8,000.[2] As best as can be determined, the £2,000 balance due was borrowed from Drummonds' Bank, which demanded collateral security that was given on 19 June 1779 (C107/65). Thus for little more than a third of the purchase price the theatre would ultimately be liable for £15,960, plus the loss of up to thirty-eight paid admissions per night for twenty-one years—which could amount to a hypothetical total of nearly £1,000 per annum or an additional £20,947 over the whole term. Most of those entitled to free admission would not, of course, have bought tickets every night, but the long-term loss to the theatre was substantial.

For the opera to make its expenses was a chancy business. To expect its income to cover large sums of interest and principal for a speculative purchase was unreasonable. To mortgage future income was a dangerous violation of the policy established in 1767 by the previous owners Gordon, Vincent, and Crawford 'not to incumber the Theatre with any *Renters Shares*, without the joint concurrence of all parties'.[3] Crawford reportedly protested in a letter of 14 October 1778, but to no avail. Sheridan and Harris were legally entitled to do what they did. They had not been parties to the 1767 agreement, and they owned five-sixths of the business. They could legitimately point out that Covent Garden and Drury Lane regularly raised capital by selling renters' shares. The fact remains that encumbering the future income of a business with so questionable a balance sheet was a profoundly bad idea.

### Theatre Capacity and Opera Income c.1778

To assess the logic of Sheridan and Harris's purchase one needs to try to calculate the potential gross income that could be generated by the opera-house. Income came from three sources: season subscriptions for places in the boxes; nightly sales of tickets for pit and gallery seats; and rents paid for

---

[1] C12/195/32 reports in passing the assignment of annuities no. 24 and 27 to Jonathan Garton by Wallis on 2 Oct. 1778.

[2] O'Reilly, *An Authentic Narrative*, 7.

[3] Ibid. 3–4; following reference to 7–8.

use of the coffee-house and some small houses on the theatre property. Rents appear to have produced only a few hundred pounds per annum. Subscriptions produced 20 guineas (£21) per head for fifty performances. If more than fifty were given, then some subscribers might re-engage for the remainder of the season (10–20 nights). A key limitation on the theatre's potential income was the number of box seats in the house.

The seating capacity of the King's Theatre between the alterations of 1709 and those of 1782 has been a subject of great confusion. Nalbach took it to be about 1,230; Langhans calculated '*c.*700–950', but believed that it had been increased to '2,000 by 1735'.[1] A recent reinvestigation, however, demonstrates that the normal 'comfortable' capacity of the theatre was about 400 in pit and boxes, roughly 350 in the two galleries, or a total of some 750. With extreme crowding as many as 200 more might be squeezed in.[2] How many boxes and box seats the theatre held we do not know. In the pit and galleries benches permitted crowding if attendance were high.

According to testimony in C12/2012/53, the boxes yielded 'no more than £3000 per annum' before Sheridan and Harris took over in 1778. During that summer they revamped and redecorated the auditorium, increasing the yield from subscriptions by £1,000 per annum (C12/578/30). Taylor testifies in the former suit that as of 1781 subscriptions produced about £4,700. We interpret these figures as meaning that in 1777–78 subscription income was only £3,000 (implying about 140 subscribers, though the theatre could hold more) and that Sheridan and Harris increased box capacity and sold about 225 subscriptions (225 × £21 = £4,725). Taylor claims to have added thirty-six boxes in the renovations of 1782 to make a total of 100. The number of seats in the sixty-four boxes available from 1778 to 1782 is not known, but at a guess there were at least 290 places in them, with about 78 per cent sold for the season to generate the reported £4,700 box income.

No figures are known for pit and gallery ticket sales during the 1770s. Figures from the 1780s suggest that subscriptions and ticket sales tended to be roughly equal, which would imply a gross income for the opera-house of roughly £10,000 per annum under Sheridan and Harris. Very crowded houses for all sixty-five nights of the 1778–79 season would have generated £11,500 in pit and gallery income, but both earlier and later figures imply

---

[1] Nalbach, 26–7; Edward A. Langhans, 'The Theatres', in *The London Theatre World, 1660–1800*, ed. Robert D. Hume (Carbondale: Southern Illinois University Press, 1980), 64–5.

[2] See Milhous, 'The Capacity of Vanbrugh's Theatre in the Haymarket', and discussion above, Ch. 1, sect. IV.

that 60 per cent attendance was doing well for walk-in trade. An estimate might therefore allow £4,700 subscription money plus £1,400 for nights 51–65 (probably overgenerous), to which could be added £6,900 in nightly ticket sales (at 60 per cent capacity). This would have generated a total of £13,000 gross income, plus a bit from rentals. Any more would be astonishing; decidedly less seems probable. As we shall see, the actual annual income appears to have been about £10,000.

Scholars have heretofore possessed virtually no documentation on the receipts and operating expenses of the theatre at this time. What is beyond doubt is that an annual rent of £1,260 was owed on the theatre, and that £75 per night was allowed for routine daily expenses; virtually no performers' salaries are recorded.[1] A manuscript recently bought by the Pennsylvania State University from Richard Macnutt is cryptic in a number of respects, but apparently sheds considerable light on the subject. Its origin and purport are not explained except in a filing title: 'Opera Account 1778 & 1779'. It consists of a single page, listing money received, money paid, cash held, and bills owing. The King's Theatre is nowhere named, but cash in hand is said to be held by 'Mr Garton', that is, Jonathan Garton, Harris's treasurer at Covent Garden.[2] The manuscript makes no sense in relation to that theatre. Our best guess is that Garton was doing double duty at the King's Theatre, and that this manuscript represents a state-of-the-venture report at the end of two seasons under the new management. 'Receipts, as per Cash Book' are given as £17,889. 17s. This presumably includes both subscription income and ticket sales. An additional £1,250 is listed as received in payment for five 'shares'. 'Payments as per Cash Book' come to a total of £23,129. 17s. 7½d. and four tradesmen's bills totalling £156. 16s. 8d. are entered as paid. Twenty additional obligations totalling £1,738. 2s. 5d. are entered under the heading 'To Pay' set against a cash 'Balance in Mr Garton's hands' of £1,853. 2s. 8½d.[3] A shortfall of some £5,885 is covered by £6,000 'Received of Messrs Blackwell & Co.', evidently a loan. If our interpretation of this document is correct, the company's operating income for two seasons was some £18,000, its outgo £25,000, and its cumulative loss

---

[1] Taylor, *A Concise Statement*, 36; Master Hett's third report (C38/715) treats the annual rent as £1,240. According to testimony by Taylor in C12/2012/54, the normal allowance for daily expenses was £75.

[2] For the little known of Garton, see *Biographical Dictionary*, vi. 116–17.

[3] Among the bills awaiting payment were £306. 13s. 7d. to 'Scott, Copper Laceman' and £603. 9s. to 'Mountford, Carpenter'. The latter probably included charges for scene-shifting, to judge from Mountford's later bills to the Pantheon company.

£8,000 (plus the cost of auditorium renovation). By the standards of the 1780s expenses were low: £18,000 was supposed to be the bare-bones budget to which the trustees of 1783–85 were bound (see below, sect. III), and no one ever suggested the possibility of a budget under £16,000.[1] The operating expenses for 1778–79 were probably around £13,000, but income at the time did not even come close to covering costs.

Sheridan and Harris definitely ended the 1778–79 season some £7,300 in the red. Since the alterations of summer 1778 are reported to have cost about £4,000, we may hypothesize that even after a substantial increase in subscription income the theatre operated at a £3,000 loss for the year.[2] In June 1779 Sheridan and Harris were forced to ask for an extension of the time in which they were to pay the first £3,000 instalment on their mortgage (C12/578/30). During the summer of 1779 Harris decided he wanted no more of this: he was a tight-fisted but competent manager and, unlike the feckless Sheridan, recognized the predicament in which they had landed themselves. The two agreed that Harris would turn over all his right and title in the concern to Sheridan in return for Sheridan's assuming all joint debts and taking future responsibility for the operation, though no written agreement was drawn up until the summer of 1781.[3] Sheridan may not actually have assumed sole control until December 1779.

Little is known about the Sheridan and Harris administration. They never intended to handle daily management themselves. According to the *Biographical Dictionary*, there was a newspaper announcement that 'Mr. Le Texier is to superintend the opera' as early as 15 March 1778—more than three months before the sale was consummated.[4] Thus from very early on the plan was for Antoine Le Texier to run the opera company. He was a curious choice—a notorious social climber whose hot temper had contributed to a chequered personal history. In 1790 he was to publish *Ideas on the Opera*, but in 1778 his practical experience was apparently minimal. He brought Pacchierotti to England for the first time (probably at considerable expense), but he never really established artistic control. How competent he

---

[1] £16,000 was proposed by Peter Crawford for 1785–86 (LC 7/3, fo. 298ʳ).

[2] These figures are derived from testimony by Sheridan and Harris in their answer to Gallini of 2 Dec. 1780 in C12/578/30.

[3] Testimony by Harris in C12/947/18 on 5 May 1782; assignment of the opera-house from Sheridan to Harris on 23 Aug. 1781 as indemnity against debts due (in C107/64).

[4] *Biographical Dictionary*, ix. 257–60. Unfortunately, the reference the authors give to the *Morning Post* cannot be correct: 15 Mar. was a Sunday. We have not located the report, but assume that the substance of the citation is accurate.

was financially is anyone's guess. Whether the reason was personal, financial, or extraneous, Le Texier ceased to be employed by the theatre some time during the winter of 1779–80 when there was an unexpected managerial upheaval.

### Gallini's Take-over Bid and the Advent of William Taylor

The immediate cause of this upheaval may have been an offer from Gallini to buy the theatre from Sheridan and Harris.[1] Gallini (1728–1805) was a dancer who had come to London about 1753 and prospered. He performed at Covent Garden and the King's Theatre in the 1750s and 1760s, became a fashionable dancing-master, accumulated a fortune, and about 1765 apparently married the eldest daughter of the Earl of Abingdon.[2] (In the spring of 1788 he received a papal knighthood, after which he is often referred to as 'Sir John' Gallini.) Whether he was outbid in 1778 or lost out for other reasons is unknown, but his unremitting efforts to acquire the opera-house loom large in the history of its next decade.

On 11 December 1779 Gallini offered Sheridan and Harris what they had paid, plus the cost of their repairs and improvements, guaranteeing 'to fulfill all Engagements they have made with any Performers'. This was a generous offer, and they would have done well to take it. Harris wanted to accept; Sheridan flatly refused. Harris apparently refrained from selling his moiety to Gallini in return for Sheridan's accepting all responsibility as of the end of the previous season. O'Reilly states in his 1791 pamphlet that when Sheridan became 'sole possessor' of the opera-house 'He immediately engaged Mr. Crawford as Deputy Manager'.[3] Le Texier was sacked (exactly when is not clear) and Crawford took over daily operations. Unfortunately, Crawford was unable to pay the theatre's bills in full, let alone to meet Sheridan's mortgage obligations.

On 25 March 1780 the late mortgage payment of June 1779 was 'peremptorily' due but could not be paid (C12/578/30). According to Harris and Sheridan, they met with Gallini in April 1780 at Drury Lane, at which time Gallini renewed his offers. Harris was ready to accept; Sheridan again

---

[1] Gallini's formal letter of offer to Sheridan and Harris of 11 Dec. 1779 is recited in their reply of 2 Dec. 1780 to his bill of complaint in C12/578/30.

[2] On Gallini, see the *Biographical Dictionary*, v. 444–9, and Richard Ralph, 'Sir John Gallini', *About the House* (Summer 1979), 30–7.

[3] *An Authentic Narrative*, 8. Many of the letters and documents quoted in this pamphlet prove that O'Reilly was in possession of Peter Crawford's papers (see esp. 9–14). This fact adds immensely to the credibility of its financial details.

refused. Gallini thereupon 'told this Defendant [Sheridan] with some warmth that he knew how he could & would get at the Opera house or to that Effect & immediately left the Theatre'. On 12 May Gallini's solicitor wrote to Sheridan and Harris, informing them that Gallini 'has taken an assignment of £12,000 Mortgage upon the Opera House & he is ready to treat with you upon Fair Terms for your remaining Property therein' (C12/578/30). In other words, Gallini had bought the mortgage from Brooke and the others.[1]

Gallini needed leverage. Sheridan asked for another nine months to pay the overdue mortgage; Gallini refused, and on 26 May 1780 he sued, demanding payment or possession.[2] By autumn 1780 Sheridan was in serious financial difficulties. He was £6,000 (plus interest) behind in mortgage payments now due to Gallini; and according to testimony by James Brooke on 8 November 1780, Sheridan was also in arrears with the rent on the theatre and had failed to pay 'several of the Performers' (C12/578/30).[3] Gallini was demanding that Sheridan be turned out of the theatre and, in the mean time, that the court appoint a receiver to look after all receipts and disbursements. In modern terms, one would say that the King's Theatre was the target of a hostile take-over bid by Gallini. Unable to pay his bills but unwilling to yield possession, Sheridan scrambled to find an expedient that might help stave off disaster.

In December 1780 Sheridan started discussions with William Taylor about selling part of the property (C12/2012/53), and on 5 January 1781 these negotiations produced a written agreement by which Taylor would purchase a one-quarter interest in Sheridan's five-sixths of the theatre for £5,500.[4] £2,500 was to be paid in cash while £3,000 was 'to be paid by [Taylor] in discharge of one fourth part of the said Mortgage of £12,000'. Whether any cash actually changed hands is doubtful.[5] Sheridan's aim was to reduce his paper obligations without losing control of the theatre. According to the terms recited in C12/947/18, Taylor accepted full responsibility for a quarter

---

[1] The indenture is preserved among the papers in C107/66, 11 May 1780.

[2] C12/578/30 (bill of complaint).

[3] This testimony is reinforced by newspaper items. The *Public Advertiser* of 9 Dec. 1780 prints a formal denial by Peter Crawford of reports impugning the company's credit, and on the 11th the same paper carries a protest against rumours concerning the company, and the offer of a 20-guinea reward to anyone who identifies the person who has been sending anonymous letters to performers, warning them that they will not get their money.

[4] Recited in their further agreement of 25 Aug. 1781 (preserved among the papers in C107/66).

[5] O'Reilly, *An Authentic Narrative*, 42, says none did.

of Sheridan's opera-house debts: why he should have had to pay for the privilege is hard to see.

In January 1781 Sheridan informed Crawford that Taylor would henceforth have 'entire controul of the money matters'. Horrified, Crawford wrote an expostulatory reply on the 29th, protesting that he was personally liable for contracts he had signed and stating his intention 'to withdraw totally from the Opera House' if his objections were not met.[1] Needless to say, they were not. On Taylor's testimony (always a suspect source for unverifiable assertions) he found debts of more than £4,000 to performers; £1,260 rent due; £3,000 due on a bank loan; plus the Gallini mortgage—and the encumbrance created by the renters' shares of 1778 (C12/2012/53). In addition the theatre was charged with the 1778–79 debts run up by Sheridan and Harris, plus the operating loss for 1779–80. Gallini, meanwhile, was raising a clamour in the Court of Chancery, and on 17 February 1781 Sheridan silenced him for a time by signing a fraudulent document that he had no intention of honouring. The 'Articles of Agreement' of that date signed between Sheridan and Gallini state that if Sheridan does not pay £6,600 on the mortgage by 1 May 1781 (plus interest on the remaining £6,000) then Sheridan will 'sell Assign and make over the said Opera House' to Gallini for £22,000, the price to be adjusted to reflect 'improvements', diminished ground lease, renters' shares and so forth.[2] In return Gallini agrees to drop all pending legal proceedings against Sheridan and to withdraw his request that a receiver be appointed. The agreement takes no account of the deal with Taylor the previous month (though he was present at the signing— C12/947/18). Sheridan testified a year later that he considered the agreement 'falsely drawn and unreasonable' but signed because he thought he would be able to make the stipulated payment and ignore the terms.[3]

Sheridan and Taylor immediately set to work to block execution of the agreement with Gallini. According to Taylor's own admission, he 'prepared a Plan or proposal for raising the Sum of £12,000 by way of Mortgage on the said Theatre, by dividing the same into 24 Shares of £500 each to become a perpetual Charge upon the said premises at an Interest or Annuity of 5% together with a transferrable ffree Admission Tickett' (C12/2012/53). Taylor names twenty-four subscribers to this scheme, including the Duchess of Marlborough and the Earl of Buckinghamshire. They were to pay 30 per

---

[1] O'Reilly, *An Authentic Narrative*, 10–12.

[2] The agreement is preserved among the papers in C107/65.

[3] C12/947/18 (answer of 17 Jan. 1782).

cent immediately, 20 per cent on 5 June 1781, 25 per cent on 1 January 1782, and the final 25 per cent on 24 June 1782. In the event, Sheridan and Taylor collected only about three-quarters of the money pledged, but it was enough to let them offer Gallini most of what was due to him. Of that, more shortly. One should note, however, that Sheridan and Taylor wilfully encumbered the opera with a 'perpetual' charge of £600 per annum (plus twenty-four more free admissions) in order to forestall Gallini.

Between 30 April and 16 May 1781 Sheridan and Taylor made repeated attempts to pay Gallini the first two instalments of the mortgage (that is, through 24 June 1780). Gallini, however, wanted possession, not his money; consequently he raised every imaginable objection to receiving the late and incomplete payment he was offered. The whole process as described in C12/2012/53, C12/947/18, and especially C24/1883 is quite comic: Gallini's lawyers balked at all forms of receipt that he was asked to sign, with the result that Sheridan wound up paying £7,112 principal and interest to Messrs Hoare (bankers) in escrow. On 21 July 1781 Gallini sued Sheridan for non-payment (C12/947/18). Ten days later, in a letter quoted in his answer of 17 January 1782, Sheridan bitterly protested that 'the Money is now and has ever since lain ready for you in the Hands of Mr Hoare'. But Gallini knew full well that he was being offered money raised against the property; he wanted control of the opera-house and saw no reason to let Sheridan get away with such shenanigans.

From later lawsuits one learns that the opera company was failing to pay its bills in the spring of 1781,[1] and over the summer Harris evidently pressured Sheridan to carry out a formal disentanglement of their affairs. The paperwork is positively dizzying, but the gist of the matter is that in an agreement of 23 August 1781 Harris assigned all his interest in the King's Theatre to Sheridan in return for Sheridan's accepting full responsibility for the £12,000 mortgage plus some £7,343 in specified debts jointly contracted in 1778–79.[2] Harris was now out of the picture *if* Sheridan could fulfil his engagement to hold his former partner 'harmless', as the legal phrase has it.

---

[1] Joseph Hayling (the tinman who provided lighting) states that he was owed £121. 7s. at the end of 1779–80 and an additional £806. 14s. 7d. at the end of 1780–81 (C12/2147/14).

[2] John Manners £2,500; Messrs Drummond, Bankers, £2,000; Albany Wallis, £805; Mr Wood, £300; sundry tradesmen, £1,738. 2s. 5d. The agreement is described by Harris in C12/947/18 (answer of 5 May 1782). On 21 Aug. 1781 Harris had assigned Sheridan his interest in the opera-house as part of an indemnification guarantee that Sheridan would be responsible for all debts (C107/65; also in C107/66; cited in C38/722).

By the end of the autumn, however, Sheridan had handed over the whole concern and its mounting liabilities to William Taylor.[1]

## II. The First Taylor Regime, 1781–1783

For the next thirty-two years William Taylor was to be centrally involved in the administration of the King's Theatre, most of that time as proprietor and manager. His accession to this position is astonishing; his clinging to it successfully for more than three decades is hard to understand, the more so because he spent significant stretches of that time in debtors' prison and under the rules of King's Bench. The authors of a 1784 pamphlet state that Taylor 'had been the clerk of Messieurs Mayne and Graham [a banking-house that went bankrupt in August 1782], and, the transition . . . was one of those singular adventures in private history, for which this town is famous'.[2] The generally reliable 'Veritas' says sourly that Taylor 'never knew a note of music or a word of any tongue but English'.[3] He was about 28 years old in 1781 and, though he had no theatrical experience, he did possess great aptitude for financial jiggery-pokery. Whether he had any capital of his own is doubtful. In essence, he became proprietor of the King's Theatre simply by assuming responsibility for its debts. Chauvinism entered this peculiar transaction: any Englishman was preferable to an Italian dancing-master. In staving off Gallini's hostile take-over attempt, however, Sheridan pretty well ensured the ruin of the opera company.

### Taylor's 'Purchase' of the Opera-House

On 25 August 1781 Sheridan and Taylor signed an indenture increasing Taylor's share from one-quarter to one-third of Sheridan's five-sixths interest 'for the further sum of £833. 6s. 8d.' or a total of £7,333. 6s. 8d.[4] Taylor was free to sell, but only if he first offered his interest to Sheridan. As of this date

---

[1] The account of Taylor's acquisition of the theatre in the *Biographical Dictionary*, xiv. 380, is unfortunately quite inaccurate.

[2] *The Case of the Opera-House Disputes*, 5. In C12/2012/53 Taylor charges that Gallini 'employed and hired one William Allen and one [blank] Jackson [later 'Johnson']' to write this 'most Scandalous ffalse and Malicious Book or Pamphlet' and paid them £100 for 'writing or ffabricating the same' and causing 'several hundred Copies thereof to be given to and dispersed Amongst the Nobility and Gentry'. Its accuracy is formally attested by W. Allen (identity unknown), T. Luppino (the opera 'tailor'), and H. Reynell (publisher of the pamphlet and many librettos).

[3] *Opera House*, 51.

[4] Indenture preserved among the papers in C107/66.

the £22,000 price held, and Sheridan was clearly still hoping to regain possession. By November even Sheridan realized that he needed to bail out. A Deed Poll of 7 November endorsed on the 25 August agreement states that Sheridan has agreed to sell out to Taylor for just £5,000 (confirmed in C12/947/18). Some of this money may actually have been paid. But so far as one can tell from the documents, Sheridan sold a third of his interest for £7,333. 6s. 8d., and then later the same year sold the other two-thirds for £5,000. He was obviously anxious to extricate himself, and Taylor was willing to give him a bond of indemnity against rent of the opera-house (preserved in C107/65) and to guarantee assumption of other debts. Judging exactly what transactions passed between them is the more difficult in that they were manifestly falsifying and misrepresenting the record. Taylor wanted 'proof' of his rights of ownership; Sheridan was anxious to buttress those rights so as to get out from under his own obligations. On 22 April 1785 Taylor went so far as to testify that he bought Sheridan's entire interest for £22,000 in January 1781, recorded in an agreement *without date* signed by both of them and placed in the custody of Albany Wallis (C12/2012/53). Such a paper may have been concocted, then or later, to throw up a smoke-screen against Gallini's suit, but even if found, it would hardly prove anything. Likewise the 7 November 1781 Deed Poll 'records' receipt of £3,333. 6s. 8d. from Taylor, but the rent indemnity of the same date states that Taylor still owes Sheridan £2,000. On present evidence there is no way to disentangle real and fictional sums in their dealings. The crux of the matter is simply that Sheridan handed over the King's Theatre to Taylor—lock, stock, and unpaid bills. He may have received no money, but then he had not exactly invested any of his own when he took title himself.[1] Taylor was an unhappy choice as proprietor of the opera-house, being both penniless and clearly unfitted to handle the direction of artistic affairs. Personnel and repertoire decisions for the season of 1781–82 may well have been made by Peter Crawford, who announced the company roster on 15 October 1781 in the capacity of 'acting Manager' (*Morning Chronicle*). In February 1782, however, Taylor delegated artistic management to Domenico Angelo, the famous riding- and fencing-master.[2] Unlike William Taylor, he could at

---

[1] The *London Courant* of 17 Nov. 1781 reports that Sheridan has sold the opera-house to Taylor for £37,000. This is an absurdity, though roughly this figure could be obtained by adding estimated losses since 1778 (see below, sect. V) to the purchase price paid by Sheridan and Harris.

[2] The contract they signed on 20 Feb. is preserved among the loose papers in C107/65 and is printed and analysed below in Chs. 3 and 5.

least speak Italian, but how well he carried out the job, and how long he held it, is unknown. His appointment was odd and inauspicious.

## Gallini's Renewed Take-over Bid

The mortgagee had by no means abandoned his determination to possess the property, and he was aggressively pursuing his attempt to foreclose—as reference in Angelo's contract to Gallini's possible success 'in the suit now depending in the Court of Chancery' serves to remind us. Sheridan, however, was a master of legal delay, and court records are full of his pleas to be allowed more time before putting in an answer. He stalled on replying to Gallini's bill of 26 May 1780 (C12/578/30), finally responding only when Gallini's lawyer obtained a 'Commission of Sequestration' to seize Sheridan's 'personal Estate and the Rents and Profits of his real Estate untill he shall fully answer' on 27 November 1780. On 20 July 1781 we find Gallini asking for a subpoena to compel Sheridan to a further answer, and on 31 July 1781 a new order of sequestration was requested. As of 30 October Sheridan was petitioning for more time 'to perfect' his answer.[1]

On 2 March 1782 Sheridan and Taylor won a major victory: without ruling on the merits of the case, the court ordered that Gallini must accept the £7,112 tendered.[2] Then on 11 December 1782 the court quashed Gallini's claim to 'an assignment and Conveyance of ye Premises'.[3] The reasoning was evidently that only £6,000 of a £22,000 equity remained due to Gallini, and that the value of the premises was sufficient security for the money, even though some of it remained overdue. Gallini doggedly continued to pursue his suit to reclaim the remainder of his money (C12/947/18); he also set about buying back shares of the mortgage from the £500 investors, and he bought up what opera-house debts he could, seeking to swell his total claims on the enterprise.[4] For the moment, however, Taylor was left firmly in charge of the opera-house.

Whether Taylor was solvent or would remain solvent was another question. He claimed to have grossed as much as £26,000 during the season of

---

[1] C33/455, fos. 138ʳ, 526ᵛ, 527ʳ, 583ʳ.

[2] C12/947/18 (reply of William Taylor, 24 May 1782). Gallini received the money on 19 Mar. 1782 (C38/708).

[3] C33/459 (Decrees and Orders, 1782A), Part I, fos. 101–6.

[4] In the Master's Report of 16 July 1785 Gallini is said to have 'repurchased £2375' of the mortgage debt, and to have 'paid off or purchased . . . Debts amounting to the Sum of £7326. 12s.' in addition to the £4,282 still owed him on the 1778 mortgage (£3,000 plus interest). Thus the court acknowledged some £14,000 owed to Gallini among the opera-house obligations of the highest priority. See C38/722.

1781–82,[1] but this figure was unquestionably padded to impress potential investors, and his expenditure is unknown. His recorded liabilities at this time (excluding money due for the current season) were something in excess of £21,500,[2] and he owed £1,360 per season to holders of renters' shares and 'perpetual' mortgage shares. From a lawsuit of 1783, however, one may deduce that by July 1781 Taylor was already borrowing money from shady brokers on bad terms. C12/133/13 is a suit by Joseph Smith, coach-maker, against Taylor and one Thomas Rowntree, 'a Money Scrivener Broker or Procurer of Money or Negotiator of Bills Bonds Notes or other Securities'. Rowntree reportedly advertised in the newspapers, but he testifies that his client Sheridan had personally introduced and recommended Taylor. He appears to have arranged for the loan of large sums of money to Taylor from various sources (including the unlucky Mr Smith), charging a premium above 'the usual discount of five Pounds per cent'. Rowntree admits to having handled about £30,000 on Taylor's behalf, and he is extremely skittish about his fees, admitting that he 'may possibly' have taken more than the legal fees and interest, declining to answer because he might incriminate himself. Smith states that Rowntree 'obtained great Influence over the Conduct and Opinions' of Taylor, and that he 'never paid or gave the full value or amount of such Securities in Money'. In short, as early as the summer of 1781 Taylor was paying more than legal interest for borrowed money of which he received only part. Any cash Sheridan actually got out of him was probably borrowed and charged to the opera-house.

In May 1782 Taylor made a strenuous effort to raise a substantial amount of money and regularize his debts. On 10 May he signed an indenture with his lawyers, Burton and Wallis, granting them the right to issue forty renters' shares of £20 each for fifteen years at £210. Taylor signed a receipt for £8,400 (the face value of the grant); whether he received it, or what proportion of actual sales he received, is unknown.[3] The cost to the theatre would be £800 per annum, plus loss of ticket sales. Less than three weeks later, on 29 May, Taylor granted another forty renters' shares of £20 each per annum. In this case he made the grant to one Maurice Lloyd as security for

---

[1] O'Reilly, *An Authentic Narrative*, 36.

[2] £7,300 debt inherited from Sheridan and Harris; £6,000 plus interest still due to Gallini; £4,000 unpaid to performers and house servants; £1,260 in back rent; £3,000 to bankers; plus unknown losses in 1780–81 and those of the current season.

[3] The indenture is preserved among the loose papers in C107/66.

a loan of £6,000 obtained to cover and consolidate various specified debts.[1] Had all these new shares been sold, Taylor would have been liable for £2,960 per annum out of theatre receipts until 1797—an alarming total indeed. He would also have been obliged to allow free admission to as many as 142 persons per night. By any rational calculation Taylor was a fair way down a slippery slope towards irretrievable insolvency. His plan was evidently to cover his obligations by increasing the theatre's gross.

## The New Auditorium of 1782

In the summer of 1782 Taylor had the interior of the King's Theatre gutted and drastically revamped the auditorium. The thirty-six new boxes added at that time reportedly helped increase subscription income from £4,700 to £8,000 per annum (C12/2012/53). He states that the alterations cost him more than £4,000 and nearly as much for materials: where he got money to finance this venture is not explained. The alterations of 1782 were designed and carried out under the direction of the machinist and architect Michael Novosielski. The architectural evidence and implications have been analysed in Chapter 1; the issue here is finances. In essence, Novosielski increased the width of the auditorium by building corridors and box access outside the walls of the original building. And he increased auditorium depth by removing vestibules at the rear and reducing the depth of the stage. The result was a theatre comprising 100 four-, five-, and six-person boxes,[2] and capable of accommodating some 480 subscribers in all. Taylor's claim that these boxes were immediately taken may be true: during the next five years minor alterations were carried out to shoehorn in sixteen more boxes, and this would not have been done if there were vacant boxes on offer.[3] The increase in the number of box places available for subscribers was of particular importance in raising the potential gross income of the theatre. Roughly speaking, subscriber income appears to have tripled between the mid-1770s and 1782–83.

In various documents promulgated in the hope of raising money Taylor claimed that 'rents and profits . . . have of late years produced together yearly one year with another the sum of twenty nine thousand Pounds', while salaries and expenses 'have of late years amounted together yearly to between nineteen and twenty thousand Pounds', leaving a profit 'of nine

---

[1] Preserved in C107/66.    [2] See the 1782–83 box-plan, British Library 639.e.27 (5).
[3] See *A List of the Subscribers . . . 1788*, preserved at Harvard.

thousand Pounds or thereabouts'.[1] This could not be even close to the truth—or Taylor would have paid off his debts and accumulated a fortune. The potential gross income of the opera, however, had genuinely soared. Even before the sixteen additional boxes were added, Taylor might legitimately have hoped to take in upwards of £11,500 from subscriptions in the course of a season of sixty-five nights (including end-of-season resubscriptions). Assuming that ticket sales tended roughly to equal subscriptions (as they did in the later 1780s), that would generate an income of about £23,000 for a season, which would be a startling increase on what Sheridan and Harris apparently grossed.

### *Taylor's Bankruptcy and the First Deed of Trust (March 1783)*

Taylor carried out his improvements under constant harassment. Gallini was raining writs and subpoenas on him;[2] in consequence Taylor positively had to come up with £3,000 on the mortgage, which he did on 25 June 1782, according to testimony by Henry Hoare (banker and trustee) in C12/947/18. Other problems were snowballing. In June 1782 Joseph Hayling, the tinman who had handled lighting for the theatre since 1768, submitted substantial bills that Taylor was unable to pay, whereupon Hayling took out writs against him in August (C12/624/2). Hayling was demanding more than £1,000, and the following spring his tenacity was to topple the beleaguered proprietor into bankruptcy and public disgrace. For the moment Taylor stalled. The same month Mayne and Graham (the banking firm for which he had once worked) went broke, forcing Taylor to cover a £1,050 note with an emergency loan from Rowntree.

The season of 1782–83 brought Taylor to ruin. On 31 December we find him negotiating a £1,200 loan from Rowntree (C12/133/13); by 14 March he was reduced to borrowing £50. Hayling had obtained a King's Bench execution, and Taylor was forced to accede to a weekly instalment plan to stave off seizure of the theatre.[3] Recognizing his jeopardy, Taylor arranged with Sheridan to institute a 'friendly Execution' on the theatre to block Hayling's unfriendly one (C12/2012/53).

By mid-March 1783 Taylor realized that he was in an untenable position and endeavoured to execute a tricky side-step. On 17 March he signed a

---

[1] Taylor makes these claims in his deed of trust of 17 Mar. 1783 (preserved among the papers in C107/65) and repeats them many other places.

[2] e.g. C33/457, fos. 254$^r$, 308$^r$ (permission for Gallini to attach).

[3] C12/624/2 (answer). Instalments started on 27 Jan. 1783.

deed of trust conveying the entire opera-house concern to Albany Wallis and Richard Troward.[1] He claimed an income of £29,000, an expenditure of £20,000 and a yearly profit of £9,000. Taylor listed £16,000 of debts to be paid off under the trust: £2,000 to George Grant, £4,800 to William Davis, £3,200 to Sir John Lade, and £6,000 to James Grant. All of them appear to have lent money at interest.[2] The terms of the 'trust', however, are decidedly suspicious. Wallis and Troward are to receive the income of the theatre for four years, pay salaries and tradesmen's bills, and use the surplus to satisfy the named creditors—who must either agree to refrain from bringing suit or be 'forever debarred of the benefit of the trust'. Taylor did not, however, have any intention of letting the business out of his hands. The 'Declaration' says 'that nothing herein contained shall extend or be construed to extend to debar or preclude the said William Taylor from conducting managing and carrying on the Business of the said Theatre and Entering into Engagements with and employing all and every of the singers dancers musicians painters artists tradesmen servants and others', setting their wages, and so forth. Taylor is to retain 'all such powers privileges and Authorities with respect to the management and conduct of the said Theatre as he at any time heretofore had or now hath', except that he is not to 'intermeddle' with the receipts. He also specifies that he retains the power to give order for free admission to any person up to the number of ten in the pit and ten in each of the galleries every night.

Trying to persuade his creditors to accept this arrangement, Taylor offered to give them a transferable right of free admission to the opera-house for every £400 of debt they agreed to place under the conditions of the trust.[3] By the beginning of April, however, Taylor's position was crumbling and he was being hounded by hordes of creditors.[4] On 8 April 1783 Taylor executed a further agreement with Wallis and Troward, authorizing

---

[1] Preserved in C107/65.

[2] Davis and Lade held seats in box 83, according to the *Morning Herald* of 5 Feb. 1783. The Grants do not appear to have been subscribers.

[3] See, for example, the paperwork on such an agreement made by Wallis and Troward with James Grant on 20 Mar. 1783 (preserved in the Theatre Museum, V&A).

[4] He had private problems as well. On 14 Mar. Maria Prudom died. She was an opera singer of moderate distinction who had been living with him. (See Pl. 6.) Thomas Luppino later testified that he did work for her on Taylor's orders; he provided £28 worth of mourning garments at the time of her death, and 'attended the Funeral as a Mourner' at Taylor's request. Luppino states that he 'hath been informed and believes the said Complainant [Taylor] was married or constantly cohabited with' Mrs Prudom (C12/2171/23, answer). This relationship was not known to the authors of the *Biographical Dictionary*, xii. 193–4.

them to 'receive . . . all sums of money' due to the opera company and to use them to pay 'the performers and others employed in the Carrying on the Amusement and business of the said Theatre' (C107/66). At a meeting of his creditors on the 16th Taylor offered to grant free admission for every £400 of debt to all creditors, and Wallis and Troward (acting as his attorneys) started collecting signatures in the hope of getting Taylor 'discharged out of Custody in respect of the Actions . . . commenced against him'. Several copies of these proposals, signed by various creditors, are preserved in C107/65. Early in April 1783 Taylor's treasurer, William Jewell, was removed from office and Peter Crawford was recalled—a move designed to reassure the performers, who trusted him.[1] One thing that slipped in the transition, unfortunately for Taylor, was the weekly instalment payment owed to Hayling, who received his money on 5 April but not a week later (C12/2147/14). Hayling already held King's Bench writs and used them. Within a month the Sheriff of Middlesex auctioned off the contents of the King's Theatre to satisfy Hayling's claims. The buyer, curiously enough, was Thomas Harris, who paid just £1,430.[2] Harris explained his purchase in a long newspaper notice, stating that he had bought the opera's costumes, scenery, and properties in the hope of keeping the venture together so that the company would have a chance to give performances and earn some money (*Morning Chronicle*, 24 May 1783).

On 10 May Mlle Théodore, a popular dancer, addressed the audience in pathetic terms from the stage of the King's Theatre, begging their support for charity benefits on behalf of the unpaid performers and servants.[3] Harris authorized the loan of scenery and costumes for performances at both the King's Theatre and the Pantheon, and the season petered out in confusion and acrimony. Meetings of Taylor's creditors were held on 20 and 30 May and 6 June (*Morning Chronicle*). On 6 June the *Morning Herald* printed a list of some £4,200 of unpaid salaries, and asserted that debts for the season amounted 'to £10,000 and upwards', a total vigorously denied the next day, when an unspecified authority assured the paper that this was 'a gross imposition on the public; there being not really due one third of the sum, pretended to be claimed'.

---

[1] O'Reilly, *An Authentic Narrative*, 18.

[2] The auction occurred on 14 May 1783; the bill of sale to Harris is dated 22 May and is preserved in C107/65. Harris was also the buyer in a further auction of Taylor's property on 28 May (bill of sale for £60 also in C107/65).

[3] The text is printed in *An Authentic Narrative*, 19–21.

Who would pick up the pieces? Gallini was the obvious candidate, and he was willing and ready. On 5 June Harris (ever the practical businessman) struck a deal with Gallini.[1]

It is this day agreed betwixt Thos. Harris & Mr Gallini, that Mr Harris shall resign to Mr Gallini all his property, interest & right whatever in ye Opera House & premises & put the said Mr Gallini into peaceable possession thereof on the consideration of two thousand guineas in hand paid, and also the sum of £1490 being the purchase money paid to the Sherriffe for the furniture of ye said Opera House & Mr Taylor's interest therein—and Mr Gallini agrees to take on himself the payment of all debts and other charges for which Mr Harris is now responsible on account of the said Opera House & premises & likewise to indemnify him against ye rent of the said premises.

J. Palmer witnessed Harris's and Gallini's signatures to this document.

Letting Gallini take over made extremely good sense. He was the opera's principal creditor; he knew the business from the inside; and he had the money to pay its bills. On 21 June 1783 Gallini served formal notice on Taylor's trustees that he was prepared to 'repay . . . all such sums of money, as are due' on account of the trust, and to accept responsibility for other debts.[2] The offer was ignored, but Gallini quite reasonably presumed that he was now duly in possession, and set about laying plans for the season of 1783–84. Between mid-June and mid-July he made a trip to France to hire Vestris, jun., and other dancers, and by about 20 July had embarked for Italy to hire singers.[3] William Taylor, however, had other ideas.

## III.  Interregnum: Gallini versus Taylor's Trustees, 1783–1785

In summer 1783 the affairs of the King's Theatre fell into a spectacular state of disarray. Gallini obtained possession of the theatre, but Taylor conveyed legal right to it to six trustees—and both parties proceeded to start hiring performers for the next season. Most of the autumn was occupied in sorting out the mess that resulted, and the season of 1783–84 was chaotic from beginning to end.

### *Taylor's Second Deed of Trust (July 1783)*

The Sheriff's sale that dispossessed Taylor was carried out without regard to the trust grant to Wallis and Troward back in March—and in February

---

[1] Folger MS Y.d. 587 (1). There is a copy in C107/66.
[2] Printed in O'Reilly, *An Authentic Narrative*, 22.
[3] *Morning Herald*, 19 and 22 July 1783.

1784 the Court of King's Bench was to hold that the sale had been illegal, however dodgy that deed of trust.[1] In July 1783, however, Taylor was penniless, dispossessed, and liable for an enormous array of unpaid debts. His solution was to execute a second deed of trust. This would, he hoped, regain him technical possession of the theatre, give him an income, and keep him out of debtors' prison.

The deed of trust of 17 July 1783 (preserved among the papers in C107/66)[2] is a massive tripartite indenture comprising eight parchments and a lot of redundant legal verbiage. The gist of the agreement was as follows. William Taylor, with the consent of Wallis and Troward, made over all his property right in the opera-house to six of his creditors, in trust for all creditors who would accept the terms of the document. The duration of the trust was to be four years, extendable if Taylor's debts had not been paid off in that time. Taylor claimed an average annual income of £26,000 for the opera-house, and annual expenditure of between £19,000 and £20,000. In contrast to the previous arrangement, the trustees were to have complete operational control of the theatre: they were to hire performers, set salaries, select repertoire, and receive all moneys due. They were limited to a total expenditure of £18,000 per annum. The trustees were given 'full power and authority to appoint and employ Peter Crawford Esquire or such person as they shall in their Judgment think competent and fit to carry on conduct and manage the Business of the said Theatre', and to pay such manager 'any sum of Money not exceeding . . . £200' per annum. Taylor stipulated that he himself was to be paid £200 a year in quarterly instalments, and that he was to retain the right 'to admit or give orders for the admission of any person or persons into the said Opera House to see Gratis any public Entertainment to be therein Exhibited'—though the number of such free admissions was now reduced to four in the pit and four in each gallery every night. Preference of employment was to be given to past singers, dancers, and other employees to whom money was owed—if they signed the agreement. Any creditor who did not sign within ten days of receiving notice of the trust was debarred from any benefit thereunder. Anyone signing trust

---

[1] The King's Bench judgment of 2 Feb. 1784 is quoted in C12/592/17. Court processes were slow. Taylor sued for damages, but not until after the fire of 1789 did he win a verdict: 'Mr. Taylor, of the Opera-House, has recovered a verdict against the Sheriff of London, for £500 damages, for being dispossessed of the Opera-House from May 1783 to February 1784' (Theatre Cuts 42 [fo. 39ʳ], with MS date of 25 July 1789). A long report of the case was printed in *The Times* of 24 July 1789.

[2] Another copy is preserved in LC 7/3, fos. 217–34.

papers thereby consented to refrain from suing William Taylor, arresting him, or attaching his goods.[1]

This deed of trust was indisputably genuine: Taylor removed himself entirely from the management and finances of the opera-house. The trustees were as oddly assorted a group as could readily have been found. George Grant and James Sutton were shady business friends of Taylor's who knew no more of the opera than that they had lent money to it at interest. A contemporary pamphlet states that Sutton and the dancer Simon Slingsby—a man with 'a careless head and a light pair of heels'—had been bankrupts.[2] Michael Novosielski was a talented designer, machinist, and architect—but also a very extravagant man without experience as a manager. Leopoldo De Michele, although a lifelong minor singer and now head music-copyist, was not an experienced manager. Giovanni Siscotti was a tradesman in lace who spoke too little English to make sense of the trustees' meetings.[3] This ill-sorted crew certainly needed the help of someone like Peter Crawford, who had good financial credentials. Whether the principal trustees (Grant, Novosielski, and Slingsby) were scoundrels or merely inexperienced and spendthrift could be debated. The fullest account of this episode in the history of the King's Theatre, Haymarket, is in an anonymous, quasi-allegorical pamphlet, *The Testament, or Will, of Mr. William Taylor*, where they are treated as thieves.[4] How the trustees might have succeeded if left to themselves is anyone's guess: government by committee rarely works. But far from enjoying 'peaceable possession' of the theatre and a chance to run it, the trustees had first to sort matters out with Gallini.

---

[1] For a list of signatories and the sums claimed, see App. II. In 1799 Taylor presented a memorial requesting extension of the theatre's ground lease in which he listed some of his debts from 1783, construction costs associated with the new theatre of 1791, etc. For a copy of this important document, see PRO CRES 6/121, 328–39.

[2] *The Case of the Opera-House Disputes*, 18–19. Slingsby denies the charge convincingly in the *Morning Post* of 1 Jan. 1785, admitting that debts contracted during his management of Mrs Cornelys's private opera in Soho Square (c.1770–71?) had brought him to the verge of bankruptcy.

[3] William Taylor—who had appointed him a trustee—describes Siscotti in C12/2012/53 as a 'fforeigner and almost totally ignorant of the Laws and language of this Kingdom and a Credulous timid Man easily alarmed and imposed upon'.

[4] London: no publisher, 1785. We have used the Huntington Library copy. The author obviously knew a great deal about the internal workings of the opera house. He creates transparent disguises for the names of the principal villains and turns the opera-house into a 'farm', but gives most names unchanged (for example, Gallini, Crawford, Luppino). So far as the factual details can be checked, they appear quite accurate.

## The 'Florence Accords' and the Battle for Possession

On 11 August 1783 Crawford and De Michele set out from London to recruit performers for the coming season.[1] Arriving in Italy, they found that Gallini had already signed up most of a company, and on 9 September De Michele sensibly struck a compromise with him (ratified by Crawford on the 10th—he had been ill). What may be dubbed the 'Florence Accords' are recited in full in C12/592/17. The document starts with an admission that Gallini's possession is in legal dispute and says that pending a resolution the two sides 'have amicably and mutually agreed' as follows. First, Crawford and De Michele 'shall desist from collecting and engaging their intended Company', and 'shall avail themselves of that Company which he the said Mr Gallini has already collected'. Second, 'That there shall be appointed in London two Managers or Superintendants that is to say each party shall appoint one', until the courts decide who should be in charge. Third, that as soon as Gallini returns to London 'he shall be secured and guarantied' against payment 'for all those Engagements which he may have entred into', and he will be 'reimbursed all the expences of his Journey, the Purchase of Music and advance he may have made of Salaries'. Fourth, regardless of the court's decision, Gallini is entitled to use opera performers at a series of twelve concerts in Hanover Square as specified in the contracts he has signed with them.[2]

While this sensible if awkward bargain was being struck in Italy, a veritable civil war was being fought in London. On 1 September the trustees announced Crawford's appointment as manager, reported several performers 'already engaged', and called a meeting of the opera's creditors for the 3rd (*Morning Herald*). On that day, however, the same paper printed a reply from the Gallini camp, flatly denying that anyone but Gallini was in charge of the opera, and insisting that the performers named by the trustees were in fact contracted to Gallini. On 5 September the *Morning Chronicle* gave an extended report of the creditors' meeting, where those attending were told that Gallini had no claim to possession but the remaining mortgage payment of £4,170, which the trustees were prepared to pay off at any time. On the 9th the trustees explained their grounds for thinking the

---

[1] C24/1929 (Crawford).

[2] This last clause is particularly important because it shows that Gallini had the written agreement of Taylor's trustees to do something for which Taylor hounded him in court over the next six years.

Sheriff's sale invalid and gave a history of the new trust. On the 10th Gallini's forces fired back contradiction and defiance, demanding that the trustees identify themselves publicly, and asking if they had a licence and what performers they had under contract.[1] At some point the trustees succeeded in ejecting Gallini's servants from the theatre and taking possession.

The month of October was devoted to intense infighting. On the 25th a notice appeared in the *Morning Chronicle*: 'The Trustees of the Opera having amicably adjusted all differences with Mr. Gallini, the Nobility, Gentry, Subscribers to the undertaking, are respectfully desired to make their applications to Mr. Crawford, Treasurer to the King's Theatre. J. Gallini, P. Crawford.' On 5 November, however, Gallini published a retraction, saying that he had 'signed such an advertisement in hopes that an amicable adjustment between us would then immediately have taken place', but that no agreement had been reached. On the 6th Crawford printed a notice denouncing Gallini's perfidy in agreeing to, delaying over, and finally 'insidiously' rejecting 'proposals not less founded in generosity than justice'. Gallini apparently went so far as to float a rumour that he would 'exhibit Operas at the Rooms in Hanover-square, in which undertaking he is promised countenance'.[2] Not until 22 November was 'An amicable and final accommodation' announced (*Morning Chronicle*).

### The Truce of November 1783—and its Collapse

The season got under way on the basis of an agreement signed on 19 November 1783.[3] The terms were these:

—First, Gallini is to be paid £525 for his 'Expences, loss of time and trouble in his Journey to Italy . . . including five Spartitas of Operas and Fifty Guineas to Mr Louvterini for his trouble'. He is also to receive £1,435 to reimburse him for advances on performers' contracts, purchase of music, and rent. The trustees are to receive £810 from subscription monies to reimburse the travel costs of Crawford and De Michele and other expenses 'they have been put to in preparing for opening the theatre'.

—Second, Gallini is to be given a bond 'to indemnify him against the engagements he has entered into with several performers for the ensuing season'.

—Third, 'Mr Crawford on the part of the trustees and Mr [Henry] Johnson on the part of Mr Gallini to be appointed joint Treasurers'.

---

[1] Both statements are in the *Morning Chronicle*.      [2] Theatre Cuts 41, fo. [99ʳ].
[3] Preserved among the papers in C107/65. Also recited in C12/592/17.

—Fourth, money is to be withdrawn from the bank only 'upon the joint Draft' of designated representatives of both parties.

—Fifth, money taken each night is to be locked in an 'Iron Chest under two Locks. The Treasurer of one Party to have the Key of one . . . and the other Treasurer to have the Key of the other Lock.'

—Sixth, 'Mr Gallini to undertake the management and direction of all matters . . . relating to Music and Dancing at the Opera House; and all other matters relative to the Business of the House to Mr. Crawford on the part of the Trustees and Mr. Gallini.'

—Seventh, performers needed but not yet hired are to be chosen and engaged by the trustees, with Gallini's approval.

—Eighth, Gallini is 'at Liberty to avail himself of that part of the Contracts entred into by him with several of the singers' for performance at Hanover Square, provided he does not schedule concerts on opera nights.

—Ninth, 'in consideration of Mr Gallini's trouble in superintending the Music and Dancing . . . He be allowed two clear Thursday Nights' (that is, benefits without paying charges).

—Tenth, 'such performers as are Creditors under the Trust' are 'entitled to a preference of engagement if in England'.

In other words, Gallini was to manage the front legs, the trustees the hind legs of this panto horse. Not surprisingly, the act came apart in a hurry.

From hopeful beginnings to chaos took less than two months. The Lord Chamberlain was reluctant to issue a licence to so makeshift an operation. Only after some of the performers wrote to him, stating that they were content with the security offered for the payment of their salaries, was a licence forthcoming.[1] It was granted jointly to Gallini and Crawford on 29 November, the first night of the season. By January 1784 Taylor was protesting non-payment of his annuity (C12/1546/73) and the trustees found themselves forced to borrow money from the bankers Ransom, Morland, and Hammersley (C12/602/50). On 24 January De Michele resigned as a trustee, and Siscotti followed suit about two weeks later.[2] On 2 February the Court of King's Bench set aside the Sheriff's sale (C12/592/17); on the 6th neither the trustees nor anyone else succeeded in paying Gallini the £4,170 due on his mortgage.

[1] The performers' letter is quoted (without date) in C12/592/17. The office copy of the licence is in LC 5/162, p. 329 (29 Nov. 1783). According to *The Testament, or Will, of Mr. William Taylor*, 19, Gallini had to 'give a security of ten thousand pounds to the Lord Chamberlain' before the theatre was allowed to open.

[2] C12/602/50. For proof of De Michele's written resignation, see C24/1929 (Parkhurst). On 8 Mar. 1784 De Michele published notice of his resignation in the newspapers (for example, the *Morning Chronicle*) as a bulwark against legal liability for the opera's mounting debts.

On 2 February—the day of the King's Bench verdict—the trustees sent Crawford a peremptory order to turn all receipts over to them, and on the 8th Crawford and Gallini protested against this usurpation and violation of agreements in a vehement letter to the Lord Chamberlain.[1] On the 14th Crawford ejected Gallini's employees and displaced Henry Johnson as joint treasurer.[2] On 9 March, however, the trustees '*ordered* . . . the Ticket Sellers, to bring their whole receipts to Mr. Novosielski's house, in Market-lane', and Crawford left the Treasurer's office in disgust.[3] By all accounts Peter Crawford was an honest man, and he seems finally to have realized that the trustees did not intend to conduct the opera in a businesslike way.

The rest of the 1783–84 season is a tangle of overlapping legal actions. On 11 March Gallini complained that his treasurer was illegally ousted and that receipts were not being paid into the bank (C31/231, no. 322). On 27 April he demanded that the court appoint receivers, which it did on 21 May (rejecting the trustees' nominee).[4] On the 24th the receivers complained that the ticket-sellers were giving the money to Novosielski and Mac-Mahon, not to them; on the 28th the trustees replied that tradesmen and orchestra members must be paid before the receivers could be given the balance.[5] Gallini had lost a battle and been deprived of a foothold in the theatre but, given the state of affairs under the trustees in the spring of 1784, he believed that he would soon regain possession by default. On 21 June he wrote to Earl Cowper, saying 'The Court of Chancery having granted me a Receiver on the Opera House & the opposite party not being able to touch the money or to discharge some very considerable incumbrances now necessary leaves great room to believe they will not be able to hold out much longer.'[6] To let Gallini take charge had made perfect sense a year earlier and did again now. As usual, however, logic had little to do with the tangled affairs of the Haymarket opera.

## Continued Infighting and the Season of 1784–85

In the summer of 1784 Gallini presented a 'Memorial' to the Lord Chamberlain, asking for an opera licence (LC 7/3, fos. 209–10); simultaneously he

---

[1] Both are printed in O'Reilly, *An Authentic Narrative*, 25, 26–7.

[2] Various forms of this story are in C12/592/17, C31/231, no. 322, and LC 7/3, fos. 209–10.

[3] *An Authentic Narrative*, 28.

[4] They nominated Parkyns MacMahon, a shady character whom they had hired to serve as a public-relations expert (C38/715, Hett's report of 21 May 1784).

[5] C31/231, no. 670 (27 Apr. 1783); C33/461, fos. 294ᵛ–295ʳ (28 Apr.); C38/715 (21–2 May); C31/232, nos. 196, 251 (24 and 28 May).

[6] Gibson, 'Earl Cowper', 241.

petitioned in Chancery for the right to manage the opera company on the grounds that he was the principal creditor and the most competent person to take charge. In a long Chancery affidavit of 15 July 1784 Gallini reviewed the stormy history of the venture since 1778, listed his expenditures, vehemently objected to Taylor as manager, and expressed fears that the next season could not be mounted and that subscribers would withdraw if a new management were not installed.[1] The remaining trustees and their minions counter-attacked vigorously. On 16 July Parkyns MacMahon (secretary and publicity director) denounced Gallini for extravagance, claiming an unnecessary increase of £20 per night in the constant charge, criticizing the singers hired, and saying that the trustees had reduced the expense of the orchestra by seven guineas per night (C31/233, no. 322). On the 20th Novosielski charged that receipts were very low at the beginning of the 1783–84 season, and increased after he became manager in February. He went on to insist upon the legality of the trusteeship, and the competence of their stewardship, and to ask the court to ratify its management of the theatre (C31/233, no. 348). On the 30th Novosielski and Slingsby attacked Gallini again, claiming that they had put money into the enterprise (C31/233, nos. 489–90). Four years later Novosielski testified that in August 1784 he offered to pay Gallini the £4,200 residue of his mortgage and that Gallini refused to take the money.[2] We must remember that Gallini was owed a great deal more than the mortgage money (and had little hope of collecting it from the trustees)—but clearly what he wanted was control of the opera-house.

The company had lost quite a lot of money under the trustees during 1783–84. Why were they so determined to retain power? The answer seems to be that they were intent on milking the venture for whatever they could get out of it. This is certainly the picture given in *The Testament, or Will, of Mr. William Taylor*. A legal and financial history of the opera-house evidently drawn up for the Lord Chamberlain in August–September 1784 spells out the whole disastrous history; it surveys the doings of the trustees and concludes frostily that 'The view of these trustees undoubtedly is to keep possession of the theatre to get the subscription money and pay themselves only for they discover no intention of justice to any other creditors.'[3]

[1] C31/233, nos. 314 (history) and 315 (request to manage).
[2] C31/249, no. 355 (1 July 1788).
[3] LC 7/3, fos. 215–16. This document was probably the work of William Sheldon.

This was a fair assessment. But against logic and probability, the trustees managed to cling to power for another season.

During the autumn of 1784 Gallini clamoured for possession. The courts continued to order him paid but refused to let him foreclose, and the Lord Chamberlain dithered. The trustees had unquestionably exceeded the £18,000 they were legally entitled to spend and were clearly violating the trust provision specifying that creditors who were signatories of the deed were entitled to preference in employment. The Lord Chamberlain's office received a flock of angry protests from performers and servants who were dismissed by the trustees before the season of 1784–85.[1] But these people had no immediate legal standing. Consequently, though the authorities fumed and warned, they did not intervene effectually. The Lord Chamberlain finally granted a licence on 10 December 1784—but only for six weeks—and inserted the name of the banker Thomas Hammersley on the theory that he could guarantee payment of salaries.[2] The opera company limped through the season under the trustees but continued to lose money at a disastrous rate. Both facts should be emphasized because of errors and misunderstandings in the introduction to the 1784–85 season in Part 5 of *The London Stage*. Hogan states that 'This season was a prosperous one . . . even at the debt-ridden King's.' He is under the misapprehension that Gallini was managing the theatre. And he says that 'In November . . . the temporary receivers *or trustees* who had been appointed the previous season were discharged by a decree of the Court of Chancery.'[3] What happened on 19 November was that the Court of Chancery ordered the trustees to pay Gallini the £2,849. 18*s.* he had advanced on contracts, discharged the temporary receivers appointed in May, and 'confirmed' the trustees 'in their right of managing the property for the benefit of the creditors'. In other words, the

[1] For example, from Rachele D'Orta Giorgi (singer) *c.* Sept. (?) 1784; Revilly (*figurant*), 15 Sept.; John Butler (ticket-seller), 30 Sept.; William Lee (under-treasurer), 12 Nov.; Francis Debaulieux (*figurant*), 12 Nov.; Barthélemon and his wife (musician and singer), 18 Nov.; Antonio Piccini (*figurant*), *c.* Dec. (?); Joseph Giorgi (harpsichordist), *c.* Dec. (?); Louis Simonet (dancer and former ballet-master), *c.* Dec. (?); Anthony Sala (*figurant*), *c.* Dec. (?). See LC 7/3, fos. 194–5, 288, 312, 313, 211–12, 284–85, 246, 249–50, 252, 280–1.

[2] The licence is in LC 5/162, p. 341. Renewals were granted on 1 Feb. and 29 Apr. 1785 (O'Reilly, *An Authentic Narrative*, 30). On 1 Feb. the name 'Martindale' appears among the licensees: he had bought Crawford's one-sixth of the venture. One wonders what Crawford succeeded in getting for his interest in this tottery enterprise.

[3] *The London Stage*, Part 5, ii. 727–8 (emphasis added).

trust was *not* dissolved, and Gallini's exclusion from management was upheld by the court.[1]

In November Gallini made yet another attempt to foreclose, bundling together all his various claims on the opera-house—but his case was summarily thrown out on technical grounds. The Court of Chancery had established a hierarchy of claims on the opera, the foremost of which was the residue of the £12,000 mortgage of 1778 (now held by Gallini). Gallini claimed to hold a total of some £24,000 of debts owing from the opera company, but almost all of it came very low in the list of claims. Consequently Gallini could obtain court orders for payment of the first mortgage, but was not allowed precedence in claims beyond that. So the trustees squandered another chance to retrieve the company's fortunes. As early as 10 December the newspapers were reporting that they had 'pawned' their subscriptions for the season, that is, had been forced to pledge subscription money in order to raise operating cash at the beginning of the season.[2] By the end of the spring, the Lord Chamberlain was fed up. Something had to be done. But what?

## Mismanagement by the Trustees

On 2 June 1785 Luigi Cherubini wrote a newsy letter to Earl Cowper, discussing 'the impending revolution in the affairs of this theatre'. 'Taylor's creditors will never be paid', he asserts, 'and the debts of the theatre instead of getting smaller, are forever growing, on account of the continuing lawsuits and the swindles of the said trustees.'

Now the most significant news is that the trustees have received a letter from the Lord Chamberlain which forbids them to contract with any person for the coming year; and they must give up the account books to be reviewed, which they have promptly taken to the Vice-Chamberlain. . . . With this encouragement various gentlemen have proposed a scheme to undertake the direction of the entertainment, guaranteeing in case of loss to pay £2,000 a year to satisfy the creditors and in case of profit to continue with the same purpose. All this is not certain, but the project seems genuine.[3]

Nothing was to come of this scheme until 1790, but the Lord Chamberlain

---

[1] See C31/234, no. 106, Master Graves's report of 12 Nov. 1784 (C38/715), and commentary in the *Gazetteer* 20 and 25 Nov. 1784; *Morning Post*, 25 and 27 Nov.; *Public Advertiser*, 29 Nov.

[2] *The Case of the Opera-House Disputes*, 34–5.

[3] Gibson, 'Earl Cowper', 243.

spent the summer and autumn of 1785 trying to find a taker for the opera other than the ever-hopeful Gallini.

Testimony from various sources is extremely damaging to the trustees. On 17 December 1784 De Michele sued his erstwhile partners, requesting reimbursement for his Italian trip and other expenses, arrears of salary, and immunity from debts run up after his resignation. He charges that they acted without consulting him or listening to him, though 'he did neverthe-less very many times and in many cases express his disapprobation & endeavour to dissuade them from engaging several persons they afterwards engaged as Performers', and that these were 'extravagant Engagements' of 'Persons who were not nor could be useful at the said Theatre'. De Michele states that the trustees 'did manage & conduct the Affairs & Trusts of the said Opera house in so extravagant a manner and so very contrary to the Oeconomical plan proposed to be followed', that their expenses ran to '£23,000 a Year & upwards' and De Michele thought himself 'in danger of being ruined'. He says he could have 'conducted . . . the said Season . . . for at least £3000 less'. When he found that the other trustees were not depositing receipts with Messrs Drummond as agreed, but 'used such monies for their own private purposes', he sent in his resignation, which was accepted at a meeting of 31 January 1784.[1] John Siscotti's answer admits that it is true the trustees 'have in many instances conducted the affairs of the said Opera house extravagantly & improperly, and very contrary to the oeconomical plan proposed', and consequently he too resigned, 'entirely disapproving of their management & having frequently remonstrated with them to no purpose'. On 30 April 1785 Grant, Novosielski, and Slingsby replied that Gallini's contracts were excessive and cost several thousand pounds more than they should have for bad performers. They deny all extravagance and say that De Michele 'hath always been employed upon the Theatre as the most inferior Performer in Comick buffoonery' and is 'totally Incapable of Conducting or Superintending a Concern of such great Import with propriety'. They admit spending more than the agreed £18,000, but say they cannot give details because their books are all in the hands of a Master in Chancery for an audit.

De Michele was by no means the only person to charge the trustees with mismanagement—or worse. William Taylor sued them on 5 March 1785 (C12/1546/73), charging 'mismanagement and ffraudulent and Collusive

---

[1] C12/602/50 (bill).

conduct', and complaining that during 1784–85 in particular they had 'entered into several improvident Contracts and Collusive engagements for the payment of very large Salaries and sums of Money to and with each other and to and with divers other Persons their Relations and Dependants'. Taylor is not very specific, and he must be regarded as a prejudiced party. Similar charges, however, were published in the anonymous *Case of the Opera-House Disputes* in December 1784. The authors of the pamphlet describe the July 1783 deed of trust in detail, and recount the resignations of De Michele and Siscotti. The trustees, they say, 'have not only exceeded the sum allotted for defraying the annual, necessary, and incidental expences; but there is strong presumption of the receipts and profits of the theatre, having been misapplied to private purposes . . . extravagant disbursements have been encouraged; salaries have been unnecessarily increased; useless places have been created'.[1] They charge specifically that when Novosielski visited Italy in 1784 'for the purpose of engaging performers', he was accompanied by his wife and one '*Father Antonio*', Le Picq, and Le Picq's mistress Signora Rossi—all at company expense to the tune of £1,500. Novosielski's salary as designer and machinist was £300; 'His present salary is *seven hundred and fifty pounds*, beside the allotment of an house, coals, candles, and the frequent advantage of joining in the public dinners at the theatre, provided by the trustees at the expence of the creditors.' Novosielski's wife 'hath an additional salary of one hundred and fifty pounds for superintending the candles; and, that an ample provision may be made for every branch of the family, her father is complimented with a salary of two hundred pounds as the superintendant of something, but what that something is, heaven only can tell'. An unnecessary position has been created for one Parkyns MacMahon to handle advertising and publicity at a salary of £150. The pamphleteers complain that while these salaries are regularly paid, others are not. 'Is it not a scandalous abuse, that many of the dressers and door-keepers should not, to this moment, have received their salaries of last year. . . . Is this management? Is this honesty?'

Taylor complained that Gallini paid to have this pamphlet written against him, and perhaps we may suspect bias against the trustees as well. We have also, however, the testimony of Peter Crawford. Deposing on 22 October 1788, well after he had sold out and removed himself from opera affairs, Crawford specifically confirms De Michele's claim that he had

---

[1] *The Case of the Opera-House Disputes*, 16–17. Following information from 26–32.

disapproved of and protested against the trustees' management, and says that De Michele 'often expostulated with them'. Crawford also says

That he this deponent having been Treasurer Steward & Manager of the affairs of the said Opera house from the year 1780 . . . by that means became well acquainted with the Conduct of the proprietors thereof from time to time and saith that in his . . . Judgment & opinion the Defendants the Trustees in the deed of the 17th of July 1783 did not manage & conduct the affairs of the said opera-house upon that Oeconomical plan as was proposed & intended by the said deed and entred into Engagements with several performers that in this Deponents Judgment & opinion were totally useless & consequently Created an unnecessary expence and in particular this Deponent well knows that they engaged Signior Rauzzini as a first Man at salary of 200 a year tho they at that time had a first man named Pacchierotti and they the said defendants the Trustees also engaged Segnora Carnivali as first woman at £200 a Year altho' they had at that time a first woman of superior talents named Segna. Uttini. And they also engaged Mons. Le Texier for the management of the Opera of Golcondor notwithstanding they had already a Composer & the assistance of this Deponent to Conduct such Opera and this Deponent therefore Concieves all such additional Engagements & expenses to have been unnecessary & extravagant.[1]

Crawford was a man of long experience; he had been hired by the trustees themselves, and his personal probity was widely acknowledged at the time. This testimony is fairly damning. And in so far as we possess financial details for the two seasons of the trustees' management, the figures demonstrate their complete failure to carry out their mandate. The task was probably impossible in the best of circumstances, but their extravagance and bungling made a bad situation worse.

### The Financial Picture in Summer 1785

Any attempt to calculate the financial results of the trustees' management between July 1783 and July 1785 is complicated by some disturbing contradictions among the available primary sources. The set of figures in which one may have at least partial confidence is an accounting conducted by Master in Chancery William Weller Pepys. In 1788 he reported to the court that in two seasons the trustees had received a total of £36,488. 1s. and disbursed a total of £44,798. 0s. 3d.—a cumulative loss of £8,309. 19s. 3d.[2] This

---

[1] C24/1929 (Crawford).

[2] C38/745 (7 May 1788). Where the balance came from is not altogether clear; some of the money may have been from the trustees, but much of it was evidently borrowed. *The Testament, or Will, of Mr. William Taylor*, 35–7, says that £4,500 of the total was supplied by

audit strongly suggests that the trustees had actually paid out £44,798. Whether they took in more than they admitted is hard to say.

*The Case of the Opera-House Disputes* claims that the receipts in 1783–84 totalled £24,000, but that 'mismanagement' occasioned a deficiency of £3,000.[1] This implies expenses of £27,000. The implications of these figures for the next season, however, are difficult to credit. Could the theatre have taken in a mere £12,500 while spending £17,800 in 1784–85? This seems improbable—and yet William Taylor testifies that receipts in 1783–84 totalled £23,419,[2] and the usually reliable O'Reilly pamphlet gives £22,856.[3] Either the Chancery audit figure for receipts is very low, or three apparently independent sources are too high—or the trustees found ways to hide income and keep it out of the books they presented in Chancery.

The most detailed statement about income in 1783–84 is to be found in an affidavit by Novosielski of 20 July 1784 (C31/233, no. 348). He names five segments of income, giving reasonably exact figures for four of them: (1) Crawford and Johnson 'received jointly upward of seven thousand pounds of subscriptions'; (2) Crawford and Johnson collected door receipts for the first twenty-nine nights of the season—said to be 'hardly enough to pay the nightly Expences of the said Theatre' (roughly £95 per night?); (3) late subscription money totalled £672; (4) receipts taken by Novosielski over the next nineteen nights totalled £4,422; (5) receipts collected by the receivers appointed by the court in May totalled £3,000 'and upwards' in the last fourteen nights of the season. The gap in category no. 2 is awkward, but if one allows £150 a night (compromising between Novosielski's very low implied figure and that obtaining the rest of the season), the result is a total income of about £19,500 for 1783–84. This figure makes sense in the total context of 1780s finances (discussed in sect. v, below). The final piece in this little tangle is a marvellously detailed 'Memorandum of the Expences of the Season of Operas 1784' printed and analysed in Chapter 3.[4] The total for the year is £20,684. Assuming this to be the basic outlay for 1784–85, we offer the conservative hypothesis that income and expenditure in the trustees' two seasons were not enormously out of balance. (For a conjectural breakdown

Robert Mawley.

[1] *The Case of the Opera-House Disputes*, 9, 20.

[2] C31/248, no. 285.

[3] *An Authentic Narrative*, 28.

[4] Bedford Opera Papers, 2.A.29. This gem of a document seems to have been put together by someone in the Lord Chamberlain's office from the accounts the trustees were forced to supply in the summer of 1785.

TABLE I. *Receipts and expenditure under the trustees (£)*

| Season | Receipts | Expenditure |
|---|---|---|
| 1783–84 | *c.* 19,500 | *c.* 24,000 |
| 1784–85 | *c.* 17,000 | 20,684 |
| [KNOWN TOTALS] | 36,488 | 44,798 |

of the totals, see Table I.) Some income may have been hidden or successfully misappropriated. Novosielski may have paid some bills for the Royal Circus (in which he was a partner) out of opera receipts,[1] and some of the bills may have been padded or inflated to fund kickbacks. Even allowing for a certain amount of chicanery, however, the bottom line of the Chancery audit suggests that the trustees were unable to make their expenses, let alone pay off huge debts with their profits. Had expenditure been held to £18,000 a year as stipulated, and had income remained the same, the venture would more or less have broken even.

By June of 1785 the failure of the trustees had become increasingly obvious. Debts were piling up; Gallini was conducting aggressive guerrilla warfare in the courts; Taylor had brought suit against them from the other side (C12/1546/73, filed 5 March 1785). The state of the enterprise was summed up in an interim report by the highly competent accountant Pepys, issued 16 July 1785 (C38/722). His summary of the financial history is a masterpiece of concision. Ignoring claims not made under the July 1783 deed of trust, he notes that not all claimants have yet come forward; hence the totals are incomplete. The debts he certifies and grants priority are £4,282 to Gallini on the 1778 mortgage; £9,000 to the 1781 stock purchasers; £1,900, £400, and £1,060 to three classes of renters; £7,326 to Gallini (debts paid on Harris's behalf), and £1,700 to Messrs Davis and Grant—a total of £25,668. To this must be added the trustees' £8,000 loss and all the tradesmen's bills and salaries to performers and servants left unpaid by Taylor in 1783, not to mention most or all of the £16,000 intended to be secured by the March 1783 deed of trust. The total debts as of summer 1785 were not readily calculable then or now, but they were unquestionably more than £60,000. Under these circumstances one can well understand Master Pepys's terse

---

[1] This charge is made in *The Case of the Opera-House Disputes*, 25.

statement that 'the said Trustees are willing and disposed to resign their Trust and give immediate possession of the premises to the said John Andrew Gallini or any other person the Court shall approve'. Lord Chamberlain Salisbury, however, was still determined to use all the power of his office to block Gallini's take-over.

## IV. Gallini in Command, 1785–1790

To understand how Gallini finally got partial control of the opera-house and the circumstances in which he managed it during the last four seasons of the 'old' Haymarket, we must make a brief excursus into the subject of theatrical licensing. Beyond that, our concern will be with the nature of the operation Gallini put together and with the precarious solvency he was able to achieve. Less is to be learnt from lawsuits than for the earlier part of the decade, but because Gallini was forced to manage under the supervision of the Court of Chancery some kinds of records do survive. They permit us to make some overall season hypotheses and comparisons that help put the condition of the opera in perspective throughout the eleven seasons at issue.

### The Licensing Dispute of 1785

A theatre operating in London after the Licensing Act of 1737 required either a royal patent or a licence. As we have explained in Chapter 1, the King's Theatre itself never received a patent. After 1740 its proprietor or manager needed to obtain a fresh licence at the beginning of each season. This was normally pro forma: whoever was in charge simply asked for the licence and received it.[1] If, however, the opera company was unable to pay its bills, and the Lord Chamberlain was being deluged with petitions and complaints, then he had the power to withhold the licence. The Earl (soon to be Marquis) of Salisbury had become Lord Chamberlain on 26 December 1783 and was very much interested in the opera. The three short-term

---

[1] The usual form of the licence granted permission 'to have Italian Operas performed at The King's Theatre' (PRO LC 5/162, p. 234, for 1778–79). In 1780 Lord Chamberlain Hertford added a clause: '. . . and do not allow that any other species of Entertainment, whatever, shall be Exhibited there, without application specifying the Nature of such Entertainment, being previously made to and Permission obtained from me for that purpose' (ibid., p. 251). The point of the addition was to force the managers to obtain a separate licence for every concert or masquerade held in the King's Theatre.

licences he issued to the trustees during 1784–85 were an innovation: Salisbury was not a *laissez-faire* overseer of the public entertainments.

Salisbury was clearly irked by the chaos the trustees' management created, as well he might be.[1] Why he did not simply dump the whole mess in the lap of the wealthy Gallini cannot be stated with certainty. To judge from the papers in LC 7/3, Salisbury held Gallini in contempt: he referred to him contemptuously as 'Bowkit' in a letter of 15 October (LC 7/3, fos. 299–300) and fiercely resisted all requests for a personal interview. He may well have shared William Taylor's personal prejudices in this regard. In a lawsuit against Gallini filed on 22 April 1785, Taylor describes him as a 'Dancing Master . . . an Italian of very low extraction and well acquainted with most of the Dancers Singers and other persons of equally mean Birth and Education' (C12/2012/53). Or Salisbury's prejudice may have been more personal: he reportedly 'inserted' Carnevale's name in the opera licence for 1788–89 'to restrain abuses'.[2]

The trustees had had enough, so something would have to be done. The plan reported by Cherubini for subsidy by 'gentlemen' soon evaporated—so much for Scheme 1. Scheme 2 was announced on 19 August 1785:

Lord Chamberlain's Office, August 18, 1785

A great Many Complaints having been made to the Lord Chamberlain, by several persons interested in the Opera-House, that the present managers thereof have conducted the same very improperly, and application having been made to them to put the management into other Hands, and they having refused so to do, Notice is hereby given, that by his Majesty's Permission, the Operas for the ensuing season, will be at the Theatre Royal in the Haymarket, under the direction of the Lord Chamberlain, where every possible care will be taken to accommodate the old Subscribers with Boxes, as far as the House will admit; and the profits are intended to be applied in discharge of the debts due on the Opera-House, according to the priority to be ascertained by the Master's Report to be made in the Cause concerning the Opera-House, now depending in the Court of Chancery. Timely notice of the Opening of the House will be given in the public papers. (*Morning Post*, 19 August 1785)

Salisbury evidently fancied himself as General Intendant of the opera. A

---

[1] Among the papers preserved in LC 7/3 are a large number of manuscripts from the Lord Chamberlain's office pertaining to the state of the opera in 1784 and 1785, and to the licensing dispute in particular. For a check-list, see Judith Milhous and Robert D. Hume, 'An Annotated Guide to the Theatrical Documents in PRO LC 7/1, 7/2 and 7/3', *Theatre Notebook*, 35 (1981), 25–31, 77–87, 122–9.

[2] *The Times*, 9 Feb. 1789.

week later, however, the *Morning Herald* announced that the plan 'of cramming the Opera House, and all its contents into Colman's [that is, the Little Haymarket], is entirely laid aside' (27 August). Probably someone had done the basic arithmetic and realized that so small a theatre could not pay the bills for the sort of opera company London subscribers were accustomed to.

Other rumours were already abroad. On 22 August the *Morning Herald* reported both the possibility of a new trust and that a manager might be appointed 'in whose name a licence might be granted with safety; two candidates have started—the veteran Crawford with his antediluvian integrity to recommend him, and Mons. Le Texier, a man of real taste and genius; but nothing was settled—we wish for a coalition of both'. The problem lay in financial guarantees. Le Texier was apparently in no position to supply working capital; Crawford may have been, but evidently declined to accept the risk as an individual. Gallini jumped in ahead of Crawford by accepting the financial liability. Both men proposed terms to the trustees (discussed below), and on 14 September 1785 Gallini signed a memorandum with them agreeing, in essence, to assume the management of the opera-house as sole trustee (LC 7/3, fos. 239–40).

This was not what Gallini wanted, but it was a step in the right direction. A codicil to this agreement dated 16 September 1785 acknowledges that on this day 'Personal Possession of the Opera House Furniture and Premises' was given to Gallini by George Grant, who 'delivered up the Keys and quitted the Premises leaving Mr. Gallini in the Possession'. After five years of infighting and litigation, and two years after he thought he had won control, Gallini was finally in charge of the opera-house—albeit only as trustee and managing director.

On 17 September 1785 Gallini wrote to the Lord Chamberlain to say that he had assumed management of the opera and to ask for a licence.[1] Salisbury replied on the 23rd in discouraging terms. He demanded 'An Attested Copy of all the Contracts' (with salaries specified); an explanation of the 'Security' Gallini would post; a copy of his agreement with the trustees, and an explanation of why they broke off negotiations with Crawford. Salisbury also stated that the total 'expenses of the ensuing season must not exceed £16,000', and that he would appoint a 'Treasurer and Receiver' to handle all money, adding that if such person were 'interrupted or molested in his

---

[1]  LC 7/3, fos. 182–3.

office upon any pretence whatsoever' the licence would be withdrawn.[1] Salisbury thereafter refused all requests for a personal interview and communicated with Gallini only through secretaries.

The next two and a half months were occupied by a violent row over whether Gallini should or should not receive a licence. The large cache of papers from the Lord Chamberlain's office preserved in LC 7/3 shows that every effort was made to find grounds on which to block the licence, and to discover flaws in Gallini's legal claims on the theatre.[2] Gallini, on his side, raised a clamour, asked noble friends to intervene on his behalf, and flatly refused to accept the £16,000 ceiling. He threatened to abandon the enterprise altogether (LC 7/3, fos. 242–5). On 15 October Salisbury wrote to his adviser on operatic affairs William Sheldon in some alarm, to say that he had received private information that 'Gallini has told his friends he shall have Ground for an Action' against Salisbury if he is not granted a licence (LC 7/3, fos. 299–300).

On 28 October Gallini won a major victory. At the start of the Michaelmas term, the Court of Chancery accepted Master Pepys's report of the previous July and then proceeded to endorse Gallini's 14 September 1785 agreement with the trustees.[3] By mid-November Salisbury was forced to agree to issue a licence, but stipulated on 20 November that it be for only six weeks at a time—a provision Gallini rejected.[4] The licence itself is apparently not preserved (even in the Lord Chamberlain's letter-books), but we deduce that it was finally issued to Gallini around 13 December for the full year (LC 7/3, fo. 262). All the doubt and delay, however, meant that the opera was not actually able to open for business until 24 January 1786, two months later than usual.

### Gallini's Articles of Agreement with the Trustees (September 1785)

Both Gallini and Crawford proposed terms to the trustees: a comparison shows why Gallini's offer was preferred despite the Lord Chamberlain's intense hostility to him. Crawford outlined his proposal in a document sent to Salisbury with a letter of 19 September 1785.[5] Crawford demanded 'full & absolute power to engage & contracting in his own name with all the

---

[1] LC 7/3, fo. 256. Drafts of this letter, and a memo about licence terms (evidently prepared by William Sheldon) are in LC 7/3, fos. 274, 315–18.

[2] See particularly LC 7/3, fos. 184–5, 188–9, 213–14, 257–8, 271–2, 301–2.

[3] C33/463, fo. 709. See also C12/592/17.

[4] LC 7/3, fos. 203–4, 289–90.

[5] LC 7/3, fos. 198, 298.

singers, dancers, musicians, and all other persons', accepting a budget cap of £16,000 on condition that the trustees would indemnify him if receipts fell below that sum. He insisted on a £2,000 penalty if the trustees 'interrupt him or oppose him during the said season'. He asked only £350 for his services as manager and treasurer, and agreed to pay two assistants out of that sum. He wanted any surplus income put in escrow 'subject to the order of the Honorable Court of Chancery'. He asked that the trustees be 'limited in regard to the number of orders they are to give for admission to the operas'. And he agreed to pay Taylor his £200 stipend. Annotations on this paper show that the trustees objected to indemnification, to the £2,000 penalty, to the escrow provision, and to the limitation on free orders of admission. They naturally wanted any profits applied first to their debts, the views of the Court of Chancery on priority of claims notwithstanding—a demand Gallini was willing to meet.

The agreement Gallini signed with the trustees is dated 14 September 1785.[1] Because most of the conditions held until the theatre burnt in 1789, we give the terms in full.

Memorandum agreed as follows / Opera House and Premises. Mr. Gallini to have possession as Trustee for all Parties interested in the property, and carry the Opera on at his own Risk.

To be the Manager at the Salary of £600 a year and to have two Nights in the Season rent free not on Tuesdays or Saturdays at his own expence, not to be subject to be removed but as the Court may direct.

To pass his Accounts Annually before the Master in the Cause Harris agt. Crawford as Trustee as soon as possible and attend the Master De die in diem. To consent for himself that the Balance which may appear by the Masters Report to be obtained due to the Trustees shall be paid out of the first profits to be made under Gallini's possession not exceeding Eight Thousand Pounds without Interest if the Balance exceeds that Sum Eight Thousand Pounds to be taken in full but if the Court shall refuse to give such preference Mr. Gallini not to be bound to make such payments good and in that case he shall account before the Master and deliver back the possession upon being repaid the Expences incurred by this Agreement and also indemnified against the Engagements that he may have made so as not to exceed the Annual Disbursements of Eighteen Thousand Pounds.

After paying that Balance then the Profits to be applied as the Court shall direct.

Not to exceed in management the Annual Sum of Eighteen Thousand Pounds including therein the Rent Taxes Expence of Performers, his own and under

[1] LC 7/3, fos. 239–40.

93

Managers Salaries Servants Wages Repairs of the Premises and expence of Scenery and Wardrobes and all expences in carrying on the Operas.

If Gallini quits possession it shall be in the Month of August and give three Months previous notice and when he shall have quitted such possession he shall revert back to the same situation he was in before this Agreement was made and stand upon the same Security and priority.

To carry on the Operas for two years certain and not to be compelled to carry them on longer than that time.

The Parties not to prosecute any Suit to interrupt this Agreement or the Business of the Theatre under this Agreement.

To permit Gallini to keep possession of the Theatre and Premises thereto belonging upon the terms above mentioned until he shall be compleatly paid or such less time as he shall think proper to carry on the Business of the Theatre, for not less than two years.

The Trustees to receive all Arrears due in respect of subscriptions and Rents up to Midsummer last and clear off all rent and taxes to that time and include same in their account.

Their Accounts to be passed before the Master in the Cause Harris & Crawford.

The Licence to be obtained in Gallini's Name so long as he continues in possession, but for and as Trustee for the purposes of this Agreement.

Gallini not to be personally liable to any of the Incumbrances other than as to such Balances as may appear due from time to time by the Masters Reports and then only as the Court shall direct. The Chancery Bill Taylor against Gallini and others to be dismissed, and the Cause in the Common Pleas Taylor against Harris & Gallini to be released. Taylor's costs of those Suits to be paid by Gallini to Taylor.

Gallini to pay Taylor out of his own pocket Two Hundred Pounds a year for so long [a] time as he continues possession and carries on the Operas provided Taylor lives so long in lieu of the Two Hundred Pounds a year now paid by the Trustees to commence the 24th June past.

The Parties to execute such Deeds and Instruments and consent to such Orders of Court as shall be advised and thought requisite by Counsel to carry the above Terms into execution at the Expence of the Trust.

Witness our Hands this fourteenth Day of September One Thousand Seven Hundred & Eighty Five.

Signatories to this agreement were Andrea Carnevale, George Grant, Gallini, and Taylor; William Davis signed as witness for 'Self & Co. Trustees'. Several points about this agreement are noteworthy. In essence, Gallini agreed to become trustee for Taylor, replacing the remains of the Gang of Six. Gallini accepted full individual responsibility ('at his own Risk'), agreed to limit expenditure to £18,000, and agreed 'for himself' to pay any surplus to the trustees until their personal losses were reimbursed. Gallini was to get £600 per annum plus two free benefits, but was to pay Taylor's £200 out of his own pocket.

Why did Gallini accept such terms? The salary was negligible to a man of his wealth, and any visible profits would go to the former trustees for the foreseeable future. (In the event, the Court of Chancery interfered and enforced its hierarchy of claimants, with Gallini at the head of the list.) Clearly Gallini wanted the position and prestige enjoyed by the proprietor of the opera company. He probably also calculated that however unsatisfactory these terms of possession, he might make them a stepping-stone towards better things.

## 'Uneasy lies the head': Gallini under Fire

Because Gallini was able to pay his bills, less is known of his regime in some respects than of the seven seasons conducted by his predecessors. The Court of Chancery continued to be flooded with opera-related cases, but most of them had their origin in the early 1780s. By no means, however, was Gallini enjoying 'peaceable possession' of the opera-house.

One of the conditions of the agreement under which Gallini became trustee and manager was that current litigation against him would be dropped. On 19 December 1785 Taylor's counsel moved that since 'the matters in difference between the Parties are since Accommodated', Taylor's bill of complaint should 'stand dismissed'.[1] This terminated C12/2012/53, but hostilities can hardly be said to have ended, for by this time Taylor was again sniping hard at Gallini. The same day that case was dropped, Taylor tried to have Gallini arrested for non-payment of costs (C33/466, fo. 55). Indeed, hostilities had recommenced even before the truce was signed. On 31 October 1785 Taylor wrote a nasty letter to Gallini, denouncing his plans for management and warning him 'not to attempt to Employ in this House any of the wretches who have been instrumental in Destroying my reputation and involving my affairs in difficulties and distresses', threatening to resist by carrying 'a remonstrance to the foot of the Throne and implore his Majestys protection against such unexampled Cruelty and Oppression'.[2] (Taylor specialized in hyperbole and self-pity.) On 14 November Taylor sent the Lord Chamberlain a list of favoured creditors entitled to employment under the terms of the deed of trust.[3] Taylor was violently hostile to

[1] C33/466, fo. 326ᵛ.    [2] Taylor recites this letter in full in C12/2012/54.
[3] LC 7/3, fos. 320, 332, 360.

Carnevale, who was Gallini's choice as assistant manager, and the employment of Carnevale added fuel to the fire.[1]

Gallini's first season was only three weeks under way when Taylor filed an affidavit denouncing his management in blistering terms.[2] Taylor complained that the season opened late, that the company was weak, and that receipts were lower than they had been in 1782—none of which was either surprising or Gallini's fault. On 18 February 1786 Taylor demanded the reinstatement of creditors sacked from the theatre's payroll by Gallini, which was legally a valid claim, though not necessarily in the company's best interests (C31/239, no. 233). Three days later Taylor's lawyers asked the court to exercise close supervision over Gallini's receipts (C31/239, no. 286). Not until 13 April 1786 did Taylor get round to bringing a new suit against Gallini (C12/2012/54), claiming that Gallini was acting as if the 17 July 1783 deed 'determined ceased and became void' when the 14 September 1785 agreement was signed. Gallini wanted to be proprietor, not trustee, and was acting as though he had succeeded. Taylor's suit, however, had little object beyond harassment.

While fending off Taylor on one side Gallini found his other flank in danger. The Lord Chamberlain had given him a licence under threat of legal action, and Salisbury immediately started looking for any convenient way of dispossessing him. On 23 March 1786 Salisbury's minion William Sheldon called a meeting of the luckless subscribers to the block-Gallini mortgage fund—the twenty-four subscribers of £500 who had put up the money in 1781 that prevented Gallini from foreclosing on Sheridan and Taylor. What Sheldon proposed was that they foreclose on their unpaid shares and get Gallini thrown out.[3] In concert with William Taylor, of all people, they initiated such proceedings, though the matter did not come to a hearing until 1788. Guerrilla warfare continued, but no pitched battles were fought for two years.

In May 1788 Taylor asked the Court of Chancery to dismiss Gallini as manager on the grounds of wilful neglect and misconduct (C31/248, no. 286). The shareholders of 1781 supported this motion (C31/250, no. 211). The Lord Chancellor heard the case in Lincoln's Inn Hall in early July 1788. The fullest information on the case comes from two quite contradictory

---

[1] Taylor wrote to Gallini on 19 Nov. 1785, protesting vehemently against the employment of Carnevale (C12/2012/54).

[2] C31/239, no. 206 (15 Feb. 1786).

[3] C31/250, no. 211.

newspaper accounts.[1] Taylor and his allies charged that Gallini was using opera-house money to pay singers he was also using at Hanover Square; that he was not submitting full accounts to the Master in Chancery; and that he was taking a cut of the performers' benefit receipts. The Lord Chancellor was evidently inclined to believe the first two charges and tightened up the financial scrutiny exercised by the court. He refused, however, to remove Gallini on the grounds that 'Sir John had a large property [that is, financial interest] in the house, and the persons who endeavoured to turn him out of the management had not thought of offering any indemnity, nor any security, nor even of mentioning a person properly qualified to succeed him'. This was indeed the rub: what wealthy person would care to manage the opera entirely at his personal risk, with any profit he might make handed over to the innumerable creditors? Gallini had the money, and he wanted the job—so he kept it. One result was a vicious smear campaign against him in the spring of 1789. The newspapers were full of slurs and digs. An item in the *Morning Post* of 6 July, for example, dubs him 'the most industrious man alive', instancing a string of activities that concludes with holding 'a meeting of the persons engaged and employed for him in his smuggling business'.

As we shall see when we get to the discussion of Gallini's receipts, he actually contrived to make a small profit. He did so, however, by economizing ruthlessly in ways that gradually roused public ire—and fed newspaper hostility. In the spring of Gallini's last season in the old theatre the audience rioted twice. A brief account of their initial outburst is printed in *The London Stage* from the *Public Advertiser* of 10 February, but longer descriptions are worth quoting. *The Times* of 9 February 1789 reported:

The strains of Marchesi had only the power to soothe while they were heard! the first *Divertissement* received some marks of disapprobation; but the concluding dance had scarce begun, when from all parts of the House 'Gallini's' name was uttered, and his presence required on the Stage.—Gallini trembling to meet the unanimous tribunal, fled from the House; and the rumor of his retreat reaching the Boxes, Carnivale was called for, in whose hands the management was principally the last two seasons:—Mr. Carnivale appearing, was, when the confusion had subsided, called to by Mr. Greville from the Duchess of Marlborough's Box; whose enquiries in effect were—'whether the subscribers might hereafter expect better

---

[1] Both are preserved in Theatre Cuts 42, fo. [10]. The first of these is virtually identical with an account in *The Times* of 3 July 1788; the second (dated '9 July' in MS) describes the court as far more hostile to Gallini. However, both say that Gallini was left in charge because no one else could be found to assume financial liability for the opera.

dancers?' Mr. Carnivale 'assured the audience, that it would be a happiness to him to contribute to their entertainment, by any means in his power, but that at this time he was not in the least concerned in the management;—and though his name was inserted in the Lord Chamberlain's Licence to restrain abuses, he had no power to make any engagements'.

The stage being filled by young men of fashion, and numbers rushing at this time from the boxes and pitt, the ladies became extremely terrified; and their apprehensions encreased when they beheld a demolition of the scenery and other havock in these mimic regions. The Prince of Wales seeing the Dutchess of Devonshire in a state of alarm, hastened to her box, and conducted her Grace to her carriage;—and other ladies retreated as well as they could.—Some few, however, were such heroines as to sit it out.

By the interference of the Prince, the total destruction of the house was prevented;—and had not some Ladies timely interfered, the chandeliers would have been destroyed.

A *light-heeled* courier who was dispatched to Paris last Monday, will, it is hoped, enable *Gallini*, who is to appear on Tuesday—for so Lord Sefton and others have undertaken,—to give such promise, as may suspend further resentment.

On 23 February 1789 *The Times* reported bad attendance at the opera and delivered some trenchant commentary:

The total want of variety at this once elegant Theatre, the wretched dancers, and the insipidity of the dances, have driven away those who used to make it a point to see and be seen. The subscribers, indeed, making the best of a bad bargain, fill the boxes as usual, but that will not fill the treasury. The Divertissements had their usual accompaniment of hisses, and *Sir John* very wisely kept out of the way. Dreading the just vengeance of the audience, he had all the scenery lifted away, and locked up. We only wonder that the public should so long continue to be insulted by such a miserable management.

A month later, before the new dancers had appeared, the audience again protested.

Opera Fracas.

Various imputations having been circulated, charging Mons. Noverre with neglect in his department, as Ballet-Master, and these being artfully intended to involve him in the disgrace which attends Gallini, he came forward on Saturday evening at the close of the Opera, [hiatus in cutting]

While Mr. Noverre was giving this explanation, Gallini stood near him, and when he had concluded, the Manger was pressed, by a large assembly of gentlemen, who ranged across the stage, to make his defence.—The powerful *hissings* of the audience, however, prevented this; and Gallini endeavouring to retreat, was *jostled* by the party on the stage, and treated with very proper marks of contempt; except in the instance where an attempt was made to throw him in to the Pitt.

The *Sardonic Grin* which Gallini put on while Mr. Noverre was speaking, heightened the resentment his past conduct had created.—The presence of *Delpini*, and another *contemptible Buffoon*, who forgetting both season and circumstance, came forward as the *Jocham* and *Boaz* of Mr. Gallini, added not [to] his claims for favor, and thus situated, his escape became so extremely perilous, that several Ladies exclaimed, 'Don't kill him!'—others fainted away—the Dutchess of *Rutland* was one of these; and a third class '*smiled* on the tempest, and enjoyed the storm!' *Gallini* in the midst of this tumult got off, and his retreat was covered by the scene-shifters.

The *heroes* from *Fop-Alley* who paraded the stage, were now called upon to withdraw, and off! off! off! was the exclamation from Box, Pit, and Galleries.—These champions retired for a time, but returned with amazing *prowess*, and five leaders brought up in battle array,—attacked—'Turk *Gregory* never did such feats!'—attacked the *Patent Lamps*—and extinguished every *wick*! each little flaming orb was *eclipsed* by this *quintriple alliance* of Shadows,—and all was dark!

What was the object of this proceeding, ye GIGANTIC-PIGMIES?—What is there to qualify such an insult to an assembly of the first fashion and beauty?— After this merciless havock on the *lamps*, several of the scenes were pulled down and trampled on the stage; and here the outrage ended. (Theatre Cuts 42, fo. [40])

Gallini did hastily hire new dancers from Paris (notably Mlle Guimard), and the company got through the rest of the spring without another riot— but clearly the audience wanted a theatre that operated on the star system. How a bankrupt opera-house with an £18,000 cap on its annual expenses was to provide costly international stars was a very good question.

## Gallini at the Little Haymarket (Spring 1790)

Solvency *per se* was not Gallini's most pressing problem in the spring of 1789. Writing to Earl Cowper about May 1789 he commented that he needed to recruit a 'first-rate' company for the next year, 'otherwise things will go badly, like this season, when everything foundered—opera and ballet'.[1] At the time of the fire of 1789 Gallini occupied a deteriorating position at the King's Theatre, Haymarket: the public was grumbling, but the £18,000 cap meant that higher receipts could not be spent on better singers, dancers, costumes, and scenery. O'Reilly reports that at this time Gallini 'frequently expressed his wish to withdraw himself from the management, to dispose of his interest, or to engage with some other person in the

[1] Gibson, 'Earl Cowper', 249.

conduct of the concern'.[1] In the same letter quoted above he queried Earl Cowper about the possibility of his becoming the London 'correspondent' for 'The court of Rome', though he appears to have been willing to serve without salary and we doubt whether such an appointment would have debarred him from continuing to run the opera. This suggestion came to nothing, and Gibson comments that in consequence 'it appeared that Gallini would have to remain in the opera business for another season'. This seems very misleading: Gallini was under no compulsion but his own vanity and ambition. He was a wealthy man and he continued to run a prosperous concert series in Hanover Square.

The fire of 17 June 1789 certainly offered Gallini a convenient exit if he wanted one. Far from washing his hands of the opera, he immediately set about scheming to build a new opera-house. He observes in a letter of 18 August 1789 to Earl Cowper, 'I hope myself, if I succeed with his Majesty to add no inconsiderable ornament to this City in my new Opera house which I think will rival any in Europe.' At this time Gallini and O'Reilly were negotiating with Salisbury for the right to abandon the old site and its debts, and to build a new opera-house under their own aegis in which to make a fresh start.[2] How that partnership fell apart in December 1789 is not immediately germane to present concerns, which have to do with Gallini's management. Two points are vital: he had every intention of carrying on as manager of the Italian opera, and for the season of 1789–90 he moved his company to the Little Haymarket.

Relatively little is known about Gallini's occupancy of the Little Haymarket in 1790: he paid his bills, so there are no scandalous reports in the newspapers and no lawsuits full of juicy details. There is, however, an obvious question: how could Gallini run an opera season in so small and inadequate a theatre? The Lord Chamberlain had backed off such a plan in 1785, and the Pantheon proprietors suffered grim receipts when their company moved to the Little Haymarket after the Pantheon burnt in January 1792. Why run an opera season at all in spring 1790?

When Gallini began making arrangements after the June 1789 fire for an interim season at the Little Haymarket, he was assuming that in 1790–91 his company would be moving into an elegant new theatre and that the venture would start with a clean slate, unhampered by William Taylor and the debts

[1] *An Authentic Narrative*, 46.
[2] For a detailed account of the tortuous negotiations, schemes, and counter-schemes of summer and autumn 1789, see vol. II, Ch. 1.

of the old opera. Gallini had the money to offer an interim season, and doing so added to his claim to head the new opera venture. In his letter of 18 August 1789 he tells Earl Cowper that he has already received a licence for the Little Haymarket for the next season, and sketches his plans. 'I propose opening with a Burletta . . . it is possible I shall not bring out any serious opera's till after the Carnival. If I cannot engage Marchesi & Mara, who I am now treating with, I think of substituting Senesino [identity uncertain] & Banti in their Place & have begged of Mr. Cecchi to apply to them for me.'[1] Gallini's plan was clearly to hire some front-rank performers to keep the audience happy, but to offer a relatively inexpensive and unambitious season—which made perfectly good sense.

The company he finally engaged featured Marchesi, Madam Mara, and Nancy Storace (the first two not appearing until 6 April). Marchesi cost £1,150 and Mara £850 plus a free benefit for just over three months—steep prices for so small a house.[2] Some of the lesser singers appear to have been marginal, and the tenor, Mussini, received savage reviews.[3] Recollecting the riot of the previous season, Gallini took care to provide a respectable roster of dancers, headed by the locally popular Mlle Hilligsberg and also featuring Duquesney and Laborie, all of whom were present throughout the entire season. In an advertisement of 7 January in *The Times* Gallini 'pledges' that the company will 'be superior to any other than ever performed in England'. This is not entirely hyperbole: considering the circumstances, the company was an ambitious and expensive one.

Nothing could make the theatre more than an unsatisfactory makeshift. *The Times* of 8 January says that 'The objections to the Theatre are innumerable; but as Mr. Gallini had only Hobson's Choice . . . we shall forbear to comment.' A preliminary notice of 4 (?) January 1790 observes that 'The arrangements are of necessity in *miniature*, yet as far as we can judge, the effect will not be unpleasant. . . . Two new boxes are gained on the stage, and the middle gallery is subdivided with much neatness. . . . The Band is a selection from that of the late Opera-house. The choice made by the Manager on this occasion has caused some discontent.'[4] We deduce that finding accommodation for subscribers was a terrible struggle, with some of

---

[1] Gibson, 'Earl Cowper', 250.

[2] These salaries are reported in the *World* of 12 Jan. 1790.

[3] A notice of 27 Feb. 1790 calls him 'miserably inferior' in 'taste'; one of 14 Mar. calls him 'the very *epitome* of affectation and insufficiency! . . . execrable' (Theatre Cuts 42, fo. [27]).

[4] Theatre Cuts 42, fo. [19ᵛ].

them stuffed into boxes carved out of former gallery space, and that the whole of the King's Theatre orchestra could not be crammed into such space as could be spared for it in the Little Theatre, necessitating a reduction in the size of the orchestra for the season.

The relatively sparse collection of reviews from this year suggests adequate if undistinguished performance standards, and better could hardly be expected under the circumstances. Without any information about either income or expenses, there is no way to estimate the magnitude of Gallini's losses. He could, however, afford it. Since he was using some of the same performers for his Hanover Square concert series, and there is every likelihood that it was profitable, those profits could offset, or at least diminish, losses on the opera.

We can only guess at Gallini's expectations in June 1790. He applied for a licence for 1790–91 and was refused on 30 June.[1] O'Reilly states that this application was 'for another Licence for the little Theatre', but that cannot be all Gallini had in mind. He knew that Taylor was rebuilding the King's Theatre and hence that by the spring of 1791 the Little Haymarket would be untenable as the home of an Italian opera company. Gallini probably hoped to rent the new King's Theatre, perhaps using his mortgage as leverage on terms. Failing that, he probably assumed that some kind of partnership bargain could be struck with Taylor. As of June 1790, at any rate, Gallini was showing no inclination to remove himself from the opera business.

The interim season at the Little Haymarket in the spring and summer of 1790 represents an attempt to continue the management pattern established by Gallini at the King's Theatre. One cannot help wondering what might have happened had Gallini actually found himself in charge of a grand new theatre in Leicester Square (as he imagined in August 1789 he would be), or even had he simply succeeded in dispossessing Taylor and operating the new King's Theatre for the next decade or more. O'Reilly had little idea what he was doing at the Pantheon and ran the venture into immediate ruin in highly competitive circumstances. Taylor—concerned mostly with a complicated financial juggling act—had no artistic policy beyond the star system. Gallini, by contrast, actually had the knowledge to make informed artistic judgements and the experience to put aesthetic choices into practice. Nor is this contrast a matter of financial acumen versus artistic sensibility for, as we shall see, Gallini was a sufficiently competent businessman

---

[1] O'Reilly, *An Authentic Narrative*, 64.

actually to have succeeded in bringing the King's Theatre's expenditures in line with its income—a unique achievement in this period.

## Receipts under Gallini

When Gallini took charge of the opera company in the autumn of 1785 he was forced to agree to limit all expenses to £18,000 per annum. He was personally liable for any additional expense, and likewise for any deficiency caused by a shortfall in the receipts. These conditions gave him a powerful motive for limiting expenditure, even at the cost of artistic quality—a factor that must be borne in mind when judging his management.

Gallini was required to pass his books under the scrutiny of a Master in Chancery, and did so. Unfortunately, they do not survive, and law-court records reveal less than one might hope. Obviously Gallini had every reason to conceal income above £18,000. And if his genuine expenses could be reduced below that level, then he had equally good motivation to pad them up to that point. Taylor accused him of various forms of skimming and concealment. How true any or all of these charges might be is difficult to say—but Taylor was an expert in financial duplicity, and Gallini had strong motives for indulging in such tricks.

Taylor's interrogatories for Gallini of 7 May 1788 implicitly charge him with at least three dodges:[1] (1) remitting benefit charges for performers in return for a personal cut of the proceeds; (2) selling tickets privately, not reporting the income, and letting the ticket-buyers into the theatre through a back door; (3) concealing income from masquerades. In the first of his new round of lawsuits, Taylor also charges that Gallini had Henry Johnson (his treasurer) sell tickets and pocket the income, putting the tickets down in the books as performer comps (C12/2012/53).

In the realm of padding expenses, Taylor says that Gallini has 'furnished various articles for the use of the Wardrobe of the said Theatre, namely tinsel foil of different Colours, tinsel Gold and silver laces French Sattins, lawns, & laces, for which he directed Bills to be made out . . . in fictitious or supposed names . . . and the prices charged . . . were very high and extravagant'.[2] This was an old trick, and one Gallini might well have employed, the more especially as he was apparently in the habit of smuggling such goods through customs.[3] In another affidavit Taylor charges

---

[1] These interrogatories are preserved among the loose papers in C107/201.

[2] C31/251, no. 207.

[3] On two occasions customs officials seized contraband on Gallini's premises—once in

Gallini with having Mr Almon, his printer, pad his annual bill by more than a hundred pounds, for which he collected a large kickback.[1] In the same affidavit Taylor gives numerous details of alleged false billing and other kickbacks. Taylor is not the most reliable of sources, but under the circumstances in which Gallini was operating one could hardly be surprised if he decided to cook his books—or at least to adjust them for his own convenience.

However shady Gallini's bookkeeping, there is overwhelming evidence that he made a profit of some £4,000 during his first three seasons, for he put the money into escrow for disposal by the Court of Chancery.[2] Beyond this bottom-line figure, gross income totals survive for all four seasons of Gallini's management (the last of them disputed). For the first three seasons there is testimony as to the total amount collected from subscribers to boxes. And for the seasons of 1786–87 and 1787–88 there are daybooks recording ticket sales for pit and gallery for every performance of the season. Since all these figures fit together tidily, one can be reasonably certain of the visible income of the theatre in these years—and that it was covering expenses. Gallini may well have padded bills and siphoned off all the income he could hide, but even so the theatre was making a small profit.

Much may be learnt from the account-books for the two middle seasons preserved in the Beinecke Library at Yale. The daily totals were reported long ago in *The London Stage*, and Petty has reproduced somewhat more detail from them, but no one has heretofore offered even a general analysis of what they mean—in part because without the subscriber income, they are virtually impossible to interpret. The account-books record for each day how many tickets were printed for the first gallery, the second gallery, and the pit, how many were sold, how many were 'returned' unused to the treasurer, how much cash was received for each area, and what the total cash take was for the day. In 1786–87 there were fifty performances, and the cash receipts totalled £8,763, or an average of £175 per night. About £130 of that sum was generated by pit sales (at 10s. 6d. each), the remainder by the galleries (at 5s. and 3s. respectively). Looking at the figures day by day, however, reveals drastic variations in attendance. Saturday performances drew

the opera-house itself, once in Hanover Square. See Theatre Cuts 42, fo. [14ʳ]. For discussion, see Ch. 7, sect. V.

[1] C31/253, no. 249.

[2] Grant and Novosielski claim that Gallini had made more than £4,000 by 27 June 1788 (C31/249, no. 303), and the next day their lawyer moved the court for payment of £4,656 (C31/249, no. 316). Matters proceeded slowly: on 19 Nov. 1788 some £4,317 was shifted to a trust account, pending further action by the court (C38/745).

TABLE 2. *Receipts under Gallini, 1785–1789 (£)*

| Season | Box Subscriptions | Ticket Sales | Season Total |
|---|---|---|---|
| 1785–86 | 8,966 | ? | 18,690 |
| 1786–87 | 9,160 | 8,763 | 18,766 |
| 1787–88 | 10,185 | 10,297 | c. 21,200 |
| 1788–89 | ? | ? | 19,001 or 17,500 |

far better than Tuesday. On Saturday, 20 January 1787, the theatre sold 324 pit tickets and 331 for the gallery (£247 total); on Tuesday the 23rd it sold 86 pit and 72 gallery tickets (£60 total). The overall figures for 1787–88 are a bit better. In fifty-two nights the total take was £10,297, or £198 per night. About £142 of that average was generated by pit sales—which is 72 per cent of the total (as against 75 per cent the previous year).

By themselves, these figures have little more than curiosity value, save for what they reveal about the capacity of the theatre. Various papers in Chancery records, however, allow one to add the total for box subscriptions and calculate season gross totals as a cross-check.[1] Adding these figures to those from the Yale manuscripts, we present the results in tabular form. (See Table 2.) The 'season total' includes some incidental income—for example, rents on houses near the Haymarket, income from the coffee-room, and so forth. Overall, however, one can see that season subscriptions and daily ticket sales tended to run in parallel, each providing upwards of 50 per cent of the total cash flow. This figure emphasizes the vital importance of the company's mounting a series of attractive new productions throughout the season. In 1786–87 walk-in sales ranged from a low of £43. 14s. 6d. on 2 January to a dazzling £371 on 17 March. No genius was needed to see the moral for managers: unpopular shows would have a devastating effect on income if not dropped immediately.

That Gallini siphoned off some income and kept it out of the theatre's books is highly likely. He regularly claimed to be doing 'badly' and even to be losing money,[2] but the Chancery figures prove otherwise. If one adds up the proven receipts above £18,000 in the first three seasons, the total is some £3,938, which is quite close to the '£4,000' that Novosielski and Taylor said

---

[1] Box subscription totals are to be found in C107/201, interrogatories of 27 May 1789; season totals for Gallini's first three years are stated in C31/249, no. 303; contradictory totals for 1788–89 are given in C31/253, nos. 325 and 384.

[2] For example, in letters to Earl Cowper of 1 May and 26 June 1787.

Gallini had made above his expenses. Gallini himself admitted on 5 March 1789 that since assuming the management he had 'made a profit of upwards of £4,000'.[1] The results of the season of 1788–89 are unclear: Gallini claimed a loss, and certainly the audience was ill-disposed. But if Gallini more or less broke even his last season in the old theatre, he would have made at least £1,000 on average throughout the four years. On a budget of £18,000, this is a 5.5 per cent profit—not at all bad in the light of the previous seven seasons. As reference to known salary figures shows, Gallini accomplished this feat by means of ruthless cost control.[2] He hired the occasional superstar (Rubinelli, Marchesi) and had to pay accordingly, but overall he brought salaries down with a bump, especially those of the dancers. Audience reaction to these economies has already been reported.

Gallini's results prove that a knowledgeable and hard-headed manager could balance the books, even in decidedly difficult circumstances. In a deposition of 5 March 1789 Gallini stated that he 'found it very difficult to Engage performers for the said Theatre at almost any rate, by Reason of the disgrace into which the said Theatre hath fallen, through the Difficulty which Several performances [performers] have for some years previous to this Deponents management met with in the payment of their salaries'.[3] Gallini had restored order and paid current bills, despite constant legal harassment by Taylor and the unremitting hostility of the Lord Chamberlain. What neither he nor anyone else could do, however, was to disburden the opera-house from the monstrous debts with which Sheridan and Taylor had encumbered it. Gallini balanced his own books, but paid nothing towards what was owed the £500 mortgagees and the numerous renters, let alone unpaid performers and tradesmen from previous seasons.

## V. A Summary of Opera Company Finances, 1778–1789

Before this investigation of Chancery records, most of what was known about opera finances in the 1780s came from O'Reilly's *An Authentic Narrative* (1791). Because he was violently hostile to Taylor—the point of the pamphlet was to discredit him—scholars have looked on its figures with distrust. In fact, they derived largely from Peter Crawford and for the most part appear to check out against lawsuit sources. They are treacherous in

[1] C31/251, no. 301.
[2] See 'Opera Salaries', 48–53, for a summary of figures from various sources.
[3] C31/251, no. 301.

TABLE 3. *Income and expenditure, 1778–1789 (£)*

| Season | Income | Expenditure | Result |
|---|---|---|---|
| 1778–79 | [*c.* 10,000?] | [*c.* 13,000?] | lost 3,000[a] |
| 1779–80 | [*c.* 8,000?] | [*c.* 13,000?] | [lost *c.* 5,000?] |
| 1780–81 | ? | ? | [unknown loss] |
| 1781–82 | '22,236' or '26,000' | ? | [unknown loss] |
| 1782–83 | '22,380' or '26,000' | ? | bankruptcy[b] |
| 1783–84 | *c.* 19,500 | *c.* 24,000 | lost 8,500 |
| 1784–85 | *c.* 17,000 | *c.* 21,000 | lost 8,500 |
| 1785–86 | 18,690 | *c.* 18,000 | made 4,600 |
| 1786–87 | 18,766 | *c.* 18,000 | made 4,600 |
| 1787–88 | *c.* 21,200 | *c.* 18,000 | made 4,600 |
| 1788–89 | '17,500' or '19,001' | ? | [broke even?] |

[a] Plus about £4,000 for auditorium alterations.

[b] Season loss unknown; Taylor spent *c.* £9,000 on major building alterations in the summer of 1782. He claimed £26,000 annual receipts in his July 1783 Deed of Trust, but in C31/248, no. 285, he stated gross receipts for 1781–82 as £22,236 and for 1782–83 as £22,380—more plausible, though probably still on the high side.

one important regard. O'Reilly (or Crawford) maliciously takes some of Taylor's claims at face value, and doing so considerably inflates alleged income in the early 1780s. Table 3 presents information for the whole range of eleven seasons at issue. Most of these figures are probably reasonably accurate, with the notable exception of income for Taylor's seasons, 1781–82 and 1782–83. The figures offered for 1781–82 in particular are simply not credible. It was an artistically distinguished season, but before the box enlargement of summer 1782 subscriber income could be little more than £5,000. At various times Taylor claimed income of £24,000 to £26,000 (and even more), but this was puffery to attract unwary investors: the Yale manuscripts suggest that ticket sales over about £17,500 would be virtually impossible, despite the enlarged auditorium. Even the lower figures reported in C31/248, no. 285 are difficult to credit.[1] We doubt that Taylor actually grossed more than £20,000 in either season.

[1] Taylor claimed 'Receipts at the Doors' of £14,702 in 1781–82 and £14,553 in 1782–83.

Calculating a total balance sheet (as O'Reilly attempted to do) is virtually impossible: income and expenditure are unknown for several seasons; some of the debts may be 'suppositious', and many are certainly padded by usurious fees. Let us, however, try to show what is known and what can be reasonably hypothesized.

Sheridan and Harris lost about £7,000 in 1778–79, some £4,000 of it for auditorium alterations. Taylor inherited this debt when he took over in 1782, plus Sheridan's operating losses from 1779–80 and 1780–81. The latter is unknown; if we have interpreted the manuscript report for '1778 & 1779' correctly, the loss for 1779–80 was a startling £5,000. Taylor also accepted responsibility for a £3,000 mortgage balance and some £4,000 in miscellaneous debts. On this basis he took over at least £15,560 in debts and more probably £18,500. He stated the total as £20,000 when testifying in 1785 about the circumstances in which he assumed ownership, and that figure could be true.[1] Taylor also assumed liability for renters' shares, and spent some £9,000 on the 1782 alterations. In other words, Taylor needed to cover debt service on upwards of £30,000 while maintaining a cash flow that would meet current operating expenses.

Since these debts went unpaid, and since Taylor was unable to meet his payroll and current expenses, the probability seems high that he was losing money steadily during the seasons of 1781–82 and 1782–83. His unpaid bills from those seasons total some £18,500.[2] The £9,000 bill for alterations should have been offset by the £8,610 (minimum) that Taylor received for renters' shares. One must assume, therefore, that the £18,500 shortfall represents current debt service and operating losses. It does not include any allowance for unpaid renters' shares and mortgage payments, which had accumulated to the impressive total of £36,351 by 1790.[3]

O'Reilly makes two separate calculations in *An Authentic Narrative*, which must be treated differently. On pages 36–41 he cleverly and maliciously totals Taylor's known (and claimed) income from various sources (£79,883. 7s. 11½d.), and sets that sum against known payments (£32,774. 13s. 5½d.). One can hardly imagine, however, that Taylor somehow made off with the £47,109. 14s. 6d. left 'unaccounted for'. A fairer estimate of

---

[1] C12/2012/53.

[2] We calculate this figure from information given in O'Reilly, *An Authentic Narrative*, 39: £3,160 unpaid rent; £8,453 unpaid to singers, dancers, and others who signed the July 1783 deed of trust; £6,877 in arrears to performers and others.

[3] Calculated from *An Authentic Narrative*: £5,100, £3,663, £3,351, £1,911, £8,166, £7,600, £6,560.

income would omit loans of various sorts, and would put season receipts at a more realistic level. If one assumes £19,000 for 1781–82 and £22,000 for 1782–83 (which may be generous), and adds £8,610 for sales of renters' shares, the total 'receipts' are no more than £50,000. Taylor's expenses for those seasons cannot have been much under £40,000, to which must be added £9,000 for the 1782 alterations and some £20,000 of inherited debts—a total of at least £69,000 owed, if not paid. This ignores money due on renters' shares, and actual income and expense figures may have been worse than is assumed here.

The second calculation offered by O'Reilly is 'A State of several Incumbrances affecting the Opera-House, from the time of the purchase from Yates and Brooke'. These figures are to be taken much more seriously. The grand total is £89,861. 17s. 11½d. This comprises some £36,000 in unpaid interest and renters' shares; the £12,000 mortgage of 1778; the £7,326 debt Harris and Sheridan had run up in 1778–79; £21,949 said to be secured by the July 1783 deed of trust; £7,333 purchase money from Taylor to Sheridan (charged against the theatre); and just £4,900 secured by the March 1783 deed of trust (though its face value was £16,000). Taylor's 'purchase money' was probably a blind, and the supposed sum involved was a cover for Taylor's assuming debts for Sheridan from 1779 to 1782. And since there is no way to calculate the overlap between the two trust deeds, one cannot tell whether £4,900 is high or low. But all in all, the £89,000 total is a plausible figure— to which must be added some £8,500 for losses under the trustees. The accumulated debt was therefore upwards of £100,000. One might analyse this debt as follows: £22,000 for the 1778 purchase; £4,000 for 1778 alterations; £3,000 for 1778–79 operating losses; £7,000 for operating losses in 1779–80 and 1780–81;[1] £9,000 for 1782 alterations; £8,500 trustees' losses; £36,000 for unpaid interest and renters' shares. The balance of roughly £10,000 represents Taylor's operating losses. In his 1799 memorial Taylor admitted to debts at the time of the fire that 'did not amount to less than £70,000' and elsewhere in that document he lists claims totalling some £84,000.[2] Even the latter sum appears to ignore losses under the trustees 1783–85 and to understate the sums owed to mortgagees and renters.

Is it frivolous to speculate about what would have happened had Gallini rather than Sheridan been the successful purchaser in 1778? Gallini could have paid cash for the opera-house. Whether he would have had the

---

[1] This is an interpretation of Taylor's 'purchase money'.
[2] PRO CRES 6/121, pp. 329, 337–9.

imagination to rebuild the auditorium and increase subscriber capacity as Taylor did in 1782 is anyone's guess. That Gallini operated at a modest profit between 1785 and 1789 is certain. Whether he was helped or hindered by the spending cap of £18,000 is hard to say. The probability seems high, however, that if Gallini had been proprietor starting in 1778, the opera company would have been solvent at the time of the 1789 fire. There is no reason to think that he would have borrowed sums beyond the capacity of the venture to pay, or that he would have tolerated deficits that remained permanently unpaid. Without Sheridan's leveraged buyout, the opera might well have arrived at the nineteenth century in a much more flourishing state—not hamstrung by accumulated debts and permanent feuds.

*These figures imply that in the 1780s the King's Theatre ought to have been able to operate in the black.* This is a startling and original conclusion. Everyone has known that the venture went bankrupt, and conventional wisdom says that opera never pays. But though the King's Theatre lost money, this was not a necessary and ineluctable state of affairs. It lost a fortune because Sheridan's ill-advised purchase plunged it into a sea of debt from which it had no chance of ever escaping. The problem lay in debt service and bad management: income and expenses were actually in good balance. The theatre could clearly draw £20,000 per season, and that sum would cover first-class performers and a high production standard. A manager who could avoid undue extravagance and waste could keep the venture afloat entirely on its own income.

Instead, there was debt, mismanagement, and chicanery. Operating as trustee, Gallini brought stability to the company, but his profits could not even pay the interest on the accumulated debts. At the time, few people realized just how hopeless the situation was. Lacking the possibility of corporate bankruptcy, the venture had no way to clear its slate and start afresh. The fire of 1789 might have offered a kind of *de facto* termination for a venture that could never hope to right itself, but Taylor's brilliant and successful manœuvring to regain power had the unintended result of leaving opera to stagger along under the permanent burden of its past misfortunes. Unless the government granted a licence, no one could start up a rival venture unencumbered by debts. Public sentiment held that the creditors of the King's Theatre were entitled to their money, and that hence the theatre must be continued in its monopoly so that it could earn the money to pay off its debts. That so glamorous and seemingly prosperous an operation could not even cover the interest on those debts was simply not understood.

The King's Theatre could have been prosperous in a way that few opera companies in history have been prosperous. Its ruin has seemed natural, but was in fact the very reverse of what ought to have been a time of unexampled prosperity.

The reasons for this extraordinary state of imaginable solvency are not far to seek. London was a wealthy and growing city, and the Licensing Act prevented any proliferation of theatres. The Italian opera was the social centre of the gentry: everyone who was anyone took a box, as the lists of subscribers in 1782–83 and 1787–88 amply prove. The Prince of Wales and other members of the Royal Family attended with great regularity. The result was that management could sell a season ticket for virtually every box seat it could cram into the theatre. In 1787–88 Gallini's subscriptions were as much as Sheridan and Harris's total income for 1778–79—about £10,000. By rights, the 1780s should have been the beginning of a golden age for opera in London.

# CHAPTER 3

# *Daily Operations and the Production Process*

═══════

THIS chapter is a detailed study of how the company managed its business and staged its shows. Some of these problems have been raised in Chapter 1, but before plunging into particular seasons and their operas and ballets we need to try to convey some sense of the internal organization and dynamics of the company, its hierarchies and administrative procedures. The basics of performance circumstances also need to be explained. What follows is all pertinent to the succeeding chapters on the opera and ballet repertoires. If the discussion of such matters as scenery, machines, and lighting sometimes seems fragmentary, that is the nature of the evidence available.

## I. The Structure of the Company

Who was responsible for what? Near-total lack of operational records for the King's Theatre makes some of the answers speculative, while the gulf between twentieth-century assumptions and what appears to have been eighteenth-century reality complicates any attempt at explanation. Two points are crucial. First, the 'proprietor' might stand in very different relationships to the artistic and financial management of the company: Sheridan, Taylor, and Gallini carried out such different functions that to treat each simply as 'proprietor' seriously distorts the nature of operations in their respective regimes. Second, regardless of who stood at the top of the management chart, daily operations were radically departmentalized. Seen at the level of production, the King's Theatre comprised a loose confederation of departments rather than a unified and centrally directed company.

*Proprietors and Managers*

The history of opera in eighteenth-century London provides at least four organizational models on which opera companies were run:

1. The impresario. Vanbrugh had built the Queen's (later King's) Theatre with the idea of being both owner and General Intendant. Owen Swiney (before he decamped in 1713), Heidegger from 1713 to 1717, Crosa in the later 1740s, and Giardini in 1763–64 had all functioned this way. The obvious disadvantage was that financial responsibility rested on one person of no great fortune.

2. The board of directors. The Royal Academy of Music had operated in this fashion in the 1720s, and so had the Opera of the Nobility in the mid-1730s. Large (if temporary) subsidies were obtained from the sponsors, though amateurism, irresponsibility, and squabbles among the participants had proved disastrous.

3. Partner-impresarios or managers. The terms of financial responsibility for the 'Second Academy' (1729–34) are not known, but during this period Handel and Heidegger worked in tandem. As best one can judge, Handel served as artistic director while Heidegger functioned as business manager. This is clearly a good model, always supposing that the partners worked smoothly together and could agree on financial limits—as Taylor and Crawford failed to do in the early 1780s.

4. The noble patron. Lord Middlesex in the 1740s is the obvious example. In this case, the patron involved himself actively in daily management, functioning as much as impresario as patron. No man of fortune came forward again to accept personal responsibility for the opera company until Bedford and Salisbury did so in 1790, though Gallini invested a lot of his own money in the company during the 1780s.

During the 1750s and early 1760s management devolved upon a series of performers and speculators, none of whom managed to establish a stable company (the third pattern described above). Between 1767 and 1778 the King's Theatre was owned by a shifting group of genteel enthusiasts and speculators. During this time the company fell into the pattern of essentially autonomous departmental organization that prevailed in the 1780s. If the results were uneven the system did at least keep the business going through bankruptcy, operatic civil war, lawsuits, and eventually even fire.

When Sheridan and Harris bought the company in 1778 they must have understood that they could not manage it themselves. Both were in charge of theatres that performed six nights a week much of the year; neither was a musician; and neither could read or speak Italian. They were to be proprietors, not managers. The one-sixth of the business that they had not been able to purchase belonged to Peter Crawford, who had worked in the treasurer's office of the King's Theatre in various capacities since about 1740, and as treasurer since about 1749 (how continuously is not known). Crawford naturally became what could be called a business manager. As largely absentee owners, Sheridan and Harris chose to appoint Antoine Le Texier as 'manager'—or as one would now say, artistic director. This was a genuine innovation. Le Texier was a cranky character who lasted little more than one season, and with the benefit of hindsight one can easily see that he was the wrong man for the job. The idea, however, was not wrong. Le Texier had artistic vision and was prepared to shake up a stodgy institution. The singers were appalled when he wanted to stage operas involving both *seria* and *buffa* personnel,[1] and he had little luck in trying to integrate dance into operas. However, some of the principles he was to enunciate a decade later in his *Ideas on the Opera* (1790) make a great deal of sense.

Le Texier argued for an opera company run by a 'good administrator' who was musically competent, could speak and write English, Italian, French, and German, knew enough history and mythology to prevent blunders in librettos, scene design, and costumes, understood painting and perspective, understood theatre machinery, and was himself a good enough speaker and actor to 'administer advices' to the performers about their acting.[2] Le Texier's artistic and managerial ideas are clearly modelled on the great polymath Metastasio but, considered as a reaction against the status quo of the King's Theatre in the 1780s, they give a good idea of what that company was like. Le Texier wanted to impose centralized control over departments that had become personal bailiwicks. Even more drastically, he wanted to subordinate individual display in music and dance to broader artistic and aesthetic principles. Probably the Archangel Gabriel could not have made this work at the King's Theatre in the 1780s, and certainly the quarrelsome Le Texier could not—but the idea was by no means foolish.

When Le Texier was fired during the season of 1779–80 at least some of his duties must have been taken over by someone else—but by whom? In all

---

[1] Susan Burney, fo. 18.      [2] See Le Texier, *Ideas on the Opera*, 37–8.

likelihood Crawford handled yet more of the administration.[1] Although Harris withdrew, Sheridan continued as an absentee proprietor, creating problems in the process. Susan Burney reports Wilhelm Cramer, the leader of the opera orchestra, as saying

many of the Performers who have been here half a year have never yet seen either Mr Harris [whose departure from management was not public knowledge] or Mr Sheridan—I have written three letters to Mr Sheridan at different times, but never have received any answer—I have called 20 times, but never have been admitted. —About half a year ago I met him accidentally in the street, & took the opportunity to speak to him—Very well, Mr Cramer—said he—But we can settle nothing here—Come & Dine with me to morrow & we will talk the Matter over—very well sir—At what o'clock?—at four—accordingly the next day at four I went—I was shewn up stairs, & told Mr Sheridan was not yet come home—Well I waited till half an hour past *five*, a full hour & half—but as Nobody came near me & I was then *extremely hungry* I went away—& since that time I have never seen Mr Sheridan—& did he send no apology?—Never. (fo. 41ᵛ)

Susan Burney likewise reports Pacchierotti's experience of Sheridan: non-payment of salary, no answer to his letters, dazzling personal charm exerted when cornered, and finally the realization that 'he *lies*, as usual'. Even then, Pacchierotti says, 'I am at a loss to take Measures against him because I believe he has a good heart—& he is a Man of such a pleasing demeanour—so gentle—*tanto Amene*, that whenever I see him I always have the hope that he is going to change.'[2]

Sheridan seems to have been only rarely in the King's Theatre and had no effective operational control over its affairs. One of the few recorded occasions on which he actively intervened was in January 1781 when the tenor Ansani was feuding with Sacchini and the librettist Badini, and wanted a scene added to *Mitridate*. The other house poet Andrei duly wrote the scene, whereupon Ansani had to have it translated into English, so Sheridan could read it. The proprietor's approval did not, however, result in co-operation between poet and composer.[3] Sheridan did possess at least some practical experience in administering a theatre, which was more than could

---

[1] Crawford signed contracts with singers and dancers and bore at least partial responsibility for their payment. See O'Reilly, *An Authentic Narrative*, 10–12. Crawford testified in 1788 that he had served as 'Treasurer Steward & Manager of the affairs of the said Opera house from the year 1780' (C24/1929, Crawford).

[2] Susan Burney, fos. 81, 127, and 153–4.

[3] Ansani's long account of opera-house infighting and his reasons for withdrawing in mid-season is in the *Morning Herald* of 3 Feb. 1781.

be said for his successor William Taylor when he abruptly became principal manager in early 1781 and then proprietor the following autumn—a position he was to hold with one major hiatus for more than thirty years. Lacking not only knowledge of Italian and music, but any experience of theatre management, Taylor was inevitably dependent on the expertise of others. He was cocky, aggressive, and probably a quick study, but especially in the early years he cannot have exercised much daily control over the theatre's offerings.

Taylor states in a 1785 lawsuit that early in his regime he relied on Henry Johnson (assistant treasurer) for help in determining reasonable salaries.[1] He must have been acutely aware of his shortcomings and naturally sought assistance. On 20 February 1782 he signed a contract with Domenico Angelo to serve as manager for seven and a half years at the princely salary of £500 per annum.[2]

The said Dominico Angelo for the Considerations aftermentioned doth promise and agree to the utmost of his skill and Ability to superintend and manage the Operas and other Entertainments to be performed and exhibited at the said Theatre under the Direction of the said William Taylor; To attend all Rehearsals of Operas and Dances and to manage both singers and Dancers in the best manner possible according to the utmost of his skill and ability for the Benefit of the said William Taylor and for the purpose shall give due attendance at the said Theatre at all proper times of practising and rehearsing by the several Performers, and also all publick Performances and Exhibitions and direct manage and conduct the same and treat with and correspond and use his Endeavours to procure singers Dancers and other Performers from abroad or elsewhere as he shall be instructed by the said William Taylor who reserves to himself the right of making confirming and executing all Engagements whatever And shall and will in General do and perform and use his skill knowledge and Endeavours to conduct manage and carry on the Business of the Theatre and use his Endeavours and Exertions to promote the success of the Theatre in all respects according to the best of his skill and knowledge In Consideration whereof and for that he the said Dominico Angelo may on Account of this Employment be obliged to decline his present Business of Riding and Fencing or a part thereof He the said William Taylor doth promise and agree to pay or cause to be paid to the said Dominico Angelo the yearly sum of Five hundred

---

[1] C12/2012/53.

[2] C107/65 (loose papers). Either party could terminate the contract on six months' notice, but if Taylor did so he would owe Angelo a £500 fee. The contract also specifies that if Gallini 'shall succeed in the suit now depending in the Court of Chancery so as to oust the said William Taylor' the agreement 'shall be void'. A perquisite not mentioned in the contract is the accommodation of Angelo's fencing-school in opera-house facilities. On 5 Jan. 1782 a Mr Picasse announced in the *Morning Chronicle* that his school had moved from there to Chancery Lane.

Pounds by four quarterly Payments clear of all Deductions . . . This Engagement to be for seven years and a half. . . .

The managerial functions specified here are (1) recruitment of singers and dancers; (2) superintendence of rehearsals; and (3) attendance at performances. Nothing is said about choice of repertoire, and Taylor specifically reserves the power to approve or disapprove all contracts (and hence to set salaries). Taylor intended to function as business manager. Interestingly, he did not sign his name to the company's 'season' announcements in the newspapers during the early 1780s. Angelo was perhaps the most famous riding- and fencing-master in Europe but had no known experience in opera.[1] He could speak French and Italian, but why Taylor thought he would be a good manager is hard to say, and to what extent Angelo actually attempted to carry out the job is not determinable.

The initial arrangement for 1783–84 (before Gallini was forced out) split managerial responsibility in an obvious way. Point 6 of the agreement between the trustees and Gallini was 'Mr Gallini to undertake the management and direction of all matters . . . relating to Music and Dancing at the Opera House; and all other matters relative to the Business of the House to Mr Crawford'.[2] Here is spelt out the division of labour between artistic director and business manager. Division of responsibilities under Taylor's trustees in 1783–84 and 1784–85 is largely unknown. Lawsuit testimony suggests that the scene painter Novosielski made repertoire decisions,[3] though De Michele (during his brief term) certainly understood opera from the inside and Slingsby had long been a premier dancer.

Among the reigning heads of company in these years only Gallini was competent to run the business himself—though he was greatly hampered by having to serve in the awkward capacity of Taylor's trustee. Had he been able to force the mortgage foreclosure he so long pursued and taken over possession in his own right, Gallini might have operated very differently. The profits made in the later 1780s prove that Gallini was financially competent: he knew what things should cost and was able to keep a budget under control. Though Gallini was old-fashioned in his view of dance, he had an enlightened operatic policy, which he implemented with great skill and vision. Of the company's 'proprietors' in these years, only Gallini was in a position to manage the King's Theatre both artistically and financially.

[1] See J. D. Aylward, *The House of Angelo* (London: Batchworth Press, 1953).
[2] C107/65 ('Heads of Agreement' of 19 Nov. 1783).
[3] Novosielski claims that his wise choice of operas proved financially advantageous to the company in 1783–84 (C31/233, no. 348).

## The Departmental Structure

One indication of the company's operations is the season advertisement or announcement that was customarily published shortly before the theatre opened each autumn. Performers are usually grouped in three separate lists: serious singers, comic singers, and principal dancers. The first two categories often overlapped. In the 1782–83 advertisement, for example, Bartolini, Schinotti, Signora Gherardi, and Signora Pollone appear in both groups (*Morning Chronicle*, 16 October 1782). This reflects the fact that opera *seria* and *buffa* were beginning to converge, both musically and dramatically, as is explained in Chapter 5. No 'Director of Operas' is ever advertised, which leaves unexplained certain key responsibilities. Two or more composers were usually advertised, being responsible for new commissions and arranging or adapting particular operas, which they then directed from the harpsichord. One seems usually to have specialized in providing additional music and rewriting where necessary, and supervising revivals. Composers were rarely responsible for repertoire choices, though there is evidence that Sacchini, Cherubini, and Storace were given some leeway in choosing librettos. At what date the custom of paying someone as 'harpsichord' originated is unknown, but by the early 1780s Muzio Clementi was employed in this capacity, and by the end of the century the position had become well paid.[1]

At the beginning of the period under consideration, there were two harpsichords in the orchestra pit, one played by the composer or arranger, the other by his assistant, who was primarily responsible (with the principal cellist) for accompanying the recitative. Giardini was responsible for having one of the harpsichords removed, while the remaining instrument was played less and less, finally coming to serve as little more than a music desk for the composer-conductor. The orchestra itself was directed by the first violinist, with different persons for opera and ballet respectively. Judging from comments by Cramer to Susan Burney about Le Texier trying unsuccessfully to insist on changes in orchestral personnel,[2] the leader had a good deal of authority over the constitution of his orchestra. A comment in the *Morning Chronicle* of 23 April 1784 implies that the leader was not obliged to participate during the playing of dance music: 'we must be allowed to protest against this privilege, assumed by the first violin, of sitting

[1] In 1796–97 Vincenzo Federici was paid £200 per annum for this service. See 'Opera Salaries', 61.

[2] Susan Burney, fo. 41ʳ.

unoccupied during the dance, and deputing the conduct of it to inferior players'. Here again is a symptom of compartmentalization.

The hierarchy of the dance company itself is much clearer. The ballet-master was expected to create new *ballets d'action*, revive old ones, and supply enough variety to keep the audience happy. *Divertissements* and *pièces d'occasion* were sometimes farmed out to another choreographer, though only rarely is a second person formally credited with such responsibility.[1] The principals normally fell into three sets of couples, though they were not generally advertised that way.

Three further heads of department are commonly advertised: the painter, the tailor, and the leader of the band. Sometimes the person who directed the orchestra during the dances (termed the 'leader of the dances') is named, but often he is not. How much the painter and tailor had to do varied drastically with the season and the production. Most productions used old scenery and costumes, and these had to be selected, refreshed, and refitted. In a relatively prosperous season many new ones might be called for, but in a tough year few or none. Managements differ in whether they advertise such matters. Since fancy scenic display was an important part of some operas and ballets (and is commented upon in the papers), someone had to supply the skills of a 'Machinist'. Novosielski was advertised as 'Painter and Machinist'; whether other scene-painters likewise doubled as machinists is uncertain. Much of what is known about costume design and the costume shop comes from a lawsuit filed by Thomas Luppino (the long-time tailor) against William Taylor, and is discussed below in section IV. Luppino certainly provided costumes—apparently for principal singers and dancers as well as extras and *figurants*.

The choice of repertoire was presumably exercised by the proprietor if competent to do so (for example, Gallini), by the artistic director, if any (Le Texier), or by whoever served as deputy manager in the absence of such a superior. What about co-ordination? There was probably less of it than modern prejudices would suppose necessary: witness the persistent complaints by reviewers of excessive length.[2] Cuts in both operas and ballets

---

[1] In 1782–83 an early announcement notes: 'The Ballets to be composed by Monsieur Le Picq. The Dances and Divertissements by Monsieur Simonet' (*Morning Chronicle*, 16 Oct. 1782).

[2] On the need for cuts, complaints about late starts, and excessively long intervals, see e.g. *Public Advertiser*, 4 Mar. 1785 and *Morning Herald*, 26 Jan. 1786; *Daily Universal Register*, 15 Jan., 26 Apr., and 10 Dec. 1787; *World*, 10 Dec. 1787; and *The Times*, 2 Mar. 1789. The *Public Advertiser* of 4 Mar. 1785 denounces a thirty-five minute delay in drawing the curtain and

after public performance were commonplace: apparently no one could time the rehearsals and insist on necessary trimming before performance—or at least no one did, and encores could drag things out. Performers, of course, had the right to substitute arias in old operas, and they negotiated changes and additions with composers in new ones. There was no 'director' in the modern sense, and no evidence shows how elementary blocking was carried out for operas.

An interesting picture of production practice is contained in Peter Crawford's testimony concerning Rauzzini's *La regina di Golconda* (1784).[1] This was in the style of an *opéra-ballet*, which was not a form the King's Theatre was used to dealing with, so the trustees hired Le Texier for the startling salary of £150 to stage this single piece. He was apparently expected to perform some of the functions now considered directorial, but Crawford could see no point in this and testified that hiring Le Texier was needless extravagance, since the company already had the services of the composer (Rauzzini) and of Crawford himself. Did composers help with what we should now call stage blocking? More likely, the singers were expected to apply standard conventions and deal with the matter themselves. From Crawford's point of view, a new opera could come to the stage with only a musical arranger and the treasurer as midwives. This need not imply a lack of acting on the part of the singers, but it points to a rather static and uncoordinated concept of stage presentation.

Lights were provided by an outside contractor (see below, sect. v). Music-copying was handled within the company by Leopoldo De Michele, who employed at least two or three apprentices or journeymen, and perhaps more.[2] Publicity was handled through the treasurer's office, which arranged to print both 'great bills' for public display and handbills for distribution to favoured individuals, and sent advertising copy to several newspapers. The appointment of Parkyns MacMahon as 'Secretary' under the trustees in 1783–84 at a salary of £150 per annum was an innovation that drew fire from the indignant authors of *The Case of the Opera-House Disputes*, who protested against 'the creation of a place for this same Parkyns Mac Mahon

a 'no less preposterous delay between the first Act and the Dance . . . no less than twenty minutes'.

[1] C24/1929 (Crawford); discussed at length in Ch. 5, sect. III.

[2] C24/1929 (depositions by Mazzinghi, Thomas Walker, and John Wiber). Walker worked as journeyman from 1782 to 1787; Wiber says he had worked for De Michele 'for many Years'.

TABLE 4. *Budget categories in the season of 1784–85 (£)*

| | | | |
|---|---|---|---|
| principal singers | 3,900 | scene designer/machinist | 300 |
| principal dancers | 4,365 | treasurer | 300 |
| *figurants* | 975 | secretary | 150 |
| orchestra | 1,711 | dressers/nightly servants | 561 |
| costume shop | 900 | lights | 559 |
| scenery/scene-shifting | 700 | music-copying | 150 |
| composers | 530 | printing | 345 |
| poets | 150 | office and music porter | 40 |
| nightly guards | 135 | | |

. . . as puff-master-general', commenting that 'Dispatching the bills and advertisements of the theatre to the public prints was formerly the business of the treasurer, and of course the present salary was saved.'[1] MacMahon—an opportunist, to judge from his lawsuit testimony—seems to have functioned as a kind of public-relations director.

The 'Memorandum of the Expences of the Season of Operas 1784' (1784–85?) preserved in the Bedford Opera Papers provides a rough sense of the proportional costs of the various departments of the company.[2] (See Table 4.) We say 'rough' since there is no way of telling how typical this season may have been (or how accurate this report may be). The total (£20,684) is inflated by £2,948 for 'Sundry Salleries', which probably reflect extravagance and graft on the part of the trustees. Items such as house rent (£1,400), taxes (£240), and coal (£50) contribute to the total. Whether or not this is exact or typical, these figures give a sense of what various parts of the business cost, and what budget categories the company recognized.

Opera, ballet, and orchestra were autonomous units, as were the painter/scene shop and the tailor/costume shop. Lights and some music-copying were jobbed out, though the persons responsible must have spent a lot of time in the building, especially the lighting man. The treasurer handled money and administration, supervising the housekeeper, dressers, box and house staff, and after 1783 the 'secretary'. The assignment of boxes was a duty almost as touchy as collecting arrears on subscriptions. Gallini testified in 1789 that he 'always left the direction of the Boxes to Mr Johnson the Treasurer and the Receipt of the Subscriptions for such boxes to Messrs

---

[1] *The Case of the Opera-House Disputes*, 30–2.    [2] Bedford Opera Papers, 2.A.29.

Ransom Morland and Hammersley'—in other words, subscriptions were paid directly to the opera's bankers, but the actual assignment of boxes was handled in the treasurer's office.[1]

Least clear is how the proprietor exercised or delegated the authority that made the separate departments work together at all. At times, managerial authority clearly broke down. Susan Burney reports insubordination and chaos under Sheridan, and this picture is confirmed by other sources.[2] The *Morning Chronicle* of 27 and 28 November 1780 claims that *L'arcifanfano* was 'chosen against' the 'consent' of the 'present director', and says that consequently Sheridan cannot be held accountable for it—but the report does not make plain who had the power to bring it to the stage. In 1781–82 and 1782–83 Taylor was at least on the spot but had to delegate artistic authority or rely on advice. When Gallini took over in 1785 he replaced Crawford and MacMahon with Carnevale, Badini, and Henry Johnson. What were their jobs? Johnson was treasurer; Badini served as poet, translator, and probably as 'puffmaster';[3] Carnevale served either as head of the opera department or as deputy manager/liaison between Gallini and the opera performers. The *Morning Herald* of 16 September 1785 says he has been chosen as 'pilot' by Gallini, whatever that means. The announcement of his benefit in the *Morning Herald* of 27 May 1786 terms him 'Deputy Manager', and in 1789 he is described as the person 'in whose hands the management was principally the last two seasons'.[4] Gallini was qualified to serve as his own artistic director but was a busy man who might well have wanted to delegate responsibility for rehearsals and routine administration. Carnevale, who served through 1787–88, is praised in the *Daily Universal Register* of 25 December 1787 for managing 'the whole conduct of the scenic business . . . with great ability'—which may imply responsibility for co-ordination of staging, since he was certainly not the scene designer. In 1788–89 Carnevale was replaced by Ravelli, who was owed £150 and a benefit as 'deputy manager'.[5] This case provides occasion to remark that one cannot be certain who had (and who actually took) benefits. *The London Stage* contains no hint of the production intended for Ravelli's benefit in June 1789—for the good reason that the theatre burnt down the night before it was to have taken place.[6] Unfortunately, advertisement of a benefit does not

---

[1] C107/201, Gallini's answer of 21 July 1789.   [2] Susan Burney, fo. 65.
[3] See Da Ponte, *Memoirs*, 212–13.
[4] Theatre Cuts 42, fo. [40ʳ], dated in manuscript 9 Feb. 1789.
[5] 'Opera Salaries', 53.   [6] *The Times*, 11 June 1789.

prove that the beneficiary collected (let alone how much); nor does lack of an advertisement prove that none was granted. Benefits were usually but not invariably advertised (see Pl. 7*a*), and specially designed and printed tickets were customary (see Pl. 7*b*).

This survey of departments and administrators shows that the King's Theatre tolerated a remarkable degree of autonomy among its component parts. Gallini may have kept a reasonably tight grip on all parts of the company, especially the opera, for which there is considerable evidence of a conscious artistic policy. With the exception of the ill-fated Le Texier regime in the late 1770s, the company seems to have lumbered along doing business as usual. Different proprietors created different deputy and liaison arrangements, but these did not alter the essentially independent nature of departmental operations. The King's Theatre was not so much a kingdom as a loose confederation of moderately co-operative baronies.

## II. Recruitment and Salaries

Only recently has much information come to light about these subjects, and our knowledge is still far from satisfactory. Hiring principal performers was a perennial headache for the management of the King's Theatre. Stars quickly waned in a company that staged eight or ten operas over fifty or sixty nights per season—the more so in that the numerous and influential subscribers attended night after night. At Drury Lane or Covent Garden a principal performer might stay for decades, but hardly anyone attended every performance, and the theatres mounted fifty or sixty different mainpieces over a season of 180–200 nights. The opera audience flocked to see new celebrities, but soon lost interest. This had always been true, and it remained a problem.[1] In the spring of 1787 Gallini commented glumly: 'With regard to Robinelli and Mara—the public no longer listen to them. One needs novelty.'[2] The King's Theatre consumed new performers at an alarming rate, and the subscribers were always clamouring for more. Recruiting was not easy. London was a long way from the Continental opera circuit; the cost of living was high; the climate was feared. None the

---

[1] Writing nearly two generations earlier, Cibber comments dourly that the 'best Voices' are merely flowers that 'bloom but for a Season, and when that is over are only dead Nosegays', adding that not so long after Farinelli took London by storm he was 'singing to an Audience of five and thirty Pounds'. See Cibber, *Apology*, ii. 88.

[2] Gallini to Earl Cowper, 1 May 1787; printed in Gibson, 'Earl Cowper', 247.

less, performers knew that fortunes had been made in London, and some were eager to come—but they wanted top-of-the-line salaries.

## The Process of Recruitment

For a season that generally started in November and ended around the beginning of July, recruitment needed to begin by April, if not earlier. In most seasons, recruitment was carried out by correspondence. The post was erratic, and many weeks might be lost in an exchange of letters. The dancer Le Picq was hired by post from Naples for the 1782–83 season as early as the previous January.[1] In February 1789 William Taylor stated in an affidavit that Lent was 'the proper and usual time of engaging performers . . . particularly singers'.[2] In a set of interrogatories for Gallini the same year, Taylor asked 'Why . . . or how did it become necessary for you to take a journey into Italy' for recruitment 'when you knew or ought to have known that such a journey had never been usual and that the business abroad had been handled invariably by a correspondence and might have been transacted by you in that manner or by agency abroad as formerly?' Taylor then expressed his suspicion that Gallini had chosen to make the trip to see his 'relations and friends' at the theatre's expense.[3] Gallini would not have been the first. In the summer of 1784 Novosielski made a recruiting trip, accompanied by an entourage that included his wife and a personal chaplain, at a reported cost of £1,500.[4] Gabriel Leone's itemized expenses in 1763 came to £505. 18s.[5] More efficient trips cost less: Crawford was paid £200 in 1783 (including remuneration for his trouble), and Gallini charged only £100 in expenses for a trip to Paris.[6] Gallini justified his Italian trip by saying that the subscribers had demanded the engagement of Marchesi, and that he had been 'obliged to go to Milan in Italy to prevail on him to come to England'.[7] Considerable light on the practice of recruitment by mail is shed by letters from Gallini to Earl Cowper in Florence during the 1780s.[8] Lord Cowper was no doubt an atypical 'agent', a wealthy expatriate and fanatic

[1] *Morning Herald*, 9 Jan. 1782. He arrived in time for the last two months of the 1781–82 season. Negotiations with top performers might take place over many months. On the case of Le Picq, ballet-master in 1782–83, see the *Morning Herald* for 24 Apr. 1781.

[2] C31/251, no. 207.

[3] C107/201, interrogatories for Gallini, 7 May 1788.

[4] *The Case of the Opera-House Disputes*, 27–9.

[5] *The Impresario's Ten Commandments*, 20.

[6] See C12/615/9 (on Crawford); C107/201, interrogatories for Gallini of 7 May 1788.

[7] C31/249, no. 45.

[8] These are quoted and discussed in Ch. 6.

music lover who obliged with advice and assistance for the pleasure of meddling in such matters.[1] Even a well-connected and well-informed native Italian had to depend heavily on advice from abroad. Who was good? Who had succeeded recently? Who was available? Price ranges could be specified, but in many instances the local agent would have to be trusted not only to select the performer but to negotiate the salary. Travel expenses often had to be paid,[2] and advances arranged—not an easy matter in the financial world of the 1780s. The usual method was to establish a line of credit with a merchant firm that had foreign branches or correspondents who would honour its bills of exchange. In one of his letters to Lord Cowper, Gallini mentions his being known to several Florentine bankers, 'but particularly Mr Orsi' (autumn 1785).[3] The firm of Orsi had been doing business with the King's Theatre for more than thirty years, and in troubled times was willing to guarantee salaries to nervous performers—for a 2 per cent fee.[4] In Paris the firm of Perregaux transacted the King's Theatre's business—and was to act for the Pantheon as well.

The London manager (or his deputy) thus kept in touch with a variety of agents in Italy, France, Austria, and elsewhere. The Italian community in London had been a rich source for news and gossip when Giardini was manager, and probably still was. Recruitment by post was feasible unless it was left too late. Gallini and two representatives of the trustees set off (separately) for the Continent in late summer 1783 because the chaos attending Taylor's bankruptcy completely disarranged the usual procedures. After the fire of 1789, Gallini dispatched Robert Bray O'Reilly to Italy to sign up a company. The recruiting trip about which the most is known was that undertaken by Gabriel Leone for Giardini in 1763—starting in mid-July.[5] One cannot take that star-crossed venture as typical, but it illustrates some of the obvious problems. Leone was given detailed instructions (preserved in full), but Giardini started hiring people in London, got all sorts of advice, and fired off orders that he countermanded by the next packet. The post

[1] Perhaps a more normal agent was Owen Swiney, who served the Royal Academy in the 1720s—and had considerable difficulty collecting his fees. For his letters of advice to his masters, see Elizabeth Gibson, *The Royal Academy of Music, 1719–1728* (New York: Garland, 1989), App. C.

[2] To judge from the Pantheon papers, travel allowances from Paris ranged from £10 to more than £100, depending on the rank of the performer.

[3] Gibson, 'Earl Cowper', 244.

[4] See Elizabeth Gibson, 'Italian Opera in London, 1750–1775: Management and Finances', *Early Music*, 18 (1990), App. A.

[5] See *The Impresario's Ten Commandments*, 3.

proved maddeningly slow; almost everyone Leone approached had already signed for the coming season or wanted more money than he had authority to spend. Leone was an inexperienced agent; Giardini was an underfunded impresario—the result was a mess that wound up in court. But the case gives a vivid picture of the difficulties of late recruitment by agent.

Certain problems recurred regularly. Singers or dancers might wish to come, only to find themselves prevented by contracts elsewhere or obligations to noble patrons. Thus we find Le Texier writing to Lord Cowper, lamenting that 'We were expecting to have Signor David this year . . . but I have just learnt that . . . Signor Campigli has personally opposed his leave [from Rome]'.[1] Gardel and Vestris jun. were denied royal permission to go abroad in 1787.[2] Singers often arrived late or fell ill, and late replacements were not uncommon. The *London Courant* of 7 November 1781 carries a notice saying

The Opening of this Theatre is unavoidably deferred on account of the indisposition of some of the Performers, lately arrived from abroad. . . . Signora Maccherini, who is engaged as First Serious Woman for the ensuing Season, being detained by her Engagement abroad until the end of the present Month, Signora Prudom, hoping for the Indulgence of the Public, will in the mean time undertake the First Serious Part; and the Second Soprano engaged at this Theatre, being taken ill at Boulogna [Boulogne? Bologna?], on his Way to England, Signor Manzoletto is re-engaged for the ensuing Season.

Emergency substitutes might be hired if they could be found, but seldom gave satisfaction. Singers were much too expensive to allow duplication, and understudies were unknown. One can see why versatility was valued and Gallini might want a serious woman who could do *buffa* roles if needed. Illness might force postponement (*Morning Chronicle*, 12 November 1782), or the company might resort to desperate expedients. 'Signor Morigi being unable to perform on Saturday night [he was in gaol], Signor Cremoni [Cremonini] was obliged to read his part, and to personate in that aukward and deficient manner the protagonist of . . . *Il Tutor Burlato*' (*Morning Herald*, 19 February 1787).[3] For the next performance 'Calvesi . . . took the part of Martufo, and though entirely out of his cast, conceived and executed it remarkably well' (*Daily Universal Register*, 23 February 1787). During his

---

[1] Letter of Oct. 1779 (printed by Gibson, 'Earl Cowper', 239).

[2] *Daily Universal Register*, 3 Jan. 1787.

[3] For Morigi's otherwise unrecorded stay in the Fleet prison, see PRO PRIS 10/23 (17 Feb.–29 Mar. 1787).

regime, Gallini introduced a policy of fractional engagements, whereby principal performers would be heard for half a season, that is from after Easter until the beginning of July. This had the advantage of allowing singers such as Marchesi to complete lucrative Carnival seasons in Italy before travelling to London.

## Salaries and Benefits

No season salary lists appear to be extant, but from newspaper reports, documents filed with the Lord Chamberlain's office, and Chancery testimony a considerable number of salaries can be recovered.[1] The concern here is to establish a sense of the salary scale. Probably every company had such a scale, whether or not formally spelt out. In the instructions to his agent in 1763, Giardini stipulated exactly what he was prepared to pay for a *primo uomo*, a *prima donna* (substantially less 'if middling'), a bass, a tenor, a composer, two good dancers, and so forth, and he added a 'Rule of Augmentation' to specify how much higher the agent could go if necessary.[2] Deriving so tidy a scale from the 1780s figures is difficult for several reasons. Newspaper gossip may be sensationalized; different managers worked in different circumstances; singers came for varying lengths of time. Gallini's salaries are a special problem because (contrary to usual practice) he signed singers to perform both at the King's Theatre and at his concert rooms in Hanover Square and, as an unhappy Master in Chancery reported to the Court, there is no way to determine what percentage of the salary should be assigned to the opera-house.[3] Taylor was profligate and allowed excessive salaries in 1782–83.[4] Contrariwise, in 1785–86 Gallini started late and in chaotic circumstances, and severely squeezed down top salaries. Rubinelli came for a season and a half for £1,700, serving at both venues. All such untidinesses aside, standard practice for principal singers and dancers is reasonably clear. The company had three salary spans (which may be dubbed 'upper', 'middle', and 'lower'), plus a top category that could be invoked for major stars. Varying a bit from season to season, these categories were £100–£200 at the lower end, £250–£500 in the middle, and £600–£1,000 at the upper end.

[1] Almost all of them are listed, season by season, in 'Opera Salaries'.
[2] *The Impresario's Ten Commandments*, 27, 40–3.
[3] C38/754.
[4] A writer in the *Morning Post* of 4 Jan. 1785 commented that 'it is very well known that the salaries given by Mr Taylor were much greater than the property could pay, even in the most successful season', instancing Le Picq at 1,700 guineas (but see below), Mlle Théodore at 900, and Pacchierotti at 1,200.

Only very occasionally did anyone earn £1,200; £1,500 to Marchesi in 1788–89 is the highest salary recorded in this period. No principal received less than £100. The key issue in any season budget was how many people went above the middle range. In a tight year, not many did. Benefits are a complication to be dealt with in due course.

At the lower end of the scale, £100 would hire Clementina Cremonini (1784–85), Giovanna Sestini (1785–86), or Vincenzo Calvesi (1786–87). Quite a few singers made £150 or £200.[1] In the middle scale Rachele D'Orta made £500, Luigi Tasca £350, Vincenzio Bartolini £300, and Angelo Franchi £250 in 1784–85. At least two or three singers had to be hired in the upper bracket each season in order to provide the stars demanded by exigent subscribers. Even in the economical season of 1785–86 Gallini hired Madam Mara at £800, Rubinelli and Babbini at £700, and Anna Laschi (who failed to come) at £600. Stars naturally tried to negotiate superscale salaries. In this decade very few were given. Pacchierotti and Marchesi are reported at £1,200 and £1,500, and Mara proved popular enough in 1785–86 that she was able to demand £1,200 for the following season (provoking a loud protest by Taylor against Gallini's extravagance).[2] Newspapers loved to trumpet top salaries and frequently exaggerated them. Even actual contracts were sometimes padded. The report of Master in Chancery Hett concerning finances in 1783–84 notes that Dauberval and his wife Madame Théodore had returned £105 to the company, 'their nominal agreement being £945 though they were in fact to receive only £840', and that Pacchierotti had likewise returned '£50 being one third part of what he agreed to return his Nominal Contract being for £1150 though he was to receive only £1000'.[3]

One gets a fairer sense of normalcy from the relative number of principal singers in the lower, middle, upper, and superscale categories. In 1784–85, for which there is a nearly complete list of principals' salaries, no one was paid more than £850, and there are three 'upper' salaries, four 'middle' salaries, and three 'lower' ones. In 1786–87 (a fairly prosperous year, with another lengthy list of salaries) only Mara received more than 'upper' scale, and the three normal categories had two, four, and two occupants, respectively. Note, however, that none of the 'middle' salaries was higher than

[1] Clara Pollone (1784–85, 1785–86), Eliza Wheeler (1785–86), Vincenzo Fineschi, and Paolo Torregiani (1788–89) made £150. Lodovico Simonetti and Andrea Morigi (1785–86), Cecilia Giuliani (1787–88), Clementina Graziani, Marie Pieltain, and Giovanna Sestini (1788–89) made £200.

[2] C107/201, interrogatories for Gallini, 7 May 1788.

[3] C38/715, Hett's third master's report, 12 Nov. 1784.

£350. In 1788–89 Marchesi received £1,500, but only Cecilia Giuliani enjoyed an upper-level salary (£891); there were four 'middle' salaries (only one above £260) and seven salaries of £150–200. Incomplete as the figures are, the number of singers receiving more than £300 or £400 a year was very small indeed. Returning singers appear to have earned pretty much the same salary from year to year; how much chorus members were paid is unknown.[1] They were probably hired on an occasional basis. Other than Madam Mara's 50 per cent rise for 1786–87, the only instance of such a jump in the extant records for these years was Nancy Storace's leap from £350 in 1786–87 to £800 for 1787–88—again provoking a loud complaint from Taylor.[2]

Salary patterns for principal dancers are harder to judge since there were fewer dancers, and the situation is complicated some years by supplements for the ballet-master, joint salaries for partners, and the like. None the less, the picture is essentially similar. Le Picq is reported to have earned £1,700 in 1782–83, but part of that was probably for his dancing in May and June of the previous season; £300 was for serving as ballet-master; and the remainder may have included the services of his partner, Geltruda Rossi. In 1784–85 (a more straitened year) Le Picq collected £800 or £850 as principal dancer and ballet-master, while Rossi received another £500. Normal top of scale for dancers appears to have been about £900, and most stars received £600–£800. The prodigy Vestris jun. received only a 700-guinea salary for 1780–81 despite his extraordinary popular success, but was able to get £1,200 for 1785–86.[3] In 1784–85 Nivelon had £700, Carolina Angiolini £650, Madame Rossi and Slingsby £500 each, Madame Dorival £350, and Mons. Frédéric £160. So far as can be judged from scanty records, this is a representative spread. In 1788–89 the fabled Noverre (ballet-master) received £735, Didelot got £600, Mlle Adelaide £400, five others £100 to £300—and Mlle Guimard was engaged late in the season (in response to audience riots), reportedly for £1,500 but actually for £670 plus board, lodging, a carriage, and other perquisites. *Figurants* contributed to the expense of the dance establishment. At least sixteen of them were considered necessary,[4] at

---

[1] This was very much the pattern between 1796 and 1808, when fairly complete salary lists for most seasons are preserved. See 'Opera Salaries', Table 8.

[2] C107/201, interrogatories for Gallini, 27 May 1789.

[3] LC 7/3, fo. 207ᵛ.

[4] In C31/233, no. 322, MacMahon and Slingsby testified that in 1783–84 the ballet-master had 'declared that several of the said Figure Dancers [hired by Gallini] were unnecessary and others, particularly the Apprentices of the said John Andrea Gallini unequal to their parts, and that Sixteen persons only were sufficient in that Capacity'.

prices ranging from £30 or £40 to £80 each—not so very much in salaries, but all of them had to be costumed. The usual salary for a ballet-master was £300. Gallini testified in 1788 that in 1785–86 'he engaged Mr Dagville as Ballet Master at the Salary of £50 being a very small and inadequate salary for such a person (£300 being the usual and accustomed Salary)' and therefore allowed him the profits from a masquerade.[1] As a rule ballet-masters were performers as well, which makes the salary hard to disentangle. The £735 (plus benefit) paid to Noverre in 1788–89 was particularly large when one remembers that he no longer danced.

Evaluating the salaries for other personnel is even harder than for singers and dancers, but once again some clear and consistent patterns emerge. Pay for several of the jobs varied drastically with the season's offerings. If costumes and scenery were being scrimped on, the tailor and scene-designer might be paid less than usual. Writing to Lord Cowper, Gallini said in August 1789 'I shall not want any composer 'till the next season, 1790[–91], at the new Opera as the present one is too confined'—by which he meant that he did not intend to concentrate on new operas at the Little Haymarket (only Federici's *L'usurpator innocente* was newly commissioned); he relied instead on revivals and arrangements.[2] Such variables notwithstanding, customary salaries are reasonably clear.

Badini was paid £100 as poet in 1784–85 but got a rise to £150 in 1785–86, eliciting a complaint from Taylor.[3] Gallini replied that Badini had undertaken to serve as translator as well.[4] This may be legitimate: accounts audited by the Court of Chancery for 1783–84 appear to show about £50 paid to 'Mr Molini Translator of the Operas'.[5] Leopoldo De Michele received £150 as music-copyist in 1782–83 and again in 1783–84. This probably covered administrative services; he billed the theatre separately for supplies and the cost of his subordinates' labour. As of the end of the 1782–83 season De Michele claimed to be owed a total of £513. How much—if anything—Taylor had paid him during 1781–82 and 1782–83 is not known, but obviously a substantial amount more than the copyist's salary was at issue.[6] The leader of the band received £150 per annum. Susan Burney quotes Wilhelm Cramer as saying 'You give me £150 for leading your band' in 1779–80, and he apparently received the same sum in 1783–84. The leader's

---

[1] C31/249, no. 45.    [2] Gibson, 'Earl Cowper', 250.
[3] C107/201, interrogatories for Gallini, 7 May 1788.
[4] C107/201, Gallini's answers of 21 July 1789.
[5] C38/715, Hett's third master's report, 12 Nov. 1784.
[6] C24/1929, interrogatories of 20 Oct. 1788.

salary remained unchanged when Cramer headed the orchestra at the Pantheon in 1790–91.[1]

The arrangements for 'painters' (scene designers) are more variable and complex. According to a Lord Chamberlain's list, Novosielski was owed £300 for 1784–85. The pamphleteers of 1784 state that Novosielski's salary was 'formerly' £300, that he had offered his services for 1783–84 for £250, and that he was collecting £750 in 1784–85.[2] The difference was presumably managerial supplement and graft. In 1785–86 Marinari received only £100, but £250 went to Biagio Rebekah for 'decorations', making the total £350 for the season. Marinari got £190 in 1787–88. Gallini may well have chosen to pay per opera rather than grant a flat annual salary. Like the tailor and the copyist, the painter was expected to employ assistants and to bill the theatre for supplies. Records of these expenses are very rare, but accounts audited for Chancery imply that the additional 'painters' bill for 1786–87 was £164, while 'carpenters' came to £440. The latter included not only construction of scenery but scene-shifting during rehearsals and performances. In 1787–88 'carpenters' came to £512, 'timber merchant' to £96, and 'painters' to £281.[3]

The tailor in most of these seasons was the vastly experienced Thomas Luppino. William Taylor fired him in 1782, and the resulting lawsuit contains contradictory details about what he was owed and for what duties: Sheridan had hired him to do work for Drury Lane as well and had charged at least part of his salary to that budget. The gist of the complaint, however, is that he had a contractual salary of £200 per annum and was owed reimbursement for his costume-shop assistants and all materials.[4] This salary accords precisely with later, unrelated Chancery litigation involving Gallini, where Luppino is said to have been owed £200 in 1785–86.[5] The 'tailors' bill came to £323 in 1786–87 (including Luppino?), with another £297 for 'mercers and weavers'. The following year 'tailors' totalled £597; there is no separate fabric bill in the figures preserved (C38/754).

---

[1] Susan Burney, fo. 41ʳ (20 Nov. 1779). C38/715, Hett's third report. Bedford Opera Papers, 2.A.34. Giardini temporarily supplanted Cramer in 1782–83, reportedly for the startling salary of £400 (*Morning Herald*, 25 Oct. 1782), but to judge from the evidence printed in App. II he collected almost none of it.

[2] LC 7/3, fo. 191. *The Case of the Opera-House Disputes*, 29.

[3] C38/754 (master's report of Mar. 1789). Figures are rounded to the nearest pound.

[4] C12/2171/23.

[5] C107/201, interrogatories for Gallini, 7 May 1788.

The treasurer Henry Johnson received £150 in 1785–86 and again in the next two seasons. Deputy managers seem to have made at least £150 per annum, as Carnevale did in 1785–86 and Ravelli in 1788–89. Taylor charged that Gallini had extravagantly given Carnevale £250, but he also claims (apparently without foundation) that Badini was getting £220.[1] When one reaches the realm of house servants, not only the salaries but most of the names are unrecoverable. When one looks at the personnel of a better-documented company (the Pantheon, for instance), one realizes how small a percentage of the King's Theatre's employees is now known. Occasionally, a name surfaces. In May 1783 the housekeeper was a Mrs Rogers—a fact known only because she later testified in Taylor's suit against the Sheriff of London (*The Times*, 24 July 1789).

Composers' salaries are a problem. The only individual season salary we have for the King's Theatre in these years is £224 for Cherubini in 1785–86, but this includes service at Hanover Square. In 1786–87 the Chancery Master's accounts list a payment of £63 to Stephen Storace. Lawsuit testimony shows that this comprised not salary but 25 guineas each for two pasticcios and 10 guineas reimbursement for music bought in Germany.[2] Taylor complained bitterly about Arnold's being paid £105 for *Giulio Cesare* in 1786, stating that the usual rate for a pasticcio was only 10 guineas.[3] This may have been the bottom rate for piece-work, though in May 1782 Tommaso Giordani sued successfully for £30 (and another £30 in costs) for having 'got up' an opera called *La contadina bizarra* that the King's Theatre had not produced.[4] 'Composers' are known to have received a total of £530 in 1783–84, and the Pantheon paid Mazzinghi £300 for his services in 1790–91. A house composer could expect about £200 for composition and performances; perhaps half that sum was paid to the person or persons later designated 'harpsichord' (sometimes the same person), and operas from other composers could cost anything from £10 to £100 each.

All salary figures must be considered in the light of possible benefit receipts. Here one encounters a thicket of difficulties. Benefits were not always advertised and were sometimes 'sold' back to management for a flat fee. Dauberval, for example, reportedly sold his 1784 benefit for only £150,

---

[1] C31/239, no. 206 (15 Feb. 1786).

[2] C38/754, Mar. 1789, and C107/201, Gallini's answer of 21 July 1789.

[3] C107/201, interrogatories for Gallini, 7 May 1788.

[4] James Oldham, *The Mansfield Manuscripts and the Growth of English Law in the Eighteenth Century*, 2 vols. (Chapel Hill: University of North Carolina Press, 1992), i. 370–1.

though it is said to have grossed 'near £700'.[1] Lacking the theatre's account-books, one must turn to newspaper speculation, which tends towards the sensational. But because of the sums involved, which could easily match or surpass the annual salary, one cannot afford to ignore benefits as a fundamental part of the economics of opera in this period.

Occasionally a benefit became a major public occasion, as Vestris jun.'s did in 1781. The newspapers freely asserted that he had made as much as £3,000 or more; even the sceptical Horace Walpole estimated £1,400—a truly staggering sum.[2] Early editions of *Grove* (relying on Capon's *Les Vestris*, 1908) report the take at 12,000 guineas, which is ludicrous. Even after considerable enlargement in the summer of 1782, the King's Theatre held a total of about 1,800 people, jam-packed. Some 700 of these places were in the galleries. Basic arithmetic shows that at face prices (10s. 6d. in pit and boxes, 5s. and 3s. in the galleries) the total gross would not exceed £800. A generous patron might, to be sure, give the beneficiary more than the face value of the ticket, which makes Walpole's £1,400 figure possible in 1781 only if we assume that every place was taken and that all of the occupants paid an average of roughly double the normal price for their tickets: £1,400 is a great deal but remains a far cry from 12,000 guineas.

The *Morning Chronicle* of 6 March 1784 says that Pacchierotti's benefit 'was a very full one, as we should guess above seven hundred pounds'. Allowing something for expenses, this is perfectly possible. On the following 20 April the same paper had adjusted its estimate down to £650, but adds some others: 'Vestris about £700.—Rossi £500.—D'Auberval near £700 . . . Mad. Simonet had above £500.' Benefits were not part of the subscription season: if subscribers chose not to buy tickets, the beneficiary would not make much money. If one did not feel popular, or did not cultivate many friends, or needed cash but hated the process of flogging tickets to acquaintances, then one might prefer to sell the benefit back to the house and avoid the risk and trouble.

For most benefits the recipient had to pay 'house charges' to cover the cost to management. 'Free' benefits were given with great reluctance, for the obvious reason that the entire cost came straight out of the proprietor's pocket. The long-standing procedure was for the treasurer to deduct £30 for house rent plus various constant and incident charges (for example, lights)

---

[1] *Morning Chronicle*, 20 Apr. 1784.
[2] *St. James's Chronicle*, 22–24 Feb. 1781; Walpole, *Correspondence*, xxv. 134 (letter to Sir Horace Mann, 26 Feb. 1781).

from cash received, turning the balance over to the beneficiary. Taylor tried to change this procedure, demanding that beneficiaries accept direct responsibility for all bills—and thereby precipitating a series of lawsuits. The testimony preserved in C24/1939 is quite confusing, but is considerably clarified by Peter Crawford, who explains that while the recipient was responsible for expenses and house rent, these had always been paid by the manager and the total deducted from the proceeds. Unfortunately, no figures show actual benefit deductions, but £75 was the customary per diem allowance for routine orchestral and non-performer costs,[1] and adding £30 for rent would bring the chargeable cost of a benefit to £105. By way of comparison, one may note that the rent for use of the Hanover Square concert room was 25 guineas per night.[2]

Benefits were probably most profitable for popular stars at the top end of the salary scale, but any performer might hope for as much as his or her annual salary and, while profit was by no means guaranteed, lower-paid beneficiaries might enjoy an even greater windfall. One can see why Marie Pieltain and Giovanna Sestini were offered £200 *or* a benefit as remuneration for 1788–89: a half-full house would have yielded upwards of £300 after deductions. A complication is Taylor's charge that Gallini was granting some benefits only on the condition that he receive a portion of the take under the table. Taylor is not the most trustworthy source, but the details he offers carry some conviction.[3] He claims that Gallini had extorted kickbacks from Carnevale (£200) and Babbini (£70) on free benefits for which the house paid expenses. Taylor further says that he has seen a contract with Forlivesi entitling Gallini to half the profits of concerts arranged for him, as well as half the receipts of his opera benefit. This charge is apparently confirmed by Forlivesi in a notice published in the *Morning Post* of 9 July 1789. Kickbacks are not a modern invention.

### III. House Management

Much of the daily operation of the theatre is now unrecoverable, but from a variety of scraps some sense of it can be constructed: subscriptions, box assignments, the coffee-room, the printing of librettos, royal patronage, and so forth.

---

[1] C12/2012/54.    [2] C31/249, no. 45.
[3] C31/253, no. 249 (affidavit of 11 July 1789).

*Arrangements at the Beginning of the Season*

Some time in November or December (only very occasionally as early as October or as late as January) the 'season advertisement' appeared (Pl. 8)—a genteel invitation to subscribers to pay in their money at the company's bank. Though never mentioned, the customary price for a single place in the boxes was 20 guineas, which entitled the purchaser to attend all but benefit performances to the end of the regular subscription season (normally fifty nights).[1] Four hundred subscribers, fully paid, would generate 8,000 guineas, upwards of half the sum required for a minimum annual budget. Unfortunately, not everyone paid in full at the beginning of the season: three instalments were considered routine (to judge from the Pantheon), and credit was extended, however reluctantly. Debtor box-holders had been a problem in Handel's time and remained so for the Pantheon.[2] Evidence for the period at issue is scanty, but an official notice signed by Henry Johnson and Jonathan Garton states 'that between six and seven hundred pounds of the subscriptions of the two last seasons remained due at the commencement of the present season, independent of many of the boxes not having given the full number' (*Morning Chronicle*, 11 December 1780). The problem may have been worse in 1780–81, for at the outset of the next season a newspaper asserts that 'it is a known fact that near a thousand pounds of the subscription of last year remains still unpaid'.[3] Presumably the King's Theatre had similar problems throughout the decade.

Houses were usually thin until well past Christmas.[4] The substantial

---

[1] In some seasons a further subscription was offered (for example, eight additional performances for three guineas—see a printed notice of 15 May 1792 in the Little Haymarket folder for 1792, Enthoven Collection, Theatre Museum, V&A). If there were additional performances but no further subscription, box-holders could reserve their usual places by informing the treasurer's office by noon on the day of a performance. See the *Morning Herald*, 20 June 1785.

[2] See Judith Milhous and Robert D. Hume, 'Handel's Opera Finances in 1732–3', *Musical Times*, 125 (1984), 86–9. At the end of the 1791–92 season the Pantheon company's accounts showed £589 in 'Subscriptions Outstanding', by far the largest part owed by the Prince of Wales and his brother the Duke of York. Six people had failed to pay their £21 subscriptions, and others lesser sums. See Bedford Opera Papers, Box 3, Book VIIIa. Polite letters from Trancart to various debtors are preserved in the Bedford Opera Papers, 3.A.1–5. The company went so far as to have its solicitor threaten Lady Essex with legal action if she failed to pay (1.C.3).

[3] Theatre Cuts 41, fo. [70ʳ], undated but part of a notice of the performers for 1781–82.

[4] The *Morning Herald* of 11 Jan. 1782 notes that the theatre has been unusually well attended even before the Queen's birthday, 18 Jan., which 'has always been considered as the

amount of subscription money collected at the start of the season permitted the company to make the 'first payment' to employees in late January or thereabouts. Rank-and-file members of the orchestra and 'house servants' were paid weekly (if possible), but performers and senior staff received their annual salaries in three instalments, due roughly 1 February, 1 May, and at the end of the season. References in Gallini's accounts prove, as expected, that the King's Theatre had to supply a fair number of salary advances as well as travel money long before the 'first payment'.[1]

### Box Arrangements

The best boxes were much coveted, and management had a perennial problem keeping people happy. One person (very often a woman) held the box and determined who would be the other occupants. Boxes seated from four to six persons (six only with crowding), and they were not as fixed an entity as one might suppose. Management periodically revamped the auditorium to squeeze in more premium seating. Lady Mary Coke's complaint about reduction in box size for 1778–79 was quoted in Chapter 1. Taylor's alterations in 1782 were yet more drastic: on 1 September Lady Mary wrote

with regard to the Opera the House is altering and our Box is to be again reduced. None as I am informed are to remain for six Persons four are to be the Number. Lady Ailesbury tells me She has proposed to You that we should take one in the front which to me is the worst part of the House the best thing I should think that we could do would be to get one Lady and Gentleman additional and take two Boxes together where ours was for surely it was the best situation in the House. Lady Betty Mackenzie I should think would like to subscribe and I imagine there will be no difficulty in finding another Gentleman.[2]

In the course of the next several years an additional sixteen boxes were crammed into the auditorium. The *Morning Post* of 17 January 1785 comments snidely: 'The boxes erecting at the Opera are to have new appropriations . . . a *beaufet* for refreshments, and a *water closet*; six chairs to each box have been proposed, but the ladies think *conversation* may be carried on with more spirit upon a couch.'

commencement of the opera season'.

[1] See C38/715, Hett's third report, for numerous instances of salary advances 'on account' and travel money paid by Gallini. The Pantheon's books show that it had to supply numerous advances, and even to help performers pay foreign debts before they could leave for England.

[2] The *Morning Herald* of 5 Feb. 1783 lists Lady Ailesbury as holder of Box 3, with Lady Mary Coke, Lady Strafford, Lord Hertford, General Conway, and Horace Walpole as the other occupants. Presumably they could not all attend on the same night.

Subscribers sometimes carried box lust well beyond the bounds of civility. A notable disagreement that culminated in the interruption of a performance occurred in 1783 and was celebrated in *The Opera Rumpus* (quoted in Chapter 1). An even greater row erupted in 1785, and is described by Lady Mary Coke:

Mrs Hobart who has generally quarrels upon her hands, is at this time in dispute with Lord and Lady Salisbury about her Box at the Opera, for as She some time ago determined to go Abroad Lord Salisbury paid the Money and took the Box for Lady Salisbury and the key was given. Mrs Hobart came to Town and says She also paid the money for the Box and demanded it, they told her Lady Salisbury had the Key and was not in Town, this happened last Saturday, and She was contented to sit in some other Box, but at that time meditated revenge and laid her plan of operation which was executed soon after I came into the House. Mrs Damer and I heard a great Knocking and Noise and directing our eyes from whence it came found it was from the contested Box and after the blows had been three or four times repeated with great violence the door flew open and in came Mrs Hobart and Mr North triumphant. The Prince of Wales went to them seemingly to congratulate their success, upon which I observed to Mrs Damer that I thought the Prince had better have been neuter, as this is an Affair which will certainly be much talked of. H R H soon after came to the side of our Box and said he was present when the door was forced, and that after Mr North had made two or three attempts, Mr[s] Hobart to encourage him, said one kick more, and it will do. What is to be the consequence of this business I really don't know. (5 January 1785)

The consequence was the hurried erection of six or eight new boxes (and the consequent diminution of the rest), accompanied by a flood of newspaper commentary ranging from the amused to the outraged.[1]

Boxes were normally rented by the season but could be leased for longer terms. Leasing boxes on multi-year contracts was a good way of raising cash—though at the price of diminished receipts in the future. The complexities of box rights are well illustrated in a long-running dispute between Taylor and the Mr Broadhead who had contested Lady Jersey's occupation of his box. Broadhead had been so foolish as to buy three renters' shares in the King's Theatre about 1781, and when he was not paid what was owed him, he decided unilaterally to start applying the money due against his box obligations—a solution Taylor found unpalatable. The fire of 1789 merely

---

[1] See particularly the *Morning Post* of 6, 8, 10, 12, 14, and 15 Jan. 1785, and Lady Mary Coke's entry for 15 Jan. The *Morning Herald* of 10 Jan. says that six new boxes have been added in just three days, and that they will make a great deal of money for the theatre. The *Morning Post* of 12 Jan. reports eight new boxes. Eight further boxes were added for 1787–88 (*Daily Universal Register*, 10 Dec. 1787).

complicated the situation: Broadhead was not happy with the location of the box he was offered in the new theatre. He sued; Taylor countersued.[1] The details do not matter: the point is the passions roused in subscribers by rights to boxes, and the legal and financial complications that followed.

## *The Coffee-Room and the Fruit Concession*

The social appeal of the opera is evident in the custom of printing subscriber lists, as has been noted in Chapter 1. The publisher of the subscriber pamphlets, from the Pantheon list for 1790–91 to at least 1806–07, was William Lee, long-time holder of the King's Theatre's coffee-house concession. He clearly knew everyone and had the tact and manners necessary for running what was in essence a fashionable club. He is first encountered in a letter he sent to the *Public Advertiser* of 7 November 1775, stating that he had served refreshments in a room at the King's Theatre with a passage to the boxes and had done so since 1772, being charged £60 per annum and paying for light and fires himself; now the managers are charging him £160 per annum rent, while fires and light cost him an additional £80. Lee was also employed as box manager or box bookkeeper at the King's Theatre, and he was appointed manager of the boxes at the Pantheon at £50 per annum. The coffee-room was more than a gathering place before and after performances: it seems to have been a social centre throughout the evening. The *Morning Post* of 31 March 1785 says that it was 'heretofore the *rendezvous* of the Ladies, and the place of *relief* for the beaux from dull music' but 'is now used for more *serious* purposes', instancing transaction of business there—a subject picked up satirically in the issue of 2 April. Commenting on the Little Haymarket arrangements for 1789–90, the *Public Advertiser* of 9 January 1790 says 'The new Coffee room [built for the opera season] is a large well-proportioned room; but it will be found at an inconvenient distance from the boxes.' Le Texier waxes sardonic on the subject, inveighing against the numerous opera patrons who wander in 'towards nine or ten o'clock' after dinner, applaud a song or ballet, and camp 'in the coffee-room, with that common topic of conversation, politics and horses', remaining there 'till the end of the Opera brings the whole of the polite company'.[2] In the later 1790s the coffee-room concession was held by Da Ponte's wife Nancy.[3]

---

[1] See C12/195/32 (*Broadhead* v. *Taylor*) and Taylor's countersuit, C12/661/3.

[2] *Ideas on the Opera*, 33.

[3] Sheila Hodges, *Lorenzo Da Ponte: The Life and Times of Mozart's Librettist* (New York: Universe, 1985), 144.

A notice in the *World* of 7 January 1790 from M. Harris, 'Book and Fruit Woman to the Theatre Royal Covent Garden', informed the public that 'she has undertaken to supply the Opera-House with Books, Fruits, and Refreshments', hoping that the public will reward her forty years' experience and help her 'to support the Seven Children of her late unfortunate Son'. The *World* of 25 February 1790, puffing the proposed opera-house in Leicester Square, reported that 'the sum of £400 has been offered for the liberty of selling fruit in this new Theatre'. This is probably a great deal more than the privilege had commanded at the old King's Theatre, but fruit and other refreshments were for sale during performances—and no doubt subscriber lists and books of the opera and ballet as well.

## Advertising

As printers' bills for the Pantheon suggest, the King's Theatre printed two sorts of playbills in addition to newspaper advertisements. 'Great Bills' were poster-size statements of the day's attractions meant for public display in the street. Handbills were miniature versions of the poster, dispatched to individuals. Whether they were systematically distributed to all subscribers who lived within a reasonable distance of the opera-house is not known: the newspaper advertisements should have been sufficient notice, but possibly a personal touch was considered necessary. Justifying steep printing-costs, Gallini reportedly testified that he regularly sent opera bills to schools in the vicinity of London.[1] Late changes to the programme were apparently announced by distributing handbills, if the alteration was too late for the newspapers. The *Morning Herald* of 21 June 1785 reports that *The Deserter* could not be given because Mlle Dorival was unexpectedly unable to appear: 'hand-bills had been given out to apprize the public' but not everyone had taken the trouble to peruse them; a fuss ensued in the theatre, and Le Picq had to come forward and deliver an apology (in French).

The principal mode of communicating the company's offerings was naturally newspaper bills. These almost always appeared in the top left corner of the first page of the several papers favoured with the company's business each season. (See Pl. 7*a*.) Very often more space was devoted to the ballets than to the opera, though the opera came first. Advertisements almost

---

[1] Taylor responded with a complaint about this 'useless and unnecessary expence' (C31/253, no. 249). A satire on puffing in the 28 Jan. 1782 *Morning Herald* described '*Literary opera glasses*', which make twenty people look like 2,000 and magnify 'boarding-school boys' into 'foreign Ambassadors'; perhaps Gallini was not the first to distribute bills to schools.

always specified 'serious' or 'comic'; the title was given; the composer was named (or some of the composers drawn upon for a pasticcio). If the composer was not in charge, a formula was often employed, for example, 'The Music entirely new, composed by the celebrated Signor Sarti, under the direction of Signor Anfossi' (*I rivali delusi*, 7 February 1784). Singers of 'Principal Characters' were often named, though their roles were rarely specified. The titles of the ballets were given, together with a list of the principals; again, roles were hardly ever listed. The choreographer (to use the modern term) was named far more regularly than the composer of the dance music. New scenery and costumes were occasional treats, and tended to be advertised. The prices were always listed, however familiar and unchanging—10*s.* 6*d.* for the pit, 5*s.* first gallery, 3*s.* second gallery. Starting time was routinely announced, since it varied. The doors opened at 6.00 or 6.30, and the performance was due to commence an hour later.

*Librettos and Scenarios*

The texts of a large majority of the operas were printed, as a rule in dual-language form with Italian and English on facing pages. The singers and their roles were almost always given; substantive dedications or prefaces were a rarity. Unlike new plays, new operas were put in print immediately —in time for the première, if possible. Only a company in a state of wretched confusion failed to get its librettos published promptly: most members of the audience could not understand Italian, and the auditorium was sufficiently well lit to permit one to follow along in the books during performances (see below, sect. v). During the 1780s the standard price of a libretto rose from 1*s.* to 1*s.* 6*d.*, a change eliciting angry legal challenges from Taylor, who demanded to know why Gallini had allowed Badini to raise the price and keep the extra money: the house and the poet had formerly been entitled to 3*d.* each (the printer presumably took the other 6*d.*), but now Badini was allowed 9*d.* from each copy sold.[1] From time to time the opera

---

[1] C107/201, interrogatories for Gallini, 7 May 1788. 'Veritas', *Opera House*, 21, states that at this period 'The poet, or prompter, had also the perquisite of the Opera books, estimated at £500 per annum.' At 9*d.* per copy, this would require sales of more than 13,000 copies, a figure difficult to credit. Whatever his income, Badini was by his own admission thinking of declaring bankruptcy in 1789 when he was sued by John Gallerino, apparently a member of the opera orchestra who had arrived from Italy three years earlier (C12/471/7, bill filed 11 Mar. 1789). Gallerino charged that Badini had borrowed twelve guineas from him, and then induced him to sign documents in English that he could not read, making him liable for another £35.

advertisement says something like 'Books of the Ballets to be had at the Theatre, price 6*d.*' (*Morning Post*, 30 January 1784), but only a handful of such scenarios survive.

### Applause and Disapprobation

Audience appreciation was expressed with clapping and often with cheers.[1] For singers the key indicator of success was the encore: the newspapers report with great regularity who and what received encores, and lack of audience demand for them was felt to indicate a cool reception. What are now termed 'curtain calls' were clearly a custom by 1779–80, when Susan Burney reports her hero Pacchierotti's behaviour on such an occasion. Describing the end of a performance of the pasticcio *L'Olimpiade* for Pacchierotti's benefit on 9 March 1780, she says

When all was over, & he came forward with the usual *ceremonies* to bow—there was such an applause as I scarce ever remember—he bowed & bowed, & bowed again—& could scarce get away—the colour rose in his face . . . had he not at last retired, the applause for ought I know might have lasted till now, as nobody seemed inclined to give up. (fo. 76ʳ)

Applause was usually for singers and dancers but began to extend to others. Noverre modestly refused a curtain call in 1782 and was criticized for accepting one in 1788 (see Ch. 7). But by 3 June 1789 the *World* remarks that the audience was so enthusiastic about *La generosità d'Alessandro* 'that they did as is done in foreign Theatres—they gave the *Composer* specific applause—"Bravo *Tarchi*"—"Bravo *Maestro*"—and they encored a Trio, ten minutes long'.

The newspapers regularly accused management of filling the galleries with friends who entered free on 'orders', though the managers naturally denied it. 'Philharmonicus' observed in the *Morning Post* of 16 March 1778:

The Managers . . . think to command [success] by cramming the upper part of the house with a set of miscreants, (the sweepings of every Italian warehouse in town &c. &c.) whose only payment is by *palms of hands*, and *lungs*. These vermin . . . are ever keeping up an incessant jabber, during the music, to the total prevention of

---

[1] The *Morning Post* of 30 Dec. 1780 reports a query from a correspondent 'whether instead of clapping hands, it would not be more consonant to delicacy, for ladies to express their approbation at the theatre by striking with their fans on the breast-work of the box. . . . Such an expression of approbation would be correspondent to a gentleman's striking the floor with his cane. Though a lady may plead custom for clapping a favourite author, or player, nothing would excuse the indelicacy of her hissing.'

those who would attend to it, and think they discharge their part of the contract, if at the end of each song indiscriminately, they thunder out a *brava,—Ancora, Ancora!* and promote a rapid circulation of blood in their fingers-ends.

Management huffily denied the charge on the 17th, asserting that 'very few' orders are ever given out, but Philharmonicus replied tartly on the 19th: 'With respect to the "very few orders issued", no body who has staid two minutes to change a guinea at the gallery door can have failed to observe the excess of proportion the *paper currency* [that is, orders for free admission] always bears to that of *hard money.*'

Occasional riots and general inattention notwithstanding, the audience seems generally to have been good-humoured. It quickly became very familiar with each season's performers and treated them with a fair degree of tolerance and often with affection. When offended, however, the audience could be fierce and made its feelings known with groans, jeers, and whistles. Even a favourite might offend them. A notable instance occurred in May 1784, when Vestris jun., a great pet of the public, refused to perform in a revival of *The Deserter* because he was not given the principal part. When he next appeared 'the pit and boxes . . . thundered forth, in hisses and other marks of indignation' (*Morning Post*, 19 May)—and the newspapers thundered forth themselves, heaping contempt and recrimination upon the recalcitrant dancer, who hastened to make a public apology in the theatre and to assure the audience 'that he would in future perform his part in the Deserter, though greatly beneath his dignity and pre-eminence as *premier Danseur absolu*', as the *Morning Post* reported on 21 May.

### Royal Patronage

George III attended the King's Theatre only occasionally. Mount Edgcumbe noted that Arnold's pasticcio *Giulio Cesare* in March 1787 'answered the end proposed: The king came two or three times to hear it', and Gallini commented specially on the King coming in a letter to Lord Cowper.[1] The King was a music-lover and a Handel fanatic, but not an opera-goer, and hence little help to the King's Theatre's social prestige, even before the first of his episodes of 'madness'.[2] The Prince of Wales, however,

---

[1] Mount Edgcumbe, *Musical Reminiscences*, 54–5; Gibson, 'Earl Cowper', 247.

[2] Etiquette is implied in a rather huffy recommendation to the opera managers in the *Morning Herald* of 30 Jan. 1781 that they 'take care the orchestra are all ready to strike up immediately' when the Prince enters the house '(as when the King is there) and not to offend him by the noise of their crouding in and tuning their different instruments, which was the

quickly became an habitué after attaining his majority.[1] The newspapers avidly reported his presence, and the amount of space Lady Mary Coke devoted to him suggests the degree to which even the nobility and gentry enjoyed gawping at royalty. He wandered from box to box, spent evenings socializing in the pit, womanized, and eventually flaunted his domestic relations with Mrs Fitzherbert for all the audience to see.[2] Some of the newspapers found the spectacle unedifying, but one must suspect that the Prince sold more tickets to the opera than Parkyns MacMahon ever did.

## IV. Scenery, Properties, and Costumes

The importance of scenery to both opera and ballet in the 1780s is beyond doubt. The company spent substantial sums of money on it, and newspaper commentary (however maddeningly unspecific) · demonstrates the high degree of audience interest in it. When William Hodges failed dismally as the scene-designer at the Pantheon in 1791 the newspapers hounded him out in mid-season.[3] In hard times skimping on scenery, 'that great ornament of a Theatre', drew loud complaints.[4] Scenery and fancy machine effects had been one of the special attractions of opera in London from its semi-opera origins in the late seventeenth century. English opera had been the vehicle by which the Italian transformation stage came to England, and its magical effects had taken deep root in the pantomime that formed an important part of the offerings at Covent Garden and Drury Lane. To the 1780s audience, scenery and machinery were vital parts of opera and ballet. For the twentieth-century scholar the subject is highly problematical because virtually no direct evidence survives. Not a single scene design for the King's Theatre is known for the period 1778–91, nor even a list of stock scenes in the company's possession. Quite a lot more is known about Continental practice, and a relatively large number of scene designs are preserved. The chances are high that the King's Theatre used very similar scenery. London was part of an international circuit, and the principal scene-designers in London in the 1780s (Novosielski and Marinari) trained and worked on the

case on Saturday evening'.

[1] See the *Morning Chronicle*, 15 Jan. 1781.

[2] The *Oracle* of 2 Apr. 1792, reviewing Paisiello's *La discordia conjugale*, noted that 'The Prince sat with Mrs Fitzherbert, *La concordia conjugale*, visible enough.'

[3] See Curtis Price, 'Turner at the Pantheon Opera House, 1791–92', *Turner Studies*, 7 (1987), 2–8.

[4] See, for example, the *Morning Post* of 15 Mar. 1786.

Continent. Likewise, the King's Theatre's scenery was undoubtedly similar to that at Covent Garden and Drury Lane, where both Novosielski and Marinari also worked. None the less, the present discussion is confined primarily to evidence pertaining directly to the opera-house in the years at issue.

### Changeable Scenery

The wing-and-shutter system in use at the King's Theatre in the 1780s had obtained in all London theatres since the introduction of changeable scenery by Davenant in the 1660s. The classic discussion remains Richard Southern's.[1] The exact details of the King's Theatre stage are not known, but its basic principles are clear enough. Scenery was done in co-ordinated sets of wings, shutters, and borders (valances). They were changed in full view of the audience and could provide dazzling shifts of location and transformations in seconds. Like the other theatres, the King's Theatre also used 'drops', and apparently not just for backcloths: 'The scenery, except in the premature dropping of the rustic's kitchen . . . was better shifted than has been usual at this Theatre' (*Morning Chronicle*, 20 December 1784). Anyone familiar with the scenic potential of the late eighteenth-century theatre at Drottningholm (re-created by Ingmar Bergman in his film of *The Magic Flute*) will know the sorts of effects in which 1780s audiences delighted all over Europe. Unlike the Drottningholm Theatre, which powered its scene shifts with an integrated machine, the King's Theatre stayed with the old English system of large crews of scene-shifters—invisible to the audience, shoving wings and shutters in and out of view on command—but the magical results were the same. The stage floor contained a variety of trapdoors, and the flies were equipped with a cloud machine and transportation for supernatural beings from Cupid to Medea. 'Flyings' were an important part of the display. Scenery of this sort made little pretence of creating 'reality', and only the most necessary furnishings dressed the stage, facilitating scene changes. Mishaps were unconcealed, and the lack of technical rehearsal (see sect. v) cannot have helped. Reviewing Bertoni's *Il convito* on 5 November 1782, the *Morning Chronicle* observes that 'The *Scenemen* ought not to go without their Share of proper Mention;—in the last Dance, one of the Wings was near tumbling; and in the Garden Scene of the Opera, where the Count and Chevalier appear on the Stage as Statues, through the Scene not

[1] Richard Southern, *Changeable Scenery* (London: Faber and Faber, 1952).

closing on them as it ought to have done, Viganoni and Bartolini, though then in the Character of Rocks and Stones, were forced to help themselves, assume Loco-motive Powers, and go jumping off the Stage.' Such grumbles prove that oversights did occur from time to time, but they were the exception, not the rule.

Virtually everything known about scene-painting in eighteenth-century London has been conveniently assembled in a pair of books by Sybil Rosenfeld.[1] Most of the scenes were probably drawn symmetrically. Little of the evidence on such subjects as topographical and antiquarian scenery, lighting scenes, and various styles of painting has any direct connection with the opera-house, but what Rosenfeld has gleaned for other theatres probably holds true for King's as well. An extensive scene inventory survives for the Pantheon (to be discussed in vol. II), and it is very similar to the inventories discussed by Rosenfeld. Since Marinari took over from Hodges at the Pantheon, there was undoubtedly a high degree of continuity. Some of Rosenfeld's illustrations from non-opera-house sources probably give a very fair idea what the King's Theatre's sets looked like at this time. The 'Library' in Drury Lane's *School for Scandal* (1777) would have served admirably for many of the upper-class interiors (*A Short History*, pl. 16). Michael Angelo Rooker's formal garden (pl. 17), John Inigo Richards's 'Maid of the Mill' (pl. 18), De Loutherbourg's prison (pl. 21), Rooker's army camp (*Georgian Scene Painters*, pl. 13), and Greenwood's gothic exteriors for Covent Garden and Drury Lane (pls. 25 and 27) were probably of the sort used at the King's Theatre in the 1780s.

Scenery was expensive and not lightly discarded: hence it was reused in show after show, sometimes for many years. Servandoni painted some for a Covent Garden *Alceste* that could not be used when the production was cancelled; it came out of storage twenty years later for a pantomime.[2] Scenery required regular cleaning, repair, and touching up, but properly maintained it might serve for decades. Most operas at the King's Theatre were mounted from stock: the audience did not expect to see a different visual approach to each production, or even to see scenery specific to a given opera or ballet in most cases. Advertisements tended to trumpet new scenery. Thus for *Il trionfo d'Arianna* the advertisement says 'With new

---

[1] Sybil Rosenfeld, *A Short History of Scene Design in Great Britain* (Oxford: Blackwell, 1973); *Georgian Scene Painters and Scene Painting* (Cambridge: Cambridge University Press, 1981).

[2] Rosenfeld, *Georgian Scene Painters*, 28.

Scenes, painted by Signor Novosielski, New Dresses and Decorations, both for the Opera and Dances' (*Morning Chronicle*, 16 January 1784). This does not mean that *all* the scenes were new, and the newspapers are sometimes snide about these claims, but such advertising proves the importance of 'new' scenery. On the rare occasions when the company advertised 'entire new Scenes, Dresses, and Decorations',[1] it certainly expected to reuse the scenes and costumes in future operas and ballets. Most of the thirteen seasons under consideration here involved nine or ten operas each, and in 1780–81 there were twelve. Most called for a minimum of three locations, and some ran as high as seven or eight.[2] Add two or more locations for ballets, and even with a large stock of scenes the subscribers would probably find themselves over-familiar with some of the standard sets.

Except in rare instances, ballets were not integrated into operas: they shared the bill, though *not* normally the scenery. However plotless the evening's *divertissement* might be, a change of scenery usually preceded it. The vast majority of operas change scene between acts—in part, one suspects, because the scene had to be changed for the ballet anyway.[3] And logically, *The Pert Country Maid, Les Nymphes de Diane,* and *Rural Sports* ought not to be danced in any setting listed in the libretto of Sacchini's *Mitridate* (23 January 1781). Most *divertissements* needed no scenic variety, but *ballets d'action* almost always did. Staging a story ballet in a single scene was unusual enough to evoke disapproving commentary from a reviewer.[4]

A warning: rather than import information wholesale from other times, countries, and theatres, for this period one must *faute de mieux* turn to the opera librettos for descriptions of scenery and staging. They are admittedly a treacherous source. In a few cases they can be proved to be accurate and even to record decisions agreed by the production team. But librettos do not survive for all the operas produced; some are slapdash; others, especially for revivals, probably do not report the staging as it was actually carried out. Such difficulties notwithstanding, librettos collectively convey a sense of the

---

[1] 'Entire new scenes' were most commonly advertised for the first production of a season—for example, for *L'avaro deluso* (Nov. 1778), *Alessandro nell'Indie* (Nov. 1779), *Ezio* (Nov. 1781), but *Mitridate* (Jan. 1781) and *I viaggiatori felici* (Dec. 1781) were also described that way.

[2] *Erifile* took at least seven, possibly as many as nine. *Demofoonte* required seven or eight.

[3] For example, the reviewer in the *Morning Herald* of 8 Dec. 1783 praised the new scenery for two unremarkable *divertissements* which could not have used the same locations as the evening's opera.

[4] For example, the *Morning Post*, 7 Feb. 1785, concerning *Il convito degli dei*.

scenic and staging demands of these operas. Newspaper descriptions and what is known of Covent Garden and Drury Lane prove that everything called for or described in the opera librettos *could* have been done: it was within the normal capacities of the King's Theatre.

## Standard Settings

Certain locations reappear with great frequency, and the King's Theatre presumably had several exemplars of each. Mythological and historical operas posed special demands, and *seria* and *buffa* tended to have different requirements, but any opera-goer would have become familiar with stock versions of palaces, inns, taverns, city streets, harbours, temples, halls, chambers, woods, groves, gardens, and prisons. In all likelihood the company was equipped to make obvious class distinctions for several of these settings. Inns are useful for mixing classes of patrons, but even if the title character of Paisiello's *Il re Teodoro in Venezia* (1787) has fallen on hard times, that opera ought not to take place in the same setting as Sacchini's *L'avaro deluso* (1778), which is located on the outskirts of Milan and involves only lower middle-class people. The 'closet' in a Carthaginian palace called for in Bach's *La clemenza di Scipione* (1778) was presumably far grander than the 'Chamber' in the miser Don Anselmo's house in Sacchini's *L'amore soldato* the same year; the 'rustic room' in Cecchino's house in Sarti's *Le gelosie villane* (1784) ought to be yet different in style. Assuming Le Texier's complaint is accurate, such niceties might be neglected if choice of scenery were left to the convenience of the master carpenter. The complaint is about lack of supervision and taste, not resources.

How many 'palaces' the company had in stock is impossible to guess. Whether the location was ancient Rome, Gothic Spain, or Persia seems to have made little difference, though conceivably some of the decorative details and props helped specify location. The libretto of *Zemira e Azore* (1779) preserves only three signs that the palace is enchanted: the banquet table that appears without attendants, the door that opens unaided, and the 'magic picture' that allows Zemira to see her father and sisters. These tricks could have been added to any grand palace. The numerous inns, taverns, and coffee-houses of *opera buffa* would have been relatively easy to distinguish with the tables and chairs at which patrons ate, drank, read newspapers, played card and dice games, or added up accounts.

A large number of scenes occur in middle- and upper-class houses. The libretto descriptions call for reception rooms, galleries with looking-glasses, courtyards, ballrooms, formal halls for nuptials, dining-rooms, gardens. Lower-class dwellings are much rarer, and tend to involve exteriors—settings usually described as rustic rather than poor. When they demand interiors, the living-space tends to be the same as eating-space.[1] Regardless of class, interior settings were apparently provided with furniture only when it was required. Thus the milliner in *I vecchi burlati* (1783) needs a table to display her merchandise, but she also uses it to hide her elderly suitors from another caller. *Il pittore parigino* (1785) begins with a disgruntled baron lolling on a sofa at a distance from his reluctant fiancée, who is reading, and the painter's studio presupposes easels with paintings and statues for students attending a class to draw.

Generalized public settings most commonly involve military encampments, ancient and modern;[2] a city square (often with triumphal arch); harbour scenes (ships arriving were a favourite piece of scenic display);[3] and banqueting-halls, prisons, and temples galore. Gardens, woods, and groves are about as numerous as temples. Lacking a scene inventory, there is no way to tell how much variety the company tried to provide in its temples and gardens. For the latter they probably had at least a lavish formal garden and a simpler bourgeois garden. Did the same 'shady grove' serve for the lovers' tryst in Rauzzini's *Creusa in Delfo* and for Micheluccio's hiding-place in Caruso's *L'albergatrice vivace* in 1783? One can only guess. Perhaps the audience had been conditioned to believe that a grove was a grove, or perhaps it expected a different style in classical groves and *buffa* groves.

Even without much detail a number of settings are distinctive enough to be traced through several operas. Sacchini's *Erifile, regina di Zacinto* (1778) begins in 'a magnificent square richly set off for the arrival of Learchus. In front a majestic triumphal arch'. Since scene design of the time made little difference between Greek and Roman locales, this island in the Ionian Sea was almost certainly portrayed as Roman, and the set would therefore have been appropriate for Act I, Scene v of Bertoni's *Quinto Fabio* (1780), which calls for a triumphal arch in front of the gates of Rome. The sepulchre of Cimene's father in the 1783 opera that bears her name might well also have

---

[1] *Il trionfo della costanza* (1782), *La cosa rara* (1789).

[2] Found in such operas as *L'amore soldato* (1778), *Il re pastore* (1778), *Alessandro nell'Indie* (1779), *Ifigenia in Aulide* (1782, 1789), and *Armida* (1786).

[3] Found in *Demofoonte* (1778), *Alessandro nell'Indie* (1779), *Il soldano generoso* (1779), *Mitridate* (1781), *Ifigenia in Aulide* (1782 and 1789), *Il trionfo d'Arianna* (1784), *La schiava* (1784), *L'usurpator innocente* (1790), and *Andromaca* (1790). Gondolas are naturally to be found in *Il re Teodoro in Venezia* (1787).

served as the tomb of Giunia's father in *Silla* the next year and as Eurydice's tomb in *Orfeo* (1785). It might even have been pressed into service for burying Emelia alive in *La vestale* (1787).

Pagan shrines and temples are common in *opera seria*. They support ceremony, omens, and providentially interrupted sacrifice. The King's Theatre used two kinds of temple scenes: the portico/courtyard (an exterior, but within the sacred precinct) and, more commonly, the interior. The courtyard permitted a vista of the temple proper, used to great effect in Sacchini's *Enea e Lavinia* (1779), or of another element like a funeral pyre in the pasticcios *Alessandro nell'Indie* (1779) and *La generosità d'Alessandro* (1789). Giordani's *Il re pastore* (1778) calls for 'A Part of the Space surrounded by the Grand Portico of the famous Temple of Hercules, in Tyre'. The librettist or designer may have had a particular building in mind, although any grand courtyard would have served.[1] The interior of a temple was probably bland and featureless in most cases. An early description shows several conventions at work, though it must be read with caution. In *Erifile*, Act I, Scene vii, the translation says

The temple of Juno with the symbols and festoons of palms and laurels. Practicable galleries all around. In the middle is the image of the goddess, adorned with proper attributes, with a grand Altar illuminated. Mean-time the Zacinthian ladies and grandees of the kingdom prostrate themselves before the goddess, some of the priests bind and bestrew the image with flowers, and some cast perfumes upon the burning pyre.

The unspecified symbols might have related to Juno; festoons certainly did not. Although the libretto calls for practicable galleries, they are not in fact used nor are they necessary. But the free-standing image of the goddess and the illuminated altar are crucial. These features recur, whether the temple is dedicated to Juno, Diana, Concord, Vengeance, Apollo, Nemesis, or an unidentified deity (*Andromaca*, 1790). The cult statue identifies the shrine and makes an all-purpose scene feasible. This is not to say that the King's Theatre had only a single temple interior, rather that its temples were designed to be interchangeable.

Mozart's *Lucio Silla* does not use a temple, but the pasticcio *Silla* (1783) derived from it calls for two. Rather than try to differentiate the usual bland interior, the librettist set the first of the scenes outside the Temple of Jupiter

---

[1] So specific a designation is intriguing, because the opera was set 'in sight of the City of Sidon'.

Stator (Giove Statore). A religious site is not important for the action, an attempted coup, but an open, public one is. The temple interior in the second of the scenes is only metaphorically religious: in it, Silla gives up the laurels of a dictator and dispenses mercy on all those he had threatened. The description calls for a 'Temple of Vesta, wherein the Senate formerly assembled, adorned with columns, and bass-relievo. At the bottom, an inclosure, where the Vestals used to keep the sacred fire.' In this case, the shrine is what communicates 'temple'. Among the new scenes advertised for this opera might have been the designated temples. The first building is so clearly identified as to imply a recognizable picture. Piranesi included a temple of Giove Statore in three of his *Vedute di Roma.*[1] The three columns that remain would not provide a complete exterior, but they might have been enough to inspire Novosielski's design.[2] As with the unnecessarily specific references to the Tyrian Temple of Hercules in *Mitridate*, this seems to be a clear trace of conferences between designer and librettist.

The ubiquitous garden had few identifiable features, and no doubt the theatre had several in stock. The royal gardens in *Il soldano generoso* (1779) need not have been 'Persian'; the description makes clear that the setting included a prospect of the sea, so that the audience could witness a crucial shipwreck. The garden with fountains in Sacchini's *Rinaldo* (1780) would also have turned up in the ballet (1782) and in *Armida* (1786). By comparison the 'Garden behind the house, with a door leading to [the chambermaid] Dorina's rooms' in *I rivali delusi* (1784) was probably a simpler one, as might be those in such middle-class environments as *L'albergatrice vivace* (1783), *Il tutor burlato* (1787), and *Gli schiavi per amore* (1787). The two most interesting gardens are those for *Zemira e Azore* (1779), containing 'a wild spot, in which is a Den', where Azore expects to die if Zemira does not return to him; and the one for Cimarosa's *La locandiera* (1788), which involves a climbable tree. The appropriate garden would have been chosen on the basis of its degree of formality and implied class.

A garden is an extension of civilization. By contrast, a wood is wild (*Giulio Sabino*, 1786; *Il tutor burlato*, 1787; *La cosa rara*, 1789). The enchanted wood in which Rinaldo must cut down a myrtle is a special case, but hardly

---

[1] See *Piranesi: Rome Recorded* (New York: Arthur Ross Foundation, 1989), pls. 13, 22, and especially 100.

[2] Even though no pictures survive, we can hypothesize that the King's Theatre was moving towards the process of embodying familiar artwork onstage, which became common in the 19th c. See Martin Meisel, *Realizations* (Princeton, NJ: Princeton University Press, 1983).

a tame environment. Groves seem to fall somewhere in between. They may be sacred, though the signal of that status is not always clear. By implication, Lavinia prays to a statue of Faunus in a grove dedicated to him, and the god later speaks to Latinus there (*Enea e Lavinia*, 1779), but the only thing that sanctifies the grove in *L'usurpator innocente* (1790) is the fact that it leads to a temple. The grove near the inn in *L'albergatrice vivace* (1783) might well have reappeared as the grove near the Marchese's house in *La vendemmia* (1789), nor do the stage directions provide any obvious reason the same grove could not have served earlier in *L'avaro deluso* (1778) and *Alessandro nell'Indie* (1779).

## Special Settings

By 'special' we mean unusual settings required by a particular opera and representations of actual (presumably recognizable) buildings or places. The company advertised 'new scenes' for Anfossi's *Il trionfo della costanza* (1783), and one can see why: the 'cobler's stall' would be hard to convey in any of the stock scenery, though any rustic cottage would serve for the 'Glade, with a prospect of the Miller's house'. The scenery for *Enea e Lavinia* (1779) could easily have been pulled from stock: gates to the Temple of Janus; a sacred grove; a king's garden; a plain with opposing military camps; a palace. Even 'Vulcan's forge', a mythological setting of a kind then falling out of fashion, should have been available, since *Le ali d'amore* (1777) called for such a scene.

Historically specific scenes are not numerous but were probably enjoyed by the King's Theatre's relatively well-travelled and educated audience. Given the propensity of *opera seria* for Roman history, some settings were probably as historically accurate as the painters could manage—that is, copied from such sources as Fischer von Erlach's *Entwurff einer historischen Architectur* (1725) and Piranesi's *Vedute di Roma* (c.1748–78). The Forum was painted new for *Ezio* (1781) and probably reappeared in *Giunio Bruto* the following spring.

When a libretto mentions a historical site rather than 'city gates' or 'a temple', the specificity can derive from actual sources. In the case of *L'eroe cinese* (1782) one may be reasonably sure that the 'Imperial Palace', the view of 'a great Part of the Imperial City', and the 'Imperial Pagoda' had been specially painted: the probable source was Nieuhoff's *Embassy [to] China*, of which John Ogilby had published two editions in the 1670s. Likewise for *Il re Teodoro in Venezia* (1787) the setting provided important local colour.

According to one reviewer, the opera offered Marinari 'an opportunity of giving two fine aquatic views of that celebrated city; the *first*, outside of Taddeo's inn, with a prospect of the *Rialto* and its vicinage; the gondolas and people on the bridge have a very striking and novel effect; the former are worked most ingeniously, and the latter seem absolutely starting from the canvas; the other gives a view of the grand canal, upon which gondolas pass, with a variety of vessels, with a noble hall in the inn, supported by a double row of columns' (*Daily Universal Register*, 10 December 1787). Not everyone was favourably impressed. A week later a reviewer in the *Public Advertiser* carped,

The only part of the scenery which is interesting is the bridge Rialto, and this is badly executed; it looks like a pantomimic show, but not like a grand opera scene; the bridge is crowded with figurative passengers, and small gondolas appear beyond it. The first idea is a capital error, for the representation of the bridge is supposed sideways, and being covered with shops, no passengers can be seen; the latter idea of boats being placed beyond the bridge crowds the scene, and makes the bridge lose its grand appearance at a distance.[1]

Regardless of the quality of execution, part of the point of the Venetian settings was surely for people to recognize vistas typical of Venetian genre painting, if not details of what they remembered from their travels. The critic who objected to people on the Rialto bridge was applying standards of accuracy far in advance of his time, since the crowded bridges of Venice were a common genre subject. In this case Marinari chose the more animated tradition, disregarding the Rialto identification, which is not important to the drama.

Doubtless some locations were easier to identify than others. The *Morning Post* reviewer of Anfossi's *Issipile* (10 May 1784) compliments Novosielski on his scenery, 'particularly the last, representing the ancient port of Lemnos, and the ruins of the temple of Venus'. Was his identification the fruit of a classical education or merely derived from a quick look at the libretto? 'Special' settings went into storage and could be used in future shows, but they were always something of an extravagance unless readily reusable. Not surprisingly, their number falls off sharply after Gallini takes over the management in 1785, operating under a strict budget cap. Scenery was one realm in which he could safely economize.

[1] A possible source is Antonio Visentini's engravings after Canaletto, *Prospectus Magni Canalis* (1735).

While some scenes in the King's Theatre stock were merely pretty pictures, stage directions may specify that the hallway of an inn has four usable doors (*L'avaro deluso*, 1778), that a house 'on a summit' has a window and door (*Le gelosie villane*, 1784), that a temple of Diana or a saloon in an Italian inn has 'folding doors' (*Ifigenia in Aulide*, 1789; *L'albergatrice vivace*, 1783). In the thirteen years surveyed here the number of 'working' elements increases significantly—or at least so the stage directions imply.

One strong argument that the practicable units called for in printed librettos were real is their repeated use. A hyperbolic stage direction might not have been edited out of the first translation in which it appears, but if variations on it continue to turn up, the company probably staged what is described. Not all stage directions in the librettos were necessarily followed, and proscenium doors and balconies might be used when practicable elements were required. This would have been quite easy in *La governante* (1779) and *Giannina e Bernardone* (1787), for example. But not all cases can be explained away: where action depended on a layout, the theatre probably provided something like what was described. The by-play in *La locandiera* (1788) includes Polidoro's climbing a tree and Mme Brillante's pursuing him with pruning-shears.

'Bridges' appear several times. In *Alessandro nell'Indie* (1779), Greek soldiers march over a bridge that spans the Hydaspes as it runs through the countryside (Act II, Scene ii). Five years later in *La regina di Golconda* the same kind of setting is emphasized by a long description of the programme of the symphony that opens Act II (the morning star, warbling birds, gentle breezes). The symphony shows off 'a cottage on one side, and on the other side an elegant country seat. A bridge formed of trunks of trees thrown over a small river'. Because this idyllic scene is a replica of the place where Alina and Alberto fell in love years before, it is important to the plot, and Alberto is captivated when Alina makes her entrance over the bridge. The structure of the bridge might well have been the same in the two operas. Since the King's Theatre had used a practicable bridge as early as 1720, one would be astonished if they had merely faked it in these cases.[1] In the last month of

---

[1] See Judith Milhous and Robert D. Hume, 'A Prompt Copy of Handel's *Radamisto*', *Musical Times*, 127 (1986), 316–21. Covent Garden had long used a practicable bridge. When it collapsed with nearly thirty men on it during a rehearsal, *The Times* (16 Apr. 1790) reported that the carpenters 'thought the bridge was *safe*, as it had lasted forty years without an accident'.

the old King's Theatre's life a pair of reviewers commented on a bridge episode in Tarchi's *La generosità d'Alessandro*:

The audience had what pleased them better than any excellence of composition:—Scenery and singing. Among the first of these, with regard to stage effect, we ought to mention the demolition of the Bridge at the beginning of the second act. . . . (*Diary*, 3 June 1789)

The reviewer in *The Times* the same day went so far as to say that 'the Battle with the Broken Bridge is equal to any thing in the Drury Lane *Richard*' —that is, in John Burgoyne's *Richard Cœur-de-Lion* (October 1786), a production famous for its elaborate staging.[1]

Sacchini's *Enea e Lavinia* (1779) provides an example of elaborate scenic and lighting effects that were probably representative of what was routinely feasible at the King's Theatre. Early in the opera priests of Janus dressed in white vestments and carrying incense enter in procession

between the Colonades of the Portico, advancing through the Centre towards the Steps of the Temple, on which are seen the Statue of Janus, at the Foot of which Discord, Fury, Hatred and War, lie bound. . . . Flashes of lightning are seen, and claps of thunder heard, the gates of the temple are burst open, and the temple appears as if on fire. . . . The statues . . . become animated by the interposition of Juno. They break their chains, and run to light their torches in the temple, spreading terror and devastation every where.

Having practicable steps for the animated statues to mount is by no means essential, but an already striking scene becomes far more effective if they are provided.

In Martín y Soler's *La cosa rara* (1789), Lubin tears a branch from a tree in order to knock Tita down, which implies a trunk substantial enough to support detachable pieces. The 'thick Myrtle' in the enchanted wood that Rinaldo must attack in order to free himself from Armida's toils was presumably a free-standing unit that split open to allow the sorceress to emerge, her evil nature at last revealed. The same stage direction occurs in librettos of both the 1780 *Rinaldo* set by Sacchini and the 1786 *Armida*, a pasticcio based on Mortellari. Librettos regularly call for climbable hills, and

[1] Several of the elements mentioned in the stage directions of *La generosità d'Alessandro* occur in slightly different combinations in three contemporaneous designs attributed to Loutherbourg. The sketches have been assigned to an undated late 18th-c. production of *Richard III*; they might also relate to designs by Marinari for Sheridan's *Pizarro* at Drury Lane in 1799. See Christopher Baugh, 'Three Loutherbourg "Designs"', *Theatre Notebook*, 47 (1993), 96–103.

while they may not always have been provided, they were necessary for the opening scenes of both *Rinaldo* and *Armida*, during which Ubaldo fights his way up one side of the magic mountain, while Clotarco leads the attack on the other. Criticism of Noverre's *Adela of Ponthieu* (1782) proves that the knighting scene took place on an incline (on which see discussion in Ch. 7).

Some of the most complicated stage directions during these years involve ships. Between 1779 and 1790 no fewer than nine operas feature the arrival or departure of ships, from which people disembark or which they board. A whole fleet at anchor could easily be painted on wings and would require no comment. Several operas, however, have much more explicit stage directions and imply practicable elements. For example, Anfossi's *Il trionfo d'Arianna* (1784) begins on the coast of Naxos, where a large ship has just arrived. Two early disembarkation scenes could be handled by simple entrances, but Act II, Scenes ix and x would seem to require something more elaborate.

Night, the Moon rising. A view of the seacoast. Tents scattered here and there, one of which is larger and more magnificent than the rest, and is placed before them. Soldiers, who in great silence, to the light of a few torches, are taking down, folding up the tents, and carrying them on board the ship, which with the sails loose is ready for sea. Ariadne sitting in the large tent . . . falls asleep. . . . Theseus . . . seemingly in suspence, approaches Ariadne, and finding her asleep, talks softly to two centinels, who having heard his orders, go to prepare planks for getting on board. [Theseus collects Phaedra from another tent and] conducts her resolutely on board the ship, which weighs anchor, and immediately sails. . . . [Following a dance that represents Ariadne's nightmares, she wakes, discovers that she has been abandoned, and exits, lamenting.] Ariadne being gone, a sprightly symphony of drums, tymbals, and other oriental musical instruments is heard at a distance towards the sea, which encreases gradually, as a naval squadron approaches the shore. The vine leaves, flowers, garlands and other emblems shew it to be the victorious fleet of Bacchus.

Admittedly, the tents could be struck and carried offstage in the direction of the ship, and the fugitive lovers could simply exit after the soldiers, board the mobile ship in the farthest wing position upstage and be trucked across the back of the stage. Bacchus could mount the same unit, or another rigged as an 'Indian' ship, and reverse the process, disembarking into the wings and making his entrance at the same point where Theseus and Phædra departed. But the description is vivid and specific, and there is nothing here beyond routine staging conventions of Drury Lane and Covent Garden at this period. The opera was very likely staged as the libretto implies, with visible embarkation and a movable unit capable of carrying passengers.

Likewise in Nasolini's *Andromaca* (1790), which begins and ends in 'The port of Buthrotus with Grecian ships', there is a good case for accepting what the libretto says. At the conclusion Oreste, Pilade, Astianatte, and Ermione board a ship to flee. Probably they do not cast off (since Pirro forgives all and offers Ermione his heart, a gesture praised by the final chorus), but the action described strongly implies that the fugitives are on a different level from Pirro—that is, that the ship was a sufficiently practicable unit to allow singers to climb up into it.

Practical elements can be hard to introduce and remove in a hurry: the more elaborate, the more cumbersome. A report in the *Morning Post* of 25 March 1789 comments that Marchesi had requested the revival of Cherubini's *Ifigenia in Aulide* only to be told by Gallini 'that on account of the scenes for the new ballet *Les jalousies du serrail*, it would be impossible to have the view of the sea with the boats . . . in the serious opera'. Marchesi protested, demanding instead that a different ballet should be scheduled. Building up the practicable ship in *Ifigenia in Aulide* apparently blocked enough of the upstage wing and shutter positions on one side that the ballet scenery could not be deployed until a lengthy process of deconstruction had been carried out.[1]

Cumulatively, the evidence suggests that the King's Theatre increased its efforts to add dimension to spectacle, to make parts of the scenery functional, and to vary the levels available to stand on. In so doing, it was merely following the lead of the patent theatres. As Paul Ranger has shown in his study of the staging of Gothic drama, by the 1780s Drury Lane was routinely able to display effects much more elaborate than any described in the opera librettos under consideration here. He points out that in the design for *Richard Cœur-de-Lion*

the principal feature . . . was the variety of levels on which the action took place: these consisted of a raised terrace, a moat, trucks on either side of the stage supporting fortifications spanned by a drawbridge and to stage left a high tower topped by a parapet.[2]

---

[1] The execution may not have been perfect in any case. The reviewer in *The Times* of 26 Jan. 1789, though mostly rapturous, is quite caustic about 'Achilles and his Myrmidons . . . being seen walking from behind the scenes in the midst of the waves, in order to get in the ship'. The opera and the problematic ballet were in fact done together on 28 Mar., without delays exciting comment.

[2] Paul Ranger, *'Terror and Pity reign in every Breast': Gothic Drama in the London Patent Theatres, 1750–1820* (London: Society for Theatre Research, 1991), 44–5, where he prints an

Stage directions imply that at least three levels besides the stage floor were usable in this production. Pure spectacle had grown increasingly important in late eighteenth-century drama, and when the theatres expanded in the early 1790s it rapidly became more so. The range of physical actions singers were asked to perform in these librettos remains limited—indeed, clearly more limited than that expected of actors in Gothic plays. But like the patent theatres, the Italian opera was moving in the direction of more elaborate, three-dimensional scenery.

### Properties

Evidence about properties comes almost entirely from a few scattered references in librettos and from the records of Joseph Hayling, the tinman who supplied lighting for the theatre.[1] Hayling was only responsible for the properties a tinker might make, so his contributions do not give a complete picture, but they help anchor in reality what can be deduced from librettos. Props were evidently kept to a minimum, though of course librettos tend to notice only distinctive properties and those necessary to the action. Operas called for official papers and private correspondence to mishandle; rings for lovers to exchange; bundles for runaways and merchants, baggage for travellers; unidentified gifts for hostesses, newly-weds, and monarchs; and plenty of pagan religious paraphernalia. One finds telescopes (usually associated with astrologers); spinning-wheel and distaff to mark the industry of country folk; garlands and crowns that help ensorcel Rinaldo, and which he must tear off to get free; the rose tree whose flower, once cut, entitles Azore to demand the merchant's daughter in exchange; a raree-show and hurdy-gurdy in *Ninetta* (1790). The King's Theatre had a whole armoury of weapons with which to equip choruses of soldiers, 'Roman' or contemporaneous, and courtiers out hunting. Joseph Hayling notes such items as 'Sixteen Spears to order'; 'Mending four Tin Locks to Wood Guns'; 'Twelve Shields'. In *Giannina e Bernardone* (1787) a gun was apparently fired offstage, and *La cosa rara* (1789) calls for the prince to fire a pistol, which flashes in the pan. Most weapons, however, like the axes Hayling repeatedly tinned, were threatening but unused. Daggers were carefully spring-loaded. Probably the most dangerous weapons Hayling supplied were the 'Flambeaus for Furies' prominent in *Medea and Jason* and constantly in need of repair. Two librettos mention live animals. Pasquale, 'riding at the head of

engraving of the scene.

[1] On Hayling and his records, see below, sect. V.

several horsemen', was said to come down a hill in *Il trionfo della costanza* (1782), which was physically feasible if not really necessary. Given the real trees and shrubberies of the setting for *L'omaggio* (1781), the lamb and kid offered to the count and countess were probably also real.

Food is much discussed but not much consumed in these operas, at least by principals. One may doubt whether rolls for the hunters' picnic in Piccinni's *Vittorina* (1777) actually included the prosciutto specified by the librettist, or whether coffee was usually served in operatic coffee-houses (though evidence earlier and later suggests that real wine was drunk onstage). Fruit just harvested or for sale in market baskets was artificial and therefore durable. According to a contemporary satirist, when an opera called for a banquet there was 'a complete entertainment and desert in the *property man's* room, elegantly carved in *wood*'.[1] The banquet was presumably more suitable to the Count's feast at the end of *La vendemmia* (1789) or the social-climbing world of *Il convito* than to the rustic settings of *Il trionfo della costanza* (both 1782) or *La cosa rara* (1789), but perhaps there was a country feast in the prop room as well.

Hayling's detailed notes make clear the amount of work that went into mounting and maintaining productions. He is forever picking up 'A Glew Pot' for the carpenter, making 'a new Rose to a Water pot and Handle', or supplying 'Six Dressing Room Candlesticks'. Sometimes the work he reports can be assigned to a particular production. For example, 'Three 3 spout Lamps to Vauses fitted up with Chains' added to the pagan spectacle of the 'Tempio sotterraneo illuminato da antiche lampade' in *Mitridate* on 23 January 1781. The 'Block [black?] Tin Vause or urn to Silver pattern' and 'Large raised Bason' listed a month later cannot be assigned, but the 'two pair of Tin Garden Sheers' the same day must have been for *The Country Diversions*, a ballet. Among his more startling charges are those for the bells and mouthpieces for French horns—but somebody must fix broken instruments, and a tinman ought to have the equipment. Hayling's list supplements what the librettos mention and shows just how fragile the theatre and its stock were.

More properties are included in stage directions at the end of the decade than earlier, probably because librettists were trying to paint clearer word-pictures for their readers. Sacchini's *La contadina in corte* (1779) sets the opening scene with a spinning-wheel and distaff, used by the second

---

[1] *The Opera Rumpus*, 11 n.

woman, not the first. In *Il re Teodoro* (1787) Nancy Storace, as the daughter of an innkeeper, not only serves coffee but sings a song with other serving-girls while she irons and they work at other domestic tasks. *Opera seria* includes many temples with burning altars (*Erifile, Mitridate, Medonte*). Perhaps it is no coincidence that the one depiction of a King's Theatre scene known to us in the later eighteenth century is the burning altar at the end of *L'Olimpiade* in 1769.[1] Versions of this opera were mounted at the King's Theatre in 1779 and 1788: that both scenery and burning altar came straight from the company's store-rooms is very likely. In contrast, the demands of *opera buffa* tend strongly towards the everyday and the realistic.

## Costumes

The King's Theatre expected to provide new costumes for new principals each season, but, like scenery, most costumes tended to come from stock. Librettos seldom describe costumes, because apart from making class dis-tinctions, what people wore was not important. Only when costume had a dramatic function was it likely to be mentioned. Conspirators in *Erifile* (1778) were distinguished by red shoulder-belts, but the libretto for *L'Olimpiade* (1788) gives no clue as to what castrati wore when participating in the Olympic games—presumably the ubiquitous 'Roman' costume. Ways of distinguishing the exotic receive some attention. The formality of aristocratic Spanish dress is exploited, sometimes as a contrast to 'Turkish' dress, at others for comic effect. The captives in *Il soldano generoso* (1779) are identified as Spanish, and *Cimene* (1783) takes place at the Spanish court, where the title-character's mourning sets her apart. While Spanish attire complete with long whiskers makes a comic disguise in *I vecchi burlati* (1783), 'tremendous whiskers' are a means of distinguishing a German lover from a Spanish lover in *I due castellani burlati* (1790). Turkish costumes also provide disguises in *L'albergatrice vivace* (1783) and *La schiava* (1784). The latter calls for four black slaves to unload wedding gifts, and identifies other slaves as 'Turkish', though one may doubt whether the first woman's appearance as a slave extended to skin colour. However, in *La villana rico-nosciuta* much is made of the blackamoor disguise of the *primo buffo*

[1] Printed in Allardyce Nicoll, *The Garrick Stage*, ed. Sybil Rosenfeld (Manchester: Manchester University Press, 1980), pl. 72 (p. 103). Nicoll identifies the picture as an 'Engraving by Walker after Gravelot, issued with the Italian–English libretto, January 1770' and credits it to the Bodleian Library (p. 178). Unfortunately, the Bodleian has no record of its owning this libretto or any other with such an illustration. We have been unable to locate the illustration there or elsewhere.

*caricato*, who changes places with a 'Turco fedel' or 'faithful African' to escape arrest. When a dethroned sultan in *Il re Teodoro* wants an incognito, he disguises himself as an Armenian. *La regina di Golconda* (1784) probably indulged in appropriate dress to go with its 'Asiatic' architecture, as well as to provide a contrast between the present and the re-creation of the English countryside from the lovers' past. For *L'eroe cinese* (1782) Hayling supplied Luppino, the tailor, with fourteen 'Front Pieces for Caps' and 'Tops for Ditto'. These were helmets for *chinoiserie* soldiers, not the pointed 'Mandarine cap' for the courtier Siveno complained of by the *Morning Herald* on 18 March 1782, which 'being no ways proportioned to [Pacchierotti's] size . . . only put us in mind of old *Mother Shipton!*' The reviewer prefaced this quibble by saying that the costumes were 'uncommonly magnificent', though he could not vouch for their advertised authenticity. Ghosts occur in several of these operas, but the word was enough to identify them to the original readers of librettos and they are not further described. A certain number of gods and goddesses appear, similarly undescribed, but recognizable from their attributes (Bacchus' vine leaves, Diana's half moon, etc.). A trace of a convention is evident when, after Rinaldo attacks the myrtle tree, Armida 'comes out of it, all dishevelled, and in a black suit', with a magic wand in her hand (*Armida*, 1786). The disorder, the colour, and the weapon are specified as a contrast to her earlier appearance. No doubt many such traditions lie hidden behind the bland façade of the librettos.

The only convention clearly identifiable in these descriptions concerns participants in pagan rituals. They wear white, which apparently distinguishes them from non-participants, and are often crowned with flowers, especially if they are sacrificial victims. *Demofoonte* (1778), *Enea e Lavinia* (1779), *Creusa in Delfo* (1783), *La vestale* (1787), *L'usurpator innocente*, and *Andromaca* (both 1790) all demonstrate this convention, so probably *Ifigenia in Aulide* (1782, 1789) and *L'Olimpiade* (1788) employed it too. *La vestale* plays on colour. Emilia is inducted into the society of virgins wearing white and crowned with flowers; but when the gods reveal that her heart has known love, her white veil is changed for a black one before she is locked away in a tomb in the Infamous Fields reserved for vestals who fell from grace. When Jove's mercy saves her, mortal acceptance of divine will is shown by the removal of the black veil.

Costumes were supplied by the company tailor, a functionary responsible both for design and for supervision of what would now be called the costume shop. Virtually the only direct evidence about this vital part of the company comes from the lawsuit in which Thomas Luppino sued William Taylor for back salary, workmen's wages, and goods he had paid for directly.[1] Luppino also worked for Drury Lane, but was tailor to the King's Theatre most seasons for many years. Sestini was advertised in 1784–85, 1788–89, and 1789–90, but Luppino's pre-eminence in the field is clearly signalled by his appointment at the Pantheon in 1790–91. Taylor had tried to hire a cheaper substitute in 1781–82, but Luppino testified that even 'whilst there was another person employed' as tailor, he 'almost daily Attended at the said Opera House . . . to assist and Advise in the performing and executing the several dresses necessary for the appearance of the several characters performing in the several Opera's and ballets'. Luppino says that his replacement, a Mons. Simon (otherwise unknown), was dismissed on account of 'incapacity and want of ability . . . to conduct and manage the Taylors business . . . with that kind of propriety and Taste which was required'.[2] Costumes were made on the spot, not jobbed out. The 1783 inventory of the theatre in C107/65 lists both a 'Wardrobe Room' and a 'Taylors Room', and notes further costume storage along several hallways. Discussing his 1781 demotion, Luppino says that 'he . . . having in his Possession the Keys of the Wardrobe belonging to the said Opera House', the proprietor came to him 'in the Taylors Shop in the said Opera House and desired him to deliver up' the keys. The tailor was an employee of some status, not just an anonymous outside contractor.

The 'Schedules' that Luppino submitted to the court suggest rather casual bookkeeping and are frustratingly limited as evidence of how the costume shop worked, but several points emerge. He claimed £200 per annum salary from the King's Theatre and laid out a lot for supplies ('Paid for Thread Tape Silk and Pins £2. 3s.'; 'Paid for 36 yards of Pink Crape Gauze £5. 8s.'), expecting the theatre to reimburse him, but most fabric bills went directly to the treasurer. He bought items like stockings and hats ready made ('Paid for Eighteen Chip Hats for the Dancers and Performers £2. 15s.'). The costume shop presumably had some regular assistant tailors who were paid weekly wages, but Luppino hired temporary help as well ('Paid six Workmen for Doing the Work Eleven days at 2/6 a Day £8. 5s.'; 'Paid for

---

[1] C12/2171/23.

[2] The importance of taste is referred to in the *Morning Chronicle* of 26 Jan. 1782, which says that 'if Mons. Noverre shewed his skill in composing the dances [for the 24 Jan. masquerade], he did not betray less taste in devising the dresses, which were extremely well executed by the new taylor Mons. Simon'.

Victuals and Tea for ffourteen People who were at work all one Sunday in order to get ready for a new Opera £1. 5s. 9d.'). Refitting and refurbishing old costumes was a large part of the job.

How much say did performers have about what they wore? One can hardly imagine that stars would not expect new finery and demand to be consulted about it, but the tailor could more easily attempt co-ordination in new productions than in revivals. A hint of personal fancy appears in a snide report in the *Morning Chronicle* of 4 December 1780: 'Ansani chose it [*Ricimero*], because the character he played, always appears in chains, which it seems he considers as a favorable situation for a performer.' On the 21st the *Morning Post* added, 'Signor Crotchetti refuses his part, unless the Poet makes him appear every act in chains.'[1] The 11 January 1782 *Morning Herald* credited Morigi with having 'dressed, sung, and acted' the German soldier in the ever-popular *Buona figliuola* 'with a degree of humour peculiar to himself'. Morigi is also credited with dressing his character in *La contadina in corte*, but that production too was a revival (*Morning Herald*, 4 March 1782). Management could not hope to exercise tight control over revivals, or over every performer.

Because Luppino's bills for goods comprise only a few miscellaneous purchases of his own, they do not permit an estimate of the total costume budget. Costumes were, however, expensive, particularly for ballet and *opera seria*. Appropriate clothes for princes and generals required plenty of fancy trim, necessities imported from the Continent and subject to stiff import duties, as a dispute Gallini had with customs agents in the spring of 1789 shows. On 31 January *The Times* published a list of more than twenty-five parcels seized in raids on Gallini's house and the theatre. The 'sattin wrought with gold', 'Silk and velvet steel-trimmed, with white silk Blois lace', or crape and 'tiffany pettycoats painted' might imaginably have been for private consumption or re-sale, but metallic braid, tassels, foil stamps, foil-backed 'stones' to represent jewels, eleven parcels of copper spangles, eighteen pounds of tinsel, 7,600 sheets of foil, and five kinds of copper lace were clearly meant to be used on costumes. The sheer quantities involved are noteworthy.[2] Gallini, like many other people, knew ways to slip such

[1] The *Ricimero* chains came from stock, but on 18 Feb. 1782 Hayling supplied 'Five Slaves Chains at 4s. 6d.', altered them on the 20th, and painted them red on the 23rd, probably for *Rinaldo and Armida*.

[2] Comparison with the list of goods Giardini asked his agent Leone to smuggle in 1763 is instructive. The only item explicitly destined for the stage was 'a Stomacher of false Stones second hand for the Theatre set in Silver'. The rest, which included items made of tortoise-

materials in without paying the duty, and ordinarily no questions would have been raised about the origins of the 'tinsel and other ornaments for the use of the opera, which could not be purchased in England' (*The Times*, 2 February 1789).

How satisfactory were the costumes? As with scenery, reviewers' comments are seldom specific enough to help the historian. That Adriana Ferrarese's dress for *Demetrio* was 'particularly magnificent' or that all the costumes for *L'usurpator innocente* were 'magnificent' but the scenery lacking in 'grandeur' tells us little. An occasional comment is revealing: in *Ifigenia in Aulide*, Torregiani as Chalcas 'performed with his long white beard, and solemnity of *recitative*, great dignity, and frequently put us in mind of Homer' (*Morning Post*, 28 January 1789). Many of the comments are negative. A paragraph in the 29 May 1786 *Morning Herald* regards Mlle Baccelli's feather-trimmed petticoat for *L'amour jardinier* as 'singular', because 'in the *front center*, a plume, as striking as the *princely crest*, continues in *wanton motion* at every step!' The reviewer for the *Daily Universal Register* in 1787 similarly complained that a disguise in *Il re Teodoro* 'might have been made more contributing to the laugh it was intended to create' (10 December) or that the transformed beast in *Zemira and Azor* is 'too meanly *attired* in the concluding scene—his dress bespeaks rather the *neatness* of a *running* footman, than the magnificence of an *Eastern* Prince' (3 March). The same reviewer took exception to Cremonini's hat in *Giannina e Bernardone*: 'such a *nab* would be scouted in *Field-Lane*—let him not wear it then on the stage of *Theatre Royale*' (15 January 1787). Such particular objections notwithstanding, the company apparently put most of its costume budget into flashy clothes for principals and let others get by with an assortment of hand-me-downs. The *figurants* cost time, if not a lot of money, given their numbers and the need for at least two full sets of costumes for every performance. A reviewer in the *Morning Herald* of 8 January 1787 commented, 'Accustomed as we have been to see the *Corps de Ballet*, or figurants dressed in a slovenly or at least careless and unmeaning manner, it was no small satisfaction to us to see them not only decently clad, but uniformly habited, and with due attention paid to the characters they had to represent.' Extras also had to be dressed from stock.

One misapprehension must be cleared up concerning costume changes and dressing-rooms. Writing about the temporary move of the Drury Lane

shell, gold trinkets for watch chains, oil paintings, and more than seven dozen rings, seem to have been bought for re-sale. The list, from PRO C12/517/16, is reproduced as plate 3 of *The Impresario's Ten Commandments*.

company to the new King's Theatre in 1791, the *Oracle* of 25 August said: 'A dilemma has arisen from the want of Dressing rooms for the Performers. It appears that the Italians always dressed at home previously to their appearance on the Stage.' This has been taken literally by some modern scholars, but we doubt that it means quite what it says. Can Pacchierotti have been expected to arrive at the theatre in his *habit à la romaine*, carrying his plumed helmet? *Figurants* would not have traipsed through the streets of London all winter wearing flimsy stage costumes—and they could hardly afford coaches. In fact, the Dumont plan of the pre-1778 King's Theatre contains 'Chambres ou les Acteurs s'habillent' and the Soane Museum plan for the 1782 alterations (discussed in Ch. 1, sect. IV) includes 'Dressing Rooms'. The inventory of 1783 in C107/65 specifies men's and ladies' dressing-rooms for the figure dancers and at least eight other dressing-rooms, all of which were heated, not to mention the wardrobe and the tailor's shop. The old and new King's Theatres may have had fewer single or double dressing-rooms than Drury Lane, but one cannot suppose that no costume changing was done on the premises.

## Conclusions

However incomplete the evidence, a reading of librettos and newspaper reviews makes some trends plain. In the course of the thirteen years under review here opera settings tended to become increasingly specific, even realistic, and the theatre began to use more three-dimensional settings. Magical transformation scenes were still enjoyed, but they were going out of fashion. This meant more concern with creating plausible illusions of reality on stage. Conventions and expectations were changing, albeit slowly. In an earlier day, the audience probably did not think twice about the scene in *Quinto Fabio* (1780) that starts out as a private interview between the emperor and his son-in-law but transmutes into a public display of Quinto Fabio's submission when the tent suddenly lifts up to reveal the army and people gathered round (Act II, Scene vii). Pacchierotti's choice of this piece as a benefit vehicle at the Pantheon in 1791 was decidedly backward-looking: he was a singer nearing the end of a distinguished career and indulging in the conventions of earlier years.

    *Opera seria* was in its nature remote from the mundane settings of the present time. Reviewing Tarchi's *Il disertore* (admittedly a very special kind of *opera seria*) on 2 March 1789, the *Morning Post* commented: 'The serious Opera will not admit of modern characters, and the dresses of these times. Poor Marchesi's dignity was quite destroyed—he appeared exactly like a

*Valet de Chambre.*' But even what remained of *opera seria* was affected by the trend towards the historically and nationally 'correct'. Back in 1755 Roger Pickering had written concerning tragedy that 'there should never be such a *Scarcity* of *Scenes* in the *Theatre*, but, that, whether the Seat of Action be *Greek, Roman, Asiatic, African, Italian, Spanish*, &c: There may be one *Set*, at least, adapted to *each* Country'.[1] Writing at about the same time, Count Algarotti demanded not only stylistic differentiation but a serious attempt on the part of scene designers to base their work on genuine research into the styles and customs of antiquity. He maintained that the architecture of Greece, Rome, and Egypt should be studied (for example, in Norden's *Travels in Egypt and Nubia*, 1757) and properly represented; that Chinese gardens should be drawn from knowledge of what such gardens were actually like; and that particular places and buildings, ancient and modern, ought to be faithfully represented.[2] Algarotti's pioneering essay was translated into English in 1767. He was ahead of his time and no doubt the King's Theatre vacated its rut slowly and reluctantly—but it could hardly ignore what De Loutherbourg was doing to the concept of topographical scenery in the 1770s and 1780s at Drury Lane. If there was growing interest in what is now termed 'romantic' presentation, there was simultaneously a sharp rise in concern for historical and stylistic accuracy and the presentation of 'real' as opposed to conventionally stylized settings.

## V. Lighting and Special Effects

Until recently almost nothing was known about opera lighting at the King's Theatre in the eighteenth century. The discovery of Joseph Hayling's daily accounts for the seasons of 1780–81 and 1781–82 vastly increases understanding of the subject.[3] Hayling was an outside contractor and, when unpaid, he sued to collect. William Taylor counter-sued, charging excessive prices, and in response Hayling provided the court with a copy of his daily records of goods and services supplied to the opera-house. Hayling attended rehearsals and performances; supplied oil; cleaned, filled, and lit the lamps; provided

[1] *Reflections upon Theatrical Expression in Tragedy* (London: W. Johnston, 1755), 76.
[2] *An Essay on the Opera*, 71–86.
[3] Unless otherwise credited, information is from C12/2147/14 (filed 15 Mar. 1787). This is the second of three lawsuits by Taylor against Hayling; all were dismissed, with costs to the defendant. Hayling's 'schedules' are reproduced in App. III, below. For a more technical analysis of this material, see Judith Milhous, 'Lighting at the King's Theatre, Haymarket, 1780–82', *Theatre Research International*, 16 (1991), 215–36.

special effects that involved live fire; and served as resident tinker. Because he had been in the business a long time, Hayling offers a certain perspective. He describes his arrangement with the theatre as follows:

for the space of thirteen Years or thereabouts before the said Complainant [William Taylor] became concerned or had any Share in the said theatre [that is, since about 1768] he this Defendant (being by Business a Tinman) was engaged or employed to light the Lamps and make the Illuminations at the said Theatre and also to supply the said Theatre with Oil on any Particular Occasions and also with other Materials and to do such other business as was Necessary . . . in the Way of his said Trade.

Hayling explains that he charged a set fee for providing a specified amount of light for each performance. In response to Taylor's complaint that light cost far more than it had in earlier seasons Hayling replies:

And this Defendant saith that in the Year 1775 the Common number of Lights used in lighting up the House on Common Nights of the Operas was 1,332 but in the Year 1777 forty lights were added which made the Common Number to be lighted 1,372 but in the Year 1779 when the said Thomas Harris and Richard Brinsley Sheridan were Managers 552 Lights and some blinds were added which with a Charge for the Mens Labour in fitting Reflectors to Lamps made the Common Nightly Charge to them for that Year £5. 10s. 6d. for each Night.

In 1780–81 Hayling began with the same price for 1,844 lights, but early in the season 100 were added, and later another forty. In 1781–82 Taylor increased the number to more than 2,000.[1] This is extremely important information. The trend is towards a very substantial increase in opera illumination: in 1781–82 there were 50 per cent more lights than there had been six years earlier.

How much light was this, and how did it compare with other theatres in London and opera-houses abroad? Relatively full if not strictly comparable records exist for the Comédie-Française and for Covent Garden and have been well analysed by Bergman.[2] Other theatres of the time for which there are good records primarily used candles, which makes comparison virtually impossible. Bergman reports that in 1783 the Paris Opéra was lit by 100 oil lamps with eight wicks each, or 800 flames in all, each of which was reckoned to produce twice as much light as a wax candle. How these flames

[1] Taylor states the number as 1,984 each night in 1780–81 and 2,060 each night in 1781–82 in his interrogatories for Hayling of 11 Nov. 1789 (C24/1940).

[2] Gösta M. Bergman, *Lighting in the Theatre* (Stockholm: Almqvist & Wiksell, 1977). On oil lamps in particular see F. W. Robins, *The Story of the Lamp* (London: Oxford University Press, 1939).

compared to Hayling's there is no way to tell, but one gets the impression that the King's Theatre was quite well lit, especially after the massive increases of the late 1770s and early 1780s. The usual charge for an opera night was about £6. By comparison the lighting at concerts for the benefit of 'Decayed Musicians' on 19 April 1781 and 25 January 1782 cost only £3, while that for masquerades ranged from £27 to £84 and averaged £45 on ten occasions. Masquerades were *very* brightly lit throughout the whole house: Hayling charged by the thousand lights rather than by the hundred. Masquerades also went on for many hours; they involved special decorations and lighting effects, and many of the lights had to be specially rigged and then removed.

At the beginning of his accounts for each season, Hayling specifies what may be called his 'basic hang' for an opera night. Thus on 25 November 1780 for *L'arcifanfano*, he supplied the following:

| | | |
|---|---|---|
| Stage Lamps, 214, 2 lights each | 428 | |
| Front Lights three Rows, 150 each | 450 | |
| Passage Lamps and all over the House | 494 | |
| | 1,372 | (£3. 18s. 0d.) |
| Extra Lamps to move about instead of Candles Vizt | | |
| On Blinds, 61, 2 [lights] each | 122 | |
| Fills, 110, 2 each | 220 | |
| Ground Blinds | 130 | |
| | 472 | (£1. 12s. 6d.) |
| [TOTALS:] | 1,844 | (£5. 10s. 6d.) |

For Hayling, a salient point was whether a light was stationary or movable. He employed the term 'blinds' to refer to movable equipment used to light wings, backdrops, and perhaps free-standing pieces of scenery. He did not specify the placement of 'fills' (fill lamps), which came in 4d. and 8d. sizes. Service bills show that they had replaceable backs; some fitted into sockets while others hung from leather straps (which had to be bought in bulk and were frequently replaced).

At the beginning of 1781–82 more movable lamps were added onstage. The figure of 1,372 for fixed lights remains unchanged, but the entry for *Ezio* on 17 November 1781 specifies in addition:

Extra Lamps behind the Scenes to move about instead of Candles Vizt

| | | |
|---|---|---|
| Ground Blinds, 4, ten each | 40 | |
| Ditto, 6, fifteen each | 90 | |
| One Row more front Lights | 150 | |
| Stage Lamps added, 40, 2 lights each | 128 | |
| 24 Lanthorns about the House | [no figure] | |
| Fills Lamps, 120 each | 240 | (£2. 2s. 6d.) |
| | ——— | |
| | 648 | |

Thus in 1781–82 the total charge for light on an 'ordinary' night began at £6. 0s. 6d.; after some changes were made, the cost settled at a steady £6. 2s. 6d. Hayling explained to the court that 'he was not employed to find and provide the Oil merely but to light the Lamps themselves for which he charged and was paid at a rate by the hundred Lights according to the Price of Oil at the beginning of each Season'. The price was fixed for a given number of lights, regardless of the length of the evening's entertainment. Some 494 of the lights (evidently plus 24 'Lanthorns' in 1781–82) supplied illumination for the auditorium. Granting some spill from the stage lighting, this implies approximately three times as much light for the stage as for the auditorium. None the less, the level of auditorium light had risen significantly since mid-century, when Fielding describes the use of a personal candle to read a libretto at the King's Theatre.[1]

Many of the lights were fitted with reflectors. Hayling rarely used the term but did supply them. Thus on 10 December 1781 he charged for 'Four dozen and half Backs for Fills Lamps 8d. [each] . . . £1. 16s.' and 'Three Ditto of Lamps and Backs compleat 16s. [per dozen] . . . £2. 8s. 0d.'. Hayling provided large numbers of oval, round, square, and diamond-shaped reflectors for masquerade lights, but nowhere in these accounts is there reference to any form of reflector fancier than a simple tin mirror.

One of the key discoveries from Hayling's records is that once the light level was set for a season, it changed almost not at all. Comic operas, serious operas, and ballets of all kinds got precisely the same set of lights—though movable lights might be altered during a show. The amount of light charged for has no reference to any particular production. Once the basic

---

[1] 'He procured her a Book and Wax-Candle, and held the Candle for her himself during the whole entertainment'—an oratorio, we should note, not an opera. Henry Fielding, *Amelia* (1751), ed. Martin C. Battestin (Oxford: Clarendon Press, 1983), 189.

hang and charge were established for a season Hayling simply noted 'The like this Opera Night' for each performance. Occasionally there was an accidental variation. On 9 January 1781 '4 Back Blinds 96 Lights' remained unlit, an oversight for which Hayling reduced the charge by 5s. 6d.

Unlike ordinary opera nights and singers' benefits, dancers' benefits often have an extra charge for supplementary lighting. Hayling usually just jots down 'extra oil', but on 22 February 1781 he offers an explanation for the most expensive night that season: 'Benefit Monsr Vestris [jun.] . . . 1 Row more front Lights added and Lamps burning longer than usual', for a total of £7. 1s. 6d. The highest price throughout these two seasons was £7. 12s., charged on 11 April and 9 May 1782—which by no coincidence were the benefit nights for Noverre and Gardel. For obvious reasons dancers were more conscious of light than singers.

How much variation in the light was there during performances and how was it achieved? Stage directions in librettos and ballet scenarios imply the necessity of changing light levels, and this was certainly done at Drury Lane and Covent Garden.[1] Footlights could be mechanically dropped below stage level. Chandeliers could be raised or pulled into the wings. Even lights on wings could be masked. Darkness was not possible, but the relative amount of light could be quickly and precisely controlled, if not with the speed or totality possible with a rheostat. However, the painted night scenes and passing storms in the operatic *Rinaldo* (23 December 1780) or *Ifigenia in Aulide* (25 May 1782) must have been appropriately lit. *Il trionfo d'Arianna* (1784) shows the painter co-ordinating with Hayling's successor to heighten the contrast between a penultimate 'Night Scene' and a final palace of Bacchus, created with transparencies (*Morning Herald*, 19 January 1784). Hayling testifies that Taylor let 'his Machinist go into greater Expences than had been before usual'—perhaps implying that the designer, Michael Novosielski, was responsible for specifying what lights were to be moved, coloured, masked, and unmasked in the course of a performance. Hayling does not say that moving and masking the lights were among his duties: the likelihood is that these jobs were carried out by the numerous 'carpenters' who shifted the scenes, with the prompter responsible for co-ordinating the changes.

[1] For example, the *Morning Chronicle* of 1 Nov. 1782 complains about a failure to lower lights in a performance of *The Grecian Daughter* at Drury Lane: 'This evening, it is hoped, Mr Younger will ring the lights down in the Scene in which Phocian comes out of the tomb, and at length recognizes his Euphrasia. If the business of the Scene in question was meant to be transacted in all the glare of stage illumination, the incident is totally irreconcileable to probability.'

A particularly valuable feature of Hayling's accounts is the documentation they provide on special effects. Operas and ballets frequently call for elaborate storm scenes. Sacchini's *Rinaldo*, for example, opens with 'Winds blowing, thunder and lightning'; the second scene of Bertoni's *Ifigenia in Aulide* (1782) involves 'Ships and harbour; preparations for sailing. Altar. Storm at sea, incessant flashes of lightning, dark clouds, and thunderclap which falls on the altar'.[1] Hayling regularly provided lightning (and charged extra for it). His bill includes 'Ten Lightning Flashers three foot long tubes', and repeated entries for wire and 'Six pound Ground Rossin sifted fine', 'A Quart Boyler for Spirits', 'A pan for Spirits 3 feet 8 inches long', and 'Two pans to burn Spirits and altering the other'—suggesting that the theatre cooked up its own sparklers.

Before its destruction in 1789 the King's Theatre freely employed fireworks on stage, and they appear in Hayling's accounts. Noverre's *Medea and Jason*, first staged in London by Vestris sen. in the spring of 1781, apparently had Medea's dragon chariot depart in a shower of fire, though the full effect may not have been ready for the première. The framing for the fireworks does not appear in Hayling's accounts until the fourth performance, 7 April. The results were apparently memorable: a newspaper comment on the Queen's birthday ball a year later refers to it (*Morning Herald*, 4 January 1782). Some effects do not appear in the accounts—for example, the 'inscription written in letters of fire' that dooms Admetus in Noverre's Alcestis ballet, *Le triomphe de l'amour conjugal.* It was probably done routinely, much like the illuminations Hayling provided for royal birthdays. Light and fire were important features of such climactic moments as the 'hell scene' at the end of the ballet version of *Rinaldo and Armida* (1782), to be discussed in Chapter 7. Hayling's accounts lend credence to the descriptions of such special effects in librettos. In the following season, for which no comparable accounts survive, the theatre continued to exploit the dangerous medium, though for less serious dramatic purposes. The first act of *Il convito* and the second act of *L'avaro* both end in fires.

The accounting and payment system reported by Hayling is worth attention because it was probably representative of how the theatre dealt with a number of its contractors and department heads. Hayling kept three accounts. Once the basic charge for the season was approved, he 'used every Week to Deliver in his Bills of the Common Business done in lighting the

---

[1] *Rinaldo* (London: E. Cox, 1780); *Ifigenia in Aulide* (London: H. Reynell, 1782).

said Theatre to the Treasurer'. In other words, he expected to be paid weekly, though in fact he was not. The second set of accounts was for masquerades and other special occasions, and he delivered his bills 'when the Business was done' but did not expect payment until the end of season reckoning. The third account was 'his General Bill as a Tinman' which he 'delivered at the End of the Season'. In 1780–81 Hayling's bill was £432 for seventy opera nights, a concert, and £24 worth of rehearsals; the masquerade bill was £315; extra oil and tinkering came to £60—for a grand total of £808. In 1781–82 the figures were £519 for eighty-four opera nights; £141 for three masquerades; and £176 for tinkering, extra oil, and rehearsals—a total of £836.[1] His totals for light were less than the charge for 1784–85 in Table 4 above (p. 121).

## Lighting for Rehearsals

Hayling's lighting schedules prove that most new operas were staged with little or no technical rehearsal.[2] When *Ricimero* (a new serious opera) had to be completed and staged in haste early in the 1780–81 season, the schedule lists only 'Stage Lamps, 70; Fills Ditto, 40; Ground Blinds, 40; Five Gallons Oil used to Ditto, £1. 10s.' and 'The like Four Gallons and half oil used, £1. 7s.' for two rehearsals (29 November, 1 December 1780). Hardly any opera rehearsals enjoyed more than a minimum of light. If the flies did not need to be lit, they stayed dark. The dress rehearsal on 28 March 1781 of the next day's benefit for Vestris sen. required

| | |
|---|---|
| Stage Lamps, 100, 2 lights each | 200 |
| Fills Ditto, 120, Ditto | 240 |
| Front Lights one Row | 150 |
| Top of the House 1 each | 70 |
| Ten Lanthorns, 2 each | 20 |

This is about a third of the light provided at an actual performance, but clearly more than an opera rehearsal got. The total was 680 lights at £4. 9s. for two rehearsal sessions ('ditto lighted again'). Since the scheduled opera was a revival, the rehearsal probably concerned only the ballets, *Les caprices de Galatée* and *Medea and Jason*.

---

[1] Hayling says he was asked to put rehearsals in the tinkering account this season.
[2] Musical rehearsals are discussed in Ch. 4.

Some special stage effects no doubt required rehearsal, but the clear implication of the Hayling accounts is that most operas could be staged without bothering. A major *ballet d'action* was a different proposition. Hayling's entry for Noverre's *Rinaldo and Armida* on 20 February 1782 has all the earmarks of a difficult technical rehearsal (discussed in detail in Ch. 7). At more than £6 for light, this rehearsal cost nearly as much as a public performance. Noverre apparently insisted on getting the effects in his ballet just right. Ballet rehearsals naturally needed space, and hence a lot more stage time than operas, but the cost in 1780–81 seems to have been scant in terms of light. The huge increase in Hayling's rehearsal charges for 1781–82 is probably attributable to Noverre and his celebrated attention to detail. In general, rehearsal does not seem to have been one of the King's Theatre's strong points.

A great deal remains unknown about opera-house lighting in this period, but Hayling's schedules are invaluable. For its time, the King's Theatre had quite a high level of light. The total level of illumination increased by approximately 50 per cent between 1775 and 1782—from 1,332 lamps to 2,060. Their precise placement is not determinable, but each of the 214 'Stage Lamps' had two lights, and there were three, sometimes four, rows of 'Front Lights'. Movable lamps, replacing candles within recent memory, varied from 472 to 648 or more on 'Blinds', 'Ground Blinds', and as 'Fills' (two lights each). The basic cost was about £6 per night; by custom, repairs, special effects, and rehearsals were billed separately. Illumination could be increased, but save for dancers' benefits, rarely was. Alterations in lighting must have been achieved largely by shifting the 'movable' lamps and sinking the footlights.

## VI. Some Notes on Performance Practice

Few issues are as vexed as that of 'acting style'. How did the singers try to convey emotion? What were the conventions? How did those conventions differ from ours? These questions are not really answerable within the limits of the present investigation. Newspaper commentators regularly praise or criticize performers for their acting but almost never in terms useful to the historian. They say that a singer acted well or badly, that a portrayal was convincing or wooden—but nothing about what made it so. Contrary to the wisdom of textbooks, there is excellent reason to believe that in the English playhouses a substantial amount of what would now be called 'direction' had been exercised for many decades—most often by the author in new plays, by a manager or his deputy in old ones.[1] There is powerful evidence that someone handled blocking, explained character and motivation to actors, and coached the performers on how particular speeches were to be made and with what kinds of gestures. Lack of evidence hampers our knowing how much of this was done in Italian opera. Acting in opera was probably formulaic: classical *seria* and *buffa* were extremely standardized both in construction and conventions. There was also, of course, the language barrier. Susan Burney comments of Bertoni's *Quinto Fabio*, 'I like the Drama very much indeed, & if the Italian language was better understood, I doubt not that it would add very much to the success of the Opera—particularly as Pacchierotti feels every word of his parts, & will give it all the expression it admits of' (fo. 64ᵛ).

Conventional gesture helped communicate both action and feeling. In the course of the previous century and beyond, a complex language of gesture had been developed and was widely current all over Europe. It was employed in French and English tragedy and almost certainly was routinely employed in opera, whether in Italy, France, or England. Handbook after handbook catalogues such gestures, and adaptation of them in twentieth-century performances has proved surprisingly effective. Anyone wanting further pictorial examples, analysis, and bibliographic references to the large number of eighteenth-century sources for this material should consult Dene Barnett's massive study of the subject.[2]

Many of the gestures remain familiar from the stage, and some even from daily life. 'Shame in the extreme sinks on the knee and covers the eyes with both hands.' 'Hanging down of the Head is the Consequence of Grief and Sorrow'; '[The hands] are clasped or wrung in affliction.' A more complex example is welcome for an unexpected friend, when 'the foot takes a step backwards, at least the body leans backwards in astonishment, while the arms already begin to stretch towards the guest in heartfelt welcome'. Aversion takes time and two gestures to express: 'first the hand held vertical is retracted towards the face, the eyes and head are for a moment directed

---

[1] For discussion, see Judith Milhous and Robert D. Hume, *Producible Interpretation* (Carbondale: Southern Illinois University Press, 1985), ch. 2.

[2] Dene Barnett, *The Art of Gesture: The Practices and Principles of 18th Century Acting* (Heidelberg: Carl Winter Universitätsverlag, 1987). For a particular discussion of the impact of changing acting theory and practice upon opera, see Daniel Heartz, 'From Garrick to Gluck: The Reform of Theatre and Opera in the Mid-Eighteenth Century', *Papers of the Royal Musical Association*, 94 (1967-8), 111–27.

eagerly towards the object, and the feet advance. . . . Then suddenly the eyes are withdrawn, the head is averted, the feet retire, and the arms are projected out extended against the object, the hands vertical.'[1] In addition to these 'expressive' gestures there were commencing and terminating gestures, those of address and emphasis, and many other possibilities. Given the availability of bilingual librettos, the familiarity of many opera stories, and the highly expressive gestures that were part of the common grammar of tragedy and opera in performance, one may presume that the audiences usually knew more or less what was happening, language notwithstanding. Nuances may not have come across so well.

Barnett makes clear that the system was capable of great subtlety, but only if applied with taste, control, and precision. Individual performers chose and rehearsed their gestures in private. How the cast co-ordinated their interactions depended on their alertness and commitment to a production. In one of the few specific published criticisms of a singer's acting from the period, a reviewer chastised Calvesi, saying that

did he attend more to the *cunning* of the *scene*, [he] would be better entitled to a favourable report; Calvesi seems to have all the *material* requisites—then why so *cool* to the love inspiring Benini—a little more *warmth* and *attention*—the eyes less *directed* to the pit, and more to the stage, will be acceptable, good Signor Calvesi. (*Daily Universal Register*, 29 January 1787)

Calvesi had neglected what Barnett would call a 'gesture of address', the one most frequently documented by theatre practitioners.[2] Such a gesture 'could be performed cajolingly or imperiously, so that it would also express flattery or pride'. By concentrating on the orchestra, Calvesi left the attraction between the characters less convincing than it might have been, and the critic, used to better, was able in this instance to say just what was missing.

The roster of principals changed substantially from year to year, as did the repertoire. Even when an opera appeared in two successive years it usually underwent substantial changes in response to new personnel. Speaking of his forthcoming benefit in 1780, Pacchierotti says 'I shall have *the favourite Opera of the Olimpiade*—but it will be almost new, as only Pozzi & myself remain of last years Company.'[3] Same title, same story—but perhaps very different constituent parts and a lot of different music.

Another factor to be noted is pressure of time. Illness or injury might force the company to cancel a successful opera or ballet without notice:

[1] Barnett, *Art of Gesture*, 67, 42–3, 68, 59–60.
[2] Ibid. 247. Following quotation from 84.        [3] Susan Burney, fo. 69ᵛ.

hurriedly mounting a new show was easier than finding a substitute performer. Even without such mishaps new operas and ballets often had to be rushed to the stage. This company did not follow Handel's pattern of running each opera until it ceased to attract audiences but, when a show failed, the hole in the repertoire had to be filled quickly. To judge from comments by Susan Burney, operas were sometimes written (or assembled) under forced draft and rehearsed as the bits became available. Thus Bertoni rides in a carriage with Pacchierotti, but cannot get out to chat with the Burneys because 'he is obliged to refuse himself the pleasure of seeing you, in order to write the comic Opera, as he is very much pressed' (fo. 89$^r$). Operas and ballets were worked up over many weeks, if possible, but in a pinch one could be done in less than two weeks—thus Susan Burney commiserated with Pacchierotti over 'it having been necessary for him to get an entire new part in twelve Days' (fo. 43$^r$).

Under such pressure, one might expect bumpy performances, and indeed the newspapers regularly complain about mishaps. 'The performers . . . had not sufficiently rehearsed, and were not quite perfect in the recitative; the Prompter, though not ostensible, as he formerly was, took care from his centry-box, to let the audience know that he was not idle. We hope, however, that this defect will be fully remedied by the next representation.'[1] Given the number of new operas, the high degree of re-shaping, and the necessity for cuts even after the première, the prompter must often have been a vital crutch as the company struggled through the first performance or two. Reviewers were occasionally tetchy about such things. One wrote of a performance of *Silla* (29 November 1783), 'we would recommend . . . to the actors, to get more perfect in their parts; or the *Suggeritore* to prompt them in a lower key, as his voice was often heard above that of the performers.'[2] A description of the rebuilt auditorium in the autumn of 1782 shows that at this time the position of the person 'holding the book' was changed:

The *Frontispiece* is formed by two large Corinthian Pillars, which advance some Feet on the Stage, and in their *Base* contain the *Prompter*, who through a small Aperture in each Pillar, communicates with the Persons on the Stage.—A great Improvement this, from the old Trap-door in Front, which ought to have been execrated by us, as it is in some Parts of Italy. (*Morning Chronicle*, 5 November 1782)

Were the *suggeritore* and the 'prompter' the same person in the King's Theatre? The prompter would hardly have found a position under the

---

[1] *Morning Post*, 16 Apr. 1784.     [2] Theatre Cuts 41, fo. [101$^r$].

forestage a convenient place from which to run performances prior to 1782. Whether the change was permanent is to be doubted, for the *Daily Universal Register* of 25 December 1786 complains that 'The Prompter has again made his appearance at the Opera-house, in a trap-door on the stage as formerly. We imagined this custom had been entirely laid aside. We know not from what circumstances of convenience it is recalled, but it must ever prove disgusting to a British audience.' Virtually nothing is known of prompters at the King's Theatre in the eighteenth century, but one hint appears in a paragraph in *The Times* on 8 May 1789: 'On Wednesday night the prompter of the Opera House, who had been in that situation 40 years, after eating an hearty supper, fell from his chair, and expired immediately.' A long-serving prompter was no doubt a vital cog in the well-oiled machine that had put operas on the stage decade in and decade out, upheavals and bankruptcy notwithstanding.[1]

A variety of commentators report that many members of the audience came and went, moved about, and talked with their neighbours during performances. In this regard audience behaviour was probably more typical of twentieth-century football matches and baseball games than the Bayreuth-like reverence that is now considered appropriate to opera and ballet. At times the audience was no doubt hushed and riveted, but at others it was inattentive and noisy.[2] Newspaper reviewers complained about this, particularly when the theatre was crowded. The critic for the *Morning Chronicle* of 26 January 1784 reported a full house for the première of Anfossi's *Il trionfo d'Arianna*, and complained that the audience 'utterly disregarded' the opera.

The Opera Band, perhaps as complete as any in the world, is overpowered by the noise and nonsense on the spectator side of it, and even Pacchierotti himself cannot sufficiently, without impaired effect, make his way to those who are happy in hearing him. . . . The house was very crouded, and we who frequent the Opera, 'Not for devotion, but the music there', much less to see than to hear, could not uninterruptedly hear a dozen bars together!

On 10 May 1784 a critic in the same paper commented of the première of *Issipile*, 'A house so full as that of Saturday is probably as serviceable to the

---

[1] The identity of this long-time prompter is unknown, but he might have been Signor Serafini, a singer known only from a 29 Jan. 1754 role. A Joseph Serafini was among Taylor's creditors in 1783 (C107/66).

[2] Audience members occasionally pursued private quarrels, which could interrupt the performance: the *Morning Herald* of 2 Jan. 1782 reports the forcible eviction of an American patriot who had been making a nuisance of himself in the theatre.

dancing, as it is apt to be destructive to the singers. The incessant buz of crouded benches is such an accompaniment, as few singers find themselves able to still, or to struggle under.' When the stage itself began to fill with auditors, the dancers too were discommoded. 'The Ballet was in some sort maimed in its progress by the number of people on the stage.—They were hissed a little by the audience and yet more annoyed by D'Auberval who in Skirmish, seemed to do some real execution among them when he brandished and discharged a chair.'[1] Playbills regularly repeated the injunction, 'By COMMAND of THEIR MAJESTIES, No person to be admitted behind the Scenes', but as a complaint in the *Morning Post* of 26 March 1784 tells us, the command was honoured principally in the breach. Susan Burney reports that when discussing the forthcoming première of *Rinaldo* with Dr Burney, Pacchierotti

said he hoped his Friends would exert themselves to procure silence the first Night. My father said the *Gallery* was the only place where it could be commanded or was generally met with. The *lower* Gallery, said he [Pacchierotti], I believe—but the other—Indeed the people they often behave abominably—there are the *Italian rascals* there, who only go to do mischief. (Susan Burney, fo. 94ᵛ)

Some of the noise may well have been deliberate sabotage, or so the partisan Susan Burney believed. During the performance of Sacchini's *Rinaldo* on 29 April 1780, she reports, 'there were some Beasts in the House (Tenducci I *saw* & firmly believe to have been one of them) who blew their Noses, cough'd, spit, & did every thing possible but *hiss* during every one of his [Pacchierotti's] songs, in a shameful manner—they meant to disturb him & make him sing ill & out of tune, to prevent people from hearing him' (Susan Burney, fo. 114ʳ).

In the course of Chapter 4 Susan Burney will be quoted extensively about a number of operas. She makes a marvellous commentator: knowledgeable, sensitive, enthusiastic, musically educated, and comfortable in French if not entirely so in Italian. In these respects she was no doubt a decidedly atypical member of the audience. By way of contrast, we conclude this prelude with an assortment of opera comments from Lady Mary Coke over the dozen years with which this book is concerned. She was a great lady who knew everyone in the world of titled box-holders, a traveller thoroughly familiar with the Paris and Vienna operas, and a person with decided likes and dislikes. She regularly attended concerts but never public

---

[1] *Morning Chronicle*, 22 May 1784.

performances of plays, and she had long held one of the 'best' boxes in the King's Theatre (indeed, George III borrowed it once in 1778). She paid enough attention to find some operas 'silly' and to approve or disapprove voices and acting. She wrote her letter-journal to another long-time opera-goer, which makes the dearth of particular commentary the more striking. She never names a ballet, and rarely an opera. Singers and dancers are approved or disapproved, but save in rare cases she refers to them only by function—'the new first man' or 'the new first woman'. She displays no interest at all in who wrote the music. Much of her attention is on who was present and the gossip of the day. She likes both opera and dance, but she attends the King's Theatre as part of a social ritual. She is a very different auditor from the Burneys, or the fiery Italian gallery partisans. Lady Mary was probably representative of a substantial component among the subscribers who kept the King's Theatre in business, and the twentieth-century critic would be foolish to ignore her outlook.

I am going to the Opera for the first time this year & their Majesties have taken our Box. I was starved at the Opera & not much amused, very little company indeed. (3 January 1778)

I went this evening to the Opera for the first time. . . . The musick I think good & the first Man as remarkable fine, & I think a pleasing singer, the Woman has an agreeable voice & is a very fine Actress. [References appear to be to *Demofoonte*, with Pacchierotti and Signora Bernasconi.] The Audience was not numerous. (2 January 1779)

Tis so cold I have accepted a private party at Lady Gowers & given up the Opera. (7–8 January 1780)

The new dancer [Vestris jun.] is excessively admired. He is Son to one I have often seen dance at Paris who perhaps is as extraordinary as any person ever was. She [probably Mlle Baccelli] is a remarkable bad figure short, & broad, with a large head, yet when She dances She is inimitable. (21–24 December 1780)

This evening there was a new Opera and a very pretty one it is. The Dowager Albemarle desired a place in the Dutchess of Richmonds Box not to see the Opera but the Prince of Wales who goes there constantly. (19 December 1782)

Lady Ailesbury has just now been with me. She says She has not been well but 'tis a disorder that probably will carry itself off tho' very inconvenient to go Abroad with.

She was obliged She tells me to leave the Opera being much pressed and tho' 'tis a natural and not an unreasonable want yet still one feels unwilling to confess it in a great company. She seems very well satisfied with the first Woman at the Opera [Signora Lusini]. She has a good voice and a pleasing figure but the musick of the Opera She does not like. (3–4 December 1783)

I went this evening to the Opera and liked it very much I think the first Woman has one of the finest voices I ever heard and one of the most pleasing the dancing is delightful. You will find a great change in the dress few sacks are seen, so far it pleases me as I always liked a night Gown, but these Air balloon hats which have wafted themselves over from France are a real nuisance in a public Place, yet you will see numbers of them at the Opera and at Assemblies. At the play House they are very wisely excluded, the Ladies who have gone there in them have been civily desired to go back as they were determined not to admit them. (20 December 1783)[1]

If the Weather continues so cold tomorrow I shall not go to the Opera. (29 December 1783)

I did not go last night to the Opera nor shall I till there is some change in the weather. (30 December 1783)

The Ugly frost is returned and with it the cold face of Misery however I go to the Opera and Lady Sackville goes with me. . . . Our Opera was thin of Ladies but a good many Men the Prince of Wales appeared as if he was drunk he was five or six times in and out of the Pitt. . . . The new Man and Woman in the Comic Opera [Signor Tasca and Signora D'Orta] are both good ones, I mean their Voices for as to the Person of the Lady it is not agreeable. (6 January 1784)

There is an opposition forming again to the Operas, Lady Mary Duncan, Lady Mount Edgcumbe and Lady Brudenal have withdrawn their subscription and want to set up a Consort which I think is not so good entertainment, so they shall not have my support. (29 December 1784)

Mrs Damer went with me to the Opera it was, I rivale Delusi one of the last year and very pretty, but the dancing in my opinion inferior to what we had the last winter. (5 January 1785)

---

[1] Lady Mary adds two weeks later on 4 Jan. 1784: 'you will laugh I am sure when you see the hats at the Opera, for you'll have no reason to cry as they can't come before our Box. They are of all forms and put on in all sorts of ways and some has one hat growing out of the other.'

It has been particular satisfaction to me to hear you intend being in Town after Christmas and that you will belong to Our Box at the Opera. Alass I was there but four or five times last year but this winter I hope to go often. (27 September 1785)

There will be no Operas till after Christmas and then as I am told there will be something patched up, which probably will not be very good as all the best performers will then be engaged. (30 November 1785)

This evening I went to the Opera but I can't give a good account of a bad thing some of the music is pretty but the Opera is sillier than any I ever heard and the performers are not too good, but Vestris is if possible better than ever tis a pleasure to see dancing in such perfection tis pity there is no Woman that approaches his excellence to dance with him. (28 January 1786)

The crowd at the Opera on Tuesday was beyond what I ever saw it. Hundreds were sent away and when I came it was with difficulty I passed the passages to get to Lady Townshend's Box. A pick pocket was discovered in the Pit to all appearances a Lady but supposed to be a Man in Women's Clothes. (27 May 1786)

When I went last night to the opera it thawed but during the night it froze harder than ever. . . . The opera was far from full and far from pleasing, one or two songs excepted it was very dull. Rubinelli and Mara were very fine but Maras songs were not good. The dances were terrible and only two dancers that are worth looking at, two women [Mlle Mozon and Mme Gervais Perignon], and no man that is tolerable to dance with them. The Duke of Cumberland has the box he had before he went abroad but he was often in the pit. The Prince of Wales seemed restless and stayed nowhere long, I don't know whether Mrs Herbert [Fitzherbert] was there or not, he went for a little while into Lady Lansdale's box it appeared to be for Lady Arskine as he talked only to her. (24 December 1786)

Lord Charles Spencer brought his eldest son to our box he is just come from abroad and very handsome. . . . The dances are improved but the opera does not grow better upon acquaintance, we are to have a new one on Tuesday. (6 January 1787)

We had at the opera Mr Pitt and the two Secretaries of State the Prince of Wales has taken again his box and was in it for some time but when Lady Broughton comes to Town he allows her to sit in it. The comic opera is better than the serious one tho not very excellent. The new woman [Signora Benini] has a very pretty voice but not enough for that theatre. (10 January 1787)

The opera very hot. (24 May 1788)

This evening I went to the opera [at the Little Haymarket] the music is pretty and the new singer [Signora Laurenti] has a good voice but is a bad actress upon the whole it is better than I expected. I subscribe for two tickets and shall be happy at any time to give you one and have the pleasure of your company in the box. The Duchess of Bedford has a small box below stairs just by fops alley. Sir James Peachy said she looked like a great spider that was catching at all the flies. The Duke of Orleans has a box not far distant from Ours his mistress Madame de Bufton is very pretty, the Prince of Wales made her a low bow from the Pitt and afterwards went into the box as did the Duke of Queensbury but the Duke of Orleans never left her, a caution that perhaps is necessary. (7 January 1790)

Turning to an account of the operatic repertoire from 1778 to 1790, the reader would do well to remember that there were undoubtedly a lot more Lady Mary Cokes in the audience than Susan Burneys.

# CHAPTER 4

# *Opera under Sheridan (1778–1781)*

Between the *Drama*—the *Composition* & his performance I was—absolutely *melted*—I cried as I did at the first serious opera I heard, when Guadagni performed Orfeo.
—Susan Burney on Pacchierotti's performance in *L'Olimpiade* (1780)

RICHARD BRINSLEY SHERIDAN'S regime as proprietor of the King's Theatre (1778–81), despite its dire consequences for the long-term financial stability of Italian opera in London, was artistically a continuation of previous practice. No one commented on any radical change in production style or in the calibre of the performers engaged. There was perhaps a slight shift towards more lavish productions with choral-ballet scenes in the first season or two, such as Sacchini's *Enea e Lavinia* (1779) and his *Rinaldo* (1780), and there was the occasional experiment encouraged by the new owner-manager—*La governante*, for example, Bertoni's burletta based on Sheridan's English opera *The Duenna*. But there were no striking innovations, no decisive break with the past, and certainly no attempt to reform the conventions of *opera seria*. Why should there have been, when Italian opera in London was enjoying its greatest popularity of the century? Sheridan had little difficulty in engaging leading singers, such as Roncaglia, Danzi, Adamberger, Pozzi, Ansani, and Pacchierotti. The dominant King's Theatre house composer throughout the 1770s and during Sheridan's management was Antonio Sacchini, greatly admired both in England and on the Continent. Sacchini provided London with a high-profile international opera composer absent since Handel headed the 'Second Academy' in the 1730s. Perhaps the full measure of the esteem he was afforded by London society is that his portrait was painted by Sir Joshua Reynolds in 1775. (See Pl. 9.) Johann Christian Bach was also still active at the King's Theatre, composing his last London opera, *La clemenza di Scipione*, just before Sheridan took over the management. In 1779 the immensely experienced Ferdinando Bertoni joined the theatre as house composer, filling the gap left by Bach's temporary removal to Paris. The choice of revivals and new productions of works that had already been performed on the Continent also reveals discerning judgement on someone's part: Paisiello's *La frascatana*, Piccinni's *La schiava*, and Grétry's *Zemira e Azore*, to name but three. There is a basic integrity and quality to almost all the music produced under Sheridan's auspices that is often lacking in later seasons. Sheridan was an incompetent and perhaps actually a dishonest businessman, but Italian opera thrived under his management. How much of the credit actually belonged to him is another matter.

## I. The Musical Establishment under Sheridan

This politician, playwright, and impresario was a busy man and, though involving himself in the details of opera production from time to time, he probably had little real influence on the choice of repertoire or on the general artistic direction of the King's Theatre. During the 1778–79 season (and part of 1779–80), Sheridan and Harris delegated the day-to-day artistic management to Antoine Le Texier but, despite the increased newspaper attention to the King's Theatre that began at about this time, his duties within the musical establishment of the company are but sketchily reported. Even the identity of 'the Director of the Opera' who authorized the general announcement of the 1778–79 season is not revealed, though it was presumably Le Texier.[1] The printed librettos, the 'Larpent' manuscripts submitted to the Lord Chamberlain's office, and the abundant collections of *Favourite Songs* give a fairly complete picture of the texts of the works themselves from this period, even in the absence of many full scores. The inner workings of the music department under Sheridan are not as well understood as during Gallini's regime (1785–9) or at the Pantheon opera-house (to be discussed in vol. II), but, thanks mainly to Susan Burney's letter-journal, quite a detailed picture can be painted, at least for the first two seasons.

### Le Texier as Sheridan's Director of Opera

The Burneys were intensely interested in the management of the King's Theatre and eagerly sought information about Sheridan, who was already rumoured to be in financial trouble by late 1779. They were keen to

---

[1] The announcement appeared in the *Morning Post*, 14 Nov. 1778.

establish good relations with the new opera-house officials, who were a potential source of free tickets and admittance to rehearsals. So much did the Burneys crave knowledge of *new* music, they found rehearsals more desirable to attend than premières. Susan and her novelist sister Fanny had some acquaintance with the previous managers of the King's Theatre, Mrs Mary Ann Yates and Mrs Frances Brooke. Fanny was puzzled why the latter, 'a woman of Character & reputation' as a *femme de lettres*, should have become intimate with Mrs Yates, 'one whose fame will bear no scrutiny'.[1] The Burney sisters were guests of Mrs Brooke at Venanzio Rauzzini's London début on 8 November 1774. In her diary Fanny recorded how at the opera-house they

were led up a noble stair case, that brought us to a most magnificent Apartment, which is the same that belonged to the famous Heideger, & since his Time, has always been the property of the Head manager of the Opera. Here we saw Mrs Yates, seated like a stage Queen surrounded with gay Courtiers, & dressed with the utmost elegance & brilliancy.[2]

This vignette partly explains why so many people were willing to risk so much to gain control of the King's Theatre. With Sheridan's acquisition of the opera-house, the Burneys found themselves on the outside, having to rely on Pacchierotti, Bertoni (the singer's inseparable friend and mentor), and especially on the gossip Wilhelm Cramer, leader of the opera orchestra, for news from behind the scenes.

Ominously, even these key performers seemed to know little about the management. Sheridan and Harris had appointed Antoine Le Texier 'to superintend the opera and all matters of spectacle' in March 1778.[3] Le Texier had been a professional reciter in France, and upon his arrival in England in 1775 established himself as a would-be impresario, reportedly with encouragement from Garrick. In league with Gallini, he had clashed with Mrs Yates and Mrs Brooke over breach of contract in an attempt to sublet the opera-house. Because of his flair for literature, he had also been a house guest of Hester Thrale, but the two had apparently parted company by the time Mrs Thrale took Fanny under her wing, for neither of the Burney sisters had any direct contact with him.

---

[1] Fanny Burney, *Early Journals and Letters*, ii. 55.
[2] Ibid. ii. 55–6. Fanny was later in correspondence with Mrs Brooke (see 163).
[3] *Biographical Dictionary*, ix. 258.

Susan's letter-journal provides the best available account of Le Texier's stint as opera manager. She leaves unexplained the reason for his dismissal in early 1780, but it is easily guessed. The first sign of trouble was Pacchierotti's strong disapproval of Le Texier's plan (which Susan reports on 20 October 1779) to offer a double bill of an adaptation of Sacchini's comic opera *La contadina in corte* coupled to a one-act serious pasticcio to be assembled by Bertoni. According to Pacchierotti, 'the Public after being once indulged by hearing the serious & comic singers on the same evening will never be satisfied with their former fare' (fo. 18ʳ). (Could Pacchierotti really have been unaware of the earlier practice in Italy of performing serious operas with comic intermezzi?) But of greater concern to him was the prospect of having to 'perform twice instead of only once a week', that is, on Tuesday or Thursday in the double bill and then again on Saturday, the usual night for *opera seria*. Le Texier did little to improve relations with Bertoni when he cancelled the double bill (which Susan reported on 8 November) because he had not been able to engage enough *buffi* to mount *La contadina in corte*; Bertoni's work on the one-act pasticcio was now useless.[1]

Besides being late for rehearsals, Le Texier had offended the *prima donna seria* Franziska Danzi (who married the oboist Ludwig August Lebrun in 1778). The orchestra leader Cramer, noted for his tact and diplomacy, reported to Susan on 20 November 1779 that he had offered to mediate between the opera manager and Madam Lebrun:

I therefore . . . took all the pains I possibly could, *indeed*, to set every thing right between them—& if Mr. Tessier wd. have only spoke to her at the Rehearsal to ask *how she do* I am sure she wd. have been quite satisfied without any further apologies.—But you saw Ma'am [that is, Susan] . . . He never came near her—never paid her the least civility—I told him afterwards He could not expect to be on good terms with the Performers if he behaved in such a manner—but he said *Mr. Le Brun* is this & that & t'other. (fo. 40ᵛ)

Such behaviour seems to have been characteristic of Le Texier. Cramer reported that the director of opera had wanted to sack the entire orchestra. The violinist agreed that with the possible exception of the oboist 'Einfort' (Philip Eiffert), the wind-players were 'insufferable' and should at least have their salaries docked. A general meeting of the orchestra was called. As Cramer recalled,

---

[1] It was, however, rescheduled for 14 Dec. 1779.

I believe there never was more noise at the House of Commons.—*No* was cried out by all united—at last he [Le Texier] was obliged to give it up—as indeed almost all his schemes—I heard yesterday he intended to give up the management—but I don't know how it will be, or who will *succeed* him—for Many of the Performers who have been here half a year have never yet seen either Mr. Harris or Mr. Sheridan. (fo. 41ᵛ)

The authors of the *Biographical Dictionary* (ix. 258) state that Le Texier 'resigned or was discharged on or after 27 December 1779'. But Susan Burney, who was in daily contact with one or more King's Theatre performers, does not report his downfall until 28 March 1780: 'both Bertoni & Pacchierotti think a change will very shortly take place in the management of the Opera House [they were wrong]—& I heartily wish it may, for tho' Tessier is now out, nothing can be worse than the conduct of the present Proprietors' (fo. 83ᵛ).

Le Texier may have hung on until March 1780, but he had become isolated and ineffective at least two months earlier. On 19 January Susan recorded Pacchierotti's comment that the theatre, which was badly in need of repair, was a '*Republic*, as Mr. Sheridan wd. not act, & there was therefore no *Cheif*' (fo. 65ʳ). Continuing in French, the language to which Pacchierotti usually switched for his most bitter personal complaints, he said that the low-ranking singers Rovedino and De Michele had treated Bertoni and him with 'grossiertés affreuses'. As the second season progressed, Sheridan did become involved in production matters: he interceded in a dispute between the poets Andrei and Badini over the libretto of Sacchini's *Rinaldo* (discussed below) and even offered advice on musical matters. But the proprietor expended at least as much effort trying to avoid Cramer, Pacchierotti, and other performers whose salaries were badly in arrears. A ringing testament to the strength of the 'well-oiled machine' described in Chapter 3 is that Sheridan's neglect and irresponsibility made hardly any immediate or visible difference to the company's operation.

### Composers and Conductors

Through close contact with Pacchierotti, Bertoni, and Cramer, Susan Burney gained intimate knowledge of the duties and responsibilities of the King's Theatre's composers and conductors. The organization she describes generally resembles that which existed under later managers and probably differs little from earlier practice, except for being rather more chaotic. Contrary to modern assumptions, there was no single director of music, except the manager—first Le Texier and then, by necessity, Sheridan himself. Le Texier apparently decided on a production plan over which even the *primo uomo* had little control except in the choice of work to be produced for his benefit night and the right to substitute arias (but this process was subject to negotiation with other singers). By contrast, Luigi Marchesi, whose engagement at the King's Theatre in 1788 caused a frenzy of excitement, had considerable influence on the choice of repertoire. Le Texier instructed one or both of the house poets, Carlo Francesco Badini and Antonio Andrei, to consult with whatever composer had been selected to set a particular work. They would then hammer out a libretto, often in consultation with the principal singers. There was considerable animosity between the poets, who evidently had the final say on the text of an opera. During the preparation of *Rinaldo*, Badini finally gained the upper hand over Andrei and then contemptuously refused to include some verses that Pacchierotti wanted Sacchini to set as a *rondò*.[1]

Composers signed annual contracts with the manager and, while none survives for Sheridan's regime, one may assume that the terms were roughly in line with those granted by earlier and later managers: in return for a salary ranging from £200 to £400 (modest in comparison even with those of middle-ranking singers and dancers),[2] the composer was expected to write one or two operas as instructed by the manager, to attend all rehearsals, and to conduct all performances of his own works from the harpsichord. In 1780–81 Giovanni Battista Bianchi may have been employed as conductor/arranger and general dogsbody, as Joseph Mazzinghi was during Gallini's management, working closely with the house music-copyist in preparing scores and with special responsibility for conducting pasticcios. The start-of-season announcements of engagements were often misleading, particularly with regard to composers. For instance, the one that appeared in the *Morning Post* on 13 November 1779 mentions the appointment of no fewer than six house composers: Sacchini, Bertoni, J. C. Bach, Paisiello, Giuseppe Giordani,[3] and one 'Ponto', as yet unidentified but perhaps Giuseppe Ponzo. This list raises immediate suspicion, because of these six, only Sacchini and Bertoni actually composed anything for the King's Theatre during the following season. Susan Burney sheds light on this matter. She spent

[1] Susan Burney, fo. 92ᵛ.
[2] See 'Opera Salaries', 45–53.
[3] Perhaps the father of the King's Theatre composer Tommaso Giordani; see *Biographical Dictionary*, vi. 216–17.

part of the evening of 16 November 1779 in conversation with her father and the singer Gabriele Mario Piozzi,

talking awhile of the Opera, & cutting up Mr Tessier very notably. . . . I suppose you have seen Tessier's impudent puff in the Morng. Post where he names 7 or 8 Composers for the Opera this season, out of which number *but one* has been engaged by the Managers.—He begins wth. Sacchini, who has nothing to do this year—then Bertoni, who alone is engaged—he adds *Bach*, who is at Paris, Paisiello, in *Russia*, & 3 or 4 more but not *Philidor*—it seems as if *that* scheme was given up, which I much rejoice in. (fo. 33ᵛ)

In order to attract subscribers, Le Texier had simply made up a list of the most famous opera composers he could think of. The lack of a firm engagement for Sacchini by this date (the season opened on 27 November, just eleven days later) is surprising, as is the manager's ignorance of Bach's whereabouts.[1] By all indications the composers attached to the opera-house, even the famous Sacchini, received but scant respect from the managers and were often treated as little more than lackeys. The retiring Bertoni was particularly abused. As mentioned above, his serious pasticcio was abruptly cancelled and then rescheduled at very short notice. Some of the singers treated him with contempt and, because of Sheridan's poor planning, he was left with nothing to do for a month at the end of the season.[2] During rehearsals, which are discussed in detail in the next section, the composer was in charge of the singers and anything happening on stage that had a bearing on the music, except the ballet, which was conducted by the main répétiteur. Pasticcios were conducted by the composer who had undertaken the arrangement, but in such works his authority was often undermined by the singers. For example, Pacchierotti complained when Madam Lebrun decided to introduce a substitute aria into *Alessandro nell'Indie*, conducted by Bertoni, without so much as a day's notice, thereby spoiling the integrity of an important scene (discussed below).

Although practice varied considerably from regime to regime, two harpsichords were normally used during Sheridan's management, one played by the composer and the other by an assistant; in 1779–80 the second player was no less a figure than Muzio Clementi. During one of the periods when he was music director of the King's Theatre, Giardini, who detested the

---

[1] The aborted plan to bring over François-André Danican Philidor from Paris, apparently unrecorded elsewhere, seems almost incredible, since his operas were unknown and unperformable in London.

[2] Susan Burney, fo. 153ᵛ.

instrument, reportedly 'prevailed on the manager to remove *one* of [the harpsichords], and the performer not to play on the *other*'.[1] But even by the late 1770s the use of two harpsichords was an anachronism, and the trend was towards the composer as conductor in the modern sense of waving a baton or a scroll of paper. The assistant was left the job of helping the cellist accompany the simple recitatives.

The orchestra, in effect a separate department of the opera-house and something of a law unto itself, was directed by the principal violinist, Cramer. Unlike the composer, he was in absolute control of the band, members of which were customarily addressed only through him. Much of the responsibility for maintaining the pace and continuity of a performance rested with Cramer, and such was his authority that an opera, even a première, could be adequately performed in the absence of the composer. Unlike the house composers and most of the singers and dancers, Cramer was supposed to have direct access to the managers, though Sheridan became increasingly elusive as the season progressed and his financial problems worsened.

## Rehearsals

Susan Burney attended many rehearsals at the King's Theatre in 1779 and 1780. Although the incidents and production methods she describes differ little in general terms from contemporaneous reports of Continental practice or indeed from what happens in many opera-houses today, hers is by far the most vivid and detailed account of opera rehearsals in London during the eighteenth century. Her letter-journal is all the more valuable because these are informed observations. Susan had usually read the libretto or discussed the plot with Bertoni and Pacchierotti in advance. She had a good idea beforehand what pieces would be included in a pasticcio. The King's Theatre conducted basically two kinds of rehearsals, private and public. The first were held at the opera-house in various public rooms: the theatre had no dedicated rehearsal space, though the coffee-room was the usual venue.[2] These private rehearsals concentrated on the simple recitative or individual arias and ensembles and were accompanied only by the harpsichord (later fortepiano) or a few instruments. In the company of her stepmother and Pacchierotti, whom she met by chance alighting from his carriage in front

---

[1] The *Morning Post*, 9 Dec. 1789; see also Judith Milhous and Curtis Price, 'Harpsichords in the London Theatres, 1697–1715', *Early Music*, 18 (1990), 39.

[2] See, for example, the *Morning Post* of 21 Feb. 1789.

of the opera-house, Susan attended the first rehearsal of Bertoni's comic opera *Il duca d'Atene* on Wednesday morning, 3 May 1780. The première was less than a week away, that is, Tuesday, 9 May. Serious operas, especially those offered early in the season when the company was green, required more rehearsal time, as explained below. Though delighted to see her, Pacchierotti tried to warn Susan off: 'It is . . . but the first Rehearsal, & I am afraid there will be a great many *Da capos* which will tire you!' (fo. 117ʳ). By 'da capos' he meant of course that pieces would need to be repeated in order to set things right. But Susan would not be deterred:

He went with us into the Room where the Rehearsal was to be & I was sorry to find it was *quite* private—No Women at all but the singers, & the Room a much smaller one than the Coffee Room where Rinaldo was first Rehearsed—I shd. not have had courage to have sat it wth. anybody but my Mother, & was very glad that Pacchierotti got seats for us, tho' sorry enough that the Room was so crowded, being small, & so hot that he went away quite to the Door of it, so we had no more conversation.

Bertoni was at the harpsichord and Cramer was also present, though whether he was leading a small band of instrumentalists is not clear. Yet Susan does note that when she arrived 'The Overture was over & the opera began', which implies the participation of at least some members of the orchestra. Besides herself, Mrs Burney, and Pacchierotti, Susan counted only three other persons in the tiny audience. Although this was 'the first Rehearsal', Bertoni had been at work on the opera since at least 13 April (see fo. 89ʳ), and the singers had probably received copies of their arias and learnt the recitative before the run-through on 3 May. Nevertheless, this account confirms that comic operas were typically simple, straight-forward productions that could be got up very quickly by an experienced troupe of *buffi*. *Opere serie*, especially those with integrated ballet scenes, were an entirely different matter, as will be seen in the case of Sacchini's *Rinaldo*.

The second type of rehearsal was a complete run-though with orchestra in the theatre itself, what Germans would call the *Generalprobe*. At the King's Theatre this was often well attended by box-subscribers, professional musicians, and anyone else who could wheedle his or her way past the door-keepers. Apart from the stage and orchestra pit, the theatre was completely dark and even in winter unheated to save expense. Susan describes Pacchierotti jumping up and down between arias to stay warm. On Friday morning, 19 November 1779, Esther Burney, her husband Charles Rousseau

Burney, and Susan attended the general rehearsal of the pasticcio *Alessandro nell'Indie*, the first full rehearsal of the season. It was chaotic, and the première, scheduled for Tuesday, 23 November, had to be postponed until Saturday the 27th.[1] Susan was 'a little *entremblant*' that the Burney party would be refused admission, but upon dropping her father's name, they were 'very civilly allowed to pass'. Her account of this rehearsal is important, for it reveals hitherto unknown details about how a pasticcio was assembled and directed. The theatre had announced that the opera was to be under the direction of Bertoni,[2] but Susan understood that he had composed nothing original for it. She further deduced that he had introduced no more than three or four old numbers of his own: 'This I supposed by observing that He did not stand forwards as *Direttore* . . . all the singers acted as *Maestro* during their own songs' (fo. 36ʳ). In other words, each singer gave the orchestra the tempo and character of his or her own arias, a practice which suggests they had some part in deciding the musical content of the opera. For one of Madam Lebrun's songs, her husband ('who looks a conceited fop') gave the tempo, which Susan took as a certain sign that he was also its composer.

The rehearsal of *Alessandro nell'Indie* did not go smoothly. With no one in overall control, pacing was often badly awry. In the third act Antonio Tozzi's bravura aria 'Già via ed in lontananza', sung by Signora Pozzi, was taken so fast 'that before she came to the end of it, she *non poteva più*, & was obliged to stop for breath Lery for merry' (fo. 37ᵛ). Cramer then stepped in and with 'his accustomed good humour' started the aria again at a slower tempo. Susan noted his 'Gentlemanlike' manner in addressing the orchestra, but later in the morning his patience snapped:

the Wind Instruments were all out of tune, & tho' I pited poor Cramer 'twas impossible not to laugh—After repeatedly desiring the French Horn Players to make their Instruments sharper, at last he called out in a voice wch. proved that he wth. difficulty cd. repress a degree of Indignation—& with his foreign accent— '*Gentelmen* [sic] . . . *You are not in tune At all?*—'*Its a very sharp Morning* Sir', said one of them—'We shall do better another time'—Another sd. that the *Crook* he used was right—but Cramer desired he wd. try the other—He did so—'Why that is *better*'—sd. Cramer, as indeed it clearly was— '*Very well sir*', sd. the stupid Earless wretch. '*I'll be sure to use it.*' (fo. 38ʳ)

---

[1] *The London Stage*, Part 5, i. 298–9. Susan also mentions that some dancers had not yet arrived in London: see fo. 47ᵛ.

[2] Ibid. 299, and repeated on the title-page of the libretto (London: W. Mackintosh, 1779).

In the same piece Cramer was again forced to stop when the bassoonist 'was dreadfully & ridiculously out of tune' (presumably he overlooked a change of key signature in his part). To illustrate his mistake, Muzio Clementi at the second harpsichord (and something of a wag, as Susan reveals elsewhere) 'play'd over the passage wth. natural notes in the treble, & flat in the Bass'.[1] At Pacchierotti's suggestion, Cramer ordered the bassoonist to omit the passage altogether. These scenes will be all too familiar to anyone who has been involved with opera production, but the fact that *Alessandro nell'Indie* should have been in utter shambles four days before the scheduled première shows what could happen when the 'well-oiled machine' stood idle over the summer. These minor disasters should not obscure the fact that the division of responsibility between the composer directing the singers from the harpsichord and the principal violinist controlling the orchestra worked perfectly well most of the time. And even when Sacchini was too ill to conduct the first performance of *Rinaldo*, the musical part of the opera went smoothly enough; the serious mishaps, which left Pacchierotti bruised and humiliated, had nothing to do with the composer's absence; rather, as is explained below, they resulted from inadequate rehearsal and a lack of co-ordination between singers and dancers in a complex scene.

Susan Burney's account of the 1779–80 season is packed with information about the operas she attended. Much of what she says about compositional process and production technique probably applies to other seasons as well. Only for the Pantheon opera-house (1790–92) do we possess so much information, but of a very different kind: mostly financial records. Susan Burney provides insight into the human and technical aspects of opera that almost no one else cared to comment on. And she does ultimately answer the key question about whether the King's Theatre had an artistic policy, at least during the second season of Sheridan's regime.

The remainder of this chapter is largely devoted to a season-by-season account of selected operas produced under the Sheridan–Harris management. The emphasis is on the works themselves, though notice is also taken of finances and other managerial matters when they can be shown to have affected recruitment of performers and other artistic personnel. Most of the operas examined here are in varying degrees adaptations; even the newly

---

[1] She was hindered at this point in her explanation by Fanny's evident ignorance of music theory: 'I don't know whether you can understand what I mean, but it had the most dissonant & comical effect & produced the best imitation of their accompt. that can be conceived' (fo. 38ᵛ).

composed works by Sacchini and Bertoni were subjected to the pasticcio process during production. But they are treated as musico-dramatic entities rather than constantly examined to see how they differ from models or previous productions; they are analysed as they were performed and not simply as they appear on the page. We have heeded Susan Burney, who believed that even a pasticcio could have an overwhelming emotional effect if planned and executed with due regard to the drama. Coverage of revivals is generally omitted and detailed discussion is reserved for premières of original works or those for which substantial musical sources and contemporary criticism survive. To set Sheridan's regime in context and to compare it with the relatively stable and prosperous company he bought into, we need briefly to consider the season before he assumed control of the opera-house.

## II. The 1777–78 Season: The Co-Managers' Swan-Song

Repertoire:[1]

*Le due contesse*, Paisiello, libretto by Petrosellini, 4 November 1777 (7 performances); orig. Rome (Valle) 1776

*Creso*, Sacchini, libretto by Pizzi (revised), 8 November 1777 (16 performances); orig. Naples (S. Carlo) 1765

***Vittorina***, Piccinni, libretto by Goldoni, 16 December 1777 (2 performances) (p. 200)

*La vera costanza*, Anfossi adapted by Giordani, libretto by Puttini, 20 January 1778 (8 performances); orig. Rome (Dame) 1776

***Erifile, regina di Zacinto***, Sacchini, libretto by De Gamerra, 7 February 1778 (8 performances) (p. 197)

*L'amore artigiano*, Gassmann adapted by Giordani, libretto by Goldoni, 3 March 1778 (6 performances); orig. Vienna (Burg) 1767

*Il marchese villano*, pasticcio with numbers by Piccinni and Paisiello, libretto after Goldoni, 26 March 1778 (1 performance)

*La buona figliuola*, Piccinni, libretto by Goldoni, 2 April 1778 (3 performances); orig. Rome (Dame) 1760. London 1766, 1767, 1768, 1769, 1770, 1771, 1772, 1773, 1774, 1775, 1776, 1777

***La clemenza di Scipione***, J. C. Bach, librettist unknown, 4 April 1778 (8 performances) (p. 195)

***L'amore soldato***, Sacchini, libretto by Andrei after Tassi, 5 May 1778 (8 performances) (p. 199)

*Il re pastore*, T. Giordani, libretto after Metastasio, 30 May 1778 (2 performances)

[1] Information given in the following order: composer (conductor or arranger); librettist (or adapter); date of first performance this season; number of times performed this season; place and date of original production (for those works that have been only moderately revised); earlier London productions of this particular version. The operas are listed in order of first performance this season, and principal works discussed are shown in ***bold italic*** type. Note that within each season operas are not necessarily discussed in chronological order.

The final season of opera managed by Mesdames Brooke and Yates was, notwithstanding Fanny Burney's doubts about the latter's character, one of the most successful artistically in the later history of the King's Theatre. It was also apparently profitable, since there were no reports of unpaid performers. All but one of the eleven operas in repertoire this season were London premières, and six works were commissioned specifically for the King's Theatre. This level of creative initiative was not matched by any later manager. Apart from an informed and well-aimed complaint about the butchering of Gassmann's *L'amore artigiano* by inverting the order of the first two acts,[1] press reception was unusually positive. In a perceptive article in the *Public Advertiser* of 6 April 1778, an anonymous writer congratulated Brooke and Yates for securing the services of 'two of the best Composers now existing for Serious Operas', namely Antonio Sacchini and J. C. Bach: 'the Managers of the King's Theatre, by engaging both, have occasioned an Emulation between them, and given a Spur to their Invention, which cannot fail of adding considerably to the Amusement and Satisfaction of all Lovers of Music.'[2] The managers should really have been complimented only on the Bach commission, because Sacchini had been house composer since 1772 and had enjoyed unprecedented and almost uninterrupted success. But his invention and stamina were beginning to wane. Bach, by contrast, had not composed a full-length opera since *Carattaco* in 1767 and, according to Dr Burney and some recently discovered letters, had never been in favour with the London opera establishment, which was dominated by Italians.[3] Although Bach was for this season strictly speaking a 'house composer' and undoubtedly conducted *La clemenza di Scipione* from the harpsichord, he remained aloof from the King's Theatre and generally did not associate with its employees.[4] *Scipione* was well received, being

---

[1] *Morning Post*, 16–17 March 1778.

[2] This article is reprinted in *The Collected Works of Johann Christian Bach*, ix, ed. Ernest Warburton (New York and London: Garland, 1990), pp. xv–xvi.

[3] See *A General History*: the failure of *Adriano in Siria* (1765) 'seemed matter of great triumph to the Italians, who began to be jealous of the Germanic body of musicians at this time in the kingdom' (ii. 869); 'perhaps by the assistance of Italian politics, [Vento] had the honour of defeating Bach' (ii. 884). See *The Impresario's Ten Commandments*, 3, 48–51, for an earlier King's Theatre manager's indifference when Bach returned to the Continent in 1763.

[4] Pacchierotti, as Susan Burney reports, was offended when he was snubbed: 'I thought Mr Bach very Unkind, particularly as I brot. a letter of earnest recommendation with me from a Nobleman abroad to whom he owed a great deal' (fo. 66ʳ). Pacchierotti was also surprised to learn that Dr Burney did not have free admission to the Bach–Abel concerts and thus hardly ever attended them.

performed seven times after its première on 4 April 1778, which came too late in the season to permit a longer run. (Sacchini's *Creso*, which came out unusually early on the previous 8 November, achieved sixteen performances this season.)

## *Bach's* La clemenza di Scipione

Purely in terms of musical quality, Bach's *La clemenza di Scipione* represents the high-water mark of Italian opera in London during the second half of the eighteenth century. It would have been matched only by Haydn's *L'anima del filosofo*, which was of course unperformed. The King's Theatre was also fortunate during the 1777–78 season to have three capital singers: the tenor Valentin Adamberger, later to be Mozart's first Belmonte in *Die Entführung aus dem Serail*; the *prima donna seria* Franziska Danzi, who had established her reputation in her native Mannheim, and was now at the peak of her career; and Francesco Roncaglia, the soprano *primo uomo*, who, while perhaps not as esteemed as the other two, was nevertheless re-engaged for the 1780–81 season. Roncaglia never attained the fame enjoyed by Pacchierotti, who rather spiked his London career. The 1777–78 season is further distinguished by the publication of full orchestral scores of two works, Bach's *Scipione* (omitting the simple recitatives) and Sacchini's *L'amore soldato* (lacking finales and recitatives). These were almost the last Italian operas to be issued in London in any other than *Favourite Song* format or as collected excerpts. *Scipione*, which was printed by Welcher, is an exceptionally handsome and meticulous score. The cessation of the publication of substantial parts of Italian operas is partly a consequence of the rapid development of the ensemble finale about 1780, most examples of which were far too long and complex to interest music publishers who catered almost exclusively to an amateur domestic market. The absence of any monumental printed opera score after Bach's *Scipione* is also a tacit acknowledgement of a decline in the musical quality of Italian opera produced in London. It is unlikely that any masterpiece slipped through the hands of those printers who trawled King's Theatre scores in search of *Favourite Songs*.

Mesdames Brooke and Yates maintained a rough balance between serious and comic opera: that is, 4:6, if we disregard the revival of Piccinni's *La buona figliuola*, which was canonized by constant staging at the King's Theatre and should therefore probably be excluded from any statistical analysis of repertoire. Yet the emphasis in terms of effort and expense was, as always, squarely on *opera seria*. This is confirmed by the article in the *Public*

*Advertiser* quoted above, which is concerned only with the serious works: 'La Clemenza di Scipione, is the third new Serious Opera produced this Season at the King's Theatre: They are all excellent in their Kind.' Any comparison between Bach and Sacchini would be, as the anonymous journalist admits, invidious. Yet both composers, whilst writing to formula, are exquisitely sensitive to the drama; and both tailor their music to individual singers. But Sacchini adheres rather too strictly to formula; the chromaticism and flashes of counterpoint, which distinguish him from other Italian opera composers of his generation, are restricted mostly to the middle section of ternary-form arias and are rarely integrated with the whole. His melodies can be as memorable as Mozart's—for about two bars, after which they tend to lose their way, repeat themselves, and remain locked in the tonic key. His choruses, though dramatically introduced and conducive to noisy performance, show only rudimentary part-writing skills, but perhaps they were written this way purposely to reduce rehearsal time.

*La clemenza di Scipione* overcomes the potential tedium of *opera seria* purely on the strength of its music.[1] Bach's melodies are perhaps no more memorable than Sacchini's, but they are always beautifully phrased and directed by strong and varied harmonic progressions. The vocal passage-work, sometimes instrumentally conceived, is never mindlessly mechanical; instead, the roulades, scales, and arpeggios essential to *opera seria* are always controlled by the logic of the phrase, not pasted on as extensions, as is often the case with Sacchini's virtuoso arias. Furthermore, Bach's simple embellishments are completely idiomatic of what we now call the Viennese Classical Style. It has been claimed that Arsinda's *scena* in Act III, Scene iii, 'Ah si vada—Ma il piede vacilla', influenced the construction of 'Martern aller Arten' in *Die Entführung aus dem Serail*.[2] Perhaps there could be no greater accolade than to say *Scipione* 'sounds like Mozart', but this would be to abrogate responsibility to assess Bach's achievement in the context of Italian opera in London.

*Scipione* is a modified Metastasian drama with a 'simplified story line and the consequent brevity of the recitative',[3] but lacking the climactic action finales typical of the more radically modernized librettos that were beginning to be popular in London. The anonymous libretto was reportedly the

---

[1] For an introductory discussion, see *The Collected Works of Johann Christian Bach*, ix, pp. xv–xvii.
[2] Ibid., p. xvi.
[3] Ibid.

work of 'a Foreign Minister' residing at the English court.[1] With all attendant Roman military pomp, the opera depicts the proconsul as a hero
whose benevolence and wisdom are thrust upon him by circumstance rather
than found within himself by trial. Scipio wants to extract allegiance to
Rome from the conquered Princess Arsinda and Prince Luceio. Finally persuaded by the depth of their love for one another, he lifts the threat of execution. His famed clemency has the effect of shaming the lovers into
pledging their loyalty to Rome. The high points of the drama which best
lent themselves to Bach's music are a series of contrived farewells preceded
by anguished soliloquies, the clichés of Metastasian opera. The result is an
opera that seems an act too long.

## Sacchini's Erifile

Sacchini's *Erifile, regina di Zacinto*, to a libretto by Giovanni De Gamerra
(première 7 February 1778), is a far more interesting drama, well outside the
Metastasian mould, but with parallels to *Scipione*. It is a highly complex,
well-plotted story of treason, conspiracy, and, perhaps worst of all, hypocrisy. The regent of Zacynthus, Learco (sung by the tenor Adamberger),
hopes to gain the throne by murdering all members of the royal family
except Queen Erifile (Fräulein Danzi), whom he hopes to marry. Standing
in his way is Cleomene, Prince of Naxus (Roncaglia), Erifile's betrothed.
Learco and his fellow conspirators seize power in the midst of the first-act
finale, which has seemed set to culminate in the wedding of Erifile and
Cleomene in the Temple of Juno—a wild scene framed by a chorus of
priests and an early example of a multi-sectional action finale. Unfortunately, no music for this finale survives in *The Favourite Songs in the Opera
Erifile* (Bremner). In the second act Learco compounds his crime by pretending to be the people's choice for king. Having indignantly exposed his
hypocrisy, Erifile is condemned. She responds with 'Lieta quest'alma
amante', one of Sacchini's most remarkable arias, written to order for Franziska Danzi and the virtuoso oboist Lebrun, whom she was to marry later in
the season. As if to defy Learco's sentence of instant death, Erifile stands by
in silence during a 58-bar orchestral introduction, in which the oboist must
display technical prowess including difficult tonguing and finger-work and
an exposed high $f'''$.[2] The singer then duplicates this feat up to the

---

[1] *Public Advertiser*, 6 Apr. 1778.

[2] Le Texier commented in his *Ideas on the Opera*, 'those long and tedious ritornellos
should be suppressed, during which, a personage worked by the most violent passion has

197

modulation to the dominant, at which point she is joined in thirds by the oboe before she too achieves the 'Queen of the Night' high F. Madam Lebrun was later criticized for her instrumental precision and timbre, which supposedly resulted in a lack of passion, but this duet 'had a prodigious fine effect'.[1] The dungeon scene in Act II, Scene vii anticipates nineteenth-century Gothic opera: 'Pale ragged prisoners' sing a chorus from the 'bottom of a subterraneous prison with a glimmering light'.[2] The second-act duet-finale begins as Erifile drinks what she believes to be poison and then seems to die in Cleomene's arms. A reviewer noted that this scene was 'much more pathetic than is generally found in operas'.[3] Sacchini's setting, which is included in *The Favourite Songs*, is an accompanied recitative and Largo in B flat major, a concise duet that is almost the antithesis of the typical *seria* finale, in which anguish and torment are spun out to diminishing effect. Here, Erifile's simple tune is quickly coloured by D flats as the 'poison' begins to take effect, and the accompanying strings become more agitated. After a similarly panicky response to her distress, Cleomene repeats Erifile's original melody; she joins him in thirds punctuated by diminished seventh chords as the duet and the second act end with a whimper. In the reactionary world of *opera seria*, this was daringly irregular.

Beginning about 1780, London productions of revised Metastasian operas were often cut down to two acts, the third act having been rendered a redundant denouement by the weight given to the second-act finale. But the third act of *Erifile* is anything but anticlimactic. After Cleomene's despairing soliloquy sung over Erifile's tomb, 'Palpitante, e disperato', the appearance of the ghost of the murdered Egianeo and the revival of Erifile, who has only drunk a sleeping draught, the usurper Learco is stabbed during his own coronation, dying on stage in full view of the audience. Such explicit violence (apart from suicide) is well outside the etiquette of Metastasian drama and rare enough even in post-reform *opera seria*.[4] Unfortunately, not enough of the score survives to enable one to judge how Sacchini

---

time enough to walk two or three times round the stage, before he can give vent to his rage or despair' (18).

[1] *Public Advertiser*, 9 Feb. 1778.

[2] *Erifile* (London: T. Cadell, 1778).

[3] *Public Advertiser*, 9 Feb. 1778.

[4] See, however, Marita P. McClymonds, '"La morte di Semiramide ossia La vendetta di Nino" and the Restoration of Death and Tragedy to the Italian Operatic Stage in the 1780s and 90s', *Atti del XIV congresso della Società Internazionale di Musicologia*, iii (Bologna, 1987), 285–92.

depicted the blacker side of the drama (a lot would depend on the choruses, which were not included in *The Favourite Songs*), but the duet at the end of Act II, by its self-effacing brevity, does suggest a composer prepared to take big chances.

## Sacchini's L'amore soldato

Sacchini was the quintessential *opera seria* composer, fortunate to be employed by a theatre that was a bastion of the genre. But he also occasionally ventured into the very different world of comic opera, as with *L'amore soldato* (première 5 May 1778). The libretto is a revision by the house poet Andrei of a text by Niccolò Tassi.[1] It is a rather feeble story of an old miser (Don Anselmo) and his attempt to marry off his daughter and niece advantageously. The opera is set against the background of Belgrade under siege, and there is much military colour and comic by-play over the miser's cowardice. The published score (Bremner) includes eighteen numbers, but lacks most of the recitatives and all three finales. It graphically illustrates the huge gulf that then existed between the serious and comic styles of Italian opera. Sacchini's music is simple to the point of impoverishment. Although he employs basically the same forms as in his serious operas—rondeaus, cavatinas, and so forth—his comic pieces are diminutive by comparison. *Passaggi*, the life-blood of *opera seria*, are severely curtailed, and the text declamation is largely syllabic. Chromaticism is found only in the modulating sections of ternary arias, and any counterpoint (as near the end of the duet 'Piano un po', non tanto ardore' in Act III, Scene vii) wakes one from slumber. But such easy criticism misses the point of this and similar lyrical farces: the music is rarely more than the means by which the *actors* declaimed their words. In most cases, these works are more fairly judged as plays than as operas. Interest lies almost exclusively in the drama, the acting skills of the *buffo* cast, and the pleasant effect of the *primo basso*'s patter-like delivery and the occasional catchy tune. How the King's Theatre audience, almost completely ignorant of the Italian language, could have tolerated such works for most of the second half of the eighteenth century is one of the wonders of opera history.

*L'amore soldato* is a straight farce, in that it has no semi-serious characters. Of the original singers, only Maria Prudom (Semplicina) and Leopoldo De Michele (Pasquino), *terza donna* and *ultima parte*, respectively, of the

---

[1] See *The London Stage*, Part 5, i. 169; see also Sartori, nos. 1747–58.

company, also performed serious roles this season. The opera was mainly a vehicle for the *basso* Antonio Rossi, the *primo buffo* who acted the miser. Guglielmo Jermoli (tenor) and his wife, as Don Faustino and Lisandrina, were the romantic leads. The best of the pieces that have survived is probably Don Anselmo's 'Vedrai con tuo periglio' in Act II, Scene vi. It begins *maestoso* in D major, with two trumpets and oboe augmenting the ubiquitous strings, bluster meant to reinforce the miser's feigned courage. His cowardly asides produce a complete change of style, with sinuous unison writing knotted with augmented melodic seconds. With the obligatory shift to *allegro assai*, Sacchini was able to generate sufficient energy to propel Signor Rossi into an applauded exit. To judge the whole opera by such unrepresentative snapshots is, however, grossly unfair, because the enormous finales are omitted from the printed score. A note at the end of Don Faustino's prolix aria in Act II, Scene xi, 'Non crediate, o luci care', states almost apologetically, 'to be continued', which is a marker for the missing finale. The loss of the second-act finale is especially regrettable, because the libretto suggests an unusual design. Don Faustino and Pasquino have organized a late-evening serenade for Lisandrina and Semplicina. When Don Anselmo appears in a night-gown to complain about the noise, one expects the crescendo of confusion and misunderstanding that characterizes at least 90 per cent of all second-act *buffa* finales. But the pairs of lovers and would-be lovers, during the course of their quartet, persuade Anselmo to go back to bed; chaos is thus averted and the act ends quietly. Pleasant but hardly challenging sums up this opera.

## Piccinni's Vittorina

A much more substantial drama is to be found in another comic opera offered this season, *Vittorina* (première 16 December 1777). It seems to have attracted no contemporary comment or scholarly attention, despite being the only work that Niccolò Piccinni, the most successful opera composer of the age, wrote especially for the King's Theatre. Mystery surrounds this commission. In 1763 Felice Giardini while manager tried to recruit Piccinni as a house composer, offering him quite exceptionally the chance to choose his own libretto: 'This may give him credit and acquaintance in this Country, which may prove very beneficial to him against he comes over himself.'[1] Piccinni never came to England, yet *La buona figliuola*, which was first

---

[1] *The Impresario's Ten Commandments*, 14.

performed in London on 25 November 1766, was to become the most frequently revived of all Italian operas at the King's Theatre, achieving 107 performances by 1796, more than twice the number of its closest rival during roughly the same period.[1] What contacts Piccinni may have had in London are unknown, but evidently Mesdames Brooke and Yates or someone closely connected with the opera-house was in correspondence with him. Postal commissions were not unknown at this time; for example, Paisiello's *La locanda* was composed especially for the Pantheon opera-house in 1790–91, though Paisiello never crossed the English Channel. *Vittorina*, to a libretto by Goldoni, was performed only twice, and none of the music was published. A manuscript of Acts I and III survives in the Naples Conservatorio library.[2]

Although the libretto has all the cynical wit and depth of character that one would expect from Goldoni, the story was simply a restirring of a stock plot: the Baron of Sarzana and the Cavaliere (father and son) discover they are in love with the same girl, Vittorina; their puzzlement at why they should find a mere chambermaid so desirable is explained when Vittorina turns out to be of noble birth. But Goldoni fashions this into a *dramma giocoso* that includes two serious parts, the Count of Ripalta (sung by Giuseppe Coppola from the *seria* troupe) and the Marchesa (Maria Prudom). Goldoni gives the story a twist that would have elevated this opera well above the usual King's Theatre fare: Donna Isabella, fallen on hard times and living in the country, has entrusted her daughter (Vittorina) to the care of her cousin, the Marchesa, who treats the poor girl like a servant. When Vittorina proves more popular with the gallants and more socially astute than her guardian, the Marchesa's vicious snobbery is thus exposed. Without studying the score, one can only speculate on why this opera seems to have misfired completely in London. Until about 1785, when Gallini began to introduce semi-serious Viennese operas such as Paisiello's *Il re Teodoro*, the King's Theatre repertoire was largely polarized into *opera seria* and broad farce. *Vittorina* fell somewhere in between, and its bitter attack on class hypocrisy may not have appealed to subscribers, the large majority of whom were aristocrats.

To sum up the last season of Italian opera under the old management, one finds a company that was healthy, both financially and artistically. The dynamic co-managers were probably concerned more about engaging great

[1] Petty, 363.
[2] Dennis Libby *et al.*, 'Piccinni', *Opera Grove*, iii. 1004.

singers than great composers. Yet the concentration of new works by Sacchini, Bach, and Piccinni in this one season can hardly be a coincidence, and the extent to which *Erifile* and *Vittorina* exceeded the norms of their respective genres is remarkable if not audacious. The opera company had only one notable weakness: the *primo uomo* Roncaglia was not a singer of the first rank and certainly no match for the technically dazzling Fräulein Danzi. Roncaglia was not directly criticized, but neither did Bach or Sacchini lavish their best efforts on him. When Sheridan took over the management, he simply preserved the *status quo* in most respects but was fortunate to have the services of a *primo uomo* who could, if necessary, carry the entire company on his shoulders.

## III. The 1778–79 Season: Pacchierotti's Début

Repertoire:

*L'avaro deluso*, Sacchini, libretto after Bertati's *Calandrano*, 24 November 1778 (5 performances)

**Demofoonte**, pasticcio arranged by Bertoni, libretto by Andrei or Badini after Metastasio, 28 November 1778 (14 performances) (p. 205)

*La frascatana*, Paisiello with additions by Perez, Anfossi, and others, libretto after Livigni, 22 December 1778 (6 performances); orig. Venice (S. Samuele) 1774. London 1776

*Artaserse*, Bertoni, libretto after Metastasio, 23 January 1779 (5 performances); orig. Forlì (Nuovo) 1776

*Zemira e Azore*, Grétry, libretto trans. of Marmontel, 23 February 1779 (11 performances); orig. Fontainebleau 1771 (p. 212)

*Enea e Lavinia*, Sacchini, libretto by Bottarelli, 25 March 1779 (8 performances) (p. 207)

*La buona figliuola*, Piccinni, libretto by Goldoni, 29 April 1779 (3 performances); orig. Rome (Dame), 1760. London 1766 → 1777

**La governante**, Bertoni, libretto by Badini after Sheridan, 15 May 1779 (7 performances) (p. 216)

*L'Olimpiade*, pasticcio arranged by Bertoni(?) with numbers by Gluck, Paisiello, and Bertoni, libretto after Metastasio, 29 May 1779 (6 performances). London (pasticcios based on the same libretto) 1765, 1770, 1774

The first season of Sheridan's regime, despite having to follow the co-managers' brilliant swan-song, does in retrospect feel like a promising new beginning. Paradoxically, Sheridan retained almost all the singers from the previous season; this continuity is noteworthy in itself, because there was almost always a significant turnover of higher-ranking performers from year to year at the King's Theatre, regardless of manager. But the effect of the new broom was felt in the appointment of Gasparo Pacchierotti, who replaced Roncaglia. With the new *primo uomo* came Bertoni who, despite his age (he was born in 1725), heralded a simpler, clearer musical style, capable of being both nobler and more cloying in its harmonic and contrapuntal *naïveté* than that of Sacchini. But the most interesting feature of the new regime, at least from a historical perspective, was the attempt to inject non-Italian elements into the repertoire: this season saw the first production of an *opéra-comique* at the King's Theatre, Grétry's *Zémire et Azor* (albeit in Italian translation as *Zemira e Azore*), while Bertoni's *La governante* was based on an English model, Sheridan's *The Duenna*. Both were striking innovations. Perhaps the former was produced at the behest of Le Texier, who knew well the merits of *opéra-comique* and had the full measure of Grétry and Marmontel's success in their own country. But the driving force behind this extraordinary production might equally have been Sheridan, who had produced an English adaptation of Grétry's opera by Sir George Collier, *Selima and Azor*, with music by Thomas Linley sen. at Drury Lane (where Sheridan was proprietor and manager) in December 1776.[1]

All the virtuoso male sopranos engaged by the King's Theatre had attracted highly partisan supporters and detractors. Only a few were re-engaged for more than two or three seasons: earlier in the century Senesino had been exceptional for remaining popular with London audiences over a number of years. In the second half of the century, frequent and rapid changes in vocal style within the otherwise reactionary formal structure of *opera seria* required a constant supply of strong new voices. Castrati quickly wore out their welcome in London and were not rehired. Susan Burney paints a sad picture of the once revered Giusto Ferdinando Tenducci, now a pathetic hanger-on at the opera-house, joining in with other detractors who did everything but hiss during Pacchierotti's arias (fo. 114$^r$). On another occasion Pacchierotti sung 'so *perfectly* in all particulars, that I had malice enough to rejoice at the mortification [Tenducci] must have felt' (fo. 119$^r$). Venanzio Rauzzini was another castrato cast out at a fairly young age by the King's Theatre and forced to turn to teaching and composition. Pacchierotti acknowledged his 'great merit & talents', but believed that he had become shop-worn in London. He advised Rauzzini to go back to Italy, 'where in many places he would be received with open arms, & that in a few years he might return here with added splendour' (fo. 65$^v$). This is a ploy that Pacchierotti himself later used, as he made two triumphal returns to the King's Theatre. But he also enjoyed the longest continuous period of popularity in

[1] See Roger Fiske, *English Theatre Music in the Eighteenth Century*, 2nd edn. (Oxford: Oxford University Press, 1986), 327 and 419.

London of any castrato during the second half of the century. Whether he was, as the Burneys believed, the greatest singer of the age is questionable, but he was certainly durable, adaptable to changes in style, generally good-tempered, and a fine musician.

Needless to say, Pacchierotti's reputation had preceded him. The exact circumstances and negotiations that led to his engagement at the King's Theatre are unknown, but he had been one of the leading castrati on the Italian circuit since the early 1770s, and reports of his singing had been published in England. Burney cited a passage in Patrick Brydone's *A Tour through Sicily and Malta* (1773) as being particularly influential in mobilizing public opinion. Letter xxxiv describes the opera-house in Palermo. His main subject, the *prima donna* Caterina Gabrielli, came to the King's Theatre in 1775–76, so London audiences could judge Brydone's account:

The first woman is Gabrieli; who is certainly the greatest singer in the world: and those that sing on the same theatre with her, must be capital, otherwise they never can be attended to. This indeed has been the fate of all the other performers here, except Pacherotti [*sic*]; and he too gave himself up for lost, on hearing her first performance.—It happened to be an air of execution, exactly adapted to her voice, which she exerted in so astonishing a manner, that before it was half done, poor Pacherotti burst out a crying, and ran in behind the scenes; lamenting that he had been prevailed on to appear on the same stage with so wonderful a singer; where his small talents must not only be totally lost, but where he must ever be accused of a presumption, which he hoped was foreign to his character.

It was with some difficulty they could prevail on him to appear again, but from an applause well merited, both from his talents and his modesty, he soon began to pluck up a little courage; and in the singing of a tender air, addressed to Gabrieli in the character of a lover, even she herself, as well as the audience, is said to have been moved.

Though Pacchierotti's engagement was greeted with the usual hoop-la and his success in London was immediate, the former *primo uomo* Roncaglia had in no sense been sacked or disgraced. Susan Burney knew as early as November 1779 that Roncaglia was to be re-engaged at the King's Theatre for the 1780–81 season (fo. 28ʳ), which she accepted as *fait accompli*, though of course she and the rest of the Burneys preferred Pacchierotti. On 10 February 1780 she reported that

Ly. Mary Duncan [a great supporter of Pacchierotti's and reputedly his patron] & Ly. Edgcumbe (by my *Father's* advice) set on foot a *Petition* lately to the Managers, wch. has been sign'd I believe by almost every subscriber to the opera, to beg that after next year, when *Roncaglia's* engagement must take place, they wd. reengage Sigr. Pacchierotti to return here for two years more. (fo. 69ᵛ)

This obviously partisan act does not necessarily imply the subscribers thought Roncaglia a bad singer.[1]

## Demofoonte

Pacchierotti's London début on 28 November 1778 in the pasticcio *Demofoonte*, and indeed even the first general rehearsal at which he sang *sotto voce* with a heavy cold (welcome to England), are vividly described by Dr Burney.[2] But what of the opera itself? It was a safe, conservative choice. Pasticcios—which could be put together quickly and, if the constituent numbers were well chosen, could guarantee a box-office success—often opened a season. This was a good way to ease Pacchierotti and Bertoni, who arranged and conducted *Demofoonte*, into the London system. The choice of this Metastasio libretto—adapted anonymously, but probably by either Andrei or Badini—is significant. It is an old-style, three-act *opera seria* without extended finales, whose static aria 'plateaus' made it ideal for substitutions. The libretto also had the advantage of not having been used at the King's Theatre since 1766 (in Mattia Vento's setting). It is a powerful drama about a king (Demofoonte) who, in secretly trying to protect his daughter (Dircea) from his own irrational and unjust law, causes his supposed son and heir Timante to believe he has committed incest. This libretto afforded Pacchierotti (Timante) several opportunities to display the anguished pathos for which he was famous. There are also the obligatory *bravura* arias, such as 'Non temer bell'idol' in Act II, Scene iv (set by Bertoni), but Pacchierotti was not known for vocal fireworks. Mount Edgcumbe, who also attended the first performance, immediately recognized the singer's strengths. His report was echoed by countless later critics and opera fans. Pacchierotti was

conscious that the chief delight of singing, and his own supreme excellence, lay in touching expression, and exquisite pathos. . . . As an actor, with many disadvantages of person, for he was tall and awkward in his figure, and his features were plain, he was nevertheless forcible and impressive: for he felt warmly, had excellent judgment, and was an enthusiast in his profession. His recitative was inimitably fine, so that even those who did not understand the language could not fail to comprehend, from his countenance, voice, and action, every sentiment he expressed. (*Musical Reminiscences*, 13–14)

---

[1] See also Burney, *General History*, ii. 890.    [2] Ibid. 887–9.

To build anticipation, the first appearance of the *primo uomo* was usually delayed until well into the opening act. But in *Demofoonte*, Timante begins the opera—in simple recitative. Nor is recitative minimized elsewhere; the libretto includes pages of the stuff, and even the important second scene of Act II, in which Timante pleads with Demofoonte to spare his beloved Dircea (whom he has secretly married), is conducted entirely in recitative.

The title-page of the libretto (G. Bigg, 1778) states that Bertoni composed 'the most Part of the Music', which may have been true. But only three of the seven pieces included in *The Favourite Songs in the Opera Demofoonte* (W. Napier) are ascribed to him. The other composers are Mysliveček, Monza, and Sarti. The best of Bertoni's contributions is probably the aria for Pacchierotti in Act I, Scene ii, 'Sperai vicino il lido', the first of a series of pleas that Dircea be spared the sacrifice that hangs tediously over the entire plot. In F major, evidently Pacchierotti's favourite key, the introductory *andantino sostenuto* is reworked as one of the themes in the main *allegro* section. (See Ex. 4.1.) As a whole, the aria is rather static harmonically, and the vocal passage-work mechanical. Only in the coda, which exploits Pacchierotti's ability to leap between his tenor and soprano ranges, does the aria show any signs of life. (See Ex. 4.2 on page 208.) A somewhat better piece for Pacchierotti was 'Misero pargoletto' by Carlo Monza, which is introduced at the climax of the drama in Act III, Scene iv, when Timante addresses his son Olinto, having just been told that the child is the product of incest. The pathos of this aria, especially the purple setting of the word 'misero', is as gratuitous as parading the child itself around the stage, but was apparently very effective on the night.

In an entirely different class from Bertoni's arias are the two by Mysliveček for Dircea, sung by Antonia Bernasconi, who replaced Madam Lebrun as *prima donna seria* for the 1778–79 season. 'In te spero' (Act I, Scene i) and 'Padre, perdona' (Act I, Scene iv), though introduced too early in the opera to have had much dramatic impact, are rich harmonically, with difficult but well-integrated vocal ornaments and tight motivic connections between various sections. 'In te spero', which Dr Burney thought highly enough of to teach to Queeney Thrale in summer 1779,[1] has a sophisticated formal structure, with a chain of distinctive melodies developed in the manner of Mozart. These arias may have been wasted on Signora Bernasconi, whose reputation was eclipsed by the return of Madam Lebrun in 1779, but they

---

[1] Susan Burney, fo. 6ᵛ. See also Valerie Rumbold, 'Music Aspires to Letters: Charles Burney, Queeney Thrale and the Streatham Circle', *Music & Letters*, 74 (1993), 24–38.

Ex. 4.1. Ferdinando Bertoni, 'Sperai vicino il lido', from *Demofoonte*

set a high standard for the rest of the season and suggest that this pasticcio was assembled with some care for both music and drama.

## Sacchini's Enea e Lavinia

*Demofoonte* was merely a warm-up for Pacchierotti and a pot-boiler for Bertoni. The main serious attractions of the season were Bertoni's reworking of Metastasio's *Artaserse* (première 23 January 1779) and Sacchini's *Enea e*

Ex. 4.2. Bertoni, 'Sperai vicino il lido', from *Demofoonte*

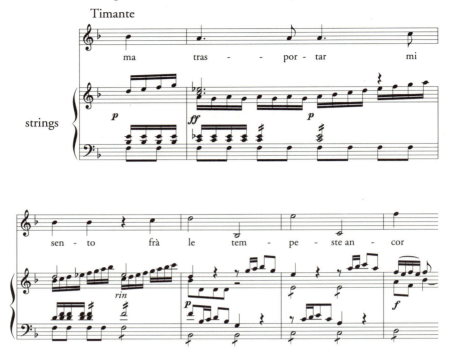

*Lavinia* (25 March 1779). By far the more sophisticated and challenging of the two was the Sacchini, a spectacular entertainment with lavish décor, choral scenes (involving priests of the Temple of Janus, furies, companions of Discord and War, fauns and dryads, bacchants, Rutulian and Trojan soldiers). There are also three extended ballet sequences, the second and third being directly incorporated into Bottarelli's fine libretto while the first is allegorically related to the action of the opera *per se*. The work seems to have attracted little if any commentary in the newspapers, but Pacchierotti, Susan Burney, and her friends were still talking enthusiastically about it and singing arias from it a year later (see below). *Enea e Lavinia* is a full-blown, post-reform *opera seria* with a sextet finale in Act II, rage arias, and other conventional features. Yet it also departs from the model not only in the inclusion of integral ballets and supernatural effects but also the anachronistic *deus ex machina* (Juno appears and even sings in Act I, Scene iii, and Act III, Scene vii). Much of this is of course taken from the twelfth book of the *Aeneid.* Bottarelli and Sacchini portray Aeneas (Pacchierotti) not as a

conventional *opera seria* hero, but as Virgil's opportunistic and easily manipulated protagonist. In suing for the hand of Lavinia and thus effectively trying to usurp the kingdom of Latium, Aeneas is plagued by his disastrous
past. This equivocal characterization indirectly adds an important dimension to Queen Amata (Signora Pozzi), who would otherwise be a conventional villainess plotting to prevent her daughter (Lavinia) from marrying
the man she loves. But in the opera, the queen's opposition to Aeneas is
based on knowledge of his treatment of Dido at Carthage. Perhaps the most
dramatic episode (there are many to choose from) is Act II, Scenes i–iii, in
which Lavinia sings herself to sleep ('Placido sonno vieni'),[1] then 'The stage
becomes dark, and the ghost of Dido appears to Lavinia in a dream'.
Recounting the circumstances of her horrible death, Dido warns Lavinia
that Aeneas is a perfidious coward. Only by the sheer beauty of his singing
in Scene iii ('Serene tornate') does Aeneas regain Lavinia's confidence,
which provokes the queen to solicit the help of a chorus of bacchants. They
enchant Lavinia into rejecting Aeneas in favour of Turnus.

The second-act finale, just before which Aeneas and Turnus agree to settle their differences in a single combat, is a typical scene of alarm and confusion. But, quite extraordinarily for London operas, it incorporates an
extended ballet sequence with music advertised as being by Carl Stamitz.
He was in London from 1777 until about 1779 and could have composed
new music for this ballet, though it may have been put together from his
instrumental works, some of which had just been published there.[2] In the
ballet the myth of Mars and Venus is adapted so that Vulcan, after being
caught in the net he designed for his adulterous wife, forgives Venus, who
then orders the Cyclops to make a suit of armour to protect her son Aeneas
in his combat with Turnus. Although it concludes with a general country
dance, the ballet never loses sight of the drama. The last act is an anticlimax
(as it almost always is in three-act serious operas), despite the impressive
machines erected to facilitate the battle. Turnus is perfunctorily killed during a symphony (which does not survive), and Juno blesses the union of
Aeneas and Lavinia in the final ballet.

*The Favourite Songs in the Opera Enea e Lavinia* (W. Napier) includes
just four pieces by Sacchini, three of which are taken from the episode in

---

[1] A stage direction states that she sits down to sing (G. Bigg, 1799).

[2] *The London Stage*, Part 5, i. 243; see also Jennifer M. Pickering, 'Printing, Publishing
and the Migration of Sources: The Case of Carl Stamitz', *Fontes Artis Musicae*, 38/2 (1991),
130–8.

Act II discussed above: 'Serene tornate' (Enea—Pacchierotti); 'Non più le vie secrete' (Amata—Pozzi with chorus); and 'Incerto è il mio core' (Latino—Adamberger). This is good Sacchini, though the aria with the bacchants, a *maestoso* in G major, is disappointing: the strophic construction of the aria is a too facile way of achieving closure, and the homophonic, rapidly declaimed choruses are a limp response to the stage direction: 'After this chorus the Queen runs backwards and forwards over the stage, and at last stands still.' Both arias for Pacchierotti are simple andantes of some beauty. The middle section of each exploits his tenor voice, which was extraordinary in a castrato with a serviceable top *c ′′′* and even, when just fooling around, *f ′′′*.[1] For his part, Sacchini achieved pathos with the simplest of means. In 'Rasserena i tuoi bei rai' (Act III, Scene vi), for instance, he often lets the singer pick up a line in mid-phrase, as if choked with emotion. (See Ex. 4.3.) That so little of the score survives is unfortunate, despite the probable pastiche composition of the ballet accompaniments, because these arias are well in tune with Bottarelli's libretto and not merely showpieces for the singers.

Susan Burney's 'most favourite of all Duets', 'Non parli? In me si gela' from Act I, Scene vii, was still quite the rage in 1780 amongst the Pacchierotti-ites. At Lady Clarges's soirée concert in April of that year, the company called for the castrato to sing the duet with their hostess. But Lady Clarges demurred, claiming the soprano part was too high for her, and gave way to the promising young amateur Louisa Margaret Harris: 'in consequence of this it was half murdered'. Miss Harris

lost all her courage the moment she began wth. Pacchierotti, & sung so low one cd. scarce hear her, & in no respect well—husky, frightened, tremulous, & in short in such a manner as to pain all that had Ears for her. Pacchierotti, who now sung the part of Bernasconi, was obliged to keep an eternal check on himself in order not to overpower his *compagne*, & to transpose several passages wch. were too high for him—so that the poor Duet was indeed sadly spoil'd. (fos. 108ᵛ–109ʳ)[2]

---

[1] Susan Burney gave Fanny an account of an informal evening when Paccheriotti 'played all sort of tricks wth. his voice—running up & down as high & as low as he could. I knew his compass to be such that he cd. sing *Tenor* songs, but did not before *suspect* he could vie wth. Agujari & Danzi in their *alt-itudes*—Will you believe me when I assure, & with great truth, that in one of his runs he ran fairly up to the highest F of the Harpsichord', that is, *f ′′′* (fo. 44ʳ).

[2] On another occasion Miss Harris sang Bernasconi's 'Placido sonno' well enough to make Susan suspect that she had been having lessons with Sacchini, a renowned vocal coach, 'but *no* teaching however constant or excellent cd. do much wth. her, for she has no soul' (fos. 77ᵛ–78ʳ).

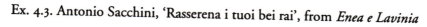

Ex. 4.3. Antonio Sacchini, 'Rasserena i tuoi bei rai', from *Enea e Lavinia*

Pacchierotti himself was disparaging about the opera and its composer. On 13 January 1780 *chez* Burney, he sang 'the Rondo of *Enea e Lavinia*, much against the grain I believe, & he took himself off in it in a ridiculous style, tho' I fancy he only meant to cast his *ridicule* on *M. Sacchini*'s *air* as he call'd it. He don't love him *too* much!' (fo. 63ʳ). These and other anecdotes nevertheless point to the opera's success, but Lady Mount Edgcumbe and 'a hundred more people' complained that it lacked a *cantabile* for Pacchierotti, that is, a slow, sustained cavatina or other short piece. The singer himself, presumably out of loyalty to Bertoni, refused to let Sacchini 'make him a Cantabile' in *Enea e Lavinia*.[1] We should note, however, that these remarks were made at least a year after the event and may be unreliable. Nothing is known about the compositional process or the première, except that Sacchini was too ill with gout to conduct, so 'there was no *Maestro*!' (fo. 98ᵛ).

### Grétry's Zemira e Azore

The French influence on *Enea e Lavinia*, especially evident in the mixing of chorus and ballet, had been noticeable in earlier King's Theatre productions. But Grétry and Marmontel's *Zémire et Azor* (2 February 1779) was something completely new. This *opéra-comique* had already attained unprecedented success throughout Europe, becoming the French equivalent of Piccinni's *La buona figliuola*. Often performed in Italian, it was just as often adapted with totally new music.[2] But the King's production, whilst using Mattia Verazi's Italian translation[3] and with new recitatives (replacing the spoken dialogue), is 'remarkably faithful' to the original (Charlton). Since the 1730s the repertoire of the King's Theatre had been strictly Italian, so the production of an *opéra-comique* was a radical departure. In 1779 the company was clearly divided into comic and serious troupes, and the singers were highly specialized, with only one or two middle-ranking performers comfortable in both *opera buffa* and *seria*. But Grétry's music for Azor (Azore), Zémire (Zemira), and Sander (Sandro) is technically too difficult and too overtly sentimental to have appealed to the rude talents of the King's *buffi* and too lacking in passage-work and *cantabile* arias to have

---

[1] According to Lady Clarges, as reported by Susan Burney, fo. 76ᵛ.

[2] See David Charlton, *Grétry and the Growth of Opéra-comique* (Cambridge: Cambridge University Press, 1986), 100.

[3] First heard in Mannheim in 1776 with music by Jommelli (see Sartori). Interestingly, in this production Francesco Roncaglia sang Azor and Franziska Danzi sang Zemira; neither singer was engaged at the King's Theatre during the 1778–79 season.

interested the *virtuosi*. Grétry's orchestration was far subtler and more complex than anything Cramer and his band had ever coped with, at least in the opera-house, with the exception of Bach's *La clemenza di Scipione*; one shudders to think what the notoriously poor wind section did to the delicate scoring of the famous 'magic picture' scene in Act III. And the drama, Marmontel's wonderful rendition of *La belle et la bête*, with its multi-layered symbolism and magic, was like nothing ever seen at the King's Theatre. In short, this opera fell so squarely between stools that one is amazed it was even attempted, let alone presented with so few alterations.

Table 5 on pages 214–15, which compares the original disposition of numbers with that of the 1779 King's Theatre production, shows a high degree of correspondence, when one considers that virtually every other London production of a Continental work underwent extensive revision. Details of the London libretto show that the King's Theatre production was based on a copy of Marmontel's original, which was rearranged into three acts. For example, Ali's first aria (no. 1), in which he tries to convince himself that the storm has passed even though it still rages in the orchestra, has the following footnote: 'The accompanyment does not agree with the words.' The most important change to the original not shown in Table 5 is that Azor, created for a tenor, was sung by Angiolo Monanni, called Manzoletto, the King's Theatre's *secondo uomo*, and almost certainly a castrato.[1] Further changes involved the addition of 'Vanne ma ti rammenta' to the second act. This is a duet for Azore and Zemira, which replaced the spoken dialogue that ends Grétry's third act. Though perhaps no improvment on the original, the duet underscores the importance of the ring that Azore gives to Zemira to release her from his power but also to symbolize their as yet unspoken love. The King's Theatre production made two substitutions, neither very disruptive of the drama: Azor's aria (no. 21) was replaced by 'Ah! sì, l'ho ancor presente' (sung by Sandro), a kind of mad song in which he sees the flaming chariot that brings Zemira back home; and 'Senza te bell'idol mio' in Act III, Scene iii, which replaced Azor's soliloquy (no. 23). This Italian aria was moved from its original position in the last scene about a week before the première, as can be determined from Larpent MS 469. The Italian version of no. 23, which was discarded, began with the words 'Tu, Zemira, che adorai'.

---

[1] The company normally carried only one tenor, at the time Adamberger, nearly always identified as such in librettos and newspaper advertisements. The *secondo uomo* traditionally sang middle-ranking roles in *opera seria* and the romantic lead in *opera buffa*, despite being a soprano or alto. Susan Burney found Manzoletto a pale imitation of Pacchierotti (fo. 37ʳ).

TABLE 5. *Comparison of numbers in* Zémire et Azor *and* Zemira e Azore

| | Fontainebleau 1771 | | London 1779 |
|---|---|---|---|
| | Act I.i | | I.i |
| (1) | L'orage va cesser (Ali) | = | Il tempo è accommodato |
| (2) | Le malheur me rend (Sander) | = | Sol m'avanza la mia costanza |
| (3) | Les esprits, dont on (Ali) | = | Degli spirti al mondo mai |
| (4) | Le tems est beau (duet) | = | Non piove più |
| | I.ii | | I.ii |
| (5) | La pauvre enfant (Sander) | = | Ah! non potea—Sapere allor |
| (6) | Ne vas pas me tromper (Azor) | = | Pietà non troverai |
| (7) | Symphonie qui exprime le vol du nuage | = | Symphony which expresses the the flight of a cloud |
| | II.i | | I.iii |
| (8) | Veillons, mes sœurs (trio) | = | Vegliam, vegliamo |
| | II.ii | | I.iv |
| (9) | Rose chérie (Zémire) | = | Rosa vezzosa |
| | II.iii–iv | | I.vi |
| (10) | Plus de voyage (Ali) | = | Per me certo più non viaggio |
| | II.v–vii | | I.viii |
| (11) | Je vais faire (Sander) | = | [recitative] |
| | II.viii | | |
| (12) | Je veux le voir (duet) | = | Vederlo io vuò |
| (13) | Entr'acte | = | [entr'acte] |
| | III.i | | II.i |
| (14) | Ah! quel tourment (Azor) | = | D'amor penando |
| | III.ii | | II.ii |
| (15) | Rassure mon père (duet) | = | Al padre, deh vola! |
| | III.iv | | II.iv |
| (16) | Entrée des Genies | = | dancing genii and fairies |
| | | | II.v |
| (17) | Du moment qu'on aime (Az.) | = | Se amore l'inspira |
| | | + | Genius of instrumental music |
| (18) | La fauvette (Zémire) | = | L'usignuolo che al nido |
| | III.vi | | II.vi |
| (19) | Ah! laissez-moi (ensemble) | = | Ah per pietade, oh Dio! |
| | | + | Vanne ma ti rammenta (duet) |

TABLE 5 *continued*

| | Fontainebleau 1771 | | London 1779 |
|---|---|---|---|
| | III.vii | | |
| (20) | Entr'acte | = | ? dance |
| | IV.i | | III.i |
| (21) | J'en suis encore (Azor) | *repl. by* | Ah! sì, l'ho ancor (Sandro) |
| | IV.ii | | III.ii |
| (22) | Ah! je tremble (quartet) | = | Ah se a noi venisse oh Dei! |
| | IV.iii | | III.iii |
| (23) | Toi, Zémire, que j'adore | = | Tu, Zemira, che adorai[a] |
| | IV.iv | | III.iv |
| (24) | Azor! en vain ma voix (Zém.) | = | Azor invano |
| | IV.v–vi | | III.vi |
| (25) | Amour! quand ta rigueur (cho.) | = | Amor fallace |

[a] This aria appears in Larpent MS 469 but is replaced by 'Senza te, bell'idol mio' (Azore) in the printed libretto. According to the Larpent manuscript, 'Senza te' appeared originally in the last scene, eight lines before the final chorus.

The substitute aria 'Senza te, bell'idol mio' is included in *The Favourite Songs in the Opera Zemira e Azore* (W. Napier), 15–21, attributed to Bertoni. The five other pieces in this collection (Grétry's nos. 8, 9, 14, 17, and 19) are virtually identical with those in Houbaut's full score (Paris, [1772]), except for the new Italian words. Bertoni's substitute aria for Manzoletto does the composer little credit. It is a big two-part piece in E flat major (a ternary-form *allegretto* coupled to an *allegro*), melodically impoverished to the point of embarrassment. The only other major interpolation was in Act II, Scene v of the London libretto, where Zemira is entertained in Azore's palace by the geniuses of the arts. Still terrified by his monstrous appearance, she hears an enchanted melody played by the Genius of Instrumental Musick, listed in the *dramatis personae* as 'Signor Hochbrucher'. This was the composer Christian Hochbrucker who, according to the advertisements, played the pedal harp in this scene.[1] This instrument was very popular for accompaniments in London Italian operas during the 1780s and 90s. *Zemira e Azore* became a perennial favourite of the King's Theatre audience and took its

[1] *The London Stage*, Part 5, i. 236.

place among the top twenty most frequently revived operas up to 1815.[1] All the more puzzling, then, is the lack of contemporaneous comment, for it could simply not have been dismissed as just another *opera buffa*.

### Bertoni's La governante

Another anomalous production of the first year of Sheridan's regime was Bertoni and Badini's *La governante*, which was brought out rather late in the season (première 15 May 1779). It still managed to achieve seven performances and should therefore probably be considered a success, though it was never revived. Badini wanted to curry favour with the new owner-manager and obviously hoped to capitalize on the tremendous popularity of *The Duenna*. He dedicated the libretto 'To the author of The Duenna'[2] and advertised its connection with the English opera. In an explanatory preface (a rare feature in late eighteenth-century London librettos) he mentions some difficulties encountered in adapting the model:

The Ground of this Opera is taken from the admired Duenna of Mr. Sheridan. It was my intention to make a literal translation, or at least to preserve the principal beauties of the original; but the *peculiar delicacy* of the Italian Stage, and some other whimsical circumstances, absolutely compelled me to alter the plot, to cut off the humourous scene of the Friars, and to over-turn the whole Opera twice. This, I hope, will be a sufficient apology for all the false steps of my Muse; for it is no wonder, if bound in the fetters of prejudice, she does not move with the grace she ought. . . . I flatter myself, however, that *The Governante*, as it is, will be deemed above the vulgar standard of Italian Operas, and not unworthy the usual kind indulgence of an English audience.     Badini

His 'intention to make a literal translation' is evident in much of the first act, which follows Sheridan fairly closely, but then the two dramas diverge sharply. Leaving aside the begged question about the 'delicacy' or 'vulgar standard' of Italian opera (Badini wants it both ways), he had not appreciated that *dramma giocoso* and English opera are basically different creatures of the theatre. The functions of *recitativo semplice* and spoken dialogue on one side, and arias and airs on the other, are not really analogous. *The Duenna* is a spoken play in which the actors are from time to time able to reflect on their actions in simple, brief songs. In *opera buffa* of this period, some arias are also short, tuneful, and dramatically inert, but they more often advance the plot, develop character, and are allowed to have a musical

---

[1] Petty, App. II.     [2] R. Ayre, 1779.

life of their own. But the biggest difference between the two genres lies in the finales to which in Italian opera all the action gravitates. In English opera, including Sheridan, they are little more than part-songs or musical dialogues in which characters sing in succession rather than in counterpoint. As Badini approached the end of the first act of *La governante*, he seems suddenly to have realized the impossibility of a 'literal translation' and abandoned his plan, producing a finale and two further acts of pure *opera buffa*. While never entirely losing sight of the original plot, the rest of the opera bears only a superficial structural resemblance to the model.

This broken-backed plan produced a very curious first act, with many arias being direct translations or free adaptations of Sheridan's sparkling lyrics (see Table 6 on page 219). Because Badini took pride in his verse translations, he provided English versions of his own free Italian translations of Sheridan's lyrics. In throwing Sheridan's own altered verses back at him, Badini was clearly inviting comparison. Here is a typical example of this curious procedure:

|  |  |
|---|---|
| *Sheridan* | *Badini's translation* |
| Tho' cause for suspicion appears, | If the least cause for suspicion appears, |
| Yet Proofs of her love too are strong | All the curses of hell are in my fate, |
| I'm a wretch if I'm right in my Fears, | But after all, were I wrong in my fears, |
| And unworthy of Bliss if I'm wrong. | My ingratitude would appear too great. |
| What heart-breaking Torments from | What heart-breaking torments from |
|     Jealousy flow, |     jealousy flow, |
| Ah None but the jealous, the jealous | Ah none but the jealous, the jealous |
|     can know! |     can know! |
| When blest with the smiles of my Fair, | |
| I know not how much I adore | |
| Those smiles let another but share, | |
| And I wonder I priz'd them no more! | |
| Then whence can I hope a relief from | |
|     my woe, | |
| When the falser she seems still the | |
|     fonder I grow? | |

*Badini's Italian version*
Se m'inganna il caro bene,
Chi di me più sventurato!

> Ma serei, s'io fossi amato,
> Un ingrato a dubitar.
> Nel pensier che mi confonde
> Non so più trovar consiglio,
> Veggo ovunque il mio periglio,
> Già mi sento vacillar.

The Italian text does not in this instance seem to have been inspired by Sheridan's original, though Badini's translation clearly was.

Larpent MS 483, submitted to the Lord Chamberlain by Harris and Sheridan on 7 May for an intended première on 11 May (delayed to 15 May), bears all the marks of Badini's struggle. One of the most heavily altered of all Larpent librettos, it is a working copy in which some scenes have little correspondence with the printed libretto. A complete account of all the changes and cancellations would require a separate study, but a brief look at some of the last-minute changes to Act I is revealing. 'Via canaglia, via ciurmaglia' in Scene ii is a love duet for Lucinda (Louisa in *The Duenna*) and Antonio, which is constantly interrupted by Don Girolamo (Jerome) issuing threats of violence. Though based on 'What vagabonds are these', the trio was in fact a late addition to the libretto, as was 'Se m'inganna il caro bene' for Chiaretta (Clara) in Scene iv. By contrast, other arias not drawn from *The Duenna* were cut. But the most extraordinary afterthought is the long finale, 'Disgraziata, scellerata', which was inserted into the libretto on fresh pages, fair copied, but towards the end cut to ribbons and rewritten in the margins and anywhere else space could be found.

Badini's farthest departure from *The Duenna*, the second-act finale, a courtroom scene with Lucinda disguised as the Chief Justice, also underwent extensive revision in the Larpent MS. This scene helps to compensate for the curtailment of the friars' subplot (which Badini mentions in the preface to the libretto). Lucinda sentences the Jew Giuseppe (Isaac Mendoza in *The Duenna*) to the punishment of having his nose cut off.[1] Other features were also drawn from *buffa* stock, such as Girolamo's catalogue aria in Act II, Scene vi, 'Sia l'allegro, sia l'andante'. He lists his daughter's musical skills, including a voice 'Che sembra Senesino, o Caffarello'. In the Larpent MS these lines read: 'Un suon di voce la sì canoro e bello / Che sembra *Pacchierotti* o Caffarello'. Perhaps this substitution is the first sign of the disagreement between Badini and Pacchierotti that flared up in 1779–80.

---

[1] Badini considerably intensifies the anti-Semitism of the original play. Sheridan's 'mainly good-humoured' fun (Fiske, *English Theatre Music*, 414) turns very nasty.

TABLE 6. *Comparison of arias/airs in Act I of* La governante *and* The Duenna

| La governante | | The Duenna | Comment |
| --- | --- | --- | --- |
| **I.i** | | | |
| Chitarrino fa pianino | = | Tell me, my lute | |
| Care luci, i rai | = | The crimson dawn | |
| Amorosa melodia | | — | |
| **I.ii** | | | |
| Via canaglia, via ciurmaglia | = | What vagabonds | lines omitted |
| **I.iv** | | | |
| Se m'inganna | = | Tho' cause for suspicion appears | shortened |
| **I.v** | | | |
| Tutto 'l mondo | = | Thou canst not boast | second verse repl. |
| **I.vi** | | | |
| Ogni tenera donzella | | — | |
| **I.vii** | | | |
| Avete mai sentito | | — | |
| **I.viii** | | | |
| Una putta è un grand'imbroglio | = | If a daughter | uses first verse only[a] |
| **I.x** | | | |
| Spiegar talor si vede | | — | |
| [no other matches in Act I] | | | |

[a] Sung by Catterina, not Jerome.

Bertoni's music was well received, and *La governante* was even compared favourably to *La buona figliuola*.[1] William Napier published the music of the first production in three volumes in *The Favourite Songs in the Opera La Governante by Sigr. Bertoni*, together with 'Con tenerezza' (Act III, Scene v), originally sung by Signora Pozzi as Chiaretta, but in this version assigned to a tenor.[2] The hit of the opera was 'La verginella', sung by Giovanna Sestini (Lucinda), who had just returned from a season in Dublin.[3] The aria was

[1] See the *Gazetteer*, 17 May 1779.
[2] 'Con tenerezza' seems to have been prepared by a different engraver and may be from a later production. The British Library copy (H.2815.1) is only a fragment. A complete copy is in the John Ward collection, Cambridge, Massachusetts.
[3] See *Biographical Dictionary*, xiii. 265.

widely published,[1] and the reasons for its popularity are easy to see. It is an imitation Scottish folk-song, of the sort that Sheridan and the Linleys had selected for *The Duenna*.[2] A cavatina that, uncharacteristically for Bertoni, manages to leave the tonic key occasionally, its most endearing feature is a Scotch snap just before the main cadence. 'Tutto 'l mondo' is also a good piece (in the same key, F major), but it betrays no obvious folk-song traits. From these two examples one would be unwise to conclude that Bertoni, like Badini, was nodding in the direction of native English opera.

That this ramshackle opera by Bertoni and Badini should have received more performances than Sacchini's setting of Bertati's *L'avaro deluso*, which opened the season on 25 November 1778, is surprising. Sacchini's music, none of which survives, was described as 'masterly' by one critic, yet 'sunk under the weight' of Andrei's adaptation by another.[3] Although both first- and second-act finales are well handled, the stock plot to trick an old miser (Calandrano—sung by Antonio Rossi) out of marrying a bright young maid (Zerbinetta—sung by Signora Sestini) is threadbare and would have held few surprises for the London audience. To Andrei's credit, Calandrano's avarice is hardly mentioned, in contrast to later King's Theatre operas on the same theme in which miser jokes are driven into the ground. But the main weakness of the plot is that, after the expected confusions of the first-act finale, Zerbinetta precipitously consents to marry Gervasio (Jermoli) in Act II, Scene iv, thereby forestalling any further development of their relationship. At about the same time, Calandrano gives up his design to marry Zerbinetta (Act II, Scene vi), at which point the opera could just as well finish. With the prospect of a stillborn third act, Andrei introduced a disguise plot, in which Gervasio and the chambermaid Modesta pretend to be French grandees. But this fails to save the opera, and the subplot is mentioned here only because it may have influenced the creation of a character in Bertoni's *Il duca d'Atene*, the *succès de scandale* of the next season.

## IV. The 1779–80 Season: Le Texier's Downfall

Repertoire:

***Alessandro nell'Indie***, pasticcio arranged by Bertoni, libretto adapted by Andrei from Metastasio, 27 November 1779 (8 performances). London (earlier operas based on this libretto) 1762 (Cocchi), 1775 (Corri) (p. 222)

---

[1] For a facsimile, see Petty, 389–90.    [2] See Fiske, *English Theatre Music*, 415.
[3] *Morning Post* and *Morning Chronicle*, both of 25 Nov. 1778.

*La contadina in corte*, Sacchini, libretto after Tassi, 14 December 1779 (8 performances); orig. Rome (Valle) 1765. London 1771 (p. 227)

*Il soldano generoso*, pasticcio arranged by Bertoni, libretto by Andrei, 14 December 1779 (8 performances) (p. 227)

*Quinto Fabio*, Bertoni, libretto by Andrei after Zeno's *Lucio Papirio*, 22 January 1780 (13 performances); orig. Milan (Interinale) 1778 (p. 230)

*L'amore soldato*, Sacchini ('With Improvements'), libretto by Andrei after Tassi, 8 February 1780 (9 performances); orig. London 1778

*L'Olimpiade*, pasticcio arranged by Bertoni with numbers by Paisiello and Gluck, libretto after Metastasio, 9 March 1780 (3 performances). London (pasticcios based on this libretto) 1765, 1770, 1774, 1779 (p. 246)

*Rinaldo*, Sacchini, libretto by Durandi adapted by Badini, 22 April 1780 (10 performances); revision of *Armida*, orig. Milan (Regio Ducal) 1772 (p. 237)

*Il duca d'Atene*, Bertoni, libretto by Badini, 9 May 1780 (7 performances) (p. 243)

*La buona figliuola*, Piccinni, libretto by Goldoni, 25 May 1780 (2 performances); orig. Rome (Dame) 1760. London 1766 → 1779

*Orfeo* (concert performance), Bertoni, libretto after Calzabigi, 31 May 1780 (1 performance); adaptation of orig. Venice (S. Benedetto) 1776

Coverage of this season is the most detailed of any of Sheridan's regime, thanks largely to the existence of Susan Burney's letter-journal. We have already seen how the director of opera, Le Texier, fraudulently announced the engagement of several composers, some of whom he was unlikely ever to have been in touch with. Again, the serious and comic troupes remained largely the same as the previous season, the only notable changes being the return of Madam Lebrun (whom Susan seemed prepared to hate) and the departure of the tenor Adamberger, replaced by Giuseppe Trebbi, who received a mixed reception in London. Le Texier had hoped to engage the famous tenor Giacomo Davide and, when the singer could not be released from an engagement in Rome, the manager wrote to Lord Cowper in Florence, asking him to intercede.[1] The most significant 'new' work was Sacchini's latest setting of *Rinaldo*, the composer's last success in London, though with cracks already beginning to show. The season also saw a noticeable increase in the reliance on pasticcios, which in itself is an indication that the company was being driven more from below by the singers than from above by the managers. In her unforgiving critical assessment of these pasticcios and, not insignificantly, her meticulous attention to attribution and originality, Susan Burney charts this minor artistic crisis, to which her friends Bertoni and Pacchierotti contributed their share, and records the poetic justice finally meted out to Le Texier.

---

[1] The letter is printed in Gibson, 'Earl Cowper', 239.

## Alessandro nell'Indie

Le Texier planned to open the season with a double bill of Sacchini's comic opera *La contadina in corte* and a pasticcio to be assembled around a new libretto by Antonio Andrei entitled *Il soldano generoso*. Although neither Bertoni nor Pacchierotti approved of this venture, work had begun by 20 October towards a late November opening.[1] But by 8 November Bertoni had stopped work on the pasticcio because, as Pacchierotti explained to Susan Burney, 'The Comic Opera that was intended to be performed with the serious cannot appear—because there will not be singers enough—there are as yet here but three comical performers' (fo. 26ᵛ).[2] The late arrival of singers and dancers had long been a problem for London managers, and star performers were often indulged in some tardiness. Nevertheless, this lack of discipline amongst the *buffi* is indicative of Le Texier's shaky authority. In a panic at the prospect of not being able to begin the season in the last week of November as the subscribers expected, the opera director 'was making new regulations, *in such manner* that a serious Pasticcio must be got ready to begin with' (fo. 26ᵛ). It was to be a setting of one of Metastasio's most famous (and most malleable) dramas, *Alessandro nell'Indie*, as adapted by Andrei.[3] Eleven days later, on Friday, 19 November, Susan attended the first general rehearsal (which was described above), though the opera still lacked a second-act finale and other items had yet to be fixed. As this was the first opera of the season and was to star her friend Pacchierotti, Susan took a keen interest in every aspect of its preparation, leaving a unique account of the London pasticcio process. Her view of the opera seems to have been formed by this single rehearsal, for other commitments prevented her from attending any of the eight public performances this season. *Alessandro nell'Indie* was advertised as being 'under the Direction of Bertoni', but it was put together in such a hurry that Susan believed 'he can have composed nothing purposely for it' (fo. 36ʳ). Authorship mattered to her, and she was indefatigable in ferreting out from the director, the singers, the orchestra leader, her father, or anyone else with inside information who had composed each piece. Comparison of her enquiries and hunches with documented attributions in the printed librettos and *Favourite Song* collections of this and many works shows her to have been almost 100 per cent

[1] Susan Burney, fo. 18ʳ.

[2] In the *Morning Post* of 13 Nov. 1779, Le Texier nevertheless announced a full company of *buffi*.

[3] See a cutting in the New York Public Library, printed by Petty, 167.

accurate.[1] Before the rehearsal Susan had studied the libretto, presumably a copy in the *Opere drammatiche* of Metastasio in the family library.[2] She knew it sufficiently well to be disappointed, upon arriving late, that she had missed Poro's first piece, 'Vedrai con tuo periglio' (Act I, Scene ii, in Metastasio); later she discovered that this aria had been cut, 'which I regretted infinitely' (fo. 36ᵛ), though she had no idea whose setting she might have heard. But the loss of this text was more than compensated by Pacchierotti's first aria (as Poro), the cavatina 'Se mai più sarò geloso' in Act I, Scene iv, by Piccinni: 'It is Elegant, charming Music, & admits of all those refinements & graces in which Pacchierotti so peculiarly excells—& He *did* sing it like a very Angel' (fo. 36ᵛ). As for the rest of the opera, 'I confess I have heard few that seemed to me possessed of a smaller number of fine, or even *pleasing* airs.' She objected to Madam Lebrun's voice ('a bad imitation of an Instrument') and her choice of arias (in the role of Cleofide), which lacked variety. She was offended that Le Texier should have advertised the inclusion of 'many songs of Handel';[3] whereas there were only two, 'one of wch. ["Mio ben ricordati" in Act III, Scene iv],[4] being sung by Manzoletto, may be fairly said to be *too Many*'. The other was Pacchierotti's rendition of 'Return, O God of Hosts!' from *Samson* with new Italian words, 'Ah, non voler mio ben!' in Act II, Scene ii, which she allowed to be 'in its solemn & antique style a fine song' (fo. 37ᵛ).

During the first interval, Pacchierotti came into the box occupied by the Burney party and discussed the piece he had just sung, a big duet for Poro and Cleofide (Pacchierotti and Lebrun) that Susan did not like, even though it was also by Piccinni: 'It is in the beginning old fashioned—& in the end Incoherent—difficult, & unpleasing—*selon moi*, & indeed *selon* every body but one I have heard mention it' (fo. 37ᵛ). Charles Rousseau Burney 'then began cutting up the Duet' (fo. 39ʳ) and asked Pacchierotti why in a pasticcio, where the *primo uomo* was under no obligation to sing something he disapproved of, such a bad piece had been inserted. The singer was more than a little indignant. The duet, which he claimed (incorrectly) to be Piccinni's last work, was '*Une Musique qui n'a pas été intendû encore—et belle en verité*'. He admitted that it had been badly performed and hoped Mr Burney would come to appreciate its quality.

[1] She ridiculed a Mr Southwell's ignorance of what *Alessandro nell'Indie* would include, particularly because he 'means to pass for one of the *Conoscenti*' (fo. 48ʳ).

[2] Later in 1780 Bertoni looked 'over a Vol. of Metastasio' *chez* Burney in search of words to set for Madam Lebrun (fo. 130ʳ).

[3] See *The London Stage*, Part 5, i. 299.

[4] Taken appropriately enough from *Poro*.

Two days later, on Sunday, 21 November, Pacchierotti called on the Burneys in the evening and, after some music, Susan and he had a long and fascinating conversation about the first-act duet-finale in *Alessandro nell'Indie*. Still worried that the Burneys, whose opinion he respected, did not like the duet 'Se mai turbo il tuo riposo', he tried to explain its importance to the overall design of the first act of the opera. In her account of the discussion Susan reminded Fanny of the crux of the drama: Poro's jealousy. Having been twice defeated by Alessandro and puzzled by the invader's clemency towards his sister Erissena, Poro accepts his beloved Queen Cleofide's offer to plead for his life. Cleofide will pretend to dote on Alessandro, but Poro does not trust her to remain faithful should the conqueror reciprocate. When Cleofide offers him 'the strongest proofs' of her attachment, Poro replies, chastened, with the aria 'Se mai più sarò geloso / Mi punisca il sacro nume, / che dell'India è domator' (May the god that conquered India punish me if I am ever jealous again). When Cleofide finally decides to pay her respects to Alessandro, she must again try to reassure Poro of her constancy in the aria 'Se mai turbo il tuo riposo'. Poro then overhears Cleofide pretending a little too convincingly to make love to Alessandro, and in a state of extreme agitation he launches into the duet-finale with her earlier words 'Se mai turbo il tuo riposo', and she in turn repeats his—'Se mai più sarò geloso'. And so, as Susan states succinctly, 'they insult each other with their former protestations' (fo. 47ʳ). Susan told Fanny that the two arias and the duet obviously 'ought to be the Composition of the same Master'. (For a list of sources, see Table 7.) In Piccinni's second setting of the libretto, in which Pacchierotti had created the role of Poro at the Real Teatro di S. Carlo in Naples on 12 January 1774,[1] his cavatina in Scene iv, Cleofide's aria in Scene v and the duet all begin with the same theme, making the connection between the pieces absolutely clear—a tradition that extends back at least to Handel's *Poro* (1731). Furthermore, his Cleofide for the Neapolitan première had been the great soprano Anna Lucia De Amicis Buonsolazzi, and the two singers ironically imitated each other's 'maniere de chanter' when repeating their earlier promises in the duet. Pacchierotti told Susan, 'Ce qui a fait un effet que je vous assure que je ne puis vous dire' (fo. 47ʳ).

But performing with Madam Lebrun in London was a different matter. He approached the *prima donna* with all due respect for her abilities and

---

[1] See Sartori, no. 812; the score is in the library of the Conservatorio di Musica S. Pietro a Majella at Naples. Pacchierotti had also sung Poro in Carlo Monza's setting for Milan in 1775.

TABLE 7. *Attributions in* Alessandro nell'Indie

| | |
|---|---|
| Piccinni: | Se mai più sarò geloso (Poro—Pacchierotti), I.iv |
| | Se mai turbo il tuo riposo (Cleofide—Lebrun), I.v |
| | Se mai turbo il tuo riposo (duet), I.vii |
| Bertoni: | E prezzo leggiero (Gandarte—Manzoletto), I.i |
| | Non sarei si sventurata (Gandarte), II.i |
| | Costante e fedele (Gandarte), II.iii |
| Handel: | Ah, non voler mio ben! = Return, O God of Hosts! |
| | (Poro—Pacchierotti), II.ii |
| | Mio ben, ricordati (Gandarte), III.iv |
| Alessandri: | Non tradisca il core oppresso (Cleofida—Lebrun), II.ii |
| Anfossi: | Che fà il mio bene! (Cleofida), II.iv |
| Sarti: | Tremate empi tremate (Trio: Poro, Cleofida, and |
| | Alessandro—Trebbi), II.v |
| Durán: | Serbati a grand'imprese (Alessandro), III.ii |
| Mysliveček: | Cara ti lascio, addio (Alessandro), II.iv |
| | Affretta i passi o caro (Cleofide), III.iv |
| Tozzi:[a] | Già via ed in lontananza (Erissena—Pozzi), III.v |
| Molza:[b] | Affetti teneri (Poro), III.vi |
| Anon.: | Vil trofeo d'un'alma imbelle (Alessandro), I.iii |
| | Chi vive amante (Erissena), I.vi |
| | Ma qual virtù non cede (Timagene—De Michele),[c] II.i |
| | Serva ad eroe sì grande (final chorus), III.vii |

[a] Antonio Tozzi, *Hofkapellmeister* at Munich from 1774.
[b] Unidentified.
[c] When De Michele, the *ultima parte*, was singing, Susan Burney said 'il faut ecouter les Instrumens' (fo. 39ᵛ).

reputation and, without asking 'her to sing an air disagreable to her', suggested that, to preserve the integrity of the drama, she should sing Piccinni's setting of 'Se mai turbo il tuo riposo' in Scene v. This she agreed to do at a meeting in the evening of 18 November, but at the rehearsal that Susan had attended on 19 November, 'sans me dire un seul Mot', she surprised Pacchierotti by singing a completely different aria, which he supposed was by her husband the oboist, since he 'a donné le ton', that is, gave the key or stood forward as conductor. Susan tried to calm Pacchierotti down by complimenting him on the recitative that leads into the duet, but he would not be deflected: 'Eh le Duo aussi est beau je vous assure Madlle', adding that with all the jealousy, caprice, and caballing he had to put up with in London, he sometimes wished he had never gone on the stage. What did Madam Lebrun sing in Act I, Scene v of *Alessandro nell'Indie*? The printed libretto (W. Mackintosh, 1779) records that it was Piccinni's 'Se mai turbo il tuo riposo'.[1] Had Pacchierotti prevailed? At the general rehearsal Cramer told Susan that he too did not like Lebrun's arias and that she was planning to sing yet another in the same style; 'however I persuaded her to change one of them' (fo. 41ʳ). Perhaps the ever diplomatic Cramer also persuaded her to reinstate the Piccinni before the première on 27 November. Some opera historians have viewed the pasticcio as the bane of the Italian opera in London and, indeed, there were many more slipshod productions than Bertoni's arrangement of *Alessandro nell'Indie*.[2] But this conversation between Pacchierotti and Susan Burney helps to overturn received opinion: principal singers could introduce arias of their own choosing, but there were limits to that choice besides the dictates of style and fashion. Metastasio's dramatic irony actually mattered to Pacchierotti.

This stopgap production received mixed reviews,[3] though it survived for a further seven performances this season. The printed libretto records the attributions listed in Table 7, most of which were corroborated by Susan Burney before the première. Napier published three arias in *The Favourite Songs in the Opera Allessandro nell'Indie*: Piccinni's 'Se mai più sarò geloso' (sung by Pacchierotti in Act I); Anfossi's 'Che fà il mio bene' (sung by Madam Lebrun in Act II); and Mysliveček's 'Affretta i passi o caro' (Lebrun in Act III). With its simpering triadic melody and lazy pedal-points, one wonders why Pacchierotti stuck his neck out for 'Se mai più sarò geloso'. Of the three pieces only that by Mysliveček ever rises above banality. In instrumental rondeau form, the simple and touching G major melody contrasts with the more agitated and harmonically adventurous development sections. But even this piece was probably selected for the *Favourite Songs* because it is easy to sing.

---

[1] No Larpent copy survives for this opera, presumably because the licenser would not have bothered to read a pasticcio on such a well-known libretto.

[2] See Curtis Price, 'Unity, Originality, and the London Pasticcio', *Harvard Library Bulletin*, NS 2/4 (1991), 17–30.

[3] See Petty, 167.

*Sacchini's* La contadina in corte *and* Il soldano generoso

Le Texier's *serio-buffo* double bill was postponed but not forgotten. On 20 November Pacchierotti's head was full of *Il soldano generoso*,[1] and Cramer reported that it had been rehearsed on Friday morning, 3 December. Despite Pacchierotti's already cited doubts about mixing the two genres on the same evening and his worry that in consequence he would have to perform twice instead of once a week (which proved to be the case), Cramer 'spoke very highly indeed of the Music [of *La contadina in corte*]—but said that it was pity to add the Sultano [*sic*] Generoso to it'. Both works together made a very long evening. When Susan Burney finally saw the production on 1 February 1780 (the last performance), she formed exactly the opposite view: 'As the Contadina in Corte rather disappointed, The Soldano Generoso exceeded my expectations—& I never felt so much the great preference of the serious to the comic operas & performers' (fo. 68ᵛ). The divergent opinions almost certainly stem from the ambiguous tone of the works themselves, yet another sign of Le Texier's (or perhaps Sheridan's) willingness to experiment with the King's Theatre repertoire. Sacchini's *La contadina in corte* was in itself an odd choice, a two-act comic opera that had but one performance in 1771 'under the direction of Signor Giordani', Sacchini presumably being indisposed, and had not been revived since. No music survives from the first production, but the anonymous libretto is worth reading for several reasons. It is a skilful blend of two familiar plots: the consequences of droit de seigneur, and the shepherdess turned princess. Prince Rinaldo's seduction of Sandrina (the *contadina*) is treated seriously, as are its effects on both his wife, Clarice, and on the victim herself. The climactic assignation in a darkened room between the prince and Sandrina, who changes places with the princess, anticipates in many respects the similar scene in *Le nozze di Figaro*. The strongly moralistic tone is confirmed when Sandrina decides to return to the country with her *contadino* Menichino, while Rinaldo and Clarice almost reconcile their differences in a non-love duet, 'Deh, mia cara in questo istante', in Act III, Scene iii.

Sacchini's 1779 version of *La contadina in corte* cannot be considered a revival, being rather a complete reworking of the original libretto into what the title-page calls an 'operetta giocosa' (W. Mackintosh, 1779). At first glance it appears to be a botched job: the original cast of seven has been

---

[1] Susan Burney, fo. 39ᵛ. Following quotations from fo. 57ʳ.

227

reduced to four: Ruggiero (Rinaldo in 1771), Sandrina, Berto, and Tancia. With the removal of Clarice also went the discordant noble marriage and, repugnant for anyone who knew the original, Ruggiero/Rinaldo's seduction of Sandrina succeeds; she prefers the life of a baroness to that of a country washerwoman. But this too is a very moralistic drama, as Sandrina's volte-face can be traced back to Act I, Scenes vii–viii, when her betrothed, Berto ('a Cunning Peasant') slaps her face for accepting the purse tossed by Ruggiero. Berto deserves to be jilted. The assignation in the darkened room is here replaced by an elaborate masquerade in which Berto, disguised as 'Count Zappadolce', tests Sandrina's already weakened fidelity, as the princess had tested her husband's in the 1771 version. Susan Burney mentioned this scene in her letter-journal, but was (uncharacteristically for her) mistaken about why it had been added:

Sacchini has new set a Masquerade scene wch. is introduced now I believe to save Prudom [who sang Tancia, 'a country Girl in love with Berto'] from appearing in Men's Cloaths—however the whole is so *vilely* performed, that it gave me pain to hear so pretty a composition murdered—Bernasconi [Sandrina], who is the best of them, sings her pretty songs very ill indeed. Trebbi [Berto, a tenor part] was as usual, a Buffoon without humour—Rovedino [Ruggiero][1] beyond measure ridiculous in the fine Gentleman, & Prudom all insipidity. I shall grieve for all who have to work this year for the Comic Opera. (fo. 68ᵛ)

As no *Favourite Songs* were published for either version, one can only speculate how much of the original music Sacchini retained: the opening spinning trio 'Gira, gira maladetto' seems to have been expanded into a quartet; Fabio's 'Vaghe le selve sono' (Act I, Scene iii in 1771) may have been reassigned to Ruggiero in the 1779 version (Act I, Scene ix), and both first-act finales begin with the line 'Verdi campi, care selve'. Otherwise, these productions should really be listed as two different operas.

*Il soldano generoso*, 'a serious dramatical performance . . . Written by Signor Andrei, the Music by Signor Ferdinando Bertoni, Except some Airs of other eminent Composers', is one of the strangest pasticcios of the era. It is a slight drama in one act, obviously designed as a show-case for Pacchierotti, with music by Giordani, Mysliveček, Traetta, Salieri, and of course Bertoni. One wonders why, then, the composer/director complained of having put so much effort into it.[2] As in *La contadina in corte*, there are only

---

[1] The printed libretto lists De Michele in this role, which is evidently a mistake, since he nearly always played minor parts and never, at this stage of his career, leads.

[2] Indeed, one might also ask why, with at least one postponement, Sheridan and Harris did not submit copies of the librettos to the Lord Chamberlain's office until 14 Dec., the day

four singers. Isabella (Madam Lebrun), who has been hijacked by pirates, resists the tender entreaties of her captor, the Sultan Osmano (Manzoletto), because she is pining for her distant lover. The man in question, Ferdinando (Pacchierotti), just happens to be shipwrecked nearby. When the sultan witnesses the lovers' joyous reunion, he magnanimously withdraws his suit and blesses them. Without any dramatic conflict, the *raison d'être* for this opera is the shipwreck in Scene iii: 'While the storm, accompanied and expressed by the symphony, encreases, a vessel is dashed by the impetuosity of the waves against the shore.'[1] Unfortunately, Susan Burney had absolutely nothing to say about this scene, but such effects were to become increasingly elaborate and realistic during the course of the 1780s at all three London theatres; Badini and Haydn even planned a shipwreck as the climactic catastrophe of *L'anima del filosofo*.

Besides Bertoni, the score included music by Giordani ('Caro bene, al pianto rio' in Scene ii), Mysliveček ('Agitata in tanti affanni' in Scene iii), Traetta ('Palpitare il cor mi sento' in Scene vi),[2] and Salieri ('Ah se agli affetti miei' in Scene viii). *The Favourite Songs in the Opera Il Soldano Generoso* (W. Napier)[3] includes only the Salieri and two pieces by Bertoni, which were presumably written especially for this opera. 'Aure che lusingate', sung by Madam Lebrun in the first scene, an *andante cantabile* in B flat major scored for flutes, horns, and strings, is redolent of the pastorale; at least this is one way of accounting for the absurdly long pedal notes decorated by lazy subdominant harmony. Apart from having the middle strings depict the wind rustling in the shrubbery by which Isabella sits, Bertoni expended little effort on this atmospheric piece. The A major duet for Isabella and Fatima (Signora Pozzi) in Scene iii, 'Ogni oggetto che de setto [*sic*; diletto]', in which the captive lady pours out her anguish to a sympathetic slave girl, takes little notice of the drama. Rather, this piece simply allowed the singers to demonstrate their skill with passage-work in thirds and to test the audience's tolerance of unchanging tonic harmony. The third piece in the *Favourite Songs*, Salieri's 'Rondo & Duet in one' (as Susan Burney described it, fo. 69ʳ) is altogether finer than either of Bertoni's contributions. In the libretto this piece is marked with virgole, normally a sign that it was cut in performance, but this would seem unlikely both because of the publication

of the first performance; see Larpent MSS 502 and 503.

[1] This stage direction does not appear in Larpent MS 502, but its omission can hardly mean that the spectacular scene was a late addition.

[2] Probably a last-minute insertion, as the text is squeezed into Larpent MS 502.

[3] Copies in the Brotherton Library, University of Leeds, and the John Ward collection.

of the music and because it forms the climax of the opera. In the score published by Napier, the parts for Pacchierotti and Lebrun are curiously labelled 'Iseo' and 'Semele', respectively. These names allow us to trace the origins of the duet to Salieri's serious opera *L'Europa riconosciuta*, which inaugurated the new ducal theatre at Milan, called La Scala, on 3 August 1778.[1] In that production Semele was sung by Madam Lebrun, while Pacchierotti created the role of Asterio, switching to Isseo (originally Rubinelli's part) in London. The accidental retention of characters' names from the earlier opera suggests that Napier was working from an unaltered score that Pacchierotti or Lebrun had brought from Milan. Yet the *duetto rondò* is joined directly to Bertoni's finale with no intervening recitative, a sign that some care was taken to splice in the pre-existing music. Though conceived for another opera, the duet works well in this scene, in which the long-separated lovers slowly rekindle their affection for one another. Isabella's hesitancy is heard in the agitated interstices between Ferdinando's warm, sentimental melody, which is flawed only by Salieri's tendency to anticipate the tonic chord a bar before cadences. Susan was generous in her praise. This piece was 'charmingly calculated to shew both singers to advantage. Indeed I came home delighted wth. this Act' (fo. 69ʳ).

### Bertoni's Quinto Fabio

Dr Burney's daughter was not Bertoni's only supporter in London; all his works had received at least polite notices in the newspapers since his arrival at the beginning of the previous season. 'La verginella' from *La governante* was even awarded the surest mark of popularity—a set of English words.[2] But Bertoni had been consistently overshadowed by Sacchini and had yet to write a major new *opera seria*, the acid test for an Italian composer in London. The opportunity finally came at the height of the 1779–80 season in the form of Andrei's alteration of Zeno's drama *Lucio Papirio*, under the title *Quinto Fabio* (première 22 January 1780). The first Susan Burney heard of the opera was on 13 January when Pacchierotti and Bertoni called on her in high spirits after the first rehearsal. The composer 'very good naturedly promised to send me a Book of it to read. Pacchierotti too promised to let us know when the next Rehearsal shd. be either by a note or calling on us' (fo. 62ᵛ). The preparations seem to have been more careful than for previous productions this season, for there were further rehearsals on 20 and 21 January, though the day before the première 'Bertoni had not yet put the

---

[1] See Sartori, no. 9431.    [2] 'Tell me o cruel maid'. See *BUCEM*, i. 104–5.

last stroke to his overture' (fo. 63ᵛ); but he did find time to send Susan a copy of the libretto.[1] Pacchierotti was enthusiastic:

He read to me before Fanny came in several of his favourite scenes from Quinto Fabio, very charmingly—I like the Drama very much indeed, & if the Italian language was better understood, I doubt not that it wd. add very much to the success of the Opera—particularly as Pacchierotti feels every word of his parts, & will give it all the expression it admits of—indeed he is full of feeling & intelligence. (fo. 64ᵛ)

Upon reading Andrei's fine adaptation of Zeno's drama, one can understand why Susan was worried that the efforts of both Pacchierotti and the dramatist might not be appreciated. It is an old-fashioned three-act *opera seria* with only moderately extended finales. The plot, which was admirably summarized in a newspaper review,[2] turns on the chagrin, envy, and humiliation of the Roman 'emperor' Lucio Papirio when his son-in-law Quinto Fabio, despite having been ordered not to fight, routs the Samnites in battle. The climax of the opera occurs in the middle of the second act: Quinto is willing to apologize for his rash act, but only in a private audience with the emperor. As he kneels in supplication in the royal tent, Lucio gives a sign and the tent suddenly lifts up to reveal the army and the people gathered round. Humiliation is thus avenged by humilation. Act III is concerned with Princess Emilia's attempts to secure a pardon for her condemned husband Quinto.

Susan Burney, who was a friend of the composer but by no means uncritical of his music, wrote a long account of the final dress rehearsal (fos. 66ʳ–67ᵛ). She concludes that 'Quinto Fabio is a charming opera, & infinitely superiour I think to any thing I have heard of Bertoni's since his arrival in England . . . The Drama is a very good one as far as I can judge, & the words often extremely well expressed.' She was apparently unaware that this was the third opera on the subject that Bertoni had produced in as many years: the others were staged at the Teatro Interinale at Milan and at Padua, both in 1778.[3] In the latter production Pacchierotti created the title-role, while the great tenor Giacomo Davide sang Lucio Papirio. That Bertoni

---

[1] In the third act of Larpent MS 509, the copyist seems to have left over-large gaps for aria texts to be written in later (one of them, 'Tremo fra dubbi miei', is in a different hand), a sign of haste. Fausta's 'Se respirar poss'io' is a replacement for an aria beginning 'Se la speranza'. The manuscript does not have a date of application, which tends to confirm the rush.

[2] Reprinted by Petty, 168–9, from an unidentified cutting in the New York Public Library.

[3] See Sartori, s.v. *Quinto Fabio*.

would have retained Pacchierotti's arias and adapted Davide's for Trebbi (the tenor in London) is quite likely, though at least some of the music for Madam Lebrun (Emilia) was composed afresh to include a virtuoso oboe part for her husband. This is certainly the case for 'Tremo fra dubbi miei' in Act III, Scene v: although the aria does not survive, a note in pencil in the British Library copy of the printed libretto reads 'accompanied by Le Brun on the Hautboy'.[1] Susan's high opinion of the music in this opera is confirmed by the pieces included in *The Favourite Songs in the Opera Quinto Fabio by Sigr. Bertoni* (W. Napier), which was issued in two volumes.[2] All but two are substantial arias in which Bertoni attempts the near-impossible task of addressing the serious issues of paternal envy and ritual humiliation, while keeping the audience entertained with implacably jolly, major-mode music.[3] Emilia's first aria, 'Va crescendo il mio tormento' in Act I, Scene iii, which Susan Burney called 'one of the best in the Opera, & a charming one' (fo. 66ᵛ), illustrates this aesthetic paradox. The only feature of the opening B flat major *allegro* that could possibly be construed as depicting the singer's despondency, besides her words, are the rapid shifts in dynamics and the huge melisma on 'che temere e palpi*tar*'. This passage-work even overruns the main cadence in the dominant, F major. The middle section of this modified sonata form is more characteristically expressive, with a slight increase in chromaticism and dotted rhythms, but the appearance of a new theme in E flat major is purely a musical idea unrelated to the structure of the verse. Susan Burney's praise of this aria had a sting in its tail: the best piece in the opera, perhaps, but '*strongly* in Sacchini's manner—rather too much, not for the song but the Composer' (fo. 66ᵛ). This is the first of many suspicions she had about Bertoni's originality.[4] The musical and dramatic high points of the opera coincide felicitously in Pacchierotti's *scena* in Act II, Scene viii, 'Ma pria ch'io rieda al campo', Quinto Fabio's complex reaction to his exposure during the act of supplication. Susan rightly described this 'Great Air' after just one hearing as containing

---

[1] W. Mackintosh, 1780 (pressmark 11714.cc.4). Confirmed by Susan Burney and a contemporaneous advertisement; see *The London Stage*, Part 5, i. 313.

[2] A complete copy is in the John Ward collection.

[3] One of Emilia's printed arias, 'Ah dolci affetti teneri' in Act II, Scene iv, may have been a last-minute substitution. In Larpent MS 509 an aria text beginning 'Ai dolenti affanni miei' is cut and the new text written in the left margin. The same text is marked with crosses in the British Library copy of the libretto.

[4] See also fo. 72ʳ: 'My sister as well as I, was more than ever struck wth. the resemblance it bears to Sacchini's songs.'

5 different Movements—It begins Majestically—then breaks out wth. vehemence—falls into a *Cantabile 'Sposa, tu piangi!'* &c returns I think to the first subject, & ends as an Aria Parlante full of Passion.—'Tis a very fine & difficult song, & Pacchierotti exerts himself in it amazingly—& is so delicious in the slow part of it that I am dying for him to have a cantabile throughout, in Millico's Style—What *can* be his objection? It exhausts him too much I believe. (fo. 67ʳ)

After the striking opening, in which the voice descends through a dominant seventh chord in simple crotchets, Bertoni relies on similar clichés of operatic passion such as Neapolitan-sixth chords and chromatic appoggiaturas. Far more remarkable is that the most expressive passages of this aria exploit Pacchierotti's ability to sustain minims and semibreves in the lower range, even down to *A*. (See Ex. 4.4 on pages 234–5.) This aria is thus curiously inverted in its dialectic: the instrumentally conceived bravura passages that explore the stratosphere (in this instance up to *b* flat ‴) are dramatically neutral, mere shows, while more complex emotions are conveyed by what is in effect the natural male voice: the tenor.

Many critics and musicians in northern Europe were beginning to complain about the artificiality of the castrato voice, which was, however, still the accepted medium for operatic heroes in Italy and England. But Bertoni, and to some extent Sacchini, seemed to prefer Pacchierotti's extended *lower* range. Susan Burney wrote, 'I knew his compass to be such that he could sing *Tenor* songs' (fo. 44ʳ), which he sometimes did at private concerts. Dr Burney often 'heard him sing Ansani's and David's *tenor* songs in their original pitch, in a most perfect and admirable manner, going down to sometimes as low as Bb on the second line in the base'.[1] In *Quinto Fabio*, both singer and composer were acknowledging the inevitable demise of the castrato and its replacement by the tenor in the more naturalistic modern form of *opera seria*. In London, this first happened definitively in 1791 with Giacomo Davide, with whom Pacchierotti had sung in the 1778 Paduan production of *Quinto Fabio*. There can be little doubt that Pacchierotti's extraordinary durability was in large part owing to the power and effectiveness of his tenor range and to Bertoni's ability to invent arias in which the climaxes come in the expressive middle sections rather than in the spectacular high *passaggi* towards the end. *Quinto Fabio* may therefore be an

[1] *General History*, ii. 889. Marchesi was also reported to possess high, medium, and low voices: 'l'acutissima di soprano, quella di mezzo di contralto robustissima, e la più virile e toccante di tenore'. See John A. Rice, 'Sense, Sensibility, and Opera Seria: An Epistolary Debate', *Studi musicali*, 15 (1986), 101–38.

Ex. 4.4. Ferdinando Bertoni, 'Ma pria ch'io rieda al campo', from *Quinto Fabio*

early signal of one of the most important developments in opera history—the replacement of the male soprano by the tenor.

Yet the flaws in *Quinto Fabio* are manifold, as Susan Burney knew only too well. The arias for secondary characters were perfunctorily written and badly performed. She was relieved that De Michele, 'Dieu soit benit, has only 3 or 4 lines of Reca. as high Priest to sing' (fo. 67ʳ). A more basic problem with the design of this opera must be laid at Bertoni's feet: failure to overcome the obvious and fundamental incompatibility of the three-act *opera seria* and the new, lighter musical style. Librettists could choose either to allow the central conflict to spill over into the last act or, as was more often the case during the dying days of the old Metastasian formula, to treat the third act simply as a denouement. In *Quinto Fabio* Andrei took the first, more difficult, path, leaving the threat of execution hanging over the protagonist's head until the very last scene, in which Quinto's father also betrays his son. But Bertoni's duet for Quinto and Emilia, 'Teco resti, anima mia', which comes in the penultimate scene, has all the feel of a premature denouement.[1] It begins incongruously with a pretty, four-square tune in E-flat major that conveys none of Quinto's inner turmoil; the only acknowledgement of the surrounding drama comes with Emilia's entrance at the words 'Tu mi lasci', which are set as accompanied recitative. In the obligatory concluding *allegro assai*, the voices join limply in thirds for the drive to cadence. One has to allow for the dominance of musical over dramatic structures at certain points in all opera, but Bertoni could find no way of delaying the musical denouement to coincide with Lucio's final act of clemency, which is inspired by the protests of a 'Chorus of the People'.

On Saturday evening, 22 January, Susan Burney attended the première of *Quinto Fabio*, which was a great success by all accounts. In a passage that Fanny later cancelled, she recorded that she avoided having to go into the five-shilling gallery with her friend Miss Kirwan, who later said Sacchini sat behind her. Susan's account adds little to the unusually comprehensive reviews of the opera,[2] which complimented Bertoni on being more than a compiler of pasticcios. Although his voice faltered at first, probably owing to a severe case of stage fright to which he was prone, Pacchierotti astonished the audience as much by his acting as by his singing—apart from a

---

[1] The text of this duet is not completed in the Larpent MS, which suggests that Bertoni left it (like the overture) till the last minute.

[2] See Petty, 168–70, who prints excerpts from an unidentified cutting in the New York Public Library, the *Public Advertiser*, and a letter from Thomas Twining.

group of 'Italian Rascals' (fo. 94ᵛ) who hissed him from the three-shilling gallery. These detractors were to plague his every public appearance this season. Madam Lebrun also had her detractors, but even Susan Burney had to admit 'I never heard her sing so well as in this opera throughout' (fo. 67ᵛ).

## Sacchini's Rinaldo

*Quinto Fabio* can thus be judged a success by all the normal criteria; it achieved fourteen performances this season, more than any other opera, and was twice revived for Pacchierotti's benefit, in 1781 and 1791. But the opera that received the greatest acclaim during 1779–80 was Sacchini's *Rinaldo*, which is also the most important from the musical point of view. It was clearly intended to be the main attraction of the season, and more resources and rehearsal time were invested in it than any other production. Sheridan took a personal interest in its creation, which was nearly enough to sink the vessel before it left port. Pacchierotti finally allowed Sacchini, who was ill during much of the composition of *Rinaldo* and was even forced to miss the première, to write him a *cantabile*, which received a huge ovation. This took the shine off Bertoni's *Quinto Fabio* and clearly put a strain on his relationship with the singer. *Rinaldo* had its première on 22 April 1780, but Susan Burney first heard indirectly about its preparation near the end of March. During a gathering at the Burney house when Bertoni was momentarily separated from the composer, Pacchierotti 'shewed *privily* . . . 2 songs to Fanny from the Opera of Armida [that is, *Rinaldo*] wch. Sacchini is now setting'.[1] But the libretto (even the title) had yet to be fixed. Sacchini complained to Pacchierotti before a recitative rehearsal on Monday, 27 March that

he had been abominably plagued in composing it, owing to Mr. Sheridan—that Andrea, the Author or compiler of the words, had brot. him a note from Mr. Sh: to acquaint Sacchini it was *his* opera he was to set—2 days after Badini came to him wth. a note in the same hand to tell him *Badini* was to write the words!—What conduct! (fo. 83ᵛ)

Sheridan was obviously floundering without an opera director, as Le Texier had now been sacked; but Pacchierotti understood that Badini had backed down and agreed to let Andrei write the libretto. This was by no means the end of the squabble. After attending a full rehearsal on 12 April, Susan heard

---

[1] Because of a gap in the letter-journal just before this passage (fo. 82ʳ), the exact date when Pacchierotti showed Fanny the songs cannot be determined.

from Pacchierotti that Sheridan had turned against Andrei, and Badini was reinstated as librettist, being 'among the Italians his only favourite' (fo. 92ᵛ). Susan was surprised to hear this, because previously Badini had specialized in comic opera and Andrei in serious. But now Badini was throwing his weight around and even refused to include some words that Pacchierotti had specifically requested that Sacchini set for him. Only much later, at the end of April, did Susan learn that *Rinaldo* was '*not* Badini's but merely *sewn together* by him' (fo. 113ᵛ). The libretto is in fact a poor adaptation of Durandi's fine drama *Armida*, first set by Anfossi for Turin in 1770 and then by Sacchini for a production at Florence in 1772, when the roles of Armida and Rinaldo were created, respectively, by Tenducci and the English soprano Cecilia Davies.[1] Perhaps Badini, Andrei, and Sheridan should share the blame for the continuity problems in the London libretto (E. Cox, 1780),[2] for example, in Act II, Scene i, and especially in Scene ix, in which Rinaldo reports that Armida has saved Ubaldo from the treacherous Idreno before this has happened. Yet these and other weaknesses did not prevent Sacchini from composing (or at least adapting) some excellent music that was universally applauded.

Various members of the Burney family attended at least three rehearsals, and from the first Susan and her father predicted a 'great success' (fo. 94ʳ). But then Pacchierotti fell seriously ill in mid-April, was slow to recover, and, when Sacchini also took to his bed, the first night had to be put off indefinitely.[3] Yet rehearsals continued, because this was a complicated production with choruses and three ballets. Susan, who, like her father, loathed dancing, was irritated when she arrived at the opera-house on Wednesday morning, 19 April, and had to wait for Baccelli and Guiardele (the choreographer) to finish rehearsing a dance. On this occasion there was no conductor: 'Poor Sacchini [is] confined wholly to his Bed with the Gout . . . fretting himself to death' (fo. 98ᵛ). Despite Cramer's sterling efforts, 'nothing seem'd to go so well as at the Rehearsal in the Room of last Week, owing to carelessness in some of the performers, & forgetfulness in others' (fo. 99ʳ). Pieces were omitted and the recitative (of which there was an

---

[1] Sartori, no. 2687, and Marita P. McClymonds, 'Haydn and his Contemporaries: *Armida abbandonata*', in *Proceedings of the International Joseph Haydn Congress* (Munich: Henle, 1986), 325–32.

[2] Dedicated by Badini and Sacchini to Mrs Cecilia Sheridan.

[3] Sheridan was so far ahead with this production that he submitted a copy of the printed libretto to the Lord Chamberlain's office instead of the usual manuscript (see Larpent MS 520).

exceptional amount for a London production) was not rehearsed. This lack of co-ordination was to prove disastrous on the opening night. At the final dress on 21 April, Susan found Guiardele's dances tedious, and she reported that Pacchierotti was tired and 'very pale indeed', because he had to remain on stage 'owing to *3 Dances* besides those interwoven in the piece being rehearsed' (fo. 100ᵛ).

Susan was unable to attend the first night with her father, who reported a packed house and a performance marred by Pacchierotti singing flatter than usual and an incident in the penultimate scene: here Rinaldo, surrounded by furies and other monsters, cuts down the myrtle to break Armida's spell. Some of the furies' torches 'went out, wch. set many fools laughing & so disturbed Pacchierotti that he cd. scarce sing a Note, & this vexatious circumstance ruin'd the effect of the Reca. & air ['Dei pietosi, in tal cimento'] with which I was so struck at the Rehearsals' (fo. 102ʳ). When the unfortunate singer called on Tuesday morning, 25 April, Susan discovered that the incident was more serious than it had appeared to her father sitting in the auditorium. The singer recalled

'four *disgraziate Furie!—Ungraceful Furies*, they came out, & by their bad actions & ridiculous manner they made all the People laugh, & indeed I could not tell how to go on—& all the time they kept beating me like a Martyre—You see Ma'am my face how it is bruised'—(I then found that a large discolour'd spot on his chin which I had taken for *dirt*, was the effect of a blow given him by these careless & awkward Beasts!—You'll exclaim as I did—especially when he went on & told us that he had had another blow on his head, wch. yet pained him extremely, & *several* on his shoulders & Back—'Yet, sd. he, I spoke to them in every language I knew & bid them stop—*it is enough—Basta—C'est assez*—Indeed when I found they wd. not desist, I had a great will to strike them myself, I felt such . . . such *rabbia—Rage*—Indeed—& then in the Newspaper the next day they put it in that I was *embarassed*, & sung too much at the private Concerts—Now on a first Night I never exert myself so much—I never felt more *impegno* . . . *premura* . . . more desire to succeed—but these *dirty scrubs* . . . Indeed they quite made me mad'. (fos. 103ᵛ–104ʳ)

Although this sounds suspiciously like a hired cudgelling, an extraordinary rehearsal was called for the following Friday to correct the problem with the furies, which Pacchierotti blamed on 'the Dancing Master', that is, Favre Guiardele: 'if this had been properly rehearsed before the time of performance, nothing of this sort cd. have happened' (fo. 104ʳ). Susan finally attended a public performance on Saturday, 29 April, when Sacchini sat at the harpsichord but was still so light-headed that he told Rauzzini there 'was *a very bad house*' when in fact the theatre was crowded (fo. 116ʳ). Everything ran smoothly, and the dazed composer 'continued after the curtain was let down to be applauded till he had left the Orchestra' (fo. 115ᵛ). The scenery, to which Susan was usually indifferent, must have been exceptionally elaborate, because she admitted it to be

very good, & *machinery* not bad—I like all but some *Monsters* who in the first scene are supposed to terrify Ubaldo from pursuing his way to Armida's enchanted Palace, but who appear so very *tame*, that one longs to pat their heads & caress them like a good natured Pomeranian Dog—The scene of the Furies went off Extremely well—there were *twelve* of them & they kept *a respectful distance* from Pacchierotti, & seem'd only inclined to *guard the Myrtle*—not to beat him again like a Martyr. (fo. 113ᵛ)

She later dilated more critically on the last scene, to which the furies, thunder, and lightning in her opinion added little to the effect of the music, which had moved her more at the first rehearsal in the coffee-room: 'It reminded me of the Witches in Macbeth, whose speaches when they are *read* freeze one with horror, but when repeated on the stage lose all their effect & become even ludicrous by the absurd appearance of gestures of the Actors' (fo. 115ᵛ). Dr Burney judged an opera on the score alone, his daughter on the dramatic effect of the music as performed.

On 8 June 1780 Susan was surprised to hear a rumour that Napier 'does not intend printing a note of that sweet opera', presumably because of the turmoil into which London had just been thrown by the Gordon Riots.[1] She was therefore grateful to receive from Lady Clarges manuscript copies of several arias, which would consequently be all the more valuable. The rumour proved to be correct: Napier did not in fact print any music from *Rinaldo*, but Bremner brought out *The Favourite Songs in the Opera Rinaldo Composed by Sigr. Sacchini* a year later, after the opera had been revived on 23 December 1780. The delay in publication of extracts from this very successful work, which would normally have appeared soon after the première, might be explained by a disagreement between Sacchini and Napier. But in light of the long-standing practice that an opera became the property of the King's Theatre, any disagreement more likely arose between the managers and the music publisher. The Bremner print is in fact a conflation of

---

[1] The letter-journal includes one of the best eyewitness accounts of the anti-Catholic riots.

TABLE 8. *Contents of* Favourite Songs in . . . Rinaldo

---

1780 première:

   'Calma la pena amara' (Rinaldo—Pacchierotti), II.iv, the famous
     *cantabile*

   'Dolce speme' (Rinaldo), II.vii

1780–81 revival:

   'Se tu seguir mi vuoi' (Zelmira—Lorenzini), I.ii

   'Torni la pace amica' (Idreno—Manzoletto), II.ii

   'Dolce speme' (Rinaldo—Roncaglia), II.vii, second setting

   'Cara, sarò fedele' (Rinaldo & Armida), I.viii, duet-finale

   'Non partir, bell'idol mio' (Armida—Lebrun), II.viii, which evi-
     dently replaced 'Non partir, mio ben tesoro' in the 1780 version

---

numbers from the first production and those composed or adapted for the 1781 revival in which Roncaglia replaced Pacchierotti and Caterina Lorenzini replaced Anna Pozzi. (See Table 8.) Almost all this music merits the praise it received. A possible exception is Armida's 'Non partir, bell'idol mio', a cheery E flat major *andante* with an independent bassoon part that might have rendered Armida's rage comical when she discovers Rinaldo's discarded garland, a symbol of her power over him. The rest is inventive, sophisticated music well tailored to the drama. The *cantabile* for Pacchierotti played to his strengths: long-held notes rising in a simple scale, with Armida's tears being later conveyed by touches of chromaticism. A comparison of the two settings of 'Dolce speme'—the one a G major *rondò andantino* for Pacchierotti, the other an *andante espressivo e grazioso* in the same key for Roncaglia—reveals no pronounced difference in approach, though the latter is slightly more daring harmonically. The first, however, is preceded by a dramatic *recitativo accompagnato* that seems to exploit Pacchierotti's superior acting ability. The enharmonic shift at the words 'pria che m'uccida il barbaro dolore' is almost inspired. (See Ex. 4.5 on pages 242–3.) The most substantial of the numbers that survive from *Rinaldo* is the duet at the end of Act I, 'Cara, sarò fedele', in which Sacchini succeeds in differentiating the two characters musically, even though Armida answers Rinaldo with essentially the same melody (but with different words). As she becomes more passionate, Sacchini reharmonizes the melody with a bass that descends chromatically by semitones. (See Ex. 4.6 on page 244.) The

### Ex. 4.5. Antonio Sacchini, 'Dolce speme' (first setting), from *Rinaldo*

final bombastic section finds both singers up high in thirds; but such clichés are powerfully directed towards the cadence, and his writing for Roncaglia shows there was still a market for thrilling top notes.

To compare the reception of *Rinaldo* and *Quinto Fabio* is not very meaningful, since both were successful. Yet, while this may have been Bertoni's best score, Sacchini, even when laid up with the gout, was a far better composer. (No wonder Bertoni did not attend the first, triumphal rehearsal of *Rinaldo*, as Susan Burney reported, fo. 88ᵛ.) But *Quinto Fabio*, in its equivocal treatment of the *primo uomo* as a character able to shift to his unnatural 'natural' voice when the emotion of the drama demanded, was a milestone on the path to the heroic tenor. London was still a long way from *opera seria* without castrati, and Sheridan's successors spent a lot of money trying to engage the ideal *primo uomo*. In Pacchierotti, Susan Burney and her friends saw a fine singer who happened to be a castrato rather than vice versa, and there is no evidence that their fascination with his tenor voice had anything to do with a desire to reform serious Italian opera.

### Bertoni's Il duca d'Atene

As in the previous season, Sheridan and Harris commissioned a new comic opera from Bertoni, *Il duca d'Atene*. On 28 March 1780 Susan Burney reported that the composer was setting 'Il finto Principe' (its working title) and that by 12 April he was 'very much pressed' to finish it for the first rehearsal on 25 April (fos. 83ᵛ, 89ʳ). It opened to very positive reviews on 9 May.[1] The original libretto (E. Cox, 1780) was written by Badini, who explained in a preface that the plot was drawn from a *commedia dell'arte*

[1] Petty, 171.

Ex. 4.6. Sacchini, 'Cara, sarò fedele', from *Rinaldo*

device, 'Arlecchino finto principe', as well as from the 'induction' or first scene of *The Taming of the Shrew*, to which the opera bears only a vague resemblance: as a jape to divert melancholy, the Duke of Athens orders the peasant Cappochio, who is unconscious from drink and exhausted after a long journey, to be dressed in fancy clothes and carried to a fine bed. When he awakes, the servants treat him like a duke. It is a crude, unsubtle drama, Badini's only refinement being that Cappochio and his betrothed Giochiglia are not duped by the charade but knowingly play along with it, while the duchess never feels threatened by her husband's half-hearted attempt to make love to the peasant girl. To this semi-serious plot Badini added several farcical diversions, including Monsieur de L'Allumette, 'a humorous Frenchman', who is superfluous to the main action and obviously grafted on. In his prefatory comments Badini drew attention to the buffoon by denying a rumour that the character was based on 'a certain foreigner'. L'Allumette's Italian is laced with French, and he describes himself as a 'director of bagatelles'. At the first rehearsal Susan Burney and indeed everyone present immediately saw the parody, wickedly exaggerated by Pietro Gherardi, the new *buffo*:

Badini has made him a *Monsr. Tessier* [that is, Le Texier]—he sings French songs—begs for *protection* in his *subscription*—offers to procure amicable Ladies for any seigneur—& says he was brot. up to the trade of *a Barber*—at the first scene there was a Roar of Laughter from all sides—but Cramer at last told me he was afraid 'twas too strong, & carried to an unjustifiable length tho' he *deserv'd* a great deal. (fo. 117ᵛ)

Cramer's diplomacy may have prevailed yet again, because L'Allumette's part as printed in the libretto is innocuous and has few if any of the bald allusions Susan mentions.[1] (Unfortunately, no Larpent MS survives for this opera, perhaps because it was censored and returned to the managers.) Shortly after the première, Pacchierotti spent a morning with Sheridan, who 'had defended Tessier in the Duca d'Atene, in which Gherardi takes him off . . . like a *Man of honour*, & a *Generous* Man' (fo. 127ʳ). The singer was incredulous that the slippery Sheridan could disclaim all responsibility for the attack, but conceded that it was 'impossible not to feel the *ascendancy* he was capable of gaining over the Minds of those he conversed with'. No

[1] After he left the opera-house, Le Texier organized a *fête* for his own benefit that 'was *manquée* in every particular, except in the size of the Audience—He was call'd for at 3 & a second time at 5 in the Morng. to offer some excuse for imposing so vile an attempt at entertainment on the Public' (fo. 88ᵛ).

music was printed for *Il duca d'Atene*, but Gherardi's catalogue aria 'Nella prima galleria' in Act II, Scene iii, in which L'Allumette lists all the instruments in the orchestra he has assembled for a mock wedding, was singled out for praise in the *Public Advertiser* of 11 May. Interestingly, the send-up of Le Texier was not mentioned in the press. Other Italian comic operas of the period probably included similar parodies and topical allusions, but Badini's revenge would have gone unrecorded save for Susan Burney, who was exquisitely attuned to such undercurrents; she had, for instance, quickly identified the hits in Sheridan's *The Critic* (fo. 34ʳ).

## L'Olimpiade

To conclude this discussion of the 1779–80 season, some mention should be made of the pasticcio *L'Olimpiade*, which Pacchierotti chose for his benefit night. The source libretto is one of Metastasio's happiest creations and was clearly selected as much for its compelling drama as for the lingering popularity of the production in the previous season, which was also a pasticcio. After all, many substitutions could be expected. *L'Olimpiade* illustrates an important point: an *opera seria*, even a pasticcio that would probably comprise a string of well-known arias, needed a strong libretto—ideally one with which the audience was familiar. On 19 February 1780, nearly three weeks before his benefit night, Pacchierotti announced his choice of libretto, but added: 'it will be almost new, as only Pozzi & myself remain of last years Company' (Susan Burney, fo. 69ᵛ). As Table 9 shows, the 1780 production in fact retained three singers from the previous season but, because no libretto survives for either, the disposition of parts cannot be determined precisely.

After the first rehearsal, Susan Burney made a comprehensive record of the pieces she had heard, though she was aggrieved that the drama had been 'so curtailed & mauled' (fo. 74ʳ). The reconstruction of the 1780 version in Table 10 can be only conjectural, since the contents of the previous production, on which it was based, are not precisely known. Pacchierotti's benefit proved so advantageous both to him and to the theatre that Sheridan took the unusual step of announcing a further performance on Tuesday, 14 March.[1] But Madam Lebrun, who also wanted to have this opera for her benefit in April, believing that another performance so soon 'would be very prejudicial to her interest if it was made common before time', feigned

---

[1] *The London Stage*, Part 5, i. 324.

### TABLE 9. *Singers in* L'Olimpiade

| 1779 | Character | 1780 |
|---|---|---|
| Pacchierotti | Clistene? | Pacchierotti |
| Adamberger | Megacle?[a] | Trebbi |
| Coppola | Licida | Manzoletto |
| De Michele | Aminta | De Michele |
| Pozzi | Aristea | Lebrun[b] |
| Bernasconi | Argene | Pozzi |

[a] In some versions of the opera, Megacle is the castrato role.
[b] Lebrun, the *prima donna*, probably sang Aristea.

illness and refused to sing (Susan Burney, fo. 78ᵛ). Sheridan was forced to back down, and *L'amore soldato* was got up instead. Madam Lebrun's benefit duly followed after a decent interval on 27 April. This opera was a chocolate-box selection but it moved Susan as much as Guadagni had in J. C. Bach's famous adaptation of Gluck's *Orfeo* in 1770 (fo. 75ᵛ). Though

### TABLE 10. *Contents of* 'Pacchierotti's' L'Olimpiade *(1780)*

| Piece | Composer | Act | 1779 | Comment |
|---|---|---|---|---|
| overture | Bertoni? | — | yes | 'excessively pretty' |
| 'duet' (Lebrun & Pacc.) | Gazzaniga | I? | yes | |
| 'quintetto' | Sarti | II? | yes | |
| aria from *Scipione* | Bach | II | no | replaced 'Tu me da me stesso' |
| Se cerca, se dice (Pacc.) | Sacchini | II | yes | |
| Tu da mi divvidi (Lebrun) | Bertoni | II | no | |
| 'air' | de Majo | ? | yes | transferred from Coppola |
| Superbo di me stesso (Pacc.) | ? | I | yes | |
| Misero me! che veggo? (Pacc.) | ? | II | ? | |
| Ti seguirò fedele (Pacc.) | ? | II | ? | a *rondò* |

'mauled', *L'Olimpiade* was a 'sweet pretty Pasticcio' that did manage to convey the essence of Metastasio's 'divine' drama.

Sheridan was already in serious financial trouble when the Gordon Riots broke out in the first week of June 1780. Though the King's Theatre remained open through the terrifying nights of destruction happening just a few streets away in and around Leicester Square (among other places further north and east), Susan Burney, an eyewitness to these events, reported that few people dared go out to the Haymarket. Many of her Italian friends and other Roman Catholic acquaintances were so frightened of being attacked by the mob that they removed their name-plates from their front doors; Giardini even took the extra precaution of daubing '*no Popery*' on his door (fo. 141ᵛ). But Pacchierotti, a big man with a heroic reputation to project, refused to remove his name-plate and even walked about the streets at night during the worst of the violence. When order was finally restored and General Gordon locked up in the Tower, opera-going returned to normal within a few days, but the loss of income was a serious blow to the King's Theatre. By 16 June, as the season was drawing to a close, Pacchierotti became increasingly worried that Sheridan would not pay him. The manager audaciously upbraided the *primo uomo* for writing him '*a shocking Letter*': 'Mr. Sheridan tell me he was disappointed himself to have some money paid him, but that very soon he would satisfy me' (fo. 153ʳ). The singer was not the only one whose salary was in arrears. Bertoni had missed '*a very good opportunity to travel with a Gentleman into Italy*' because he was waiting idle in London to be paid (fo. 153ᵛ). Susan remarked that "twas quite a new thing here that there shd. be so much trouble for the Performers to get their salaries paid', and Pacchierotti agreed that he had never heard of any problem at the King's Theatre in the past. Through her acquaintance with Mrs Brooke and with regular attendance at the Italian opera from the age of about 15, Susan can be regarded as a reliable authority on this matter. And, indeed, there seems to have been no major problem with unpaid opera salaries since Giardini's unsuccessful 1763–64 season. By 18 June 1780 nothing had been settled yet, though Peter Crawford, who was to become the official director of opera in place of Le Texier for the 1780–81 season, was acting for Sheridan. Pacchierotti told Crawford that unless he and Bertoni were paid by Wednesday, 21 June, they would hire a lawyer 'who is to have the charge of reimbursing himself as soon as possible *by Lawyer's means*' (fo. 160ᵛ). Sheridan's partial solution was to extend the season beyond 30 June, the date when Pacchierotti's contract expired. Over the singer's protests, the last

performance was on Saturday, 1 July (fo. 168ʳ), when he and the other performers earned Sheridan the money he already owed them. Since the final
entry in Susan Burney's letter-journal for this year is 21 June, we do not
know if Pacchierotti was paid his full salary but, at their last recorded meeting, she found the singer in good spirits and looking forward to a holiday at
Spa before travelling on to Venice for his next engagement.

## V. The 1780–81 Season: Ansani versus Roncaglia

Repertoire:

*L'arcifanfano*, pasticcio arranged by Bianchi with numbers by Scolari, libretto after Gol-
doni, 25 November 1780 (1 performance); orig. Lisbon (rua dos Condes) 1770 (p. 254)
*La buona figliuola*, Piccinni, libretto by Goldoni, 28 November 1780 (1 performance); orig.
Rome (Dame) 1760. London 1766 → 1780
*Ricimero*, pasticcio arranged by Bianchi, one number by Guglielmi, librettist unknown,
2 December 1780 (5 performances)
*Le serve rivali*, Traetta arranged by Bianchi, libretto after Chiari, 19 December 1780 (5 per-
formances); orig. Venice (S. Moisè) 1766. London (as *I capricci del sesso*) 1777
*Rinaldo*, Sacchini (revision of *Armida*), libretto by Durandi adapted by Badini, 23 December
1780 (9 performances); orig. Milan (Regio Ducal) 1772. London 1780
*Mitridate*, Sacchini, anonymous libretto adapted by Badini, 23 January 1781 (7 perform-
ances) (p. 250)
*Il barone di Torreforte*, Piccinni, arranged by Bianchi, librettist unknown, 22 February 1781
(16 performances); orig. Rome (Capranica) 1765 (p. 254)
*Zemira e Azore*, Grétry, libretto trans. from Marmontel, 8 March 1781 (2 performances); orig.
Fontainebleau 1771. London 1779
*Piramo e Tisbe*, Rauzzini, libretto by Calzabigi after Coltellini, 29 March 1781 (10 perform-
ances); orig. London 1775
*La frascatana*, Paisiello, libretto after Livigni, 5 April 1781 (10 performances); orig. Venice (S.
Samuele) 1774. London 1776, 1778
*L'omaggio*, pasticcio with numbers by Rauzzini, Giordani, and Bianchi, librettist unknown,
5 June 1781 (4 performances)
*Euriso*, Sacchini ('with Improvements'), libretto by Pizzi, 23 June 1781 (4 performances); orig.
as *Creso*, Naples (S. Carlo) 1765. London ?1774, 1777

The straitened financial condition of the King's Theatre at the end of the
1779–80 season is seen most obviously in the repertoire of the next. Of the
twelve works mounted, only Sacchini's *Mitridate* was newly commissioned,
and that production was beset with difficulty. The only conspicuous success
this season was an adaptation of Piccinni's comic opera *Il barone di Torreforte*, which received sixteen performances. But Sheridan relied principally
on safe revivals, such as Grétry's *Zemira e Azore* and Sacchini's *Rinaldo*. His

intention to commission an opera from Bach came to nothing.[1] Lack of money and poor planning are also reflected in the singers engaged for this season. By previous arrangement, Roncaglia returned as *primo uomo*; Madam Lebrun, whose star was now waning in London, was re-engaged as *prima donna seria*. Bertoni's place as arranger, harpsichordist, and conductor of pasticcios, if not 'house composer', seems to have been taken by Bianchi.[2] In order to fill the void left by Pacchierotti's return to the Continent and to help re-establish the position of *primo tenore* left vacant since Adamberger's departure two seasons before, Sheridan hired the highly touted Giovanni Ansani. His mishandling of this temperamental singer could only have hastened Sheridan's decision to give up the King's Theatre. The bitter dispute between the tenor and his rival Roncaglia, which quickly engulfed Sacchini and the two house poets Badini and Andrei, was more than just a little local difficulty: the fundamental issue that lay beneath the unseemly squabble was the inability of *opera seria* to adapt quickly enough to the changing position of the *primo tenore* relative to the *primo uomo*.

## Sacchini's Mitridate

The dispute, which soured the whole 1780–81 season for the opera company, centred on Sacchini's *Mitridate* (première 23 January 1781) and involved two other works, Bianchi's pasticcio *Ricimero* and the revival of Sacchini's *Rinaldo*. To help the reader follow this complicated story, here are the bare facts: Ansani, who had been singing the role of Ubaldo in *Rinaldo*, withdrew from the production on 20 January, citing as his reason a disagreement with Sheridan. When he was replaced by the *tenore buffo* Trebbi on 22 January, Ansani suddenly broke his contract with the King's Theatre and proceeded to give a series of successful concerts at the Pantheon. After being criticized in an article in the *Morning Chronicle* of 22 January, which claimed that *Rinaldo* was better without him, Ansani responded in the *Morning Herald* on 3 February 1781 with a very long explanation of his actions. This highly spirited and at times vitriolic defence should not be accepted uncritically, but the account of his dealings with Sheridan and particularly with Badini are so similar to Bertoni's and Pacchierotti's of the previous season that Ansani seems generally credible. That there was already trouble brewing between him and Roncaglia can be

---

[1] See the pre-season advertisement in the *Morning Herald*, 3 Nov. 1780.

[2] This was probably Giovanni Battista rather than the better known Francesco Bianchi. See *Biographical Dictionary*, ii. 107.

inferred from a review of the première of *Ricimero* in the *Public Advertiser,* 4 December 1780: the castrato 'seemed hurt at sharing with Ansani those marks of public Favour. We exhort them both to remember that Persons of their superior Talents ought to lay aside every petty Prejudice and personal Animosity.'

Ansani traced their differences back to a season at Florence when Roncaglia, as *primo uomo,* wanted to initiate a production of *Mitridate.* This was almost certainly Giuseppe Sarti's *Mitridate a Sinope,* given at the royal theatre in autumn 1779.[1] Ansani claimed that Roncaglia used his influence at Florence to procure him the title-role in this projected opera, which the tenor then rejected, because it was 'much out of his usual cast of parts'. It was sung instead by the tenor Carlo Angiolini. As suggested below, the probable reasons for his refusal, which caused Roncaglia great offence, lay more in the drama itself than in his envy of the castrato. That there was something about the subject of the opera *per se* that Ansani objected to is shown by his chagrin when in London Roncaglia with 'envious spirit' prevailed upon Sacchini to choose *Mitridate* as his *opera seria* for the 1780–81 season. Ansani reluctantly agreed to sing in it, but only after Sheridan had promised (in the presence of Crawford and Luppino the opera tailor) that the drama would be altered in accordance with the tenor's wishes. (Ansani was angry that Roncaglia had prevented him from introducing any substitute arias into *Ricimero* that might have allowed the public to form a 'proper judgment' of his talent.) Hoping that Sacchini's *Mitridate* would include a part that would show his full potential, Ansani was shocked upon receiving his music to see that it bore none of the alterations Sheridan had promised.

He then turned to Badini—according to Ansani '*a character not less known in Italy than in England*'—to write an extra scene for him in Act III, an insertion he assumed would not require any adjustments elsewhere in the opera. But Badini produced a scene 'totally different from that to which Mr. Sheridan had agreed, and as disagreeable as the original scene of which he had complained'. The tenor then approached the other house poet Andrei, who was naturally reluctant to get involved, having had his fingers burnt over the libretto for *Rinaldo* in 1780. But Andrei did, according to Ansani's account, finally write a scene that was 'translated into English, for

---

[1] This was not the same as the famous Cigna-Santi libretto that Mozart used for his first Italian opera in 1770, but one should recall that he too had trouble with his tenor, Guglielmo d'Ettore, in the title-role.

Mr. Sheridan's perusal'.[1] That Sheridan ever approved of Andrei's substitute scene, as Ansani claims, is doubtful, given the manager's previous favoritism towards Badini. The printed libretto (no publisher, 1781) suggests that Sacchini set the opera as originally planned, with no big scene for the tenor (Mitridate) in the last act.[2] Ansani was ready to quit the King's Theatre immediately but, since Sheridan was out of town when the storm blew up, his partner William Taylor persuaded the tenor to stay on for two more performances of *Rinaldo,* presumably those on 13 and 16 January.[3] But when the opera-house announced his further appearance in *Rinaldo* on 20 January, Ansani abruptly left, publishing a brief explanation in the *Morning Chronicle* of the same day. Later, in trying to spike various rumours, Ansani revealed that he was contracted to receive £600 plus a free benefit this season (an upper-middle range salary and half what a *primo uomo* of Pacchierotti's stature would have received); that he had been given no advance in Italy; that he had covered his own travelling expenses; and that he had received £200 by Christmas 1780.

Sacchini was incensed that Ansani should blame him for any part of the dispute. In the *Morning Chronicle* of 27 January 1781, the composer published his version of events:

I have ever made it my object and ambition to do every thing in my power to oblige and satisfy the performers I have composed for, as well as to deserve the generous protection and encouragement I have met with from my employers and the public in general. With regard to Mr. Ansani, I repeatedly offered to recompose any Song he objected to in the Opera of Mithridate, and he has often professed himself satisfied with the part, and promised to perform it after the Opera of Ricimero should have been got up for his first appearance, which was consented to by the manager, solely to gratify him, to the delay of my Opera and the great inconvenience of the Theatre.

What has since influenced Mr. Ansani to break his engagement at the Opera, and to pretend to lay the fault on me, I am at a loss to determine; but the public will easily decide when they are informed, that he had, contrary to his articles,

---

[1] Sheridan's evident inability to read Italian is surprising in one who chose to meddle with the librettos he commissioned. Perhaps Le Texier was thinking of Sheridan when he included in his list of the prerequisites of a good opera manager a knowledge of foreign languages. See *Ideas on the Opera,* 37. One should note in this context that manuscript librettos submitted to the Lord Chamberlain's office were rarely accompanied by English translations.

[2] Larpent MS 544 does, however, seem to reflect these difficulties, as it includes only the first act, in fair copy.

[3] This is the earliest mention of Taylor's direct involvement with the artistic affairs of the King's Theatre. He became joint manager with Sheridan in Jan. 1781; see C12/2171/23.

engaged himself with the Proprietors of the Pantheon, at the very time he was affecting to solicit unreasonable alterations in the Opera of Mithridate, and requesting permission from his real employers to Depart for Italy.

We must stress that this dispute did not turn on Ansani's ability as a performer: Dr Burney said he 'had one of the best tenor voices I ever heard on our opera stage';[1] Mount Edgcumbe added that he 'was a spirited actor, and in the first opera, called Ricimero, sustained the most prominent and important part'.[2] Rather, at issue here was the dramatic structure of the libretto as set by Sacchini, which is not based directly on Cigna-Santi, though both have a common source in Racine's play about father-and-son rivals for the same woman. The opera opens with the prospect of a double wedding: King Mitridate will marry the beautiful Greek Princess Almira, and his son Farnace, Princess Irene. But Farnace (the castrato part) and Almira (Madam Lebrun) are secret lovers, and the first scene is an assignation between them. The opera explores how Mitridate (the tenor) reacts to the discovery that his son is his rival in love. In Sacchini's version the king, who suspects the truth as early as Act I, Scene v, decides to test his suspicion in Act II, Scene iii. He brings Farnace and Almira together and tells them (without being certain) that he already knows they are lovers. When they confess, Mitridate is forced to dissemble a blessing. His following aria, 'Ti lascio al ben che adori' (for which no music survives) is delivered entirely as an aside—a potential *tour de force*. The rest of the opera is basically concerned with Farnace's guilt towards his father, which is assuaged only in Act III when Mitridate proves to be a coward in the face of battle. Neither character achieves moral supremacy; each remains flawed, though one can easily understand why Ansani wanted a different ending—probably a scene of redemption in place of his panicky attempt to torch the city in advance of the Roman invasion. But Sheridan (or perhaps Badini or Sacchini) was right to resist this alteration. The equivocal nature of the drama depended on a rather weak *primo uomo* and a strong, though not overpowering, tenor. There is no shining hero in *Mitridate*, no moral pecking-order or rank determined by the difficulty or beauty of the music. This subtle characterization would have been difficult to maintain with a virtuoso castrato such as Pacchierotti or Marchesi as Farnace. Casting a fine singer like Ansani as Mitridate would have helped to assure a balance between the two characters.

---

[1] *General History*, ii. 891.　　[2] *Musical Reminiscences*, 18.

More than a month after the 3 February première, in which Trebbi had replaced Ansani, a satirical letter appeared in the *Morning Herald* highly critical of Sacchini, whose faculties were said to be impaired by age, and Roncaglia, who was no better than a 'second man'. Besides missing the point about the delicate relationship between the castrato and tenor roles in the opera, the writer's opinion of Sacchini is not supported by the five numbers that appeared in *The Favourite Songs in the Opera Mitridate* (Bremner). All are notable for a lack of vocal passage-work—perhaps understandable in the four pieces that included Roncaglia, but unexpected in 'Adorata mia speranza' for Madam Lebrun (Almira) in Act II, Scene v. This is not flashy but deceptively sophisticated music. Roncaglia's 'Io parto ben mio', which Farnace sings just after his beloved Almira has been taken from his arms later in Act II, Scene v, begins with an incongruously carefree F major tune decorated with triplet quavers, but the augmented- and Neapolitan-sixth chords traditionally expressive of anguish are merely delayed until the end of the A section of this modified *da capo* aria, in itself rather archaic for Sacchini in 1781. By far the most impressive piece in this collection is Farnace's *rondò* 'Resta in pace' from Act III, Scene ii. This is probably the scene that Ansani feared would eclipse him in the role of Mitridate. The main theme in A major is purposely awkward, starting and stopping, thus rendering as ironic the words 'Resta in pace amato bene e conservami 'l tuo cor'. (See Ex. 4.7.) Farnace's consternation at being caught between loyalty to his father and love for Almira finally breaks through in the fourth section of the aria, *molto agitato*, with a new melody that begins in A minor, then modulates to C major before working its way back through E major to the main theme. (See Ex. 4.8 on pages 256–7.) Though this piece is in the conventional five-section form, with the *rondò* theme energized for the drive to final cadence, it is admirably concise, reflecting its position late in the drama, yet resisting any tendency towards a premature grand finale.

## L'arcifanfano *and Piccinni's* Il barone di Torreforte

Less imagination and sense of purpose are evident in the comic operas offered this season, the first of which was a pasticcio conducted by Bianchi (also presumably the arranger) called *L'arcifanfano* (25 November 1780). It was 'universally disapproved of' and not repeated.[1] Such utter failure was rare, even later under Taylor and the trustees when the King's Theatre was

---

[1] *The London Stage*, Part 5, i. 390.

Ex. 4.7. Sacchini, 'Resta in pace', from *Mitridate*

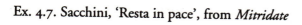

Ex. 4.8. Sacchini, 'Resta in pace', from *Mitridate*

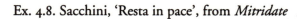

drifting out of control. Bianchi's concoction comprises three short acts, each with an extended ensemble finale.[1] A review in the *Morning Chronicle*, 27 November 1780, is damning and also hints that Sheridan had failed to exercise his authority:

The Italian Comic Opera, call'd *L'arcifanfano*, represented last Saturday night at the King's Theatre in the Hay-market, was originally written by Goldoni.[2] The

[1] The only known copy of the printed libretto is Sartori 2405, in the Staatsbibliothek Preussischer Kulturbesitz, Berlin. We have worked from Larpent MS 538.
[2] First set by Giuseppe Scolari for Lisbon in 1768; see Piero Weiss, *Opera Grove*, iv. 272. For an important study of Goldoni's works in England (including opera), see Jackson I.

subject is in itself exceedingly insipid and dull, but rendered infinitely more so by the bad choice of the music, that was adapted to it for the Opera-House. We could not perceive a tolerable air in the whole score, excepting the rondeau written by Giardini, and sung by Miss Prudom in the second act.[1] As we are well-wishers to the proprietor of the Opera-House, we would advise him to lay all pasticcios aside, and to endeavour to bring out new subjects set by able composers, or at least to revive some of those old operas that have met with universal approbation and are now quite sunk in oblivion, as *Il bacio*, *Le pazzie d'Orlando*, *Il carnovale di Venezia*, *Il duca d'Atene*, &c. We believe our opinion in this matter coincides with that of the present director, and that the condemned opera of *L'arcifanfano* was chosen against his consent. We hope therefore that this gentleman in future will enforce his authority, and that the performers, for their own sakes, will patiently submit to his judgment.

A very similar, though less detailed, review was run the same day in the *Public Advertiser*, complete with the attack on the pasticcio as a threat to the manager's authority, a coincidence suggesting that both reviews were placed by someone on the theatre's behalf. The ever-popular *La buona figliuola* was immediately brought on to fill the repertory gap.

The other new comic production this season fared much better, Piccinni's *Il barone di Torreforte*, also arranged and conducted by Bianchi. First performed at Rome in 1765, it would seem an odd choice for revival in London. But early Piccinni, especially *La buona figliuola*, was more popular than the more recent music, which even Susan Burney found 'incoherent' and 'difficult'. The opera, written to an anonymous libretto, also offered two other features that would have appealed to the King's Theatre subscribers: a strong plot and a gimmick. The baron's attempted abduction and rape of Lucinda is protracted skilfully over nearly two full acts and is finally thwarted only during the course of the second-act finale. The gimmick is Armidoro's magic-lantern show (complete with slides of camels and the King of Morocco), which occupies part of the first-act finale. The opera was considerably adapted: one of the original characters, Don Gallarino, was dropped entirely, and Larpent MS 547 shows three last-minute aria substitutions: 'Siete una figlia amabile' (Serpina—Signora Prudom)[2] replaced 'Si lo giurò o ninfa bella' in Act I, Scene v; Giordani's 'Sento che in seno'

---

Cope, 'Goldoni's England and England's Goldoni', *MLN*, forthcoming.

[1] Presumably Garbata's 'Zitto che' in Act II, Scene i, though the *Public Advertiser* of 27 Nov. 1780 singles out her aria 'Dite amor', which does not appear in the Larpent copy.

[2] So indicated by the speech prefix in the printed libretto (E. Cox, n.d.), but probably sung by Armidoro (Trebbi).

(Lucinda—Signora Sestini) replaced 'Amato mio bene' in Act II, Scene ii; and 'Dalla saetta, dalla rovella' (baron—Gherardi) in the printed libretto was apparently replaced by 'Vedete che ridicolo' in the Larpent copy, in the same scene. Other changes and revisions are also evident in the manuscript libretto. Another new production this season that requires little comment here was *L'omaggio*, a plotless pastoral medley of music by Bianchi, Rauzzini, and Giordani offered four times in June as a prelude to a masquerade. It will be discussed in Chapter 7.

Surveying the Italian opera of the Sheridan regime, one sees the innovative and highly varied first season and the personal triumphs for Sacchini, Bertoni, and Pacchierotti in the second give way to an uninspired and patchy third. There are signs that this decline was the result of economy measures. Only one new *opera seria* was commissioned in 1780–81, *Mitridate*, and it required no exceptional scenic effects or chorus. The absence of a first-rank castrato (who normally received some £1,200 per season) also saved Sheridan some money, though Roncaglia was paid £1,000, as was the *prima donna seria* Madam Lebrun. But, as is known from later lawsuits, Sheridan was unable to meet the full contracted salaries of many of his performers: for example, Roncaglia was owed £100 and Madam Lebrun £200.[1] The 1780–81 season also seems to have lost its way artistically. Bertoni, for all his shortcomings as a composer and lack of authority in the orchestra pit, had given the King's Theatre repertoire an air of respectability, if not quality, which Bianchi, clearly a mediocrity, failed to provide. Yet the most significant musical event of this last season is the beginning of the end for Sacchini. *Mitridate* may have been weakened by the Ansani–Roncaglia dispute, but the opera lacked the varied spectacle of *Enea e Lavinia* and the integrity of *Rinaldo*. The concerted campaign to discredit Sacchini, the first salvo of which was the mock letter in the *Morning Herald* quoted above, soon escalated into public allegations of plagiarism. The King's Theatre thus began a five-year artistic decline but, with the prospect of Bertoni and Pacchierotti's return engagement for 1781–82, perhaps only Sheridan, who was about to wash his hands of the whole affair, could foresee the dark times ahead.

[1] C33/455, fo. 5.

# CHAPTER 5

# Opera under Taylor and his Trustees
# (1781–1785)

FEW periods in the history of the King's Theatre can match the four seasons between 1781 and 1785 for managerial chaos and artistic indirection. The emergence of William Taylor in autumn 1781 as the principal proprietor in succession to Sheridan and the series of unmitigated financial disasters that followed have already been discussed in Chapter 2. Their effect on opera production was not, however, straightforward and did not prove immediately disastrous. The major musical events of this period of management—Sacchini's decision to leave London amid accusations of plagiarism, the re-engagement of Pacchierotti, and the fruitful tenure of Pasquale Anfossi as house composer—seem to have been unrelated to the upheavals in the business office. But other developments clearly were connected: the come-back of the apparently washed-up singers Tenducci and Rauzzini (the first as performer, the second as composer-arranger and later performer); the augmentation of the orchestra in 1782 and the cut-back only a year later; the emergence of the former singer Leopoldo De Michele as a key figure in the company; the entanglement of opera-house affairs with the Hanover Square concerts; and, most obviously, the international scandal of the performers' unpaid salaries at the end of the 1782–83 season.

One should not be too quick to heap all the blame on the management for what might today be perceived as a decline in the quality of opera offered by the King's Theatre during these troubled years. The mess that Taylor and his immediate successors made of the company coincided with two general, and conflicting, stylistic changes which Italian opera was undergoing at the time right across Europe. First, in *opera seria* the last traces of counterpoint and structural chromaticism that once characterized the Neapolitan style were being washed away, and the music began to emulate the lyrical sentimentalism that had already affected *opera buffa*. Sacchini, who resisted the worst excesses of what might be called the 'new simplicity', nevertheless defended this change. In an important conversation with the oboist Ludwig August Lebrun over lunch in London about 1780, Sacchini responded to the allegation that modern Italian music does not modulate enough:

We do modulate in church music. Because the attention is not distracted by theatrical incident, it can more easily follow artistically integrated changes of key. But in the theatre one must be clear and simple; one must touch the heart but not disturb it; and one must make oneself comprehensible to less practised ears. The composer who can write contrasting arias without changing key shows far more talent than the one who changes it every few moments.[1]

Sacchini's own Italian arias are harmonically adventurous compared with the numbing stasis of Bertoni, Anfossi, or even the mature Paisiello, but his defence confirms the harmonic and contrapuntal emasculation of *opera seria* about 1780, especially at the King's Theatre where, if the heart was often moved, the intellect was hardly ever disturbed. No wonder there was such a craze for Pacchierotti's *cantabile* cavatinas, so often at odds with the surrounding blood and thunder of the post-Metastasio finale.

The second major change was in comic opera, which was becoming much more sophisticated, both dramatically, with librettos by the younger generation including Da Ponte, and musically: witness the later works of Paisiello and Martín y Soler in which the weight of the music was finally coming into balance with the psychological and social realism of the drama. London, still wedded to the old-fashioned *primo uomo / prima donna seria* system, was caught unprepared for this new aesthetic: towards the end of the 1780–81 season, Taylor's agent was writing frantically to Italy in search of an accomplished *primo buffo*, the comic troupe having previously been regarded as almost an afterthought. The first King's Theatre manager who realized he would need both first-class serious and comic singers was Gallini in 1785–86. Before this, under Taylor and the trustees, the opera company was inherently biased towards expensive serious singers, and comic opera suffered as a result.

With the company directed by a succession of proprietors who had little or no knowledge of the musical side of opera—Sheridan and Harris,

---

[1] This anecdote, which is the thesis of a chapter of E. T. A. Hoffmann's *Kreisleriana*, was first published in Ernst Ludwig Gerber's *Historisch-biographisches Lexicon der Tonkünstler*, 3 (Leipzig, [1792]), cols. 361–2. See *E. T. A. Hoffmann's Musical Writings*, ed. David Charlton (Cambridge: Cambridge University Press, 1989), 152.

Crawford, Taylor and, initially, even Gallini himself—responsibility for the repertoire and to some extent performers' engagements devolved downwards; Taylor, however, even after handing over to his trustees, tried to retain the right to make engagements. During Sheridan's last season Sacchini was allowed to choose his own libretto, a prerogative that other managers jealously reserved for themselves. Towards the end of Taylor's first regime, the power vacuum was, perhaps surprisingly, filled by the bass and former *ultima parte*, Leopoldo De Michele, who had retired from the stage after the 1781–82 season. He became the official house music-copyist; soon thereafter he was also appointed a trustee (partly because he was one of Taylor's creditors). De Michele even accompanied Crawford to Italy in the summer of 1783 on their ill-fated recruiting trip. This was a lot of responsibility for the lowly former singer. De Michele was what would now be called a 'dramaturge': he often determined the final form of librettos, prepared scores for production, helped assign parts, and even arranged arias and composed simple recitative. Later, during Gallini's tenure when more music specialists were hired, De Michele was still in effect the music director. He also oversaw the sale of music to publishers, this being a source of considerable income. Once ridiculed as a third-rate performer, De Michele found himself for a time at the centre of the company.

No organization, particularly one devoted to art, can function without proper leadership. In his *Ideas on the Opera* of 1790, Le Texier, who knew from experience, laid all the blame for what he called the deplorable quality of recent King's Theatre productions on the lack of 'good administration'. Under Taylor, the opera company was almost totally out of financial control. In retrospect, one can see that it was also teetering on the brink of artistic bankruptcy, though the King's Theatre was often filled to capacity during these difficult years. The Italian opera in London would eventually be saved from greater degradation by Gallini, but his hard-won battle for control of the theatre was immediately vitiated by everyone from Taylor to the Lord Chamberlain himself.

## I. The 1781–82 Season: Sacchini's 'Disgrace'

Repertoire:

*Ezio*, pasticcio arranged by Bertoni with numbers by Anfossi and Sacchini, libretto after Metastasio, 17 November 1781 (16 performances). London (earlier pasticcios on this libretto) 1765, 1767 (p. 268)

*I viaggiatori felici*, Anfossi, arranged by Bertoni, libretto by Livigni, 11 December 1781 (28 performances); orig. Venice (S. Samuele) 1780 (p. 270)

*La buona figliuola*, Piccinni, libretto by Goldoni, 10 January 1782 (9 performances); orig. Rome (Dame) 1760. London 1766 →1780

*Giunio Bruto*, pasticcio arranged by Bertoni, libretto by Pindemonte, 12 January 1782 (3 performances) (p. 273)

*La contadina in corte*, Sacchini (revised), libretto after Tassi, 2 March 1782 (13 performances); orig. Rome (Valle) 1765. London 1771, 1779

*Quinto Fabio*, Bertoni, libretto by Andrei after Zeno, 7 March 1782 (2 performances); orig. Milan (Interinale) 1778. London 1780

*L'eroe cinese*, Rauzzini, libretto after Metastasio, 16 March 1782 (10 performances) (p. 276)

*Il bacio*, T. Giordani, libretto by Badini, 9 April 1782 (3 performances) (p. 278)

*Ifigenia in Aulide*, Bertoni, libretto by Cigna-Santi altered by Andrei, 25 May 1782 (1 performance); orig. Turin (Regio) 1762 (p. 283)

The first season of Taylor's regime brought critical acclaim, an excellent subscription for a varied and adventurous repertoire, and several distinguished engagements, including the return of Pacchierotti 'who every body says is much finer than when he was [here] two years ago'[1] and, much more important, the first engagement at the King's Theatre of the great balletmaster Jean Georges Noverre (see Ch. 7). As with Sheridan's management three years before, few opera-goers would have known the company was being run by someone with no previous experience of Italian opera—indeed by someone almost completely unfamiliar with the theatre world, ignorant of music and all foreign languages. Yet at the beginning of the season, Lady Mary Coke reported that 'every body this year seems satisfied both with the musick & dancing' (25–26 November 1781).

Even more than Sheridan, Taylor delegated the artistic management of the company; at the end of the previous season, he apparently asked a subscriber, one W. A. Crosbie, to write to Lord Cowper at Florence to help find a *buffo caricato* to replace Pietro Gherardi. Crosbie first requested (22 May 1781) that Cowper treat with the *basso* Giovanni Morelli and later (27 June 1781) with the famous Francesco Benucci. Crosbie was aiming very high, especially considering the miserly offer of £300 for the season (the salary Gherardi, a much inferior performer, had received).[2] Morelli did not come to London until 1787, Benucci not until 1789. Instead, for the 1781–82 season the affable buffoon Andrea Morigi, who had last sung at the King's Theatre in the early 1770s, was re-engaged. Taylor's company was substantially intact by 27 October 1781, when a general notice was placed in the *Morning Chronicle*. Once again, the venerable J. C. Bach was listed among the house composers, but he died on 1 January 1782. A more immediate

---

[1]  Lady Mary Coke, 4 Dec. 1781.
[2]  Letters printed in Gibson, 'Earl Cowper', 239–40.

problem for Taylor was the engagement of Signora Macchierini as *prima donna seria*. She was probably responsible for the failure of *Giunio Bruto* in January, after which she was advertised for no further operas.

To what extent Taylor, locked in a continuous legal and financial battle with Gallini for possession of the opera-house, was involved in making any of these engagements is unknown. The only clear evidence of his direct involvement with the artistic side of the company this season is the presence of his signature on the applications to the Lord Chamberlain for licences for *Giunio Bruto* and *L'eroe cinese*.[1] (Taylor's signature is in fact extremely rare amongst the hundreds of documents relating to opera in the 1780s and 90s, perhaps an indication of his slippery legal mind.) Taylor desperately needed an opera manager, someone who could deal with French dancers and Italian singers, write letters of engagement, mediate among librettists, composers, and performers, and generally supervise production. The two most able persons in London for the job were probably Le Texier, Sheridan's now discredited manager, and Gallini, who was of course completely hostile to the present management. Instead, Taylor turned first to Peter Crawford as 'Acting Manager' to get the company up and running in the autumn of 1781, and then signed a formal contract with Domenico Angelo on 20 February 1782.[2] This curious document gave Angelo considerable responsibility and almost no authority. He was 'to procure singers Dancers and other Performers from abroad or elsewhere', to attend all opera and ballet rehearsals, and to manage these and other entertainments. He was to report directly to Taylor, who reserved the right 'of making confirming and executing all Engagements whatever'. In other words, Angelo's decisions could be overruled at any time. The contract is only of academic interest, since Angelo seems to have left almost no trace of his activities and was soon effectively supplanted by Crawford, who was assisted in musical and linguistic matters by De Michele.

### The Rauzzini–Sacchini Controversy

The absence of strong musical direction probably did little to temper the infamous dispute between the house composers Sacchini and Rauzzini. This bitter wrangle, which clouded the whole season, was at the time confined to the newspapers, but the consequences for Sacchini were serious enough for Burney to ruminate on the affair in his *General History* (1789). Sacchini, he writes,

---

[1] Larpent MSS 581 and 588.  [2] Printed above, Ch. 3, pp. 116–17.

remained too long in England for his fame and fortune. The first was injured by cabals and by what ought to have increased it, the number of his works; and the second by inactivity and want of œconomy. Upon a difference with Signor Rauzzini, this singer from a fond friend became his most implacable foe; declaring himself to be the author of the principal songs in all the late operas to which Sacchini had set his name; and threatening to make affidavit of it before a magistrate. The utmost I could ever believe of this accusation was, that during Sacchini's severe fits of the gout, when he was called upon for his operas before they were ready, he might have employed Rauzzini, as he and others had done Anfossi in Italy, to fill up the parts, set some of the recitatives, and perhaps compose a few of the flimsy airs for the under singers. (ii. 894–5)

This scrupulous statement is misconstrued and expanded in the *New Grove*: 'Faced with the threat of imprisonment, Sacchini left England in 1781 [actually 1782] and went to Paris.'[1] The only effective legal recourse open to Rauzzini at the time would have been through the Court of Chancery: had Sacchini published Rauzzini's music as his own (which he did not do), then Rauzzini could have sued for damages, citing *Bach* v. *Longman and Lukey* as precedent.[2] The Court of Chancery had no power to order imprisonment in cases of plagiarism. It was in fact Rauzzini, not Sacchini, who went to gaol—to debtors' prison in May 1782 and again in January 1783.[3]

The dispute was sparked by Rauzzini's setting of Metastasio's *L'eroe cinese*, which achieved a respectable ten performances this season. Press notices were suspiciously glowing. The *Morning Herald* of 18 March 1782 mischievously prefaced its review with some gossip 'that the operas attributed to a certain mercenary, but celebrated composer [that is, Sacchini] were done by Rauzzini'. The paper declined to confirm or deny the rumour, but went on to declare that 'S[acchini] in his former idiom never composed in a better style than the author of *L'Eroe cinese*'. The *Morning Post* of the same day went so far as to risk a libel: the excellence of *L'eroe cinese* confirms 'that Rauzzini has been the main instrument upon which Sacchini's pretentions to musical reputation have been principally founded'. Burney suggests that Rauzzini may have assisted the master during his frequent illnesses and implies that at the very least Rauzzini did not deny these reports though, as far as can be determined, neither composer said anything publicly at the

---

[1] David Di Chiera, 'Sacchini', *New Grove*, xiv. 370, a mistake repeated in *Opera Grove*, iv. 114.

[2] See John Small, 'J. C. Bach Goes to Law', *The Musical Times*, 126 (1985), 526–9; and David Hunter, 'Musical Copyright in Britain to 1800', *Music & Letters*, 67 (1986), 269–82.

[3] PRO PRIS 10/51, pp. 29 and 41.

time. While not enough of Rauzzini's music for Italian operas survives to allow a fair comparison, that which does suggests he was a mere pygmy to the giant Sacchini.

The last notable case of musical plagiarism in England had been the Lotti madrigal scandal of 1731, which left Giovanni Bononcini humiliated and discredited.[1] That centred on a false claim of authorship of one piece; the Rauzzini–Sacchini controvery, by contrast, called into question a sizable portion of a composer's *œuvre*. Originality was of growing interest in late eighteenth-century English intellectual circles; the issue for literature was first comprehensively addressed by the poet Edward Young in *Conjectures on Original Composition* (1759),[2] and applied to music by several later writers, including Hawkins and Burney. Originality in music was also being defined legally: the implications of the judgment in the case of *Bach* v. *Longman and Lukey* in 1777, which finally brought music under the protection of the Copyright Act, were beginning to sink in. Musical ideas could be very valuable commodities indeed.

Susan Burney, who was well acquainted with both parties in the dispute over *L'eroe cinese*, was also interested in the question of originality in music. There are hints in her letter-journal of 1779–80 of the later troubles between Rauzzini and Sacchini, though her worries primarily focused on her friend Bertoni. In 1780 the three composers saw each other frequently and showed the greatest courtesy towards one another in public. Sacchini was regarded as a truly great figure against whom all other opera composers were to be measured. For instance, while Susan admired Bertoni's aria 'Va crescendo il mio tormento' in *Quinto Fabio*, she noted upon first hearing it that it is '*strongly* in Sacchini's manner—rather too much, not for the song but the Composer' (fo. 66ᵛ). From the context, one can see that Susan was concerned not merely about stylistic similarities but whether Bertoni had stolen from Sacchini. Probably because of her partisan feelings for Pacchierotti, she did not particularly like Rauzzini, a potential rival, and tried to avoid him (see, for example, fo. 25ʳ). She did, however, record a revealing conversation amongst a group of friends and admirers who gathered round Sacchini after a rehearsal of his opera *Rinaldo* in 1780.

[1] See Lowell Lindgren, 'The Three Great Noises "Fatal to the Interests of Bononcini"', *Musical Quarterly*, 61 (1975), 560–83.

[2] *Conjectures on Original Composition. In a Letter to the Author of Sir Charles Grandison* (1759): See George Buelow, 'The Case for Handel's Borrowings: The Judgment of Three Centuries', *Handel Tercentenary Collection*, ed. Stanley Sadie and Anthony Hicks (London: Macmillan, 1987), 71.

'Il est a son quatre vingtieme Opera', cried Rauzzini, who had been declaring him [Sacchini] *Unique* to Mr. Harris—'J'espere qu'il y ajoutera encore quatre vingt, et puis nous le permethons de rester tranquille—et il Mourra a son *cent soixantieme* opera.' (fo. 88ʳ)

Susan added rather cynically that, in Rauzzini's claim that *Rinaldo* was Sacchini's eightieth opera, '*Pasticcios* are inserted however'. Excluding revivals, arrangements, and known pasticcios, this was more like Sacchini's *fortieth* opera, but according to Susan he bore Rauzzini's possibly ironic flattery with 'so becoming & graceful a Modesty as was really very worthy [of] admiration'.

Yet Sacchini's energy and inspiration were beginning to flag as bouts of illness became more frequent. He had to withdraw after the first performance of the 1781–82 revival of his comic opera *La contadina in corte*, deputing 'his harpsichord to Bianchi'.[1] With this much altered revival of the 1779 two-act version—most of the changes made to accommodate a new character, the Latin-spouting Dottor Stoppino, sung by Morigi—the press began to turn against Sacchini, who had perhaps indulged the performers too much. But, given the widely accepted practices of adaptation—cutting, borrowing, and aria substitution—one is surprised by the vehemence of the attacks on Sacchini, which amounted to a concerted smear campaign. On 8 March 1782 the *Public Advertiser* ran a report about how the *prima buffa* Signora Allegranti tried to acquire the rights to this revival—if true, a unique instance of such a manœuvre by a singer:

the Manager had agreed to pay Sacchini Forty Guineas on the Production of a Comic Opera; the larger Part of a Comic Opera, the Airs and some of the Recitative, were produced according to the Agreement, and rehearsed;—their Value was immediately found to be greater than was expected;—the greatest Expectations of Success were then universally formed.

*Allegranti*, it may be presumed, partook of this general Interest, for before any farther public Progress was made, before any additional Music was consigned by the Composer to the Copyer, Allegranti opened a sudden Treaty with Sacchini, and giving him 100 Guineas, got from him the original and only Copy of the *Score*.

On this Copy being remanded, an Offer was made to reimburse Allegranti the 100 Guineas;—but in Addition to that, she required the farther Advantage of a *clear Benefit*.—That the Manager refusing, the Event was, that a new Score was composed, the old Score was supplied and supplanted, and Allegranti, in course, *lost* her 100 Guineas!

---

[1] *Public Advertiser*, 7 Mar. 1782.

The second part of this story—that Taylor forced Sacchini to make changes in order to regain the rights to the score—is plausible, but the whole report must be questioned in light of the error about *La contadina in corte* being a 'new Opera' and the long-standing custom that the King's Theatre assumed ownership of the scores it produced.

With such leaked reports, the opera-house managers themselves seemed to be paving the way for Pasquale Anfossi, several degrees Sacchini's inferior as a composer, but a better exponent of the 'new simplicity'. Some of Anfossi's music was inserted into one of Signora Allegranti's arias in *La contadina in corte*, and Bertoni included a prominent piece by him in the pasticcio *Ezio*. Allegranti also reputedly instigated the production of Anfossi's burletta *I viaggiatori felici*, which proved the outstanding success of the 1781–82 season and probably led to the composer's engagement at the King's Theatre the next year. Whatever Sacchini's reasons for leaving London at the end of the 1781–82 season, the tide had turned against him. Anfossi's arrival in London was reported on 5 September 1782, nearly two months before the King's Theatre opened for the new season, so he had probably been engaged even before Sacchini took his leave in summer 1782.

The production pattern of the 1781–82 season followed almost exactly that of Sheridan's regime. The season opened on 17 November with a Metastasian pasticcio, *Ezio*, arranged by the reliable Bertoni as a showcase for Pacchierotti's return engagement. The major *opera buffa* was probably intended to be Sacchini's update of *La contadina in corte*, with the inserted scenes for Dottor Stoppino and a new second-act finale but, as we have seen, it was overwhelmed by the unexpected success of Anfossi's *I viaggiatori felici*, mounted on the cheap early in the season as a vehicle for the enchanting new *prima buffa* Signora Allegranti. Also in emulation of Sheridan's practice, the expensive new serious works came late in the season, Rauzzini's *L'eroe cinese* (in March) and Bertoni's *Ifigenia in Aulide* (in May), both of which were overshadowed by Noverre's scenically lavish ballets. Perhaps the most daring and innovative opera of the season was Bertoni's pasticcio *Giunio Bruto*, which, however, misfired.

## Ezio

The pasticcio *Ezio* was based on one of Metastasio's most popular librettos, one that survived particularly well the late eighteenth-century process of cutting and adaptation. The poet himself had approved the introduction of the second-act ensemble-finale into Sacchini's setting (Naples, 1771).[1] The arranger of the 1781 London production, Bertoni, had also set the libretto, first at Venice in 1767 and again in Lucca in 1777.[2] Since neither score seems to survive, one cannot tell whether Bertoni drew on these earlier versions when he returned to the libretto in 1781. Other recent settings were by Guglielmi (London, 1770, and Rome, 1774), Traetta (Mantua, 1775), Mysliveček (Naples, 1775), Mortellari (Genoa and Milan, 1777), in which Pacchierotti sang the title-role, and Anfossi (Venice, 1778). As explained below, the 1781 London version may have incorporated arias from the Anfossi and Sacchini scores. There is some doubt whether the shy and reticent Bertoni conducted the London pasticcio from the harpsichord, which would have been his right as arranger. On 23 November 1781, the *Public Advertiser* reported several changes to the orchestra, and commented that 'this year . . . there is no Second Harpsichord, and Clementi did *not* play the Instrument which remains'.

In Bertoni's version Emperor Valentiniano's resentment of his general Ezio's victory over Attila the Hun, their subsequent rivalry for the hand of Fulvia, and her father Massimo's unbridled treachery are, despite severe cuts to the recitative, still intelligible; but, to an audience that had been fed a steady diet of similar love-and-honour plots since Handel's day, it must have seemed a tired formula. The libretto had not been used in London since 1770 (that is, Guglielmi's setting), but the theatre was apparently not expected to submit a copy to the Lord Chamberlain's office for censoring (no Larpent copy survives). Haste or carelessness best explains the awkward placement of the scene in Act II in which Valentiniano commands his sister Onoria to marry Ezio as well as the superfluous mention in the recitative of the villain Emilio, a character who never appears. Bertoni contributed the most effective piece in the opera, the trio 'Superbo, minacci?', the second-act finale in which Massimo reacts violently to Fulvia's declaration of love for Ezio.[3] A compelling depiction of torment and confusion, the trio attempts to distinguish the three characters musically: Massimo's indignation is expressed in pompous C major bravura, Fulvia's utter misery with a shift to C minor, and Ezio's pathetic anguish in E flat major. When the voices are joined in the drive to a climax, Massimo (sung by the tenor

---

[1] See Don Neville, 'Ezio', *Opera Grove*, ii. 98.

[2] See George Truett Hollis, 'Bertoni', *Opera Grove*, i. 456; Sartori, s.v. *Ezio*.

[3] This piece is in *The Favorite Songs in . . . Ezio* (Bremner [1782]), where Massimo's part is incorrectly labelled 'Onoria'.

Ansani) is all agitated quavers, while Fulvia (Signora Prudom) and Ezio (Pacchierotti) soar above him in thirds. The boisterous stretta comprises basically new music, though Bertoni takes care to inject motifs and figures from earlier sections. Also noteworthy is his version of 'Recagli quell'acciaro' in Act II, Scene ii, a two-part, through-composed aria, with the jagged setting of the opening line serving as a refrain. Bertoni altered the expected slow–fast *rondò* formula: the opening section, marked *sostenuto* despite its flashing scales and roulades in the orchestra, gives way to a legato melody with sustained accompaniment. While this exactly reflects the drama, the aria also gave Pacchierotti a chance to display his famed *cantabile*. Subversion of expectation also characterizes Anfossi's setting of 'Pensa a serbarmi, o cara' in Act I, Scene ii, which may have been dragged into this production.[1] The sweet G major opening is followed by Ezio's D minor outburst against Valentiniano; the opening lines then return, but set to new music.

*Ezio* must be regarded as a triumph for Pacchierotti, but the newspapers were also unanimous in their praise of the tenor Ansani. Cast as the villain, he showed he could after all work with a castrato *primo uomo*, thereby vindicating his walk-out the previous season after his quarrel with Roncaglia (see Ch. 4). Signora Prudom was also complimented, especially for her *andantino* in Act 3, 'Son spietate le mie pene'.[2] But here one suspects that the newspaper was merely being polite to Taylor's mistress, because Bertoni's brief, sentimental aria, set incongruously in A major, comes nowhere close to capturing Metastasio's expression of anguish. Only Mozart could achieve pathos with such simple materials.

## Anfossi's I viaggiatori felici

The new *prima buffa*, Teresa Maddalena Allegranti, who had been singing in Venice the previous season, was well received at the King's Theatre, despite reports of unreliable intonation, poverty of ornament, and what Burney called a 'not very powerful' voice.[3] The long-time Covent Garden oboist and memoirist, William Thomas Parke, disagreed with Burney in his unusually detailed account of her first season at the King's Theatre. According to Parke, Signora Allegranti

---

[1] It is not included in the *Favorite Songs*, but an aria of this title was published in the *Mannheimer Monatschrift*, Jahrgang 2 (Brach & Heumonat, 1779), 20–2.

[2] See the *Morning Herald*, 19 Nov. 1781.

[3] See Burney, *General History*, ii. 892; *Biographical Dictionary*, i. 62; Roland Würtz, 'Allegranti', *Opera Grove*, i. 93–4.

possessed a rich, clear, and powerful soprano voice, of extensive compass, blended with exquisite taste and expression. She was a great favourite with the English public, who bestowed on her universal applause. This charming singer, who exhibited no shake, made her closes with so much elegance and effect, that the most fastidious did not regret the absence of that hitherto essential ornament in singing. What then was not the surprise of the frequenters of the Italian Opera when, at her benefit at the latter end of the season,[1] she, for the first time, displayed in her cadences, &c., a shake the most liquid, brilliant, and perfect imaginable! This beautiful ornament she had probably kept in reserve, relying on her other powerful requisites, in order to afford her admirers an agreeable surprise on that occasion.[2]

Allegranti's appearance in *I viaggiatori felici* was, as Burney reported, 'universally admired', and Lady Mary Coke wrote that this burletta and *Ezio* were 'so liked that they bring out people who rarely frequent publick entertainments' (29 December 1781). A news item of 5 March 1782 implies that Signora Allegranti was largely responsible for the production of *I viaggiatori felici*, since Anfossi's score 'was found accidentally in her trunk upon her arrival here'.[3] This is a plausible story: she had created the role of Bettina at the Teatro di San Samuele at Venice in 1780.[4] Livigni's libretto is a typical two-act *dramma giocoso* with father-and-son rivals for the same sparky young woman (Bettina), elopement in disguise, a strong dose of xenophobia mostly directed against the French, poetic justice, and a lot of gratuitous tomfoolery. The first act is tightly plotted and virtually self-contained; the second is much looser, makes little attempt to pick up the loose ends of the first, and concentrates instead on a series of 'party pieces'. Typical of Livigni and the new generation of *opere buffe*, the finales are enormously long. The original was considerably reworked for the London production, apparently by Bertoni, whose aria for Bettina in Act I, Scene iv, 'Se mi vedi a far l'amore', was substituted at a late stage for 'Son fedele, e son costante'.[5]

---

[1] On 18 Apr. 1782, a performance of *I viaggiatori felici*.

[2] Parke, *Musical Memoirs*, i. 19–20. In recounting this episode, the authors of the *Biographical Dictionary* believe that 'shake' or 'close shake' means vibrato—Signora Allegranti 'employed no *vibrato* in her voice'—which is clearly a misinterpretation of 'trill'.

[3] Unidentified cutting in the New York Public Library, printed by Petty, 186.

[4] Sartori, s.v. *I viaggiatori felici*.

[5] See Larpent MS 578. Quite unusually, the Larpent copy seems to show cuts that are not in the printed librettos; for example, the trio in Act I, Scene i, and the duet in Act I, Scene vi are both longer in the 1781 print than in the manuscript. The reverse is true only of the first-act finale, which has been cut in the printed version. There are two issues of the printed libretto, by E. Cox (1781) and H. Reynell (1782), identical except for their title-pages. The quick reissue of the libretto is an indication of the opera's popularity.

Much of the rewriting was necessary because Livigni's original libretto includes an Englishman, Pancrazio; Bertoni must have wondered how the King's Theatre audience would react to an 'Englishman' who sings Italian. He hit upon the clever solution of transforming Pancrazio into Patterio, a role created by the *basso* Andrea Morigi, who steps out of character from time to time to portray himself. His recitative is laced with 'well-timed Interlardation of the *Vulgar Tongue*',[1] which delighted an audience accustomed to having their noses stuck in bilingual librettos. Morigi apparently had an acceptable accent, unlike many other Italians who tried to sing in English. Thus, in *I viaggiatori felici*, Patterio, instead of being an Englishman who has to get by in Italian whilst uttering the occasional oath in his own language, became Signor Morigi, a well-travelled Italian singer and dancing-master who was able to delight his audience with interjections in their own language. At his first appearance (in Act I, Scene ii), he greeted his fans after a long absence with a patter song rich in puns:

> *Yes*, nel Buffo io son Patterio
> Ma sul serio io son Morigi,
> A vedere il bel Tamigi[2]
> Son tornato, eccomi quà.
> *How do you do*, Signori miei
> Ai palchetti io fo i rispetti,
> *Mr. Pitt*[3] mi raccomando
> Alla vostra cortesia.
> Ehi Madama Galleria
> Servitore ancora a lei:
> Compatisca, favorisca
> La sua solita bontà.[4]

---

[1] *Public Advertiser*, 13 Dec. 1781. In the second-act finale of the Larpent MS, the copyist slipped once, when Gastone calls Patterio 'Pancrazio'.

[2] That is, the Thames.

[3] Addressing both the occupants of the pit and perhaps the politician, who is known to have attended the King's Theatre.

[4] Yes, in the comic, my name is Signor Patterio, but in earnest I am called *Morigi*—I always longed to come back to my dear Old England, and here I am. Ladies and Gentlemen, how do ye do?—My humblest respects to the Boxes—Mr. Pitt, I crave your favour—Ladies and Gentlemen in the Galleries, I hope you have not quite forgot me—For my own part, I shall ever gratefully remember your incomparable indulgence. (Translation from the 1781 printed libretto.)

Morigi seems to have been a good mimic, and as Dottor Stoppino in the revival of Sacchini's *La contadina in corte* later this season he took off the serious singers Pacchierotti and Ansani as well as the second man, Manzoletto, who sang in both comic and serious operas. These impersonations met with mixed reaction, and at least one critic refused to applaud the ridicule of 'that great and favourite singer, Pacchierotti'.[1] Whether Morigi also introduced such parodies into *I viaggiatori felici* is unknown, but some of Anfossi's music for Bettina is clearly meant to send up the serious mode. In Act II, Scene iii, Isabella seeks revenge for her earlier humiliation by pretending to make love to Giannetto, Bettina's husband. Bettina responds in a grand *scena* of mock rage and indignation, comparing herself to the abandoned Dido. The E flat major *recitativo obbligato* is included in *The Favourite Songs . . . in I viaggiatori felici* published by Bremner. Obsessively repeated semi-quaver figures in the upper strings, fiery scales and other instrumental outbursts, frequent tempo changes, patently silly vocal ornaments, rapid modulations, and a high top E flat are wrought with just enough skill and restraint to allow the humour to grow from the context rather than from the music itself. (See Ex. 5.1 on page 274.) Also noteworthy in the published collection is Patterio's aria 'Voi m'amate, dite sì', evidently introduced into Act I, Scene iv, at the last minute, since it is not in the Larpent manuscript.[2] Unascribed, but possibly by Bertoni, it is unusual for being in strict sonata form. The rest of the printed music—Anfossi's 'Al mio bene d'intorno volate' for Giannetto in Act II, Scene ii, and Bertoni's *andante espressivo* added for Bettina in Act I, Scene iv, 'Se mi vedi a far l'amore'—is all exceedingly bland and simple.

## Giunio Bruto

*I viaggiatori felici* may have secured Anfossi's reputation in London several months before he arrived, but the score had obviously been thoroughly overhauled by the retiring and obedient Bertoni, whose skill as a *pasticiere* should not be underestimated. The next production of the season, the serious opera *Giunio Bruto*, could not be further from the Metastasian framework so much favoured for making medley operas. Pacchierotti, who was known for putting words and drama before music, probably had some influence in the choice of this remarkable libretto by Giovanni Pindemonte,

[1] Unidentified cutting in the New York Public Library, printed by Petty, 185.

[2] The text of the 1781 (and 1782) libretto differs considerably from that in the song collection.

**Ex. 5.1. Pasquale Anfossi, *scena* in Act II, Scene iii of *I viaggiatori felici***

(strings omitted)

which Cimarosa had set for Verona only the previous autumn. The drama apparently suited Pacchierotti. The *Public Advertiser* of 14 January 1782 reported, if a little backhandedly, that he sang 'in a Stile the most superior—superior to any Singer heard in this country since Farinelli—superior to Pacchierotti himself!' The plot is well outside the *bienséances* of late eighteenth-century *opera seria*, with unmistakable revolutionary and republican undercurrents. The *Morning Herald* of 14 January 1782 said, 'as a dramatic composition, it is beneath criticism'. After overthrowing the emperor Tarquin, the Roman consul Giunio Bruto struggles against a series of counter-revolutionary conspiracies to establish another Tuscan emperor. Tarquin's captive daughter Tullia presents Bruto with a conventional dilemma, as she and his son Tito are secretly in love. But in a shocking conclusion, Tito is discovered to be a conspirator, and Bruto sentences his own son to death to preserve the republic. Underscoring the severity of his decision, the opera ends in simple recitative without an ensemble finale. Bruto sings, 'Io perdo un figlio; / Ma salva è Roma'. It was performed only three times, and the *London Chronicle* (12–15 January 1782), while admiring various arias, missed the point of the ending: 'There is a great want of a new finale in the opera; the conclusion as it stands at present being excessively bald and uninteresting.' The *Morning Herald* (14 January 1782), while putting some of the blame for the opera's failure on Giuseppa Macchierini (Tullia), assumed the ending was botched by the stage-hands:

After the execution of his son, Brutus, the stern father, was to have returned to the Roman people, drowned in sorrow for the untimely death of the young hero, and bid them rejoice at the fall of a traitor. Figure dancers, who represented the Romans, were then to join in a dance, which in our opinion would have been the *ne plus ultra* of ridicule and absurdity, unless it had been a grand dance in character, and suited to the opera. But it did not take place on account of the curtain dropping too soon. It was drawn up again, but Brutus had now altered his mind, and had nothing to say, or else, it we may be allowed the expression, the dancers feet were *put out of tune* by the bad manœuvre of the bell-man behind the scenes.

Since none of the music of the London production was published, one cannot determine whether Bertoni borrowed from Cimarosa, though he did preserve the voice types of the main roles: Giunio Bruto (tenor) was sung by Ansani, Tito (soprano castrato) by Pacchierotti. However, Procolo, originally an alto castrato, was sung by the bass De Michele. Tullia's aria in Act II, Scene vi, 'Che farò senza il mio bene', was almost certainly borrowed from Gluck's *Orfeo*. The *Morning Post* attributed Aronte's aria 'Son fra notturni orrori' to 'Mr. Gioht' (that is, Joseph Gehot, who was living in London at the time). For a pasticcio it included relatively few arias (Pacchierotti, the star, had only three, plus a duet) yet a vast amount of recitative for a London production, especially in Act II. The high proportion of recitative is another sign that Bertoni (and Pacchierotti?) regarded the drama as paramount. That this bleak tragedy was paired with Noverre's ballet *Alceste* is probably no coincidence. In Noverre's faithful treatment of the story, the heroine kills herself out of conjugal devotion to Admetus, just as Tullia might have done to save Tito. Apollo's gracious restoration of Alceste's life in the ballet might therefore have served as a 'corrective' *lieto fine* to both works.

### *Rauzzini's* L'eroe cinese

The source of the bitter controversy discussed above, Rauzzini's *L'eroe cinese* (première 16 March 1782) was based on a Metastasio libretto that had not been used in London since Galuppi's version of 1766. The choice of subject itself must have been calculated to irritate Sacchini, for he too had set the text in 1770–71, at Monaco, a production in which Rauzzini had taken the leading role (Siveno) with Roncaglia as second castrato.[1] Now safely at the harpsichord instead of on stage, Rauzzini self-effacingly invited comparison, knowing that his version of the opera would benefit from a far greater Siveno, namely Pacchierotti. As Fanny Burney reported, the great man was 'very earnest to help Rauzzini, acting as *maestro* for him, and singing like twenty angels'.[2] Metastasio's story of humane intrigue at the imperial Chinese court during the third dynasty involves Leango (sung by the tenor Ansani), the wise old regent; Siveno (Pacchierotti), his supposed son but actually the rightful heir to the throne; Lisinga (Signora Prudom), a captive Tartar princess; and Minteo (Manzoletto), her beloved, a Mandarin. For all these transliterated names and exotic setting, they might just as well be called Demofoonte, Timante, Creusa, and Olinto, and the setting Thrace. Metastasio was careful to avoid local colour and, by all reports, there was nothing Chinese about the 1782 London production beyond the title and whatever passed for 'oriental' costumes and scenery with the London audience of the time. This conventional story of a father's supposed substitution of his own son in order to save a royal infant from the mob includes, none the less, one of Metastasio's most moving scenes, when both children are revealed to have survived as Siveno and Leango. The main weakness of the

---

[1] Sartori, s.v. *L'eroe cinese*.    [2] Fanny Burney, *Diary and Letters*, ii. 77.

original libretto is that nearly everything is revealed in the middle of Act II, then thrown into doubt by Minteo's claims that he is the true heir to the throne, so the whole process must be replayed over the remaining act and a half. *L'eroe cinese* is one Metastasio libretto that did not benefit from the addition of finales, at least in Rauzzini's version. In the last scene of Act I, just before the new duet for the lovers, Siveno is already revealed to be the true heir, which makes nonsense of the first three scenes of the next act, in which this knowledge is still supposed to be concealed. The first act is thus dramatically closed and the opera could end with the duet, except for Lisinga's nagging feeling of portending doom. The other two finales do less damage to Metastasio.

*Primo uomo* at the King's Theatre as recently as 1777 and by all accounts a refined and intelligent singer though hampered by a small voice, Rauzzini was already a controversial figure when he began to devote more time to composing. He 'also played the harpsichord neatly' but, Burney continued, these considerable talents would not have so speedily gained him public favour 'as a *great* and powerful voice'.[1] Despite a certain irony in his praise of Pacchierotti, Rauzzini seems graciously to have withdrawn from London to Bath in the late 1770s and was content to compose or arrange an occasional opera for the King's Theatre and to confine his singing to concerts. The highly partisan reception of *L'eroe cinese* was not therefore completely surprising no matter how invidious the comparison with Sacchini.[2] Rauzzini was emphatically not a great composer, but he knew how to write for singers and was a good judge of public taste. *L'eroe cinese* seems to have succeeded mainly on the audacious simplicity of arias that pandered to the vogue for folk-like 'Scotticisms'. Pacchierotti's *rondò larghetto* 'Rasserena il vago ciglio' in Act III, Scene iv, sung to comfort Lisinga, was rightly praised, in one case with the hope that it would 'be naturalized in some English musical piece'.[3] Another critic believed Rauzzini had borrowed a phrase from the ballad 'Auld Robin Gray', probably a reference to the frequent use of Scotch snaps and the contrasting middle section in the minor mode with chromatic returning chords. But it is an exaggeration to say that the 'aria is, for the most part, only an elaboration of the simpler tune'.[4] None the less there were rumblings at the time that some of Rauzzini's arias were not original. On 22 March 1782 the *Public Advertiser* printed a 'serious' impromptu:

[1] *General History*, ii. 880.
[2] For a selection of reviews, both pro and con, see Petty, 187–90.
[3] *Public Advertiser*, 25 Mar. 1782.     [4] See Petty, 193 n. 12.

For to *paste* up* *Works*, Rauzzini,
    No Person can you blame:
As you say you've taught Sacchini,
    Tell us your Real Name???

*From the Musical Phrase 'Pasticcio'.

Longman and Broderip published 'Rasserena il vago ciglio' and seven other arias from *L'eroe cinese* as separate numbers in a continuous sequence, but no surviving copy contains all eight pieces.[1] One aria sung by Signora Prudom (Lisinga), 'La costanza la in questo petto', an *andantino* in G major, is not found in either the printed libretto or the Larpent copy and must have been cut. These pieces show Rauzzini a master of classical clichés, the most sophisticated of them being the augmented-sixth chord just before a reprise. Another favourite device is to dissolve the part-writing into octaves to stress important words, as in 'Perdona l'affetto' (Act II, Scene iii); this happens so often one suspects he resorted to it when harmonic invention failed. He certainly subscribed to Sacchini's policy of simplicity, even when it rendered some of his arias inappropriate for their dramatic context. 'Sventurata, abbandonata', Lisinga's response in Act III, Scene v, to the news that her beloved Siveno has been killed, is an athletic *minuetto* in A major. Only in the B section does Lisinga's anguish show. The sudden shift to F sharp major in bar 61 of Example 5.2 conveys a delayed sense of disbelief. Of the published arias, Signora Prudom's are in fact more interesting than Pacchierotti's. Only 'Ti leggo in volto', his *andantino* in Act II, Scene v, rises above the conventional. Again, the emotion is confined almost entirely to the B section. The main theme, which is recapitulated at bar 11 of Example 5.3 on pages 281–2, is an attempt at quirky originality—namely, the misplacement of the tonic chord on to the weakest beat—which does not quite come off. Perhaps Fanny Burney was thinking of this passage when she wrote, 'there is such a struggle for something uncommon, and such queer disappointments of the ear in the different turns given to the passages from what it expects, that it appears to have far more trick than genius in the composition'.[2]

### Giordani's Il bacio

Tommaso Giordani, a Neapolitan by birth, had spent many years in Dublin as a journeyman composer of English operas before settling in London in

---

[1] The instrumental parts were issued separately.
[2] Fanny Burney, *Diary and Letters*, ii. 77.

Ex. 5.2. Venanzio Rauzzini, 'Sventurata, abbandonata', from *L'eroe cinese*

1770. He had composed the music for two earlier Italian operas for the King's Theatre (1770, 1774) and had contributed numerous substitute arias during the 1770s and early 1780s. He had also collaborated with Rauzzini on the medley *L'omaggio* in 1781, though Giordani seems always to have been near the bottom of the pecking-order of the King's Theatre composers. *Il bacio*, set to an original libretto by Badini, was by far the most ambitious Italian opera Giordani ever attempted, though it survived only three performances. The *Public Advertiser* of 10 April 1782 claimed that it would have fared better had it not had to compete with the latest version of Sacchini's *La contadina in corte.*

*Il bacio* was obviously designed as a vehicle for the old *basso buffo* Morigi, who created the role of the deaf amateur composer and cellist, Don Giovanni de' Sordini. While not the best libretto Badini ever wrote, it is nevertheless delightfully quirky and effervescent. The modern-style finales, 'in a manner each an opera itself' (*Public Advertiser*), are entirely novel. The one in the first act comprises a concert, complete with a 'piccola orchestra' placed in the middle of the stage. Conducted from the cello by Don Giovanni, the concert is chaotic from beginning to end. The romantic lead,

Ex. 5.3. Rauzzini, 'Ti leggo in volto', from *L'eroe cinese*

Fidamante (sung by Viganoni), impersonates Signor Pianissimo, a famous *musico* who sings too softly for Don Giovanni to be able to hear him. They also clash over musical directions. When Fidamante '*says* piano, D. J. *plays* forte—*when he says* adagio, D. J. *plays* presto, *and so on*'.[1] Signor Pianissimo may have been intended as a parody of certain castrati, such as Rauzzini, who were criticized for their small voices.

The second-act finale is concerned with a stock stratagem by which Don Giovanni is to be tricked into allowing his intended bride Zuccherina (sung by Signora Sestini) to marry Fidamante. But Badini found a fresh approach

[1] From the libretto, H. Reynell, 1782.

to the standard scene of revelation. The finale takes place at Rome in the Temple of the Bocca della verità, where Don Giovanni forces Zuccherina to thrust her hand into the mouth of the great round face and swear that 'nessuno ti toccò' (no man has touched you). According to legend, if the mouth detects a lie, one's hand will be bitten off. Fidamante enters just in time and impulsively kisses Zuccherina in the French fashion. With her hand in the Bocco della verità, she can then truthfully say: 'Ma salvo Monsù / Nessun mi toccò' (except for the monsieur, no one has touched me). The tables are then turned on Don Giovanni, who fails the test; the statue releases his hand only when he agrees to the marriage of Fidamante and Zuccherina. The opera ends with an extended paean to the kiss. This whimsically Gothic tale is spoilt only by a tedious running joke about Don Giovanni's deafness. No music was published but, according to the review in the *Public Advertiser* quoted above, Giordani's score was partly a pasticcio, with pieces borrowed from Dibdin's *The Padlock* and other English operas.

## *Bertoni's* Ifigenia in Aulide

One other production of the 1781–82 season deserves mention—Bertoni's setting of Cigna-Santi's *Ifigenia in Aulide*, even though it was performed only once (on 25 May 1782). The music is described in the printed libretto (Reynell, 1782) as being 'entirely New', but Bertoni had already composed an opera with this title for Turin in 1762. Since nothing of the London score survives, this claim cannot be tested. At the very least, however, Bertoni radically revised his original to incorporate a series of lavish choral scenes in the manner of Gluck. This is the traditional operatic treatment of the story of Agamemnon's sacrifice of his daughter Iphigenia; as the libretto explains, 'this Drama has, contrary to all expectations, a happy conclusion'—unless, of course, you happen to sympathize with Elisena, who drowns herself in the heroine's stead. Larpent MS 593 is partly a working draft, and decisions about which arias to include in various scenes appear to have been left to the last minute. The stage directions for the processions, sacrifice, and storm scene in Act I are unusually detailed. Furthermore, the list of *dramatis personae* (copied at the back of the manuscript) provides a description of a what would appear to be a quick-change costume:

Ifigenia Principessa Reale
Figlia d'Agamennone
La Signora Prudom, la quale nel terzo atto deve essere vestita in bianca vest[e]

e coronata di f[i]ori, per esser sacrificata a diana e tal veste deve esser facia per ve-
stirsi speditamente.

Despite a long, approving review in the *Morning Herald* of 27 January 1782,
*Ifigenia in Aulide* was probably poor stuff, but its disappearance after one
night may have owed more to a flu epidemic than to the quality of Bertoni's
music.[1] Only one other serious opera was performed as the season drew to a
close—*Ezio*, on 15 June, with a substitute for the tenor Ansani.[2]

## II. The 1782–83 Season: Taylor's *Annus horribilis*

Repertoire:

*Il convito*, Bertoni, libretto by Livigni adapted by Andrei, 2 November 1782 (13 perform-
ances) (p. 288)
*Medonte*, pasticcio based loosely on Sarti, arranged by Bertoni, libretto after De Gamerra, 14
November 1782 (10 performances); orig. Florence (Pergola) 1777 (p. 289)
*Il trionfo della costanza*, Anfossi, libretto by Badini, 19 December 1782 (18 performances)
(p. 291)
*Cimene*, Bertoni, libretto after Pasqualigo, 7 January 1783 (3 performances) (p. 293)
*Ifigenia in Aulide*, Bertoni, libretto by Cigna-Santi altered by Andrei, 18 February 1783 (2 per-
formances); orig. Turin (Regio) 1762. London 1782
*Zemira e Azore*, Grétry, libretto trans. from Marmontel, 27 February 1783 (7 performances);
orig. Fontainebleau 1771. London 1779, 1781
*L'Olimpiade*, pasticcio arranged by Bertoni (?), one number by Sarti, libretto after Meta-
stasio, 6 March 1783 (8 performances). London (earlier pasticcios based on this libretto)
1765, 1770, 1774, 1779, 1780
*I vecchi burlati*, Anfossi, librettist unknown, 27 March 1783 (7 performances)
*Creusa in Delfo*, Rauzzini, libretto after Martinelli, 29 April 1783 (2 performances) (p. 295)
*La buona figliuola*, Piccinni, libretto by Goldoni, 3 June 1783 (1 performance); orig. Rome
(Dame) 1760. London 1766 → 1782
*L'avaro*, Anfossi (revised), libretto after Bertati, 14 June 1783 (2 performances); orig. Venice
(S. Moisè) 1775

The expensive remodelling and enlargement of the King's Theatre auditorium over the summer and early autumn of 1782, Taylor's bankruptcy, and
the utter shambles in which he left the company all helped to make this season an important juncture in the history of the Italian opera in London.
But did these difficulties affect the choice of performers and repertoire? Did
the alterations to the theatre lead to a different style of production—for
example, to a demand for bigger voices? Probably not. Pacchierotti, Morigi,
and Signora Allegranti remained in the company; Bertoni got up his usual
pasticcios, and Rauzzini returned with another ambitious new opera. Two

---

[1] See *The London Stage*, Part 5, i. 526.    [2] Ibid. 530.

other new works, Anfossi's *Il trionfo della costanza* and Bertoni's *Cimene*, were as innovative and ambitious as any operas then in production at Paris, Vienna, or Florence. In spite of Taylor, London was still able to swim in the mainstream.

A report of the first night of the season (2 November 1782) claimed that 'the greatest improvement in the house, amidst the various embellishments, is that the voice is now heard with equal distinctness from every quarter'.[1] This may be a puff, but the season did indeed begin with great optimism. Dr Burney wrote to his daughter Fanny on 6 November 1782: 'the Opera house is so improved that I thought myself in Italy—There is so much symmetry & Elegance in the Whole building, that it seems to me, though *in little*, compared with the Italian Theatres, to be equal in beauty to any one I ever saw on the Continent.'[2] The *Morning Herald* of 19 October 1782 reported that all the new boxes were already taken. Taylor again delegated the day-to-day management to Crawford, and Anfossi's arrival on 5 September has about it the feel of a new broom.[3] His engagement coincided with the first major upheaval in the music department for many years. A news report appearing in late October 1782, during the final rehearsals for the opening night, asked the public to welcome these changes in the same spirit as they would the remodelling of the theatre:

1.  much more money was to be spent on the orchestra, which was to be increased by eight players (see below);
2.  Felice Giardini, the violinist and one-time manager of the opera-house, was to replace Wilhelm Cramer as leader, at a salary of £400 per annum. Cramer had been paid only £150;
3.  John Crosdill was to replace James Cervetto as first cellist.[4]

The reporter was uneasy about the last change: 'The professional ability of both these masters is indisputed: all we would say is, that for the accompaniment of the recitative no violoncello could be more perfectly excellent

[1] Unidentified newspaper cutting, New York Public Library, MWEZ x n.c. 8684 (11).
[2] *The Letters of Dr Charles Burney*, i, ed. Alvaro Ribeiro (Oxford: Clarendon Press, 1991), 352.
[3] The statement in *Opera Grove*, i. 133, that 'during the years 1782–6 he served as music director for the King's Theatre' is misleading. Anfossi, along with Bertoni and Rauzzini, was simply listed as house composer. If anyone could be described as music director for the 1782–83 season, it was Bertoni.
[4] *Public Advertiser*, 24 Oct. 1782. Taylor did not list Crosdill among those owed employment in LC 7/3, fo. 320, but we have counted him in the expansion of the orchestra. Cervetto is on the LC 7/3 list and was also one of only seven orchestra members to sign the deed of trust after the season ended, though his claim might have concerned an earlier season.

than Cervetto's.' This is an important observation that reinforces several
reports of the gradual demise of the harpsichordist as an active member of
the pit band, thereby making the first cellist solely responsible for accompanying the recitatives. Thanks to unusually detailed records of King's
Theatre personnel for this season, the orchestra roster can be reconstructed
from LC 7/3, fo. 320, and the newspapers as follows:

*violins:* Felice Giardini, leader for operas(?);[1] François-Hippolyte Barthélemon,
    leader for ballets(?);[2] Felice Chabran, *répétiteur* for dances(?);[3] Joseph Agus;
    Benjamin Blake; Luigi Borghi; William Dance; Francis Hackwood; William
    Howard, jun.; William Parkinson; Robert Rawlings; Giovanni Salpietro;
    Steiner [Daniel Stayner?]; John Baptist Vidini
*violas:* Joseph Gehot; William Shield; James Simpson
*cellos:* John Crosdill; James Cervetto; Charles Scola; James Smith;
    Girolamo Tonioli
*double bass:* Stefano Gariboldi
*flutes:* George Louis De Camp; Pietro Grassi Florio
*oboes:* Philip Eiffert; John Pope
*bassoons:* Samuel Baumgarten; John Ashbridge
*trumpets:* Thomas Hill; Thomas Kay; Thomas Leander
*kettledrums:* William Burnet
*harpsichord:* Henry Condell
*music porter:* J. Baldwin

Several members played more than one instrument, so this list represents
the maximum available band, of which probably only thirty or thirty-one
ever played at the same time. The *Public Advertiser* (4 November 1782) also
mentioned a new seating arrangement in the pit: 'The flutes, hautboys, and
bassoons, are at the back of the first violin. The tenors fill the place where

---

[1] *The London Stage* gives Cramer in its 1782–83 roster, but Giardini is listed in the season
announcement and opening-night advertisement. Newspaper articles about the orchestra
noted that Cramer would lead the Hanover Square concerts and reported the huge inflation
of Giardini's salary over Cramer's (*Morning Herald*, 14 and 25 Oct. 1782). On 30 Oct. the
same paper gossiped that 'Cramer has been shamefully betrayed and deserted, by the very
band whose interests he so firmly and liberally supported', but if so his successor did not
benefit: Giardini claimed £385 unpaid salary in the deed of trust after the season ended.

[2] After the temporary closure in late May 1783, Barthélemon was advertised as sole leader
of the orchestra (e.g. *Morning Herald*, 6 June 1783). In LC 7/3, fos. 284–5, he claims that he
took over the orchestra at the performers' behest, with the understanding that he would
become first violin and leader for the trustees, giving up an engagement 'for Life' at Vauxhall. When Gallini insisted on Cramer as leader, Barthélemon was paid £100 'to compose the
music for the Grand Ballets' in 1783–84.

[3] Listed in LC 7/3, fo. 320, only as a member of the orchestra. Having been named Noferi's replacement (*Public Advertiser*, 27 Feb. 1782), he probably continued as *répétiteur*.

the wind instruments used to sit.' This arrangement did not please another journalist, who found 'no improvement in point of musical effect; and as to appearance, the spectacle is certainly the most ridiculous that can well be conceived; the transverse direction of the tenors, &c. behind the harpsichord, resembling more a knot of Spital-fields weavers, than an essential part of the band belonging to the King's Theatre'.[1]

## Convergence of Opera buffa *and* seria

No fewer than five singers performed in both serious and comic operas this season. For many years the company had employed one or two singers, mostly of middle or lower rank, such as a *secondo uomo serio*, who could serve in *opera buffa*, usually as a serious lover. The *ultima parte* De Michele had become increasingly risible in both genres and wisely retired. This season marked a change of practice: Signora Carnevale took the title-roles in the serious operas *Creusa in Delfo* and *Cimene*, but also sang in the burlettas *L'avaro* and *La buona figliuola*. Margherita Morigi, Teresa Gherardi, Vincenzio Bartolini (a castrato), and Signor Schinotti also sang in both kinds of opera this season. Such ambiguity of character line may reflect the versatility of these singers, but crossing over from one genre to the other is also a sign of the rapid convergence of the two kinds of Italian opera. This process had already begun on the Continent, not just in the *drammi giocosi* of Da Ponte and Casti with their contemporary, semi-serious themes, mid-act ensembles, and concentration on extended finales, but also in *opera seria*: the reduction from three to two acts (which generally meant the compression of the second and third acts into one); less emphasis on classical love-and-honour plots and more on psychological realism of a less exalted, even mundane kind; and, most important, the introduction of action finales and other ensembles. London was very quick to follow these developments and, in some respects, to lead them.[2]

There was a further element of convergence of genre and style at the King's Theatre that gave it a rather dubious distinction: injection of folk-like, popular arias in increasing doses. The only real difference between some of the *buffa* finales of the mid-1780s and ensembles in English operas

---

[1] Undated newspaper cutting, but from context clearly 1782, in Theatre Cuts 41, fo. [91ʳ].

[2] London was certainly ahead of Venice. See Marita P. McClymonds, 'The Venetian Role in the Transformation of Italian Opera seria during the 1790s', in Maria Teresa Muraro and David Bryant (eds.), *I Vicini di Mozart: Teatro musicale dell'ultimo Settecento* (Studi di musica veneta, 15; Florence: Olschki, 1989), 221–40.

at Drury Lane and Covent Garden is language. If one considers only the music of the King's Theatre during Taylor's regime, especially the burlettas, one has to be depressed by the appalling taste displayed by all concerned. This was little more than foreign-language music hall with expensive scenery and costumes, incongruously performed by some of the greatest singers of the age. But if we regard these works literally as *drammi per musica* rather than concerts in costume, then some of the London operas are remarkably bold and experimental.

## *Bertoni's* Il convito

These converging trends are clearly seen in the first production of the 1782–83 season, Andrei's adaptation of Livigni's *Il convito* with music by Bertoni. Cimarosa's original setting had just been done during the Venice Carnival in 1782, and its freshness is yet another sign of the enthusiasm that followed the remodelling of the King's Theatre. Rehearsals began near the end of October (unusually early); the theatre was ready but had not yet been unveiled to the public, so rehearsals were held 'very discreetly' at 'Pasquali's room in Tottenham street'.[1] *Il convito* was designed as another vehicle for the popular *prima buffa* Signora Allegranti (in the role of Alfonsina). Cimarosa's original includes a parody of a Metastasian *scena*, 'Son Didone abbandonata', but Bertoni did not set it, presumably because it would have been too close to the similar scene in *I viaggiatori felici* of the previous season. The opera is an odd mixture of mock-pathetic or semi-serious scenes, broad farce, and pandemonium-filled finales. It is constructed to the modern two-act pattern, with each act dramatically and musically closed. But the trio in the middle of the second act, which also works up to a tremendous climax of confusion, functions like a finale, thereby giving the whole opera the feel of a three-acter.

The first act revolves round the young widow Alfonsina, whose grief is ambiguously expressed in both text and music, leaving the singer free to supply comic irony. For example, in the A major duet with her sister Giacomina (Signora Gherardi) in Scene ii, 'Ombra bella ed amorosa', Bertoni makes little attempt to differentiate between the two voices, but at least they are given separate melodies, and Giacomina's turning semiquaver accompaniment might be interpreted as her helping to tease Alfonsina out of mourning. The main interest of the first act lies in the wild finale (for which

[1] *Public Advertiser*, 24 Oct. 1782.

no music survives). It begins with a duel between Alfonsina's ridiculous suitors, the vain Massimo (Morigi) and Count Polidoro (Bartolini, the castrato), who find they quite like each other and so only pretend to fight. The first level of pandemonium is introduced by the Cavalier del Lampo (Viganoni), who has tastelessly got himself up as the ghost of Alfonsina's late husband, Niccolò. The second degree is reached when the real ghost of Niccolò threatens to burn down the palace unless his widow agrees to marry Massimo. The stretta, or highest degree of confusion, is the fire itself, which produces total chaos.

The second act, which opens with the banquet of the opera's title, adds little dramatically to the first, and the preceding holocaust is dismissed as a joke. The second finale, like that of *Le nozze di Figaro*, is a night scene with most characters in disguise. Light is finally thrown on the assembled cast, but the opera ends boldly with no reconciliation; a stage direction says merely that 'Ognuno fa l'azione indicate dalle parole che canta', but this is little help, since the text does not specify any neat pairing-off of couples. This opera, which in its early stages parodies the serious mode, now seems at the end to satirize *opera buffa* itself. Unfortunately, the brilliant libretto is poorly served by Bertoni's surviving music. Besides the duet already mentioned, the four arias in *The Favourite Songs* (Bremner) are simple, self-contained, and wholly unremarkable, with the possible exception of Bartolini's showpiece in Act I, Scene viii, 'Adesso che in campo'.

## Medonte

The first serious opera of the season was a pasticcio based loosely on Sarti's version of De Gamerra's *Medonte, re di Epiro*. The première, scheduled for 12 November 1782, was delayed by two days because Signora Morigi was ill.[1] Neither the libretto (R. Ayre, 1782) nor the *Favourite Songs* (Bremner) names the adapter, but a contemporaneous notice mentions that the opera was 'under the direction of Bertoni'. He was presumably at the harpsichord, though more than one newspaper reported that the orchestra was firmly led by Giardini.[2] Bertoni had set this libretto for Turin in 1778, when Pacchierotti sang Arsace. He also took the same role in Alessandri's original of 1775, as well as other versions later in his career. In not giving Bertoni credit for the 1782 London adaptation, the libretto probably indicates that the score

[1] *Morning Chronicle*, 12 Nov. 1782.
[2] *Morning Herald*, 20 Nov. 1782; unidentified cutting in the New York Public Library, printed by Petty, 198.

remained to some extent Sarti's *Medonte*, one of the most popular of all late eighteenth-century serious operas.

For those members of the audience with good memories, the London *Medonte* was, however, just opera soup, in which large, vaguely recognizable chunks occasionally floated to the surface. In two acts, it retained only a few of Sarti's original arias, the most notable being Selene's 'Al caro ben vicina' in Act I, Scene iv, and Arsace's 'Teco resti anima mia' in Act II, Scene vii; the latter, sung by Pacchierotti, had been used in Bertoni's *Quinto Fabio* (1780). With minor verbal changes, 'Mio ben, ricordati' (Act II, Scene xi), not attributed to Sarti, had recently been heard in *Alessandro nell'Indie* (1780). The trio 'Tremate, empi, tremate' had been used twice before at the King's Theatre: in the 1780 *Alessandro*, with one small cut and Medonte's part sung by Alessandro, Arsace by Poro, and Selene by Cleofide; and in Sacchini's *Mitridate* (1781), much altered, paraphrased, and shortened. In *Medonte*, the trio could at last be heard in something like its original context. Its popularity is easily understood. The opening B flat major *allegro* merrily blusters away and makes a sharp contrast with Selene's E flat major *largo*, 'Son questi, idolo mio', to which it is joined. But most remarkable is the stretta ('Stelle tiranne, omai'), a minor masterpiece of imitative counterpoint that Sarti manages to sustain almost to the end. Three arias, none by Sarti, were printed in *The Favourite Songs*. The most interesting is 'Ah non lasciarmi, no', sung by Signora Morigi in Act II, Scene ix. This is in fact a substitution attributed to 'Sigr. Ottani', presumably Bernardo Ottani, who was active at Turin and Bologna in the late 1770s. A two-tempo *rondò* in E flat, it begins with a piercing vocal outburst spanning a minor ninth, a striking figure that returns even more dramatically in the second section. The collection also includes 'Versate in pianto, o lumi', a simple cavatina in Act II, Scene v, which the *Morning Herald* attributed to one Schuster, probably Joseph Schuster of the Dresden court theatre.[1] Both pieces are more substantial than Bertoni's awkward *accompagnato* and aria 'Mio ben ricordati', introduced in the penultimate scene. Despite music of some merit, *Medonte* gave the pasticcio a bad name. Incredibly, it omitted the third act, which is the most ham-fisted way imaginable of pandering to the vogue for two-act operas. With little more effort, Sarti's original could have been mounted instead.

---

[1] Dieter Härtwig, 'Schuster, Joseph', *Opera Grove*, iv. 258.

## Anfossi's Il trionfo della costanza

With *Il convito* and *Medonte* the company was only marking time before the major operatic event of the pre-Christmas season, Anfossi's ambitious *Il trionfo della costanza* (première 19 December 1782). This was the rarest of King's Theatre productions: a *new* work by a librettist and composer both of whom were resident in London. Badini was certainly talented and imaginative, but not always able to carry off his more extravagant ideas. Many of his London librettos are to some extent unorthodox in that they tap sources that would have been familiar to an English audience, while still conforming to Italian forms and conventions. *Il trionfo della costanza* is no exception. As one critic noted, the plot is founded on Robert Dodsley's tale *The King and the Miller of Mansfield*,[1] but a more immediate source was undoubtedly Michel-Jean Sedaine's fine libretto *Le roi et le fermier*, which had been set by Pierre-Alexandre Monsigny in 1762. This was fashioned into a two-act *dramma giocoso* of the latest type, with interior ensembles, extended action finales, and a decidedly Gothic mix of violence and sentimentality; or, as one contemporaneous critic put it, a 'medley of serious and *Allegro*'.[2] Badini's characters have been renamed as follows: Jenny, the abducted heroine, becomes Giannina (Signora Allegranti); the villainous aristocrat Lurewel (originally a tenor) is now Baron Ripa Verde (Bartolini, a castrato);[3] the part of the gamekeeper Richard is split between Giorgio and Checco. A secondary plot involving Pasquale (Morigi), a cobbler who aspires to become a soldier, opens the opera and occupies much of the first act. The high points, at least dramatically, are the duet in Scene iv, 'Il garbato baroncino', in which Giorgio and Giannina tell the baron they love each other and so advance the plot, and the finale. The latter is a very long, complex scene that begins with the announcement of the king's arrival to hunt in the forest and ends when the baron abducts Giannina during a violent thunderstorm: 'the orchestra so perfectly imitated the noise and bursting of the clouds, that it actually spread a kind of dread, similar to that

---

[1] *Morning Herald*, 20 Dec. 1782.

[2] *Morning Herald*, 23 Dec. 1782.

[3] The *Morning Herald* of 14 Nov. 1782 says 'Bartolini's voice is so very bewitching' and 'the melodious manner in which he warbled his notes' made some members of the audience at *Il convito* offer 'to lay a considerable bett, that his part in the play was that of a woman disguised in man's cloaths; indeed his figure, which is pleasing, occasioned the mistake'—some villain!

which might have been felt from the reality itself.'[1] As in Sedaine, Giannina escapes the baron's clutches in Act II, the king gets to see how the other half lives (for example, he is served maccaroni), and, in the second finale, the baron is exposed when he breaks into the humble cottage to attempt another abduction. As in Sedaine's libretto, Giorgio is ennobled, but the baron of the London version is left completely unpunished and is not even admonished—perhaps this ending was felt more appropriate for a country that was not likely to have a revolution.

Anfossi's overture and six vocal pieces were published by Bremner in *The Favourite Songs*. Typically omitting both finales, this paltry collection frustrates any assessment of the whole opera. The reviews were uniformly ecstatic and are therefore unhelpful. The unmusical Lady Mary Coke attended the première and tersely recorded: 'This evening there was a new Opera and a very pretty one it is' (19 December 1782). Fanny Burney almost agreed with her: 'it is a pretty opera, simply, and nothing more'.[2] Anfossi, a complete master of the 'new simplicity', seems hardly to have connected with Badini's hard-edged yet often subtle drama. Take, for example, the baron's lustful aria in Act II, Scene viii, sung as he works himself up for the second abduction: 'Teneri affetti miei' is set as a simple G major *andantino affettuoso* without a trace of underlying villainy.[3] In the same vein (and key) is 'Un qualche merlotto', sung by Lisetta (Signora Pollone) the cobbler's daughter at the beginning of the second act. How this simple ternary-form ballad found its way into a serious-minded Italian opera is difficult to explain. A much more interesting piece is the same character's 'Brutta cosa fastidiosa' in Act I, Scene i. Also in three sections, its opening tune is graceful and charming; the B section is a good example of the comic patter in which Anfossi excelled, while the reprise of the A section is set to different words. Giannina's 'Voglio polvere e rossetto' in Act II, Scene iv, also illustrates a cavalier disregard of the verse structure: having set the text once clearly, Anfossi felt free to build independent musical forms. Still, he came nowhere close to matching the emotional complexity of Badini's libretto.

Two other comic operas by Anfossi from the 1782–83 season require less commentary. *I vecchi burlati* (première 27 March 1783) to an anonymous

---

[1] *Morning Herald,* 20 Dec. 1782.

[2] *Diary and Letters,* ii. 148.

[3] In Larpent MS 611, a fair copy in all other respects, Giannina's aria in Act II, Scene iii, begins with the similar words 'Teneri affetti cari vezzetti'. The printed libretto (R. Ayre, 1783) renders this 'Cari vezzetti, teneri affetti'.

libretto is a crude satire on old age, infirmity, and avarice, remarkable only for the inclusion in Act I of an aria in English, 'Dear girls, be quiet' (sung by Viganoni, not, as one might have expected, Morigi); no music was published. Near the end of the season, on 14 June 1783, an adaptation of *L'avaro*, one of Anfossi's most popular works, was mounted. Again, no music was published, and the short run of only two nights for so famous a work reflects the confused state of the management of the King's Theatre following the sale of the opera-house goods on 23 May. The libretto (Reynell, 1783) shows the effects of the usual pruning of recitative and aria substitution. One amusing episode seems to have been added specially for this production (in Act II, Scene ii). Orgasmo (Morigi), the miser of the title, courts Laurina (Signora Carnevale), trying to impress her with his musical skills: 'Tengo tutta l'orchestra nel cervello: / Scrivo cantate, e sego il violoncello.' This leads to an aria, 'I violini tutti asieme', which is merely a description of Orgasmo (or rather Morigi, stepping out of character again) singing this piece. The original libretto, by Bertati, is in three acts, fashionably reduced here to two. If we can trust the 1783 libretto, then Anfossi simply allowed the last act to be cut, so the opera ends in total confusion with the hellish fire in Orgasmo's cellar. British Library Add. MS 15981, a full score of the opera though probably not the one used for this production, shows how a two-act version can avoid such an abrupt and unsatisfactory ending. After the second-act finale, there is a duet for Stefanello and Laurina, 'Se il mio cor', and a brief chorus of the whole cast, 'Della trama dell'inganno'. The 1783 production of *L'avaro* seems to be a halfway house between a three-act burletta with denouement and a modern two-act *dramma giocoso* with two extended chaos finales, a type that would enjoy some currency next season. Whether the composer approved of or participated in these changes is unknown, but he conducted from the harpsichord.

## Bertoni's Cimene

*Medonte*, the first serious opera of the season, had been presented without a proper *prima donna seria*; the main role of Selene was assigned to Signora Morigi, not a singer of the first rank. The company had also lacked a *prima donna* during the previous season as well, though Maria Prudom had valiantly undertaken some difficult roles; but she was now ill and died on 14 March 1783. Next came Signora Carnevale, similarly underendowed vocally, who made her King's Theatre début in the demanding title-role in *Cimene* (première 7 January 1783). As Fanny Burney devastatingly wrote, 'She has all the abilities to be a great singer, and she is worse than any little one.'[1] Bertoni's first 'new' serious work of the season, though superficially just another piece of hack-work, is actually important to the history of opera in England. *Cimene* is the El Cid story, based not on Bottarelli's familiar libretto, which Sacchini had used for his extraordinarily successful version of 1772–73, but on a little-known text by Benedetto Pasqualigo, which had been set only once previously, back in 1721.[2] Though influenced by Bottarelli as well as Pizzi, the 1783 London libretto offers a distinctive treatment of the subject. None of Bertoni's music survives, though the piece was probably something of a pasticcio. Fanny Burney who, unlike her sister, held no special brief for Bertoni and was becoming increasingly grumpy about Italian opera, wrote, 'Some of the music is very pretty, some very trite, and a good many passages borrowed from Sacchini.' But she also noticed immediately what was new about this work:

The conclusion [of Act II] is a long historic [that is, event-filled or plot-advancing] finale, such as we have been only used to in comic operas; and just before the last chorus Pacchierotti [Rodrigo] has a solo air, accompanied by the mandoline, which has a mighty pretty effect; but, not being expected, John Bull did not know whether it would be right or not to approve it, and, therefore, instead of applauding, the folks only looked at one another. (*Diary and Letters*, ii. 170)

Previous London serious operas had certainly included extended finales, but the one in the second act of *Cimene* is innovative because it begins at the point of maximum dramatic tension—just as Duarte comes on stage with a bloody sword after duelling with Rodrigo. Everything that follows—Cimene's mistaken conclusion that her lover has been killed, Rodrigo's dramatic entrance, and King Fernando's humiliating blessing—was apparently set to continuous music.

Fanny Burney did not mention that the first act also had an extended action finale. Bertoni borrowed this, apparently with only verbal changes, from the previous season's *Ifigenia in Aulide*. He presumably felt that, as it had only been performed once, the finale was worth resurrecting; perhaps no one would even notice. The following comparison shows that the sex of the main singers had to be reversed:

| *Ifigenia*, Act II, Scene viii | *Cimene*, Act I, Scene vii |
|---|---|
| *Ifigenia.* Vorrei—deh senti—almeno | *Rodrigo.* Vorrei—deh senti—almeno |
| Ti plachi il mio dolor. | Ti plachi il mio dolor. |

[1] *Diary and Letters*, ii. 171.     [2] See Dennis Libby, 'Cid, El', in *Opera Grove*, i. 862.

| | |
|---|---|
| *Achille.* Taci, crudele. (In seno<br>    Già si risveglia amor.) | *Cimene.* Taci, crudele, (in seno<br>    Già si risveglia amor.) |
| *Aga.* Non irritar lo sdegno<br>    D'un Rè, d'un genitor. | *Fer.* Non merta un fiero sdegno<br>    Del regno il difensor. |
| *Ach.* Serbati in vita, o cara. | Rod. Placati alfine, o cara. |
| *Ifi.* Lascia, mio ben, ch'io muora. | *Cim.* Parti. (Che pena amara!) |
| *Aga.* Ah mi si spezza il cor. | *Fer.* Che barbaro rigor! |
| *Ifi.* Padre! | *Rod.* Senti. |
| *Aga.* Figlia! | *Fer.* T'arresta. |
| *Ach.* Ben mio! | *Cim.* Addio! |
| *a3* Ah che quest'alma, oh Dio!<br>    Resister più non sa! |     Ah che quest'alma, oh Dio!<br>    Resister più non sa. |
| *Aga.* Numi! Che feci mai? | *Fer.* Numi, che far potrei? |
| *Aga. & Ifi.* Al ben che tanto amai<br>    Fido il mio cor sarà.<br>    Fedele al ben che amai<br>    Quest'alma morirà. | *Rod. & Cim.* Di tanti affanni miei<br>    Deh senti oh Dio, pietà!<br>    Sprezzar, oh Dio, potrei<br>    Sì bella fedeltà! |
| *a3* Oh barbaro momento!<br>    Che affanno! Che tormento!<br>    Chi provò mai di questa<br>    Più fiera crudeltà? | *a3* Oh barbaro momento<br>    Che affanno, che tormento!<br>    Chi provò mai di questa<br>    Più fiera crudeltà! |

Despite the deft parody, this finale does not fit very well in its new context, because Cimene, who earlier in the act expresses love for Rodrigo despite knowing that he murdered her father, abruptly changes character and demands that Fernando avenge his death. Fortunately, substitutions that make nonsense of the plot are remarkably rare in London Italian operas of this period. The vogue for action finales apparently overrode Bertoni's (and Pacchierotti's) usually scrupulous attention to opera as drama.

## *Rauzzini's* Creusa in Delfo

Following the *succès de scandale* of *L'eroe cinese* the previous season, Rauzzini was commissioned to compose another *opera seria* spectacular: the libretto was based on Gaetano Martinelli's obscure Greek tragedy *Creusa in Delfo* with a Metastasian *coup de théâtre* (a queen is nearly poisoned by her long-lost son) and grand temple scenes with lots of stage business. The opera is in two acts with a modern first-act ensemble finale in short, rapid-fire lines expressing torment, anger, and confusion.[1] The otherwise fine libretto breaks down near the end, where the anonymous adapter attempted to graft a *deus ex machina* on to an action finale. The two devices do not mix and, in cutting the appearance of Minerva (mentioned only in the list of singers), who was presumably meant to announce that the King of Greece has been cuckolded by Apollo, the end was badly botched. Bremner published one aria from this opera, 'Spiegar non posso, oh dio!', sung by Iono (Pacchierotti) in Act I, Scene vi. It is a simple ternary-form *larghetto* in E flat major, notable only for a lack of ornament.

## The Company Disintegrates

Taylor's increasing difficulties with his creditors in spring 1783 and the stopping of salaries forced the performers to appeal to the public to support charity benefits (see Ch. 2 for a full discussion). Production ground to a halt following the performance of *Il trionfo della costanza* on 12 May and did not resume until the last day of the month, with a series of benefits for the unpaid singers, dancers, and house servants. Barthélemon, rather than Giardini, directed the old reliable *Buona figliuola* on 3 June, another sign of the company's disintegration. Appalled by Taylor's mishandling of the theatre's affairs, some patrons of the Italian opera raised a subscription for the performers' relief.[2] Lady Mary Coke declined Lady Ailesbury's invitation to join her at a benefit concert at the Pantheon for those singers 'defrauded by Mr Taylor', but she bought a guinea ticket just the same, hoping that 'if all did the same a large sum of money has been raised' (28 May 1783). Taylor later characterized the concerts held at the Pantheon and Ranelagh Gardens as a mutiny. Despite having stopped their salaries, thereby forcing them to seek other engagements, he audaciously claimed that all the performers 'were bound by certain Contracts . . . to perform at the said Opera House and at no other place in the Kingdom' without his permission. He even objected when Luppino, the King's Theatre tailor, gave his services to these concerts.[3] Taylor maintained that Gallini and his associate Carnevale, presumably the husband of the singer, were organizing these concerts and gaining from them.[4] The right of opera-house singers to perform elsewhere was

---

[1] Larpent MS 622 mistakenly attributes the libretto to Coltellini.

[2] *The London Stage*, Part 5, i. 614. The *Morning Herald* of 24 June 1783 names Sir Robert Herries as the subscription receiver.

[3] C12/2171/23.

[4] C12/2012/53.

hotly contested for the rest of the decade. Amid acrimony and confusion, Taylor thus withdrew in disgrace from the active management of the King's Theatre, not returning until 1791. He had not been a total failure: the engagements of Pacchierotti, Noverre, and Anfossi, the introduction of a new style of opera and ballet, and the improvements to the auditorium all happened during his brief tenure, whether or not at his instigation. True, he could not pay the bills, but the subscribers were still able to enjoy genuine Italian opera with some of the finest performers anywhere in Europe.

## III. The 1783–84 Season: Gallini versus Taylor's Trustees

Repertoire:

*Silla*, pasticcio directed by Anfossi, libretto adapted by Andrei after De Gamerra, 29 November 1783 (9 performances) (p. 304)

*L'albergatrice vivace*, Caruso adapted by Anfossi, libretto by Palomba, 16 December 1783 (1 performance); orig. Venice (S. Samuele) 1780

*I rivali delusi*, Sarti, directed by Anfossi, libretto after Goldoni, 6 January 1784 (21 performances); orig. *Fra i due litiganti il terzo gode*, Milan (La Scala) 1782 (p. 315)

*Il trionfo d'Arianna*, Anfossi (revised), libretto by Lanfranchi Rossi, 17 January 1784 (3 performances); orig. Venice (S. Moisè) 1781 (p. 306)

*L'eroe cinese*, Rauzzini, libretto after Metastasio, 17 February 1784 (3 performances). London 1782

*La schiava*, Piccinni (revised), directed by Anfossi, librettist unknown, 24 February 1784 (2 performances); orig. *La schiava riconosciuta*, Rome (Valle) 1764. London 1767, 1769, 1770, 1771, 1772, 1777, 1780

*Demofoonte*, pasticcio with numbers by Sarti and Handel, libretto after Metastasio, 4 March 1784 (7 performances). London (earlier pasticcio on this libretto) 1779

*Alina, o sia La regina di Golconda*, Rauzzini, libretto by Andrei after Sedaine, 18 March 1784 (11 performances) (p. 310)

*Le gelosie villane*, Sarti, directed by Rauzzini, libretto by Grandi, 15 April 1784 (3 performances); orig. Venice (S. Samuele) 1776 (p. 317)

*Issipile*, Anfossi, libretto after Metastasio, 8 May 1784 (6 performances) (p. 306)

*Le (due) gemelle*, Anfossi, libretto by Tonioli, 12 June 1784 (4 performances)

Giovanni Andrea Gallini was loathed by many members of the English establishment for being a social-climbing foreigner of low extraction. He had long made a substantial income as 'a Dancing Master attending the Children of several of the Nobility and persons of Distinction and fortune'.[1] He is chiefly remembered for being in charge of the King's Theatre when it burnt down in 1789. Musicologists have overlooked his important role in bringing Haydn to London in 1791, giving the violinist Salomon,

---

[1] C12/2012/53.

who was only the messenger, most of the credit. Gallini also hired Cherubini and Stephen Storace. He had retired as an opera dancer in 1766 and since 1778 had been working steadily, patiently, obsessively to acquire the King's Theatre. He was proprietor of the fashionable concert room in Hanover Square, among other enterprises. The *British Magazine and Review* of November 1783 declared Gallini 'the only person in this country fit to conduct Italian operas with any degree of propriety'. This was essentially true: by virtue of his nationality, experience, and society connections, Gallini was by far the best qualified proprietor-manager of the King's Theatre since Heidegger. He finally achieved his goal—or thought he had—on 5 June 1783 in a deal with Harris. In fact, he was compelled to share power with the six trustees appointed under Taylor's second deed of trust, and he was forced out of management entirely in February 1784 (for details, see Ch. 2). Most of the credit for the artistic quality of the 1783–84 season was, however, Gallini's. Purely in terms of the range and quality of works he bought or commissioned, this season was the most varied and ambitious since Sacchini was in his prime. Spectacle once again returned to the serious operas and class warfare was declared in the burlettas.

## Gallini Rebuilds the Company

The recruiting-trip fiasco of the summer of 1783 needs to be assessed in terms of its effect on performers and choice of repertoire. Most of the information about this blundering episode comes from lawsuit testimony of those trying to recover travel expenses. More was left unsaid than disclosed. For example, the reason why Gallini, on the one side, legally and very publicly in possession of the King's Theatre, and Crawford and De Michele, Taylor's trustees, on the other side, should have set sail in separate entourages to engage performers in France and Italy is not clear. That they could have done so in ignorance of the other party's plans seems hardly credible. Taylor, who was already trying to wreck Gallini's management, conceded that the former dancer, 'with his usual pains and assiduity and from his personal acquaintance and Education of fiddling and Dancing with such low and Contemptible Characters and Persons as were to be employed',[1] was at least well qualified to choose performers. King's Theatre proprietors had rarely undertaken such recruiting trips, relying instead on agents, correspondence, and word of mouth. Besides, summer was probably too late to

---

[1] C12/2012/53.

engage first-rank singers for the season that would begin the following November. How many engagements Crawford and De Michele had made by the time they ran into Gallini in Bologna in early September is unknown, but they quickly deferred to his better judgement and authority by signing the 'Florence Accords'.

Gallini's decision to travel to France and Italy was almost certainly prompted by the magnitude of the problem he faced. After the collapse of the company and the scandal of the unpaid salaries, there was an exodus of singers; rarely had the King's Theatre seen such a turnover: Giovanna Sestini, Maddalena Allegranti, Teresa Gherardi, Andrea Morigi and his daughter Margherita, Clara Pollone, and Gaetano Scovelli—practically the whole *buffa* troupe—were gone. Only Bartolini (*secondo uomo*) and Schinotti remained, as well as Pacchierotti, the star of the company, whose salary may have been guaranteed by key subscribers. Signora Carnevale also returned, but not until the season was well advanced. As far as the opera department was concerned, Gallini's most urgent tasks were to find a *prima donna seria* (a position not adequately filled since 1781, when Madam Lebrun left London) and to engage a troupe of *buffi*. No contracts survive from this season, but one can determine from lawsuit evidence that Gallini advanced a total of £3,348 to various performers in Italy.[1] He personally signed up Caterina Lusini as *prima donna seria* at a salary of £600, paying her an advance of £112. 15*s*. and travel expenses.[2] This is about half what a first-rank singer could have commanded: Pacchierotti was contracted for £1,150 but returned £150 of this.[3] Gallini also engaged Teresa Gaudenzi as *terza donna seria* at £150 and Maria Catenacci as *seconda buffa* (paying her £69 in advance); he probably also hired Rachele D'Orta as *prima buffa* and Luigi Tasca as *primo buffo caricato*. Gallini presumably auditioned these singers in Italy before offering them contracts, but even so, Signora Lusini was demoted to *seconda donna* and sued for damages,[4] while Signora Gaudenzi 'was so indifferent'[5] that she was dismissed after one performance. Minor singers had often failed to please at the King's Theatre, but the engagement of Signora Lusini as *prima donna seria* does appear to have been a major misjudgement, despite initial audience approval.

As regards music, the most important of the 'Florence Accords' was the fourth, which allowed Gallini to use the opera singers at his concerts in Hanover Square. These 'double contracts', which must have been waved at

[1] C38/715, 12 Nov. 1784.   [2] See 'Opera Salaries', 46, and C12/233, no. 322.
[3] C38/715.        [4] Ibid.      [5] C31/233, no. 322.

the singers as an inducement to travel to London but which in fact allowed Gallini to exploit them, soon became very controversial. The accords also reimbursed Gallini for the purchase of five unnamed scores.[1] Among them were probably Caruso's *L'albergatrice vivace* and Sarti's *I rivali delusi* and *Le gelosie villane.*

Doubtless because of the duplication of effort in Bologna and Florence and the resulting negotiations with Crawford and De Michele, Gallini did not return to London until October 1783, which delayed the start of the season until 28 November, almost a month later than Taylor had opened the previous year. The new manager must already have known that Signora Lusini was no *prima donna*, because he also approached the great soprano Gertrud Elisabeth Mara (née Schmeling), probably during the last week of October on his way back to London. She conveyed the details to Dr Burney in London. This important letter, dated 12 November 1783, is given here in full in the faulty French in which it was written:[2]

à Ostende ce 12 de Nov. 1783

Monsieur; l'amitié que Vous m'avés témoigné autre fois, et dont je me flattois de récêvoir de nouvelles marques cet hÿver, m'arrache l'aveu sincère que c'est avec la plus grande peine que je me vois éloignée encor par des circonstances contraires d'un paÿs, ou j'ai reçu mes premieres idées, et à qui je suis attachée dépuis de tout mon coeur![3] les propositions de mr: Gallini étoient trop dures pour pouvoir les accepter; car réellement avec toute la force de ma poitrine, je ne crois pas qu'elle auroit pu suffire à me faire entendre deux fois par sémaine pendant un couple de mois dans le grand Opera; Ajoutés-y encor qu'il a marchandé com(m)e on marchande au marché des herbes, et vous pourrés aisement comprendre que je n'aimerois pas avoir à faire à un tel Directeur, à la vérité, trop indiscrêt. En acceptant 1200 £ sterl: pour faire le double service des talents qui ont été avant moi, c'est en même tems me mêttre au dessous d'eux, et ruiner ma santé peutêtre pour jamais, si j'ai l'ambition de ne pas vouloir compromettre ma réputation. si Mr: Gallini m'avait donné 1500 £, je les aurois accepté avec les condition ordinaires, mais com(m)e il n'est pas musicien, il a crû risquer son argent qu'il aime beaucoup, et il ne s'est pas fié à ses propres oreilles. Dépuis, j'ai promis à Mr: Abel, de venir à Londre pour ses concerts, mais tant [*cancelling* depuis] qu'il a quitté Paris, il ne m'a pas donné de ses nouvelles, et j'ai tout lieu de croire qu'il n'a pas réuissi dans son projet. Je ne suis pourtant pas peu étonnée de son silence. Sachant que j'ai réfusée l'éngagement de Turin pour avoir le plaisir de passer en angletterre sous des

---

[1] C107/65, 19 Nov. 1783.

[2] Yale University, Beinecke Library, Osborn File 50.72.

[3] Like Mozart, Madam Mara had made a childhood tour of England with her father; see *Biographical Dictionary*, x. 77.

auspices bien moins avantageuses, j'aurois crû du moins, qu'il ne manqueroit pas de m'avertir à tems du succès de son entreprise. Je suis même allé jusqu'ici, en cas qu'il m'avertissoit qu'il avoit compté sur moi; mais il observe toujours le même silence sur plusièrs lettres dans lesquelles je lui ai pourtant marqué que je ne me proposois pas de passer à Londre dépuis que ses nouvelles me manquerent. On m'a dit que Mr: Gallini avoit fait imprimer l'état de son Opera et de ses sujets, si cela est, vous m'obligerés beaucoup, Monsieur, de me faire le plaisir de couper la feuile qui en fait mention, et de me l'envoÿer à Bruxelles sous mon adresse, où je compte d'aller sous peu de jours pour passer de là en Hollande.[1] Mr: Pacquieroti a dit qu'il étoit Primo Homo de l'Opera à Londre,[2] mais dépuis que je l'ai entendu, j'ai quelques peines à le croire, il a chanté à la cour de Bruxelles, où on lui a présenté une tabatiêre d'or, ou 25 Louis d'or, il a préféré l'argent, ce qu'on a trouvé très vilain d'un hom(m)e qui dit vivre de ses rentes, et chanter pour son plaisir—Il est vrai qu'il en a fait bien peu aux autres, mais com(m)e il a le caractêre intriguant il sait par des tracasseries faire valoir, ce qu'il lui manque en mérite. Il a par une basse jalousie de métier (je ne parle pas de l'art qui n'en connoit pas) soulevé tous les anglais, cette année cÿ à Spa, qui ont eu la com(m)plaisance pour lui de cabaler contre moi sans me connai-tre,—sans me voir,—et sans m'entendre; voilà ce qui désiroit Mr: Paquieroti, con-tent d'avoir renvoyé les pauvres anglais dans leurs Provinces, croyant toujours qu'apres Dieu le Père, on chante com(m)e lui. Je vous démande mille pardons de vous avoir si long tems ennuyé par cette lettre, mais j'ai jugé pourtant à propos d'instruire quelqu'un des raisons qui m'ont empechées de paroitre en angleterre. Je vous prie d'avoir la bonté de remettre l'incluse à Mr: Cramer. et apres bien des ci-vilités de mon Mari, je vous prie de croire qu'il n'y a personne avec des sentimens si distingués d'estime et de parfaite Considération

Monsieur
Votre très humble et très obéisante
Servante
Mara née Schmeling
Prémiere Cantatrice de la Reine de France

(From Ostend 12th of Nov. 1783

Monsieur, The friendship you formerly showed me, and of which I hoped to receive fresh instances this winter, draws from me the sincere confession that it is with the deepest sorrow that I find myself once again removed by some contrary circumstances from a country, in which I discovered my earliest thoughts, and to which I am attached with all my heart. Mr Gallini's proposals were too harsh for me to be able to accept them; for truly, with all the power of my lungs I do not

---

[1] The season advertisement which Madam Mara asked Burney to send her appeared in the *Morning Chronicle* ten days later on 22 Nov. 1783.

[2] The London press reported Pacchierotti's arrival from Spain in October. See *Biographi-cal Dictionary*, xi. 133.

believe that I would have been strong enough to perform twice a week for a couple of months in the grand Opera. Add to this that he haggled as they do at the herb market, and you may easily understand that I would not love to have such a truly indiscreet director. By accepting £1,200 for doing double the service of the talents who came before me, is at the same time to place myself beneath them, and to ruin my health, perhaps for ever, if I have the ambition of not wishing to compromise my reputation. If Mr Gallini had given me £1,500, I would have accepted them under the ordinary conditions, but as he is not a musician, he thought he would risk his money which he loves well, and he is not faithful to his own ears. Since then, I have promised Mr Abel that I would come to London for his concerts, but since he left Paris, I have not heard from him, and I have reason to believe that he was unsuccessful in his plans. I am nevertheless a little astonished at his silence. Knowing that I refused the Turin engagement in order to have the pleasure of going to England under his auspices which are much less advantageous, I thought at least he would not fail to notify me in good time of the success of his enterprise. I have come here precisely in case he was going to notify me that he had decided on me, but he keeps always the same silence after several letters in which I have indicated that I no longer propose to go to London before hearing from him. They tell me that Mr Gallini has had printed the state of his Opera and its performers, and if that is true, I would be greatly obliged, Monsieur, if you would be so kind as to cut out the page where it is mentioned, and to send it to Brussels to my address, where I expect to go in a few days in order to go from there to Holland. Mr Paquieroti said that he was First Man of the London opera, but after I heard him, I found it difficult to believe him, as he sang for the Brussels court, where they presented him with either a gold snuff-box or 25 gold louis, and he preferred the money, which was considered very base in a man who says he lives on his private means, and sings for his own pleasure. It is true that he has given very little pleasure to others, but given that he has an intriguing character he knows how to enhance by chicanery what he lacks in merit. He has through a low professional jealousy (I don't speak of art, which knows nothing of it) roused all the English, this year at Spa, who, in complaisance to him, plotted against me without knowing, seeing, or hearing me; there you have what Mr Paquierati would desire, content with having sent the poor English back to their provinces, still believing that he is a paragon of song second only to God the Father. I ask a thousand pardons for having bored you such a long while with this letter, but I nevertheless judged it meet to inform someone of the reasons that hindered my appearance in England. I beg you to be kind enough to hand over the enclosed to Mr Cramer. And after the good wishes of my husband, I pray you to believe that there is not anyone with such distinguished sentiments of esteem and perfect consideration as, Sir, Your humble and very obedient Servant, Mara, born Schmeling, First Singer of the Queen of France.)

Perhaps Gallini saw Madam Mara's agreement to sing in Abel's concerts as the icing on the cake, though she was clearly worried about the strain of so much singing. The most important point that emerges from all this gossip is that Gallini was willing to pay more for a *prima donna* than for the great Pacchierotti, of whom Madam Mara was obviously envious.

The avalanche of testimony against Gallini from 1784–90 has smothered almost all traces of his skill as opera manager. He was criticized for engaging the inferior Signora Lusini, but no one in London, apart from Burney, may have known that he had made a great effort to secure Madam Mara. He and Peter Crawford were also attacked for hiring 'a far greater Number of Musicians for the Orchestra than were necessary'.[1] But Taylor had already increased the size of the band significantly, probably to exploit the improved acoustic of the King's Theatre auditorium; equally likely, a larger orchestra was thought necessary to produce the tremendous burst of noise now *de rigueur* in the new-style pandemonium finales of both comic and serious opera.

The most unexpected and unprecedented charge levelled against Gallini is found in an affidavit sworn by Michael Novosielski, the architect and scene painter, one of Taylor's trustees: the King's Theatre lost money under Gallini, he claims, because of the manager's 'bad choice of Operas and other amusements'.[2] Weak sopranos, flat tenors, sloppy *figurants*, ageing ballerinas, shabby scenes, and old dresses had all been cited at one time or other as the cause of the precarious state of the King's Theatre; but to our knowledge no one associated with the opera-house had ever blamed the quality of the works themselves for poor box-office receipts. Novosielski was patently wrong, of course: the theatre was often packed during the first half of the 1783–84 season; reviews of the operas *as* operas were no more critical than before; the repertoire was the typical mixed bag filled mostly with pasticcios, and Gallini may not have been responsible for this season's failures. But this complaint about the 'bad choice' of operas at least shows that the manager was involved in the selection of repertoire. It also points to a change of aesthetic. At last someone was worried about the works and not just the singers and dancers. And two or three of Gallini's operas certainly did challenge expectation.

This overview of the 1783–84 season should mention the absence of Bertoni who, for the first time in several years, was not jointly engaged with his friend Pacchierotti. His return to Italy was not lamented in the press, and

[1] C31/233, no. 322 (16 July 1784), a hostile affidavit sworn by MacMahon and Slingsby.
[2] C31/233, no. 348 (20 July 1784).

Anfossi quickly filled his shoes as principal composer, receiving commissions for two new works—one serious (*Issipile*), the other comic (*Le gemelle*). Although Anfossi helped arrange Sarti's *I rivali delusi* and other operas this season, he was probably not so willing a *pasticiere* as Bertoni. As is shown below, the first opera of the season, *Silla*, was musically almost out of control.

Leopoldo De Michele seems to have taken over from Bertoni as principal house arranger. Affidavits filed in the case *De Michele* v. *Grant, Sutton, Slingsby, Novosielski, and Siscotti* (that is, Taylor's trustees)[1] document the ex-singer's rise behind the scenes as his career faded in front. He had become head music-copyist several years before he retired as a singer; the composer Joseph Mazzinghi testified that he was apprenticed to De Michele in 1779 as copyist and musical assistant, undertaking menial jobs around the theatre such as 'laying the books on performance nights'—what would now be called the job of orchestra librarian.[2] Besides Mazzinghi, the theatre employed two other journeyman music-copyists, Thomas Walker and John Wiber. Walker confirmed that Taylor still owed De Michele money 'for Copying and *altering* Music of [a] Musical Piece' (emphasis added),[3] which suggests that by 1782 or 1783 De Michele's duties had expanded to include arranging. Crawford (his fellow traveller to Italy in 1783) reported that De Michele's salary as copyist during Taylor's regime had been £150 per annum.[4] By comparison, Anfossi, a famous and respected composer, received only £116. 13s. 4d. for the 1783–84 season.[5] As a condition for making the trip to Italy (which lasted from 11 August to 29 October), De Michele demanded the same salary he had received from Taylor, plus £200 expenses. When he later sued the other trustees in 1786, he complained that he was still owed the £200 as well as £284. 9s. 8d. 'for copying and *composing* Music and other Performances' (emphasis added).[6]

## Silla

Once Gallini was established back in London in late October or early November 1783, a licence was granted by the Lord Chamberlain and rehearsals began for the first production, *Silla*, which opened on 29 November. It was based on Giovanni De Gamerra's famous libretto *Lucio Silla*, first set by Mozart for Milan in 1772. An indirect link between Mozart and

---

[1] C12/602/50.     [2] C24/1929 (Mazzinghi, 29 Oct. 1788).
[3] C24/1929 (Walker, 21 Oct. 1788).     [4] C24/1929 (Crawford, 22 Oct. 1788).
[5] C38/715.     [6] C12/602/50.

the 1783 London production is Rauzzini, the original Cecilio and now house composer at the King's Theatre and soon to make a brief come-back as *primo uomo*. The libretto, which had also been set by Anfossi (1774), J. C. Bach (1775), and Mortellari (1779), was adapted for London by Andrei and performed 'Under the Direction of Signor Anfossi' (libretto, H. Reynell, 1783). Since none of the music of the 1783 version was published, we cannot determine how much Anfossi took from his own score. The *British Magazine and Review* for November 1783 described the opera as 'an harmonical *pudding*—made up of various tunes, introduced *ad libitum* by the performers'. Larpent MS 639, which was submitted to the Lord Chamberlain's office only the day before the first performance, also looks like a pasticcio: gaps have been left for last-minute insertion of arias and some texts show signs of reworking. The *Morning Herald* (1 December 1783) confirmed that *Silla* was the most radical kind of pasticcio, being selected from the works of 'eminent composers . . . in a very masterly manner by the principal performers'. The former reviewer continued sarcastically 'that the sole objection which can be urged against this opera, with regard to the music, lies in its superlative excellence'. In other words, the singers, with little regard for dramatic contrast, had prepared a 'feast, where the viands were entirely of sugar, and therefore disgustful'. Lady Mary Coke wrote that Lady Ailesbury 'seems very well satisfied with the first Woman [that is, Signora Lusini] at the Opera. She has a good voice and a pleasing figure but the musick of the Opera She [Lady Ailesbury] does not like' (*c*.3–4 December 1783). After judging for herself on 20 December, Lady Mary said this of *Silla* and Gallini's supposedly inadequate *prima donna*: 'I went this evening to the Opera and liked it very much. I think the first Woman has one of the finest voices I ever heard and one of the most pleasing.'

The London *Silla* closely followed De Gamerra, even though it retained only two of the original aria texts: 'Guerrier, che d'un acciaro' in Act II, Scene i, sung by Aufidio (who had, thanks to a type-setter, become 'Ausidio'); and Celia's 'Il labbro timido' in Act II, Scene iv. Newspapers reported the music was selected from Anfossi, Gluck, Alessandri, Martín y Soler, and Giordani.[1] Only Gluck's 'Rasserena il mesto ciglio' (in Act III, Scene iv) is immediately recognizable, but Pacchierotti also introduced an aria beginning 'Al caro ben vicino' in Act I, Scene i, which is similar to one heard the previous season in *Medonte*. The Larpent copy shows that Giunia's aria in

---

[1] See *The London Stage*, Part 5, ii. 662.

Act III, Scene iv, 'Ah se perdo il caro bene', originally began with the words 'Che farà senza il suo bene', which points to another Gluck parody. Also departing from De Gamerra's original, Andrei concocted a rather limp first-act finale and tried unsuccessfully to amend the already problematic conclusion of the opera: Silla's volte-face is set in the Temple of Vesta, where the Senate informs the tyrant just how unpopular he has become.

### *Anfossi's* Il trionfo d'Arianna *and* Issipile

Anfossi produced two other serious operas this season, the first a revival of his *Il trionfo d'Arianna*, originally presented at the Teatro San Moisè at Venice in 1781. One of the most spectacular works mounted by the King's Theatre in the 1780s, it received only three performances in late January 1784. There is no easy explanation for its failure, but Signora Lusini was probably not up to the title-role. Reform works with large choral-ballet scenes such as this, while conforming nicely to the twentieth-century view of the development of eighteenth-century opera, made little impression on the King's Theatre's subscribers in the 1780s and 90s; their interest was always focused more on principal singers. Casting Pacchierotti as Teseo in *Il trionfo d'Arianna* may have added to its unpopularity. Lanfranchi Rossi's libretto is a fairly straight treatment of Ariadne on Naxos, her abandonment by Teseo, and rescue by Bacchus. In the London version (Reynell, 1784) there are abundant dances and choruses of mariners, damsels, captives, spirits, deities, and so forth, all folded neatly into the main action.

Larpent MS 644 includes a detailed description of the end of the first act that does not appear in the printed libretto; this was more than an entr'acte ballet. In effect, the action continues in pantomime after the finale as Teseo engages and defeats a group of Minos's sailors in a fiery sea battle:

Terminato il finale cambiasi istantaneamente la scena in Lido di Mare. Si vedono nell'acque, le due Navi fra di loro valorosamente combattere, e sulla Prua di esse pugnano insieme i due respettivi Comendanti. Doppo un valorosa difesa per un Colpo di Teseo, il Cretense manca di vita, e precipita nell'acque. Per tal perdita svanisce ne Cretensi il coraggio, e resta la loro nave miseramente incendiata, e sommersa.

(After the finale, the scene changes suddenly to the seaside. On the water, two ships are seen engaging in stalwart combat, and on the prows the two commanders are fighting each other. After a valiant defence, the Cretan, struck by Teseo, loses his life and tumbles overboard. This causes the Cretans to lose heart, and their ship goes up piteously in flames and sinks beneath the surface.)

# Il trionfo d'Arianna *and* Issipile

The conflagration is followed 'immediatamente' by a more peaceful scene:

Cangiata la scena in folto bosco, una quantità di amadriadi, e di silvani scaturendo di sera degl'alberghi si dimostrano spaventati dall'inteso combattimento, e con atti esprimenti la loro sorpresa, danno a conoscere la maraviglia, dalla quale sono restati occupati. Nel colmo di essa comparisce la Dea Opi sopra un Carro tirato da Leoni con veste tessuta di rami, e di erbe alla di cui comparsa tutti a terra si prostrano. Ella senza discendere dal Carro con gesti, e con cenni spiega loro quanto è accaduto, gli persuade a nulla temere, e facendoli finalmente dal suolo inalzare gli assicura della sua Protezzione e gli lascia pieni di Allegrezza, e di contento. Partita la Dea si danno subito a formare allegrissime danze analoghe al loro uso, e carattere.

Fine dell'Atto Primo

(The scene having changed to a thick wood, a group of hamadryads and fauns, streaming out in the evening from their abodes, react in fright to the fierce battle, and expressing their surprise with gestures, they reveal the spectacle that occupies their attention. At the height of this the goddess Ops appears on a chariot drawn by lions, her gown woven out of branches and grass. At her appearance all prostrate themselves. Without stepping down from her chariot she explains to them, by signs and gestures, what has happened, persuading them to have no fear, and finally causing them to rise. Assuring them of her protection, she leaves them full of joy and happiness. After the goddess leaves, they immediately begin to join in lively dances appropriate to their customs and character.)

Among the best episodes is Act II, Scene iii, when a chorus of Arianna's women ('Oh giorno orribile') raise the heroine's fears that her beloved has been killed in battle. Her anguished aria, 'Ah dello sposo amato', is dramatically interrupted by Teseo's sudden, reassuring appearance. The climax of the opera occurs in the dream sequence following his sneaky exit at dead of night:

While Ariadne sleeps, a great many phantoms appear, coming from different parts dancing, and after forming some groups and circles, they approach her with gestures, alluding to Theseus's treachery, and her desolate situation, then pursuing their dance, they in a short time retire. Ariadne, after some movements, expressive of her inquietude and trouble, sits up, her hair dishevelled, intimates the terrors and disorders of her mind.

Both these dance sequences, as well as the other ballets proper to the opera, were presumably designed by the new choreographer, Dauberval.

For most of the rest of the season Anfossi concentrated on his forte, comic opera, which left the stage clear for Rauzzini and his curious confection *Alina, o sia La regina di Golconda*, about which more later. But Anfossi did return on 8 May 1784 with a new *opera seria*, *Issipile*, which enjoyed a longer run than *Arianna*. This 'new' work, based on a tried-and-true Metastasian libretto, deployed Pacchierotti as a more conventional, assertive hero (Giasone). The report in the *Public Advertiser* (10 May 1784) is worth quoting at length:

The Event of Saturday night [that is, *Issipile*] may teach the Managers, if they are not incapable of being taught, how it has happened that their House has for these six Weeks past been almost empty, and now at last was again full. For these six weeks past the Town has been disgusted with bad Music, ill sung; with that wretched Apology for a first rate singer, Rauzzini, and that barbarous dullness which he thinks Music, his *Regina di Golconda*. On Saturday Night there was the direct Reverse of all this wretched Infamy . . . There have been few finer Operas, and none since Farinelli's time so exquisitely sung.

Though hardly Metastasio's most travelled work, the libretto of *Issipile*, first set by Francisco Conti in 1732, is certainly one of his most complicated; it ends 'irregularly' (for Metastasio) with the spectacular suicide of Learco, the villain. It was adapted in 1784 in two acts by Antonio Andrei, with a long opening ensemble and extended first-act finale. Despite her alleged shortcomings, Signora Lusini returned to the stage in the demanding title-role. *The Favourite Songs in the Opera Issipile* (J. Preston) is a substantial collection (issued in two parts) comprising a three-movement overture (arranged for piano) and seven arias in full score: 'Impalida disce [*recte*: Impallidisce] in campo' (Issipile, Act I, Scene iv; see Ex. 5.4); 'Ti vo cercando in volto' (Giasone, Act I, Scene vi); 'Povero cor tu palpite' (Issipile, Act I, Scene ix); 'Frà dubbi penosi confuso' (Giasone, Act II, Scene iv); 'Dille che in me paventi' (Learco, Act II, Scene vii); 'Io vi lascio' (Giasone, location unknown); 'Eccomi non ferir' (Issipile, Act II, Scene x). While these arias show little innovation in form (most are ternary with modified reprises), Anfossi's harmonic palette is much broader, especially in the B sections, than that of any of his London contemporaries: the music actually modulates to keys other than dominant and subdominant, such as in the G major *andante* 'Povero cor tu palpiti', where the second main cadence is in B minor. Pacchierotti's arias, mostly in his favourite flat-key *cantabile* style, are not very remarkable. One piece in this collection stands out: 'Impalida', sung by Issipile as she contemplates killing her father to satisfy Eurinome. Granted, this is an extraordinary moment for Metastasio, but Anfossi rises fully to meet it. After a long, bravura ritornello in C major for full orchestra,

Ex. 5.4. Anfossi, 'Impàlida', from *Issipile*

the singer enters *andante maestoso* with a new, sweeping melody of grand, heroic intervals. This serves as a slow introduction to the main fast section, which is based on the melody of the ritornello. A difficult passage of ornamentation reaches high C, followed by a shift to E flat major. Approaching the cadenza, the singer must hold high G for more than six bars. Yet none of this is gratuitous. This music fits the drama, as Example 5.4 shows.

### *Rauzzini's* Alina, o sia La regina di Golconda

The removal of Gallini on 14 February 1784 as co-manager and artistic director seems to have had no immediate effect on production; the season was following the usual King's Theatre pattern: an early pasticcio (*Silla*), one or two cheap and cheerful burlettas around Christmas (*L'albergatrice vivace* and *I rivali delusi*), and a major new serious production in mid-January (*Il trionfo d'Arianna*). The staging of *Alina, o sia La regina di Golconda* (première 18 March 1784) would also, at first glance, appear to fit the pattern that had accommodated Rauzzini's big *opere serie* about midway through the previous seasons. However, *Alina* directly reflected the turmoil within the company: Signora Lusini was replaced by Signora Carnevale (making her first appearance this season); a producer was hired especially for this work, advertised (somewhat inaccurately) as an 'entirely new Species of Entertainment, after the French style';[1] and the composer himself, who had not sung at the King's Theatre since 1777, took the lead role of Alberto. Honest Peter Crawford, who probably spoke for his ousted partner Gallini, later registered a strong complaint about the way this opera was produced. Taylor's trustees, who were trying to run the company, had made several 'totally useless' appointments:

---

[1] *The London Stage*, Part 5, ii. 689.

they engaged Signior Rauzzini as a First Man at salary of 200 a year tho they at that time had a first man named Pacchierotti and they . . . also engaged Segnora Carnivali as first woman at £200 a Year altho' they had at that time a first woman of superior talent named Segna. Uttini [*recte*: Lusini] And they also engaged Mons. Le Texier for the managmt of the Opera of Golcondor [*sic*] notwithstandg they had already a Composer & the assistance of this Deponent to Conduct such Opera. (C24/1929 [Crawford])

On 18 March 1784 an anonymous creditor of the King's Theatre wrote to the *Morning Post* to complain about the extraordinary expense of this production.

| | |
|---|---|
| Rauzzini | £700 |
| Signora Carnevale | 400 |
| Le Texier | 150 |
| Dauberval 'in addition to his salary' | 150 |

Why employ Rauzzini and Carnevale at such an enormous expence, when Pacchierotti and Luzini are already engaged, and surely without the least reflection upon the merits of the former, can do the parts equally well? And give Le Texier £150 for bringing on ONLY one Opera, when the old veteran Crawford, as I understand, undertook the management of the whole season, the Treasurership, and the fatigue of a journey to Italy, for £200 impossible! But the sum mentioned for D'Auberval is still more incredible, because he is engaged at a salary for the whole season; and is obliged to compose every dance and ballet that are required of him. Besides, this expensive Opera is given the first night for his Benefit, a circumstance, in itself, unheard of even in the extravagance of Operatical management![1]

The controversy which *Alina* stirred up proved Crawford right on all counts, but first let us consider the matter from Rauzzini's point of view. His new opera was a very sophisticated show with built-in choral and ballet scenes, choreographed by Dauberval and modelled on the *ballet-héroïque*. Le Texier had been director of opera when Grétry's not dissimilar *Zemira e Azore* was mounted in 1779, so his experience might have been useful. Signora Lusini had not been a great success, whereas Signora Carnevale, though not pleasing Fanny Burney, had redeemed herself in Rauzzini's *Creusa in Delfo* the year before. Hardest to justify, however, is the replacement of Pacchierotti. Perhaps Rauzzini thought himself, a permanent resident, more credible as Alberto, the English ambassador.

[1] The *Morning Herald* of 18 Mar. 1784 defended Rauzzini and Signora Carnevale on the ground that they were entitled to consideration as creditors.

The libretto (Reynell, 1784), credited to the house poet Andrei, is based on Sedaine's *opéra-ballet Aline, reine de Golconde*, which had been set by Monsigny in 1766. Surprisingly, in light of the small but growing French influence on King's Theatre productions, complaints were raised against its genre: 'It is a kind of dramatic *hodge-podge*: it is not an opera, for the better part of it consists of dancing; it is not a ballet, for it is intermixed with singing.'[1] This critic was surely just pretending ignorance, because *Alina* was hardly the first Italian opera presented at the King's Theatre that partook of *opéra-ballet* conventions. It was, however, the most radical in its suppression of *recitativo semplice* in favour of *accompagnato* and in its incorporation of chorus and ballet in a more or less continuous flow of music. The *London Magazine* of March 1784 was positive about the dance, saying that it was a 'relief to the whole' and abated 'the tediousness of the recitative'. As the following plot summary shows, Andrei was faithful to Sedaine: Alina (Aline), a former shepherdess, was once in love with the lord of the manor, Alberto (Saint Phar), but their different stations prevented marriage. Having left the manor and after many wild adventures, she became Queen of Golconda in the Indies and, in memory of the happy times with Alberto, built a replica of the village by the manor, complete with her little cottage. The opera opens with Alberto's arrival in Golconda as British (French) ambassador; the queen immediately recognizes him. During a grand entertainment at the end of Act I, he is drugged by a soporiferous nosegay and awakes in Act II in the replica village, where Alina comes to him dressed as a shepherdess. To test his fidelity, she leaves him half-dreaming and sends back word that the queen has offered her hand in marriage. When Alberto refuses the offer, Alina reveals herself as the queen, and they are married.

One scholar has suggested that a French audience, with a knowledge of Stanislas-Jean de Boufflers's racy original *La reine de Golconde*, would not have taken the idealized transcendence of love over social class seriously.[2] An English audience would probably not have understood this subtext, which Andrei certainly did nothing to bring out. Yet, while not a great librettist, he achieved something very rare in opera: the second act is brilliantly suspended between fantasy and reality, consciousness and subconsciousness, waking and sleeping, pastoral and heroic, pathos and sentimentality. Alberto is astonished to find himself transported back to the scene of his first love, yet knows perfectly well this is not magic, because

[1] *New Spectator*, no. 8 (28 Mar. 1784), 6.
[2] See Michel Noiray, *Opera Grove*, i. 88–9.

Alina appears to him in the flesh. Besides, he is able to confirm the reality with Usbeck, the grandee to whom he presented his credentials in Act I.

Rauzzini's music brings us down with a bump. The opera was published in short score by Longman and Broderip, the first two acts complete; for the third, the dances and recitative were omitted, as well as all the vocal music of the last three scenes (iv–vi).[1] Not since J. C. Bach's *La clemenza di Scipione* (1779) had an Italian opera been printed in London in any but *Favourite Song* format. The volume was by no means handsome, but the music was nevertheless dedicated to the Duchess of Devonshire and was clearly intended to be Rauzzini's monument. For the first two acts everything is included: the ballet music, the recitatives, both *stromentato* and *semplice*, as well as the ensembles. Alberto's first aria, 'Son guerriero e non pavento', a flashy A major *allegro*, shows Rauzzini still able to manage high B, but the word-setting is rather crude, with most of the passage-work falling on unimportant syllables. In her first aria, 'Per un alma (Per un core) innamorato', Alina is only allowed a high B flat, perhaps a case of one-upmanship. The *Ballo di Guerrieri*, a *menuetto* and *gavotta* danced by the two Miss Simonets and Madame Théodore, ends the act in the key in which it began, D major—all competent, bright, and utterly routine. The second act, which is much more ambitious, painfully shows Rauzzini's limitations as a composer. The rather pale and indistinct C minor sinfonia, obviously meant to be descriptive of Alberto's drugged state, gives way to bird-calls and other pastoral effects. The cavatina 'La terra, il ciel, le piante' is a rather charming invocation of the dawn; as the surroundings cause Alberto to recall Alina, the music grows more agitated until she finally appears. After this dramatic build-up, their duet 'Vive Alina sol per te' completely fails to convey either a sense of ecstasy or disbelief.[2] Whether the exceedingly simple, rustic music of the rest of the second act is meant to reflect local colour or was the result of an impoverished technique and imagination is difficult to say. In the *terzetta* for Osmino, Usbeck, and Zelina, chordal part-writing gives way to rather meaningless semiquaver passages, while Alberto's final aria in this act, 'Dolce Alina ove sei gita', returns to the pastoral vein. This

---

[1] We are grateful to John Ward for supplying us with a photocopy of the third act, which is lacking in the British Library copy.

[2] The *Public Advertiser* of 19 Mar. 1784 accused Rauzzini of stealing this duet from Sacchini and a later duet, probably 'Più di me felice amante' in Act III, Scene iii, from Bertoni. Even if the pieces in question could be identified, one would face the even more difficult task of discovering if they were actually composed by Sacchini and Bertoni or had already been lifted.

act received a favourable (though superficial) review in the *European Magazine* for September 1784.[1]

Rauzzini redeems himself in the third act (or, if one can believe the more vicious reviews, chose more carefully what music to steal), especially in the arias for the secondary characters. The big A major *bravura* for Usbeck (sung by the second castrato Bartolini), while adding little to the drama, is finer musically than anything Rauzzini wrote for himself in the opera. Even more impressive is the cavatina in Scene ii for the queen's confidante Zelia (sung by Signora Schinotti), 'Se è ver che sia tiranno', whose chromatically inflected rusticity would have better suited Alina herself. The queen's big show-piece, 'Ah no. Non m'agitate', follows in the same scene and is the longest and flashiest piece of the entire score. An exercise in hollow virtuosity, it is saved by an obbligato violin part played (with applause) by Cramer, who was required to ascend to *a '''* in the opening ritornello. The inevitable love duet for the reunited Alberto and Alina, 'Più di me felice amante' (Scene iii), is awash with equally predictable sentimentality, but the sickly sweet thirds, which occupy nearly all the second part of this *rondò*, seem entirely appropriate in context.

A less than deferential critic writing in the *New Spectator* (quoted above) hit the nail on the head by suggesting half-seriously that *Alina* would have been better sung by 'Miss Philips' and 'Miss George', that is, Anna Maria Crouch née Phillips and Georgina George, actress-singers then appearing at Drury Lane and the Haymarket, respectively. This 'high treason against taste' is an attack not so much on the vocal shortcomings of Rauzzini and Signora Carnevale, but on the nature of the music itself: except for the recitative, the first two acts would not have sounded out of place in the English-speaking theatres. The third, however, returns us abruptly to the world of Italian opera.

## Comic Operas

Despite Gallini's efforts to hire a virtually new troupe of comic singers during his travels in Italy, he failed to find a *prima buffa* for the beginning of the season. There was an early production of Luigi Caruso's *L'albergatrice vivace* on 16 December with a makeshift cast,[2] but the *opera buffa* season

---

[1] Attributed to Thomas Busby by Petty, 219.

[2] The singers portraying Don Periccio and Bartolo are not given in the printed libretto, presumably because of last-minute casting changes. Larpent MS 641, however, supplies them as Bartolini and Vincenzo Uttini, respectively.

could not properly begin until the arrival of Rachele D'Orta, who starred as Dorina in an adaptation of Sarti's *Fra i due litiganti il terzo gode* (under the title *I rivali delusi*), which opened on 6 January 1784. Though not in Signora Allegranti's league, D'Orta was well received. Despite the presence of Anfossi, an experienced hand at *dramma giocoso*, only one new comic work was mounted: *Le (due) gemelle*, brought out near the end of the season (on 12 June) almost as an afterthought. Rauzzini, who was strongly identified with *opera seria*, conducted Sarti's *Le gelosie villane* (15 April), which suggests that Anfossi was caught up in the political fall-out of Gallini's departure in February. But the dearth of new works should not be interpreted as a lack of commitment to comic opera; on the contrary, even the adaptations were full of spirit and vitality and, in two cases, decidedly provocative. The emphasis was clearly on the new-style pandemonium finale but with a new and somewhat puzzling ingredient, especially in *I rivali delusi* and *Le gelosie villane*: deliberately unresolved dramatic conflict with political overtones.

Caruso's *L'albergatrice vivace*, libretto by Palomba, had first been performed at Venice in 1780 and is perhaps one of the scores Gallini bought during his recruitment trip; since no music of the London version survives, one cannot be certain. It is crudely jingoistic, with lots of pseudo-Turkish nonsense dialogue, and dramatically inept—the second act covers much the same ground as the first. It was probably given in London substantially unrevised in the light of the vast amount of recitative that remains in the printed libretto (Reynell, 1783). The opera was performed only once, on 16 December 1783.

Anfossi's arrangement of Sarti's *Fra i due litiganti* (*I rivali delusi*) fared much better, being the most popular opera of the season with twenty-one performances. The source libretto, already an adaptation of Goldoni's *Le nozze*, was subjected to many alterations following the première at La Scala in 1782; yet the London version must be one of the most extreme. The parallels of Sarti's opera with *Le nozze di Figaro* are well known.[1] Count and Countess Belfiore quarrel over the marriage plans of the countess's maid Dorina (Signora D'Orta); the countess laments losing her husband's love: 'Ah, dove è andato / Quel dolce affetto' in Act I, Scene ii (compare Mozart's 'Dove sono'); Masotto, the count's steward (the Figaro figure), outwits his rivals Titta and Mingone (Mingotto in the London version). In Sarti's opera Masotto wins Dorina, and Titta marries Livietta, a chambermaid, as

[1] See, for example, Tim Carter, *W. A. Mozart: Le nozze di Figaro* (Cambridge: Cambridge University Press, 1987), 28.

happens in Galuppi's 1755 setting of Goldoni's original. By contrast, Anfossi's 1784 London adaptation ends in total confusion. Protesting at being unable to decide her own fate, Dorina flees into a wood, the count and countess only pretend a reconciliation, Masotto does not get Dorina, and, as a thunderstorm blows up, 'They all go off confusedly, at different parts' (printed libretto). Such nihilism had long been in vogue in first-act finales, and the lack of a happy ending was not particularly unusual, but this kind of damn-all anarchy and total lack of dramatic resolution at the end of an opera was a radical departure.

The brief overture and four vocal numbers by Sarti are found in the *Favourite Songs* (J. Preston). Quite unusually for such collections, fragments of the finales are included: Dorina's G major *larghetto* 'Che bella cosa egl'è far all'amore', at the end of Act I, and an *andante* in D major for the same character, 'Per dar fine a ogni contesa', just before the second-act finale. Also unexpected in a *Favourite Song* book is an ensemble, the *terzetto* for Dorina, Masotto, and Titta, 'Chi vi par Dorina bella' in Act II, Scene iv. Typical of Sarti's *buffa* style, this piece is highly developed melodically with intricate interplay of several distinct motifs, and even some neat imitative counterpoint, but all supported by the most primitive tonic and dominant harmony. What saves the trio is when the singers step out of character for a rehearsal (conducted in recitative):

> *Titta.*    Un' altra volta.
> *Dorina.*   Ma non si forte.
> *Masotto.*  Ed io?
> *Dorina.*   Fortissimo.

Despite the publication of this music by Sarti, *I rivali delusi* was inevitably something of a pasticcio. Dorina's aria in Act I, Scene v, 'Non s'adiri, la Dorina', was said to be by Cimarosa,[1] and Titta's long, autobiographical patter-song in Act I, Scene vi, has a touch of local colour—possibly an allusion to Rauzzini:

> Con un Musico Soprano
> Fino in Londra sono andato,
> E la musica hò imparato,
> Non credete! canterò.

---

[1] *Morning Herald*, 7 Jan. 1784.

Verbal satire, if such this be, was rare in London comic operas in the 1780s. As with Morigi's impersonation during the 1781–82 season, satire was limited to lampoons of the *primo uomo* and *prima donna seria*. However, the London librettos may have hidden allusions. A case in point is the revival of Piccinni's *La schiava* on 24 February 1784, directed by Anfossi. The opera, which had been regularly revived in London since 1767, is one of Piccinni's best *drammi giocosi*: it concerns the adventures of Armida, who pretends to be the slave of her brother, the sea captain Asdrubale. Act II, Scene viii, appears to be unique to the 1784 London version.[1] *Non sequitur* to the drama, Asdrubale suddenly finds himself bankrupt; he has lost his ship and is hounded by creditors. In a nightmare aria, 'I sbirri già m'appostano', he imagines bailiffs carrying him before a magistrate, being sent to gaol, and then granted a pardon. This sounds like a satire on William Taylor, now bankrupt, in and out of debtors' prison, and widely blamed for the present difficulties of the opera-house.

Another example of a comic opera altered to intensify chaos and avoid dramatic resolution is Sarti's *Le gelosie villane*. Tommaso Grandi's original libretto is already an unsentimental study of a cruel marquis, officious town counsellors, and obsequious peasants; but the London production changes the ending—a pat trial scene with a distasteful reconciliation—into a biting comment on class oppression quite as daring as anything in Da Ponte. In a night scene the peasants literally revolt against the marquis's deceitful womanizing. When he is unmasked, Tognino wants to strike the aristocratic villain, but the other villagers, who carry 'sticks and lights', hold his arm. The marquis declares that he loves nobody and leaves in disgrace. Instead of celebrating the success of the uprising, the villagers fall into recriminations, and the opera ends *diminuendo* as they agree only to talk about things in the morning. This finale apparently attracted no special comment, but one review did mention something besides the singers and the music: 'there is in the Opera itself *a plot* tolerably well supported, and the jealousy of the villagers displayed in all that colouring of lively and ludicrous comic which becomes the situation of the various personages' (emphasis added).[2] To call the second-act finale an unfunny peasant victory in a class struggle may be wishful thinking, but the London version of *Le gelosie villane* is one of the most astonishing of all late eighteenth-century Italian librettos.

---

[1] Not all the librettos of the earlier London versions survive. This scene is not found in the one published score, *La Schiava Opera Comica* (Bremner, 1768).
[2] Unidentified cutting in the New York Public Library, printed by Petty, 216–17.

Royal College of Music MS 569 is the first act of *Le gelosie villane* adapted by Da Ponte as *I contadini bizzarri* for the King's Theatre and first performed on 1 February 1794. With drastic cuts to the recitative, mostly shown by pasting blue paper into the score, this version included substitutions by Paisiello, Carlo Pozzi, and Vittorio Trento.[1] Carlo Rovedino sang Tognino, and the name 'Miss Rovedino' appears on the title-page of the manuscript.[2] MS 569 is clearly a fragment of the score used for the 1784 production, though badly mutilated in the process of adaptation in 1794. The marquis's aria in Scene vii, 'Se volessi far l'amore', has been literally removed from the score, but the recitative leading into it remains, though cancelled. Cecchino's 'Questa radice produce' in Scene x, a discourse on wife-beating, has also been cut, but was bound in near the end of the volume (beginning on fo. 200); below the final bar is written 'segue Finale', which indicates its original position. Many other details (including handwriting and paper types) also prove that MS 569 relates closely to the 1784 production. This is, therefore, the earliest surviving manuscript full score of a King's Theatre opera for the period under discussion. The D major finale, 'Crudo amor penar mi fai', is a routine concatenation of numbers increasing in tempo and volume, halted by Cecchino's in-set aria. Momentum is resumed with Tognino's turmoil at witnessing the marquis's lechery towards Giannina, and the crescendo of agitation and noise that results when Tognino threatens the marquis is as horrific as could perhaps be achieved in an extended D major tonicization.

The only home-grown burletta of the season was Anfossi's *Le (due) gemelle*, with a libretto by the shy cellist Girolamo Tonioli.[3] It was probably designed as a vehicle for the popular *prima buffa* Rachele D'Orta, who acted the sprightly Livietta and her much more serious long-lost twin sister, Lauretta, who does not appear until Scene vi. The comic misunderstandings are well handled, but the joke becomes a little thin spread over two acts; the twins' existence is not revealed until the middle of the second-act finale. 'They' cannot of course appear together, so Livietta, who faints when Don Tiburzio threatens to kill her, is carried off stage to a doctor. Joy and happiness otherwise reign, but, after she has occupied centre-stage for most of the opera, the lively Livietta is missed at the end. No music was published.

---

[1] See *The London Stage*, Part 5, iii. 1616, and Royal College of Music MS 569.
[2] See also the printed libretto, C. Clarke.
[3] See Susan Burney, fo. 131ʳ; Tonioli will figure in vol. II of this study.

The 1783–84 season is the first examined so far in this volume in which artistic policy, if one can call it that, was significantly shaped by managerial affairs. The difficulty in assembling a company delayed the first night. Gallini's ejection from management in February clearly affected Anfossi, who was forced to give way to Rauzzini, an inferior composer who nevertheless wanted to infuse the *opéra-ballet* style into his works. Gallini should probably not be blamed for the lack of a *prima donna seria*, but someone of Madam Mara's stature would certainly have helped the box-office. There is no direct evidence that he was also responsible for the most significant artistic development of the season—the vogue for second-act 'anarchy' finales—but one should bear in mind Novosielski's claim that Gallini's 'bad choice of operas' was the cause of the company's problems.

## IV. The 1784–85 Season: Artistic Limbo

Repertoire:

*Il curioso indiscreto*, Anfossi, anon. libretto adapted by Andrei, 18 December 1784 (8 performances); orig. Rome (Dame) 1777 (p. 323)

*I rivali delusi*, Sarti, libretto after Goldoni, 4 January 1785 (6 performances); orig. *Fra i due litiganti il terzo gode*, Milan (La Scala) 1782. London 1784

*Demetrio*, pasticcio directed by Cherubini, libretto by Metastasio adapted by Badini, 8 January 1785 (8 performances). London (earlier pasticcio on this libretto) 1762? (p. 325)

*Il pittore parigino*, Cimarosa adapted by Mazzinghi (?), libretto by Petrosellini altered by Andrei, 25 January 1785 (7 performances); orig. Rome (Valle) 1781 (p. 326)

*Nitteti*, Anfossi (revised), libretto by Metastasio adapted by Andrei, 26 February 1785 (5 performances); orig. Naples (S. Carlo) 1771; revised Venice (S. Benedetto) 1780 (p. 327)

*La finta principessa*, Cherubini, libretto based on Livigni, 2 April 1785 (6 performances) (p. 325)

*Artaserse*, pasticcio directed and arranged by Cherubini, libretto after Metastasio, 16 April 1785 (6 performances). London (earlier pasticcios on this libretto) 1772 (two separate versions), 1774

*La buona figliuola*, Piccinni, libretto by Goldoni, 28 April 1785 (1 performance); orig. Rome (Dame) 1760. London 1766 → 1783

*Orfeo*, pasticcio based on Gluck, arranged by Anfossi, libretto by Calzabigi altered by Andrei, 12 May 1785 (10 performances); orig. Vienna (Burg) 1762 (p. 329)

*I viaggiatori felici*, Anfossi (revised), libretto by Livigni, 28 May 1785 (7 performances); orig. Venice (S. Samuele) 1780. London 1781

The 1784–85 season has been the source of much confusion, partly because the would-be managers themselves did not really know what was happening. This is the closest the King's Theatre came to being rudderless. Still, between December and June, the company offered a full range of works, including a première by the new house composer Cherubini. Several scholars have assumed incorrectly that Gallini was still in charge.[1] As has been explained in Chapter 2, the company was being run with staggering inefficiency by Taylor's trustees, minus De Michele and Siscotti, who had wisely resigned. But who recruited the performers and who selected the repertoire this season? Gallini, formerly co-manager and artistic director, had already made a few engagements for the next season before he was removed in February 1784, and some of the singers he had hired in Italy in September 1783 were on two-year contracts. Worried, Gallini wrote to Earl Cowper in Florence on 21 June 1784, asking him to relay a message to his agent Andrea Campigli and at the same time trying to protect his own reputation.[2] Campigli wanted to know what Gallini 'would be willing to give the performers' to cancel the contracts. Gallini asks them to name their terms if 'I should find it necessary to stop them coming', obviously a delaying tactic, since he had hoped to foreclose on the trustees' mortgage and regain control of the theatre. 'Should my expectations be overthrown', he continued, 'I would wish to recede from my Agreements with honor without being imposed on and one thing I should wish particularly to guard against, which is, provided I was not able to use them, that they should not after I recompensed them set off for England under any Engagements with my opponents'. In other words, Gallini did not want the trustees to benefit from his hard recruiting work. Always an optimist, he ends the letter by enquiring after even more performers.

Whether the trustees were able to poach any of the singers and dancers whom Gallini had already hired is unknown. De Michele had no faith in the trustees' judgement in such matters and, before he resigned, 'did absolutely forbid them to make several & very many of the Engagements which they did make with several Performers'.[3] Novosielski is known to have travelled to Italy some time over the summer of 1784 'for the purpose of engaging performers'. The anonymous authors of *The Case of the Opera-House Disputes* (1784) also charged him with extravagance and nepotism (see Ch. 2). Exactly when Novosielski embarked on this trip is unknown, but as late as 20 July 1784 he signed an affidavit[4] claiming the trustees had 'already proceeded to engage on the most reasonable terms some of the first performers for the next Season and . . . have also written many Letters to the different

---

[1] See e.g. *The London Stage*, Part 5, ii. 736, and Gibson, 'Earl Cowper', 240.
[2] This letter is printed in Gibson, 'Earl Cowper', 240–1.
[3] C12/602/50.     [4] C31/233, no. 348.

Performers in Italy with offers which they daily expect to hear are accepted'. Furthermore, he states that the trustees are willing to take three performers whom Gallini had signed for the 1784–85 season 'and to indemnify him against their salaries'. But, as is known from his letter to Lord Cowper quoted above, Gallini was not prepared to co-operate. With the trustees busy recruiting by post, Novosielski junketing round Italy, and Gallini trying to spoil their efforts, the company came close to replaying the previous summer's recruiting fiasco. Yet, whoever was actually responsible, the trustees did manage three distinguished new engagements for the 1784–85 season: the *primo uomo* Girolamo Crescentini, in place of Pacchierotti; the soprano Adriana Ferrarese del Bene, later to be Mozart's first Fiordiligi; and the composer Luigi Cherubini. Crescentini and Cherubini were too young to make much of a mark in London but, in the light of their subsequent careers, these were shrewd appointments. Signora Ferrarese del Bene, who later specialized in *dramma giocoso,* sang principally in *opera seria* this season, though she also appeared as Bettina in a much altered revival of *I viaggiatori felici.* Once again, the King's Theatre found itself without a *prima donna seria* of star rank, and Crescentini could not match Pacchierotti, who again left London after three succcessful seasons. Crescentini's salary, £850, no doubt reflected his age and reputation.[1] The trustees may have incurred 'calamitous losses' this season, but the total performers' salary bill was probably much less than in previous years.

The *Morning Post* (10 January 1785) published 'A Complete List of the Opera Band'.[2] In fact, the trumpets are omitted.

*first violins:* Cramer, leader for operas; Barthélemon, leader for ballets; Borghi; Salpietro; Soderini; Lanzone; Vidine; Condell; Howard; Chabran
*second violins:* Dance; Blake; Hackwood; Parkinson; Gehot; Stainer [Daniel Stayner]; Augus [Joseph Agus]; Rawlins [Rawlings]
*violas:* Shields [William Shield]; Simpson; Richards; Gough
*cellos:* Coroetto [James Cervetto?]; Scola; Smith; Toniole [Tonioli]
*double basses:* Gariboldi; Hilt; Pasquali
*flutes, oboes, and clarinets:* Florio; Patria; Mahon; Brandi
*bassoons:* Beaumgarten [Baumgarten]; Lyon
*horns:* Payola; Pieltain
*drum, pipe and tabor:* Burnett
*harpsichord:* Mazzinghi

---

[1]  See 'Opera Salaries', 47.
[2]  Not included in *The London Stage,* Part 5.

Comparison with the 1782–83 list shows a net increase of five players, making a total of thirty-nine or forty-two if the omitted trumpets are included. There was considerable turnover in the wind section, which was frequently criticized in the late eighteenth century, and the violins and double basses had been reinforced. Listed as harpsichordist is Joseph Mazzinghi, formerly apprenticed to De Michele as music-copyist, whose promotion also allowed him to arrange operas this season.

No great innovation or inspiration is detectable in the choice of repertoire or production pattern. The season began more than a month late on 18 December 1784 with a comic opera rather than the usual serious pasticcio; this change of routine was probably owing to the late arrival in London of Crescentini and Signora Ferrarese del Bene. The most notable feature of the repertoire this season is the high proportion of pasticcios and adaptations, which is especially surprising given the availability of two famous and respected house composers, Anfossi and Cherubini. The pasticcio had long been a staple of the King's Theatre repertoire system and was generally approved by subscribers, singers, critics, and even composers.[1] Yet this year saw the beginning of a public debate about the artistic merits of the pasticcio, apparently sparked by an anonymous review in the *Morning Post* (10 January 1785). The writer, having observed the harpsichordist-conductor Cherubini, 'a young composer who has *genius*', during a performance of the Metastasian pasticcio *Demetrio*, advised him in his next opera 'to collate less, to compose more'. Cherubini may have taken this advice, because the next opera he conducted, *La finta principessa* (2 April 1785), was indeed his own. But a fortnight later, he was again presiding over a Metastasian pasticcio, *Artaserse*, 'the Music selected from the most eminent Composers'. On 16 April 1785, the *Morning Post* re-entered the debate on the opposite side, publishing an apologia which, though partly a puff, is also provocative:

The knowing ones in musical performances give the preference to Pasticci over Operas, the music of which is composed by one man only[;] in the latter, there is often found a sameness and monotony, which cannot exist in the former, since it is from its nature a selection of the most approved composition. The new Opera intended for the King's Theatre this evening is, we hear, in this style, and we have every reason to suppose that the airs being selected by Cherubini, who has already given ample proofs of his abilities and taste as a composer, and the Opera got up for the purpose of ushering to the musical world the new Tenor Babbini, the Pasticio of Artaserse will meet with a very favourable reception.[2]

---

[1] See Price, 'Unity, Originality, and the London Pasticcio'.
[2] Babbini proved popular enough to draw some newspaper fire: 'Babooni! Babooni!

The writer implies that the selection is best done by someone with an eye and ear to the whole drama rather than by the singers individually exercising the 'choice of the book', as happened the previous season with *Silla*. Surveys of Cherubini's opera career tend to skip over the two seasons he spent in London, where he was primarily engaged as house *pasticiere*, and this period is made even more embarrassing by the total failure of his original opera *Giulio Sabino* in 1786.[1] But the defence of the pasticcio quoted above and the acknowledgement of Cherubini's skill as an adapter contain a powerful argument in the London context: a medley opera selected afresh by a genius like Cherubini might be more 'tasteful' than a completely original work by Rauzzini. Indeed, a pasticcio might even be more memorable, more dramatic, and altogether more coherent than a revival of an original work such as *I viaggiatori felici* conducted by the composer himself (as happened this season), especially if the singers had followed the 'choice of the book', obliging the composer to spruce up his opera with new and perhaps stylistically alien arias. The debate shows what eighteenth-century musicians regarded as essential to Italian opera, at least as practised in London: a series of completely interchangeable modules, the *azione*, held together by certain key characters and events, the *accidenti*. Even in extended finales, coherence was achieved through the dramatic action and not necessarily by the music. A good work could be 'improved' by the substitution of better arias, even though the substitutes might clash with the style of the music remaining. Within this completely fluid repertoire there was only one 'unassailable' classic, namely, Piccinni's *La buona figliuola*, and even that was subjected to modest amounts of substitution. The notion of an operatic canon was a nineteenth-century development.

### Anfossi's Il curioso indiscreto

The King's Theatre's policy on pasticcios and substitution was, by comparison with other major opera-houses, extremely liberal. To insist on authorial control over a revival would probably never have occurred to Anfossi, whose reputation in England was now secure, despite his contretemps with the

Babooni! all the world running after Signior Babooni; not a monkey of fashion, or an old *Tabby* of the *Ton*, but flew to the Opera to see Signior Babooni. Signior Babooni is a tenor, and a good one—but there is one material objection—his voice is *natural*. . . . His person is diminutive, his countenance shrivelled, and as to grace and action, Signior Babooni has yet to acquire both.' (*Daily Universal Register*, 18 April 1785)

[1] Exceptions are Margery Stomne Selden, 'Cherubini and England', *Musical Quarterly*, 60 (1974), 422, and Stephen C. Willis, 'Cherubini: From *Opera Seria* to *Opéra Comique*', *Studies in Music from the University of Western Ontario*, 7 (1982), 155–82.

trustees in the previous season. *Il curioso indiscreto*, the first opera of the 1784–85 season, was eighteen years old and had enjoyed success all over Europe, including Prague and Paris. For the 1783 production at Vienna, Mozart composed three substitute arias, two for his sister-in-law Aloysia Weber Lange (K. 418 and 419) and one for the tenor Adamberger (K. 420), which Salieri persuaded him not to perform. The story behind the composition of these pieces illustrates how very differently the pasticcio process was viewed in London and Vienna. In a letter to his father of 5 July 1783, Mozart wrote that some of his friends had spread word that he 'wanted to improve on Anfossi's opera'. Fearing the consequences of such presumption and aware of Anfossi's high reputation in Vienna at the time, Mozart insisted that a notice be inserted into copies of the libretto:

The two arias on p. 36 and p. 102 have been set to music by Signor Maestro Mozart to suit Signora Lange, because the arias of Signor Maestro Anfossi were not written for her voice, but for another singer. It is necessary that this should be pointed out so that honour may be given to whom it is due and so that the reputation and the name of the most famous Neapolitan may not suffer in any way whatsoever.[1]

In London any 'corrections' were undertaken by the house poet Andrei and by Anfossi himself. In pasticcio librettos the composers of individual arias are sometimes identified, but this is rarely the case for substitutes.

The original three-act libretto (an anonymous rendering of an episode in Cervantes's *Don Quixote*) was modernized into a two-acter with extended finales. Marchese Calandrano, showing indiscreet curiosity, asks his friend the Contino Ripaverde to pretend to make love to the marchese's intended bride, Clorinda, to test her fidelity. The contino rejects his own financée in favour of Clorinda. This old plot lent itself very well to 'double-chaos' treatment. In the first-act finale the contino converses with Clorinda in Virgilian allusions to warn her that the marchese is watching them ('Didone con Enea, / E Iarba il Re de' mori, / Che ascolta i nostri amori, / Là indietro se ne sta'); in the second-act finale Clorinda takes her revenge by feigning madness so convincingly that the marchese and contino become truly unhinged. The opera ends 'Già la bomba in aria è accesa, / E fra poco scoppierà' (now the bomb in the air is lit; soon it will explode).

---

[1] *The Letters of Mozart and his Family*, ed. Emily Anderson, 3rd edn. (London: Macmillan, 1985), 853–4. Also Mary Hunter, 'Curioso indiscreto', *Opera Grove*, i. 1031, and Rudolph Angermüller, *Mozart: Die Opern von der Uraufführung bis heute* (Frankfurt am Main: Propyläen, [1988]).

## Il curioso indiscreto

The *Favorite Songs in the Opera Il Curioso Indiscreto* (J. Preston)[1] includes an overture and four slight vocal numbers. The 'duetto' for Serpina and Prospero, 'Guardate che figura', is rather a dialogue; the voices overlap for only a single semiquaver. An aria in which the marchese catalogues his sexual exploits, 'Per inventar raggini', was removed before the libretto (Reynell, 1785) was printed; the text is found in Larpent MS 677, Act I, Scene x. The only apparent cut, this could be a rare instance of the Lord Chamberlain's office exercising its right to censor Italian opera. Lady Mary Coke thought *Il curioso indiscreto* 'indifferent' (18 December 1784); by no means a masterpiece, it was nevertheless an ideal vehicle for the returning *prima buffa* Rachele D'Orta in the role of Clorinda.

### Demetrio *and Cherubini's* La finta principessa

Cherubini's London début is obscured by lack of sources. He directed the pasticcio *Demetrio* on 8 January 1785. In the catalogue of his works,[2] Cherubini listed an aria, an (accompanied?) recitative, a duet and a finale (twenty-eight pages in full score) composed for this opera. The music may be found in the Biblioteka Jagiellońska in Kraków[3] but, as no libretto of the London production survives, one cannot verify whether any of these pieces was included. The *London Chronicle* of 8–11 January 1785 reported that the text was altered by Badini, who also provided 'a translation into intelligible English'. This implies that Reynell brought out the usual bilingual edition, but apparently no copy survives. The absence of a Larpent copy is also puzzling, because the last opera based on Metastasio's *Demetrio* had been staged in London back in 1762, and Badini's version would therefore have had to be submitted for licensing.[4]

Cherubini's new opera of the 1784–85 season, *La finta principessa* (2 April 1785), is also badly preserved. No music appears to be extant,[5] and no copy of the libretto, if one was ever published, is listed by Sartori. Larpent MS 714 shows this opera to be an adaptation of Livigni's *I due fratelli Papamosca*, which had been set previously by Felice Alessandri at Venice in

---

[1] Unique copy in the British Library.

[2] *Notice des manuscrits autographes de la musique composée par . . . Cherubini*, ed. Auguste Bottée de Toulmon (Paris: Principaux éditeurs de musique, 1845), 7–8.

[3] Stephen C. Willis, *Opera Grove*, i. 836.

[4] The poet fashioned another opera from this story, *Alceste*, in 1787, for which a Larpent copy does survive—MS 751.

[5] But see Willis, *Opera Grove*, i. 836; Cherubini's *Notice des manuscrits autographes* lists a 528-page full score, now lost.

autumn 1782. The manuscript libretto provides no cast-list but, from a review in the *London Magazine* (May 1785), one can deduce that Signora D'Orta sang Rosina, Franchi sang Ruggiero, and the *basso* Tasca took the role of Don Sesto. Tasca was particularly admired for his 'burlesque of his mutilated countrymen' (*Morning Post*, 4 April 1785), which included an extended parody of Gluck's 'Che farò senza Euridice' in Act II, Scene vi. The libretto is one of Livigni's best, which makes the loss of Cherubini's score all the more regrettable.

### *Cimarosa's* Il pittore parigino

As far as comic opera is concerned, the high point of the season, perhaps of this entire period of management, was an adaptation of Cimarosa's *Il pittore parigino* (25 January 1785), based on a libretto by Giuseppe Petrosellini as altered by Andrei.[1] Within the rather conventional plot of marriage forced by threat of disinheritance is a satire on bluestocking poets, in the person of Eurilla (sung by Signora Schinotti). She is a would-be playwright (librettist in Andrei's version) who is writing an opera called 'Berenice', based on Racine. Several scenes in the first act include parodies of various aspects of *opera seria*. The libretto also satirizes the Bohemian affectation of the artist's studio. Assisting the painter, Monsieur de Crotignac (sung by Franchi), to remove the obstacles in the way of his marrying the extravagant Eurilla is her cousin Cintia (Signora D'Orta), who is disguised as an opera singer. She has formerly been engaged to Baron Cricca (Tasca), Crotignac's rival for Eurilla. Cintia's threat to expose the baron gives rise to one of the most remarkable arias in the London version, 'Perchè togliermi lo sposo', in Act I, Scene ix. In front of the baron, she tauntingly alludes to their former affair as if it had all happened in an opera:

> . . . la mia rivale.
> Comincia il ritornello, io per la scena
> Con gravità passeggio — Zitti gridano
> Zitti per carità. Solo il Barone
> Che sta in platea con vari amici accanto,
> Ride fra se comincio l'aria e canto.

[1] For a recent study of this work (which does not consider the London production), see Gordana Lazarevich, 'Transformation of an Intermezzo: Cimarosa's *Il pittor parigino* as a Reflection of 18th-Century Operatic Performance Practices', *Napoli e il teatro musicale in Europa tra Sette e Ottocento*, ed. Bianca Maria Antolini and Wolfgang Witzenmann (Florence: Olschki, 1993), 175–89.

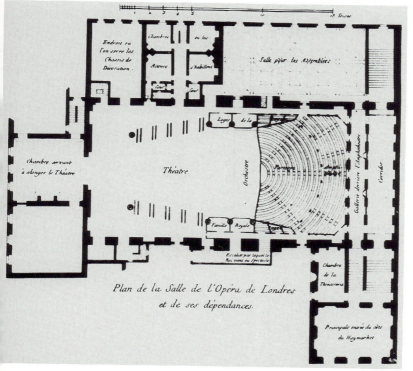

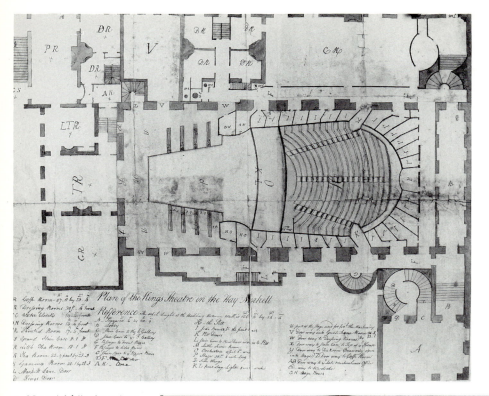

3. Novosielski's alterations
   in the King's Theatre,
   Haymarket, 1782

4. Schematic box-plan for
   the season of 1782–83

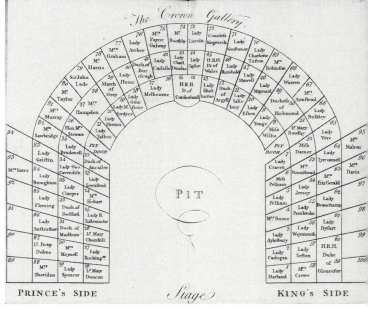

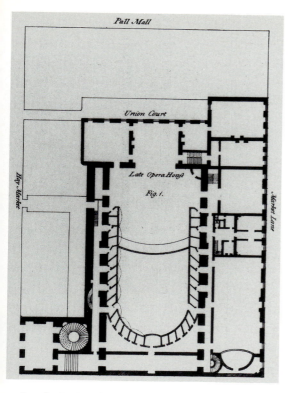

5. Saunders's plan of the
   King's Theatre,
   Haymarket, in 1789

6. Maria Prudom in Arne's
   *Artaxerxes*, 1781
   engraving by Roberts
   and Thornthwaite (*Bell's
   British Theatre*)

## KING's THEATRE.

BY DESIRE OF HIS ROYAL HIGHNESS THE PRINCE OF WALES.

For the Benefit of Monsieur GARDEL.

AT the KING's THEATRE in the Hay-Market.

THIS EVENING,

Will be presented, a new Serious Opera, in Three Acts, called,

L'EROE CINESE.

The Music entirely New, by Sig. RAUZZINI.

Principal Characters.

Signor PACHIEROTTI.

Signor ANSANI, Signor MANZOLETTO,

Signora LORENZINI,

And Signora PRUDOM.

End of Act I. an entire new BALLET, composed by Monf. GARDEL, sen. called

MIRSA,

(Taken from an American Anecdote) in which will be introduced a Minuet and Gavotte, composed by Monf. Gardel jun. who in the Concert Scene will execute a Concerto on the Violin.    Principal Dancers,

Monf. Gardel and Mademoiselle Baccelli,

Monf. Nivelon and Mademoiselle Theodore,

Signora Crespi and Monf. and Madame Simonet.

End of Act II. A new Serious Dance, composed by Monf. Noverre, called,

APOLLON & LES MUSES.

By Monf. Lepicq and Madame Simonet,

Monf. Nivelon and Mademoiselle Theodore,

Signora Crespi and Mademoiselle Baccelli.

End of Act III. an entirely new Ballett, composed by Monsieur NOVERRE, called

ADELA OF PONTHIEU.

(The Subject taken from the History of ancient Chivalry)

Principal Dancers.

Monsieur Gardel and Madame Simonet,

Monsieur Nivelon and Mademoiselle Theodore,

Monsieur Simonet and Signora Crespi,

And Mademoiselle Baccelli.

Tickets Half-a-Guinea each, to be had of Monsieur GARDEL, No. 26, Margaret-street, Cavendish-square; and of Mr. MAC MAHON, No. 80, near the Opera House.

COVENT-GARDEN.

---

7a. Advertisement for Gardel's benefit, *Morning Herald*, 9 May 1782

7b. Ticket for Gardel's benefit, 9 May 1782

## KING's THEATRE.

EVERY thing is now in complete Readiness for the Opening of the House, which will be advertised in due Time.—The following is the List of Performers engaged for the Season:

### SERIOUS SINGERS.
Signor CRESCENTINI,
Signor Bartolini, Signor Cremonini,
And Signor BABINI.
Signora SCHINOTTI,
Signora CATANACCI,
And Signora TERRAVESE.

### For the COMIC OPERA.
Signor BABINI.
Signor Banki, Signor Schinotti,
And Signor TASCA.
Signora SCHINOTTI,
Signora Pollohi, Signor Catenacci,
And Signora RACHAEL DORTA.

### COMPOSERS,
Signor ANFOSSI—Signor CHERUBINI.

### PRINCIPAL DANCERS.
| | |
|---|---|
| Monsieur Lepieq, | Mademoiselle Rossi, |
| Monsieur Nivelon, | Sig. Pitrot Ang_olini, |
| Monsieur Frederic, | Mad. Dorivall, |
| Signor Angiollini, | Signora Fusi, |
| Signor Zuchelli, | Mad. Julien, |
| Monsieur Henry, | Mad. Bithmure. |

### BALLET MASTER,
Monsieur LE PICQ.

### LEADER of the BAND,
Mr. CRAMER.

The Subscribers are respectfully informed, that the Subscriptions for the Season are to be paid into the Hands of Mess. Bansen, Moreland, Hammersly, and Co. Bankers, No. 57, Pall-mall, where the Tickets are now ready to be delivered.

N. B. The temporary Receivers appointed last Season are finally discharged, by a Decree of the Court of Chancery.

Subscribers of last Year, who have not yet signified their Intentions, are entreated to do it in the Course of the ensuing Week, as there is a great Demand for Boxes; and it is the Duty of the Trustee to see that they are disposed of before the opening of the House.

Season advertisement for 1784–85, *Public Advertiser*, 20 November 1784

Antonio Sacchini, by Sir Joshua Reynolds (1775)

10. Frontispiece to *Orfeo*
    (1785)

11. 'The Charmers of the
    Age' (Rubinelli and
    Mara), engraving by
    James Sayer (1786)

12. Giovanna Baccelli,
    engraving by John
    Jones (1784) after
    Gainsborough
    (R.A., 1782)

3. Vestris jun. as Colas in
   *Ninette à la cour* (1781)

4. The King's Theatre,
   Haymarket, site (old
   and new theatres) from
   PRO C12/958/64

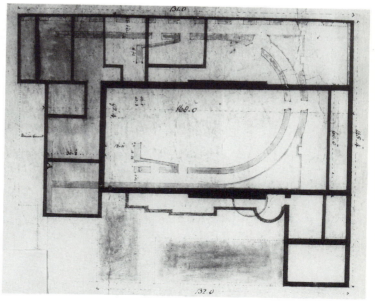

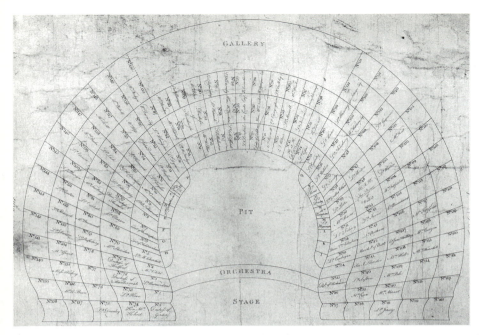

15. Box-plan for the new King's Theatre, Haymarket, September 1790

16. Michael Novosielski and his plans for the opera-house, by Angelica Kauffmann (1791)

This curious opera-within-an-opera manner of discourse is given full vent in Act II, Scene xi, when the baron, having learnt that Eurilla has jilted him, breaks into a histrionic *scena* in accompanied recitative. At the same time, Tasca (the singer) steps back from the drama to comment, Brecht-like, on the effect the music is having on him. He will die like the baron in an opera:

> Ecco che gia li vedo. — Oimè che tetra
> Orribil Sinfonia —
> Non avete paura, Figlia mia!
>
> . . . . . . . . . . . . . . .
>
> I spiriti folletti
> Al suon di dolci flauti e clarinetti.
> Addio Cintia mia cara . . .
> [aria]
> . . . Quell'oboè m'ha seccato.
> I corni m'han stordito.
> Le trombe m'han stonato.

Most of the reviewers admired Cimarosa's music—this being his first complete opera given in London—and noted a 'new style'. But the *Morning Post* (26 January 1785) found the drama 'rather tedious and insipid'. For once Lady Mary Coke almost gushed: 'it was a new one and much liked. I never heard one the first time that pleased me so much' (25 January 1785). Royal College of Music MS 131 includes a one-act opera entitled 'Il pittore parigino', but this score, which was evidently prepared for a later production, does not relate to the 1785 King's Theatre version.

## *Anfossi's* Nitteti

The major new spectacular this season was Anfossi's *Nitteti* (26 February 1785). In an implied criticism of Cherubini's earlier pasticcio *Demetrio*, the critic in the *London Magazine* (March 1785) wrote that *Nitteti* 'with truth . . . is the *first* serious Opera performed this season'. Andrei's adaptation of Metastasio is not directly related to any of the more recent settings—Paisiello (St Petersburg 1777), Anfossi, first setting (Naples 1771) or his second (Venice 1780), the last being adapted by Verazi in three acts with ensemble action finales.[1] In reducing the opera to two acts, Andrei lost the third-act finale: his version ends with a conventional chorus of celebration, while the

---

[1] Briefly discussed by Marita P. McClymonds in '"La clemenza di Tito" and the Action-Ensemble Finale in Opera Seria before 1791', *Mozart-Jahrbuch* (1991), 768.

first act has a love duet for Sammete (Crescentini) and Beroe (Signora Ferrarese). Andrei's adaptation therefore goes very much against the fashion in London for action finales, even when this meant cutting the third act and ending with the second. Andrei (and Anfossi?) also eschewed the several opportunities for choral-ballet scenes, which the libretto had by tradition offered. They did, however, preserve the two most spectacular scenes. The first is Amasi's coronation procession in Act I, Scene vi:

A large space near the walls of *Canopus*, magnificently adorned for the triumphal entrance and Coronation of the new King. A rich and elevated throne, at the foot of which, on the right, stand some Priests, bearing the ensigns of royalty on golden basons. A triumphal arch in perspective, with various lodges full of spectators.[1] A view of the *Egyptian* army at a distance. The victorious King is seen seated on a white elephant, advancing slowly under the arch, preceded by the deputies of the provinces, and a train of *Egyptian* grandees, *Ethiopian* captives, &c. He ascends the throne to the sound of symbols, sistrums, and other oriental instruments,[2] assisted by *Amenophis* and *Sammetes*.

The second is Act II, Scene vi: Sammete, against his father's command that he marry Nitteti, elopes with his beloved shepherdess Beroe as a storm gathers ('He takes Beroe by the hand, and goes towards the Beach'). Unfortunately, the London score does not survive, but it apparently included Anfossi's music for the ensuing pantomime: Beroe

faints and falls on a mass of stone. *Sammetes* attacks furiously the royal guards, and, amidst the lightning, claps of thunder, the ships through the violence of the tempest running foul of each other, flashing, dashing to pieces, and sinking, an obstinate engagement follows to the sound of a martial symphony, between the

---

[1] The Italian version of this stage direction gives more information: 'Vari ordini di loggie all'intorno popolate *di Musici*, e spettatori' (emphasis added). Stage musicians were extremely rare in late 18th-c. London Italian operas.

[2] Exotic instruments seem to have been something of a novelty this season. The *Morning Post* (10 Jan. 1785) carried the following (tongue-in-cheek?) report: 'The musical instrument, says a correspondent, on which Mr Zuchelli, in the ballet of Le Tuteur Trompé, entertained the audience at the King's Theatre, last Wednesday evening, is supposed to be one of the most antient at this period in use. Ever since the decease of poor Joan of Naples, it has been the subject of universal admiration throughout the blessed dominions of her holy successors, and is said to be, at this time, in some little vogue amongst a few private practitioners, even in our own isle. It greatly resembles a pair of inverted kettle-drums; and it is a species of *moroton*; or, at best like the hurdy-gurdy of the Cambro Britons, limited to a very small number of notes; from the loud, sudden, explosive sound of which, and from some other particulars, it originally derived the name of *Le Bomb Fidello*; though the rusticity of *John Bull* thinks proper to distinguish the same by an appellation somewhat similar, indeed, to the ear, but of a much more homely signification [bum fiddle?].'

followers of Sammetes and the Royal Guards, who at length conquer, and pursue the others off the stage. The tempest ceases gradually; the sky becomes serene; and the rainbow appears.[1]

The press rarely commented on spectacle in Italian opera, nor, for that matter, did Burney or the later musical memoirists Mount Edgcumbe, Parke, and others. The *Public Advertiser's* report (4 March 1785) of audience indifference to Act II, Scene vi, of *Nitteti* is therefore noteworthy for the implication that something out of the ordinary had been attempted: 'The music too, accompanying the represented tempest, boasted equally a good deal of contrivance and effect, passed by neglected, without a single hand in favour of Anfossi.'

## Orfeo

*Nitteti* eschewed the integral choral-ballet scenes to which it was particularly well suited, but the King's Theatre did not neglect French-style opera this season. Rauzzini, who had since *L'eroe cinese* in 1782 provided spectacular if musically controversial works each year, had apparently overreached himself in 1784 with *Alina* and was not re-engaged by the trustees. Instead, they turned to another ageing castrato, Giusto Ferdinando Tenducci, for a very different kind of production. To have used Rauzzini, who had stepped down as *primo uomo* only in 1777, is one thing, but to call upon Tenducci, who had not sung in an Italian opera in London since the mid-1760s and who had probably passed the age of 50, is quite another. The decision to revive J. C. Bach's adaptation of Gluck's *Orfeo* is also surprising. Many opera-goers, including Dr Burney and his daughters, could still vividly remember the moving performance of Guadagni, Gluck's original Orfeo. Tenducci, by contrast, had long since abandoned *opera seria* in favour of English opera and, latterly, concert-giving: he had made his greatest impression on the London stage as Arbaces in Arne's *Artaxerxes* in 1762. His return to the King's Theatre in 1785 was therefore curious in several respects; though no triumph, Tenducci's *Orfeo* nevertheless proved to be the most popular opera of the season, despite a late première.

The printed libretto (Jarvis, 1785) is itself an important historical document. (For the frontispiece, see Pl. 10.) Though perhaps available to the audience at the first performance on 12 May, it was clearly designed as a

---

[1] This stage direction is not in Larpent MS 373, which may suggest that staging details were not worked out until the last minute.

souvenir programme for Tenducci's benefit on 19 May. The preface adds to his biography and explains how the production came about:

Having concluded an agreement with the Directors of the Opera for the representation of *Orpheus*, I now take the liberty shortly to hint some things concerning myself. . . . The celebrated Caffariello, under whom I studied Music from my infancy, obtained for me, by the means of Master Cocchi, an invitation to England, as Second Singer in the King's Theatre . . . although I was then not above fifteen years of age.

After a short stay in this island, Dr. Arne introduced me as a First Singer at Covent Garden Theatre in the Opera of *Artaxerxes*. The success of this Opera . . . and the kind and favourable attention which was paid me, made me take such a liking for this country, that I thought no more of returning home. But Prince Giustiniani, Director of the Argentine Theatre at Rome, being then in this city . . . persuaded me by various arguments to accept the office of First Singer in that Theatre.

I left London with infinite regret, and as I passed through Florence, in my way to Rome, the Grand Duke of Tuscany was pleased to make a point of it that my first performance as a Singer in Italy should be in a Theatre of my own country. He himself selected the Opera of *Orpheus*, in which he chose that I should sing. The effect of this performance . . . was great, as can be attested by many English people of distinction, who were present. His Royal Highness shewed himself so much satisfied with me, that . . . he appointed me First Singer of his Band, an honour which had been eagerly sought by Manzoli, by Guarducci, and by many other capital Singers, who were actually in the service of the Grand Duke.

After this I sung in Rome, and several other cities of Italy: and I was every where treated in the kindest and handsomest manner. But . . . I felt in my bosom a great desire to return again to England . . . [where] I have resolved humbly to present . . . [to the Nobility and the Public] that same *Orpheus*, which was so much applauded at Florence. . . .

The Directors of the Opera, in conjunction with M. Lepicq, have done, and will do all in their power, that this Opera shall be worthy of your approbation.

Works in themselves truly excellent, after the lapse of some years, come to be regarded anew with favourable attention, even by Fashion itself. Hence it is that their Britannic Majesties, and so great a number of noble personages, take a delight in hearing frequently a concert of Ancient Music. In the Opera of *Orpheus*, which I have the honour to present, besides the Music of Gluck, of Bach, and of some other famous masters, there are introduced several pieces by the immortal Handel, which I hope will delight you much more than many musical compositions which have nothing new but the name. . . .

That Tenducci studied with Caffarelli is not, to our knowledge, recorded elsewhere, but this statement would help explain why he introduced an aria by this singer in the pasticcio *Attalo* at his King's Theatre début in 1758,[1] when Gioacchino Cocchi was house composer. Tenducci was certainly engaged as *secondo uomo*, but he seems to be fibbing about his age (15) at the time. This would mean that he was born in 1743; other sources suggest a date closer to 1735.[2] More interesting is the revelation that the 'Directors of the Opera', that is, the trustees, commissioned Tenducci to organize the production of *Orfeo*, not merely, as Burney suggests, that they invited him to supersede Crescentini as *primo uomo*. (Crescentini did not, however, appear again this season after the first performance of *Orfeo*.) Tenducci may have instructed Andrei in making the 'additions and Alterations' and assisted Anfossi in the musical direction. But the most remarkable claim of the preface is that *Orfeo*, even as a pasticcio, was a classic, not unlike 'a concert of Ancient Music'. This is quite different from the way in which *La buona figliuola* was viewed: namely as evergreen. *Orfeo* was clearly being advertised as a museum piece.[3] Tenducci was no stranger to the role of Orpheus, having performed in an English version of Gluck's opera in the 1770s.[4] And in 1784 he sang the role in Dublin with Mrs Billington as Eurydice. This production, which may have been the catalyst for the 1785 London Italian version, was assembled by Tenducci himself: Gluck's *Orfeo* 'is now for the first time translated into Poetical English, and I have spared no Labour to adapt the Words to the Music, without injury I hope to either'.[5] While the Dublin *Orpheus* begins like Gluck's original, it soon becomes an entirely different work.

In London a year later, Tenducci, with Andrei and Anfossi, attempted some major restoration. Though retaining a few features of J. C. Bach's 1770 version, which included twelve of the vocal numbers of Gluck's 1762 Viennese original,[6] they retrieved Orfeo's 'Cerco il mio ben' and the Dance of the Blessed Spirits, which had been replaced in 1770 by singing shades. Tenducci also included some of Calzabigi's original stage directions. Insertions by Bach and Guglielmi were cut (for example, 'Piango il mio ben così' in Act I, Scene ii). Tenducci also removed some of the most egregious of

---

[1] Burney, *General History*, ii. 857.

[2] See *Biographical Dictionary*, xiv. 392.

[3] This had been attempted before, in May 1773. The *Public Advertiser* announced a performance of Gluck's opera 'Altered [*sic*] as it originally was performed at Vienna'. As Ernest Warburton points out, 'no copy of the libretto has been found to confirm or deny the veracity of this statement'; see *The Collected Works of Johann Christian Bach*, ix, pp. xi–xiv.

[4] *Biographical Dictionary*, s.v. 'Tenducci'.

[5] *Orpheus and Eurydice, an English Musical Drama* (Dublin: J. Hunter, 1784), preface.

[6] Not seven, as stated by Jeremy Hayes in *Opera Grove*, iii. 746.

Bottarelli's and Bach's 1770 additions, namely the opening scene for Eagro (Orfeo's father) and Egina (Euridice's sister), an aria for Pluto (Act I, Scene iii), and some extra recitative after 'Che farò'. (For a comparison of the main vocal contents of the 1785 version with Gluck's original, see Table 11.) The comparison shows that Tenducci's *Orfeo* was not so much a pasticcio as a reconstruction with substitutions. The dances seem largely to have been retained, judging by the descriptions given in the 1785 libretto:

1. Funereal feasts, Act I, Scene i
2. Dance of Furies placated by Orfeo, Act I, Scene iii (II.i in 1762 original)
3. Dance of the Blessed Spirits, Act II
4. Celebrations of heroes, etc., Act III, Scene ii (sc. iii in 1762 version)

Choreographed by Le Picq, these ballets were probably the saving grace of the 1785 production. Tenducci's libretto is also unusual (if not unique for London) in printing the names of the choristers, who total twenty-six, not counting their director, a Mr Webb. Reflecting oratorio practice, the sopranos were apparently all boy trebles ('Masters Batleman [Bartélemon?], Clark', *et al.*) and the altos were 'Contre Tenors'.

Tenducci did not disgrace himself as Orfeo, though the snobbish Mount Edgcumbe described the opera as the 'performance of an old man, who had never been very capital'.[1] Parke, not always writing as an eyewitness, seems in this case not to have based his account on Burney:

The manager, being desirous of strengthening the serious opera, engaged Signor Tenducci, who had been singing with success at the Hanover Square concerts: he appeared on the 11th of May [actually the 12th] in Sir Christopher Gluck's opera 'Orfeo.' Nearly the whole weight of this opera lay on Tenducci, who, though an Atlas of former times, found his physical powers so much diminished, that he was unable to bear the pressure to the satisfaction of the public. Signora Ferrerese was not equal to the part of *Euridice*. (*Musical Memoirs*, i. 49)

In a letter of 2 June 1785 to Lord Cowper in Florence, Cherubini generally agrees, except for the reception of Signora Ferrarese del Bene. Since this important letter summarizes the 1784–85 season, we quote it *in extenso*:

There will also have been brought to your notice the unhappy position of the actors, the serious as well as the comic, and of all the operas and ballets given this year except the ballet *Le festin de Pierre* and the three operas *L'Artaserse*, in which Babbini was distinguished with universal applause; *L'Orfeo* in which old Tenducci

---

[1] *Musical Reminiscences*, 45.

TABLE II. *Main vocal pieces in* Orfeo, *1785*

| | | | |
|---|---|---|---|
| **Act 1** | | | |
| sc. 1 | Coro: Ah se intorno | = | 1762, no. 2 |
| sc. 2 | Orfeo: Cerco il mio ben | = | 1762, no. 6c |
| | Amore: Gli sguardi trattieni | = | 1762, no. 9 |
| | Orfeo: La legge accetto | = | substitute new to 1785 |
| sc. 3 | Coro: Chi mai dell'Erebo | = | 1762, no. 14 |
| | Coro: Misero giovine! | = | 1762, no. 19 |
| | Orfeo: Men tiranne | = | 1762, no. 22 |
| | Coro: Ah! quale incognito | = | 1762, no. 23 |
| **Act 2** | | | |
| | Euridice: Chiari fonti | = | substitute from 1770 |
| | Euridice: Se a un casto petto | = | substitute new to 1785 |
| | Orfeo: Che puro ciel! | = | 1762, no. 25 |
| | Orfeo: Guidatemi pietoso | = | insertion, Handel? |
| | Coro: Vieni a' regni | = | 1762, no. 26 |
| | Orfeo: Alme belle se pietate | = | substitute new to 1785 |
| | Coro: Torna o bella | = | 1762, no. 29 |
| **Act 3** | | | |
| sc. 1 | Orfeo: Vieni, segui | = | 1762, no. 30 |
| | Orfeo: Lascia pur l'ingiusto | = | substitute |
| | Euridice: Qual vita | = | 1762, no. 32 |
| | Euridice: Che fiero momento | = | 1762, no. 33 |
| | Orfeo: Che farò | = | 1762, no. 35 |
| sc. 2 | Orfeo *et al.*: Trionfi amore | = | 1762, no. 43 |

sang but only Ferraresi was honoured above the other singers, although the whole entertainment gained favour and the ballets did not displease, [and] to which the king came only once, not having been any other evening at the theatre the whole season, since he is completely offended by the management; and *I viaggiatori felici*, presented for the first time [this season] last Saturday, in which the same Ferraresi and Babbini distinguished themselves, repeating an aria each and a duet and also doing well in the rest of the drama. . . .

He then reports that the Lord Chamberlain, having lost patience with the trustees, hopes to make different arrangements for the coming season (discussed in Ch. 2). In Cherubini's opinion,

All this is not certain, but the project seems genuine and well founded enough to make the rumours trustworthy. If this project has its effect, it would bring much honour to the nobility, to the theatre and to London, since it is shameful to see so rich and noble a theatre in the hands of such scoundrels, as it has been for some years, who suffer it to be debased by defrauding of wages those who have earned them, when the profits are clearly secure in consequence of the small expense they have paid out for the dignity of the entertainment. I am preparing an opera seria (*Il Giulio Sabino*), but I believe that it will not be given this year, because the season is too advanced. It finishes after the king's birthday [4 June], at which time all the world goes to the country and Parliament closes.[1]

Cherubini was intensely interested in the managerial disputes, but he obviously did not know the half of what was transpiring between the trustees and Gallini, who was fiercely opposed by the Lord Chamberlain. Probably aware that Lord Cowper was in league with Gallini, Cherubini paints the trustees in as bad a light as he dared. That they had commissioned Cherubini to compose an *opera seria* so late in the season is surprising, given the pattern of production during the previous few years. In the event, his *Giulio Sabino* was not performed until March 1786. This letter is gold dust to the student of late eighteenth-century Italian opera, because it shows a famous composer preoccupied with the managerial and financial problems of the theatre. He brushes aside their serious effect on his composing, remains silent about his own activity this season as *pasticiere*, reporting the success of *Artaserse* (16 April 1785), but omitting to mention that he had been warmly praised for arranging and directing it.[2] Taylor's regime, followed by Gallini's abortive attempt to gain control only to be ousted by the rump of the trustees, could hardly have been more chaotic, and any attempt to deduce an 'artistic policy' from the four seasons discussed in this chapter would be futile. That the 'well-oiled machine' did not entirely seize up at the end of the 1782–83 season is surprising. On the contrary, the opera repertoire was particularly fresh and challenging during this period, which perhaps indicates that the company, lacking an independently minded artistic director, simply aped Continental fashion. At the same time, Andrei, Badini, Anfossi, Rauzzini, and Tenducci were evidently free to indulge in some audacious experiments; the repertoire under Taylor and the trustees was hardly dull. The most apparent consequence of the managerial upheaval of these years is, of course, the failure to engage enough first-rank singers for both the comic and serious opera. Recruitment had to be an Italian opera manager's highest priority. In this respect, Gallini was not to fail the King's Theatre.

[1] Trans. in Gibson, 'Earl Cowper', 242–3.     [2] *London Magazine* (Apr. 1785), 302–3.

# CHAPTER 6

# *Opera under Gallini (1785–1790)*

════════════

THE four seasons between 1785 and the destruction of the King's Theatre in June 1789 were operatically the best of any during the last two decades of the eighteenth century. London came closer to being pre-eminent in Italian opera than at any time since the 1720s. No wonder Mozart and Haydn both had hopes of crossing the Channel. Apart from the Pantheon and Little Haymarket seasons of 1790–92, more can be learnt about the management of the King's Theatre under Gallini than about any other eighteenth-century regime. Since he was effectively running the company as a trustee under an order from the Court of Chancery, an order that required him to submit the opera-house accounts for annual inspection, Taylor and all other interested parties could, by means of Chancery interrogatories, compel Gallini to justify every dubious expenditure and to explain virtually every management decision. Given this microscopic scrutiny, no one should be surprised that irregularities were discovered. But this mass of mostly unfavourable detail about Gallini's regime should not obscure his considerable accomplishments. He introduced a much more sophisticated Italian opera repertoire to London. While maintaining connections with Italy, he began to look much further afield for singers and repertoire. Thanks largely to Stephen Storace and singers from the Vienna Burgtheater, recent *drammi giocosi* of Paisiello and Martín y Soler were produced; significant amounts of Mozart were heard for the first time at the King's Theatre.

Gallini also introduced a different repertoire system. The King's Theatre had previously relied mostly on a combination of pasticcios and new works by distinguished house composers of the older generation, such as J. C. Bach, Sacchini, and Anfossi. But Gallini now commissioned only the occasional new work from house composers or those such as Gresnick and

335

Tarchi who were simply passing through London; he concentrated instead on popular recent works, minimally revised, by celebrated composers who never had a chance to come to London or who were not at the time in residence: Salieri, Cimarosa, Martín y Soler, and Paisiello. The house music director during Gallini's tenure was the local musician Joseph Mazzinghi, who became nearly as important a member of the company as the foreign house composers. A few original works were commissioned, but revivals of recent hits from the Continent, such as *Una cosa rara*, *Il re Teodoro in Venezia*, and *Il barbiere di Siviglia*, were given a much higher profile. In short, the King's Theatre began to anticipate the repertoire system of the modern opera-house.

In one of his tetchy defences against charges of managerial extravagance, dishonesty, and incompetence, Gallini stated that all his performers had been 'punctually paid . . . even in advance', so that the King's Theatre 'acquired great Credit and reputation in France and Italy as well as in England by which means [he] has been able to employ the greatest singers and the most celebrated dancers that ever appeared at the Kings Theatre'.[1] Although the quality of ballet trailed off during these years, his claim to have engaged the finest singers is fully justified. Gallini's sterling achievement as manager, especially when one recalls the £18,000 per annum spending limit imposed on him, was recruitment of virtuoso singers. Moreover, he was the first King's Theatre manager to attend equally to the *buffa* and *seria* troupes, assembling under one roof the most prestigious roster of performers of the entire century. The castrati Giovanni Maria Rubinelli (1785–86 and 1786–87 seasons) and Luigi Marchesi (1787–88, 1788–89, and 1789–90 seasons) more than filled Pacchierotti's place. Though still a celebrated singer capable of moving his audience to tears and destined to return once again to London in 1790–91, Pacchierotti was erratic (see Susan Burney's comments quoted in Ch. 4). The fashionable subscribers had turned against him at the end of the 1783–84 season. The usually generous memoirist Parke was cruel: '. . . I have frequently heard him hold a note for two or three bars below the pitch, and be enthusiastically applauded for it'.[2] Rubinelli and especially Marchesi were younger *musici* and, while lacking Pacchierotti's pathetic *cantabile*, were much more secure in a range of styles.

In 1785–86 Gallini finally hired Gertrud Mara, with whom he had treated unsuccessfully in autumn 1783. He was apparently reluctant at first

---

[1] C31/249, no. 45 (28 May 1788).  [2] *Musical Memoirs*, i. 29.

to employ her but 'was compelled at the pressing Sollicitations of several Noblemen to engage' her 'on any Terms'.[1] A somewhat stiff actress, she did not, however, disappoint as *prima donna seria* and took the London stage by storm, as she had already done the concert platform. (For Mara and Rubinelli at this time, see Pl. 11.) Though they received a less ecstatic reception, Nancy Storace and Francesco Benucci, Mozart's former singers, headed the brilliant and experienced *buffi* later in the 1780s. In retrospect, the King's Theatre lagged behind the main Continental houses only in the lack of a first-rate tenor. Giuseppe Forlivesi, while well received, was no match for Madam Mara or Marchesi. Because of the continuing dominance of *primo uomo* and *prima donna*, Gallini's serious operas were generally more conservative than those mounted by Sheridan and Taylor had been.

There are two invaluable sources of information about the operation of the music department under Gallini: a handful of manuscript full scores used in King's Theatre productions, and a lawsuit initiated by Stephen Storace, who was house composer at the time, against the publishers Longman and Broderip, by which Storace secured the rights to one of his substitute arias. The scores include a copy of Cherubini's *Giulio Sabino*, De Michele and Mazzinghi's alteration of Sarti's *Giulio Sabino*, *Gli schiavi per amore* (after Paisiello's *Le gare generose*); Mazzinghi's alteration of Cimarosa's *L'Olimpiade*; and *Il barbiere di Siviglia*. These give unprecedented insight into the process of adaptation and help to explain why some scenes were untouched and others radically revised. *Storace v. Longman and Broderip* is equally valuable, as it generated extensive testimony about the complex relationship among the manager, the house composer, the *prima buffa* Nancy Storace, the house poet Badini, the music-copyist and *de facto* musical director De Michele, and the King's Theatre's official publishers Longman and Broderip. The lawsuit also reveals how scores were acquired from Vienna, how Paisiello's music was received in London, and how attitudes towards music as intellectual property were changing.

Throughout the years when he was out of power, Taylor pored over the King's Theatre books, talked with friendly subscribers and his moles within the opera-house, and tried to glean every bit of evidence against Gallini. In their very churlishness, Taylor's complaints inadvertently reveal Gallini to have been a strong and remarkably independent manager. Taylor charged Gallini with four shortcomings:

[1] C31/249, no. 45.

1. attendance at the King's Theatre was damaged by the 'double contracts' that required leading singers to perform at the Hanover Square concerts;
2. the performers were overpaid;
3. the theatre was overstaffed with artistic assistants and singers holding the same rank;
4. the manager refused to comply with the wishes of the noble subscribers that particular operas be produced.[1]

Italian opera singers in London had always performed at public and private concerts on their nights off from the King's Theatre and in oratorios during Lent. Any manager needed to be concerned that overexposure of a principal singer outside the opera-house would affect receipts. As mentioned in Chapter 5, Taylor himself had drawn up contracts that restricted his singers' non-operatic engagements. As both manager of the King's Theatre and owner of the Hanover Square concert room, Gallini had a conflict of interest, as he freely admitted in affidavits and answers to Chancery interrogatories. Several singers signed opera contracts with him that obliged them to perform at Hanover Square, for which privilege they had to pay Gallini a nightly 'rent'. For instance, Madam Mara gave three concerts there during the 1785–86 season, for which she paid Gallini the hefty sum of 25 guineas a time.[2] He denied extortion, claiming instead 'that some of the principal performers refused to be engaged unless they might be permitted to sing at private concerts in order to make as many ffriends as possible for their benefit, the Nobility and other Subscribers to such private concerts being most of the subscribers to the Opera house'.[3] The Master in Chancery ruled that for Rubinelli to sing at Hanover Square was not in the interests of the opera-house and ordered Gallini to deduct ten guineas per night from the singer's salary. The manager adamantly denied that the concerts were detrimental to the theatre: subscriptions increased during the time when Rubinelli was singing at Hanover Square, he claimed. Besides, the two kinds of music-making were utterly different and thus the attraction to an audience mutually exclusive: 'the trouble of singing in a concert is considerably inferior to the trouble of *acting* or sustaining a part in the performance of an

---

[1] These charges are most clearly set out in C31/248, no. 285.

[2] C31/249, no. 45. Gallini claimed this was a bargain 'rent': he had charged Bach and Abel 50 guineas a night for their famous concerts; see C107/201, 24 Apr. 1789.

[3] C31/249, no. 45.

opera' (emphasis added).[1] Gallini may have been grasping at straws in trying to defend the 'double contracts', but this last statement implies that King's Theatre productions were perceived as something more complex than mere concerts in costume.

Performers' salaries rose steadily during Gallini's regime, though records from before 1785 are so patchy that one cannot say whether this was a real escalation or whether he was only restoring pay-scales to the levels established by Sheridan and Taylor.[2] Madam Mara was engaged in 1785–86 at £800 and Rubinelli at £700, on the face of it extremely economical salaries, given their fame and the fact that Pacchierotti had always received at least £1,000. But, as will be explained, these salaries were actually *pro rata* since the 1785–86 season was unusually short. In 1786–87 Madam Mara's salary increased to £1,200, more what one would expect for a singer of her reputation. But Marchesi's salary of £1,500 plus perquisites in 1788–89 was extraordinary by the norms of the 1780s. What drove the total salary bill for performers so high during Gallini's regime was the corresponding quality of the *buffi*—never as high individually as the *primo uomo* and *prima donna seria*, though Nancy Storace received £800 in 1787–88. Gallini offered a simple explanation for escalating salaries: certain influential subscribers put great pressure on him to acquire the best available Italian opera singers who, knowing the demand for their services in London, proved tough negotiators. The spending-cap imposed by the Court of Chancery meant that dealing with the likes of Madam Mara posed a dilemma: Gallini 'always endeavored to behave with proper respect and Civility towards the Nobility and Gentry Subscribers to and supporters of [the King's Theatre] and to Comply with their wishes as far as they were consistent with his Engagement and situation being limitted in his Expenditure' to £18,000 per annum. Therefore, when in 1787–88 he tried to reduce Madam Mara's salary from £1,200 to £800, 'she refused to accept' and was not employed.[3]

The charges that Gallini hired two singers of the same rank when one would have been sufficient to meet the needs of the repertoire and that he appointed too many musical assistants will be discussed later under the seasons concerned, but his defence against these charges is of interest here: Gallini was trying to provide the King's Theatre subscribers with the best Italian opera in Europe. This simple reply may be disingenuous, given the financial constraints under which he had to operate; besides, he found crafty

---

[1] C107/201, 24 Apr. 1789.    [2] 'Opera Salaries', 48–53.    [3] C31/249, no. 45.

ways to exceed the £18,000 limit and still make a profit. For Taylor's final charge, that Gallini 'refused to bring out and perform such Operas and Dances as have been by the . . . subscribers recommended to him and sollicited',[1] there is no corroborating evidence. Opera subscribers have probably always tried to influence the choice of repertoire and performers. There is no reason to assume that Gallini was more resistant to such suggestions than his predecessors, but one should note that he was opposed at a more basic political and personal level by the Lord Chamberlain, the Duke of Bedford, and other powerful figures who were soon to acquire a vested interest in the Italian opera. But Gallini's struggle against the Lord Chamberlain in particular was so courageous, even heroic, that one can imagine him taking pleasure in his artistic independence.

## I. The 1785–86 Season: Gallini versus the Lord Chamberlain

Repertoire:

*Il marchese Tulipano*, Paisiello, adapted and directed by Cherubini after *Il matrimonio inaspettato*, libretto after Chiari's *Il marchese villano*, 24 January 1786 (9 performances); orig. St Petersburg (Ostrov) 1779 (p. 346)

*Didone abbandonata*, pasticcio directed by Anfossi, arranged by Madam Mara, including numbers by Sacchini, Mortellari, Piccinni, and Schuster, libretto adapted by Badini after Metastasio, 14 February 1786 (8 performances); orig. (adapted) Venice (S. Moisè) 1775. London (earlier pasticcio on this libretto) 1775 (p. 356)

*La scuola de' gelosi*, Salieri adapted by Anfossi, libretto after Mazzolà, 11 March 1786 (11 performances); orig. Venice (S. Moisè) 1778[2]

*I viaggiatori felici*, Anfossi, libretto by Livigni, 16 March 1786 (6 performances); orig. Venice (S. Samuele) 1780. London 1781, 1785

*Perseo*, Sacchini, revised by Madam Mara (?), libretto by Aureli, 21 March 1786 (5 performances); orig. London 1774

*Giulio Sabino*, Cherubini, libretto after Giovannini, 30 March 1786 (1 performance) (p. 347)

*Virginia*, pasticcio based on Tarchi, directed by Cherubini, librettist unknown, 4 May 1786 (8 performances); orig. Florence (Pergola) 1785 (p. 351)

*L'inglese in Italia*, Anfossi, libretto by Badini after libretto set by Mazzoni, 20 May 1786 (2 performances) (p. 355)

*Armida*, pasticcio after Mortellari, libretto adapted from Durandi and De Rogatis, 25 May 1786 (6 performances); orig. Modena (Ducale) 1776 (p. 358)

The extensive correspondence involving Gallini, Taylor, his trustees, several King's Theatre employees, and the Lord Chamberlain's office (LC 7/3) has

---

[1] C31/248, no. 285.

[2] Sartori reports a copy of the printed libretto at Yale, but we have been unable to locate a copy there or anywhere else.

been discussed in Chapter 2. Details relating to recruitment and the effect of the theatre's debts on artistic policy this season are explored further here. Given the Lord Chamberlain's efforts to thwart Gallini at every turn, even after the Court of Chancery had ratified the memorandum of agreement between Gallini and Taylor's trustees on 28 October 1785, one must be surprised that there was any Italian opera at all this season, which opened extraordinarily late on 24 January 1786. Lord Salisbury very nearly succeeded in cutting off his nose to spite his face.

Within six days of signing the agreement with the trustees, Gallini wrote to Lord Cowper in Florence on 20 September 1785 'much straitened' 'from the season being so far advanced'. He desperately needed two singers, a *primo uomo* and a *primo buffo*, to complete his company; 'the rest [I] must get from [those] remaining in London' from the previous season. Evidently he had already made arrangements with Madam Mara, since he required no help in finding a *prima donna seria*. He wanted Lord Cowper to find a first castrato whose 'voice must be strong and stile different to Crescentini who has been unsuccessful here'. He left the decision to Cowper but mentioned three possibilities: Marchesi, clearly his first choice (eventually engaged for the 1787–88 season), the little-known Consoli, and Rubinelli; the last-named did in fact come to London in 1786. As *primo buffo*, Gallini wanted Giovanni Morelli 'if possible if not Benucci'. If neither was available (which proved to be the case) then he asked Cowper to engage 'the best that can be got but a very strong voice and good stile'. In a separate note Gallini added: someone 'with a strong voice who acts gracefully'.[1] Gallini wrote again three days later (on 23 September), sounding an even shriller note of alarm: 'It is absolutely unnecessary to consider the money so that I can have the best of Italy, and for the buffo Morelli or another better than Tasca.' He had to settle for Tasca, but Rubinelli was engaged for the last three months of the season, which helps explain his salary of only £700. Gallini had in fact engaged Rubinelli for a season and a half, that is, till June 1787, at a total salary of £1,700.[2] In requesting strong voices, he obviously hoped to remedy the lack of first-rate singers over the past two seasons. This concern may also reflect the increase in the size of the orchestra and the extra power needed to cut through the clamour of the new-style ensemble finale.

Had the Lord Chamberlain not stalled over issuing a licence, Gallini might well have been able to start the season in late November or early

---

[1] Gibson, 'Earl Cowper', 244. Following quotation from 245.    [2] C31/249, no. 45.

December as usual, or at least before Christmas. But Lord Salisbury, through his assistant Watson and Troward, as well as his confidential adviser on operatic matters, William Sheldon, tied Gallini up in red tape. Among other forms of harassment, they made him submit copies of contracts that had been signed and sealed. On 9 November 1785 Gallini reported the engagement of key members of the non-performing staff: Carnevale, assistant manager (£150); Badini, house poet (£150); Molini, translator of librettos (£52. 10s.); Marinari, a young painter and machinist apparently new to London (£100); and 'Mr Rebekah', that is, Biagio Rebecca, scene painter (£250).[1] In a postscript, Gallini added: 'A power [of attorney] is likewise sent to Italy for the providing different Performers and a credit sent abroad for £2,000 for engaging Signor Rubinelli to replace Marchesi, Sign. Fabiani and Signora Campioni the best Dancer's now to be had in Italy and strongly recommended by Lord Cowper.'[2]

As if the Lord Chamberlain were not causing the King's Theatre enough trouble, Taylor was trying to force Gallini to hire opera-house creditors, who under the deed of trust had 'a preferable right to situations and employments in this theatre'.[3] Now acting as Taylor's trustee under the terms of the 14 September 1785 agreement and officially recognized as 'Principal Creditor' by order of the Court of Chancery, Gallini was indeed ultimately responsible for the other creditors; but merely continuing to employ them at the opera-house would not discharge old debts. Among the musicians and other artists, the largest creditor by far was Novosielski, himself a former trustee, who was owed nearly £2,800 for work done up to the end of the previous season. He had nothing further to do with Italian opera until after the fire in June 1789.[4] But Gallini did indeed employ most of the others, including Anfossi (owed £740), Rauzzini (owed £100), and De Michele. In an important letter to the Lord Chamberlain of 26 November 1785, De Michele expanded on these circumstances:

I humbly beg leave to refer your Lordship to a Letter I took the Liberty of writing on the 7th of July Last; wherein I laid before you the state of my demands on the King's Theatre for Last Season; But I forgot therein to mention that I am also a very great Looser by Mr. Taylor in a sum of £514; which added to £412 due to me by the Trustees makes the whole amount to £926. Now My Lord a circumstance hath Lately arisen which compells me to implore your Lordship's interference and patronage. Mr. Gallini has no objection to employ me; and this I look upon as a

---

[1] Not recorded elsewhere as having worked for the King's Theatre this season.
[2] LC 7/3, fos. 207–8.   [3] LC 7/3, fo. 332.   [4] LC 7/3, fo. 248.

matter of right, not of a favour, I being a creditor of the House; but at the same time he will deprive me of the privilege, 'I ever enjoied', of printing the Musick; this is the advice, which Carnevale is giving to Mr. Gallini to hurt all the Creditors; moreover they will oblige me to sign a Writing purporting that I shall not prosecute Mr. Gallini by Law for the recovery of £150 or upwards due to me in the year 1784; when I was engaged with Mr. Gallini as well as with the Trustees. This is my Case Mylord; and I think it but justice to be continued in the same manner; and if I were so happy as to find your Lordship of the same opinion I most earnestly entreat you to take me under your protection, and consider in me a Father of a large family, and who for the long course of 24 years has been in the Service of the King's Theatre, and the publick . . . Leopoldo De Michele No. 61 in the Hay Market St. James[1]

Gallini apparently regarded De Michele's services as essential, since he employed him throughout his regime. The question of the copyist's right to sell music will be discussed in depth later; but one should note here that Gallini minimized the value of this privilege: 'the musick belonging to the proprietors . . . being of no considerable value, [I] gave the benefit of the printing of it to Leopoldo De Michele the musick copyist in consideration of his attention and services [and he] sold the same to . . . Messrs Longman and Broderip for the sum of £40 or thereabouts each season'.[2]

In regular reports to the Lord Chamberlain during the humiliating struggle to secure a licence, Gallini revealed that he was prepared to economize on certain performers and to sign false contracts to protect their reputations:

According to your Lordships desire I have sent to your Lordships Office copies of the different contracts I had entered into with the Performers as the same were signed by me, and among the rest Signora Ferrarese's which is made for £650 as your Lordship was informed by me, purposely to prevent her losing her credit in Italy should it be known she had engaged for so small a sum as £300 which I am to give her and no more, and which I likewise mentiond to your Lordship. I should esteem it a very material honor done to me by your Lordship not to let it be revealed as I should be very unwilling either to prejudice her here or abroad, but being determined to act with the utmost Candour by your Lordship I conceived it right to apprise you how the Affair stood; the rest are to be paid as their Contracts specify, your Lordship shall as I enter into any Engagements be made acquainted literally how they are to be, but it is customary with some to enter into Agreements for a greater Amount than they are to receive in order not to hurt their reputation abroad. . . . Hanover Square. . . . J. A. Gallini[3]

---

[1] LC 7/3, fo. 205.    [2] C107/201, 21 July 1789.
[3] LC 7/3, fos. 277–8 (17 Nov. 1785).

Gallini's frank disclosure that he signed fraudulent contracts necessarily casts doubt on all reported salaries before the 1791–92 Pantheon season, for which payments to performers are minutely documented. But his statement that Signora Ferrarese del Bene was a special case does imply this was not a widespread practice. After leaving London at the end of the 1785–86 season, she travelled to Milan before taking up an engagement in Vienna in October 1788, where she sang for Mozart. Her transition from serious to comic performer might have been encouraged by singing the role of Miss Nancy, the accomplished English girl in Badini and Anfossi's *L'inglese in Italia*, one of the most delightful works presented at the King's Theatre during the entire period under discussion.

Despite the manifest quality of the singers engaged this season, even without a famous *primo buffo*, Taylor complained that Gallini had not 'engaged or provided a proper or sufficient Company of Performers . . . for the present Season especially of Dancers, which have been for several years past the Principal attraction' of the King's Theatre.[1] Gallini's ambivalent attitude towards his former profession is explored in Chapter 7 and, as one will see, Taylor may have had a legitimate point about the quality of the dancing this season; but the charge against the singers was sour grapes, as was the question he put to Gallini about redundant appointments in the opera department:

Why and for what reason did you engage both Signora Feraeze [Ferrarese] and Signora [Giovanna] Sestini in the season of 1785/86 in the capacities of first buffas or comic singers when you know that it had been usual to have but one and could not this season be necessary to have more, there being the usual number of second women singers for both the comic as well as serious opera?[2]

As far as can be determined, Gallini never answered this question. When accused of the same alleged malpractice in 1786–87 in hiring both Nancy Storace and Anna Benini as *prima buffa*, he claimed that Signora Benini had failed, so he was forced to engage another; but this explanation was officially rejected.[3] Gallini might more honestly have pleaded artistic necessity; this was certainly the case for *L'inglese in Italia*, which included demanding roles for both Ferrarese del Bene and Sestini.

Gallini made other important changes in the opera department this season, motivated, so Taylor claimed, more by financial than artistic considerations. The long-serving poet Antonio Andrei, a creditor of the theatre, was

---

[1] C31/239, no. 206; see also C12/2012/54.    [2] C107/201, 7 May 1788.
[3] See below, and C107/201, 8 Dec. 1789, and C38/754, Nov. 1789.

summarily removed[1] and Carlo Francesco Badini promoted. Through Court interrogatories Taylor asked Gallini to justify Badini's salary of £150, 'when you know that the salary of the poets engaged and retained at the . . . theatre had never before your management exceeded £100'.[2] Taylor's follow-up question reveals important details about the sale of librettos:

Why . . . did you also pay to the said Badini the sum of £24. 7s. in each season for Books of Operas for the Royal Family contrary to the Custom and usage of the said Theatre in such Cases and whether you have not often refused to pay or allow the same as an Imposition on [the] part of the said Badini and intirely useless in itself? Have you not . . . allowed . . . Badini to raise the price of the Books of the Opera from one shilling to one shilling and six pence each contrary to former Custom, an Imposition upon the frequenters of the Opera in particular and on the Public at large and directly contrary to the Interest and Benefit of the said Trust Estate which is intitled to the clear sum of three pence upon each Book sold at the same time that the Interest and benefit of the Poet himself is trebled He having formerly enjoyed three pence out of each Book sold in Common with the Estate But who now enjoys nine Pence out of each Book sold?

Gallini did not respond directly but in a later answer to a similar set of questions said bluntly that Badini would not accept less than £150; besides, he added, there had previously been 'two persons in the office or quality of poet and one in the quality of a translator and Mr Badini acted' in both capacities.[3] Sacking Andrei and promoting Badini saved the opera-house money, Gallini said. He also mentioned that Badini had been first poet. This ranking probably explains why he had been commissioned to write original librettos, while Andrei had dealt almost entirely with adaptations. A final detail about the music department that emerges from the interrogatories is that, in denying he had profited from the sale of music owned by the opera-house, Gallini admitted to having 'exchanged some musick which was his own seperate [sic] property with Messrs. Longman and Broderip for a forte piano'.[4] He did not say whether the instrument was for his own private use (for the Hanover Square concerts?) or for the orchestra pit, where the piano had begun to supplant the harpsichord.

At first glance the choice of operas this season appears to conform to past practice, except for opening with a burletta, *Il marchese Tulipano* (24 January 1786), rather than a serious pasticcio. But in several respects the season was highly irregular, with striking innovations in both music and drama.

---

[1] C31/239, no. 206.
[2] C107/201, 7 May 1788, from which the following quotation is also taken.
[3] C107/201, 24 Apr. 1789.    [4] Ibid.

Madam Mara made her sensational London opera début on 14 February 1786 in *Didone abbandonata*—true, a pasticcio, but one without the customary support of a castrato Enea. The role was sung instead by the tenor Babbini. Similarly, Cherubini's long-awaited serious opera *Giulio Sabino* (première 30 March 1786) was also performed with a tenor as the male lead. Before jumping to the conclusion that Gallini had initiated the downfall of the castrato in *opera seria*, one should realize that these instances of 'natural' casting were almost certainly caused by the late arrival of Rubinelli in May. Several years would pass before London audiences would prefer a tenor to a castrato as the hero in a serious opera.

Il marchese Tulipano

Although Anfossi remained in London this season as house composer, his 'reputation was rather diminished than increased in this kingdom', as 'his resources failed him'; he was 59 years old in 1786.[1] Burney also believed that he was badly affected by the bankruptcy of the opera-house; indeed, he was owed a substantial amount of money. Perhaps for this reason, Gallini gave him ample work during his final months in London: he assembled and conducted *Didone abbandonata* and conducted Salieri's *La scuola de' gelosi*; he also presided over a revival of his own *I viaggiatori felici* and *L'inglese in Italia*, a new commission. But the limelight had already moved to Cherubini in the previous season, and now the most prestigious commissions, and those which proved historically important, were going to the younger man. The opening work of the season was *Il marchese Tulipano*, planned for Saturday, 21 January 1786 but delayed to the 24th.[2] This was a revamping of Pietro Chiari's libretto *Il marchese villano*.[3] Cherubini used as his basic source Paisiello's 1779 St Petersburg setting called *Il matrimonio inaspettato*, which was to have been the title of the 1786 London production but was changed on the Larpent manuscript copy. Little of the original remained.[4] Badini altered the libretto, the only copy of which is in the Bayerische Staatsbibliothek, Munich.[5] It is mentioned in the *Public Advertiser*, 25 January 1786: 'the English translation presents a poem more regular and ingenious than usual'. In the catalogue of his works, Cherubini listed six freshly

[1] Burney, *General History*, ii. 897.
[2] The earlier date appears in Gallini's application on Larpent MS 720.
[3] The *Morning Herald* (26 Jan. 1786) printed a detailed and essentially accurate account of the adaptation.
[4] British Library R.M. 22.1.1–2 is not related to the London production.
[5] See Robinson, *Paisiello*, i. 289.

composed insertions:[1] 'Nobile al par che bella', a duet for Tulipano (Morigi) and the Baronessa (Signora Sestini) in Act I, Scene iv; 'Madamina, siete bella' for Giorgino (the tenor Babbini) in Act I, Scene viii; 'Al mio bene, al mio tesoro' for Giorgino in Act II, Scene v; 'Assediato è Gibiltera' for Tulipano in Act II, Scene iv; 'Per salvarti, oh mio tesoro!', a *rondò* not in the libretto; and a new first-act finale, beginning 'Cosa vuole il marchesino'. The last was a substantial piece—forty pages in full score. The opera was apparently designed as a vehicle for the old favourite *basso buffo* Morigi who, as Tulipano, interjected the occasional English phrase, as he was wont to do. His battle aria in Act II, Scene v about Gibraltar is topical and mentions 'Monsù Crillon' and 'Gen'ral Elliot', that is, George Augustus Eliott, elevated to Lord Heathfield on 14 June 1787.[2] Though still a pasticcio, *Il marchese Tulipano* was tightly controlled by Cherubini, who seems to have added much more of his own original music than was customary for London. The *Favorite Songs* were published by Longman and Broderip.[3]

## Cherubini's Giulio Sabino

*Giulio Sabino* was clearly intended to be the principal new serious opera this season. But there were no significant reviews in the London press, and one must look to the *Gazzetta Toscana* of 20 May 1786 for an account of the première:

Abbiamo ricevuto avviso da Londra che l'opera in musica il Giulio Sabino, che si rappresenta in quel teatro, continua ad avere il più grand'incontro. Il sig. Luigi Cherubini, nostro concittadino, ha scritto la medesima e ha superato sé stesso e la sua età in questa nuova produzione; quello che più sorprende si è che egli ha saputo distinguersi, con tanta felicità, in un'opera in cui il suo Maestro, il celebre Sarti, molto aveva sudato per renderla una delle sue migliori composizioni. Le prime parti vengono eccellentemente eseguite dalla sig.ra Adriana Ferrarese del Bene e dal tenore sig. Matteo Babini con applauso universale.[4]

(We have received news from London that the opera *Giulio Sabino*, which is being staged in the theatre there, continues to have a very great reception. Our fellow citizen Luigi Cherubini has written it and has exceeded himself and his age in this new production; it is all the more surprising that he has distinguished himself, and with

[1] *Notice des manuscrits autographes de la musique*, ed. Bottée de Toulmon, 8.
[2] See John Eliott Drinkwater (afterwards Bethume), *A History of the Siege of Gibraltar* (London: John Murray, 1905).
[3] Copy in the Sibley Music Library, Eastman School of Music, M1505 P149 M.
[4] Reprinted in Vittorio Della Croce, *Cherubini e i musicisti italiani del suo tempo*, 2 vols. (Turin: Edizioni EDT, 1983), i. 104.

such felicity, in an opera over which his teacher, the celebrated Sarti, had laboured to make one of his best compositions. The principal parts are superbly executed by Signora Adriana Ferrarese del Bene and by the tenor Signor Matteo Babbini with universal applause.)

Nevertheless, its single performance (on 30 March 1786), the composer's departure for Paris shortly thereafter, and Burney's epitaph ('murdered in its birth, for want of the necessary support of capital singers')[1] have left a black mark on this work. Since the full score survives nearly complete, one is able to address the connected issues of quality and reception directly.

Cherubini began work on *Giulio Sabino* during the second half of the previous season (see his letter to Lord Cowper of 2 June 1785), and it was now brought out for the benefit night of Signora Ferrarese del Bene, who sang the role of Epponina.[2] The libretto was based on Pietro Giovannini's *Epponina*, first set by Giordani in 1779 and reworked for Sarti in 1781 into one of the most successful of all post-Metastasian *opere serie*. As the report in the *Gazzetta Toscana* implies, while Sarti was composing *Giulio Sabino*, Cherubini was his pupil. His teacher made him 'compose, for experience and to relieve him in his labours, all the arias of the secondary parts in the operas on which he worked'.[3] If he performed this service for Sarti's *Giulio Sabino*, Cherubini did not include any of the ghost-written arias in his own version of 1786. The libretto was a curious choice for Cherubini, since Sarti's opera was by then greatly admired; Pacchierotti and Marchesi had both sung the title-role.

The composer faced two additional challenges: to adapt Giovannini's three-act drama to the two-act formula now *de rigueur*; and to create a part for the tenor Babbini (Sabino) that would have the same weight and dramatic impact as if sung by a castrato. The libretto retained only three of the original aria texts and the recitative was brutally curtailed. In Giovannini's powerful story of conjugal devotion, Epponina has hidden and protected her husband, the failed revolutionary Giulio Sabino whom the Romans believe to be dead, by encouraging the affection of Tito, the emperor's son. This she does with the purest of motives and under the most difficult circumstances, including concealing her pregnancies from Tito by applying an

---

[1] *General History*, ii. 899.

[2] That it was prepared especially for her benefit is stated on the title-page of the Larpent libretto, MS 728.

[3] Cherubini, *Catalogue général par ordre chronologique des ouvrages composés par moi*; see Willis, 'Cherubini: From *opera seria* to *opéra comique*', 156.

ointment to make her whole body swell. In the 1786 version, Giovannini's original, which is already deeply Gothic, is turned into a melodramatic shocker, with the focus shifted away from Sabino and squarely on to Epponina; this was, after all, for Signora Ferrarese del Bene's benefit. The most stunning change is that for the first six scenes of Cherubini's opera, Epponina believes that Sabino is actually dead. Her affliction thus arises, Dido-like, from a conflict between her growing love of Tito and a widow's devotion to the memory of her dead husband. In Act I, Scene vii, during a visit to her husband's tomb, concealed deep within the ruins of his castle at Langres, Epponina is astonished when Sabino suddenly emerges from the gloom. His appearance brings the terrible realization that she was about to commit unknowing adultery with Tito. This extraordinary reunion rather blunts the effect of the extended sequence in Act II when Sabino, knowing his hiding-place is about to be discovered, prepares to murder his own children to rob Annio, Tito's general, of the pleasure. Despite several absurdities that resulted from compressing Giovannini's second and third acts into one, Cherubini was presented with a libretto that in many ways is potentially more dramatic than the one set by his teacher Sarti. This perhaps explains why he was willing to run the risk of indivious comparison.

With the very first aria Cherubini ostentatiously announces *Giulio Sabino* as a big work.[1] Sung by Bartolini, the only castrato in the opera, Arminio's 'Al mormorar del vento' is a fully scored A major *bravura* packed with *Sturm und Drang* effects, including huge vocal leaps and ample coloratura. It is also indicative of a general miscalculation on Cherubini's part: all the characters, even the inexperienced and apparently unsuccessful Eliza Wheeler (as Voadice), were provided with virtuoso music, except Babbini in the title-role. He was instead expected to exude Pacchierotti-like pathos: his passage-work is mostly limited to rather monotonous arpeggiation. This deficiency was accentuated by delaying his first aria until Scene viii, raising false expectations. But this is Epponina's opera, and her first aria, 'I mesti affetti miei' (Act I, Scene v), if making little musical comment on her widow's dilemma, is a brilliant show-piece by any standards, despite the token sentiment heard at the beginning (see Ex. 6.1 on page 350). The rest is largely *fioritura* of dotted rhythms and scales reaching up to high *e'''*.

---

[1] Copy consulted: Florence, Conservatory Library MS D.1153. This lacks the overture, though at the end of the first act the trumpet and kettledrum parts of a three-movement overture in D major are bound into the manuscript.

Ex. 6.1. Luigi Cherubini, 'I mesti affetti miei', from *Giulio Sabino*

Perhaps the biggest disappointment of the score is Cherubini's decision to set Epponina's discovery of Sabino, alive but furiously jealous, in simple recitative (Act I, Scene vii). In an opera that in other respects is very modern in its approach to action and narrative, this is a throw-back to Metastasian convention, wherein great events pass by quickly in recitative or happen off-stage and are then reflected upon in arias. Conversely, one of the short-comings of late eighteenth-century *opera seria* is the *dispositio* (or goal of musical design) of the first-act finale, which makes interior *scene* difficult to fit in. This is easier in the second act, where the finale, if one is present, is rarely developmental or climactic. What was lost by shying away from *recitativo accompagnato* in Act I, Scenes vii and viii is, however, recompensed in full by the first-act finale, a duet for Sabino and Epponina, 'Consola le mie pene'. Like Sarti's original, this is an anguished farewell taken from stock, but with a different, more complex premiss: Epponina has been in love with Tito but, understanding the reason why, Sabino apologizes for being jealous. Cherubini's simple B flat major melodies convey a sense of forgiveness, but the main point of the two-section finale is contained in the relationship between the voices. The full orchestra includes parts for solo violin and cello that expose and develop the main melodic ideas; sometimes the cello is paired with the tenor and the violin with the soprano, but they also form a quartet of equal parts with the voices. Though the finale is by no means a masterpiece, Cherubini cleverly filled in the 'missing' soprano castrato sonority with the solo violin.

The harrowing episode in the 'subterraneous vaults' in Act II is a grand *stromento* melodrama, with horror and pathos in equal measures. It begins *adagio* in G minor, with sudden dynamic changes, thick bassoon textures, and a solo oboe wailing above. Proceeding step by step, the action is accompanied by string tremolos, wild chromatic shifts, pizzicato effects—but it all smells faintly of the lamp. The problem is the failure of the orchestra—Cherubini leaves it completely subservient to the singers—to make its own statement. The overall effect is little more than orchestrated simple recitative, as contradictory as that may sound (see Ex. 6.2 on page 352).

Everything considered, *Giulio Sabino* is a remarkable music drama, especially seen in the London context where brilliant singing, from which this production did not apparently benefit, was everything. When an arrangement of Sarti's original was mounted two seasons later in 1788, it enjoyed eleven performances but owed its success almost entirely to Marchesi in the title-role. Cherubini, in his version, deftly side-stepped the problem caused by lack of a *primo uomo* by shifting the weight of the drama on to Signora Ferrarese del Bene. If she was not able to bear it, that was only partly the composer's fault.

## *Tarchi's* Virginia

The Gothic trappings of *Giulio Sabino* were as nothing compared with the real horror depicted in an adaptation of Tarchi's *Virginia*, also directed by Cherubini this season and brought out for Rubinelli's London début on 4 May 1786. It was still drawing large audiences nearly a month later when on

**Ex. 6.2.** Cherubini, excerpt from *recitativo stromento* in Act II, Scene vi of *Giulio Sabino*

27 May Lady Mary Coke reported 'the crowd at the Opera on Tuesday was beyond what I ever saw it. Hundreds were sent away and when I came it was with difficulty I passed the passages to get to Lady Townshend's Box'. Composed for Florence in autumn 1785, and therefore perhaps recom-

mended by Lord Cowper, and with Rubinelli as Icilio,[1] *Virginia*, set to an anonymous libretto (perhaps by Moretti), breaks decisively with Metastasian tradition and is one of a handful of operas composed around 1785 that aspire to true tragedy.[2] In Tarchi's original, the heroine's father, Lucio Virginio, fails to protect his daughter from the sexual advances of the villain Appio Claudio. Rather than see her violated, Lucio stabs Virginia off-stage and carries her body in during the final scene (like *King Lear*, but without the laughs). The adapter of the 1786 London libretto (probably Badini though the preface is unsigned) thought all this 'too ferocious and tragical for an Opera', and so omitted 'the catastrophe, and . . . made some alterations, which are, however, analogous to the principal circumstances relative to this historical event' (J. Almon, 1786). Though a typical chaos finale, the ending as altered for London is almost more shocking than Tarchi's original: hiding in 'Subterraneous Vaults under the Carmental Gates',[3] Virginia (Madam Mara) gropes pathetically through the darkness in search of her beloved Icilio (Rubinelli), who has been singularly powerless to help her. Her cowardly and thoroughly despicable father, who fails Virginia in her hour of need, is also present when Appio and his soldiers discover the wretched trio. The opera ends as Virginia is carried off to be raped. The critic of the *Morning Herald* (8 May 1786) reacted lamely to this historic departure from the conventions of *opera seria* as practised at the King's Theatre: 'The quartetto, at the conclusion of the Opera, is in an entirely new plan; it has a very pleasing effect, but in our opinion should be curtailed.' What would he have said if Lucio had 'snatched a knife from the next butcher's stall, and stabbed [Virginia] to the heart', the original ending as described in the preface to the libretto, which the London adapter was trying to avoid?

Rubinelli sang mostly Tarchi's music in the 1786 production,[4] but in other respects this was a pasticcio, with an overture and one or two arias by Cherubini, who conducted, and other contributions by Anfossi and Piccinni.[5] Larpent MS 731 shows a number of last-minute changes and substitutions: 'Superbo del mio fato' in Act I, Scene vi, replaced an aria beginning 'Ah, se nel febro ancora'; 'Son qual fiume' in Act II, Scene iv, replaced

---

[1] Sartori, no. 24958.

[2] See Marita P. McClymonds, '"La clemenza di Tito" and the Action-Ensemble Finale', 766-72.

[3] Compare *Giulio Sabino*, Act II; the sets were probably reused.

[4] Not, as is reported in the *Biographical Dictionary*, xiii. 131, 'written especially for him'.

[5] *The London Stage*, Part 5, ii. 882.

'Agitato per troppo contento'; and 'Idol mio quest'alma amante' in Act II, Scene vii, was substituted for 'Caro ben nel fiero istante'. Another important substitution is mentioned below. Rubinelli received the adulation that London audiences routinely afforded any half-way decent castrato at his first appearance at the King's Theatre, but Dr Burney's analysis of his voice is both detailed and admiring without quite betraying his close friend Pacchierotti.[1] Rubinelli was, too, a specialist in the pathetic style but, claimed Burney, possessed a much deeper and more reliable contralto, almost a tenor; in fact, except for a few notes above high *c* ", which he produced in falsetto 'and so much more feeble and of a different register from the rest', his range was very similar to that of Babbini, a tenor. To find a castrato admired more for his lower than for his upper notes is not a little disconcerting, but the same compelling effect and tone quality could evidently not be achieved by a tenor.

Turning to the surviving arias for Rubinelli from *Virginia*, which were published as separate numbers by Longman and Broderip, one is struck by their utter simplicity and almost total lack of coloratura. Typical is the substitute aria 'Idol mio quest'alma amante' in Act II, Scene vii, a long F major *rondò*, whose sugary melodies are decorated by lumpy arpeggios in crotchets and quavers. To depict the words 'E fra l'ombre', the music moves to the subdominant as the voice descends to the bottom of Rubinelli's range, a striking effect noticed by one reviewer: 'The sudden shift to the lower notes in the second line [actually the third line]—the address to Lucius—and the apostrophe to other faithful lovers, "Fidi amanti voi vedete"—are among the most heartfelt and delightful excitements we recollect from any musick.'[2] Longman and Broderip also published the first-act finale, a duet for Virginia and Icilio, 'Non lagrimar, ben mio', also by Tarchi, which replaced an entirely different finale in Larpent MS 731, which begins 'Ah se tu m'ami ancora'. The former is little more than a virtuoso display of singing in thirds—at one point in the *allegro* section, for ten bars with scarcely a pause for breath. As both *Virginia* and *Giulio Sabino* illustrate, *opera seria* had became extremely daring in its violation of the conventions of the classical drama on which it was based, but evidently in order to support such

---

[1] *General History*, ii. 898–9.

[2] Unidentified cutting in the New York Public Library, printed by Petty, 237. On 240 n. 16, Petty claims incorrectly that this aria is attributed to Gioacchino Albertini in the Longman and Broderip publication. It is, however, labelled 'Sigr. Tarchi'. Albertini composed 'La mia sposa' in Act I, Scene ii.

innovation and unaccustomed realism, the music had to remain 'pleasing' and 'delightful'. The dichotomy would not be removed until the nineteenth century.

## *Anfossi's* L'inglese in Italia

Shortly before he departed from London, Anfossi composed a burletta in the manner of Mozart's *Der Schauspieldirektor* and Salieri's *Prima la musica e poi le parole*, which were nearly contemporaneous (February 1786). *L'inglese in Italia* (première 20 May 1786) is a parody of Italian opera—its composers, singers, and dilettanti. Whether Badini, the librettist, knew Casti and Salieri's opera is uncertain, but there was a connection to the 1785–86 London season: the centrepiece of the Viennese spoof was Nancy Storace's take-off of Marchesi in a scene from Sarti's *Giulio Sabino*. In *L'inglese in Italia* Badini satirizes the pasticcio, nefarious recruiting practices, himself as poet, and, in the character of Sir Thomas Connoisseur, almost certainly Lord Cowper, Gallini's agent in Italy. The opera, for which unfortunately no music survives, is a delightful confection and yet another sign of Gallini's liberal and tolerant policy towards repertoire.

Sir Thomas (sung by Simonetti), a long-term resident of Naples and a 'dilettante in antiquity', has been retained by the manager of the opera in London to engage local singers and dancers ('Avuto ho l'incumbenza / Di cercar de' soggetti'—Act II, Scene ii). He becomes infatuated with a young singer, Volatina (Signora Morigi), who induces Sir Thomas 'to engage a set of performers for the Opera in the Hay-market' (from Badini's 'advertisement' or preface). But first, he must be cured of a tarantula bite with a concert organized by Don Pasticcio (played by the *basso* Tasca). The composer is discovered in Act I, Scene vi, 'composing at the harpsichord, having by him a large open trunk full of written sheets of music'. He is having trouble with a line from a duet for Lauretta and Pasquino:

> L'onda chiara e l'aura lieta,
> L'aura lieta, e l'onda chiara,
> L'aura chiara, e l'onda lieta—
> Maledetto sia 'l Poeta!
> Mio tesoro, mio bel Sole—
> Che versacci, che parole!
> Questa cosa non può andar.

(The lucid wave, and the fresh gale—the fresh gale and the lucid wave—the lucid gale and the fresh wave—Hang the poet! My treasure, my Sun—what doggerel! what words! 'tis absolutely impossible to set them.)

Unable to continue, he digs into his trunk and finds a duet 'sung by Time and Truth, who are making love together; as I am to express the affection of a new married couple it suits my purpose extremely well—but there is a note wanting here—I need but add the syllable *sì*'. Don Pasticcio thus solves a basic problem facing every *pasticiere* but one not always attended to—finding the right music to suit the drama. In the next scene, when Volatina sings over an aria about an eruption of Vesuvius, Conte Rifinito (Babbini) comments that the composer should have used 'un motivo / Un po' più affettuoso', and the singer agrees that she would prefer a rondeau. Don Pasticcio responds indignantly: 'Oh diavolo! un Rondeau / Spiegando il terremoto' (a rondeau expressing an earthquake!). When pressed, he says he will ask the impresario to decide. Any artistic integrity he might have gained from this debate is literally swept away at the beginning of the second-act finale, whose chaos is partly generated by some dock-hands who drop Don Pasticcio's trunk into Naples harbour: 'Senza baule / Non son Maestro, / Mi manca l'estro, Non so che far' (Without my trunk, I am no maestro; without my 'inspiration', I won't know what to do).

The libretto is stuffed with puns and in-jokes, none more outrageous than the appearance in Act II, Scene iii, of Volantina's mother, an old singer called La Signora Catterina Pataffia, who has in her day triumphed on the London stage, though she then suffered the disgrace 'Di non esser pagata' (of not being paid, which the libretto translation glosses to 'She met with an astonishing applause, but the manager did not pay her'). In pressing Sir Thomas to arrange a return engagement, she says that her daughter never goes anywhere without her. Adding to the humour is the fact that Signora Pataffia was sung in drag by the old *basso* Morigi, with his real daughter in the role of Volatina. The loss of Anfossi's music is most regrettable for the first-act finale, which includes Don Pasticcio's concert; one wonders how the inset arias were incorporated into the continuous flow of music. This opera should be compared with Giordani and Badini's *Il bacio* of 1782, which also included a burlesque concert.

## Didone abbandonata *and other Pasticcios*

The biggest event of the season, at least the one that helped most to replenish the King's Theatre coffers, was the hiring of Gertrud Mara as *prima donna seria.* She was by all accounts a remarkably intelligent musician with ringing high notes and neat coloratura, but whether her outstanding reception was owing as much to several years of diva deprivation as to her virtuosity is difficult to say. Not since Madam Lebrun or even Caterina Gabrielli in the mid-1770s had the King's Theatre known a female serious singer of her stature. But Madam Mara was able to demand much more than her predecessors. She was the first of a line of sopranos, including Catalani and Banti, who were to tyrannize both composers and repertoire by continuing to rely on the pasticcio so sharply satirized in Badini's *L'inglese in Italia.* For Madam Mara undoubtedly travelled with a trunk full of music and, being trained in the science as well as in the practice of the art, she was deeply involved in the selection and arrangement of the music in her pasticcios.

Her début on 14 February 1786 (which was planned for the 11th but delayed)[1] was in a reworking by Badini of Metastasio's *Didone abbandonata,* which had not—oddly enough, given London's appetite for such works— been used for a pasticcio since 1777. Though it was nominally under the direction of Anfossi, Mount Edgcumbe recalled that Madam Mara 'made a very judicious selection of songs, introducing four of very different characters'.[2] Published by Longman and Broderip, they are: 'Son regina, e sono amante' in Act I, Scene iv, by Sacchini, who never set this libretto but contributed to the 1775 pasticcio; 'Ah non lasciarmi nò', in Act I, Scene ix, by Mortellari, who set the opera in 1772; 'Se il ciel mi divide' in Act II, Scene iii, by Piccinni, whose version dates from 1770;[3] and 'Ombra cara' in Act II, Scene vii, by Schuster, whose setting dates from 1776 (this aria was also attributed to Gazzaniga). Madam Mara's selections were thus somewhat yellow at the edges, and Badini's libretto made no radical departure from the 1734 state of Metastasio's text. Regarded as a good interpreter of Handel, Madam Mara had decidedly old-fashioned tastes and manner. Nevertheless, her *Didone abbandonata* caused a sensation.[4] Even Gallini, who got off on the wrong foot with the singer during their fruitless negotiation in autumn 1783, had to acknowledge her brilliance in a letter to Lord Cowper of 25 February 1786: 'Signora Marra has made her début and has had a great success. She sings superbly well with a strong and brilliant voice, sounding the notes like a violin.'[5]

Another creaking vehicle rolled out for Madam Mara was Sacchini's *Perseo* of 1777. No libretto survives for this revival, but one journalist wished

---

[1] Larpent MS 721.    [2] *Musical Reminiscences,* 52.    [3] This is not from his *Didon.*
[4] For a selection of reviews, see Petty, 232–4.    [5] Gibson, 'Earl Cowper', 245.

'that more of Sacchini's songs had been preserved'.[1] Again, the singer seems to have done more than simply portray Andromeda. The *General Advertiser* reported 22 March 1786: 'As to the Choruses, we understand that they were under the immediate direction of Mme Mara.' Sacchini still enjoyed a warm following in London, and one critic thought the revival of *Perseo* 'to be the second best effort the Opera can make—the best would be procuring some new composition'.[2] A newspaper article that appeared soon after Sacchini's death on 6 October 1786 suggests that Gallini may have heeded this advice:

The late Sacchini, about a month before his end, had entered into an engagement with Mr. Gallini, to set a new Opera, written by Mr. Badini for the King's Theatre, and was in great hopes of re-visiting England in the course of the next season: having ever had a strong partiality for this country, though the noble generosity of the beneficent Queen of France, enabled him to move in a sphere of affluence to which he would ever have been a stranger among us.[3]

Michele Mortellari, whose music had increasingly found its way into King's Theatre productions as substitute arias, settled in London in 1785 and awaited his chance to conduct an opera.[4] This came late in the present season on 25 May 1786, when his *Armida* (Modena, 1776) was revived with alterations following a composite of two librettos, one by Durandi and set by Anfossi (Turin, 1770) and the other by De Rogatis, set by Jommelli (Naples, 1770). Madam Mara declined to sing any of Mortellari's arias, and her substitutions were announced conspicuously in the printed libretto (Stuart and Stevenson, 1786):

The first ['Che pretendi amor tiranno'] by Pugnani
The second ['Chi di valor si vanta'] by Monopoli
The third ['Adorata mia speranza'] by Sacchini
The fourth ['Non partir, mio bel tesoro'] by Mr. Scultz [Schuster]

Three of Mortellari's pieces from this production were, however, published by Longman and Broderip: the first-act duet-finale 'Ah tornate, oh dio'; 'Resta ingrata', sung by Rinaldo (Rubinelli) in Act I, Scene v; and the same character's 'Calma la pene amara' in Act II, Scene iv. The last, a D major

---

[1] Unidentified cutting in the New York Public Library, printed by Petty, 235.

[2] Ibid.

[3] Undated cutting, Theatre Cuts 41, fo. [101ʳ].

[4] See Marita P. McClymonds, 'Mortellari, Michele', *Opera Grove*, iii. 474, and ead., 'Haydn and his Contemporaries: *Armida abbandonata*', *Proceedings of the International Joseph Haydn Conference* (Munich: Henle, 1986), 325–32.

Ex. 6.3. Michele Mortellari, 'Calma la pene amara', from *Armida*

*larghetto con moto*, stands out from the others, and indeed from most of the studiously simplistic music then in vogue at the King's Theatre, for its harmonic invention, based partly on a prominent descending chromatic cell: A, G sharp, G natural, heard first in the voice part in its second bar. The main theme of the ritornello, which is simplified for Rinaldo, is somewhat irregularly introduced by the cellos (see Ex. 6.3).

Despite the Lord Chamberlain's mean-spirited attempt to deny Gallini a licence and the consequent late start, the 1785–86 season must be judged a considerable success—not just for the celebrated performers, both singers and dancers. The opera repertoire was, Madam Mara's efforts notwithstanding, intrinsically good and acutely attuned to recent developments in Italy and, more importantly for the future, Vienna. After several difficult years, the King's Theatre was once again swimming rather than floating in the mainstream of Italian opera.

## II. The 1786–87 Season: The Storaces' Return

Repertoire:

*Alceste* (*Demetrio*), Gresnick, libretto by Badini after Metastasio, 23 December 1786 (9 performances) (p. 368)

*Giannina e Bernardone*, Cimarosa adapted by Mazzinghi, libretto by Livigni, 9 January 1787 (9 performances); orig. Venice (S. Samuele) 1781 (p. 376)

*Il tutor burlato*, Paisiello (?), adapted by Mazzinghi, librettist unknown, 17 February 1787 (3 performances) (p. 378)

*Giulio Cesare in Egitto*, pasticcio after Handel arranged by Arnold, 20 February 1787 (9 performances) (p. 371)

*Virginia*, pasticcio based on Tarchi, librettist unknown, 15 March 1787 (6 performances); orig. Florence (Pergola) 1785. London 1786

*Didone abbandonata*, pasticcio arranged by Madam Mara (?), libretto after Metastasio, 29 March 1787 (1 performance). London (earlier pasticcios on this libretto) 1775, 1786

*Gli schiavi per amore*, Paisiello's *Le gare generose* adapted by Storace, libretto by Palomba, 24 April 1787 (19 performances); orig. Naples (Fiorentini) 1786 (p. 378)

*La vestale*, Rauzzini, libretto by Badini, 1 May 1787 (2 performances) (p. 375)

At the end of the 1785–86 season, the two main King's Theatre composers, Anfossi and Cherubini, left London never to return. The first was one of the most esteemed Italian opera composers of the older generation, the second was at the beginning of what many people in London anticipated would be a brilliant career. But there is no indication that anyone within the opera company regarded their departure as a blow. Singers were of far greater concern, and Gallini already had contracts with Rubinelli as *primo uomo* and, though he had to raise her salary from £800 to £1,200, Madam Mara as *prima donna seria*. Nevertheless, Gallini once again set off for the Continent over the summer holidays to look for other performers.[1] His most important foreign engagements appear to have been the tenor and composer Bernardo Mengozzi (at £350) and the *primo basso* Giovanni Morelli, a protégé of Lord Cowper, whose running footman he had reputedly been.[2] Morelli had been sought for the King's Theatre since 1781, and his salary of £305 was

---

[1] C107/201, 7 May 1788.     [2] See Kelly, *Reminiscences*, i. 112–13.

a premium for singers of his type, considering he did not arrive in London until late April 1787. Such fractional engagements, which previous managers had tried strenuously to avoid, were becoming more common: Gallini felt that the injection of new blood late in the season helped maintain audiences when the weather improved.

## The Storaces

The 1786–87 season marks a decisive move in establishing a Viennese connection. On his return from Italy in October 1786, Gallini may have called at Vienna with the specific purpose of engaging Haydn as house composer (*Morning Chronicle*, 10 October 1786). Word of the exciting developments at the Burgtheater under the impresario Count Orsini-Rosenberg, who commissioned works by Paisiello, Salieri, and Mozart, had reached London via aristocratic travellers. Of particular interest was the news that Vienna's celebrated *prima buffa* was the Englishwoman Anna (or Nancy) Storace who in 1777, at the age of 12, had sung at the King's Theatre. Her rise to first singer in Italy in the early 1780s had been watched by various travellers, including the young English architect John Soane, with growing infatuation.[1] She joined the imperial court theatre at Vienna in spring 1783, bringing distinction to a number of roles, including Rosina in Paisiello's *Il barbiere di Siviglia* (Vienna première 13 August 1783) and Susanna in Mozart's *Le nozze di Figaro* (première 1 May 1786).[2] Her brother Stephen Storace, who accompanied Nancy to Italy and studied composition for a time at the Naples Conservatory, though returning intermittently to England, joined her in Vienna once she was established. He composed two operas for the Burgtheater, *Gli sposi malcontenti* (1 June 1785) and *Gli equivoci* (27 December 1786), both with his sister as *prima buffa*.

The circumstances of the Storaces' King's Theatre engagements in 1787—why they decided to leave Vienna at the peak of their success, the negotiations with Gallini, their initial reception in London—have not hitherto been well understood, even though the Irish tenor Michael Kelly was an eyewitness to some of these events. Generally reliable when not merely self-serving, Kelly was not always precise about dates:

---

[1] See Dorothy Stroud, *Sir John Soane, Architect* (London and Boston: Faber and Faber, 1984), 42.

[2] For accounts of her career, see *Biographical Dictionary*, xiv. 294–305; Patricia Lewy Gidwitz and Betty Matthews, *Opera Grove*, iv. 553–4; and Geoffrey Brace, *Anna . . . Susanna: Anna Storace, Mozart's first Susanna* (London: Thames Publishing, 1991).

Stephen Storace at length arrived at Vienna from England, and brought with him an engagement for his sister, from Gallini, the manager of the Opera House in London, as Prima Donna for the comic opera. Her engagement at Vienna was to finish after the ensuing carnival, and she accepted it, and I wished much to accompany her, and go to Dublin to see my family. (*Reminiscences*, i. 266)

Stephen later testified that he met with Gallini in London in September 1786, just before leaving for Vienna, which contradicts the news report cited above about Gallini in Austria. The manager asked him to acquire a score of Paisiello's *Il re Teodoro*.[1] The composer does not mention his sister's contract with the King's Theatre, but he had other things on his mind at the time, namely discussions with Da Ponte about the libretto for *Gli equivoci*. Gallini was later required to justify a payment of £63 to Stephen for the 1786–87 season and to explain 'what was the nature of [his] business or employment'.[2] The manager replied in some detail:[3]

Signor Storace composed two pasticcios for which he . . . was paid 25 guineas each and he brought over some Music from Germany for which he was . . . paid ten guineas . . . Signor Storace well deserved what he so received . . . another composer [Mazzinghi or Gresnick] was also employed and paid for composing at the same time with Signor Storace but . . . Signor Storaces Music . . . [was] much admired and repaid the price paid for it. . . .

Although Gallini does not mention Nancy Storace in this context, there is no reason to doubt Kelly's report that arrangements for her return to England were in her brother's hands.

Kelly's colourful account of the Storaces' last dissolute weeks in Vienna (which Stephen described as 'one continual scene of riot') does not convey any sense of urgency to take up their engagements with Gallini in London. Besides performing at the Burgtheater and attending ridottos, Nancy sang in various concerts, including her farewell on 23 February at the Kärntnertortheater where she may have performed Mozart's *scena in rondò* for soprano, piano, and orchestra ('für Mselle Storace und mich'), 'Ch'io mi scordi di te' (K. 505).[4] Three days before there was an incident at a ridotto

---

[1] C12/1703/11 (*Longman and Broderip* v. *Storace*), Storace's answer, 17 Apr. 1788.

[2] C107/201, 27 May 1789.

[3] C107/201, 21 July 1789.

[4] H. C. Robbins Landon, *Mozart: The Golden Years 1781–1791* (London: Thames and Hudson, 1989), 187, doubts this: 'it seems unlikely that the Count [Lord Barnard] would have failed to mention Mozart's participation'. Though Lord Barnard probably saw Mozart socially on many occasions during his residency in Vienna, he does not once mention the composer in his diaries.

which, as vividly recounted by Kelly, has left a stain on Stephen Storace's character. Though 'proverbially a sober man', Storace

had swallowed potent libations of sparkling Champaigne, which rendered him rather confused. He went into the ball-room, and saw his sister dancing with an officer in uniform, booted and spurred. In twirling round while waltzing, his spurs got entangled in Storace's dress, and both she and the officer came to the ground, to the great amusement of the by-standers. Stephen, thinking his sister had been intentionally insulted, commenced personal hostilities against the officer: a great bustle ensued, which was ended by half a dozen policemen seizing Storace, and dragging him to the Guard-house, to which several English gentlemen followed him. The officer of the guard was very good-natured, and allowed us to send for some eatables and Champaigne;—we remained with him all night, and a jovial night we had.[1]

Kelly discreetly omits to mention the name of the 'officer' in question. In one of his few surviving letters, written from prison on the very night, Storace explains at length to 'J Serres Esqr.' in London his side of the story:[2]

Ash Wenesday Vienna Feby 21 1787

You might not have received a letter from me so early as this my good friend—had it not been owing to a ridiculous circumstance that happen'd last night or rather early this morning—to make short of the story—it is some hours since I have been in a guard-house under an arrest—and of course having much leisure I know no better mode of passing my time than devoting it to my friends in England—but to inform you of some of the particulars—you must know that there never perhaps were so *hard a going* sett of English in any one Town out of England—as are at present in Vienna—we have lived these last six weeks almost in one continual scene of riot *amongst ourselves*—as long as it remain'd so, nobody could find fault—but lately some of our youths—high-charged with the juice of french grapes—have made their occasional sallies & exposed themselves to the Natives especially at the Ridotta's, or Masquerades—many of which have been given in the course of the newly expired Carneval a few nights ago the Honbl Charles Lennox—Ld Clifford and one or two others—courted some Ladies—with rather too much vehemence— which occasion'd an order—that every Englishman that behaved with the least impropriety, at the ensueing Ridotta (the one last night) should be put under an arrest—It so happen'd that about three oclock this morning as my Sister was danc- ing a minuet with Ld Barnard, a Man who was standing by chose to stand in such a manner that Lord Barnard turning the corner inadvertently trod on his toe—upon which he was rather impertinent—Ld B took no notice but proceeded on again

---

[1] Kelly, *Reminiscences*, i. 275–6.
[2] Harvard Theatre Collection TS 990.1, vol. 5, fo. 79. This letter has not previously been printed, though one passage is quoted in the *Biographical Dictionary*, xiv. 307.

coming to the same corner—the Gentleman took an opportunity of advancing still further into the ring & had nearly thrown him down—upon which I who was a stander by—with more spirit than prudence—asked him 'what he meant by being so impertinent as to attempt throwing down any gentleman that was dancing'—he then immediately chose to use some very ungentlemanlike language—which I (who had rather too much Champaigne in me though far beneath intoxication) could not brook—in short words begat words—the whole rooms were presently in a confusion—the report was that an *Englishman had mis-behaved*—we were almost press'd to death by the multitudes that crowded round us—my antagonist proved to be an officer—he immediatly apply'd to the officer of the guard—who *sans cerimonie* put me under charge of a corporal's guard—and I was conducted to the guard-house— from which place I have the honor of addressing to you this epistle—as all the English have taken up this matter warmly I immagine I shall soon be liberated—and we shall strive hard to bring the aggressor to condign punishment.

We purpose leaving this place on Saturday next at 2 in the morning and proceeding through Saltzburg—Munich—Ansperg—Ulm—Strasbourgh,—& Chalons to Paris—with as much expedition as possible as the weather has lately been very fine & open—we expect to find the roads in very good order—last night my sister sung for the last time [at the opera, Martín y Soler's *Il burbero di buon cuore*]—to a very great applause, & every mark of partiality in an audience that possibly could be shewn—the people here are very sorry to lose her—she gives her benifit Friday— and as I have already observed a few hours after, we leave Vienna.—a post or two ag[o?] I asked you—through Mr Hall—to send me a letter to [Mons.?] de Forge— at Paris—inclosed in one to me directed *a la poste restante*—we expect to be in Paris ab[out] the 6th or 7th of March—I can hardly refrain from laughing at the Idea of myself *in durance vile*—relating to you the journey I am going to take of 1,100 miles—within these three days—I have made a pretty little collection of music— which my friend Dom: shall have the [indecipherable] over on our meeting. I am happy to hear that all your good family have enjoy'd their health—I hope that of your sister Hannah may be speedily reestablished—If I can be of any service to you or yours—at Paris—I desire you will command me, without reserve—as I am never so happy as in testifying how much I am yr friend. . . .

Lord Barnard, future Earl of Darlington, had been Nancy Storace's constant companion since he had met her after the opera on 6 July 1786. Supposedly on the Grand Tour, he had tarried in Vienna on and off since his arrival from Venice on 10 April 1786.[1] His diaries provide a valuable record of

---

[1] The diaries and journals of Henry N. Vane, Lord Barnard, Raby Castle, County Durham. We are grateful to the present Lord Barnard for permission to quote from these volumes. They are day-to-day summaries in French and Italian and give only the bare essentials. Excerpts in English translation have appeared in Landon, *Mozart: The Golden Years*, 187; and in Brace, *Anna . . . Susanna*, 60–3.

opera-going in several countries. Before arriving in Austria, Lord Barnard had travelled extensively in Italy, attending the opera at every opportunity except, oddly, at Venice: Florence, 28 December 1785; Pisa, 3–4 January 1786; Rome, 17, 23, 24, 29, and 30 January 1786; Naples, 8 and 11 February; Rome again, 18 and 19 February; Florence again, 27 February, and so forth. While in Florence Lord Barnard met Sir Horace Mann and Lord and Lady Cowper; opera seems to have been the main topic of conversation. On 16 March 1786, three days before leaving for Venice, Barnard wrote: 'Miladie Cowper m'a desiré si j'irai à Petersburg de faire, Marquisini, et le premier Compositeur de Musique à l'Imperatrice, me chanter un duo à sa Requête.' 'Marquisini' is probably a diminutive of Marchesi, the celebrated castrato who was in St Petersburg in 1786 to inaugurate the Hermitage Theatre; Sarti was at the time *maestro di cappella* to Empress Catherine. The Cowpers were obviously acquainted with both musicians, but Lord Barnard never got as far as Russia on his travels.

That Lord Cowper, who had almost certainly heard Nancy Storace sing at Florence, encouraged Gallini to engage her for the King's Theatre is not beyond the realm of possibility. He certainly helped with the contract for Marchesi in May 1787. Lord Barnard, for his part, was besotted with La Storace and, during the summer of 1786, following her performance in *Le nozze di Figaro* whose première he attended, he saw a great deal of her before setting off on a tour of the north German states. But this too may have been in pursuit of her. On 15 August, in the company of three English friends, he attended a performance of Stephen's *Gli sposi malcontenti* at Brunswick.[1] In the weeks before the Storaces left Vienna for good, Lord Barnard was with them nearly every day, including the infamous 20 February 1787, when he confirmed that Stephen was seized 'et mis en Prison', adding laconically, 'Je suis allé au Prince Ch. Lichtenstein; Je ne me suis pas couché de tout.'

The Storaces left Vienna at 2.30 a.m. on Sunday, 25 February, probably travelling in Lord Barnard's comfortable coach. In Kelly's sanitized version of this famous journey, the party included 'Storace, her mother, her brother, Attwood,[2] and myself, not forgetting Signora Storace's lap-dog' (Lord Barnard?).[3] In other respects the two accounts, one written en route, the other forty years later, are in substantial agreement. Lord Barnard does

---

[1] Libretto listed in Sartori, no. 22530. Storace's opera was also given this summer at Prague; see Sartori, no. 22531.

[2] That is, the composer Thomas Attwood, who had been studying with Mozart.

[3] *Reminiscences*, i. 277.

not mention the encounter with Leopold Mozart in Salzburg, but he supplies details of concerts and other musical events they attended along the way: a concert at Munich (1 March); plays at Strasburg (7 March) and Paris (11 March). They attended the Opéra several times in Paris, hearing Gluck's *Iphigénie en Aulide* (19 March), *Iphigénie en Tauride* (12 and 20 March), and 'Madame St. Huberty', that is, the soprano Jeanne Charlotte Saint-Aubin in *Alceste* (19 [21?] March). At the Comédie-Italienne they heard Grétry's *Richard Cœur-de-lion* (16 March). On 23 or 24 March, Lord Barnard left the party at Calais and doubled back to Paris for more high living. When he finally arrived in London via Brighton on 27 April, he dined with Signora Storace, but their relationship had cooled. His re-entry into the social whirl included occasional visits to the King's Theatre, and his last recorded evening there was 24 May, when he attended a performance of *Gli schiavi per amore* for Signora Storace's benefit. He saw her once more on 6 June, but by then his diary is filled with meetings with his cousin, 'Miladie Katherine' Powlett, his future wife. The Grand Tour was over.

This lengthy digression provides an informal picture of the international Italian opera circuit, of the personal relationships that helped drive singers and repertoire round Europe. While Gallini was awaiting the arrival of his new house composer and *prima buffa*, the Storaces paused for ten days at Paris, cramming in as many visits to the Opéra as possible. But experience of the works of Gluck and Grétry would have been of little direct use in the thoroughly Italianized King's Theatre, except as fodder for parody. Nor did Gallini depend on the Storaces to sustain his company through the 1786–87 season: that burden was being easily borne by Rubinelli and Madam Mara. Nancy Storace was about to enter an entirely different kind of opera company from the one she had left. The Burgtheater mounted almost exclusively *opera buffa* and *dramma giocoso*. The repertoire was tightly controlled by the Emperor Josef II himself and by the General-Spektakel-Direktor, Count Orsini-Rosenberg. There was no expensive ballet company, no *primo uomo / prima donna* system, and hence no need of the pasticcio. Nancy Storace had flourished in comic roles without serious female competition. In London, by contrast, she not only had Madam Mara to contend with but, upon arrival, found the position of *prima buffa* already filled by the soprano Anna Benini. And, unlike Signora Storace, Benini was also able to sing in serious opera and had even replaced Madam Mara in a revival of *Virginia* on 17 April 1787.[1]

---

[1] See *The London Stage*, Part 5, ii. 967.

Whereas in the previous season Gallini had had no compunction in appointing *both* Signora Ferrarese del Bene and Signora Sestini at the rank of *prima buffa*, he sacked Signora Benini shortly before Nancy Storace's first performance on 24 April in *Gli schiavi per amore*. Gallini was asked to explain: 'Why & for what reason did you agree to pay . . . Siga Storace . . . the Salary of £350 for the season of 1786–7[?] Was not Siga Benini engaged & paid a salary of £600 for the same season & for the very same Duty as Storace was engaged for'?[1] On the surface Gallini's response seems straightforward and unanswerable. He admitted that 'altho Signora Benini was . . . engaged and paid a salary of £600 for the same season as Signora Storace was engaged for, yet as . . . Benini did not give satisfaction to the public he was afterwards under the necessity of engaging . . . Storace for half' the season.[2] Yet, according to the press, Signora Benini 'gave great satisfaction' and 'was loudly encored'.[3] The Master in Chancery, William Weller Pepys, did not regard this as a sufficient explanation for Gallini's having engaged 'two persons for the same Duty'.[4] Pepys implies that Signora Benini was as much unfairly dismissed as Nancy Storace was redundantly employed. Realizing that Gallini had probably offered Signora Storace a contract as early as autumn 1786, one suspects that Gallini had planned all along to use Benini only until his star attraction arrived from Vienna.

Gallini also had to defend employing more than one composer this season, which is puzzling because the King's Theatre had throughout the century retained at least two or three composers, even during Handel's time at the Royal Academy of Music. In this case, hostility seems to have been directed at Stephen Storace himself. As we have seen, Gallini testified that he 'well deserved what he so received', adding that the popularity of his pasticcios justified the investment. Gallini had thus 'acted for the benefit of [the] proprietors by purchasing' them.[5] Whether the other composer to whom he compared Storace was Gresnick, Mazzinghi, or Arnold, all of whom were employed by the King's Theatre this season, is not clear, but we assume Gallini was referring to Mazzinghi, who did more arranging and conducting than the others.

The choice of repertoire this season seems distinctly odd and lacks the clear sense of direction that might have been provided by an Anfossi or a Cherubini. The first production of the year was *Alceste* by Antoine-Frédéric

---

[1] C107/201, 27 May 1789.   [2] C107/201, 8 Dec. 1789.
[3] See Petty, 244–5, for a selection of reviews.
[4] C38/754, report in *Harris and Gallini v. Crawford, Grant, and Taylor*, Nov. 1789.
[5] C107/201, 21 July 1789.

Gresnick, perhaps engaged at the insistence of Madam Mara, who had championed his works in Paris at the Concert Spirituel in the early 1780s and had introduced his music as substitute arias the previous season.[1] *Alceste* sustained the *opera seria* until 20 February 1787, when Samuel Arnold brought out his curious museum-piece medley of Handel's operatic music under the title *Giulio Cesare in Egitto*. Was Gallini being daringly inventive, as in 1786, or just scraping the bottom of the barrel? The cheap and cheerful burlettas offered early in the season—Mazzinghi's adaptations of *Giannina e Bernardone* by Cimarosa and Paisiello's *Il tutor burlato*—were just fillers before the arrival of the Storaces.

As far as the *opera buffa* repertoire was concerned, Nancy Storace could not have arrived in London more opportunely. The King's Theatre had already mounted two operas in which she had appeared on the Continent: Cimarosa's *Il pittore parigino* (Milan 1782, London 1785) and Sarti's *Fra i due litiganti* (Milan 1782 and Vienna 1784, London 1784 as *I rivali delusi*). During her years as *prima buffa* at the King's Theatre, most of La Storace's roles were in revivals of works she already knew: Paisiello's *Le gare generose* (Vienna 1786, London 1787 as *Gli schiavi per amore*); Cimarosa's *L'italiana in Londra* (Vienna 1784, London 1788 as *La locandiera*); Paisiello's *Il re Teodoro* (Vienna 1784, London 1788); Gazzaniga's *Le vendemmie* (Vienna 1782, London 1789 as *La vendemmia*); Martín y Soler's *Una cosa rara* (Vienna 1786, London 1789 as *La cosa rara*); Paisiello's *Il barbiere di Siviglia* (Vienna 1784, London 1789); and Bianchi's *La villanella rapita* (Vienna 1785, London 1790). More than anything else, this long list helps explain the strengthening connection between the King's and the Burgtheater; yet it may simply represent Stephen Storace's 'pretty little collection of music' carried from Vienna in 1787. As we shall see, the Storaces were not the only advocates of Mozart's operas in London.

### Gresnick's Alceste

The season opened on 23 December 1786 with Gresnick's *Alceste*. This two-act adaptation of Metastasio's *Demetrio* is, by Badini's standards, extremely conservative, with a conventional first-act duet-finale, 'Ah! ti lascio amato bene', and a perfunctory second-act choral finale wrapped up in a happy ending. Badini evidently rejected or did not know Bianchi's 1774 version,

---

[1] See Philippe Mercier, *New Grove*, vii. 704.

which included an early example of an action ensemble finale.[1] Nor was the 1786 London production very spectacular, except for Act I, Scene iv, with a throne room and perspective view of a port with illuminated ships.[2] *Alceste* was chastely Metastasian in tone if not in form, and the critic in *The Times* objected (8 January 1787):

Plot, intrigue, distress, and all the bustle of tragedy . . . Alceste has not an atom of. The hero and heroine walk coolly into the Temple of Hymen, the disappointed lover coolly gives up his mistress, and the piece coolly concludes with a grand chorus. This may suit the languor of *soft Italia*, but in the land of beef and liberty, something of characteristic opposition is wanting—to keep the audience 'tremblingly alive'.

The harrowing physical and psychological realism of *Virginia* and *Giulio Sabino* of the previous season had apparently made some impression.

*Alceste* was clearly got up as a vehicle for Rubinelli and Madam Mara, though it was not a pasticcio: all the music was apparently by Gresnick. But the Larpent copy of the libretto shows signs of pasticcio-like construction. The recitative, stage directions, and many of the aria texts were written in two fair hands, with several gaps into which aria texts were later inserted by a third, minuscule hand: 'Mar crudela' in Act II, Scene v, sung by Madam Mara (Cleonice) is one example. The *Morning Herald* (1 January 1787) was uncharacteristically critical of her execution of the coloratura in 'Quando sarà quel dì', in which she 'appears entirely out of her element'. Interestingly, in the Larpent manuscript this aria (in Act II, Scene ii) is assigned to Olinto, sung by Antonio Balelli, the *secondo uomo*. Madam Mara's mixed reception was also observed by Lady Mary Coke, who attended the opening night: 'The opera was far from full and far from pleasing, one or two songs excepted it was very dull. Rubinelli and Mara were very fine but Maras songs were not good' (24 December 1786). Things had picked up a week later: 'The opera was much fuller this evening than it was last Saturday; the Prince of Wales had so large a knot under his chin that his face rested upon it' (30 December 1786).

Longman and Broderip published the overture, arranged for piano by Mazzinghi, and six vocal numbers from *Alceste*. One of these, 'Deh t'affretti astri tiranni', sung by Madam Mara, is not in the libretto. Gresnick's music is in general much more chromatic and structurally sophisticated than that

---

[1] See Don Neville, 'Demetrio', *Opera Grove*, i. 1,118–19.
[2] See Larpent MS 751. No printed libretto survives.

## Ex. 6.4. Antoine-Frédéric Gresnick, 'Quando sarà quel dì', from *Alceste*

fa    non si - a do - lo - - - - re

of the Italian composers associated with the King's Theatre during Gallini's regime. The first act duet-finale, 'Ah! ti lascio amato bene', is a substantial piece, spoilt only by a few thudding clichés. After the opening *larghetto* in F major, the E flat major *allegro* is a tonal surprise, righted with a concluding reprise in F. The loud bravura for Rubinelli in Act I, Scene vi, 'Scherza il nocchier talora', includes modest amounts of coloratura and exploits his lower range, except for a run at the end of the first section ascending to *f* sharp ″; as Burney remarked, Rubinelli could produce these notes only in falsetto. Though her performance was criticized, Madam Mara's arias are by far the most impressive of the printed selection. 'Quando sarà quel dì' in Act II, Scene ii, is a *siciliano* in B flat major with restrained expression until the B section, which moves quite exceptionally into the parallel minor (see Ex. 6.4). The same singer's 'Se libera non sono' in Act I, Scene iv, was one of the most virtuosic bravuras heard at the King's Theatre since the days of Madam Lebrun. The passage-work includes scales, long-held notes, tricky turning figures, several *c*‴s and one 'Queen of the Night' *f*‴.

## Giulio Cesare in Egitto

The English attitude towards their national composer Handel was becoming increasingly ambivalent in the 1780s. *Messiah* was already regarded as a monument of English culture, and the recent annual Commemoration concerts at Westminster Abbey and the Pantheon, which began in 1784, had brought the public veneration of Handel to international attention.[1] Yet the music itself was heard as hopelessly old-fashioned; the Italian operas had long been dead, and the only music of Handel that had been performed

[1] See William Weber, 'London: A City of Unrivalled Riches', in *The Classical Era*, ed. Neal Zaslaw (London: Macmillan, 1989), 321–2.

recently at the King's Theatre were old favourites from the oratorios fitted with new Italian words. But with George III's professed love of Handel's music and with Madam Mara an admired interpreter who had sung at the Commemoration, Gallini decided to take a chance: he commissioned Samuel Arnold to arrange a pasticcio selected from Handel's Italian operas rather than from the publicly more acceptable oratorios. Arnold was well qualified for the task, as he was just beginning to publish an edition of Handel works, which, though never completed, ran to 180 issues over the following ten years and included five of the Italian operas. *Giulio Cesare in Egitto* (20 February 1787) is quite unlike any other pasticcio produced at the King's Theatre throughout the period, as it comprised 'Music entirely by Handel and selected from various operas set by that incomparable Composer' (title-page of the libretto, D. Stuart, 1787). It may, however, be compared with Tenducci's similarly classicizing attempt in 1785 to reconstruct the original version of Gluck's *Orfeo* (see Ch. 5).

While Handel's music, even from the Italian operas, might have been thought in some sense timeless, Nicola Haym's 1724 libretto was clearly unacceptable for the 1780s. In the preface to his pasticcio Arnold announced that because of 'a great number of incongruities, both in the language and the conduct, several material alterations have been thought absolutely necessary, to give the piece a dramatic consistency, and to suit it to the refinement of a modern audience'. In fact, the opera was virtually rewritten, turned into a two-act drama in which Tolomeo does not die and only fragments of the Parnassus scene remain intact.[1] Of Handel's music, only 'Alma del gran Pompeo', 'Da tempeste il legno infranto' (transferred from Cleopatra to Tolomeo), and the final duet and chorus were retained. Everything else was drawn from other operas. (See Table 12.) Arnold's method of arrangement can be glimpsed in the only piece of the pasticcio that was published at the time, the duet for Cesare (Rubinelli) and Cleopatra (Madam Mara), 'T'amo, sì, sarai tu quella'.[2] He added parts for horns and oboes, which play expressive appoggiaturas, and cut the B section. Judging by the other aria texts printed in the libretto, this was the only instance of a suppressed *da capo*. This type of aria had almost completely disappeared from Italian opera twenty years before, so its retention here is perhaps the

---

[1] For further discussion, see Price, 'Unity, Originality, and the London Pasticcio', 22–4.

[2] Printed by Birchall and Andrews, not the King's Theatre's contracted publishers Longman and Broderip. Arnold seems to have bypassed De Michele and made his own arrangements.

TABLE 12. *Sources for Arnold's* Giulio Cesare

| Scene | Title/Singer | Source |
|---|---|---|
| I.1 | Viva il nostro Alcide (coro) | *Giulio Cesare* |
| 3 | Voglio amare infin ch'io moro (Curio) | *Partenope* |
| 4 | Scherza in mar la navicella (Tolomeo) | *Pastor fido* (1734) |
| 5 | Agitata, parto sì (Cleopatra) | *Radamisto?*[a] |
| 6 | Sempre dolci ed amorose (Nirena) | *Berenice* |
| 7 | Alma del gran Pompeo /Affanni del pensier (Cesare) | *Giulio Cesare* |
| 8 | Con la strage de' nemici (Curio) | *Radamisto* (1720) |
| 9 | [fragments of Parnassus scene] | |
| 10 | T'amo sì, sarai tu quella (Ces & Cleo) | *Riccardo* |
| II.1 | Lusinghe soavi [più care] (Achilla) | *Alessandro* |
| 2 | Se possono tanto (Cesare) | *Poro?* |
| 3 | Non trascurate amanti (coro) | *Deidamia* |
| 4 | Rendi il sereno al ciglio (Cleopatra) | *Sosarme* |
| 5 | Da tempeste il legno infranto (Tolomeo) | *Giulio Cesare* |
| 6 | Verdi prati e selve amene (Cesare) | *Alcina* |
| 7 | Agitato da fiere tempeste (Curio) | *Riccardo* |
| 8 | Dove sei amato bene? (Cleopatra) | *Rodelinda*[b] |
| 9 | Se costretto (Nirena) | *Floridante?* |
| 10 | D'eterno allor (coro) | *Scipione?* |
| | Ritorni omai nel nostro core (coro) | *Giulio Cesare* |

[a] Attributed by Arnold to *Radamisto,* but not in Handel's version.
[b] Arnold attributes this to *Floridante.*

most surprising feature of Arnold's *Giulio Cesare*.

Gallini made a substantial investment in this pasticcio and was apparently proud of the result. He mentioned it in a letter to Lord Cowper written in mid-March 1787: 'We did an opera of *Hendel* called Giulio Cesare—ancient music but tolerably good. Mara and Robinelli's duet ['T'amo, sì, sarai tu quella'] pleases the king. I believe he will attend tomorrow evening.'[1] This account is generally confirmed by Mount Edgcumbe, who thought Rubinelli particularly suited to 'ancient music' and that

[1] Gibson, 'Earl Cowper', 247.

'Nothing could be finer than the delivery of the famous recitative Alma del gran Pompeo':

But in the inferior parts it was miserably executed, and the effect was absolutely ludicrous. It, however, answered the end proposed; The king came two or three times to hear it, and it was pretty generally liked by the public: at least it filled the house by attracting the exclusive lovers of the old style, who held cheap all other operatical performances. (*Musical Reminiscences*, 55)

William Taylor, ever vigilant for irregularity in opera-house affairs, noticed in the accounts for the 1786–87 season that Gallini had paid Arnold £105 for the score of *Giulio Cesare*. In a Chancery interrogatory he seems to challenge the pasticcio process itself, though he probably had baser motives:

Was not the . . . Music compiled or selected from the works of some other . . . master and was not . . . £105 a premium . . . considerably . . . higher than is usually . . . given to persons for compiling or selecting Music for an Opera & is not ten Guineas or the most £20 the Common price given . . . to persons furnishing or Compiling or selecting music for Operas[?]

Taylor was also concerned because he had heard that the first performance of *Giulio Cesare* was a benefit for one of Gallini's employees, of which the manager collected a percentage.[1] Gallini's response is so inept that it must contain an element of truth. When he offered less than £105 for the score and parts, Dr Arnold 'so far insisted on receiving that sum that he took away the spartito from the music copyist and refused to return the same until he was promised his full demand of £105'. Gallini agreed this was

considerably higher than is . . . commonly given to persons for compiling music for an opera . . . as the price is generally proportional to the abilities of the compiler or composer or the greatness of the work and the work in question was of great merit and much applauded and amply repaid the expence of compiling it.

Therefore Arnold deserved the money.[2] This ringing defence of Handel, Arnold, and the London pasticcio begs several questions. Why was Stephen Storace, a successful international composer, paid only 25 guineas for adapting Paisiello's *Le gare generose*, which probably involved considerable fresh composition, while Samuel Arnold, organist of the Chapel Royal and dabbler in English opera, was paid four times as much for adding wind parts to arias selected from the works of Handel? Were King's Theatre composers really paid according to the 'greatness' of their work, whether original or arranged? How much skill was required to assemble a pasticcio, or was the

---

[1] C107/201, 27 May 1789.    [2] C107/201, 21 July 1789.

*pasticiere* simply rewarded for the not inconsiderable effort of copying out the score and parts? Most of these questions are addressed in the case of *Storace* v. *Longman and Broderip*, discussed below.

Finally, Gallini freely admitted that the first performance of *Giulio Cesare* was for the benefit of his deputy manager Andrea Carnevale, claiming a manager's 'right to give what opera he pleases to any performer or other person concerned in the house'. Even the great Marchesi had to negotiate for the privilege of a benefit performance; for a deputy manager to be offered one so casually smacks of corruption. The Master in Chancery, Pepys, was rightly dissatisfied with Gallini's answer, because the manager ducked the question about whether he had collected a percentage of the 'Profits arising from such Benefit'.[1]

*Giulio Cesare* was a curiosity and in no sense represented an attempt to revive the aesthetic of classical *opera seria*. Handel's original would have been impossible to revive in 1787—for dramatic, not primarily musical reasons. Post-Metastasian serious opera was an entirely different genre. With both *Alceste* and *Giulio Cesare* Gallini had virtually abrogated any commitment to the new style of serious opera epitomized by *Virginia* and *Giulio Sabino*. The talents of Rubinelli and Madam Mara were being squandered this season.

## *Rauzzini's* La vestale

Rauzzini, who had not been heard at the King's Theatre since his embarrassing performance as *primo uomo* in his own opera *La regina di Golconda* in 1784, was recalled once again to compose and assemble the last serious opera of the 1786–87 season, *La vestale* (première 1 May). With the departure of Anfossi and Cherubini, he was, frankly, as capable as anyone then in London of organizing an *opera seria*. *La vestale* had only two performances; the serious singers were by this point being swept aside by the runaway success of *Gli schiavi per amore*. But Rauzzini's opera is still noteworthy, perhaps not so much for its music ('many of the passages . . . are not worse for being familiar to the ear'; 'part of it would establish the fame of the first composer, and part of it might have been written by any composer')[2] as for Badini's libretto. This story of Emilia, a vestal virgin, is at one level a conventional *opera seria* with a *deus ex machina*, blazing altars, anguished farewells, and a heartless tyrant, Domiziano, Emperor of Rome. At another level, *La vestale* is a witty critique of Metastasian aesthetics and conventions.

---

[1] C38/754, Nov. 1789.      [2] *Gazetteer* and *The Times*, 3 May 1787.

It ridicules the heroic conflicts that lie at the centre of classical *opera seria*. Badini's method is ingratiating. The first act unfolds a well-constructed and utterly predictable heroic plot. Emilia (Madam Mara) is inducted as a vestal, decides that she loves Celere (Rubinelli) too much to bear the cloister, and elopes. When she is captured, her father Domiziano (Mengozzi) orders her to be buried alive. The first-act finale is a model of increasing anguish and confusion, as Celere's blaspheming the gods fuels the emperor's pig-headed tyranny. In the second act, Domiziano becomes a caricature of himself, referring in recitative to the mistakes of other operatic heros such as Tito. Emilia grows in stature and develops her defence as a feminist manifesto: the laws for vestals, we are told in Act II, Scene iii,

| | |
|---|---|
| Non sarian sì severe, | Would not be so severe, nor liberty |
| Ne sarebbe per noi | In love be deem'd for us so great a fault, |
| La libertà d'amor sì gran delitto, | If man, usurper of the female rights, |
| Se l'uomo usurpator del nostro dritto | Had not assum'd th'authority to frame |
| Non dettava il divieto. | them. |

Domiziano's excesses grow ever more absurd as he insists on carrying out the wishes of the oracle, even when Celere points out how often its predictions have been wrong. After seeing Emilia enter her tomb in Act II, Scene vii, the emperor slinks off stage and does not reappear—silent ignominy. During the lovers' final embrace, the scene darkens, thunder is heard, and a cloud appears 'which gradually dispersing itself, discovers the Deities with the written Oracle', which has to be explained by Venus: 'Mora? no—che 'l Ciel non vuole!' This is of course a parody of the *lieto fine*, as Badini hints in a long, pseudo-scholarly preface to the printed libretto (D. Stuart, 1787). He observes that history is not often 'consistent with the rules of dramatic probability', but

To produce an Italian Opera absolutely free from incongruities, is a task that borders on impossibility; yet I hope I shall not be deemed presumptuous to think, that the present Opera has a better claim to the indulgence of an English audience than the operatical rhapsodies commonly imported from Italy.

### Cimarosa's and Mazzinghi's Giannina e Bernardone

Rauzzini's *La vestale* and Madam Mara's virtuosity notwithstanding, comic opera clearly was in the ascendant this season, both in terms of reception and musical inventiveness. With the arrival of Giovanni Morelli and the

Storaces in April, the balance swung decisively away from *opera seria*. This is not to minimize the importance of Mazzinghi's adaptation of Cimarosa's *Giannina e Bernardone* earlier in the season. Livigni's 1781 libretto is a tale of a jealous husband, Bernardone (Morigi), who resorts to violence: he locks his wife Giannina (Signora Benini) away in her room, probably beats her, and discharges a shotgun at his rival Captain Francone (it failed to fire at one performance).[1] None of this is in the slightest farcical: though roundly condemned for the treatment of his wife, Bernardone is motivated by the realization that her relationship with Francone is not entirely innocent. Donna Aurora (Signora Sestini), an almost completely serious character, gives Giannina cynical advice about men throughout the drama and in Act II, when Bernardone believes he has murdered Francone and Don Orlando quickly offers to marry Giannina if her husband is hanged for the crime, the tone turns nasty indeed.

Cimarosa's opera was popular and widely performed. At Vienna in 1784, during Signora Storace's illness, Giannina was sung by Luisa Laschi, who later created the role of the Countess in Mozart's *Figaro*, which will give some idea of the nature of the earlier character. The Viennese production included seven substitute arias, and the composer himself made extensive changes for the Neapolitan version of 1785.[2] Mazzinghi's alterations for the 1787 London production were also extensive: the second act was virtually rewritten. Livigni's talking-statue scene was replaced by a trial, in which Giannina, disguised as a magistrate, passes benign judgment on her husband before the forgiveness scene. There were also drastic cuts made after the première on 9 January and during the run. On 1 March *The Times* reported that the prison scene (Act II, Scene x) was omitted, adding that this prevented Signora Benini (that is, Giannina) 'from unnecessarily wearing the breeches', that is, dressing up as the judge; this implies that most of Mazzinghi's finale was also cut. Longman and Broderip published two arias: Cimarosa's 'La donna che è amante', a big *rondò* in E flat major, which was actually a substitute for 'La moglie ben trattata' in Act I, Scene vii, the latter being itself a substitute text that Haydn was to set in 1790 for a performance at Eszterháza. The other published aria, 'Ti consola amato', also sung by Giannina, is by Gazzaniga—another *rondò* and again a substitute, probably for 'Ti compiango amato bene' in Act II, Scene vii. Even before the première the opera had been cut and rearranged: several arias and whole scenes found in Larpent MS 756 do not appear in the printed libretto.

[1] *The Times*, 15 Jan. 1787.
[2] See Gordana Lazarevich, 'Giannina e Bernardone', *Opera Grove*, ii. 404.

*Giannina e Bernardone* had thus migrated both textually and musically far away from the 1781 Venetian original, but remained an exciting and provocative drama.

## Il tutor burlato

Mazzinghi performed a similar operation on *Il tutor burlato* (première 17 February 1787), librettist unknown. The music was said to be Paisiello's, but he composed no opera of this title.[1] The libretto is the flimsiest of guardian-in-love-with-his-charge stories, and one suspects this was largely a pasticcio, even though the *Morning Herald* reported on 19 February 1787 that Lord Cowper had brought 'the score from Florence, and [recommended] it to the manager in the Haymarket'. No music survives, but two of the aria texts turned up in later King's Theatre operas: 'Voi mi amate già lo vedo', sung by Rosina (Signora Benini) in Act I, Scene ii, was used in *La vendemmia* in 1789; and 'Sento che amor', sung by Lindora (Signora Sestini) in Act II, Scene iii, was reused in *I due castellani burlati* in 1790. Morigi was cast as Martufo, the 'tutor burlato', but 'an unexpected event prevented [him] from appearing. Cremonini therefore read his part'.[2] Morigi had been arrested for debt the day of the première (17 February) and was not released from prison until 29 March.[3] He was also the male lead in *Giannina e Bernardone*, the only other comic opera then in repertoire; Mengozzi replaced him in this opera, while Calvesi stepped into *Il tutor burlato*. Given Morigi's importance to the company, one may be surprised that Gallini did not bail him out; but a far better *buffo*, Giovanni Morelli, was already on his way to London.

## *Paisiello's* Gli schiavi per amore

Lord Barnard left the Storace party at Calais on 23 or 24 March 1787, and the *World* reported their expected landing at Dover on the 26th.[4] Assuming that they arrived safely in London a day or two later, Stephen thus had less than a month to adapt Paisiello's *Le gare generose*, the score of which he had presumably carried from Vienna, for his sister's début as *prima buffa* on 24 April 1787. She had sung the role of Gelinda at the Burgtheater in

---

[1] Giovanni Marco Rutini and Francesco Lenzi composed operas with this title in 1764 and 1778, respectively; see Sartori, nos. 24145a and 24148.

[2] *The London Stage*, Part 5, ii. 954.

[3] PRO, PRIS 10/23, Fleet Commitment Book, Abstract, p. 92.

[4] See Brace, *Anna . . . Susanna*, 64.

September the previous year in a version of the opera that already included two or three substitute arias and an accompanied recitative introduced especially for her.[1] But Signora Storace, in choosing this opera, did not wish merely to rest on her Viennese laurels, nor did her brother simply reproduce the earlier version: *Le gare generose* was substantially revised. The scene was shifted from Boston to the French West Indies (post-colonial America was a touchy subject in England); Miss Nab became Mademoiselle Paté (Signora Schinotti), Miss Meri was altered to Neri (Signora Morigi) and Mister Dull to Monsieur Perruque (Morigi—his first appearance since being released from prison).

There are many differences between Larpent MS 769, the printed libretto (D. Stuart, 1787), and the full score that relates directly to this production: British Library R.M. MS 22.K.12, which is inscribed 'Le Gare Generose ò Sia Gli Schiavi per Amore in due Atti Burletta in Musica del Sigr Giovanni Paisiello L. De Michele Copista del Opera in Londra'. Several hands appear in this manuscript, though De Michele was responsible for much of the simple recitative and some of the larger ensembles, except the finales, which were taken over from Paisiello with minor verbal changes. The original *introduzione*, 'Thè, Dianina tu servi un pò a me', was moved to Act II, Scene iv. In its place is a new opening trio, 'Quattro, cinque', which one might have guessed that Stephen Storace composed especially for the 1787 London production, were it not so slight a piece. Perruque, Mlles Paté, and Neri are playing 'all'oca', a dice game (see Ex. 6.5 on page 380). The counting is very reminiscent of the opening of Mozart's *Le nozze di Figaro*. This ensemble is self-contained and could, frankly, serve as introduction to any number of burlettas.

How much of the rest of the non-Paisiello music was composed by Storace is unknown; he never claimed any of it, not even the opening trio. His sister sang none of the music introduced for her at Vienna: Dittersdorf's 'Così destino e voglio' was dropped; 'Minacci avverso il fato' in Act I, Scene ix, seems to have been replaced by 'Infelice sventurata', and Francesco Bianchi's 'Per pietà padron mio caro' replaced 'Perchè volgi altrove il guardo' in Act II, Scene viii. Just before the last piece, however, Signora Storace could not resist inserting the accompanied recitative 'Ah, se voi m'affliggete' (attributed to G. B. Borghi) that she had sung in the Viennese production, though this was added at the very last moment: it appears in neither copy of

[1] For a comprehensive account of the various versions of this opera, see Robinson, *Paisiello*, i. 373–83.

Ex. 6.5. Stephen Storace (?), 'Quattro, cinque', from *Gli schiavi per amore*

the libretto. In the Larpent manuscript a marginal note says 'Qui si Altera il recitativo', and the music is found in De Michele's manuscript. The composer and tenor Bernardo Mengozzi, who sang Don Berlicco in the London production and was married to the soprano Anna Benini (just sacked to make room in the company for La Storace), also contributed two arias: 'Con un moto orrendo', added at the last minute to Act I, Scene viii, and sung by Bastiano (Morelli), and 'Donne, donne chi vi crede' in Act II, Scene iv, also for Bastiano. If Stephen Storace had hoped this opera would make his reputation at the King's Theatre, then he kept a surprisingly low profile. His name appears on none of the voluminous published music from the production—only on the title-page of the printed libretto as director. That he was in fact deeply involved in the adaptation is known only from Gallini's later testimony that he was paid 25 guineas for 'composing a pasticcio' this season.

There is so much information about *Gli schiavi per amore* and so many sources, including a full score prepared under the supervision of De Michele, that one needs to stand back to see the work's greater significance for the history of Italian opera in London. Gallini had established a connection with Vienna that would supply the King's Theatre with many operas during the next few seasons and lead ultimately to the appointment of Haydn as house composer and to the famous invitation to Mozart issued in autumn 1790. Implicit in this shift is an acknowledgement that what the poet Badini called 'the operatical rhapsodies commonly imported from Italy' would no longer do, that Mozart, Paisiello, Casti, and Da Ponte were now creating works more 'consistent with the rules of dramatic probability' and whose richer music would appeal to English taste, which was growing ever more sophisticated. This was still a long way from the glories of the contemporaneous Burgtheater, but the King's Theatre seemed on the verge of a brilliant new era under Gallini. His employment of two prominent musicians of English birth also demonstrated bold confidence in the new direction Italian opera seemed to be taking in London.

One should not overestimate the Storaces' role in this change. The pattern of adaptation exhibited by *Gli schiavi per amore* suggests neither a brilliant controlling hand of someone who had recently worked with Da Ponte and rubbed shoulders with Mozart nor a *prima donna* throwing her weight around. The most substantial parts of *Le gare generose*, the finales, were preserved. Even the sparkling *introduzione* was saved by moving it into a dramatically neutral position in the second act. And the aria substitutions were not all made at the behest of Signora Storace; the new *primo buffo*, Morelli, was also indulged. But none of the substitutes appears to have been a suitcase aria, rather they were composed on the spot for the singers involved, two of them by Mengozzi, himself a member of the cast but no celebrated *maestro*. Despite these changes, Storace, and probably Mazzinghi and De Michele, showed far more respect for Paisiello's original than did most of their King's Theatre predecessors.

*Gli schiavi per amore* was a great success, being performed nineteen times in what little remained of the 1786–87 season and thirteen times the next. Signora Storace and Morelli were both well received, but there was obviously some rivalry between them. Morelli wrote to his mentor, Lord Cowper, on 29 April 1787 about his London début:

I am writing to give you notice of our opera which was performed yesterday evening. I can assure you that I have never had applause for any part I have sung such as I have had in London. All the pieces I sang were repeated to great enthusiasm. Storace repeated only one cavatina, and the remainder of what she sang went indifferently, but it doesn't matter as she is very capable, isn't she? But they expected much more. In all, I am very happy with London. After the opera I had the honour of a compliment from the Prince of Wales, who said that in London there had never been a buffo like me and that the whole public were very pleased with me.[1]

Gallini, too, wrote to assure Lord Cowper of his protégé's success (on 1 May 1787): 'It is with great pleasure that I tell you that Morelli has done fantastically. Storace pleases very well, and I hope the opera buffa will recover the money that the opera seria has lost me.' Burney, who was also biased towards Italian singers, nevertheless gave a more measured judgement:

Giovanni Morelli has a base voice of nearly the same force and compass as Tasca's, but infinitely more flexible and pleasing. He is likewise a good actor. . . . Storace . . . though a lively and intelligent actress, and an excellent performer in comic operas, her voice, in spite of all her care, does not favour her ambition to appear as a *serious singer*. There is a certain crack and roughness, which, though it fortifies the humour and effects of a comic song, in scenes where laughing, scolding, crying, or quarrelling is necessary: yet in airs of tenderness, sorrow, or supplication, there is always reason to lament the deficiency of natural sweetness, where art and pains are not wanting.[2]

---

[1] Trans. in Gibson, 'Earl Cowper', 246; following quotation from 247.
[2] *General History*, ii. 900.

In a letter of 3 July 1787 to Sir Robert Keith, the British ambassador at Venice, Stephen Storace sounds somewhat paranoid about their reception in London:

My sisters success in London upon the whole had been much as one would expect—though she has had great opposition from the Italians—who consider it as an infringement on their rights—that any person should be able to sing that was not born in Italy—at present she gains ground very fast—we have done the *Gare Generose* under another title with very great success—it has been performed to near 20 bumper houses—she is re-engaged for the next season at an advanced salary—& likewise at the ancient concerts—I am likewise to compose an opera.[1]

If there was Italian opposition to Nancy Storace in London, resulting from anything but the vocal problems Burney mentioned, one can easily understand the source: her appointment as *prima buffa* at Anna Benini's expense. And Mazzinghi, too, though he was not of Italian birth, might have felt chagrined that Gallini clearly favoured Stephen as a composer. After the end of the 1786–87 season, several members of the King's Theatre opera company travelled to France and performed *Gli schiavi per amore* at Versailles. It was rearranged in three acts, with Signora Benini taking over La Storace's role (Gelinda), Morelli as Bastiano, Morigi as Perruque, Calvesi as Don Berlicco, and Signora Pollone as Mademoiselle Neri; Signora Nardi (Mademoiselle Paté) was the only new member of the cast.[2] Another copy of the 1787 score, a rough draft largely copied and assembled by De Michele (British Library Add. MS 16075), was used for a later production, presumably the one mounted in 1797 at the King's Theatre, when Signora Storace and Morelli returned in the principal roles.

## III. The 1787–88 Season: Marchesi Arrives; Storace Sues

Repertoire:

*Il re Teodoro in Venezia*, Paisiello, numbers by Storace and Mazzinghi, libretto by Casti,
   8 December 1787 (13 performances); orig. Vienna (Burg) 1784 (p. 385)
*La locandiera*, Cimarosa, directed by Mazzinghi, altered from Petrosellini's libretto *L'italiana in Londra*, 15 January 1788 (7 performances); orig. Rome (Valle) 1779 (p. 395)
*Gli schiavi per amore*, Paisiello's *Le gare generose* adapted by Storace, libretto by Palomba,
   5 February 1788 (13 performances); orig. Naples (Fiorentini) 1786. London 1787

[1] British Library Add. MS 35538, fos. 258–9. Storace begins this letter with a request for missing sheets from a book he acquired just before leaving Vienna. He had not noticed the omissions because of 'my ignorance of the german language'.
[2] See Sartori, no. 21226.

*La cameriera astuta*, Storace, librettist unknown, 4 March 1788 (7 performances) (p. 397)

*Giulio Sabino*, Sarti, arranged by Mazzinghi and De Michele, libretto by Giovannini, 5 April 1788 (11 performances); orig. Venice (S. Benedetto) 1781 (p. 400)

*L'Olimpiade*, Cimarosa, libretto after Metastasio, 8 May 1788 (10 performances); orig. Vicenza (Eretenio) 1784 (p. 404)

*La frascatana*, Paisiello, directed by Mazzinghi, number by Sacchini introduced, libretto after Livigni, 15 May 1788 (6 performances); orig. Venice (S. Samuele) 1774. London 1776, 1778, 1781

The most important event of the 1787–88 season—as far as opera is concerned, for Noverre returned as ballet-master—was the engagement of the soprano castrato Luigi Marchesi. He was widely acknowledged as the finest of the late castrati, and indeed proclaimed by some as the greatest serious singer of the age.[1] Gallini first attempted to engage him in 1785. The singer is frequently mentioned in his letters to Lord Cowper (see, for example, March 1787: 'If Marchese does not come I will manage with Robinelli'). When Gallini wrote to Cowper on 1 May 1787, he had already begun serious negotiations through an intermediary, Campigli, but Marchesi was keeping him in suspense and therefore preventing him from hiring supporting singers and a *prima donna seria*: 'With regard to Robinelli and Mara—the public no longer listens to them. One needs novelty and good voices—ordinary ones make me lose much money.'[2] By 7 June 1787, Gallini had decided to travel to Florence 'to fix the entire company' in person. Marchesi had still not signed a contract:

Please tell Signor Campigli to write to me in Turin of Signor Marchese's decision so that I can be settled when I see him in Italy and persuade him to be moderate so that we will both be satisfied. I have need of a good tenor and mezzo-carattere and a prima donna seria who can sing buffo if necessary. These are the persons necessary for my opera. [Singers with] beautiful voices who understand music well are essential; I will not fail to pay them according to their merits if they have good voices.

On 26 June, a few days before leaving for Italy, Gallini had still heard nothing from Marchesi. The correspondence with Lord Cowper is interrupted at this point, but in a deposition given to the Court of Chancery a year later, Gallini said he had finally engaged 'with Signor Marchesi on the best terms in his power and was obliged to go to Milan in Italy to prevail on him to come to England through the pressing Sollicitations of many of the princi-

---

[1] For a detailed account of his triumph in Milan in 1780, see Rice, 'Sense, Sensibility, and Opera Seria', 109–17.

[2] Gibson, 'Earl Cowper', 247; following quotation from 248.

pal subscribers to the Opera House'.[1] After all this effort, Marchesi did not arrive in London until early March 1788, making his début in Sarti's *Giulio Sabino* on 5 April 1788. For the remainder of the season he received £376. 13s., but this led in 1788–89 to the highest recorded salary for a King's Theatre performer to that time: £1,500 plus a benefit and other perquisites.[2]

## *Paisiello's* Il re Teodoro in Venezia

Despite Gallini's complaint about the lack of good singers this season, at least until Marchesi arrived on the scene, the *buffa* repertoire reached a peak of quality unsurpassed until the age of Rossini. Nancy Storace and 'Viennese' operas were once again featured, while Stephen received the only new commission, *La cameriera astuta*. The first opera of the season was Paisiello's masterpiece *Il re Teodoro in Venezia* (8 December 1787) which, following the success of his *Gli schiavi per amore* in the spring and summer, was 'the so long talked of *serio* comic opera'.[3] Signora Storace, a member of the original Vienna cast of August 1784, repeated the role of Lisetta. (Michael Kelly, now singing at Drury Lane, had also been in the first production.) The extent to which Paisiello's opera influenced Mozart in *Le nozze di Figaro* is beginning to be appreciated.[4] There seemed to be genuine interest in London in the plot of the opera itself. Although the story of the deposed and impecunious king of Corsica was drawn from Voltaire's *Candide*, the protagonist, Baron Theodor von Neuhof, was a real person who had come to London after his fall from power in 1736 in search of funds but, like the erstwhile manager of the King's Theatre, had ended up for a while in the Fleet Prison and eventually died in London. Casti's fine, remarkably innovative libretto, a biting comment on the folly and transience of royal power, nevertheless depicts the deposed king with great humanity. He is living incognito in Venice, hounded by creditors, fearing exposure, yet always hoping his ship will come in.

Casti was a political writer; his libretto *Cublai, gran Kan de' tartari* had in fact been banned for its satirical overtones.[5] The papal nuncio at Vienna, Garampi, reported in January 1785 that *Il re Teodoro* was intended as a satire

---

[1] C31/249, no. 45 (28 May 1788).

[2] 'Opera Salaries', 51–2.

[3] *The Times*, 10 Dec. 1787.

[4] See Wolfgang Ruf, *Die Rezeption von Mozarts 'Le nozze di Figaro' bei den Zeitgenossen* (Wiesbaden: Franz Steiner Verlag, 1977), 47–71, and Daniel Heartz, *Mozart's Operas*, ed. Thomas Bauman (Oxford: Clarendon Press, 1990), 153–7.

[5] See Rudolph Angermüller and John Platoff, 'Casti', *Opera Grove*, i. 758.

on Gustavus III of Sweden, who had notoriously indulged his love of women and oysters during a stay in Venice.[1] The main English source concerning the alleged extra-musical purpose of *Il re Teodoro* is Kelly's *Reminiscences*, but Horace Walpole knew something of this when he wrote to the Countess of Upper Ossory on 15–16 December 1787. Walpole was old and crotchety and never much liked comic opera:

I have been once at the opera, and was tired to death; and though I came away the moment it was ended, did not get home till a quarter before twelve. The learned call the music good, but there is nothing to show the humour and action of the Storace and Morelli. I bought the book to read at home, because the Emperor [Josef II] paid £1000 for the piece as a satire on the King of Sweden—how, the Lord knows. The plot is taken from Voltaire's deposed kings at Venice in his *Candide*, of whom only two are introduced, King Theodore and Sultan Achmet. The words are ten times stupider, than our operas generally are; nor do I yet know that the King of Sweden, to whom I am no more partial than Cæsar is, was ever deposed—In short, if it is a satire on any mortal, it is one on Cæsar himself for having paid so dear for such unintelligible nonsense. (Walpole, *Correspondence*, xxxiii. 586–7)

Walpole's puzzlement is partly explained by the fact that the London libretto omits most of the references to Teodoro's love of oysters. Kelly was equally circumspect about the political content, but was able to give some additional details:

Casti was a remarkably quick writer; in a short time he finished his drama. . . . It was said, Joseph II. gave him the subject, and that it was intended as a satire upon the King of Sweden, but the fact I believe was never ascertained . . . the most marked part, and on which the able Casti had bestowed the most pains, was that of Gaforio, the king's secretary. This character was written avowedly, as a satire on General Paoli, and drawn with a masterly hand. Casti declared, there was not a person in our company (not otherwise employed in the opera) capable of undertaking this part. It was decided, therefore, by the directors of the theatre, to send immediately to Venice, to engage Signor Blasi, at any price, to come and play it. (Kelly, *Reminiscences*, i. 240)

The most remarkable parts of Paisiello's score are the two act-finales, especially the first. Various characters in disguise or pretending to be someone else recognize each other in a series of asides—Teodoro sees his sister Belisa; Gafforio (Teodoro's 'prime minister') recognizes the deposed sultan

---

[1] See Derek Beales, *Mozart and the Habsburgs*, 1992 Stenton Lecture (Reading: University of Reading, 1993), 16–17.

Achmet; Achmet recognizes Teodoro as 'il Re posticcio', and so forth. Instead of mounting confusion leading to the conventional stretta, astonishment spreads quietly as one character after another exits (not unlike Haydn's *Farewell Symphony* in its effect), leaving Taddio alone on stage.[1] Not everyone saw the point. One London critic wrote:

the poet has deprived Signor Paisiello of great share of applause by badly finishing the first act; for whilst the imagination of the auditors is in an extasy with the full music of the finale, and ready to burst out in universal applause, they are prevented by the action not being over, when the music dwindles into simple notes, and cools the audience, who find no cause to applaud the latter part, and thereby the finale, which is the best part of the opera, loses all its great merit. . . .[2]

This person had obviously not read the libretto. A similar dramatic diminuendo happens in the penultimate scene of the second act, after Teodoro is unmasked and arrested. As his hopes and plans unravel, his fair-weather friends come to ridicule him and then leave one at a time, except for the loyal Gafforio. In the final scene, Teodoro is in debtors' prison. Belisa's final, ironic words of encouragement—take heart, the law favours insolvents[3] —must have chimed a chord with certain King's Theatre trustees and former managers. One wonders, in fact, if this element of the opera prompted Gallini to commission Stephen Storace to acquire a copy.

The London production was under the direction of Mazzinghi, which is somewhat surprising in light of Storace's role in delivering the score and adapting the very successful *Gli schiavi per amore* the previous season. Gallini later testified that Mazzinghi was employed in 1787–88 'to Arrange the Pasticcio [*sic*] and to accomodate any Music to ye Genius of particular performers And . . . from ye nature of his Contract [to provide] such additional Music or Songs or other of his Compositions for performance'.[4] Mazzinghi himself said that on orders from the 'managers & directors' he 'made several Additions to ye sd. Opera of Il re Teodora [*sic*]'.[5] Comparison of the London libretto (D. Stuart, 1787) with the Viennese original shows that Mazzinghi mainly thinned out the recitative and compressed a couple

---

[1] See Marita P. McClymonds, 'Crosscurrents and the Mainstream of Italian Serious Opera 1730–1790', *Studies in Music from the University of Western Ontario*, 7 (1982), 99–136, who shows that the 'finale of diminishing personnel' was invented by Verazi for *opera seria* at Mannheim. See also the first-act finale of Jommelli's *La schiava liberata* (Ludwigsburg, 1768).

[2] Unidentified cutting in the New York Public Library, printed by Petty, 252–3.

[3] Sta allegro fratello / Le leggi in favore / Son sempre di quello / Che solver non può!

[4] C24/1936, deposition sworn by Gallini on 17 June 1789.

[5] C24/1936, 13 June 1789.

of scenes in the second act. The wonderful finales were virtually untouched, as was the first act, apart from the recitative. In the second, the opening scene was truncated, the chorus of gondoliers cut, and three new arias inserted: 'Sposar voglio una zittella' (for Taddeo in Scene x),[1] 'Care donne che bramate' (for Lisetta in Scene xii, on which more later), and 'Già fatto è il colpo' (for Sandrino in Scene xiii). The first and third of these may have been composed by Corri and Mazzinghi, respectively.[2] Perhaps the biggest change was to the role of Gafforio, which Paisiello had created for a tenor but which was now sung by Antonio Balelli, a soprano castrato. This would obviously have involved some transposition and rewriting, but how Mazzinghi managed this in the finales and other ensembles is unknown.

Rarely had the London version of an opera first performed on the Continent been so little tampered with. Practically a straight revival (Paisiello himself had made more substantial changes), this production represents a radical departure from King's Theatre practice: in the past, to revive was always virtually to rewrite. Burney believed that even the minor changes destroyed 'the unity of style', because 'the certainty of there being merit of some kind or other in every composition of Paisiello, inclines lovers of Music to lament, that any of his airs should be changed or omitted'.[3] Yet we must ask why *Il re Teodoro* was preserved to such an extent. Most alterations were necessitated by the singers—roles were tailored to suit voices, not vice versa, which is modern practice. Only Signora Storace had sung in the original version of Paisiello's opera, and her new aria was an insertion rather than a substitution, as we shall see. There are two possible reasons for the fidelity of this production to the original: either Gallini was too lazy or stingy to commission the usual overhaul, a possibility that must be rejected in light of the operations Mazzinghi and the other house composers routinely carried out this season; or perhaps the manager and his principal singers recognized something in *Il re Teodoro* itself worth preserving. The second explanation is so obvious that one might easily overlook how revolutionary it really is for the history of Italian opera in London. Singers would continue to tyrannize over the repertoire, but the integrity of a few works was beginning to be regarded as sacrosanct.

---

[1] This is not in Larpent MS 788 but probably replaced 'Per onor farsi ammazzare', which is marked with virgole.

[2] See Burney, *General History*, ii. 901.

[3] Ibid.

Stephen Storace's substitute aria in Act II, Scene xii, 'Care donne che bramate', was the subject of three lawsuits, a King's Bench jury trial, and a landmark decision about music copyright handed down by the Lord Chancellor in 1789. These were long cases, complicated by legal issues unrelated to music, but because of the light they shed on the operation of the King's Theatre, the gestation of the London production of *Il re Teodoro*, and the world of Italian opera in general, they deserve detailed discussion. An outline of the Chancery proceedings is as follows:

1. C12/618/12 (*Storace* v. *Longman and Broderip*): on 25 January 1788 Stephen Storace sues the King's Theatre music publishers Longman and Broderip for issuing an unauthorized edition of 'Care donne che bramate'; he requests an injunction to stop further sales and an award of damages; Longman and Broderip reply on 4 February 1788 that they lawfully purchased the aria from the opera-house music-copyist De Michele.

2. C12/1703/11 (*Longman and Broderip* v. *Storace*): on 12 February 1788 the publishers counter-sue, claiming that Storace brought out his own edition without the permission of the King's Theatre; Storace responds on 17 April 1788 with a detailed account of how the aria came to be written and why it is thus his intellectual property; the plaintiffs issue interrogatories to several material witnesses, including Badini, De Michele, Mazzinghi, and Gallini (C24/1936).

3. C12/623/35 (*Storace* v. *Longman and Broderip*): on 14 February 1789, following a favourable verdict in the Court of King's Bench, autumn 1788, Storace restates his case for compensation; the publishers reply feebly on 18 April 1788.

4. On 15 July 1789, the Lord Chancellor dismisses Longman and Broderip's countersuit (item 2 above) and orders them to pay all legal costs; Storace is awarded one shilling in damages (C33/472, Part 2, fos. 607–8).

The main issue was the copyright of operatic music in Great Britain. The rights of composers to their own music had been definitively established in *Bach* v. *Longman and Lukey* in 1777, but the ownership of operas was much more complicated. Who owned the score of an opera, only a small part of the total production and of little use unless staged—the King's Theatre or the composer? Did a composer, whether on annual salary or paid a lump sum for each commission, have the right to publish a score or arias thereof for his own profit? The case was complicated by two further issues that had not arisen in *Bach* v. *Longman and Lukey*, where only instrumental music was at issue. Could the words of 'Care donne che bramate', which were protected by copyright, be legally separated from the musical notes? The second, far more interesting issue, was basically philosophical: does an aria introduced into a pre-existing work become a part of that work, or does it remain a discrete object? These lawsuits thus posed fundamental questions about the nature of Italian opera itself.

Much of the testimony in the lawsuits is contradictory and patently untrue, but the gestation of the London production and the circumstances behind Storace's inserted aria can be reconstructed or deduced with reasonable certainty from uncontested statements. Longman and Broderip's countersuit contains much more information than Storace's original complaint. In his response, the composer states that in September 1786, when he was about to leave London for Vienna (to write *Gli equivoci* with Da Ponte), Gallini had asked him 'to procure . . . (amongst others) a Copy of the said Opera or Musical Entertainment' *Il re Teodoro*.[1] The other scores he acquired were *Le gare generose*, the first to be produced in London, and probably *Il barbiere di Siviglia* and *Una cosa rara*, which were mounted next season. Storace goes on to say that *Il re Teodoro* was 'put into rehearsal' 'in or about the Month of December' 1787, which is probably slightly inaccurate; the first night was 8 December and, as was explained in Chapter 4, rehearsals normally lasted about a fortnight. However, Gallini did not submit the libretto to the Lord Chamberlain until 7 December.[2] A rushed production might account for the reports of scrappy orchestral playing (*Public Advertiser*, 17 January 1788) and poorly designed scenery. The delay between Gallini's acquiring the music and the production suggests that he built up a library of scores for consideration rather than being stampeded by principal performers into mounting previously successful works for their benefit, which was still happening, of course, in the choice of serious operas.

The accounts of plaintiff and defendants begin to diverge sharply when they discuss the aria in question. In response to the composer's original bill of complaint, Longman and Broderip maintained that when the opera was put into rehearsal, Signora Storace, 'to whom one of the Parts or Characters therein was allotted objected to one of the songs Introduced into her part on account of its great length and in order to Oblige her [Gallini] indulged her with the Liberty of changing the same for another', namely 'Care donne che bramate'.[3] In their countersuit the publishers expand on this claim: La

---

[1] C12/1703/11, answer.     [2] Larpent MS 788.     [3] C12/618/12, answer.

Storace objected to a particular aria because of its great length 'and the fatigue of executing' it.[1] In other words, they maintained that 'Care donne che bramate' was *substituted* for one she was incapable of singing. We now know this is not true. Signora Storace sang all of Lisetta's arias in Paisiello's original score: her brother's piece was an *insertion*, not a substitution. We also know that it was added at the very last moment. In the Larpent copy only the word 'Cavatina' appears, not Badini's new verses. But Stephen's version of events is also in part implausible: during rehearsals 'it being then deemed and considered by many Persons that the Music of the said opera was dull and heavy it was thought necessary that some lively Song or Air should be introduced therein in order to enliven it'.[2] 'Care donne' did prove to be very popular (hence the lawsuits, which are about money), and Walpole was not the only person to comment on the surprising seriousness of the drama. But whether anyone regarded Paisiello's music as 'dull and heavy' is doubtful. A likelier reason for Nancy's being indulged with the freedom to change her part emerges later in Stephen's response. He wrote the aria for his sister, expecting no 'recompence or reward but that he only lent the same for that purpose and would not upon any Consideration allow . . . [it] to be printed [or] vended . . . without his consent'. In other words, Gallini agreed to the insertion provided it cost him nothing.

Longman and Broderip claimed that the words of the aria 'were written and adapted' to the music by the house poet Badini.[3] 'Prima la musica, poi le parole. . . .' This taunt particularly annoyed Storace, who responded that Badini was, under the terms of his contract with Gallini,

engaged to write and compose all additions with respect to Words and Language which may be deemed necessary for any opera . . . and that . . . Badini accordingly by the order or direction [of Gallini] wrote and composed the words of the Song . . . Care Donne che Bramate . . . which thereupon . . . became the property of the Managers . . . the words . . . were afterwards set to Music by [Storace] and were sent by him to the said Manager.[4]

Storace clearly won this point. But the admission that Badini's words were the property of the opera-house undermined his claim to ownership: the poet later deposed that, according to his contract, Gallini 'is intitled to Print and sell ye words of all Operas and songs written by him as Poet'.[5]

---

[1] C12/1703/11.    [2] C12/1703/11, answer.    [3] C12/618/12, answer.
[4] C12/1703/11, answer.    [5] C24/1936, 17 June 1789.

These were all preliminary considerations. The case hinged on two further issues: whether the aria was a part of the opera; and, if so, who had the right to publish it. At this point the key figure in the dispute enters: Leopoldo De Michele, music-copyist and, as we have seen, the most powerful member of the King's Theatre music department. Though he testified at the request of the defendants Longman and Broderip, De Michele did not help their case by admitting that Signora Storace introduced the aria 'by permission of ye Managers'. She then 'gave ye Manuscript Copy of the said Song' to the copyist 'to be written into ye Music of ye House as forming a part of ye said Opera of Il Re Teodora [*sic*] And as a part of which it has always since been sung at every Representation'.[1] Storace never disputed the important claim that his aria, once introduced (for whatever reason), became a part of the whole. But he hotly disagreed that in allowing his aria to be copied into the full score he thereby ceded rights to his own creation. Longman and Broderip and everyone within the opera company who gave evidence—Gallini, Badini, Crawford, Mazzinghi, and of course De Michele—cited the thirty-year-long custom that 'the Property of and right of publishing and Vending all such Operas and Musical Compositions' was a perquisite afforded the music-copyist to supplement his salary. De Michele therefore sold Storace's aria to Longman and Broderip in good conscience. Prior to this, however, Storace had—quite innocently, he claims—sold the piece to Birchall and Andrews who had, by 17 April 1788, sold 'near ffive hundred Copies . . . and that he hath acquired Some Gains and profits to himself thereby'.[2] If this figure can be believed, then one can see that no trifling sum of money was at stake. Longman and Broderip claimed to have printed 100 copies by 4 February 1788, of which about fifty had been sold.[3] Storace challenged De Michele's right to sell his music on both legal and moral grounds: the copyist had 'usurped the right of publishing . . . the operas and musical and other Entertainments'. He regarded this as pure exploitation, which De Michele had been able to get away with because the composers were 'Foreigners and unacquainted with the Laws of this Country' or were 'unwilling to enter into a course of Litigation and legal controversy'.[4] Gallini and De Michele tried to deflect the charge of exploitation by pointing out that later in the 1787–88 season, when Storace was commissioned to compose *La cameriera astuta,* he acknowledged the theatre's ownership of his score: 'being desirous of printing and publishing

---

[1] C24/1936, 13 June 1789.    [2] C12/1703/11, answer.
[3] C12/618/12, answer.    [4] C12/1703/11, answer.

his . . . Opera for his own benefit he . . . applied to the . . . Managers for their permission so to do but . . . ye . . . Managers refusing Granting it to him unless upon Condition of his first paying to their Copyist an adequate Compensation'; Storace, they allege, duly paid up.[1] The implications of this last statement are chilling: the dearth of surviving music of King's Theatre productions in the 1770s and 1780s is perhaps owing to a perquisite granted to the music-copyist in lieu of salary. Even more disturbing is the possibility that this arrangement may have discouraged original opera composition in London.

The Lord Chancellor's judgment in favour of Storace is disappointing in that it contains no ringing affirmation of the opera composer's rights. The award to Storace of one shilling in damages, plus legal costs, was a token sum by which the judge signalled his belief that none of the parties had been seriously aggrieved or deprived of large amounts of money. Indeed, Storace continued to do business with Longman and Broderip once the dust had settled. And De Michele, as we know from a similar lawsuit of 1792 (discussed in vol. II), continued to plunder King's Theatre scores for *Favourite Songs*. This case exposed another dilemma for the manager of the King's Theatre: the gradually emerging right of composers to their own music and the not unrelated respect for the integrity of certain operas, such as *Il re Teodoro* and *Il barbiere di Siviglia*, clashed directly with the 'choice of the book', the practice of allowing certain singers to alter their parts at will. The attempt to reconcile these forces distinguishes Gallini's regime from that of all other late eighteenth-century King's Theatre managers.

Almost lost in this cloud of litigation was Storace's aria itself. Looking now upon the banal, G major cavatina, one may wonder what all the fuss was about (see Ex. 6.6 on page 394). The melody is pleasant enough, but it simply does not develop in any of the ways of which Storace was clearly capable. But when the piece is considered in its dramatic context, one can see that it offers light relief after Taddeo's dark and brooding nightmare aria 'Non era ancora'. 'Care donne che bramate' is still somewhat incongruous to Casti's 'dramma eroi-comico', but the King's Theatre production was to an unprecedented degree faithful to what Paisiello actually wrote. Although performed thirteen times this season, *Il re Teodoro* was not particularly well received. Lady Mary Coke was exceedingly terse: 'The opera was not full very cold and dull' (22 December 1787). A review written at the end of the

[1] C24/1936, 13 June 1789.

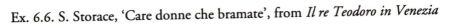

Ex. 6.6. S. Storace, 'Care donne che bramate', from *Il re Teodoro in Venezia*

initial run commented that it was 'the best music that can be produced for that kind of drama', but was scornful of the standard of performance, especially from the orchestra. Both Mazzinghi (at the harpsichord) and Cramer (the leader) were criticized for not getting the band to accompany the singers more sympathetically:

The arias of the tenor and base have been played, or rather accompany[ed], too fast, and without harmony, with the voices of Morelli and Fineschi, which being good, and they seeming to wish to sing with all possible expression, the orchestra should have accompanied accordingly. The same may be said respecting the Finale of the first act.

Madem. Storace, however, has baffled the efforts of the musicians to make her sing out of tune, quick or slow—As they fiddled, she modulated. (*Public Advertiser*, 17 January 1788)

### Cimarosa's La locandiera

The next *opera buffa* of the 1787–88 season, a reworking of Cimarosa's popular and often revived *L'italiana in Londra*, would appear, from circumstantial evidence, to have been drawn from another score that Stephen Storace brought from Vienna. His sister had performed the role of Madama Brillante at the Burgtheater in 1783 and that of Livia at Florence in autumn 1781.[1] Almost without precedent, some of the music was published in advance of the London première by J. Cooper (not Longman and Broderip). As was mentioned above, some members of the King's Theatre company went to France at the end of the 1786–87 season. The heading of 'Chi dice che le femine' in the Cooper edition is unusually informative: 'in the Opera call'd L'Italiana in Londra, Sung by Mr. Morelli at the Court of France at Versailles with Great Applause, was repeated every Night, & will be Performed this Season at the Opera House, by the same Celebrated Performer'. Cooper also published 'Se m'abbandoni mio dolce amore', attributed to the same opera and sung by Mengozzi at Versailles, but 'will be Perform'd this Season at the Opera House by Mr. Fineschi', that is, the second tenor Vicenzo Fineschi, who did indeed sing the role of Mynheer Vanderdur in *La locandiera*, though this aria is not included in the London libretto. Cooper had obviously been informed well in advance of Gallini's plans for the 1787–88 season. The published music implies that Cimarosa's *L'italiana in Londra* was, like Paisiello's *Gli schiavi per amore*, staged at Versailles, but no printed libretto of the former survives.

Obviously another vehicle for La Storace, the libretto for *La locandiera* was adapted by Badini with Mazzinghi as music director. Showing little respect for Cimarosa's original, this production reverted to bad old ways. The scene was changed from London to Amsterdam. Burney, who contrasted this production with that of the more faithful *Il re Teodoro*, was uncertain what injured the opera more—the change of setting or 'the mediocrity of most of the performers'.[2] The *Public Advertiser* (17 January 1788) offered a reason: 'as there is a stigma in [the original] on English customs,

[1] Sartori, no. 13951; Benucci sang Don Polidoro in the Viennese production.
[2] *General History*, ii. 901.

the managers have changed the name, and transported the scene into Holland, for fear of disgusting the audience, and by that means have deprived the Comic Muse of part of her rights'. So, jokes about tea-drinking and bad weather were replaced by cracks about geese and canals. The insipid plot, however, remained mostly intact.

While far from hostile, the newspaper critics were disappointed with *La locandiera* because, unlike the highly original *Il re Teodoro*, the music and drama offered little new. The review in the *Morning Post* of 16 January 1788 is typical: 'The fable, which in productions of this sort is never an object of much regard, is in this piece particularly meagre, and consists merely of love-scenes between four people, who have no obstacles to encounter, and who as usual are in the end happily united.' The libretto's saving grace is the character of Madama Brillante (Signora Storace) who, while ceding to Livia (Signora Schinotti) the honour of being the main object of masculine desire, gradually establishes control over the other characters. Signora Storace was, however, let down by the music, which, judging by the printed extracts, was simple in the extreme. The *Morning Post* review alluded to the impoverishment: 'Storace appears chiefly in *recitative*, but she contrives to exert her talents with considerable spirit.' Much of this spirit is at the expense of the fool Don Polidoro (Morelli). The most popular number of the opera was their duet in Act II, Scene iii, 'Con quelle tue manine'. This is the climax of a scene in which Madama Brillante convinces Polidoro that he is invisible by pouring water over his head and nearly cutting off his nose with the pruning-shears after he has climbed a tree in order to hide. The long G major duet, which ridicules 'the *bravura style* in singing', is interrupted by an *adagio* accompanied recitative. The only other overt signs of parody are the scale flourishes at the end of the A section and the descending chromatics before the final *presto*.

Lady Mary Coke 'was not amused . . . the music did not please me neither anything I heard or saw all went contrary to my inclination' (22 January 1788). Her inclination, like that of many of the aristocratic subscribers, was more towards serious opera. A 'Spectator' writing in the *Public Advertiser* (17 January 1788) was also lukewarm about *La locandiera* but added 'upon the whole, it will do, until by the arrival next month of the celebrated Signor Marchesi, and the serious groupe of Cantanti, the attention of the public will be more deservedly taken up'. Comic works, even those of the quality of *Il re Teodoro* and *Gli schiavi per amore*, the second of which was revived on 5 February for thirteen performances, could not satisfy the tremendous desire for virtuoso singing.

### Storace's La cameriera astuta

*La cameriera astuta* is the only Italian opera that Stephen Storace wrote for the London stage and, given the high quality of his two earlier Viennese *opere buffe*, the loss of most of the score is to be much regretted. Although commissioned at the end of the previous season (see the composer's letter of 3 July 1787, quoted above), the opera seems to have been brought out on 4 March 1788 as padding until Marchesi's début opera could be arranged and rehearsed. *La cameriera astuta* was a qualified success, running for seven performances. The second night was for Signora Storace's benefit, which confirms that the opera was designed to exploit her talents, but also suggests a lack of confidence in its ability to draw a big crowd on the first night or to last longer than a couple of performances. The libretto (D. Stuart, 1788) is anonymous. Since it includes a parody of opera and debates musical taste in the manner of *L'inglese in Italia*, one might suppose that Badini was the author. But this is unlikely: Storace and Badini were on opposite sides in the 'Care donne che bramate' lawsuits. The libretto of *La cameriera astuta* is a lively example of a modern burletta with two, self-contained acts, extended finales, and long, interior ensembles, but it is too stale of plot and flat-footed in its humour to be Badini's. The 'clever chambermaid' Violetta (Signora Storace) helps her mistress Leonora (Signora Sestini) wriggle out of an arranged marriage to the oafish marchese Don Pancrazio Garofano (Morelli). For us today the main interest of the libretto is its running debate about the relative merits of French and Italian opera, culminating in the shambolic rehearsal in Act II of a burletta called 'Didone cotta arrosto', composed by Leonora's father, the dilettante Anselmo Buonvivente (Morigi). He is a fervent supporter of the traditional Italian style, as he reveals in Act I, Scene iii:

> Non mi parlar di Musica Francese,
> Il gusto della Musica Italiana
> Ora regna anche in Francia;
> Sull'Opere del celebre Sacchini,
> Del famoso Piccini
> Fanno adesso i Francesi un grande studio,
> Ma della mia Burletta ecco il preludio.

The translation in the printed libretto, probably too inelegant to be Badini's, glosses this recitative:

Don't mention your French music to me—there's not a Frenchman of any taste but allows the superiority of the Italian music; and the best composers in that nation are now endeavouring to imitate the works of the late incomparable Sacchini, and of the celebrated Piccini. My opera is set in the true style of these great masters; I will give you a specimen of it.

Violetta, by contrast, is an advocate of the French style—at least when it suits her purpose. For instance, in Act I, Scene x, she teaches Don Pancrazio how to sing French airs as a means to secure Leonora's affections. There are also touches of personal satire in this episode: Don Pancrazio has earlier (in Act I, Scene v) made his entrance accompanied by running footmen (the former profession of Morelli, who acted this role); and the general rehearsal planned for Act II, Scene vi, has to be abandoned because the singers have not yet seen their parts ('La colpa è certamente del copista'). Perhaps Storace was taking his revenge against De Michele for stealing 'Care donne che bramate'.

Storace's music seems to have reflected and enhanced the libretto's debate about operatic style. A critic writing in the *Public Advertiser* on 6 March 1788 thought the composer had

entirely deviated from the usual plan of Italian authors. Were it not for the Recitativo, and several passages in the Arias, the whole would rather appear a French composition than any other. The Overture announces entirely a French author—and the Finales are in the German style of Gluck, loaded with harsh terrifying music of trumpeting and drumming.

The critic may have confused Storace's own style, which was decidedly Viennese, with those he was deliberately parodying.

Birchall and Andrews published four numbers from the opera: a one-movement overture in B flat major arranged for violin and harpsichord (more in the Italian than French vein), and three vocal numbers. Of the latter, the most important by far is Violetta's scene in parody of the French style, 'Beaux yeux qui causez mon trépas', in Act I, Scene x. This opens with a grand accompanied *récitatif* in G minor, fully scored, with tremolo strings and the vocal part marked '*ad lib.*', though it is largely doubled in the French manner. Sensitive to the purposely overwrought text, this is a credible imitation (see Ex. 6.7). The *récitatif* is followed by a G major *gavotte*, with which Violetta demonstrates the smooth, syllabic style of French

## Ex. 6.7. S. Storace, 'Beaux yeux', from *La cameriera astuta*

text-setting. The other published numbers are Violetta's teasing 'mad song' in Act II, Scene iii, 'E di matti questo mondo', a simple two-tempo aria with a codetta based on nonsense syllables, and the chorus that completes the quartet in Act II, Scene iv, 'Ah perche di quel ingrato'.[1] These remains are too meagre to allow us to mount a defence against the harsh criticism *La cameriera astuta* received. If 'Beaux yeux' is any indication of Storace's method in the rest of the opera, then he may have erred in making the parodies too much like the real thing.

### *Sarti's* Giulio Sabino

Reporting Marchesi's arrival in London, the *Public Advertiser* (6 March 1788) also shed further light on the circumstances surrounding the singer's negotiations with Gallini:

Signor Marchesi has strictly performed his engagements in coming here post-haste, after having acquitted himself of his duty at Turin, where (as pensioner of music in his Sardinian Majesty's service) he was obliged to sing to the end of the Carnival: but the Managers, instead of keeping every thing in readiness against his arrival, and supposing him ready for his part, (of which there is no doubt) are now waiting for the first and second woman, and for the tenor; nor is the scenery, &c. in readiness; so that the public must wait a month longer before a serious Opera can be presented.

One Signora Honorati was announced as *prima donna seria* but failed to appear. Her place was taken by the *seconda donna* Cecilia Giuliani, while the new tenor was Giuseppe Forlivesi. As noted above, Gallini claimed to have selected these singers to complement his prized *primo uomo*; but to suppose that the first *opera seria* of the season was delayed on their account is hardly credible. Instead, the gap between Marchesi's arrival in London and his much anticipated début seems to have resulted from necessary adjustments to Sarti's celebrated *Giulio Sabino*. Gallini submitted the Larpent copy to the Lord Chamberlain's office on 22 March, hoping to open on 29 March.[2] The première was then postponed until 3 April, but there were still public rehearsals on 2 and 4 April. Marchesi reportedly did not want his début to clash with Madam Mara's benefit at Drury Lane,[3] where she had been performing after Gallini failed to meet her salary demand. She and Marchesi

---

[1] In the printed libretto the text begins 'A perchè questo sguajato', and includes other variants.

[2] See Larpent MS 800.

[3] *Morning Post*, 3 Apr. 1788.

seem to have played a game of cat and mouse, because her benefit finally happened on 8 April, after the long-awaited *Giulio Sabino* had appeared on 5 April.

The opera was a clever choice. Pacchierotti had created the title-role in Venice in 1781, and this part had since been performed by Marchesi (1781) and Rubinelli (1782). The new *primo uomo* was therefore inviting comparison with the other singers; the London audience would also be able to compare the Sarti original with Cherubini's failed version of 1786. Aided by intense advance publicity, the tantalizing postponements, and the long interval since the last serious opera performance, Marchesi's London début was a sensational success. As *The Times* reported on 8 April 1788, '*Sir John Gallini* was remarkably vociferous on Saturday evening, and cursed with all the bitterness of disappointment the Architects of the Opera House, for not making it larger.' The crowd was so great that 'all parts of the House were occupied very soon after the doors were opened'; even the stage was filled 'so much that the business of the scenes was not accomplished without great difficulty'.[1] The daily accounts preserved for 1786–87 and 1787–88 fully bear out the newspaper reports.[2] Cash receipts for the night of 5 April 1788 totalled the startling sum of £473. 15s. 6d., reflecting attendance of 644 in the pit and 489 in the galleries. The second highest night in these two seasons was £386. 6s. 6d. on 5 February 1788, and cash receipts totalled £300 or more on just eleven of 102 nights in these seasons. Excitement over Marchesi's début must have been extraordinary.

The newspapers were filled with ecstatic accounts of Marchesi's singing, though both Burney and Mount Edgcumbe wrote with more circumspection after the event.[3] Although Marchesi's technical prowess, especially in the bravura style, was universally admired, Mount Edgcumbe thought his taste in ornaments suspect. Burney, by contrast, found his 'facility of running extempore divisions . . . truly marvelous'. At first Marchesi was judged inferior to Pacchierotti in the cantabile, 'that deep, searching voice of meaning and emotion'; the *World* of 7 April 1788, for example, found his

'*organic excellences* . . . prodigious. Through three octaves, from the high soprano to the deep bass, he displays himself with ease. . . . But for portamento, the carriage of his voice from ready impulse, to heart-felt effects—all the charm of

[1] *Morning Post*, 7 Apr. 1788.
[2] Beinecke Library, Yale University.
[3] See Burney, *General History*, ii. 901; and Mount Edgcumbe, *Musical Reminiscences*, 60–2.

expression on his part, and impression on the hearer, it was on Saturday in vain to search. . . . We shall be glad to hear of any body that shed a tear or raised a sigh.

Soon, however, he was able to demonstrate the pathos necessary to succeed in London.

To return to our main concern here, the opera *Giulio Sabino*, in line with the King's Theatre's emerging policy of faithful revival, closely followed Sarti's original score. But neither the heavy-weight opera critics Burney and Mount Edgcumbe nor the journalists considered this a virtue. A letter in the *Morning Post* (8 April 1788) sniffed that *Giulio Sabino* was 'rather *an old opera*, and may [be] said to be still *an older composition*'. Burney recalled that 'Several of the songs, indeed, had been previously sung here at concerts, and did not appear new.'[1] Mount Edgcumbe was more specific: 'I was a little disappointed at Marchesi's execution of [the arias in the opera], for they were all familiar to me, as I had repeatedly heard Pacchierotti sing them in private, and I missed his tender expression.'[2] The desire for novelty was a commonplace; indeed, it was the driving force behind the pasticcio. But *Giulio Sabino* illustrates the danger of Gallini's new policy towards repertoire: faithful revivals were feasible only if the works selected were of fairly recent composition.

The full score used for the 1788 London production of *Giulio Sabino* survives in the Royal College of Music—MS 570. A recent study of this important source demonstrates that it was based on the full score of the original Venice production, published some time in 1782 at Vienna, probably by Artaria.[3] Dozens of copies survive, five in London libraries alone, and the one in the Dragonetti Collection in the British Library was once owned by Venanzio Rauzzini. Royal College of Music MS 570 is the work of at least ten scribes, most prominent among them being De Michele, who copied much of the simple recitative and made alterations throughout the score.[4] The various hands and paper-types can be divided into two groups: those writing mainly on Italian paper and responsible for almost all of Act I; and those working under De Michele's supervision and mostly using paper manufactured in England by James Whatman. This patchwork suggests that

---

[1] *General History*, ii. 902.

[2] *Musical Reminiscences*, 62.

[3] Gabriella Dideriksen, 'From Manuscript to Performance: *Giulio Sabino* and London Opera Production in the 1780s', M.Mus. diss. (King's College London, 1992), to which the following discussion is indebted. The score is mentioned in Carl F. Cramer, *Magazin der Musik* (Hamburg, 1783, facs., Hildesheim and New York: Georg Ulms, 1971), i. 129.

[4] See Dideriksen, 22.

the King's Theatre probably acquired the first act from Marchesi or direct from agents in Italy. The second and third acts were compressed into one for the London production and therefore required considerable alteration —apparently undertaken by De Michele with instructions from Marchesi. The Royal College manuscript bears signs that the decision to reduce the opera to two acts was taken at a fairly late stage, because some scenes prepared by De Michele had to be renumbered: for example, Act III, Scene iii, became Act II, Scene xi.[1] In the process Epponina (Signora Giuliani) and Tito (Forlivesi) each lost an aria. Perhaps in compensation, the tenor was allowed to substitute Mazzinghi's 'Tornate nell'alma' for Sarti's original 'Bella fiamma' in Act II, Scene xi. Mazzinghi directed the performances but seems otherwise to have had little involvement in the adaptation.

Marchesi also made one substitution, in the first scene, where the original 'Pensieri funesti' was replaced by the cavatina 'Lungi dal caro bene'. The substituted text appears in the printed libretto (J. Stevenson, 1788), and the preceding recitative was altered in the manuscript to lead to G major, the key of the substitute, rather than to E flat, the key of 'Pensieri funesti'. De Michele cued the 'Cavatina' at this point but, oddly, 'Lungi dal caro bene' was not copied into the score. It was, however, published by Longman and Broderip, who accidentally labelled the voice part 'Rinaldo', thereby betraying the aria's origin in Sarti's *Armida e Rinaldo* (St Petersburg, 1786). The *Morning Post* (7 April 1788) reported that 'The first air sung by Marchesi, is said to be his own composition, and it is well adapted to display his voice.' Something closer to the truth is stated in the heading of the supplement to the Longman and Broderip edition: 'Aria Del Sigr. Guiseppe [*sic*] Sarti coll accompagnamento d'Arpa de Sigr. Luigi Marchesi.' As will be explained in volume II of this study, singers later tried to claim copyright of substitute arias by composing or having someone else compose such accompaniments. In 1792 Madam Mara took the further precaution of preventing a substitute from being copied into the full score.[2] Marchesi, undoubtedly aware of Storace's lawsuit against the music publishers Longman and Broderip, may have started this practice in London with 'Lungi dal caro bene'. In other respects Royal College of Music MS 570 accurately reflects the state of the opera as performed in April 1788 and is thus an invaluable record of King's Theatre practice. One may conclude that De Michele co-ordinated

[1] See Ibid. 32. This indecision is puzzling. The three-act Italian opera had long since been abandoned at the King's Theatre.

[2] See Price, 'Unity, Originality, and the London Pasticcio', 27–30.

the musical aspects of the production, though much under Marchesi's instruction. Sarti's music was already known to London cognoscenti through the Viennese printed score and from Pacchierotti's concerts in 1782–84. Though De Michele undoubtedly had access to the published score, he worked instead from an Italian manuscript. While the compression of Acts II and III was achieved simply by cutting whole scenes, he nevertheless had most of the new second act recopied in London by a team comprising both house copyists and freelance professionals.

Marchesi's London début was a triumph by any standards, but the popularity of Sarti's *Giulio Sabino* was short-lived. Attendance soon dropped off sharply, and William Taylor noted with *Schadenfreude* that on 22 April 1788, only Marchesi's fifth appearance, the serious opera 'brought a Receipt of no more than £124. 6*d.* in Money at the Doors whereas an Old Comic Opera [*Il re Teodoro*] often performed brought on Tuesday [6 May 1788] the sum of £161. 14*s.*'[1] While Marchesi was not particularly well supported by Signora Giuliani, whose small voice paled in comparison with the brilliant Madam Mara's, the problem was rather with the opera itself. It was perceived as old-fashioned; and, in truth, it is not as strong dramatically as Cherubini's 1786 version. Sarti's original ending—a dream-like sequence in which Sabino is spared execution by Tito's sudden change of heart—was out of step with the more realistic catastrophes of recent serious operas. However much one would like to commend Gallini's new policy of minimal adaptation, this production badly needed Badini's or Cherubini's often outrageous but always challenging updating of tired musical and dramatic material.

## *Cimarosa's* L'Olimpiade

With receipts for *Giulio Sabino* trailing off, Gallini brought out another serious opera, based on Cimarosa's *L'Olimpiade*, for Marchesi's benefit on 8 May 1788. Metastasio's famous libretto had last been used at the King's Theatre in 1783 for a pasticcio. Cimarosa's version dates from 1784 (Vicenza) and was therefore fresher than Sarti's *Giulio Sabino*. It retained many of Metastasio's aria texts and did not stray far from the basic musico-dramatic structure of the well-known settings by Caldara, Pergolesi, and Galuppi, except for the now *de rigueur* compression into two acts, the omission of the chorus, and Megacle's attempt to drown himself at the end of

---

[1] C31/248, no. 285; these figures are corroborated by the Yale manuscripts.

the original second act. The 1788 London production was also part pasticcio, under the direction of Mazzinghi. Much applauded was Megacle's farewell aria 'Se cerca, se dice' in Act II, Scene vii, previously set *parlante* by Pergolesi and *agitato* by Galuppi. Published by Longman and Broderip and curiously attributed to 'Sacchini & Cimarosa', it is an excellent C major *rondò* with an adventurous excursion into A flat major; in the middle of the *allegro* section, the opening melody, slowed down and marked 'ad libitum', returns dramatically. Mazzinghi provided a new setting of Aristea's 'Grandi è ver son le tue pene', sung by Signora Giuliani in Act II, Scene ii, and published by Longman and Broderip. Mazzinghi's aria is also a *rondò* in A major (the two sets of tempo indications are *Larghetto—Allegretto* and *Largo con moto—Allegro giusto*, respectively) but, apart from superficial resemblances, it is a quite different piece from Cimarosa's. Aristea contrasts Argene's open display of grief with her own torment, which she is forced to conceal. Cimarosa's setting conveys little sense of inner conflict, whereas Mazzinghi, by setting off certain lines harmonically and with imaginative orchestration, produced a much more overtly dramatic aria (see Ex. 6.8 on pages 406–7). Despite the gaucheness of some of the modulations and the twiddly figuration, this piece makes one wonder why Mazzinghi never managed to compose more for the Italian opera. The other main substitution was Marchesi's final aria (in Act II, Scene xiv), 'Questa non era o cara', by Sarti (and published by Longman and Broderip), which replaced Cimarosa's 'Nel lasciarti'.

British Library Add. MS 16000, a full score, may have been the starting-point for the London production, as it shows a strong correlation with the printed libretto (J. Stevenson, 1788). Act I is identical, save that the simple recitatives of some longer scenes have been thinned out, and Argene's aria 'Frà mille amanti un core' was cut. The second act did not escape so lightly. Besides the substitution already mentioned, a new aria for Aristea, 'Agitata in tante pene', was introduced, and Licida's big *scena* in the temple while a storm gathers, 'Torbido il ciel s'oscura', the high point of the act, was inexplicably truncated. Even more surprising, if one may judge from the amount of text that remains in the printed libretto, Cimarosa's ensemble finale, the first in any of his *opere serie*,[1] was reduced to a chorus. Add. MS 16000 shows none of the cutting and pasting typical of a revival or a pasticcio, and one copyist was responsible for almost all the music. The first page

---

[1] See Don Neville, *Opera Grove*, iii. 662.

Ex. 6.8. Joseph Mazzinghi, 'Grandi è ver son le tue pene', from *L'Olimpiade*

# L'Olimpiade

tan - to       ma —— di - man - di    al - men     pie -

tà       giu - sto ciel    che   rio    ci - men - to

ah     di me   che mai   sa - rà     di me   che mai   sa -

rà     che mai   sa-rà      che mai   sa - rà     Allegretto

of each act is inscribed 'Presso Bonoris-Zappi Bologna', which replaces an erased note unreadable even under ultra-violet light. Besides the première at Vicenza in 1784, the only other production of Cimarosa's *L'Olimpiade* prior to London was at Brescia in 1786. Add. MS 16000 was probably supplied by a professional copyist at Bologna and seems to have been given in London not much altered from that state. Despite the cuts and a reception rather cooler than that which *Giulio Sabino* received, this off-the-shelf version of Cimarosa's *L'Olimpiade* is impressive, especially the lengthy accompanied recitatives. Nevertheless, Marchesi hedged his bets: at the end of the opera he sang 'Generosi Britanni in lieta fronte', a song 'set to music by himself' with words by Badini.[1] As this apparently elicited no comment in the press, one must assume it rightly made little impression.

The 1787–88 season afforded Gallini a brief respite from his monumental managerial difficulties. The lawsuits over Storace's substitute aria, which have loomed large in this discussion, did not materially affect the manager and detracted little from the brilliance of the comic opera. Despite Marchesi's success, La Storace and the other *buffi* were putting the *opera seria* in the shade.

## IV. The 1788–89 Season: Apogee and Immolation

Repertoire:

*La cosa rara*, Martín y Soler, directed by Mazzinghi, libretto by Da Ponte, 10 January 1789 (10 performances); orig. Vienna as *Una cosa rara* (Burg) 1786 (p. 411)

*Ifigenia in Aulide*, Cherubini, libretto by Moretti, 24 January 1789 (7 performances); orig. Turin (Regio) 1788 (p. 417)

*Il disertore*, Tarchi, libretto by Benincasa, 28 February 1789 (8 performances) (p. 419)

*La villana riconosciuta*, Cimarosa, directed by Mazzinghi, libretto by Palomba, 24 March 1789 (3 performances); orig. Naples (Fondo) 1783

*L'Olimpiade*, Cimarosa, with added numbers by Tarchi and Sarti, libretto after Metastasio, 2 April 1789 (9 performances); orig. Vicenza (Eretenio) 1784. London 1788

*La vendemmia*, pasticcio based on Gazzaniga, directed by Mazzinghi, libretto by Bertati, 9 May 1789 (5 performances); orig. Florence (Pergola) 1778 (p. 413)

*La buona figliuola*, Piccinni, directed by Mazzinghi, libretto by Goldoni, 28 May 1789 (1 performance); orig. Rome (Dame) 1760. London 1766 → 1783, 1785

*La generosità d'Alessandro*, Tarchi, libretto by Badini after Metastasio's *Alessandro nell'Indie*, 2 June 1789 (8 performances); orig. Milan 1788 (p. 419)

*Il barbiere di Siviglia*, Paisiello, libretto by Petrosellini, 11 June 1789 (4 performances); orig. St Petersburg (Hermitage) 1782 (p. 415)

---

[1] Badini's words and translation were printed for distribution to the audience. The handout is bound at the end of the British Library copy of the libretto, pressmark 907.k.2 (4).

The final season of opera in Vanbrugh's old King's Theatre in the Haymarket began very late on 10 January 1789, was disgraced by the audience riots of 7 February and 7 March, and ended in makeshift fashion at Covent Garden after the catastrophic fire of 17 June. These disruptions naturally overshadowed the notable accomplishments of the opera department this season: the reunion of Nancy Storace and Francesco Benucci (Mozart's original Susanna and Figaro), the first London production of Paisiello's internationally acclaimed *Il barbiere di Siviglia* (largely unaltered), and the appointment of the innovative Angelo Tarchi as house composer of serious operas. All this required herculean effort from Gallini even as his position crumbled; in openly favouring opera at the expense of the ballet he showed perhaps foolhardy commitment to the revisionist artistic policy that had been developing over the last three seasons. The attempt to economize on the ballet backfired with the February riot, and he was forced to send to France for emergency reinforcements; yet the quality of opera production remained high.

As was explained in Chapter 2, Taylor nearly succeeded in having Gallini removed at the end of the 1787–88 season, largely over the manager's dubious practice of attaching a clause to some singers' contracts requiring them to sing at the Hanover Square concerts. For instance, Taylor claimed to have seen the terms of the tenor Giuseppe Forlivesi's contract: besides his duties at the opera-house, he was bound to sing at Hanover Square 'but also at every other Concert at which . . . Gallini shall procure his employment upon Condition that . . . Forlivesi shall divide equally with . . . Gallini' the fee; the singer was entitled to a benefit at the King's Theatre, but 'half of the receipts should be paid to . . . Forlivesi and the other half to . . . Gallini'.[1] Although this affidavit was filed a year after Taylor succeeded in bringing the charge of mismanagement before the Court of Chancery, the Lord Chancellor was prepared to remove Gallini in July 1788 but could find no one with the ability or financial resources to replace him. Gallini was therefore left in limbo with his old enemy the Lord Chamberlain once again prevaricating over the licence. In a manœuvre clearly designed to destabilize the opera-house, Lord Salisbury issued the licence for 1788–89 with the name of Andrea Carnevale, Gallini's deputy manager, 'incerted'. Gallini protested that Carnevale 'had been discharged' before the licence was issued.[2] Very little information survives about this power struggle, so one

[1] C31/253, no. 249, sworn on 11 July 1789.   [2] C31/251, no. 301.

cannot be certain that Gallini did not sack Carnevale as a counter-ploy. The general season advertisement, which appeared in the *Morning Post* on 17 December 1788, names no manager, but according to an account of the 7 February 1789 riot (printed above in Ch. 2), after Gallini fled the theatre, the audience called on Carnevale for an explanation. He responded that although his name appeared in the licence he was not part of the management. Carnevale was indeed replaced this season as 'assistant acting manager' by Anthony Ravelli, who received £150 and a free benefit.[1] In an affidavit sworn in 1793 when he was 52 years old, Ravelli testified that 'he was many years Deputy Manager of ye Opera House at Naples', presumably the Teatro S. Carlo.[2] Ravelli was therefore no mere hanger-on but perhaps the only person in power at the King's Theatre in the 1780s with direct administrative experience in a mainstream Continental opera-house.

Gallini's letters to Lord Cowper show that he was concerned to hire the best available singers for both serious and comic opera, though he was all too aware that the company's fortunes depended crucially on the *primo uomo*. The great Marchesi was beginning the second year of a two-year contract, and the manager hired a composer specifically to write and direct serious operas—Tarchi, who was also listed as house composer for the previous season but seems to have done little, if he was even in London then. Mazzinghi was retained as musical factotum (though not advertised as such), while Stephen Storace faded from the picture. There seems to have been a rift between the Storaces and Gallini this season. Nancy left the King's Theatre to sing in oratorios at Covent Garden in February and March 1789 and did not return to Italian opera until May. Gallini anticipated her departure in a letter to Lord Cowper of 1–3 February 1788: 'For next year [that is, 1788–89] I am lacking a good buffa . . . next year I would like three or four leading persons for the buffo.'[3] The manager's apparent dissatisfaction is curious, because Signora Storace, Morelli, and Morigi formed the core of one of the most distinguished comic troupes ever assembled. The new singers Lord Cowper may have helped to provide—Signora Margherita Delicati (*prima buffa*), Elisabetta Borselli (*seconda buffa*), Fausto Borselli (*mezzo carattere*), Luigi Delicati (*buffo carricato*), Paolo Torregiani (*buffo carricato*)—were hardly as celebrated, and the comic operas languished until the production of Gazzaniga's *La vendemmia* on 9 May 1789, when Signora

---

[1] See *Biographical Dictionary*, xii. 262.
[2] C24/1964, 9 Jan. 1793 (in *Skillern and Goulding* v. *Longman and Broderip*).
[3] Gibson, 'Earl Cowper', 248–9.

Storace and Sestini were re-engaged to complement the new *primo buffo* Benucci.

## Martín y Soler's La cosa rara

During Nancy Storace's stint as *prima buffa* at the Vienna Burgtheater, one of the most popular new productions in which she appeared was *Una cosa rara* (17 November 1786), which nearly swept aside Mozart's *Figaro*. The elegant Vicente Martín y Soler injected considerable local Spanish colour into Da Ponte's splendid libretto. La Storace took the role of Lilla, while Benucci sang that of her brother Tita; for both, the opera was a great personal triumph. Da Ponte related how the singers were at first extremely displeased with their parts, and

Nearly all of them sent back their parts to the copyist and enjoined him to tell Martín that it was not their style of music and that they would not sing it. The ringleader was the *primo buffo* who had a special grudge against the Spanish composer, as the latter was tenderly regarded by his faithless Dulcinea. (*Memoirs*, 146)

The 'first comedian' was almost certainly Benucci and 'Dulcinea' Signora Storace.[1] We wonder whether Da Ponte may have intended an element of satire in Tita's attempt to force his sister Lilla to marry the magistrate Lisargo against her will. Signora Storace's recent, disastrous marriage to J. A. Fisher was still a subject of gossip in Vienna, and the parallel in the plot may have caused some tension amongst the cast.

*Una cosa rara* probably formed part of Stephen Storace's 'pretty little collection' brought back from Vienna in 1787; the fact that it was produced at the beginning of the 1788–89 season by the new *buffi* under the direction of Mazzinghi, before the reunion in London of 'Lilla' and 'Tita', is another indication that the Storaces had temporarily fallen out with Gallini. Da Ponte's fully developed libretto, with its huge, self-contained finales and brilliant handling of the double plot of royal hunting party meddling in a tale of village love, demonstrated a sophistication previously unknown at the King's Theatre. The discrediting of the wicked Prince of Spain and his confidant Corrada was strongly reminiscent of Sarti's *Le gelosie villane*, though the attempted rape of Ghita (Act II, Scene xiii) had to be toned down for London. Martín y Soler's music—tuneful, unfailingly periodic,

---

[1] This is argued convincingly by Otto Michtner, *Das alte Burgtheater als Opernbühne* (Vienna: Hermann Böhlaus Nachf., 1970), 405. However, an affair between Benucci and La Storace has been doubted: see Andrew Steptoe, *The Mozart–Da Ponte Operas* (Oxford: Clarendon Press, 1988), 147.

and implacably cheerful—was something of a throw-back to the pseudo-folk style of Bertoni and Rauzzini, and was lapped up by the King's Theatre subscribers.

The London production (10 January 1787), under the title *La cosa rara,* was a milestone in the history of the Italian opera in London, because it was the closest thing yet to a straight revival of a Continental première. True, the recitative was somewhat reduced, which still left the opera far too long ('though the ballets were unusually short, it was twelve o'clock before the curtain dropt').[1] Quite unusually for the King's Theatre, most of the choruses were retained. The changes to Martín y Soler's score were otherwise minimal by London standards: the chorus 'Suoni pur' was not repeated at the end of Act I, Scene iv; the duet for Ghita and Tita in Act I, Scene vi, was somewhat shortened; Ghita's aria in Act I, Scene xi, 'In quegli anni in cui solea', was replaced by 'Tutti dicon che le donne'; the *introduzione* to Act II was cut; the duet for Lilla and Ghita, 'Villanelle che volgete', was cut along with much of the rest of Act II, Scene vii; and a new aria for Lubino, 'S'è bella la moglie', was added to Act II, Scene viii. There is some confusion over the music published from the London production. 'Ah perchè formar non lice' (Act II, Scene v) and 'Calma l'affanno' were published under the name of Domenico Corri.[2] Because no copy of either edition appears to survive, one cannot determine if Longman and Broderip claimed Martín y Soler's music for Corri. Lilla's aria in Act II, Scene x, 'Consola le pene', was also published by Longman and Broderip and attributed to 'Messrs Martin & Mazzinghi', though this is only a slight revision of the original.[3] The same publishers' version of Lilla's aria in Act I, Scene xiii, 'Dolce mi parve un dì', goes even further in attributing the music to Mazzinghi,[4] though it is simply the original. One suspects fraud, because other numbers from *La cosa rara* were published at the time with correct attributions.[5] That Mazzinghi claimed two of the most popular pieces in the opera is probably no coincidence. At least one critic fell into the trap, opining that the arias in *La*

---

[1] *London Chronicle,* 10–13 Jan. 1789.

[2] See Dorothea Eva Link, 'The Da Ponte Operas of Vicente Martín y Soler', Ph.D. diss., University of Toronto (1991), 213–14, 233, 295–7.

[3] In British Library G.196 (4). A note in *BUCEM,* ii. 656, says, incorrectly, 'This song is not in the German and Italian editions of the opera. It was probably introduced by Mazzinghi in the London production.'

[4] *BUCEM,* ii. 664, again states incorrectly that this is 'a new setting'.

[5] 'Un briccone senza core' (Birchall); 'Lilla mia dove sei' (Longman and Broderip); 'Dirò che perfida' (Birchall).

*cosa rara* attributed to Mazzinghi 'are infinitely superior to any in the Opera,—and Mr. Gallini cannot consult his interest better than by giving this young composer an opportunity of setting a whole Opera'.[1] When such a commission was finally proffered in 1790–91, Mazzinghi failed to fill it.[2] The favourite piece of the production proved to be Martín y Soler's duet for Lilla and Lubino in Act II, Scene xiv, 'Pace mio caro sposo', which Michael Kelly (Corrada in the original Viennese production) and Mrs Crouch had already popularized as 'Oh thou wert born to please me' in Colman's *Comus* at Drury Lane. *La cosa rara* received more performances this troubled season than any other opera and, though not revived till after 1800, made a considerable impression. Martín y Soler's 'graceful' melodies and 'sweet' harmony and Da Ponte's complex yet deeply satisfying libretto epitomized the best of Italian opera in London in the 1780s, even though in this instance the music and the drama never really fused to produce a work greater than the sum of its parts. One can nevertheless understand why both men later decided to travel to England.

Cimarosa's *La villana riconosciuta*, also under the direction of Mazzinghi, was staged on 24 March 1789 and for only two further performances. Originally a three-acter for Naples in 1783, it was reduced to two acts and performed by essentially the same singers as *La cosa rara*, but if that work was a great step forward for comic opera in London, *La villana riconosciuta* took three steps backwards. Palomba's libretto is a racist farce distinguished only by the audacity with which clichés of disguise, misunderstanding, and slapstick are strung together. The *World* (25 March 1789) reported 'it is bad music, and it is worse sung'. None of the arias was published.

### *Gazzaniga's* La vendemmia

The King's Theatre had first attempted to recruit Francesco Benucci in June 1781, though Gallini (probably influenced by Lord Cowper) did not consider him as great a singer as Giovanni Morelli. Today, Benucci appears in almost every history of opera mainly because he created the title-role in *Le nozze di Figaro*, while Morelli is virtually forgotten. Perhaps, as Madam Mara believed, Gallini was a poor judge of voices; he certainly admitted to Lord Cowper that he was unable to predict how a singer would fare in London. On 18 August 1789, having shrugged off the effects of the fire, he wrote: 'The taste at present here, runs more in favour of strong Base voices,

---

[1] *London Chronicle*, 10–13 Jan. 1789.
[2] See 'Opera and Arson', 85–9; to be discussed in vol. II.

than a finer or clearer sort. For instance, Benucci did not please much yet Morelli and Taschi [Tasca] succeeded.'[1]

The King's Theatre owned a sizable collection of scores of operas in which both La Storace and Benucci had already performed; consequently, one is surprised that Gallini chose *La vendemmia* as the medium for their reunion. While not attaching too much importance to the Mozart connection, one might have assumed that singers of their stature could have found something more substantial and up-to-date than Gazzaniga's *dramma giocoso* of 1778. Instead, they returned to this opera, in which they had both appeared at Venice in 1783.[2] Gluttony is treated as a running joke in this utterly conventional plot; there is little dramatic development in the second act, and the only notable feature is the free interaction between aristocrats and peasants, members of each group scrambling up and down their own despicable pecking-order. Furthermore, Bertati's libretto was given pasticcio treatment, a rare procedure at the King's Theatre for a comic opera.

Much of Gazzaniga's music was retained, including 'Quando vedrai chi sono' for Count Zefiro (Benucci) in Act I, Scene x, a catalogue aria and a possible model for 'Madamina, il catalogo è questo' in Mozart's *Don Giovanni*. Since none of the music of the 1789 London version appears to survive, one cannot be certain of all the borrowings, but the *Morning Post* (11 May 1789) noted the inclusion of music by Paisiello, Tarchi, Pozzi, and Mozart; Stephen Storace was also said to have contributed.[3] The Paisiello was probably 'Voi mi amate, già lo vedo', sung by Agatina (Signora Storace) in Act I, Scene xiii, which had been heard in 1787 in *Il tutor burlato*.[4] The Mozart, the first piece of his operatic music to be performed at the King's Theatre, was the duet for the Count and Susanna, 'Crudel! perchè finora', in Act III of *Figaro*. It is introduced somewhat awkwardly into Act II, Scene iv, here.[5] Interestingly, the duet seems to have been included more for dramatic reasons than to exploit Benucci's experience of Mozart's music: he sang Figaro, not the Count, while in *La vendemmia* he was cast as Count Zefiro, the glutton. Quite unusually, the *primo buffo* opens the second act with the aria 'Son vari degli uomini' (again the subject is gluttony) and, when he thinks he has been poisoned (in Act II, Scene ix), he has a mock

---

[1] Gibson, 'Earl Cowper', 250.

[2] See Brace, *Anna . . . Susanna*, 31.

[3] *Biographical Dictionary*, xiv. 308.

[4] From the pasticcio *L'amore ingegnoso* (Rome, 1785). See Robinson, *Paisiello*, i. 354.

[5] It was published by Birchall and Andrews. For a facsimile of the first page, see *The London Stage*, Part 5, ii. following 725.

death-scene, 'Se mai cerca, se domanda'. The latter was probably intended as a burlesque of Marchesi's 'Se cerca, se dice' in Cimarosa's *L'Olimpiade*, which was being revived from the previous season. Neither Benucci nor this comic pasticcio seems to have made much impression on music critics in London.

## *Paisiello's* Il barbiere di Siviglia

A pasticcio based on an old and unremarkable opera, *La vendemmia* was obviously an expedient to bring Benucci before the public as soon and as cheaply as possible. A far more significant production, and yet another landmark this season, was Paisiello's *Il barbiere di Siviglia*, performed just twice on 11 and 15 June 1789 before the fire and two more evenings in early July at Covent Garden. Probably because of the disruption caused by the fire, little is known about the early reception in London of Paisiello's masterpiece. The first night was a benefit for Signora Storace (announced as such on the Larpent copy, MS 837); she and Benucci assumed the roles of Rosina and Bartolo, for which they had been celebrated in Vienna during the period 1784–86. Michael Kelly, who was at the time a mainstay of the Drury Lane theatre, made his first appearance at the King's Theatre as Count Almaviva. He glosses over this episode in his memoirs. After the fire, which he claims to have witnessed, 'The Opera company went to Covent Garden, and finished the remainder of the season, where I played six nights.'[1] While there were indeed six nights of Italian opera at Covent Garden at the end of the 1788–89 season, Kelly withdrew from *Il barbiere* on 4 July and was replaced by Fineschi from the serious troupe on the 11th.[2]

The London production included a couple of substitutions and some minor cuts in the recitative and longer ensembles, but its most striking feature is the degree of fidelity to Paisiello's original. Petrosellini's libretto, in four acts with an extended chain finale only at the end of the fourth, was easily adapted into the two-act formula demanded in London, though to end the first half with Rosina's cavatina 'Giusto ciel' (originally in Act II, Scene xii) instead of a chaos finale would have struck the King's Theatre audience as a novel proceeding. All the numbers for which Paisiello's opera was (and is) justly famous were retained, including the yawning and sneezing trio 'Ma dov'eri tu stordito' (originally Act II, Scene v; Act I, Scene xi for London) and Bartolo's rumour aria 'La calunnia, mio signore' (II.vii =

---

[1] *Reminiscences*, i. 321.      [2] *The London Stage*, Part 5, ii. 1,171–2.

I.xiii). Given the cohesiveness of Paisiello's score, the inevitable substitutions were disruptive. Least problematic was the replacement of Rosina's 'Già riede primavera', the song that 'Alonso' (that is, Count Almaviva) is supposedly teaching her to sing, by 'Sconsolata tortorella' (III.iv = II.iv). The only insertion came later in this act when Figaro is preparing to shave Bartolo. Quite out of character and disturbing the build-up to the quintet 'Don Basilio', Bartolo sang 'Non più andrai farfallone amoroso' from *Le nozze di Figaro*, a hitherto unnoticed instance of a major piece of Mozart being inserted into a King's Theatre production. Benucci, of course, sang both roles, so this remarkable addition was probably made at the *basso*'s request. The only possible dramatic justification for the inclusion of this bellicose aria is Count Almaviva's previous disguise as a drunken soldier demanding a billet in Bartolo's house. When *Il barbiere* was revived at the King's Theatre in 1793 under Stephen Storace's direction and with Morelli as Bartolo, 'Non più andrai' was dropped.[1] British Library Add. MS 16079, a copy of the original four-act version of the opera that materially lacks only the last two scenes of Act II, seems to have been the main source of both the 1789 and the 1793 London productions, given the high degree of correlation with the printed librettos. The score was, however, cut and altered, and the various layers of revision are difficult to uncover. It is sufficiently different from both librettos to suggest that another (now lost) score must have been prepared for the 1789 production.

Kelly's quiet withdrawal from the cast of *Il barbiere* after only one performance, Benucci's lukewarm (or rather non-) reception even after singing so great an aria as 'Non più andrai', Nancy Storace's ambivalence between Italian and English opera—all these suggest that a singer who had triumphed in Vienna was by no means guaranteed success at the King's Theatre. Sheer power, technical virtuosity, and an affecting cantabile were apparently preferred to clarity and what Mozart called good taste. A great deal more was demanded of comic singers in London than in many other leading theatres, mainly because they had to compete with the serious opera, which had been abandoned at Vienna. Furthermore, the two genres were beginning to overlap both musically and dramatically. *Il re Teodoro* already occupied the middle ground, and Tarchi, the newly appointed King's house composer, was dedicated to bringing a more contemporary aesthetic to the world of serious opera.

---

[1] See the printed libretto, J. Hammond.

## *Cherubini's* Ifigenia in Aulide

The high quality of comic opera during the 1788–89 season should not over-shadow the continuing adulation of Marchesi. The choice of repertoire also marked the King's Theatre as a leading venue for experiments in new-style serious opera. With a wildly popular *primo uomo* resident in London at the beginning of the season, one might have expected Gallini to open with a show-piece pasticcio, as was the rule in Pacchierotti's time. But the trend towards faithful revival and a receptive attitude to innovation that now characterized the comic opera were also detectable in the choice of serious works. Marchesi's first appearance was in Cherubini's *Ifigenia in Aulide* on 24 January 1789. The opera was just a year old, having been composed for Turin in January 1788; it was the first stage work Cherubini wrote after leaving London at the end of the 1785–86 season. Marchesi had created the role of Achille, which he repeated at La Scala, Milan, in autumn 1788.[1] Further indication that the failure of *Giulio Sabino* was not the composer's fault and certainly no disgrace is the warmth with which his new opera was welcomed.[2] Only *The Times* (26 January 1789) sounded a dissenting note, as much an attack on Gallini's artistic policy as on the opera itself:

None of the airs throughout the opera were encored; this failure cannot be attributed to *Marchesi* or *Giuliani*, who had the greatest share, but to their extreme length,—and a sameness of stile, which must ever be the case where the Opera falls to the care of one composer; for that reason, a Pasticcio will always have the advantage in point of popularity.

Despite the final phrase, this view seems reactionary in light of the strong tendency away from medley operas, which had begun decisively in the previous season with the relatively unaltered version of Sarti's *Giulio Sabino*. As *primo uomo*, Marchesi may simply have demanded operas with which he was comfortable *passim*, rather than abuse his right to introduce substitutions, which he occasionally did, of course. But he stands in complete contrast to others, particularly Madam Mara, in not having operas mutilated just to gain 'the advantage in point of popularity'.

Moretti's libretto had been set first by Zingarelli for La Scala, Milan, in 1787. Cherubini retained the spectacular scenes as well as the opera's most remarkable feature—the on-stage suicide of Erifile, the 'real' Ifigenia. The

---

[1] See Sartori, nos. 12738 and 12739.  [2] See Petty, 265–7, for a selection of reviews.

depiction of death on stage was something of an *idée fixe* for Moretti.[1] The climactic murder or suicide of a protagonist in tragic circumstances was not unknown to the King's Theatre—one may recall especially the pasticcio *Giunio Bruto* (1782) and Tarchi's *Virginia* (1786)—but this had rarely happened in full view of the audience during the final scene. Moretti's libretto is studiedly classical in its simple rendering of the drama; there is no bombast or Metastasian psychology on display here. Rather, we find the Agamemnon and Achilles of mythology (or at least as filtered through Racine) and not stand-ins for eighteenth-century princes caught in artificial conflicts. The first-act duet-finale for the hero and heroine is, however, utterly conventional, as are the scenes of ships. The debarkation of Achille in Act I, Scene vii, was butchered in the London production, as has been described in Chapter 3.[2]

The degree of fidelity to Cherubini's original cannot be accurately assessed because so little of the music was published and, unlike *Giulio Sabino*, no manuscripts linked to the King's Theatre production appear to survive. Mazzinghi, who directed, was praised for his 'very powerful aid' in the accompaniments, which were described as 'elegant and correct'.[3] But the *Morning Post* (26 January 1789) objected: 'the accompaniments were too complicated, and overpowered the airs, and though the band had opportunity to display their abilities; the vocal Performers were proportionably circumscribed'. Achille's victory aria in Act I, Scene vii, 'A voi torno o sponde amate', sung by Marchesi and attributed to Cherubini, was published by Longman and Broderip. In D major with all appropriate military flourishes, including the introduction of kettledrums in the final section, its simple triadic melody exploits Marchesi's low range and not, as one would expect in such a piece, his brilliant high notes. Tarchi, the new house composer who had worked with the librettist Moretti at Mantua in 1785, contributed an important piece to the London production: 'Nel lasciarti amato bene' in Act II, Scene xiii. It begins as a fairly tame *rondò* in F major for Achille, who addresses Ifigenia. But the second section, an agitated *allegro*, turns into a trio: Ifigenia (Signora Giuliani) enters in F minor, followed by a tormented Agamemnone (the tenor Forlivesi), who dominates the texture till the end.

---

[1] See Marita P. McClymonds, *Opera Grove*, iii. 468, and ead., 'The Venetian Role in the Transformation of Italian Opera Seria during the 1790s', 224.

[2] *The Times*, 26 Jan. 1789.

[3] *Morning Herald*, 26 Jan. 1789.

## *Tarchi's* Il disertore *and* La generosità d'Alessandro

The first new opera of the season, evidently a commission from Gallini, was Tarchi's *Il disertore* (28 February 1789). A striking new departure for the King's Theatre, even though it had no immediate or medium-term successors, this was a *dramma serio* with a mundane contemporary setting involving ordinary people, but performed by Marchesi and other members of the *opera seria* troupe rather than the *buffi*. Louis Sébastien Mercier's story was already known in England from Badini's comic libretto based on Sedaine and Monsigny's *opéra comique* (1769), which was set by Guglielmi for the King's Theatre in 1770, and more recently from Dauberval's hugely popular ballet *Le déserteur* of 1784. The first treatment of the story as a serious opera was Bartolomeo Benincasa's libretto, set by Francesco Bianchi for Venice in 1784, on which the 1789 London version was based.[1] Given his previous interest in the subject, Badini is likely to have been the adapter, though the printed libretto (W. Bingley, 1789) is unsigned. The learned historical preface also points to his involvement, even if the libretto itself is perhaps a bit too tame and regular for his style.

The variety of new and innovative works, both comic and serious, presented during Gallini's tenure was so wide that hardly anyone seems to have noticed that Tarchi's *Il disertore* launched the King's Theatre into the modern age of opera. The idea of Marchesi, the *primo uomo*, whose roles had been confined almost completely to Roman princes and generals, Greek kings and warriors, and others of elevated rank, portraying Gualtieri, a common soldier who deserted his regiment to attend his dying mother, would have been unthinkable a few years earlier. A critic writing in the *Morning Post* (2 March 1789) saw the plot itself as a serious disadvantage:

The story of this piece is so hackneyed, having already been many years on the English stage—and having been introduced on that of the Opera House in a popular *ballet* by D'Auberval, that a composer had to struggle with great difficulties in the attempt to revive so exhausted a fable.

Tarchi has executed this arduous task with very great ability; but as the story was wholly anticipated by the audience, his music, though beautiful, had little influence over the feelings.

---

[1] See Sartori, no. 7970. In the Venice production Brigida Banti sang Adelina, Pacchierotti was Gualtieri, and Matteo Babbini was Ormondo, all of whom sang in London some time during their careers.

According to the opinion of the best critics, the music of Il Disertore is rather scientific than affecting; but this decision is perhaps made too rashly, considering that it was employed upon a subject too familiar to the feelings of the Public to be capable of much impression, even by the aid of the most pathetic compositions.

In one respect *Il disertore* closely parallels Tarchi's earlier opera *Virginia*, which was excessively bold in its depiction of cruelty and violence. In both a father (Virginio/Ormondo) is forced to administer civil/military justice to his daughter/son, with tragic result in the earlier work. In *Il disertore* Ormondo orders Gualtieri's execution by regimental firing-squad, but the prisoner is saved at the last moment by a royal pardon. Upon first reading, the pardon scene appears to have been bungled. In Act II, Scenes vi and vii, Gualtieri's faithful betrothed, Adelina (Signora Giuliani), dreams that she has obtained a pardon for her lover, of which nothing more is heard until Scene xi. While the dead march is sounded, she recovers from a swoon, desperately searching for a piece of paper, which she finds in the nick of time. The strong air of unreality about the last-minute reprieve (how did she get word to the king? why should the king pardon Gualtieri?) contrasts sharply with the rest of the opera, which is characterized by its very ordinariness. The 'magic' piece of paper can be interpreted, however, as a substitute for the *deus ex machina* of classical *opera seria*, an important link with the past that helped keep *Il disertore* within the bounds of the genre.

The première on 28 February 1789 was eagerly anticipated and, quite unusually, the first and second rehearsals, held in the coffee-room of the opera-house and not in the auditorium, were open to the public and consequently reviewed in the newspapers. The composer and leading singers were lavishly praised, though Marie Pieltain was found too young and too beautiful to be credible in the role of Belinda, Adelina's mother.[1] After the second rehearsal, the *Morning Post* (21 February) voiced a criticism common to all subsequent reviews:

If there be any thing objectionable, it is that the *recitatives* are *too long*. This is a fault generally discoverable in operas, which is tedious to the audience, and injurious as well as tiresome to the performer, diminishing the spirit and power that should be devoted to the airs. Let Tarchi shorten his *recitatives*, and his opera will augment even his great reputation.

There is certainly a lot of simple recitative in *Il disertore*—Act II, Scene ii, being an extreme example—but the opera includes no more of it than any number of contemporaneous Italian operas. The only difference here is that

[1] *Morning Post*, 19 Feb. 1789.

Tarchi, to his credit, apparently refused to cut it, thereby preserving the most remarkable aspect of this work—the plot. Had the narrative sections been reduced, even to the limited extent that Sarti's *L'Olimpiade* was trimmed the season before, *Il disertore* might have become just another *opera seria*. Only one piece from the London production was published, Marchesi's aria 'A quei cari amati accenti'.[1] This was supposed to be sung by Gualtieri to the sleeping Adelina in Act II, Scene vii (the so-called 'couch scene'), where it appears in Larpent MS 815, but was cut from the printed libretto. Marked 'Largo non tanto', it is a gentle lullaby in F major with a solo cello part. *The Times* (2 March 1789) commented on the great length of the opera and suggested that 'the whole of the couch scene might be totally omitted'. In fact the work underwent considerable revision during rehearsals, as can be determined by comparing the Larpent copy with the printed libretto. The aria in Act I, Scene vii, for Corradino (Balelli), 'Nell'età storica', was a last-minute insertion; and both finales were extensively altered before the première.

Equally popular this season was Tarchi's more traditional serious opera *La generosità d'Alessandro*. The libretto is an adaptation by Badini of Metastasio's *Alessandro nell'Indie*. Tarchi's first opera of this title was presented at Milan in 1788.[2] The London version was first performed on 2 June, survived the fire, transferred to Covent Garden, and was successfully revived in 1790. Its appeal lay not just in Tarchi's music and Marchesi's singing, both of which received exceptional praise, but also in the welcome return to Metastasian drama and a generous helping of spectacle, especially in Act II, Scene i, which featured a collapsing bridge: 'Alexander draws the sword, and goes towards the bridge, where a fight ensues betwixt the troops of *Porus* and the *Macedonians,* till some *Grecian* pioneers demolish the said bridge, and put the *Indians* to flight.'[3] Although the *Alessandro* libretto had served for a pasticcio as recently as 1780, the *Diary* (3 June 1789) felt obliged to give a detailed account of the plot.

Despite the disruption caused by the fire, Longman and Broderip published four pieces from *La generosità d'Alessandro*. The most ambitious of

---

[1] Longman and Broderip; for the location of copies of the score, whose connection to the London production has not been established, see Dennis Libby and Marita P. McClymonds, 'Tarchi', *Opera Grove*, iv. 653. Marchesi later sang Gualtieri in revivals of Tarchi's setting at Siena (1791), Vicenza (1794), and Genoa (1799); see Sartori, nos. 7975, 7978, and 7979.

[2] See *Opera Grove*, iv. 653; no libretto for this performance is listed in Sartori, though Tarchi's opera was revived at Livorno in 1791 with Marchesi as Poro.

[3] From the libretto for the 1790 revival (Hammond and Cane), substantially the same as Larpent MS 836, which relates to the 1789 production.

these is the first-act duet-finale for Poro (Marchesi) and Cleofide (Signora Giuliani), a setting of the famous text 'Se mai turbo il tuo riposo' (for a discussion of Piccinni's version, see Ch. 4). Tarchi distinguishes the two voice parts melodically, but Marchesi's coloratura, in particular, seems pasted on. Far more interesting is the long *recitativo accompagnato* that precedes the duet. The whole recitative ('Lodi agli dei') is based on and held together by the bold opening ritornello for the full orchestra. It is so dynamic that the duet which follows is rendered an anticlimax. Of the other pieces, only the trio in Act II, Scene iv, 'Son prigioneri, lo vedo', for Poro, Cleofide, and Alessandro (Forlivesi) deserves comment (the Longman and Broderip edition attributes the words to Badini). It is constructed like a finale, that is, in several sections of increasing tempo and agitation, and Tarchi tries at first to distinguish the contrasting emotions of the three singers; but later on, when the voices are joined, he concentrates on elegant, chordal part-writing at the expense of the drama. The whole trio is 'correct' and rather dull.

To claim that the destruction of the King's Theatre on 17 June 1789 cut off the golden age of Italian opera in London would be an exaggeration: Gallini's position as manager was fragile and the numerous lawsuits pending in the Court of Chancery were a string of time bombs waiting to blast him from control if the Lord Chamberlain did not succeed in removing him first. No one much lamented the destruction of the King's Theatre—even Gallini: 'Notwithstanding the unfortunate fire at the Opera House I have at length recovered my spirits and have every prospect of approaching success.'[1] Behind the intense manœuvring to re-establish the Italian opera in London is the half-spoken belief that the fire was a kind of divine retribution for greed.

Unfortunately, after the fire the Italian opera theatre no longer had the clear artistic direction that Gallini had provided since 1785, most conspicuously in his choice of performers. As *The Times* (no opera-house poodle) editorialized on 3 June 1789, 'The Opera, in its best times, has never boasted names higher in the list of fame than *Marchesi, Bennucci, Storace, Guimard, Saulnier, Nivelon,* and *Didelot*'.[2] But Gallini was also concerned about composers and repertoire. Cherubini, Tarchi, Gresnick, and Storace were far from hacks; and Gallini was the only King's Theatre manager during the second half of the eighteenth century to mount largely unaltered revivals of works of recognized quality. When he assumed control, the opera-house

---

[1] 18 Aug. 1789; see Gibson, 'Earl Cowper', 250.    [2] The last four were dancers.

was old and worn out, yet, following Taylor's renovation of 1782, the scenery worked smoothly and the auditorium had good acoustics, which especially favoured the orchestra. True, the theatre demanded singers with big voices, but it was still intimate enough to flatter the subscribers sitting comfortably in their Italian-style boxes. Much of the appeal of Italian opera in London, especially the serious variety, vanished in the flames—along with Gallini's hope to make London the leading centre for the art form.

## V. The 1789–90 Season: At the Little Haymarket

Repertoire:

*Ninetta*, Cimarosa adapted by Giardini, libretto by Palomba, 7 January 1790 (11 performances); orig. Naples as *Chi dell'altrui si veste presto si spoglia* (Fiorentini) 1783 (p. 427)

*I due castellani burlati*, Fabrizi adapted by Giardini, libretto by Livigni, 2 February 1790 (6 performances); orig. Bologna (Marsigli-Rossi) 1785 (p. 429)

*La villanella rapita*, Bianchi, directed by Federici, libretto by Bertati, 27 February 1790 (9 performances); orig. Venice (S. Moisè) 1783 (p. 430)

*La buona figliuola* (1st act only), Piccinni, libretto by Goldoni, 25 March 1790 (1 performance); orig. Rome (Dame) 1760. London 1766 → 1783, 1785, 1789

*L'usurpator innocente*, Federici, libretto after Metastasio's *Demofoonte*, 6 April 1790 (15 performances) (p. 432)

*La generosità d'Alessandro*, Tarchi, directed by Federici, libretto by Badini after Metastasio's *Alessandro nell'Indie*, 29 April 1790 (12 performances). London 1789

*Gli schiavi per amore*, Paisiello, directed by Federici, adapted from *Le gare generose* by Storace, libretto by Palomba, 27 May 1790 (1 performance); orig. Naples (Fiorentini) 1786. London 1787, 1788

*Andromaca*, Nasolini adapted by Federici, libretto after Salvi, 28 May 1790 (6 performances); orig. Venice (S. Samuele) 1790 (p. 434)

*Il barbiere di Siviglia*, Paisiello, libretto by Petrosellini, 3 June 1790 (2 performances); orig. St Petersburg (Hermitage) 1782. London 1789

By 1790 Gallini was both unpopular and embattled. At the beginning of the opera season this year Charles Dibdin the elder mounted a vitriolic campaign against him in a weekly called *The By-stander*.[1] Dibdin was no lover of Italian opera, and his prejudice against almost everyone from Handel to Nancy Storace is blatant. He approves Italian music only in being even more hostile to the 'German harmonists' (clearly Gallini's Vienna connection did not please him). Dibdin assures his readers that he cannot believe that Gallini has obtained a licence from Salisbury by bribery or personal favouritism while saying again and again that 'Mr. Gallini is the last man upon earth who ought to manage the opera-house.' He professes bafflement

---

[1] See particularly the issues of 26 Dec. 1789, and 9, 16, 23, and 30 Jan. 1790.

at the reasons for granting Gallini a licence. 'It cannot be his erudition, for he can scarcely write his name. It cannot be his taste in music, for that extends no further than the scratching of a kit. It cannot be his liberality, for the plum and a half out of which he has fooled the English are yet in his strong box.' Dibdin spends a good deal of space sneering at Gallini as an 'Italian baker turned dancing-master', and ostentatiously corrects his initial charge that Gallini had gone about with a bell and a basket, hawking muffins, explaining that he actually sold 'pyclets' (pikelets). The malice is obvious, but no doubt a certain amount of the dirt stuck to its target. Gallini had chosen to carry on, and he would have to do so in extremely unsatisfactory circumstances and subject to endless abuse.

The Lord Chamberlain had been surprisingly quick to grant Gallini a licence in August 1789, thereby allowing him to make plans for the makeshift season at the Little Haymarket Theatre as promptly as possible. As Gallini told Lord Cowper in a letter of 18 August 1789, he had decided to open the season with a burletta, delaying the first serious opera till after Carnival. But he had already started to negotiate with Marchesi and Madam Mara.[1] Despite adequate time for assemblage, the company announced in the *Morning Post* on 29 December 1789 must have seemed unpromising. Apart from the veteran Signora Sestini ('in Immortal Youth') and some second-rank *buffi* from the previous season, the list included no big names. Gallini appointed the veteran violinist Felice Giardini as 'director of music', apparently a replacement for Mazzinghi, while Wilhelm Cramer continued as leader of the orchestra. A writer in the *Morning Post* (9 December 1789) was amused at the thought of Giardini sitting at the harpsichord:

There were formerly two harpsichords in the Opera orchestra, but such was the dislike of Giardini to that species of musical instrument, that he prevailed on the manager to remove one of them, and the performer not to play on the other. The taste of Giardini must have undergone a wonderful improvement in the course of a few years, if he can resign the violin to others, and be content with an humble situation at that very harpsichord which he wished to banish from the stage for ever.

In fact, on the opening night (7 January 1790), Dance was at the harpsichord and Giardini 'was behind', that is, presumably behind the scenes, coaching the singers.[2] Marianna Laurenti from Rome, a pupil of Giardini, was appointed 'prima buffa assoluta' (apparently the first use of this inflationary title in London); her engagement was perhaps an instance of

[1] Gibson, 'Earl Cowper', 250.     [2] *World,* 8 Jan. 1790.

patronage. The *World* (8 January 1790) reported that Signora Laurenti was 'not very heavy laden with voice or figure'; *The Times* (11 January 1790) was unkinder: 'This lady has still much to acquire, and forget—ere she can be entitled to the distinction of first Buffa Assoluto' (*sic*). Lady Mary Coke remarked that 'the new singer has a good voice but is a bad actress' (7 January 1790). By the end of the month Gallini had re-engaged Nancy Storace, who assumed the female comic leads for the rest of the season. For the serious, he did in fact hire Marchesi and Madam Mara, thereby assembling a group of *virtuosi* even more splendid than that of the previous season.

Colman's Little Theatre in the Haymarket was small, utilitarian, and hardly elegant but had the advantage of location, being situated directly opposite the ruins of the King's Theatre. Knowing that at least two schemes were already well advanced for erecting a new opera-house, many of the former subscribers were willing to put up with the Little Haymarket for an interim season. At first, the gentry in the audience constituted what *The Times* (11 January 1790) called 'a private party of Ton', but old subscribers did slowly return in some numbers. The most serious complaint about the Little Haymarket Theatre concerned the so-called 'crown gallery': 'Surely some plan might be adopted to render this once favourite lounge in some degree more suitable to the price of admittance; for, as the seats are now ordered, it is absolutely impossible to see the stage without standing on the benches, and even then the Pitt is not discernable' (*The Times*, 11 January 1790). Lady Mary Coke renewed her subscription and found the opening night 'better than I expected'. She noted that 'the Duchess of Bedford has a small box below stairs just by fops alley. Sir James Peachy said she looked like a great spider that was catching at all the flies' (7 January 1790). On 16 January Lady Mary noted that the house had never been more than half full, but by 23 January the 'opera this evening for the first time was full the consequence was the being very difficult to get away'.

Free from the Taylor-inspired harassment of the Court of Chancery, Gallini was at last able to run the opera exactly as he wished within, of course, the limits imposed by the makeshift theatre, the principal performers, and the wishes of prominent subscribers. In the serious opera he continued to show a strong preference for new works by rising composers. His choice of comic works was more eclectic and hit-or-miss, but particularly noticeable was the sudden increase in the amount of Mozart introduced by substitution. This belated appreciation was not driven solely by Nancy Storace. An indication of Gallini's determination to concentrate on revivals and adaptations of comic works rather than on new ones is found in a postscript to his letter to Lord Cowper of 18 April 1789: 'I shall not want any composer 'till the next season, 1790[–91], at the new Opera as the present one is too confined, but would be glad of any one your Lordship would recommend to me for the New Theatre.'[1] That Lord Cowper would need to have suggested Haydn is doubtful.

On 9 December 1789, a month before the season began, the *Morning Post* published an article signed by 'Marcello' which is, to our knowledge, the first sustained attack on the practice of aria substitution. The advantages and disadvantages of the pasticcio had been a subject of public debate for several years, but 'Marcello' went directly to the heart of the issue that the Storace lawsuits had carefully skirted:

Of all the absurdities belonging to the Italian Opera, (and they are in number not a few) there is none greater than the priviledge allowed the principal singers of what is called the *choice of the book.*

By this claim they obtain a preposterous power over the composer, of whom, instead of being docile servants, they become imperious directors. Such tyranny no man of genius and science can bear; and in this source, perhaps, may be found the cause of that backwardness shewn by some eminent musicians to write for the lyric stage. When, indeed, a performer can say, 'I will have a *rondeau* in such a scene,—I will not have my *cantabile* in the first act,—and my *bravura* shall be after that of such a singer', and all this without having studied, or without capacity of studying, the fable, characters, and sentiments of the piece, or the general effect of the music—the composer's chance for reputation is certainly reduced to a very pitiful span.[2]

The main arguments in favour of aria substitution were that it was a means of introducing novelty into old librettos, especially those of Metastasio, or even revivals of works that had been mounted a season or two before, and that the 'choice of the book' could help assure variety of style within a given work. These arguments, so alien to modern reverence for unity and originality, were born of a theatre world in which the drama as conveyed by the libretto, the artistic independence of singers, and the adapter's skill were all singly and collectively regarded as more important than the composer's original score. At the King's Theatre, where the vast majority of operas were second, third, or fourth generation versions of works first produced on the

---

[1] Gibson, 'Earl Cowper', 250.

[2] 'Marcello' then goes on to relate Burney's story of Handel's insisting that Carestini sing 'Verdi prati' in *Alcina.*

Continent with mostly different singers, aria substitution made perfectly good sense. But Gallini's unaltered revivals of worthy originals forced critics to confront what Dr Burney had already realized about J. C. Bach's 1770 arrangement of Gluck's *Orfeo*: 'the unity, simplicity, and dramatic excellence' of the original was lost.[1]

'Marcello' went even further in claiming that the principal singers' right to make substitutions was actually deterring gifted composers from writing Italian operas. There is only empirical evidence to support this claim: revivals with substitutions far outnumbered new works in the King's Theatre repertoire; but that was true of many late eighteenth-century Italian opera-houses. 'Marcello' was expressing a minority opinion, and the pasticcio continued to be accepted practice. For example, *The Times* (13 February 1790) reported: 'Storace's engagement at the Opera does infinite credit to the liberality of the Manager [Gallini]. She is to receive two hundred guineas for ten nights—with full liberty as to the selection of her arias.' But the situation was confused. The Lord Chancellor's decision in favour of Stephen Storace in the 'Care donne che bramate' cases, which protected the composer's right to his own substitute aria, apparently did not affect the opera-singer's 'choice of the book'. Nor was there any way to know when the composer of a newly commissioned work had deliberately borrowed arias or had simply bowed to the *prima donna's* wishes. Federici was attacked in *The Times* (8 April 1790) for claiming *L'usurpator innocente* as 'a genuine composition of his own', when it included two arias by another composer. What is not known is whether Federici had any choice in the matter. Perhaps he was browbeaten by Madam Mara. Marcello's letter should be read in this context. The irony is that this season also saw the sudden influx of Mozart into Little Haymarket productions, all of it by substitution.

## *Cimarosa's* Ninetta

The first opera of the season was based on Cimarosa's popular farce *Chi dell'altrui si veste presto si spoglia* (composed for Naples in 1783). Incorporating elements of *commedia dell'arte*, Palomba's libretto and Cimarosa's music had undergone several adaptations in Italy and might have come to Gallini's attention through any number of sources. The 1790 version was prepared by Giardini as a vehicle for his pupil Signora Laurenti in the title-role. Confusion surrounds the identity of the *primo buffo* this season, one Signor Neri.

---

[1] *General History*, ii. 877.

Robert Lamar Weaver states that he was the Florentine Michele Angiolo Neri, one of the few soprano castrati of this era to appear in both serious and comic roles (*Opera Grove*, iii. 572). The *Biographical Dictionary* claims, however, the singer was Gaetano Neri, evidently a *basso buffo* since he did not take serious roles later in the 1789–90 season (xi. 10). The latter is almost certainly correct. In his letter to Lord Cowper of 18 August 1789, Gallini mentioned 'Gaetano Neri a primo buffo', and the *World* (9 January 1790) commented: 'Neri, the Buffo, is from Rome . . . [as was Signora Laurenti]. His voice is more than mezzo-basso; and in a deep tone or two, not unlike Morelli. His manner is not bad, and the people seemed to think he had some comic powers.'

Cimarosa's opera is a moderately amusing tale of the confusion arising when the maid Ninetta assumes the identity of her mistress, Baroness Stellidaura. But in the first act of Giardini's adaptation, the plot is interrupted in several places by inserted show-piece arias in which the singers virtually step out of character to display their parts. Occasionally an added aria, such as Ninetta's 'Son padrona, e sono amante' in Act I, Scene xiii, is apropos, but even this would appear a set-piece parody of Metastasio's famous aria for Didone. The only number to receive more than passing notice in the press was the so-called 'laughing Terzetto', presumably 'Con sostegno, grazia, e brio' in Act II, Scene iii. Confronted with written descriptions of their true identities, Ninetta, Martuffo (Neri), and Putifare (Signor Costa) reveal themselves. The words are only a skeleton for involved stage business, which is not described in the printed libretto (Reynell, 1790), though in Larpent MS 854 a large gap was left in the middle of the trio, apparently to accommodate a lengthy stage direction that was never written in. Three of Giardini's pieces for Signora Laurenti were published by Birchall: 'Sono dame, è son signora', a cavatina in Act I, Scene ii; 'Bei labbri che amor', a *rondò* in Act I, Scene v; and 'La Ninetta poverina', in Act II, Scene vi. In the first, Ninetta's aristocratic pretensions are rather predictably conveyed by wide, ostentatious vocal leaps. 'Bei labbri che amor' comprises pleasant enough tunes, though they are underdeveloped. And the accompanied recitative leading into 'La Ninetta' is a grand parody of the serious style. Taken together, Giardini's music is decidedly old-fashioned and might well have been composed in the 1760s. 'La Ninetta poverina' is in fact an undisguised *da capo* aria.

*Fabrizi's* I due castellani burlati

'A new Comic Opera, before the old one was well worn out' (*The Times,* 3 February 1790), *I due castellani burlati* was also adapted and conducted by Giardini and sung by the same cast as *Ninetta.* But Livigni's libretto, set by Vincenzo Fabrizi in 1785, is vastly superior, and in this instance Giardini seems to have done much less damage to the original. *The Times* (8 February 1790) thought the opposite: *Ninetta* was the superior work and *I due castellani burlati,* 'tho' considerably curtailed, is yet most insufferably tedious, flat, and uninteresting'. True, the plot is a conventional contest between rivals for the favours of a clever woman, Zeffirina, who is already secretly married; yet all the action is realistically motivated in long, well-constructed scenes with touches of genuine humour. Unlike Da Ponte, Livigni has not grossly overweighted the finales.

The most noteworthy feature of Giardini's adaptation is the inclusion in Act II, Scene v, of 'Voi che sapete che cosa è amor' from *Le nozze di Figaro.* Placed just before the beginning of the second-act finale, it was evidently chosen as much for dramatic as for musical reasons, unlike the introduction of 'Non più andrai' into *Il barbiere di Siviglia* during the previous season. Valerio (Costa) is trying to decide either to leave his ungracious wife Zeffirina (Signora Laurenti) or to forgive her for making him jealous. Despite the necessity of changing the sex of the singer, Susanna's aria is not inappropriate in this new context. The *London Chronicle* (2–4 February 1790) mentioned that Fabrizi's opera was 'enlivened by several arias by other masters, particularly one *or two* by Mozart' (emphasis added). The other piece might have been a parody of Zerlina's aria in *Don Giovanni,* transformed into the trio in Act I, Scene ii:

| *Don Giovanni* | *I due castellani burlati* |
|---|---|
| Batti, batti, o bel Masetto | Pace, pace, bel mostaccio, |
| La tua povera Zerlina | Non più guerra, Spagnoletto. |
| Starò qui come agnellina | Un di voi mi stà già in petto |
| Le tue botte ad aspettar | Questo core a pizzicar. |

How Mozart's aria was expanded into a trio is unknown (there is considerably more text in the second piece), but the similarity of the two lyrics should alert one to the possible presence of other parodies in the London repertoire. The *London Chronicle* (2–4 February 1790) reported the inclusion of an unidentified aria by Giordani. Larpent MS 858 has every appearance of a pasticcio, much of which was assembled at the last minute: there are paste-overs, cuts, and aria texts added in spaces left by the main copyist.

### *Bianchi's* La villanella rapita

The skilful introduction of Mozart notwithstanding, something was wrong with the comic opera offered so far this season. Giardini seems to have provided workman-like direction, but faith in his pupil Signora Laurenti was clearly misplaced. The *London Chronicle* (2–4 February 1790) noted:

After the comic acting that we have so lately seen by Storace and Morelli, the heart is not satisfied with Neri and Laurenti: but we hear that the Chevalier Gallini has procured in France another first man, and has thus done his utmost to enrich his comic opera.

Gaetano Neri was not replaced, but a new tenor, Nicolò Mussini, soon arrived from Paris (*The Times*, 1 March 1790). Nancy Storace was also re-engaged, simply as *prima buffa*, without the 'assoluta'. The other important change about this time was the appointment of the little-known Vincenzo Federici as house composer and director of the next comic opera, a pasticcio based on Bianchi's *La villanella rapita*, a work with strong Viennese connections. With a fine libretto by Bertati, which anticipates many aspects of Da Ponte's *Figaro*, it was first performed at Venice in 1783 and then in Vienna in 1785 with Signora Storace as Mandina, a study for Susanna a year later. The Viennese version included two brilliant ensembles freshly composed by Mozart, the quartet 'Dite almeno in che maniera' (K. 479) and the trio 'Mandina amabile' (K. 480). The finest opera presented by Gallini since *Il re Teodoro* in 1788 and a high-water mark of Italian opera in London in the second half of the eighteenth century, the 1790 London production of *La villanella rapita* retained the Mozart ensembles and probably added one or two other pieces by him. In Act II, Scene iii, Mandina expresses her contrition to Pippo (Signor Borselli, her Figaro-like financé) in an even closer parody of Zerlina's aria than the one used in *I due castellani burlati*:

> Batti, batti o bel Pippetto
> La tua povera Mandina:
> Starò quì come agnellina
> Le tue botte ad aspettar.

La villanella rapita

The opera also included near the beginning of the second finale the passionate love duet for Pippo and Mandina, 'Occhietto furbetto', which was borrowed from Martín y Soler's *L'arbore di Diana*, Act I, Scene xv. While all other signs point to Signora Storace as the driving force behind the London production of *La villanella rapita*, one should note that she had not appeared in Martín y Soler's opera, which was first performed on 1 October 1787, several months after she left Vienna. Therefore, while the basic score may have been a part of Stephen Storace's 'pretty little collection', Gallini and his house composers probably had other suppliers of Viennese music.

Though a pasticcio, *La villanella rapita* is a compelling drama. All the extra numbers are beautifully integrated, especially the two pieces Mozart himself added in 1785, both being action ensembles that advance the plot. As in *Ninetta* earlier in the season, the main comic characters are disguised as nobles but, whereas in the previous work they are ridiculed for their foppish presumption, in Bianchi's opera Pippo's impersonation 'vestito in caricatura' of a French beau is in order to save Mandina, who has been drugged in the first-act finale and kidnapped by the wicked count. Bertati's serious attack on arbitrary aristocratic behaviour is, unfortunately, compromised when the count suddenly forgives everyone in the middle of the second-act finale.

One is bound to ask: if Gallini was such an enlightened manager willing to risk a production of a challenging and controversial work such as *Il re Teodoro in Venezia* and with the Burgtheater's former *prima donna* at his disposal, why did he not offer a complete Mozart opera during his regime? The question becomes even more pertinent in light of the extraordinary review of *La villanella rapita* that appeared in the *Morning Herald*:

All the music of the opera deserving celebrity is by Mozart—and it is to the praise of Storace that so many of these have been introduced. To the merit of this favourite singer, all the success the Opera experienced is also to be attributed. The air, by Mozart, '*Bella rosa porporina*'[1] and the trio by the same master, in which Storace and Mussini took a pre-eminent lead, with another air, may be adduced in proof. In the second act, Mozart's music equally challenged approbation, particularly the quintette [*sic*], '*Dite almeno in che maniera*'. This was a beautiful composition, and Storace's superiority in it very conspicuous. Another noticeable performance was '*Ochietto forbetto*'; but this we have heard, in Allegranti's time, executed much better.[2] The composer of this popular duet is the present Martini. . . . The finales

[1] No aria by Mozart with these words is known.
[2] This would have been impossible. 'Occhietto furbetto' was composed in 1787, and

431

are pretty, but very short of Paisiello; that in the last act was best, but is like the Opera, a *Pasticcio*, and contains the music of three or four masters, oddly combined. (1 March 1790)

The writer is not so well informed that one can accept the last statement at face value—that the second-act finale was a medley of Mozart, Paisiello, and Martín y Soler; but there was precedent in London productions for such amalgam finales. The time was clearly ripe for Mozart in London, and the moderate success of *La villanella rapita* probably paved the way for Robert Bray O'Reilly's letter of 26 October 1790 inviting him to become house composer at the Pantheon, an invitation almost certainly urged by Nancy Storace.[1] But that is a story for volume II of this study. The absence of a complete Mozart opera from the King's Theatre or Little Haymarket during Gallini's regime is probably owing purely to chance: there were so many operas to choose from, most of them more successful internationally than any of Mozart's. And Gallini might also have had some doubts about how Mozart's operas would be received in London, because the former Burgtheater singers Benucci, Kelly, and even to some extent Signora Storace had not exactly triumphed in Italian opera in London. Another important factor is that Gallini had to balance three troupes of nearly equal importance: comic, serious, and ballet. If dance was occasionally allowed to slip, *opera seria* needed constant attention and substantial investment, because this was the leg on which the whole enterprise stood or fell.

### Federici's L'usurpator innocente

The clearest possible sign that Gallini regarded the 1789–90 Little Haymarket season as no mere stop-gap but rather as a launch-pad for his bid for the long-term management of the London Italian opera was the engagement of Marchesi and Madam Mara, the undisputed stars of international *opera seria*. Mara had spent two years on the Continent and had last sung at the King's Theatre in 1787, leaving at the end of the season after a disagreement over salary. Marchesi, too, had fallen out with the manager who 'had used him like a dog'[2] and returned to Milan at the end of the 1788–89 season. But, as noted above, Gallini was already negotiating with both singers in August 1789. Again, the castrato's salary was reported to be £1,500, while

Teresa Maddalena Allegranti left London in 1783 and did not return until 1799. See *Biographical Dictionary*, i. 62.

[1] See 'Opera and Arson', 68–71.

[2] According to a letter from Dr Burney quoted in the *Biographical Dictionary*, x. 90.

Madam Mara was said to have received £850 plus a free benefit.[1] Given the size of their egos, one is a little surprised that Gallini decided to commission a new opera to present this 'coalition capable of realising the fabulous wonders that are related concerning the music of the ancients'.[2] A pasticcio in which Marchesi and Mara could select their own arias would have been simpler. Federici's *L'usurpator innocente* was based on Metastasio's *Demofoonte*, which had perhaps not coincidentally served as a favourite device for London pasticcios for several decades; one critic was incensed that 'some botching pruner' had altered the title.[3] Despite the audience's familiarity with earlier settings,[4] Federici used many aria texts appropriate to the libretto, as well as others that had made the rounds in other London operas, such as 'Per lei fra l'armi dorme il guerriero' (Act I, Scene iii, sung by Demofoonte—Mussini), last heard in the 1783 *Medonte*, and 'Un tenero affetto' (Act II, Scene iii, sung by Dircea—Madam Mara), which had recently appeared in Cherubini's *Ifigenia in Aulide*. Marchesi (Timante) seems to have sung the music Federici provided for him, but Madam Mara exercised the 'choice of the book'. *The Times* complained that Federici

announces the music of the Opera on Saturday, to be a genuine composition of his own: and therefore we may fairly ask him, why the two sweetest airs in the whole . . . happen to be not only in the music, but in the very words taken from an Opera composed by the celebrated Signor *Andreozzi*? . . . the airs no doubt are divine, and they were well executed; but, Signor, you should not rob *Andreozzi* of his laurels. (8 April 1790)

The arias in question were probably Dircea's 'Nell'amarti o caro sposo' in Act II, Scene ix, an 'enraptured Rondeau' that the *Morning Herald* (7 April 1790) attributed to Andreozzi; another *rondò*, 'Se ti perdo o caro bene' in Act I, Scene ii (also sung by Madam Mara); and probably 'Che mai feci amici' in Act II, Scene iv. The last two were published by Longman and Broderip without attribution, whereas Henry Holland issued three of Marchesi's arias and the duet in the second-act finale under Federici's name. The offending announcement about the opera being 'a genuine composition of his own' does not appear to survive, except in the form of a note on the title-page of Larpent MS 868. Significantly, the printed libretto (Cane and Hammond, 1790) states simply 'The Music by Signor Frederici' (*sic*), departing from the more usual form 'The Music entirely new by . . . .'.

---

[1] 'Opera Salaries', 53.　　[2] *Morning Post*, 7 Apr. 1790.
[3] Unidentified cutting, printed in Smith, *Italian Opera*, 14.
[4] See e.g. *The Times*, 7 Apr. 1790.

Having exonerated Federici of any dishonesty, we must report that his published music from *L'usurpator innocente* is mostly poor stuff. Only Marchesi's *rondò* in Act II, Scene xi, 'Misero, misero pargoletto', with its built-in pathos (Timante is addressing his child, whom he believes to be the product of incest), rises above the mundane. The *Morning Herald*'s remarks (7 April 1790) about Federici's 'astonishing fertility', comparing him with Sacchini, seem so much puffery. Finally, one should note that Gallini dedicated the libretto to the Marchioness of Salisbury. Dedications are rare in London Italian opera librettos and, if Gallini was not being ironic (in light of his recent battles with the Marquis of Salisbury, the Lord Chamberlain), then one must assume he was attempting to curry favour in advance of an application for an opera licence in 1790–91, which was unsuccessful.

## Nasolini's Andromaca

The season at the Little Haymarket went on until 12 June, when Gallini once again moved the company to Covent Garden 'to perform the remainder of the Subscription Nights'.[1] The season did not finish until 17 July, the latest the Italian opera had ever run in London. Marchesi and Madam Mara were continuing to draw well, but to inject new blood into the summer season, Gallini brought out an adaptation of Sebastiano Nasolini's *Andromaca* on 28 May. It had first been performed only the previous February at Venice, so this was probably the fastest that any Italian opera had been transferred to London.[2] It is, however, a disgrace to Badini's skill as an adapter, not that the original offered much to work with. Nasolini's opera was based on Antonio Salvi's ancient libretto *Astianatte* of 1701, even to the extent of preserving the three-act format (though Oreste's wounding of Pirro in Act II is omitted).[3] Badini, who dedicated the libretto to the Prince of Wales, reduced the opera to two acts, cutting and rearranging the recitative, probably to accommodate Marchesi and Madam Mara, but, since no music survives from the London production, one cannot be certain. The *Public Advertiser* (31 May 1790) reported that the *primo uomo* 'sung three arias of his own composition'. Judging from his sleight of hand with an aria from Sarti's *Giulio Sabino*, this claim may be doubted, but one of Marchesi's alleged pieces might have been Pirro's 'Senza di te mio bene', a text that had

---

[1] *The London Stage*, Part 5, ii. 1262.
[2] See John A. Rice, 'Nasolini', *Opera Grove*, iii. 560; no libretto for the Venetian production is listed in Sartori.
[3] See Dale E. Monson, 'Andromache', *Opera Grove*, i. 131.

last been used at the King's Theatre in Sacchini's *Mitridate* (1781). Badini's adaptation barely hangs together: for instance, the second scene of Act I repeats in simple recitative (!) information that has already been conveyed in the first; several arias are weakly prepared and irrelevant to the drama. A number of the problems in the first act seem to have been caused by rearranging events in order to delay Andromaca's first aria until Scene viii. The most anachronistic aspect of Badini's version of *Andromaca* is that it includes no ensembles, except for the duet-finale in Act I, 'Il mio dolor tu vedi'. Yet this throw-back to pre-Metastasian *opera seria* was performed six times and sustained Gallini's company through its removal back to the Covent Garden theatre. It was, however, a limp end to five remarkable seasons of Italian opera.

## Assessment of Gallini's Regime

In terms of artistic policy, Gallini's tenure as manager of the Italian opera in London stands in stark contrast to those around it. Sheridan took only a sporadic interest in repertoire and singers and nearly always made a mess of things whenever he decided to interfere. Taylor was self-confessedly incompetent in artistic matters and left the hiring of singers and selection of operas to others, though he was always ready to complain about their choices. When he resumed control of the Italian opera in 1792, Taylor was forced to make hard decisions to balance the competing interests of comic opera, serious opera, and ballet, but he was hardly concerned with the relative artistic merit of the three forms of entertainment. At the Pantheon in 1790–91, O'Reilly put the artistic direction entirely in the hands of Mazzinghi and the even more obscure musician Luigi Borghi, who clearly acted on the whims of the financial backers of the ill-fated enterprise, the Duke of Bedford and the Marquis of Salisbury. Gallini, unlike all these people, played a key role in recruiting and in the choice of operatic repertoire, though he was doubtless influenced by certain subscribers and by Lord Cowper in Florence.

Paradoxically, the orders imposed by the Court of Chancery afforded Gallini an independence and authority that other managers had never enjoyed. Within the spending limit, he was almost entirely free to run the company as he saw fit, provided he could persuade the Lord Chamberlain to issue him a licence each year. Gallini's personal fortune would have allowed him to get out at any time, but the 'double contract' arrangement with Hanover Square and the percentage of the receipts he extracted from performers' benefits gave him a margin of profit. He could therefore take chances with the repertoire by introducing Viennese-style *dramma giocoso* and the new *dramma serio* of Cherubini and Tarchi, shifting the emphasis away from Goldonian domestic farce and the Metastasio-based pasticcio, though neither was entirely supplanted. Even more daring was his policy of offering unaltered revivals, an indirect attempt to abolish the singers' 'choice of the book'. The operatic high points of Gallini's regime are the productions of Cherubini's *Giulio Sabino*, Paisiello's *Il re Teodoro in Venezia*, Tarchi's *Virginia* and *Il disertore*, Martín y Soler's *Una cosa rara*, and Bianchi's *La villanella rapita*, the latter with substantial chunks of Mozart. Gallini was clearly moving the London Italian opera in a 'historically correct' direction that would lead to the commission of a new opera by Haydn in 1791 and the engagement of both Da Ponte and Martín y Soler a year or so later. But momentum was lost with the 1789 King's Theatre fire and the ensuing battle between Taylor and the Lord Chamberlain for control of Italian opera. Had Gallini rather than Taylor emerged as proprietor of the new King's Theatre in 1792, London might have continued to flourish as a centre for Italian opera.

# CHAPTER 7

# *The Ballet*

BALLET was at least as important as opera in the repertoire of the King's Theatre, Haymarket, during the 1780s. Enormous amounts of money were spent on importing international superstars. The company often presented the best to be had in Europe, but when it economized and failed to satisfy the audience the result could be riots. This was an exciting period in the history of ballet in London: the introduction of the *ballet d'action* was followed closely by the arrival of Jean Georges Noverre as ballet-master. However, the theatre's bankruptcy in 1783 had an ill effect on all its offerings, and the stabilization Gallini accomplished after 1785 helped the dance department less than it might have. Gallini ruthlessly limited expenditure in this realm, and his old-fashioned taste in dance did not encourage experimentation in new modes. The story that follows is largely a tale of decay and disappointment after Noverre's glorious season of 1781–82.

This chapter begins with an overview of the dance establishment at the King's Theatre in the 1780s, based on the chronological survey of developments in dance and in personnel that follows. Any history of this period is greatly hampered by the impossibility of knowing what the actual dance steps in a given production were. Although dances could be written down, and there are hints that in at least some cases they were, such notation has not been preserved.[1] When available, scenarios of the story ballets are helpful, but few survive, and in any case they do not account for the whole repertoire. The descriptive terms used to advertise dances and to review them

---

[1] Noverre discusses the practice of writing down dances, translated 'chorography' in Letter XXI of the English edition of his *Works* (London: G. Robinson *et al.* [1782–]1783), ii. 118–28. He regards it as 'a useless art', incapable of recording the complexities of contemporary ballet. For a translation from the St Petersburg edition, see Cyril W. Beaumont, *Letters on Dancing and Ballets* (1930; rpt. New York: Dance Horizons, 1966), Letter XIII.

varied from season to season and occasionally from week to week. Lacking evidence of the exact nature of most of the dances, we have used the descriptors of the time rather than rely on more standard labels, whose applicability is difficult to judge. Despite these limitations, the evidence permits study of the calibre of performers hired to dance each season, the kinds of dance the theatre advertised, and the overall reception of dancers and dances. This survey will show why *ballet d'action* took some time to become established in London.

The other major obstacle to reconstruction is the nature of the surviving music for ballets at the King's Theatre. A great deal was published between 1778 and 1790, but to survey it is dispiriting. A few works were issued more or less complete (*Il ratto delle Sabine*, two versions of *Le tuteur trompé*, *Les fêtes de Tempé*, *The Deserter*, *Il convitato di pietra*, *Les deux solitaires*, *Les offrandes à l'amour*, *Admète*, *La bergère des Alpes*, *Le premier navigateur*, *Zemira and Azor*, *Les mariages flamands*, and *The Generous Slave*), and fragments of several others survive. But all the ballets—which typically comprise an overture or introduction (almost invariably in D major) followed by ten to fifteen contrasting numbers with a finale—are pastiches printed in simple piano score, sometimes with separate violin parts. Their melodic and harmonic banality is truly astonishing, and only with great imagination can they be made to fit the printed scenarios.[1] Dancers' names are usually given (except for the 1789–90 season), but the location or dramatic function of individual numbers is rarely specified; the music that accompanied the pantomime is not generally included or is often difficult to distinguish from shorter character dances. In short, the ballet scores are strictly functional— at one extreme, workman-like narrative, and, at the other, unobtrusive and unchallenging accompaniment to virtuoso dancing. Small wonder the Burney family regarded this music as beneath contempt and always tried to sneak out of the opera-house before the final ballet began.

But these ballet scores should not be dismissed too lightly. Noferi, Borghi, Mazzinghi, Rauzzini, Chabran, and especially Barthélemon were able to invent or to select and adapt from a range of sources music of highly varied rhythmic character. Some of the big solo dances, particularly the rondeaus with variations of increasing athleticism and fiery codas, can generate tremendous energy. The best of these scores—Borghi's *Il ratto delle Sabine*,

---

[1] For an illuminating discussion of this problem as it relates to a slightly later ballet, see Roland John Wiley, 'Jean Georges Noverre and the Music of *Iphigenia in Aulis*', *Harvard Library Bulletin*, NS, 2 (1991), 31–53.

Barthélemon's *Le tuteur trompé* and *Macbeth* (both of 1785)—are no mean achievements, if one considers that the *pasticheur* and his fellow hacks were constrained by the unwritten rules that 95 per cent of ballet music had to be in the major mode and that sentimentality was expected to substitute for seriousness. Always subservient to the ballet-master, scene painter, tailor (costumer), and lighting man, the composer had to cut his music to measure. Stripped of orchestration and reduced to crude violin and keyboard arrangements, the ballet scores appear poor things indeed, but one should not underestimate the craft involved in their composition. The Burneys formed a hypercritical minority; this wallpaper music accompanied the dances that kept the King's Theatre alive during the 1780s.

## I. The Dance Company

The most crucial member of the dance department was the ballet-master. According to standard Continental practice, he would also have been the principal male dancer, but this was seldom the case in London at the time under discussion. In a well-run company, the ballet-master was the first person associated with dance to be hired, and his appointment determined most, if not all, of his employees. Ideally, he had complete autonomy, though he needed to be aware of budget constraints. In practice, autonomy varied with the stature of the individual ballet-master, the promptness of his hiring, the existence of prior contracts for dancers, and the assumptions of a given administration about the place of dance in the opera-house. After he had recruited a company or at least approved it, the ballet-master was responsible for deciding on a production schedule and co-ordinating it with the opera schedule; inventing or 'composing' the dances;[1] choosing or commissioning music; rehearsing; arranging with the tailor for costumes, and with the painter, stage carpenter, and lamp man for scenery and technical effects; providing copy if scenarios were to be printed, and plot summaries and cast-lists for advertising purposes; and deciding on substitutions or changes in repertoire as the season progressed. The authority of a Noverre, who did not dance, or a Dauberval, who seldom did, was hard to challenge, but separating composition from performance under lesser talents did open a space for dispute or at least resistance that marred some seasons. Noverre rated a deputy or assistant who composed *divertissements* and could help

---

[1] We have in some instances used the term 'choreographer' in its modern meaning to avoid confusion with music composition.

with rehearsals. A violinist called the 'leader of the dances' practised with the dancers, directed the orchestra at both rehearsals and performances, and often composed or arranged the music for the dances. Any number of other employees of the theatre might also contribute to the success of the dance department, from the call-boy to the hairdresser.

The company consisted of between four and ten principal dancers supported by a group of *figurants* that varied from fifteen to twenty-four members. At the beginning of this period principals usually came in pairs, but that pattern broke down during the decade, as individual virtuosos were hired, and partnerships were arranged after the company assembled. Some managers—or ballet-masters—insisted on differentiating between principals and 'second dancers' in advertisements as well as in documents internal to the company. The amount and quality of dancing would have made the distinction apparent to the ballet enthusiasts in the audience, but rank is not always clear in the historical record, especially at the beginning or end of a dancer's career. Principals danced longer, more difficult parts than second dancers, a difference reflected in their salaries, which were on the order of twice as large. They often received benefit performances, whereas second dancers did not; nor were group benefits standard in this period. Principals and second dancers were advertised regularly; *figurants* were not. Their existence is documented, but little is known of their identity, numbers, and function until the time of the Pantheon.

Virtually no salary figures survive for individual dancers before the season of 1788–89. The generalizations that follow are made on the basis of those figures, augmented by known salaries at the Pantheon for 1790–91 and 1791–92. An annual salary for a top star attraction might be as high as £1,200 (Vestris jun.), or more for a dancer who was also a choreographer (Le Picq reportedly had £1,400 for one and a third seasons, plus £300 for choreography). 'First dancers' were generally worth up to £500; 'second dancers' usually received between £100 and £250. *Figurants* were lucky to make £70 (perhaps with £10 travel expenses from Paris); others got about £45; at the bottom of the scale a few received as little as £25 or £30.[1]

Most of the principals and second dancers who appeared in London had received their training in France, a few in Italy. Reputations made abroad could help foreign dancers find employment in London, but they had to satisfy a fairly demanding audience. Rival styles were seldom discussed, but

---

[1] For most of the surviving figures, see 'Opera Salaries', 45–53. On pay-scales for dancers, see Judith Milhous, 'Dancers' Contracts at the Pantheon Opera House, 1790–1792', *Dance Research*, 9 (1991), 51–75.

on the whole critics seem to have preferred French-trained dancers to Italian. Criticism was as vague as the remark of 'a correspondent' in the *Morning Post* of 25 January 1785 that under the Italian-born Le Picq 'the Ballets at the Opera House are become quite pantomimical; in so much, that grace and elegance seem only secondary objects'.

So fixed was the prejudice in favour of imported dancers that fewer than half a dozen local residents became second dancers or stars during the decade, and most of those who did were of French extraction. The training that might have developed local talent was simply not available in England. Native dancers did have long, if not exactly distinguished, careers as *figurants*, though even there imported dancers often equalled them in number and were much more likely to be elevated to temporary status as second dancers. Second dancers sometimes descended to the rank of *figurant* as they got older. Male dancers at all levels had the option of teaching; there is no evidence that women did so as a regular occupation, though individuals managed to teach on a small scale.[1] If lesser women dancers helped in dancing schools, their names were not advertised.

Because the audience demanded novelty, principal dancers could not expect to be hired for consecutive seasons.[2] The ballet-master also changed virtually every year, though the most popular dancers and masters might be offered return engagements at a later date. The 'leader of the dances' seems to have been fairly secure, and some *figurants* (mostly men) can be traced over a number of years. But the advertised personnel—the dancers who attracted an audience—changed with dizzying regularity. A new company had to be taught new dances, so in most seasons there was an almost complete change of repertoire. As the decade wore on, a handful of *ballets d'action* attained the status of classics and were revived with some attention to previous productions, but *divertissements* were expected to vary, even in the rare instances when a title was carried over.

For a normal night's performance the dance department provided ballets after each act of the opera: one or two *divertissements* and a longer, or at least more demanding, ballet to finish the evening. Normally, a further

---

[1] For evidence that Mlle Théodore, Mme Simonet, and Mme Rossi taught, see the *Morning Herald*, 9 Feb. 1782, 18 Jan. 1783, 20 Nov. and 4 Dec. 1784. For a report of a client's refusing to pay Louis Simonet for teaching his mistress, Miss Harvey, and then assaulting him behind the scenes in the opera-house, see the same paper, 8, 12, 14 Jan. and 9 Feb. 1782, and Lady Mary Coke, 5 Jan. 1782.

[2] The only exception is Le Picq, and he may be said to prove the rule. He danced from the spring of 1782 through the 1784–85 season, but by the end of that time he had worn out his welcome.

production in each category would be introduced soon after the start of the season, providing the possibility of alternation. In the course of a season the company expected to present between seven and fourteen ballets, depending on their popularity, the budget, and the extent to which the ballet-master could inspire his dancers. No more than about four dances were kept in repertoire, though pieces from earlier in the season might be revived at any point. Special efforts were often made for benefit performances: the ballet-master or the recipient might put together an entire production for that night. However, in such cases the emphasis was usually on display of dance rather than on story. For example, in making up the *divertissement* for his 1785 benefit, Nivelon reused a scene that the critic for the *London Magazine* recognized from *Le seigneur bienfaisant*.[1] The reviewer was pleased

both by the exertion of the dancers, and the intrinsic merit of the performance. The most remarkable part of it is the mock minuet between Frederick and Dorival; a most laughable contrast to the graceful manner of Signora Angiolini. The concluding part of this first dance, hath, in our eyes, the greater merit by offering at one view, the three stiles of dancing united, viz. serious, demi-character and comic, performed altogether to the same music, and exhibiting the completest groupe that imagination can conceive.

The contrast of styles made a recycled ballet acceptable. The second dance that night was a version of *La rosière de Salency*, to which the same magazine devoted a plot summary but little evaluation, a hint that perhaps the story was not altogether clear from the performance. Now and then such a *pièce d'occasion* proved popular enough to enter the regular repertoire, and there are exceptional instances of major productions that originated as benefits.

Over the course of this decade the audience came to expect the repertoire to include at least one *ballet d'action*. Such productions remained the exception, however vital to the company's success. A sensible ballet-master would prefer to get acquainted with his company before launching into a major production, so they seldom came early in the season. Narrative ballets were extremely expensive to mount and difficult to co-ordinate, and they required dancers who could act. In addition, stories that could be told in mime proved surprisingly difficult to find.

A great ballet-master was one who could discover or create such stories and convey them effectively. Almost anyone could, after a fashion, put together and run a dance company; with good enough dancers, one might

---

[1] *London Magazine*, Mar. 1785, 219–20.

get by without much in the way of stories. But whether a ballet-master could contribute to the stock of *ballets d'action*—or even attempted to do so—was a measure of how seriously he regarded his profession. Surprisingly few learnt even to imitate the successful *ballets d'action* of others.[1] Of the eight ballet-masters employed by the King's Theatre in this period, the only ones who were able to extend the form while in London were Le Picq and Dauberval. Virtuoso male dancers often felt compelled to attempt some choreography, but ability to perform was no guarantee of ability to invent dances. To be fair, at least three of the men who experimented with the *ballet d'action* in London (Le Picq, Dauberval, and Didelot) went on to successful careers as choreographers elsewhere.

The limits of the evidence preserved about this period are severe. No subscriber's prospectus with proposed repertoire appears to survive. Newspaper advertisements at the beginning of the season name the ballet-master and first and second dancers, but never the *figurants*. Surviving scenarios for *ballets d'action* usually include casts, but often identify *figurants* only by category, not by name. A few lists of dancers appear in opera librettos.[2] The best documentation of the dance company comes from day-by-day newspaper advertisements, which are tricky to interpret. Their content and format changes with the theatre administration, so advertisements for some seasons yield more than for others. For example, in 1789–90 the dancers are always named in unvarying hierarchical order, whereas under ballet-masters like Dauberval and Le Picq, the order of advertisement sometimes reflects the importance of the characters or the order of the dancers' appearance in a particular ballet.

In the course of the 1780s newspapers started to carry more and better-informed reports about dance. Some were legitimate critiques; others were manifestly 'bought'; all favour principal dancers and usually ignore the rest of the company. The few extant scenarios and scores are of only limited

---

[1] In the period under discussion, most women dancers did not attempt even this. Mlle Guimard revived *Ninette à la cour* for a colleague's benefit on 14 May 1789, and she was supervising the dance component of a special entertainment when the opera-house burnt down in June, preventing the production (*The Times*, 10 and 11 June). At most women might contribute single numbers: Théodore offered a *Minuet and Gavotte* 'of her own composing' as part of her 8 May 1783 benefit, but Le Picq did the chief *pièce d'occasion* for the evening. Mlle Dorival likewise provided her own *pas seul* on 27 Jan. 1785.

[2] Such a list sometimes also records dances integral to an opera, as in the 1785 *Orfeo*, but most do not. Company policy in 1787–88 and 1788–89, for example, was to name principal dancers in opera librettos, but there is no indication that these operas contained purpose-made dances.

help. One can never recapture even a shadow of the actual work done by the dancers. However, by studying the patterns of the company's hiring and repertoire one can learn a surprising amount about what it offered and how the dancers and dances were received.

## II. The *Ballet d'action* Comes to London, 1778–1781

When Sheridan and Harris bought into the opera, London was a sleepy backwater in terms of current trends in dance. Since the 1760s Noverre had created *ballets d'action* all over Europe and, unlike most other ballet-masters, had published his scenarios; but to British audiences in 1778 dance that told an elaborate story by means of mime was only a rumour from the Continent.[1] Three seasons later Noverre himself was lured to London, where he put on a season of unprecedented distinction. Even before that the change in management affected the established patterns of dance repertoire at the King's Theatre.

### *The* Status quo *in 1778*

The resident ballet-master was Louis Simonet. A journeyman dancer with the advantage of French training, Simonet came to London in 1776 and remained a force in the dance world for more than ten years. Though conservative, he was at least competent both as dancer and as ballet-master, and his was a stable, well-regulated department. Had he been less flexible (or less generous in outlook), he might have moved or retired to teaching when he was badly treated by various managers in the mid-1780s. Instead—no doubt mindful of the fact that he had three dancing daughters to place—he remained a reliable fall-back on whom the opera depended, rather than a villain in the story that follows.

By autumn 1778 Simonet had enjoyed two seasons of routine *divertissements*, which he labelled only *Grand Serious Ballet* or *New Ballet*. He was

---

[1] On the history of the *ballet d'action*, see Marian Hannah Winter, *The Pre-Romantic Ballet* (London: Pitman, 1974); Baird Hastings, *Choreographer and Composer* (New York: Twayne, 1983); and Joan Lawson, *A History of Ballet and Its Makers* (New York: Pitman, 1964). Ivor Guest treats the period discussed below at the beginning of *The Romantic Ballet in England* (London: Phoenix House, [1954]). Although several of John Weaver's productions, beginning with *The Loves of Mars and Venus* (1717), can be considered *ballets d'action*, no tradition of such dances grew up in England, and few members of the 1778 audience could have seen Weaver's work. On Weaver, see Peggy van Praagh and Peter Brinson, *The Choreographic Art* (London: Adam & Charles Black, 1963), and Richard Ralph, *The Life and Works of John Weaver* (New York: Dance Horizons, 1985).

proud of his wife Adelaide's abilities and featured her in many of his compositions. Otherwise, the most remarkable thing about his tenure is the extent to which he was willing to share the task of composition with the principal male dancers. Vallouis, Zuchelli, and Banti all presented dances in which one of the Simonets usually participated. The size of the ballet company is unknown, but there were usually at least two principal couples and perhaps another less important one (second dancers), two or three character dancers, and a group of *figurants*. Simonet expected to begin a season with three new ballets, two of them fairly short, one rather longer. The initial dances were expected to serve with either comic or serious opera and might be repeated for several weeks.

None of the scenarios for Simonet's ballets was ever published, nor were his dances reviewed, so only the titles and occasional brief descriptions in advertisements remain.[1] Giovanni Battista Noferi's music was at this time being issued in annual collections of *Opera Dances* (published by J. Welcker), but these are simply miscellanies of brief pieces and rarely include descriptive titles or dancers' names. With the benefit of hindsight, one can nevertheless detect the approach of the *ballet d'action*. Before 1778 Simonet's work remained very much in the tradition of theatricalized social dance and character dances based on *commedia dell'arte* figures. On 4 February 1777, for example, a new comic opera concluded with 'a new *Masquerade Dance*' comprising 'a *Provençal* by Vallouy le cadet; a *Scaramouch* by Signor and Signora Zuchelli; a *Minuet* by Mons and Mme Simonet; to conclude with a *Country Dance* by all the Characters'. Not only was this assemblage unrelated to the opera, it was also easy to vary if someone was hurt or ill, since the parts had no definite relationship to one another. A similar *Masquerade Dance* was described on 3 March 1778 as 'incident to the opera' (*L'amore artigiano* by Gassmann), but for the performance a week later the audience was warned of a substitution. '*Minuet* by Simonet and Signora Jermoli in place of *Minuet de la cour and gavot*', noted the advertisement, which went on to explain that 'Mlle Baccelli being still unable to dance, Signora Jermoli [a singer], has . . . undertaken to dance a Minuet, in her character of Angiolina, with Simonet'. A letter to the *Morning Post* on 16 March 1778

---

[1] The libretto of Sacchini's *Enea e Lavinia* (1779) contains brief descriptions of the ballets made for this opera, presumably by Simonet, though he is not directly credited there or in advertisements. The most detailed account, for *Hippomenes and Atalanta*, is devoted to the background of the story rather than the action of the ballet. The third ballet, *La fête du ciel*, had no title as of the time the libretto went to press.

acknowledged that Jermoli was no Baccelli, but the fact that such a substitution was even attempted shows that a connection still existed between social dancing and the lower reaches of theatrical dancing. A performance of *La governante* on 15 June 1779 included another example of fairly direct exchange between social and theatrical dancing: Simonet's introduction of 'the *Quadrilles* danced at the Pantheon last night' by his principal dancers into the same *New Ballet* that had been in the repertoire all season.

Some ballets of Simonet's early years had more enticing titles: *La sérénade interrompue* (24 February 1778) and *La surprize de Daphnis et Céphise* (31 March 1778) at least suggest an element of drama. Most of them contained only hints of a story: *Les amusemens champêtres, Les amans unis par l'Hymen, L'amour dans la vendange, La paysane distraite, Les amans heureux; ou, L'aimable viellesse.* Amusing local customs and temporarily obstructed courtships are the obvious themes. A stage of development closer to the *ballet d'action* is a title that depends on the audience's knowing a story, as in the case of Simonet's first offering in November 1777, *Le devin du village.* If this were merely a succession of dances, there would be no gain from invoking Rousseau's *intermède.* But titles that imply a story, however promising, make up a very small part of the repertoire both in relation to other titles and in terms of the number of performances achieved. New management changed that pattern.

## Innovation by Simonet and Guiardele, 1778–1781
### Ballet Repertoire for 1778–79[1]

*Annette et Lubin,* Simonet, 24 November 1778, 'a new Pantomime Ballet' (16 performances)

*La noce hollandoise* [advertised as *La noche hollandoise*], Simonet, 24 November 1778 (18 performances)

*Les nymphes de Diane, ou L'amour faune,* Simonet, 24 November 1778, 'a new grand Serious Ballet' (13 performances)

*New Ballet,* no choreographer credited, 28 November 1778, 'connected with' *Demofoonte* (20 performances)

*Les moissonneurs,* no choreographer credited, 22 December 1778, music by Paisiello (24 performances)

*Les oiseleurs,* no choreographer credited, 23 January 1779 (14 performances)

**Ballet by Genii of the Various Arts**, no choreographer credited, 23 February 1779, part of Act II of Grétry's *Zemira e Azore* (11 performances) (p. 448)

---

[1] Dances omitted from the season repertoire in Part 5 of *The London Stage* are marked with an asterisk (*). Ballets discussed at some length are given in **bold italic**. Some titles are in French and others in English because the company was inconsistent about anglicizing titles in advertisements.

**Ballet by the Fairies of the Court of Azore**, no choreographer credited, 23 February 1779, part of Act II of *Zemira e Azore* (18 performances) (p. 448)

**Le couronnement de Zémire**, no choreographer credited, 23 February 1779, 'a new serious Ballet' at the end of *Zemira e Azore* (10 performances) (p. 448)

*Hippomène et Atalante*, no choreographer credited, 25 March 1779 (11 performances)

*Les forges de Vulcain*, no choreographer credited, 25 March 1779, 'a new Ballet, connected with' *Enea e Lavinia*, 'entirely new' music by Carl Stamitz (7 performances)

*La fête du ciel*, no choreographer credited, 25 March 1779, 'a new Serious Ballet' (8 performances)

*La bravoure des femmes*, no choreographer credited (but probably by Simonet), 15 April 1779, 'a new grand Military Pantomime Ballet' (1 performance)

*Les paysans volés*, no choreographer credited, 15 May 1779 (11 performances)

*La sérénade interrompue*, no choreographer credited, 15 May 1779, 'a new Ballet Espagnol', revived from 24 February 1778 with a *pas de deux* by Noferi (7 performances)

*New Divertissement*, no choreographer credited, 29 May 1779 (3 performances)

When Sheridan and Harris took over the King's Theatre the personnel of the dance company hardly changed. This was Pacchierotti's first season as *primo uomo*, and bringing him to London probably took a disproportionate part of the budget. Continuity limited the degree to which the dance company could change its ways, but it also proves that the abrupt shift in repertoire stems directly from the new owners. Ballets suddenly acquired titles; many more were offered during the season; and more dancers were advertised. The last change is probably just a matter of public relations. No doubt the company had had 'second dancers' all along and simply failed to publicize them, and titles alone do not make ballets. But management had obviously decided to 'promote' ballet more aggressively and systematically than before.

The variety of titles for dances implies that more money was invested in costuming them. Simonet continued to do some old-fashioned pieces like the *New Ballet* (28 November 1778), which could use almost any costumes pulled from stock. But *Les moissonneurs*, *La noce hollandoise*, and *Hippomène et Atalante* required different costumes, if not new ones. Again the departure from earlier practice is likely to have been one of degree rather than kind: Simonet had done ballets featuring classical characters, courtiers, and peasants of various nationalities before, but they are harder for the historian to identify when titles are less specific.

The most interesting production of 1778–79 shows what the dance company was reaching for. On 23 February 1779 Simonet contributed to a new production of Grétry's *Zemira e Azore* three ballets much more closely related to the opera than had been the norm. Act II contained a 'Ballet by

447

Genii of the Various Arts' that included the Zuchellis, the Simonets' eldest daughter Rosine, and 'Hochbrucher, like a Genius of Instrumental Music', playing on the pedal harp. After the second act came a 'Ballet by the Fairies of the Court of Azore', danced by Banti, Signora Tinti, Le Det, Henry, Rosine Simonet, and Mlle Baccelli, a local favourite, in her first appearance of the season. (See Pl. 12.) The evening ended with a serious ballet entitled *Le couronnement de Zémire*, which featured the Simonets, the Zuchellis, Banti, Signora Tinti, and Slingsby. This attempt to construct an integral connection between an opera and the entire evening's offerings of dance was highly unusual for London, though quite standard in Paris. It may represent Le Texier's aesthetic ideas: as company manager he was in a position to encourage the opera and dance departments to co-operate.

One danger of such integration is the greater difficulty of recycling the dance material with other operas later in the season. The allegory of artistic *genii* could presumably have been grafted on to other productions, but this one was not. The *Ballet by the Fairies*, however, was performed seven times with other operas this season. Contrariwise, one would expect performances of *Zemira e Azore* to retain the dances created specially for that opera but, at the Simonets' benefit on 15 April 1779, the coronation masque was changed to 'a new grand Military Pantomime Ballet, *La bravoure des femmes*, in which Mme Simonet, in the character of Leading Officer, will fight a Duel at Small Sword. Other Principal Parts by Mlle Baccelli, who will dance a *Minuet* with Mme Simonet'. A vehicle for virtuoso display was more important on a benefit night than aesthetic integration between opera and ballet. The Simonets' status and the importance of dance in its own right are emphasized by the fact that only Pacchierotti's benefit preceded theirs this season.

The degree to which the integration of dance and opera in *Zemira e Azore* was extraordinary is evident when one looks at the first two operas of the same season, which opened on 24 and 28 November 1778. The move towards story-ballet suggests that Simonet had been sent abroad the previous summer to learn what was happening in the French dance world. After Act I of Sacchini's *L'avaro deluso* he offered 'a new Pantomime Ballet, *Annette et Lubin*'. Dibdin had opened a one-act comic opera of this title on 2 October at Covent Garden (based on the play by Favart and Santerre), but Simonet was presumably working from Noverre's controversial new ballet, done at the Opéra in July 1778. The second-act dance made almost no pretence of story: it was a simple mélange called *La noce hollandoise.* The last dance for *L'avaro deluso* was 'a new grand Serious Ballet, *Les nymphes de Diane; ou, L'amour faune'.* The first two dances, however inappropriate, were pressed into service for the pasticcio *Demofoonte,* since it opened so soon after the comic opera. By the time Simonet got to the closing number for *Demofoonte,* the strain of opening four new ballets in a week was showing, and the piece that became the corner-stone of the year's repertoire bears only the title *New Ballet.* But dance in 1778–79 was already more interesting than in the two previous seasons, because final ballets could be alternated; and after Simonet added another entr'acte ballet, *Les moissonneurs,* on 22 December, even more combinations were possible. The difference between the hotch-potch at the beginning of the season (despite its advantages for varying repertoire) and the Grétry opera with its integrated dances is marked. That Simonet was able to galvanize the same dancers into doing vastly more work for 1778–79 than they had the previous season suggests the level of excitement felt around the house.

Nevertheless, various weaknesses and limitations are apparent. The principal dancers often preferred fairly rigid partnerships: the Simonets usually danced together, the Zuchellis almost always did. Signora Tinti's usual partner was Banti, but his health was not good, and Le Det sometimes had to substitute for him (for example, on 29 December and 29 May). There might be physical or stylistic reasons why dancers appeared together, but the hiring of couples would diminish sharply in the years ahead. Partnerships had the advantage that at least for *divertissements* couples could rehearse independently, and the performers often appear to have followed pretty much their own lines. Simonet himself danced with his wife and with Mlle Baccelli when she joined the company in late February. His eldest daughter, Rosine, appeared in the *Ballet of the Fairies* and later as Cupid in *Les forges de Vulcain.* Simon Slingsby danced Vulcan in the latter, which was 'connected with' Sacchini's serious opera *Enea e Lavinia,* in that it involved Aeneas' mother, Venus. In the serious ballet at the end of the same production, Mme Simonet portrayed Apollo and then danced in men's dress in the grand *Chaconne.* She often danced *en travesti* at the couple's benefits, though not usually in regular performances. Simonet managed to get more variety out of his company than might have been predicted from the almost unchanged roster. Sheridan and Harris, however, were evidently not satisfied, and for the next season they imported a new ballet-master.

## Ballet Repertoire for 1779–80

*Grand Serious Ballet*, Guiardele, 27 November 1779, 'connected with' *Alessandro nell'Indie*,
  'in which the celebrated *Chaconne*' by Jommelli (21 performances)
*Indian Ballet*, Zuchelli, 27 November 1779, 'adapted to' *Alessandro nell'Indie* (8 perform-
  ances)
*Pastoral Ballet*, Zuchelli and Slingsby, 27 November 1779 (24 performances)
*Il disertore*, Zuchelli, 14 December 1779, 'a new Pantomime Dance' (18 performances)
*Masquerade Dance*, no choreographer credited, 14 December 1779 (12 performances)
*Grand Ballet*, no choreographer credited, 14 December 1779, 'new; connected with' *La conta-
  dina in corte* (8 performances)
*La bergère coquette; ou, Le triomphe de l'amour*, no choreographer credited, 22 January 1780, 'a
  new Ballet, Demi-caractere' (14 performances)
*Serious Ballet*, Guiardele, 22 January 1780, 'connected with' *Quinto Fabio* (27 performances)
*The Female Warriors*, Simonet, 20 April 1780 (1 performance)
*The Serenade Interrupted, or La serenata spagnola interrotta*, Simonet, 20 April 1780, revived
  from 15 May 1779, with a *pas de deux* by Noferi (9 performances)
*La fête pastorale*, Guiardele, 22 April 1780 (9 performances)
*The Rural Sports*, Guiardele, 22 April 1780 (11 performances)
*New Serious Ballet*, Guiardele, 9 May 1780, 'to conclude with a *Grand Chaconne* of Jomelli'
  (9 performances)
*Il filosofo*, Zuchelli, 9 May 1780 (10 performances)

Favre Guiardele was a Noverre protégé, which probably explains his being hired for 1779–80.[1] The season was pedestrian and unsuccessful, in part at least because of budget constraints. Severe economies were effected in the wake of the £7,000 deficit of the new management's first season. Besides Guiardele, the only new dancer hired was Anna Tantini. Zaccaria Banti apparently left the company, and other stalwarts of the previous regime (including Simonet) were not advertised.[2] The company's offerings were not helped by Sheridan's continuing to borrow dancers regularly for service at Drury Lane.

Guiardele arrived late, so for the first night of the season he staged only the *Grand Serious Ballet*. Zuchelli deputized, providing an *Indian Ballet* to serve as one of the 'first dances' with *Alessandro nell'Indie*; and with Simon Slingsby he put together a *Pastorale Dance* for the same evening. A month later Guiardele concocted a *New Grand Ballet* and perhaps a 'grand *Masquerade Dance*', though his name was not attached to it. The company had

---

[1] See *Biographical Dictionary*, vi. 444–5. He was dancing in Milan in 1775, but his experience as a choreographer is undocumented.
[2] Simonet's presence in the company may be deduced only from his 'first appearance this
season' at his wife's benefit on 20 Apr. 1780, which he supervised, and from a petition of
about Dec. 1784 in which he claims to have been a member of the company for ten years (LC
7/3, fo. 252ʳ).

returned to generic titles. Only three of the ballets during the season appear to have had a discernible story, and two of them (*Il disertore* and *Il filosofo*) were credited to Zuchelli. The second of Zuchelli's pieces may have been assigned to him after Guiardele failed to give adequate instructions to the furies who battered Pacchierotti during the last act of *Rinaldo* at its première (discussed in Ch. 4). Despite Noverre's tutelage, Guiardele was not the choreographer for whom the King's Theatre was looking. The result of his mediocrity and a pinched budget was a dispirited season. During 1780–81 Sheridan transferred the theatre piecemeal to Taylor in return for assumption of debts, and Taylor made expensive improvements in dance.

## Ballet Repertoire for 1780–81

*New Ballet*, no choreographer credited, 25 November 1780 (2 performances)
*The Country Gallant*, Simonet, 25 November 1780 (6 performances)
*The Fortunate Escape*, Simonet, 25 November 1780 (23 performances)
*The Squire Outwitted, or Le marquis désappointé*, Zuchelli, 2 December 1780 (4 performances)
*Les amans surpris*, Simonet, 16 December 1780 (22 performances)
*Grand Serious Ballet*, Simonet, 16 December 1780 (16 performances)
*The Pert Country Maid*, Simonet, 13 January 1781, 'a new comic Ballet' (15 performances)
*The Nymphs of Diana*, Simonet, 23 January 1781, 'a new serious Ballet' [but see 1778–79] (10 performances)[1]
*The Rural Sports*, Simonet, 23 January 1781, 'a new grand Ballet half-character' (15 performances)[2]
*The Country Diversions*, Simonet, 22 February 1781, 'a new Pastoral Ballet' (8 performances)
**Ninette à la cour**, 'composed by' Vestris sen., 22 February 1781 (19 performances) (p. 452)[3]
*Les caprices de Galatée*, 'composed by' Vestris sen., 29 March 1781, 'a new Ballet Anacréontique' (10 performances)[4]

[1] On 24 Nov. 1778 the Simonets, Banti, and Signora Tinti had appeared in Simonet's 'new grand Serious Ballet' entitled *Les nymphes de Diane; ou, L'amour faune*. Of the 1781 cast, at least Vestris jun., Mlle Baccelli, and Signora Crespi were new, but there is no way of telling in what other respects the 1781 version differed from the earlier one.

[2] A ballet by this title was credited to Guiardele on 22 April 1780, with the Zuchellis, Henry, Miss Andreas, Miss Simonet, and Signora Crespi in the cast. The 1781 cast included Vestris jun., Mlle Baccelli, Henry, Signora Crespi, Traffieri, Slingsby, and Signora Tantini. How else the productions differed is unknown. Later in the decade if a ballet-master intended to copy rather than adapt and build on someone else's production, the practice would be to invoke the creator's name, but such niceties were not yet observed at the King's Theatre. Reuse of this title invited the audience to compare the versions, presumably to Simonet's advantage.

[3] The plot summary published in the *Public Advertiser* of 26 Feb. 1781 proves that the story was that of the ballet Maximilien Gardel did in Aug. 1778 at the Opéra and earlier at Choisy. To what extent Vestris sen. copied the dances is unknown.

[4] Vestris sen. was presumably copying, or improving, Noverre's one-act ballet of this title. See Spire Pitou, *The Paris Opéra: Rococo and Romantic, 1715–1815* (Westport, Conn.: Greenwood, 1985), 91–2.

*Médée et Jason*, 'composed by' Vestris sen., 29 March 1781, 'a new Ballet Tragique', music by Noferi (21 performances) (p. 455)[1]
*[Dances in] *L'omaggio*, Vestris sen., 5 June (4 performances)

The ballet-master named in the 1780–81 season announcement,[2] Traffieri, did not arrive until January, so Simonet was restored to that position. Money had been found to hire a rising star from the Paris Opéra, Vestris jun. With him came his father, still known as 'le dieu de la danse', and now increasingly committed to choreography. Together they changed the course of dance, and incidentally of dance criticism, in London.[3] Vestris jun. was far superior to any dancer seen in England since Dauberval in 1764. Skilful promotion turned him into a celebrity. He was highly paid, sought after by everyone, commemorated with souvenirs of all kinds, and even rioted over. Unfortunately, dance criticism in the newspapers was not yet up to recording many details of what made him so successful—though merely competent dancing, however well promoted, could not have achieved the same effect. More important in the long run, Vestris father and son were able to produce *ballets d'action*.

Simonet was duly credited with providing most of the ballets of the season—the requisite *Grand Serious Ballet* and a classical excursus, *The Nymphs of Diana*, as well as happy peasant dances worked into minimal courtship stories with titles such as *The Rural Sports* and *Country Diversions*. With great tact Vestris sen. made himself available to stage and perform in one of the productions at his son's benefit, and William Taylor, trusting in his experience, agreed to underwrite a genuine *ballet d'action* for the occasion. London had never seen the like.[4]

The show-piece of Vestris jun.'s benefit was *Ninette à la cour* ('Nancy: or, The Country Girl at Court'), a three-act 'grand Pantomime Ballet' credited in newspapers to Vestris sen. (but in fact following Maximilien Gardel). Mlle Baccelli danced the title-role; Vestris jun. was her lover, Colas; Vestris sen. and Mme Simonet were the Prince and Countess; and Simonet

---

[1] Vestris sen. was again following Noverre.

[2] *Public Advertiser*, 3 Nov. 1780.

[3] The following discussion is based on Judith Milhous, 'Vestris-mania and the Construction of Celebrity: Auguste Vestris in London, 1780–81', forthcoming in *Harvard Library Bulletin*.

[4] The 18 Feb. 1783 *Public Advertiser* dates 'the first introduction of the ballets called *d'Action*' from when 'Vestris held the sceptre of Terpsychore at the King's Theatre'. Rumour put the investment at £1,200 (*Public Advertiser*, 22 Feb. 1781). For the full text of Vestris jun.'s contract, see Milhous, 'Vestris-mania'; Vestris sen.'s contract is known only from the report in the *Public Advertiser* of 3 Mar. 1781 that he would perform in his son's benefit and on a limited schedule thereafter.

appeared as the Dancing-Master.[1] Eight other dancers were named in the cast-list, which includes up to sixteen 'Figure Dancers', some of whom no doubt doubled as the Captain of the Prince's Life Guards, two Equerries, four Pages, four Waiting Women, two Notaries, and the Dancing-Master's Attendant (*Public Advertiser*, 26 February 1781). This ballet was far more ambitious in scale than had been customary at the King's Theatre—'the most splendid Entertainment of the Kind ever exhibited in England', the head-note to the plot summary called it. This hyperbole may not be much of an exaggeration: the production was apparently much more elaborate than had been the norm for dance. In the future scenarios would often be published for *ballets d'action*, either with operas or as separate pamphlets, but until this date none had been necessary.

*Ninette* was easy for the audience to follow because Sacchini's opera *La contadina in corte*, most recently revived in February 1780, used a version of the story. However, the plot of the ballet took a different turn. In the opera, class proves no barrier to Sandrina, who marries the baron. Her country lover goes back home with a former girlfriend. The stakes are higher in the ballet, however: the noble hunter who falls in love with Ninette in Act I is not a baron, but a prince, and one for whom an appropriate marriage has been arranged with a countess. To punish Colas after a lovers' quarrel, Ninette, unaware of the countess, accepts the 'protection' of the prince. Unlike Sandrina, in the second act Ninette does not assimilate to the court, though she learns to pass for a lady well enough to fool Colas when he comes looking for her. Making an alliance with the countess, she switches places with her so that the prince unwittingly pursues an assignation with his fiancée. When all is discovered, Ninette of course returns to Colas, and the third act features their country wedding, attended by all their friends as well as the prince and countess.

The story allows for several crowd scenes such as the court ball, providing spectacle, but its effectiveness depends on the acting abilities of Ninette, Colas, the Prince, and the Countess. The greatest opportunities in this ballet go to Ninette, who not only has the most stage time and the most control over the action, but is the character who must embody in succession all the social gradations to be found in the ballet, returning at the end to her

---

[1] While the casting was determined in part by competence of the available dancers, it also embodied a compliment to Simonet and possibly to other dancers. Compare the cast in the 1778 Gardel scenario: King—Vestris [sen.]; Countess—Mlle Heinel; Fabrice—Gardel cadet; Colas—Dauberval; Ninette—Mlle Guimard; Dancing-Master—Gardel l'aîné.

comfortable 'country' self. The only reviewer to comment on the dancers particularly noticed the skill with which Mlle Baccelli imitated an unskilled dancer. He appreciated her 'Display of that rural Naivete, which forms the Character [of Ninette]. . . . We thought her as inimitable in her affected Aukwardness in attempting the Minuet, as she is, when her Part requires of her the Exertion of those extraordinary Abilities which speak her one of the first Women of her Profession.'[1] This discussion of the meta-theatrical dimension of the performance shows that London had its connoisseurs, though they seldom wrote for the newspapers.

Eighteenth-century scenarios focus on telling the story and on elaborating unspoken motivations. Mime is apt to generate detailed description, whereas the more extended a display of dance technique, the less space it receives in the scenario. The proportion of stage time devoted to dance cannot be estimated from a scenario, because mime dominates the narrative. Unfortunately, the more detailed the description of the mime, the more likely it is to seem cliché-ridden. No doubt the dance was equally convention-bound but, lost in silence, it seems more alluring. The scenario for *Ninette*, although competent and energetic, demonstrates these limitations. The most extended passage of dancing in the noble style, in the fanciest costumes, takes place at the ball in the middle of Act II. More space is devoted to the entrance and exit than to the dance. The entire description reads: 'The Scene changes to a Ball-Room, to which Nancy [Ninette] is conducted by her Pages. The Prince and the Countess supervene followed by all the Court. After various Dances, the Ball ends with a March.' Yet the reviewer commented, 'Nothing can equal the Elegance and Graces [Vestris sen.] displayed in the Minuet de la Cour but the exalted Merit of his Partner, Mme Simonet.' Aesthetically, this was the high point of the ballet.

Emotionally, the evening belonged to Ninette, who survived the intrigues of court and won Colas back. The lovers' quarrel that led to the whole adventure lends itself to description much better than either the ball at court or the third-act celebratory dances:

The Prince's Feelings being naturally hurt by the Preference she gives to Colas; he retires, and leaves her with her beloved Swain. But Colas, being now possessed with jealous Phrenzy, is far from thinking his Mistress innocent; he bitterly upbraids her Conduct, and to give the greatest Proof of his Indignation, he tears out of his Hat the Ribbands and the Flowers he had received from her as the Pledges of their

---

[1] *Public Advertiser*, 26 Feb. 1781.

approaching Wedding, and then leaves her. She runs after him, trying every Method to soothe his groundless Rage, but he rebukes her more severely than ever, and endeavouring to get rid of her, inadvertently pushes her down. When he sees her fall, he instantly repents the Rudeness of his Usage; helps her to rise, and throws himself at her Feet, imploring her Pardon. The beautiful Shepherdess pouring forth a Deluge of Tears, in all the Storm of Grief, reproaches her Swain with his unaccountable Cruelty; and meditates a Revenge. The Prince appearing this Moment, she does not miss the Opportunity.

On the printed page the rejected love tokens and kneeling apology may seem formulaic; the vengeful woman is certainly a stereotype. There is no way to recapture what made the performance so charming. Vestris jun. had already established his considerable sex appeal, which this role exploited, even though it gave him less stage time than one might expect for a beneficiary. Because his role was comparatively small, he had to work hard to keep from being overshadowed by his father or Mlle Baccelli, since most of his scenes were with her. One of the two 'official' pictures of Vestris jun. from this season is in the role of Colas, and there is reason to think this is how he chose to be remembered. (See Pl. 13.) Whether *Ninette* served Vestris jun. well or not, it paved the way for the introduction of multiple-act ballet in London. Except in the number of costumes, the ballet made no unusual technical demands on the theatre. *Ninette*, which enjoyed nineteen performances during the season, was a great success.[1] The second venture in this new direction would not be so easy for the theatre or for the audience.

### Vestris sen.'s Staging of Médée et Jason

For his own benefit on 29 March 1781, Vestris sen. staged *Les caprices de Galatée*, featuring Mlle Baccelli, and for himself and Mme Simonet he produced London's first version of *Médée et Jason*.[2] The latter was performed twenty times in the twenty-eight opera nights after it had its première, a reflection of its popularity with both the audience and the dancers. That

---

[1] Estimates of what the benefit earned range from £1,400 to £3,000. Vestris sen. kept tinkering with the production, a practice that, however typical, can seldom be documented. On 27 Mar. he added a dance entitled the *Devonshire Minuet*, a gracious compliment to the duchess, and on 5 May unspecified 'improvements' were advertised for a command performance.

[2] Following contemporary London practice, Vestris sen. took credit for these ballets, though, as some papers were quick to point out, they had been created by Noverre. See the *Morning Herald* of 29 Mar. 1781. (The likely source of this information was Noverre's brother, who lived in London.) Credit for dances had not been important until this time and is another indication of how the *ballet d'action* changed the public's perception of dance.

Vestris was able to sell this tale of vengeance to an audience that expected dancers to embody little more than happy peasants or benign classical deities is testimony both to the effectiveness of Noverre's scenario and to the growing sophistication of the London audience.

Although Vestris followed the basic outline of Noverre's scenario, he changed certain details of the story and perhaps the proportions of some of the dances, for reasons that will be taken up below.[1] At a reception at the court of Corinth, Medea's jealousy is aroused when Creon repeatedly arranges for Creusa and Jason to be together. Afterwards, Creon offers Jason his throne and his daughter. Medea nearly retrieves Jason's loyalty by begging him to kill her rather than desert her, but then Creusa reappears. Jason repudiates the startled Medea in favour of the modest, infatuated Corinthian princess (a scene commemorated in a print issued by Boydell that captures Vestris sen. at his haughtiest).[2] Medea retreats to a cave and summons furies, who aid her in concocting fatal presents for her enemies. She threatens her children but decides instead to use them to deliver the gifts. The scene again changes, showing 'on the left, the Entrance to the Palace of Creon', in the background 'the Prospect of the City of Corinth', and 'on the right an open Country'. Creon abdicates his throne in favour of Jason, then pledges his former subjects to his successor. A celebration follows, during which 'the people, by their dances and other marks of joy, testify their approbation' of their new king. Jason is about to drink a nuptial toast to Creusa when Medea and the children arrive. Creon accepts the golden casket 'and retires to lay it by, little thinking of the destructive flames it contain[s]'. Medea pins the nosegay to Creusa's wedding dress, wishes the couple well, and, after mutual embraces, departs, gloating at her successful deception. The celebration resumes, but Creusa is soon stricken by poison inhaled from her nosegay. Jason is appalled but helpless. Medea reappears in her dragon chariot, the corpse of one son at her feet. Despite Jason's entreaties, she kills the other child, then throws Jason the dagger. He means to

---

[1] We are very grateful to John Ward for giving us access to what appears to be the only surviving copy of a scenario for this production, an anonymous pamphlet, *Historical Account of the Grand Tragic Ballet Called Medæa* (London: G. Bigg, 1781). Vestris sen. created the role of Jason in Noverre's original production in Stuttgart in 1763, and he had participated in revivals and staged his own version several times in the intervening years. See Lynham, *Chevalier Noverre*, 167.

[2] The *Catalogue of Political Satires . . . in the British Museum*, no. 5910, dates this print 3 July 1781, but does not identify Creusa or relate the print to this moment in the ballet. The Harvard Theatre Collection owns a separate picture of Mlle Baccelli as Creusa, drawn by Roberts, engraved by Albanesi, and published by Harris on 7 Jan. 1782.

stab himself, but is prevented by the furies. Medea throws them a lighted torch with which to set the palace on fire. Jason 'wrenches from one of the furies the dagger, with which he puts an end to his wretched existence', and Medea flies away, 'rejoicing at the dire effects of her relentless, inhuman revenge'.

Thirteen of Giovanni Battista Noferi's dances for this ballet were published by James Blundell in *The Celebrated Dances Performed by the Messrs. Vestris &c. at the King's Theatre*, Book III (1781). What is printed seems a little short for the entire score; Ivor Guest has suggested to us that this may be because the music for the mime sections was excluded. A French-style march and an exceedingly long *chaconne* are highly characterized and were therefore probably designed to reflect the choreography.[1] However, one would be rash to assign the music specific functions within the ballet.

Unlike the sorts of dances that had long predominated at the King's Theatre, *Médée et Jason* required elaborate props, scenic effects, and technical rehearsals. Joseph Hayling's accounts document the production process. On 15 March 1781 he entered in his tinkering account 'A large Square planish'd Box & altering several times . . . 15s.', which is almost certainly the casket prepared for Creon.[2] Three days before the ballet opened Hayling prepared 27 'Furies Trunchions or Machines for the Lightning', and they required repairs throughout the rest of the season. He also provided four spring-loaded daggers a week before the première, as well as four tin daggers on 28 and 29 March. Hayling records only one rehearsal, on the 28th, but it included half-light in the 'Top of the House' to permit practice with Medea's chariot and the fireworks. Since the lights were all extinguished and relighted, the company probably took a break and then went through at least the ending again. A contemporary description reports flippantly that 'Flames seiz'd on *Creon*'s hall, / And one promiscuous blaze envellop'd all.'[3] Even so, adjustments continued after the production had opened. On 2 April Hayling entered a charge for 'Nailing Eighteen Sheets of Tin for Fire Works' and on the 7th he added 'Twelve Plates wired at bottom / Stays for ditto and fixing to Wood for fire Works / Twenty four plates nailed on

---

[1] Blundell also published a five-page keyboard arrangement of *The favorite Overture to the celebrated Tragic Dance of Medee et Jason . . . Composed by Sigr. Gluck*. This is actually the overture to the opera *Iphigénie en Aulide*.

[2] This and subsequent references to Hayling's records are to C12/2147/14. See App. III. Both casket and 'empoison'd bouquet' are referred to in *An Heroic Epistle, from Monsieur Vestris, Sen: in England, to Mademoiselle Heinel in France* (London: R. Faulder, 1781), 23.

[3] *An Heroic Epistle*, 23.

Wood', along with 'A Man for two days Work'. (This mechanism had to be repaired on the 14th.) The rhetoric of a (planted?) paragraph in the *Public Advertiser* of 6 April 1781 may be exaggerated, but it documents crucial details: 'The Downfall of Creon's Palace is rendered more gloomy by the excellent Painting of Signor Novosielski, and the Rain of Fire introduced into the Midst of the general Devastation, is a very great Addition to the Performance.'[1]

The scenario shows that Vestris made several changes in the story, some of which might have been dictated by local conditions, but which had the overall effect of drawing focus away from other characters and towards Jason.[2] He retained the role he had originally created, which left Auguste no part in the story, since he could hardly play Creon or stoop to being a fury. Thus the most popular dancer in London made only a cameo appearance as a prince in *Médée et Jason*. Louis Simonet was the right age to play Creusa's father, and Noverre's account of the last scene gave Creon the first death, dramatically sprawled over the steps of the throne he had just vacated. Rather than share the last scene with him, Vestris sen. implausibly directs that Creon retire to put away his present, having him die offstage and unremarked, even though Medea had elaborately shut up 'the most devouring flames' in the casket (and the company had spent money on a functional prop). Jason spends less time with Medea than with the Corinthians, so it is perhaps not surprising that the early scenes are intact, but Medea's conjuring scene is reduced. The London scenario gives details of her interaction with only four furies, rather than the six Noverre includes. This lessens the tension built up in her ritual preparation of the weapons of her revenge. In the simplified last scene, Jason, having failed to succour Creusa, is also powerless to prevent Medea from killing the second child, but he does not immediately stab himself in despair. Rather, furies intercept the dagger and torment him. No death could compete with Medea's exit in a dragon chariot, but Vestris delayed it as long as he could. After the palace begins to burn (and the court presumably flees, as in the Noverre version), Jason is allowed to dispatch himself and Medea to depart. While the Vestris scenario is too derivative to be considered an independent creation, it is no worse a distortion than twentieth-century versions of the *ballets blancs* have sometimes been.

---

[1] Virtually the same paragraph appeared in the *Morning Chronicle* on the same date.

[2] Comparisons are to Noverre's scenario in *Recueil de programmes de ballets de M. Noverre* (Vienna: Joseph Kurzböck, 1776), British Library 11739.a.7.

Much of the audience would have had no basis of comparison for the production and may have been well satisfied with what Vestris presented. Because *Médée et Jason* had its première on a benefit night, editorial policy precluded the newspapers from reviewing it, nor did they comment on later performances. The effect, especially in contrast to enthusiasm earlier in the season, is a stunned silence in the historical record.[1] One sign that the audience found the work difficult, however fascinating, is the demand for scenarios. All they had to go on the first night was a cast-list and a paragraph summarizing the story, a single sheet at the back of the libretto of the night's opera, *Piramo e Tisbe*. Only after two more performances did a scenario become available, 'By desire of the Frequenters of the Opera House' (*Public Advertiser*, 7 April 1781). The King's Theatre, recognizing a potential source of revenue, did not offer this scenario to the newspapers, as had been done with *Ninette*. But the company was just learning to estimate demand for such ephemera. Three issues were necessary before the end of the season, yet only a single copy appears to survive.[2]

Three other responses to the ballet show that not everyone was prepared to take it seriously. Boydell's satirical print portrays not one of the more climactic moments in the ballet, but one of the more clichéd. As part of a campaign against the Vestris as highly paid French dancers the print was intended to ridicule, not endorse, their accomplishments. A more immediate response was a burlesque that took place at a masquerade at Hanover Square on 8 June 1781, the second night of *L'omaggio*. The reporter for the *Public Advertiser* (11 June) missed the performance, but noted that the participants were unnamed 'Gentlemen and Ladies who paid the full Price for their Admission, and who of themselves had previously formed the Party'. The amateur origins of this burlesque may explain why the *Lady's Magazine* carried an unusually full report on it.[3] Creon became a Justice of the Peace, his daughter a 'Boarding-school Miss', Medea a Gypsy with 'Parish Children', who was aided by a Butcher (the Demon of Revenge) and Chimney-sweepers (Nurse, Priest, Furies). Jason was merely himself: Vestris sen.

---

[1] Patrons of the King's Theatre were ill prepared for Noverre's willingness to depict violent death on stage, since opera plots lagged behind dance in this respect. See Marita P. McClymonds, '"La morte di Semiramide" . . . and the Restoration of Death and Tragedy to the Italian Operatic Stage', 286–7.

[2] The *Morning Herald* of 26 Apr. 1781 and the *Morning Chronicle* of 22 May report second and third 'editions'.

[3] *Lady's Magazine; or Entertaining Companion for the Fair Sex*, xii (June 1781), 303–4. We owe this reference to the kindness of John Ward.

needed no alternative character. Vestris jun. was concealed among the anonymous courtiers. The action followed that of the scenario very closely except for the end, which replaced the dragon chariot and shower of fire with a good fairy to revive 'Kings, Queens, Lords and Commons' so they could 'join, one and all, in a country-dance'. The performers could have attended *Médée et Jason* as many as fourteen times; they had ample opportunity to select postures and gestures to imitate. With some musical quotations, the story should have been quite recognizable to fellow opera-goers. The public display of this elaborate private jest is apparently unique in the period and could only have happened before *ballets d'action* had become a familiar part of the opera season. Gallini sponsored the masquerade, which was catered by Claridge of St James's Street. Both reports indicate that the burlesque was extremely well received. George Colman the elder treated ordinary theatre-goers to a professional burlesque at the Little Theatre in the Haymarket, beginning 8 August 1781, in which Punch represented Creon, Pierrot played Jason, and Medea was presented as the traditional English witch, Mother Shipton. Such attention from the summer theatre indicates how topical the ballet remained.

Vestris sen. unquestionably brought ballet at the King's Theatre to a height it had never before achieved. The difference between the story-ballets in the repertoire in the mid-1770s (*Apollon et Daphne, Pigmalion amoreux de la statue, Le triomphe d'Euthime sur le génie de Liba*) and *Ninette à la cour* or *Médée et Jason* is difficult to define precisely from extant evidence. However, the London audience could readily distinguish between the 'real' *ballet d'action* and unsatisfactory imitations of it. The amount of comment in the newspapers (at a time when arts coverage was generally skimpy or non-existent) and the extraordinary benefit for Vestris jun. testify to the degree to which dance in 1780–81 had surpassed anything with which the audience was familiar.

Vestris sen. was, however, essentially reproducing Gardel and Noverre artefacts. His own limitations as a choreographer are evident in *L'omaggio* (5 June 1781). The 'story' of vassals paying their respects to their lord includes no conflict: it is merely a pretext for songs and dances, without dramatic tension or development. The first performance was priced at two guineas to keep the masquerade or 'fête' exclusive, since the decorations were more elaborate than usual and in this case perishable.[1] Reviews said little about

---

[1] According to the *Morning Chronicle* of 6 June 1781, 'From the end of the side boxes to the extreme of the stage, the whole was disposed after the manner of a French garden, —dec-

the musical component, but reported that 'The dances were such as might be expected, when composed by Vestris, actuated by the *point d'honneur* of his profession. Amongst others, a quadrille and a minuet, figured by twelve couples were greatly applauded, particularly the minuet, as much from its novelty, as from the merit of the performers' (*Morning Herald*, 7 June 1781). Vestris sen. could successfully restage Gardel's and Noverre's stories, but he evidently had difficulty constructing one himself. None the less, with his guidance ballet had claimed an unprecedented share of audience attention. The company's final performance of the season, on 3 July 1781, seems emblematic: it began with *Ninette à la cour*, went on to a single act from Sacchini's opera *Euriso*, and concluded with *Medea and Jason*. Noverre himself had not yet arrived, but the *ballet d'action* was already there.

## III. Noverre in London, 1781–82

Europe's leading choreographer served as ballet-master for 1781–82 and brought dance at the King's Theatre to the pinnacle of its achievements in the eighteenth century. Noverre was available because of the vicious infighting and theatrical politics that characterized the dance company at the Paris Opéra in these years.[1] Who managed to recruit him is not known, but presumably William Taylor (in sole charge by December 1781) either initiated or approved the move. What did London have to offer that was more attractive than other places Noverre might have gone? His salary is not recorded, but it was no doubt high. Perhaps as important, he appears to have been offered a free hand, and his brother could assure him that local conditions were tolerable. Noverre was, in truth, past the peak of his career, and this visit might have been a disaster. In the event, it was a triumph; the disaster was to come in 1789. Conditions in 1781–82 were decidedly favourable: Taylor was full of great plans (and not yet in the throes of insolvency), so Noverre was able to put together a very fine company and could spend freely on his productions.

orated with green latice-work, and filled with evergreens, and pots full of the most seasonable flowers, and illuminated with a countless number of lamps of variagated colours, fancifully disposed. The *coup d'œil* on entering the house was singularly new and agreeable. Nor was vision the sole sense gratified, the house, contrary to the custom of theatres, being extremely fragrant.'

[1] Lynham, *Chevalier Noverre*, remains the standard study, but must be used with caution.

## Noverre's Company and its Repertoire

### Ballet Repertoire for 1781–82

*Pastoral Dance*, Simonet, 17 November 1781 (23 performances)

*Divertissement Dance*, Noverre, 17 November 1781 (33 performances)

*Les amans réunis*, Noverre, 17 November 1781, 'a new Tragi-Pantomime Ballet' (11 performances)

*Les petits riens*, Noverre, 11 December 1781, 'a new Ballet Anacréontique'; music by Barthélemon, 'entirely new' (13 performances)

**Le triomphe de l'amour conjugal, ou Alceste**, Noverre, 10 January 1782, 'a new Serious Dance' (22 performances) (p. 466)

*New Divertissement Dance*, Simonet, 7 February 1782, including a 'grand *Chaconne*' by Piccinni (20 performances)

**Rinaldo and Armida**, Noverre, 23 February 1782, 'a new Pantomime Ballet'; music by Lebrun (*Public Advertiser*, 25 February 1782) (14 performances) (p. 470)

*La rosière de Salency*, Noverre, 19 March 1782 (8 performances)

**Adela of Ponthieu**, Noverre, 11 April 1782, 'an entirely new Ballet',[1] music 'entirely new' by Lebrun (11 performances) (p. 474)

**Medea and Jason**, 'as originally composed by Noverre', 11 April 1782, overture by Gluck, rest of music by Noferi (*Public Advertiser*, 12 April 1782) (7 performances) (p. 473)

*Apollon et les Muses*, Noverre, 2 May 1782, 'a new dance, the first time' (9 performances)

*New Dance*, 'demi-character', Noverre, 2 May 1782 (12 performances)

*Mirsa*, originally by Gardel sen., local choreographer not named, 9 May 1782, 'with entirely new Music', overture by Carter (3 performances)

*Apelles and Campaspe*, Noverre, 5 June 1782, 'an entirely new heroic Ballet' [though actually created in Vienna in 1773] (7 performances)

Noverre brought several dancers with him, and even without Vestris sen. and jun. the company was decidedly high-powered. Those new to London were Bournonville, Pierre Gardel, [Jean-Marie?] Léger, [Louis-Marie?] Nivelon, Raymond, Mlle Théodore, and Mlle Dumont—to whom were added Olivier[2] and, for eighteen performances between 2 May and 29 June, Le Picq, who became ballet-master the next season. Continuing in the company were Henry, Simonet, Slingsby, Mlle Baccelli, Signora Crespi, Mme Simonet, and Rosine Simonet. Gardel was less charismatic than Vestris jun. but was a very steady alternative. Bournonville and Nivelon were strong additions to the company; Slingsby and Mlle Baccelli were local favourites; Théodore was a glamorous novelty. Noverre employed Simonet as deputy choreographer and built his major productions around Mme Simonet, his former pupil.

---

[1] But created in Vienna in 1773, according to Lillian Moore, 'Unlisted Ballets by Jean Georges Noverre', *Theatre Notebook*, 15 (1960), 15–20.

[2] Olivier appears to have been a *figurant* temporarily promoted: he was advertised only between 19 Mar. and 23 Apr., without any special designation.

Noverre chose to feature Mme Simonet where reputation might suggest that Mlle Baccelli or Mlle Théodore would take precedence. Thus in *Le triomphe de l'amour conjugal* Simonet was Alceste, Théodore was Hebe; in *Rinaldo and Armida* Simonet was Armida, Théodore and Baccelli the spirits who distract Rinaldo's fellow knights; in *Adela of Ponthieu* Simonet was Adela while Théodore, Crespi, and Baccelli were simply grouped as Ladies of the Court; in *Medea and Jason* Simonet was Medea, and she was Campaspe to Le Picq's Apelles.[1] Mlle Théodore was listed before Mme Simonet in the company's season announcement, and her benefit was earlier (19 March as opposed to 30 April), but Théodore had fewer and less important roles.[2] Mme Simonet was probably the better actress, and at least at this point in their respective careers had more range as a dancer. Certainly her parts consistently require more acting than Théodore's. Noverre treated Mme Simonet as the ranking ballerina of the company, a prominence she was never again to enjoy. Towards the end of the season the papers occasionally suggested that the younger women be given a chance, but that decision had to await a new ballet-master. Mme Simonet does not seem to have appeared in *La rosière de Salency*, mounted for Théodore's benefit on 19 March, but she had been quite ill while it was rehearsed, and there is no report of tensions between them.

Other members of the company appear to have worked together harmoniously, despite obvious potential for trouble. Gardel and Nivelon took the male leads undisputed. Late in the spring, Le Picq arrived to visit with his old master Noverre and begin meeting people towards the next season, but he did little dancing. Mlle Baccelli was much less prominent than she was accustomed to being in this company. Signora Crespi was regularly featured as a second dancer (though William Taylor later disparaged her); so was Henry (whom Taylor later championed). Bournonville (father of the great Bournonville) was also regularly advertised—more often than the local hero, Slingsby, who was ill or injured for long periods. Noverre managed to

---

[1] Casting is reported in *The London Stage* under the dates of premières except in the following cases: *Rinaldo and Armida* (Cambridge University Library Hib. 7.782.11); *Adela of Ponthieu* (Harvard Theatre Collection TS 5278.459); Medea is documented in *Opera Rumpus*, 17 n.

[2] The season announcement is in the *Public Advertiser* of 19 Oct. 1781. Baccelli comes last in the list, without a partner; but the list is incomplete. Théodore's position may indicate that she made a higher salary, but that would not have obliged Noverre to give her leading roles. Her salary was rumoured to be £400 and her benefit 1,000 guineas or more. See the *Morning Herald* of 23 Mar. 1782.

keep the peace. Indeed, complimenting his use of Slingsby, one chauvinistic reviewer moralized early in the season that 'Base envy, and national prejudice had retarded the progress of representation under former ballet-masters [Guiardele?], but the real man of genius, will ever act with that liberality which distinguishes Mr. Noverre, who knows how to set a proper value on extraordinary abilities wherever he can meet with them' (*Morning Herald*, 12 December 1781). The ballet-master probably defused rivalries by keeping all the principals fully occupied.

On 2 March 1782 the opera-house ran an advertisement: 'An Academy is established at this Theatre, for the purpose of bringing up Dancers for the Stage. Under the Direction of Mons. Léger, a professed Master of Dancing and Member of the Royal Academy in Paris.—Young Persons, willing to become pupils, may see the Plan and Conditions of the Academy, by applying to Mons. Léger, at the Theatre' (*Morning Herald*). This notice suggests that the King's Theatre management was interested in implementing the 'French model' in London to help sustain new developments in dance. Léger's association with Noverre went back a long way: he had participated in the 1763 revival of *Renaud et Armide*. He may have been hired partly for teaching services, both within and outside the company. Unfortunately, the experiment seems to have been short-lived: the school could not have been a paying proposition, and the opera-house was to go bankrupt the next season in any case.[1] But the attempt to found a dance academy in conjunction with the theatre is a measure of the excitement dance was generating at the time.

Surveying the repertoire, one finds that only one of the four productions that supported the season with twenty performances or more was a *ballet d'action*: *Le triomphe de l'amour conjugal, ou Alceste* (performed 22 times). A *Divertissement* (33), a *Pastoral Dance* by Simonet (23), and a *New Divertissement* (20) were the other three staples. The adaptability of such dances, both in length and in personnel, is easier to document this season than is sometimes the case. Simonet's *Pastoral Dance* received its première 17 November; on 2 February four new dances were added to it, which Noverre had made for a masquerade on 24 January; and on 28 February it reverted to its original form. Perhaps because of the instability of the *divertissement* casts, the editor of Part 5 of *The London Stage* often fails to list these dances in summaries of the season repertoire. That omission falsifies the amount of work

---

[1] Aylward, *House of Angelo*, 144, mentions the academy without citing a source and without noting that it was a school for theatrical (not social) dancing.

done by dancers during the season: the *Pastoral, divertissements,* and the *New Dance* of 2 May account for eighty-eight performances, whereas all ten other ballets total 105. Three dances with more individual titles operated only slightly above the level of *divertissements*: *Les petits riens* (performed 13 times), *Les amans réunis* (11), and *Apollon et les Muses* (9). With more stable casts and more in the way of story-lines, this second level of the repertoire provided variety without, apparently, making enormous technical demands.

The most popular of the *ballets d'action* turned out to be the first, *Le triomphe de l'amour conjugal, ou Alceste*. It had some advantage from its January première, but must also have worn well. The other major productions, in order of total performances, were *Rinaldo and Armida* (14); *Adela of Ponthieu* (11); Mlle Théodore's benefit piece, *La rosière de Salency* (8); *Medea and Jason* (7), which obviously suffered from prior exposure; *Apelles and Campaspe* (7), which came very late in the season because it was made for Le Picq, but was shown at all but two of the remaining performances; and *Mirsa* (3), which was got up for Gardel's benefit, presumably by Pierre Gardel himself, following his brother's production. The titles alone convey no hint of the scope of some of these productions, which were far more demanding than those the company had offered just the year before. By the end of April they could offer five different *ballets d'action* in the same week.[1] These halcyon days were cut short by an influenza epidemic, but they still represent an astonishing accomplishment for the company.

Noverre had much to offer London but took time to test the company before embarking on the course that would lead to that glorious week in April. Soon the dancers would do anything for him, and the management fully supported him. Despite widespread enthusiasm, pockets of resistance remained in the audience, both to dance itself and to its use in serious stories. Vestris sen. had already shown *Medea and Jason* to audiences for whom it had been quite a stretch. There were still casual references to it in newspapers in January of 1782, but spectators associated it more with the Vestris, whom they had seen, than with its creator, Noverre. Not everyone was willing to concede that ballet was an art, and even among those who enjoyed it, some remained committed to a more purely aesthetic form of dance. The backward-looking 'Bowkitt' in a letter in the *Morning Herald* of 1 January 1782 raised the question whether ballet was an appropriate medium for serious stories. After reviewing 'panegyrics' that favour religious dance from

[1] Between 23 and 27 Apr. 1781 the schedule was *La rosière* and *Rinaldo* on Tuesday, *Alceste* and *Medea* on Thursday, and *Alceste* and *Adela* on Saturday.

many cultures, mostly ancient, he admits that '*dancing* is of infinite use to the human frame, like all other exercises, taken in moderation'. But finding its association with religion 'truly preposterous', he looks for a less august origin, which in turn delimits the art:

*Dancing*, in its true natural state, seems to be the offspring of genial warmth, which flowing through the veins of youth, and acting upon the animal spirits, produces elastic motion, adorned with grace, and expressive of chearfulness. By this natural species of *dance* we may express love, a certain degree of solicitude, and infinite good humour. It seems most apposite to a pastoral life, and may be used to advantage in the most exalted situations. The attitude required by the step and motion of a minuet, are highly advantageous and ornamental; but to extend the practice beyond the limits of those probable boundaries is inconsistent with common sense.

Having outlined acceptable limits, he then challenges other conventions. 'Can any thing be more ridiculous than to die *dancing*?' he asks and goes on to answer:

The gloom of suicide, the rage of jealousy, or the perpetration of murder, require a combination of all the faculties and all the senses, and when attempted to be expressed by the *dance*, however elegantly performed, lose their sublimity. The ballets [that is, performance, not choreography] of the younger *Vestris*, *Slingsby*, and *Baccelli*, are beautiful, and inoffensive to the nicest distinguisher. . . . At the exhibition of *Medea, and Jason*, or any other tragic history, however we may admire the pantomimic powers of the performers, we must secretly lament the depravity of public taste, and the absurdity of the exhibition!

Published nine months after the Vestris production opened, this letter shows how entrenched a resistance Noverre had to overcome. What he was able to achieve at the King's Theatre is evident in the following accounts of three of his *pièces de resistance*.

Le triomphe de l'amour conjugal

Noverre made a canny choice by offering *Le triomphe de l'amour conjugal, ou Alceste* as his first major production in London. Lynham describes it as a mere 'divertissement', because it is shorter and less complicated than other versions.[1] The ballet constitutes Noverre's adaptation of earlier versions of

---

[1] Lynham, *Chevalier Noverre*, 170, with a tentative reference back to a Stuttgart production of 1761. In a review of *Rinaldo and Armida* on 25 Feb. 1782, the *Morning Herald* calls that ballet 'the *Corps de Reserve* of the ingenious *Noverre*' and says 'he had hitherto trifled in miniature'. But that comment means only that the *Alceste* was shorter, not that it was underproduced.

the Alcestis story to the conditions under which he was working in London. Viewed as preparation for more demanding productions there, it is more important than Lynham recognized. The scenario was published with the libretto for *Giunio Bruto*: they had been intended to appear together, the ballet leavening the tragic end of the opera.[1] *Giunio Bruto* is mentioned in the newspapers on 11 December 1781 as a coming attraction, without reference to a ballet. Although *Alceste* (as it will be referred to for convenience) did not receive its première until 10 January 1782, both were intended for a date before Christmas. The last rehearsal recorded by Joseph Hayling in December 1781 took place on the 17th, but *Alceste* was the next production to open and did so without further rehearsal. Since *Giunio Bruto* and *Alceste* were meant to be produced together, one must ask why they were performed separately. The problem was Signora Macchierini's voice: even before the public rehearsal, one newspaper was recommending a substitute for her.[2] The rehearsal convinced management that *Giunio Bruto* could not open for some time, and then Pacchierotti fell ill. The opera was announced for 8 January 1782 but again postponed indefinitely on the 7th, to sardonic comments in the papers. By that date the *Morning Herald* described *Rinaldo and Armida* as being 'in forwardness', so if *Alceste* was to have any value as preparation for later work, it had to appear immediately—and there was no telling when the opera might come out. Hence the ballet was offered free to subscribers on a double bill with *La buona figliuola*, by way of apology for the delay in expanding the operatic repertoire.[3]

The title of the ballet encapsulates the sentimental message underlying the story of Alceste—the faithful wife volunteers to die in place of her husband, Admetus, and is brought back to life as a reward for her generosity. Earlier in his career, Noverre had set a version of the story that started with Alceste's abduction by Licomedes. Admetus was wounded in the attempt to rescue his wife (though nothing explains why he should be offered the option of a substitute to die in his place). To judge by the translation of *La mort de Licomede* from *Recueil de programmes de ballets de M. Noverre* (1776)

---

[1] The opera ends in a square in Rome, where *figurants* formed part of the crowd that was bidden to celebrate the salvation of the city (see the *Morning Herald*, 14 Jan. 1782). 'Roman' and 'Greek' costumes were indistinguishable at this date, so as soon as the scene had been changed from a square back to the previous scene for the opera, the Temple of Concord, the same *figurants* could easily accompany Admetus and Alceste to the temple to celebrate their wedding anniversary.

[2] *Public Advertiser*, 13 Dec. 1781. See also Mount Edgcumbe, *Musical Reminiscences*, 30.

[3] *The London Stage* notes the free performance without attempting to explain it.

that appeared in Noverre's *Works* (1783) as *Alceste, or The Triumph of Conjugal Love*, the earlier ballet involved several more named characters, multiple scene changes, and a much longer story. This was not, however, the ballet that was given in London.

*La mort de Licomede* is an elaborate machine play: Alceste is abducted by ship; when Hercules and Admetus lay siege to rescue her, Admetus is fatally wounded; Apollo announces the arbitrary test of loyalty; Alceste dies in place of Admetus but is duly restored to him. In *Alceste* Noverre follows Euripides and thereby gains dramatic cohesion, the curse on Admetus requiring no explanation. Admetus and Alceste have no previous history. They are celebrating a wedding anniversary when an 'inscription written in letters of fire' appears in the sky: 'Admetus must instantly die—or another for him!'[1] Panic naturally ensues. The core of the earlier ballet was reused: the near-fatal decline of Admetus while Alceste searches for a substitute; her acceptance of the role and subsequent suicide; his recovery and realization of her sacrifice; her restoration. Some of the means of telling the story were different, however.

To play Alceste, Noverre had a fine actress, Mme Simonet, but neither of his technically brilliant principal male dancers, Gardel and Nivelon, was ideally matched to her. The story offered little for his other principal women, Théodore and Baccelli, to do. *La mort de Licomede* had included at least three strong male roles to the single important female role. In London, named characters include only two men, but three women. The new story obviously focused more on Alceste, and there was comparatively little interaction between male and female characters. Admetus (Gardel) is given a death scene but cannot participate in the search for a substitute, nor does he know what Alceste decides to do. After her death, he reacts in an extended scene, at the end of which he collapses. Only a god can resolve this stalemate, and Noverre sends Apollo (Nivelon), aided by Hebe and Iris (Théodore and Baccelli) along with Cupid and Hymen, to restore order. Comparison of the two scenarios shows that Noverre not only adjusted the story to the talents of his dancers but integrated the ending better in London.

In the more complete version, when Admetus finds that his recovery has cost him his wife, he tries to kill himself but is disarmed by Hercules. Enraged, he lashes out at all around him, especially Hercules. Admetus tears

---

[1] The scenario was printed in the *Morning Herald* of 11 Jan. 1782.

his hair, rends his garments, and eventually collapses from exhaustion. Thereupon, a miracle: the tomb of Alceste opens, and she returns to life. After the couple is reunited, they thank Hercules for preserving Alceste from Licomedes and then Admetus from himself. In a separately numbered scene Apollo appears and 'Admetus and his queen humbly prostrate themselves at the feet of the beneficent deity, and offer their vows of love, respect and gratitude'. The ballet ends with everybody dancing in celebration.

For reasons not entirely clear, Hercules did not figure in the London production, though he may have been intended to at first.[1] Once Admetus has fallen 'motionless in the arms of his courtiers', Apollo 'appears carried in a cloud, accompanied by Hebe, Iris, Cupid, and Hymen. The latter holds an extinguished torch'. Although the scenario does not say so, Noverre presumably gave these deities an introductory dance, both to display the three principals involved and to direct attention to the next incident. When Hymen re-lights his torch from that of Cupid, Alceste reawakens. 'She sees Admetus; their eyes meet; yet they seem to doubt their happiness, but convinced at last of its reality, they fly into each other's arms. Then, falling prostrate before their protecting deities, they express their gratitude and supreme felicity. A general dance ensues and concludes the entertainment.'[2] The reunion takes place before the gods who brought it about, rather than just to the accompaniment of thunder and lightning, and the thanksgiving develops naturally rather than requiring a separate scene. Without going to the histrionic excesses of a full-length tragedy, *Alceste* provided the principal dancers with a useful exercise and the audience with a pleasing tale well told—which the King himself applauded 'in a most particular manner' at the première.[3]

---

[1] On 14 Jan. 1782 the *Morning Herald* commented in a partisan review, 'We are sorry to find that Mr Slingsby has been prevented, through indisposition, from taking upon him the part of Hercules, who is fabled to have brought Alceste from the infernal abode. Mons. Noverre had judiciously pitched upon him for a character which required all that manly execution for which that excellent performer is so justly admired; we hear, however, that as soon as his health permits the above improving addition will be made to this Ballet.' However, Hercules had been eliminated by the time the scenario was printed and there is no evidence that he was ever restored to the London production.

[2] The day before the première, Joseph Hayling lacquered two 'Tin Flambeaus to order'. They cost 4s. 6d. apiece, a shilling less than the 'Flambeaus for Furies' he had made up the previous February. The coincidence of dates and the 'to order' distinguish these from the earlier torches. They are almost certainly the torches for Hymen and Cupid.

[3] *Morning Herald*, 12 Jan. 1782. The following autumn, the same paper records *Admetus and Alcesta*, 'a grand Tragic Ballet', at the Royal Circus (4 Nov. 1782).

## Rinaldo and Armida *and the Finale of* Medea and Jason

English audiences had been seeing versions of *Rinaldo and Armida* in the opera-house since 1711, and as Noverre acknowledged in his 'Preliminary Discourse' to the 1782 scenario (reprinted in App. IV), the story was extremely familiar. Although it grows increasingly serious, the plot is much less grim than that of *Medea and Jason*. Noverre apologized gracefully for not having had enough time to 'study the taste of the Public' in London: 'three months are not sufficient to please at once sensations diametrically opposite'. Aware of resistance to the more esoteric reaches of his art, he nevertheless had a reputation to maintain that required larger-scale work.

As is often true of Noverre's scenarios, the plot is presented in a series of clearly visualized interchanges among the principals. Rinaldo (Gardel) is first lured across the magic threshold to an island in the Oronte River. After he is put to sleep by the followers of Armida, she (Mme Simonet) comes forward intending to kill him.[1] Strangely attracted to him, she transports him on a cloud to her palace to worship Venus instead of Pallas Athena. His comrades Ubaldo and the Danish Knight (Mons. Simonet and Nivelon) manage to follow him with the aid of a 'golden wand'. Resisting dalliance with the nymphs who impersonate their ladies (Mlle Baccelli and Mme Théodore), they take advantage of Armida's momentary absence to confront Rinaldo. Ubaldo

holds up to him the enchanted shield. No sooner does the young hero cast his eyes on this faithful mirror, whose peculiar use is to show vice and weakness in their natural deformity, than he starts back with shame and horror, the sight of his effeminate accoutrement inflames him with wrath, he tears his apparel, stamps on his crown, plucks off the garlands of flowers, and divests himself of those childish ornaments and inglorious garments.[2]

Armida, returning, tries to win him back. A second exposure to 'the truth-disclosing mirror' is necessary, but Rinaldo then steels himself to be the

[1] Lynham states erroneously that Mlle Théodore 'achieved a great personal success' in 'the role of Armida' (*Chevalier Noverre*, 103): both the scenario and the review in the 25 Feb. 1782 *Morning Herald* name Mme Simonet as Armida. The review compliments Mlle Théodore warmly, but does not specify her role. The scenario contains a cast-list, to which the review in the *Public Advertiser* of 25 Feb. adds that 'the Cupids were the *Niece and Daughter* of Simonet'.

[2] Hayling had prepared 'A Planish'd Shield with Looking Glass and Foil &c' for 10s. 6d. as early as 15 Feb. It was either replaced or repaired on 22 Feb., when 'Six pieces of looking Glass' were 'soldered on a Shield'.

'lover who sacrifices inclination to obey the calls of glory', and the three knights leave.

Only a page and a quarter of the eleven-page scenario is devoted to the last scene, but the description plus Joseph Hayling's records show that the finale required the most rehearsal. When Armida, who has apparently fainted, recovers enough to find herself abandoned,

she gives way to those sentiments which despairing love alone inspires. She calls to her assistance the hell-born Deities of Hate, Fury, and Revenge [Messrs Léger, Bournonville, and Henry]. . . . The Princess breaks to pieces the quiver and arrows of the God of love,[1] tears off his bandage, and wresting from the goddess of Revenge, her flaming torch,[2] sets fire to her own palace; the thunder roars, swift lightning flashes through the clouds, a river of fire issuing from the mouths of two frightful dragons, rolls along with the utmost impetuosity. [Armida and her assistants escape in a chariot.] Some of the Demons precipitate themselves into the burning fluid, others sink into the fiery abyss, and that spot which was before, the abode of enchanted beings under the most pleasing forms, now becomes the dreary mansion of wild beasts, and shapeless monsters.

Noverre took the King's Theatre a long way beyond happy peasant dances.

His demons and dragons seem to be reflected in the surviving music for the ballet: *The favorite Dances for the Year 1782 called Armida Composed by Monsr. Le Brunn*, published by J. Blundell, 'Music Seller to their Majesties and all the Royal Family'. The oboist Ludwig August Lebrun's music includes six pieces, half of them gavottes. No dancers are named nor is location or dramatic function specified, but these pieces are unusual in that all include *minore* sections, even the 'Prince of Wales's Minuet'; the first, a gavotte in B flat major, has two of them, showing increasing pathos and chromaticism and a coda marked 'smorz'. Music of this seriousness and intensity is rare in the surviving ballet scores for the King's Theatre; indeed, many an *opera seria* from the period contains less minor mode music than do these six pieces. Blundell's publication exists in another state, identical to the first except for the title-page: *The favorite Dances in the Opera of Armida* . . . (copy in British Library, b.51.i). This is puzzling. Sacchini's *Rinaldo* had been revived during the 1780–81 season and, although it includes extended ballet sequences (discussed in Ch. 4), Lebrun is not known to have

[1] On 12 Feb. Hayling had made and lacquered a 'Quiver Case to take off in half' (5s. 6d.); on the day before the ballet opened he provided five more.

[2] On 15 Feb. Hayling provided 'Thirteen Fluted Furies Truncheons', painted red (£2. 12s.), and repaired and repainted twenty-four old ones. These fragile torches required constant overhauling, especially once *Medea and Jason* entered the repertoire.

composed them. This second title-page would therefore appear to be a mistake corrected by *The favorite Dances for the Year 1782*.

The technical demands of staging *Rinaldo and Armida*, while not innovative, were formidable, and Noverre expected to get exactly what he wanted. To judge from newspaper commentary, he was given a free hand, and this impressionistic evidence is borne out in Joseph Hayling's accounts, which document no fewer than five rehearsals for the ballet, at charges running from a mere 6s. on 13 February to £6. 1s. 6d. on the 20th. The most expensive rehearsal, attended by patrons including the Prince of Wales, incognito, went on for at least four and a half hours. It was disrupted by an unfortunate occurrence: the leader of the dances, Noferi, had a stroke, which proved fatal a week later.[1]

But this rehearsal was exceptionally long and difficult for technical reasons too. At some point after the scenario went to press, a decision was made to change the dragons and river of fire into a single hell-mouth.[2] The *Morning Herald* reviewer felt that 'The jumping of the dancers into the monster's mouth had a very good effect' and the *Public Advertiser* noticed 'the Conflagration Scene with the Dragon's Mouth' (25 February 1782). Neither mentions a river of fire, and Hayling's accounts confirm the change. In his records for the 20 February rehearsal, which was meant to be the final one before the première, Hayling lists 'Putting together Eighteen Strong Tin plates and fitting to Figure Head to fire works'; 'Altering the above, two men to Ditto and refix it'; 'Fourteen Plates to Ditto fixed for Fire Works, two men Nails &c to ditto'. On 22 February an only slightly less expensive rehearsal (£5. 10s.) was held to be sure that all effects were functioning.[3]

---

[1] See the *Morning Herald* of 21 and 28 Feb. 1782. Noferi's absence was affectionately regretted in the *Public Advertiser* of 25 Feb., and two days later that paper noted that he had been replaced by 'Monsieur Chapron', that is, Felice Chabran, who later became leader of the dances for the Pantheon opera. The fact that his appointment was considered news is evidence of the importance of the leader.

[2] In the Milan version the finale of the scenario reads: 'Armide en revoyant la lumière ne peut plus douter de l'inconstance de son Amant. . . . Elle s'arme du flambeau de la Vengéance, elle embrase son Palais. Le tonnerre gronde, les éclairs percent la nue, une pluie de feu le détruit entierement; elle monte sur un char: la Vengéance, la Haine, & la Fureur se grouppent autour d'elle; elle se fraye une route dans les airs. Dans cet instant tout le Palais s'écroule, et l'on n'apperçoit qu'un desert épouvantable habité par des Monstres.' See Jean Georges Noverre, *Renaud et Armide, Ballet Heroique* (Milan: Jean Montani, 1775). Copy used: British Library, pressmark 906.e.3 (2).

[3] There is no way of knowing how many rehearsals the ballet-master held separately, though *Rinaldo and Armida* had been described in the *Morning Herald* as being 'in forwardness' on 7 Jan. 1782. However, between 8 and 22 Jan. Simon Slingsby, who was probably in

After many delays, some caused by an injured dancer, *Rinaldo and Armida* was performed publicly on 23 February. Running fifty-five minutes, it was clearly a major ballet.

Amidst the generally admiring newspaper commentary, two complaints are of interest. The reviewer in the *Morning Herald* of 25 February objected that 'the cloud in which Rinaldo and Armida are supposed to be carried off is excessively mean. Surely so powerful an enchantment ought to command a better one; we therefore wish to see this nuisance removed in the next representation; when compared to the other parts of the scenery, it looks like a dirty spot on a sumptuous garment.' This request for a change may have been met: on 2 March the theatre explained that 'alterations in the machinery' would delay *Rinaldo and Armida* until the next week (*Morning Herald*). Hayling's records show no rehearsal, implying that only the cloud front, not the mechanism, was adjusted.

The *Morning Herald* reviewer also complained that 'The scenes, especially the back ground in the hell scene, wants more light, nor should the *lightening blowers* be so sparing of their breath. . . . [The tumbling of the devils] borders too much on the ludicrous in so awful a scene'. Another writer in the same issue of the paper found them less amusing: he opined that the '*infernal spirits*' should not have 'approached so near the stage-boxes as to terrify the ladies', while at the same time he enjoyed having 'so many *lovely faces*' 'rendered more conspicuous by the proximity of light'. The notice in the *Public Advertiser*, contrariwise, suggested that 'The last Scene will make "Feu de l'Opera" [a fabric colour fashionable the previous season] glow again, and with an *Eclat* which it never had before.' Torch-bearing furies could easily be told to stay further from the boxes, but Hayling's records show no adjustment in light level, if any was made in response to these criticisms.

Noverre was evidently worried by the degree of overlap between this finale and the rather similar one in *Medea and Jason* that Vestris had produced with such success the previous season. The focus seems to be less on Armida's Medea-like flight than on making manifest the hell in which

the cast, did not perform at all. On 6 Feb. 1782 the ballet was advertised for the 14th, but on the 12th it was delayed by Slingsby's indisposition (see the *Morning Herald*). Shortly thereafter Slingsby was replaced (possibly by Léger, who took his role in *Les amans réunis* on 9 Mar.; if so, Slingsby's role would have been Hatred). Rehearsals that involved technical staff did not begin until 13 Feb. They then occurred on the 17th, 18th, 20th, and 22nd, according to Hayling's records.

Rinaldo was so nearly trapped. As the second piece for his benefit on 11 April, Noverre produced *Medea and Jason* 'as originally composed'. Familiarity with the Vestris version provided the audience with a unique perspective on the ballet. The 12 April 1782 *Public Advertiser* was rhapsodic:

The Dance as it now stands *gains* some Advantage over the last Year's Performance of it, by the Introduction of Mad. Theodore, and . . . there is not as much *lost* as we expected, from the Change of the Elder Vestris to Gardel [Jason], and the Young Vestris to Nivellon [Young Prince]. Mad. Simonet [Medea] was greater than usual; she out-did herself![1]

But since this was a benefit, the reviewer made no comment about the staging. One of the few documentable changes comes from Hayling's records. It concerns efforts by Noverre and Hayling to intensify the visual effect of Medea's escape. On 10 April fifty-seven plates were 'wired and riveted together to fix across the stage for Fire Works'.[2] There is no comparable entry in the lighting accounts for the 1781 production. The span of plates would at least have doubled the shower of fire with which the ballet ended, and it proved memorable. Nearly a year later the mock-heroic poem *Opera Rumpus* referred to it, and as late as 1790, when John Palmer took over the Royal Circus, he advertised a 'Grand Spectacle' version of *Medea and Jason* with the 'Dance of Furies' and 'a Magnificent Shower of Fire'.[3] Again, we find Noverre taking the trouble to improve old productions, vary his effects, and differentiate his works.

Adela of Ponthieu

A story of true love braving obstacles of decorum and chivalry was the production Noverre put most work into for his benefit on 11 April 1782.

---

[1] Théodore probably appeared only in the dances, not in a mime role, as was the case in the revival Noverre staged at the Opéra in Jan. 1780. See Pitou, 391 and 518. In the *Morning Herald* of 11 Apr. 1782 Gardel declared that he had accepted the role of Jason 'by no means with a view to set himself upon a level with Mons. Vestris; it would be a presumption of which he is far from being capable; the more so, that the celebrated dancer alluded to had two months to prepare for a part, which Mons. Gardel has been compelled to get up in the space of a week'. This statement is useful as documentation of the length of rehearsal period for a *pièce d'occasion*, though as Gardel had also appeared in the ballet at the Opéra (Pitou, 238), Noverre need hardly have worried about being disgraced by him. The paragraph is essentially an exercise in public relations.

[2] Hayling repaired the old mechanism on 5 Apr. 1782, so there is no way to tell whether the larger one is an extension or a separate effect. A new 'coffret' to give to Creon had to be made: on 8 Apr. Hayling listed 'Altering a Box holes punched in the top and a hole in the Bottom'.

[3] *Opera Rumpus* (1783), 14, and *The Times*, 5 April 1790.

Newspapers suspended their rule against reviewing benefits: *Adela of Ponthieu* 'convinced the spectator that without calling up *Hellfire* to his assistance, the ingenious Ballet Master can move our feelings, and excite our admiration' in a delightful 'gothic' setting as well as in pagan vales (*Morning Herald*, 15 April 1782).

Renaud, Earl of Ponthieu (Simonet), has arranged a prestigious marriage for his daughter Adela (Mme Simonet) with Alphonso, a Spanish knight (Gardel). Just before the public announcement of the betrothal, Adela realizes that she is in love with Raymond of Mayenne (Nivelon), who is still only an esquire. Adela refuses to give her hand to the foreign knight and faints; Alphonso immediately suspects a rival. When he interrupts a tête-à-tête, he loses his temper and makes such a scene that the uproar draws the Earl. Alphonso insults his host; Raymond offers to fight on the Earl's behalf; and a combat is arranged. In order to legitimize the fight according to the rules of chivalry, Raymond is knighted in an elaborate ceremony. Alphonso is killed in combat, and the lovers are united.[1]

The scenario sets the knighting in a 'superb saloon, adorned with trophies, and other military attributes', but reviews state that it took place in an outdoor setting, on a hill. The *Morning Herald* reviewer of 15 April 1782 thought the hill 'superb', but after the second performance the same paper complained that 'When Raymond kneels to Renaud, in order to be knighted, he is *brought so low*, that Simonet's sword looks like the rod of an angry Pedagogue, going to punish the naughty school-boy. This might be altered for the better, by Raymond standing within arm-length of Renaud' (17 April). Such awkwardness suggests insufficient rehearsal time with scenery. Hayling's records show rehearsals on 2 and 10 April, with most of the latter devoted to *Medea and Jason*.

The story allows for much pageantry: a court betrothal, a knighting, assembling for the combat, and rejoicing at the end. There is also room for fine acting on the part of all the named characters. How much the story was elaborated in mime is difficult to say, but two features of the scenario deserve comment. The French version has an interesting footnote on the dramatic use of silence; and new information is available about the fight as staged in London.

In his production Noverre made deliberate use of silence, which he apparently felt called upon to explain when he published the scenario in his

---

[1] The cast is printed in the scenario, *Historical Account of Adela of Ponthieu, a Tragedy-Pantomime Ballet, Composed by Monsieur Noverre, and Translated from the French by Parkyns Mac Mahon* (London: H. Reynell, 1782).

*Recueil de programmes* (1776). The two knights are called to the list by 'une musique'. They kneel and agree to the rules. Then 'Les Parreins leur présentent des armes égales: ils placent les combattans aux deux extrêmités du Champ-clos: on ferme la barrière. Un nouveau silence regne.* Cette moment tranquille & effrayant annonce celui du combat et redouble l'effroi d'Adele'. The footnote marked by the asterisk says,

L'orchestre, se tait dans tous les instans du combat. Il est remplacé par le roulement des tambours à sourdine. Les Timbales et les Trompettes, ainsi que les autres instrumens ne sont employés, que dans les momens qui annoncent le combat, ou dans ceux qui annoncent le triomphe. Cette cessation de musique donne un clair-obscur à l'action, et sert, pour ainsi dire, de repoussoir aux effets brillans de l'orchestre: le combat n'étant point subordonné au mouvement reglé et uniforme de la musique, devient d'aileurs plus chaud, plus vrai et plus interessant. Il est quelque fois avantageux de se passer un Instant de la musique: les yeux gagnent alors, ce qui est enlevé à l'oreille; et cette espèce de fourberie de l'art, employée à propos, ne peut manquer de produire le plus grand effet.

This footnote is not included in the English translation. Had Noverre won his point? An alternative explanation might be that the translator was protecting his readership from discussion of technical matters. In any case the footnote indicates how deeply Noverre had considered his artistic choices in the decade before this trip to England.

Some details of the fight itself are clarified by entries in Hayling's tinkering account. On 3 April 1782 he charged 3s. 6d. apiece for twelve shields and 18s. 6d. for as many tin spear-tops. No doubt knights formed part of the parade before the combat, and their number is a hint at the scale of the production. The dozen shields were, however, decorative rather than practical. Three days before *Adela* opened, Hayling charged 3s. for 'finishing 2 Iron Shields'. These were supplied by somebody else and only decorated by Hayling. The low cost, compared with the tin ones, and the lateness of the charge suggest that the iron shields had been used in rehearsals until close to time for the dress-rehearsal. On 10 April Hayling tinned two axes, and the next day he repaired them. Nowhere in his records does he list swords, helmets, gauntlets, breastplates, or anything that could be armour, which must have come from a professional supplier. The combat was planned to look—and sound—real, and Gardel and Nivelon ran real risks in performing it. The *Morning Herald* noted that 'besides their already acquired abilities', Gardel and Nivelon 'had received some instruction from *Mr. Angelo*. The fall of Gardel was surprisingly great; struggling against death itself, he seems to collect all his remaining strength, to push at his fortunate adversary, but life forsakes him in the attempt' (17 April 1782).

The English version of Noverre's scenario describes the fight, which, after the preliminary ceremonies, occurs in two stages:

Armed cap-à-pie, the hatchet in hand, the two knights run furiously at each other. After several blows, aimed with vigour, but parried off with equal adroitness, they at last cut asunder the braces that fastened their respective armours. They tear them off, and cast away, in a disdainful rage, their hatchets and shields, and attack each other with sword in hand.

The first blow from Alphonso falls with mighty force on Raymond's helmet; he staggers, and is ready to drop. The acclamations of the multitude, a piercing cry from Adela, who sinks expiring in her father's arms, revives the courage of Raymond. As swift as lightning he flies to his adversary, who, unable to withstand the powerful attack, receives a mortal blow. (Noverre, *Works* [1783], 90–1)

The iron shields were probably needed as much to make the battle sound dangerous as to protect the fighters. Is one really to believe that the braces of their armour had to be cut? Some kind of unhooking that could be managed in a clench seems much more likely, but however it was managed, for maximum effect both breastplates should come off. Alphonso is then vulnerable to Raymond's broadsword, and Raymond is disencumbered so Adela can embrace him after the fight. The hatchets were not particularly dangerous, but they took a lot of punishment. Hayling may not have known until the dress rehearsal how strong the axes had to be, but he only records repairing them once.

The combatants were no doubt presented swords as part of the arming procedure, and here one must be allowed some licence in interpretation. Although the *Recueil* version of *Adela* uses the word *épée* in this passage, it must be taken in the most general sense of sword. The only appropriate weapon for the fight described is the broadsword. This second stage of the fight presumably also involved some feints, or at least some practice swings for both men, before the blow that finishes Alphonso. The lover's recovery, the crowd's inspiring roar, and Raymond's attacking with new energy all focus attention on Raymond rather than his victim. These distractions sanitize the fact that society takes a terrible vengeance on Alphonso, the outsider, for having lost his temper. They also serve to prolong the fight while controlling the danger to which the company's leading dancers exposed themselves. The direct combat may well have been one of the attractions of the ballet for dancers. On the whole this production cannot have demanded as much of the company as *Medea* or *Rinaldo and Armida*, but Noverre seems to have been fond of it.

At about this time, William Forster, 'Music seller to his Royal Highness the Duke of Cumber[lan]d', began to publish a new up-market series of dance music, featuring a distinctive title-page within an elegant circular device. The earliest item we know of in this series is *The Favorite Airs, in the Grand Ballet of Adel de Ponthieu Composed by Monsieur Le Brunn*, Book I (the title-page of the British Library copy is dated by hand '1782'). This comprises a sinfonia, eleven dances, and a brief finale—all pleasant and competent, but entirely lacking the rich pathos of Lebrun's memorable gavottes for Noverre's *Rinaldo and Armida*.

## Noverre's Impact

At the end of *Rinaldo and Armida* the applause of the audience 'continued for some minutes after the dropping of the curtain'. Indeed, according to the *Morning Herald* of 25 February 1782, 'a circumstance happened, which though very common abroad, never took place in this country, at least within our recollection: *Noverre*'s name was echoed from all parts of the house; he was called forth to receive in person, the flattering marks of public approbation; but the modest artist, content to have deserved, thought proper to decline the proferr'd honor'.[1] Here is the unprecedented phenomenon of choreographer as superstar: the audience clearly recognized that Noverre was the *fons et origo* of exciting new developments in dance.

Studying the performance calendar and the extant evidence of reception, one can see just how extraordinary Noverre was. He had a good company in 1781–82, but there is some question how well either of the Simonets, for example, would have withstood comparison to the troupe at the Opéra. Noverre could get amazing results from less than star-quality material, given enough rehearsal time and decent technical support for his productions. Part of his competence, especially compared with some of the lesser ballet-masters who preceded and followed him in London, was his ability to get co-operation from the large number of people whose help was necessary to mount productions on the scale he could envisage. That he got such results in London just two years after the Guiardele season is testimony to his methods and to his tact. Whatever simplification of actual dances may have

---

[1] This previously unnoticed report of Noverre's adherence to local custom is particularly interesting because in 1788, when he did appear to receive applause for *L'Amour et Psiché*, at least two newspapers chauvinistically denounced the display.

been necessary, Noverre preferred to stand by the scenarios he had worked out years before. He could, however, adjust to circumstances, as *Alceste*, among others, proves. He left behind a company that believed it could do what he wanted and that had already worked with his annointed successor. He had showed London how *ballet d'action* ought to be done. Whether the company could continue to do it, let alone improve on it, remained to be seen.

## IV. Le Picq and Dauberval, 1782–1785

Noverre did not return to King's Theatre for a second season in 1782–83. He was succeeded by the 38-year-old Neapolitan Charles Le Picq, a former pupil. Le Picq was a brilliant principal dancer and at least a competent choreographer, but he had to try to live up to heightened expectations under conditions that were deteriorating rapidly. When the theatre fell into bankruptcy in the spring of 1783, the normal response would have been to depart, but Le Picq remained, probably for personal reasons.[1] In 1783–84 Jean Bercher Dauberval came to the King's Theatre as choreographer, joining his wife, Mme Théodore, for a moderately successful season.[2] Le Picq followed Dauberval for 1784–85 and then left London.

### Le Picq succeeds Noverre, 1782–83

### Ballet Repertoire

*New Divertissement*, Simonet, 2 November 1782, advertised as *La bergère constante* on 5 November only; contents fluctuated markedly (42 performances)
*Apelles and Campaspe*, Noverre, revival by Le Picq (?), 2 November 1782 (17 performances)
**Il ratto delle Sabine; or The Rape of the Sabines**, Le Picq, 12 December 1782, 'a new grand Ballet', music by Borghi (9 performances) (p. 481)

---

[1] By July 1783 Mme Rossi had apparently left her husband (the *figurant* Dominic Rossi) and moved in with Le Picq: she signed Taylor's deed of trust in her own name and in 1783–84 she and Le Picq used the same address, no. 31 Pall Mall, for his dancing lessons and her benefit tickets. Although gossip paired them off as early as 18 Jan. 1783 (see the *Morning Herald*), the *Morning Post* of 7 Feb. 1785 referred to the liaison as if it were news.

[2] A letter from Paris in the *Morning Herald* of 10 May 1783 reports that a faction led by the reigning ballerina Mlle Guimard had blocked Dauberval's appointment as director of the dances at the Opéra, though Ivor Guest believes he 'had made up his mind some time before to leave and was only hanging on to secure advantageous pension rights' (private letter, 10 Mar. 1994). The *Morning Herald* of 14 Dec. 1782 described the Daubervals as married (cf. *Biographical Dictionary*, iv. 161). Thereafter her name appears in various permutations: Mlle Théodore, Mme Théodore, Mme Théodore Dauberval. Henceforth we shall employ the second of these forms.

*Le tuteur trompé; or The Guardian Outwitted*, Le Picq, 11 January 1783, 'an entirely new Ballet', music by Borghi (34 performances) (p. 484)

*\*Pastoral Ballet*, no choreographer credited, 13 February 1783 (1 performance)

*Les épouses persanes; or The Persian Wives*, Le Picq, 15 February 1783, 'an entirely new ballet of Serious, Comic, and Demi-characters', music by Borghi (?) (7 performances)

*Il riposo del campo; or The Recreations of the Camp*, Le Picq, 13 March 1783, 'an entirely new Divertissement' (19 performances)

*La bégueule; or She Wou'd and She Wou'd Not*, Le Picq, 13 March 1783, 'a new Ballet' (12 performances)

*The Amours of Alexander and Roxana*, Le Picq, 10 April 1783, 'an entire new Ballet', music by Barthélemon, 'entirely new composed' (1 performance)

*Le déjeuner espagnol*, Simonet, 1 May 1783, 'an entirely new ballet' (1 performance)

*Les ruses de l'amour*, 'originally composed by Noverre', 1 May 1783 (2 performances)

*La dame bienfaisante*, Le Picq, 8 May 1783, 'an entire new Ballet, Tragi-Comic', music by Floquet (1 performance)

*The Four Nations*, Le Picq, 28 June 1783 (1 performance, but performed at the Pantheon on 17 and 24 June)

Although Le Picq began with great good will and wonderful connections established during his visit the previous spring, the company assembled for 1782–83 could only be an anticlimax. Most of the money went to Le Picq himself.[1] The other principal men were Slingsby and Zuchelli; the principal women were Geltruda Rossi, whom Le Picq had arranged to bring from Naples, and Mme Théodore. Simonet was again hired to make *divertissements*, though he was credited with only one; Mme Simonet danced for £10 per night when called.[2]

Comments in the papers make clear that some part of the audience was tired of the Simonets; whether management led or followed in this case, their changing status caused tensions in the company. Illness and injury were rife: Mme Rossi was out in the latter half of December, Mme Théodore in late January and early February, and Slingsby in February and April. The season comprised seven ballets, including Simonet's *New Divertissement*; only one, *Il ratto delle Sabine*, could imaginably be called a *ballet d'action*, and few require any comment at all. Six other advertised dances

---

[1] The *Morning Herald* of 24 Apr. 1781 reported a rumour that he had been hired at a salary of £1,500, but he was denied leave and did not come (ibid., 8 Apr. 1782). Mme Théodore said Le Picq's salary was 1,400 guineas as dancer, 300 as choreographer, and his benefit was estimated at over £500 (*Morning Herald*, 13 May 1783). On 20 June 1783 when he joined the lawsuits against William Taylor, Le Picq swore an affidavit that he was owed £867 (see App. II, Taylor's Creditors).

[2] According to the *Morning Herald* of 13 May 1783, Simonet was paid only £250 for *divertissements*, whereas the previous season he had been paid £400. For Mme Simonet's terms, see the *Morning Herald*, 31 Dec. 1782. Since both of them taught dancing, they were not entirely dependent on the theatre for their income.

were strictly *pièces d'occasion*, put together for benefits. Given the declining budget and the personnel available, Le Picq did as well as might be expected, but he cannot be said to have advanced the cause of the *ballet d'action* or the company's standard of performance. Forster's up-market series of dance scores for this season comprises music largely by the violinist Luigi Borghi, implying that he was 'leader of the dances', though this status is not certain.[1] The four volumes that appeared in 1783 include the music of three complete ballets: *Il ratto delle Sabine*, *Le tuteur trompé*, and 'La sposa persiana', that is, Le Picq's *Les épouses persanes*.

Opera productions appear to have been given priority this season: three were mounted before Christmas. Le Picq had to begin with a revival of *Apelles and Campaspe*, featuring Mme Simonet, because Mesdames Rossi and Théodore arrived too late for him to stage a major ballet.[2] Delays on *Il ratto delle Sabine* multiplied until a whole month had been wasted in saving Mme Rossi's début for that piece. On 30 November Le Picq worked a *pas de deux* for the two of them into the *New Divertissement*. When *Il ratto* was ready, newspaper commentary—probably planted—emphasized Mme Rossi's versatility: 'Now an innocent rural nymph; then a Sabine Princess shewing her yielding companions the example of all those virtues that should shield the weaker sex, from the vile attempts of seducing man. Here, grave and heroic; there, playful and sportive; in both, equally engaging, easy and graceful' (*Morning Herald*, 12 December 1782). Even if this was managed publicity, it points up Rossi's value: Mme Simonet's abilities were chiefly dramatic and Mme Théodore's chiefly *demi-caractère*.

*Il ratto delle Sabine* told the story of Romulus and his fellow colonists carrying off the women of the neighbouring Sabine tribe in order to populate the future Rome. No copy of the published scenario appears to survive, but among the incidents mentioned in the reviews were 'the wrestling; the gladiators; the defeat of the Sabines; the besieging of Rome by the latter, their reconciliation with the Romans'.[3] To personalize this rather general

---

[1] *The Celebrated Opera Dances, as Perform'd at the King's Theatre,* 'Printed by W. Forster Violin Violoncello Tenor & Bow maker to their Royal Highnesses the Prince of Wales and Duke of Cumberland also Music seller to his Royal Highness the Duke of Cumber[lan]d. Dukes Ct. in St. Martins Lane'.

[2] The *Morning Herald* reported Rossi's arrival on 14 Oct., Théodore's on the 29th; the season opened on 2 Nov.

[3] This and the subsequent quotation are from the *Morning Herald*, 13 Dec. 1782. The wrestling sequence constituted a novelty, according to the same paper the next day: 'The wrestling . . . was supported, if we may be allowed the expression, with true Roman spirit. Mons. Degville formerly Ballet-master at the Winter Theatres, gave such proofs of his

account Le Picq introduced 'an episodical scene, in which Ersilia [Mme Rossi], the principal of the Sabine women, is supposed to have been betrothed to Aoronte [Zuchelli], who is afterwards slain by Romulus [Le Picq]'. This triangle allowed him to set up a scene both 'truly pathetic, and . . . exquisitely performed', in which 'the Sabines in the new ballet, with hair dishevelled, and concern painted in every look,—rush between the combatants, and in a supplicating posture, beg them to suspend their hostile purpose, and be reconciled to the Romans' (*Public Advertiser*, 14 December 1782). Mme Rossi's acting was praised, in particular 'her inward struggles between anger, love, and duty, to herself and country. . . . But the *Dancer* soon rose superior, if possible, to the *Actress*; and Mme Rossi, in her *Chacone*, soon convinced us, that altho' great things had been said of her as a serious dancer, they fell far short of the real truth' (*Morning Herald*, 13 December 1782). The only other reported details concern spectacle. The *Morning Herald* of 18 January 1783 complained of reviewers' 'silence' concerning 'the Temple of Jupiter, the concluding scene in the new grand ballet of the Sabines, in which there is a pleasing mixture of that magnificence which suits the awfulness of the place, and that neat simplicity which could not but attend even the grandest edifices amongst the Romans at that early period of their infant state'. Novosielski had apparently attempted to convey the fact that colonial Rome was not imperial Rome. A more dynamic comment comes from the *Morning Herald* of 17 December 1782: 'The peculiar merit of the new ballet and which must eminently distinguish it from all representations of that kind we have seen hitherto, is, that the principal performers are always in action, and fill the scene in a manner much more agreeable than the figurers could ever be supposed to do.' Even after we allow for exaggeration, the key point remains the word 'always'. The passage reflects the fact that Italian dance was more athletic than the French school. It also suggests that Le Picq's control of the *figurants* was less good than that of Vestris sen. or Noverre.

Given the generally high quality of Borghi's score (*The Celebrated Opera Dances*, Book IV, 1783), the loss of the scenario is particularly regrettable. Among the sixteen surviving pieces are two or three simple but overtly dramatic numbers obviously designed with a narrative purpose. For example, no. 7, a fast and furious *allegro* in D major, with unison flourishes and a

strength and agility, as made him acquire the surname of the *modern Hercules* bestowed upon him by all the spectators, who were delighted at the novelty of the exhibition.'

grumbling bass line, might have accompanied the Sabines, 'hair dishevelled', rushing about the stage. Borghi also seems to have been unusually concerned with the overall structure of his score; the various pieces are organized in a logical sequence of keys, with a good balance between sharp-side and flat-side, culminating in a huge *chaconne* in E flat major that relates back to lyrical pieces in the same key.

In the two previous seasons, when the company was busy assimilating change and not pinched for cash, personal rivalries were channelled productively or even forgotten. This season was different. Tensions between old and new dancers were such that an anonymous letter in the *Morning Herald* accused Simonet and the dancing-master Vallouis of publicly hissing Mme Rossi at the second performance of *Il ratto*. Simonet made a dignified protest, saying that 'He and Mr. Vallouis can produce witnesses of such a credibility, as will convince the *Subscriber* and the public, that the former was certainly misinformed. They at the same time can not sufficiently wonder how so aggravating a charge could be brought against them, under an anonymous signature, and invite the writer to disclose his real name, that they may have an opportunity of undeceiving him and the public.'[1] The undercurrent remained a factor in commentary throughout the season. Unfortunately, Mme Rossi fell seriously ill after the second performance, with the result that *Il ratto* never regained its momentum and accumulated only nine performances.

Finances inevitably affected dance as well as opera, though they were never spoken of in the papers. The first pay-day was probably late if scheduled for the end of December, as in 1780–81; and although Le Picq was paid that instalment in full, not everyone was. On 31 December 1782 Taylor borrowed £1,200, either for current expenses or to pay debts.[2] Two days earlier, Slingsby, who was having health problems, had announced his intention to retire (though he stayed on for two more seasons). In July he swore an affidavit that he was owed £680.[3] Mme Théodore's salary was reported in the *Morning Herald* of 13 May 1783 as £900. Well before the last pay-day she swore an affidavit that she was owed £373, and being short-paid may explain her dropping out of certain dances for long periods. An indication of unrest among the dancers is the refusal of some to perform the specially created

---

[1] See the *Morning Herald* for 19 and 23 Dec. 1782, and the attempt on 31 Dec. to end the debate over the dancers' merits.

[2] C12/133/13.

[3] PRIS 2/48, no. 4,778. On Taylor's creditors, see App. II.

'Prince of Wales's Minuet' at the masquerade on 23 January 1783. According to the *Public Advertiser* of 25 January, 'The Public were in Expectation of Quadrilles by the principal Performers; but some of them having made Demands in money, contrary to the Custom and the Tenor of their Engagements, the Dances were suppressed.' The report goes on to exonerate Le Picq, Slingsby, Henry, Rossi, Théodore, and Crespi. The only genuine 'principals' left would have been the Simonets; Zuchelli and Caterina Sala might have made another couple. Ordinarily such insubordination would have meant dismissal, but so many creditors, past and present, were clamouring by then that this small incident went almost unnoticed. The Simonets were the less expendable because Mme Théodore had just suffered a serious fall.[1]

Le Picq's most successful ballet for the season was *Le tuteur trompé*, which received its première on 11 January 1783 and enjoyed thirty-five performances during the season. Manifestly derived from Paisiello's *Il barbiere di Siviglia*, which had yet to be seen in London, it depended largely on the virtuoso dancing of Le Picq and Mme Rossi for its appeal.[2] However amusing, this ballet provoked comments that admit in a roundabout way to Le Picq's lesser accomplishments in choreography. The *Morning Herald* sounded a conservative note:

Those dances where mirth and a display of agility are the chief requisites, are likely to be restored to their former consequence by Mons. Le Picq undertaking to compose that kind of lively ballets which keep a medium between the insignificant *divertissement*, and the sublimity of the *ballet d'action*. 'In medio virtus', says the old adage, and we think it here very applicable. The above middling stile of dancing is to a Serious ballet what a pleasing entertaining novel is to the loftier strain of historical gravity; the latter may move the passions, the former is sure to please them by inspiring the spectators with that lively pleasure which dancing is originally meant to convey. (11 January 1783)

---

[1] The *Public Advertiser* of 27 Jan. adds that 'When Performers meet with such unlucky Accidents they are not only entitled to the utmost Indulgence, but have a just Claim to public Concern; and here it may not be improper to observe to those who so clamourously inveigh against the large Salaries allowed to Foreign [i.e. French] Dancers, that in their Country if disabled by accidental Misfortunes they are sure of a certain Income for Life; whereas here they have only the Chance of a small Portion of Pity and Compassion, without any other Recompence.'

[2] Reviews in the *Morning Herald* and *Public Advertiser* on 13 Jan. 1783 acknowledge the source. Together with the *Public Advertiser* of 10 Feb. 1783 they make clear that Le Picq was Almaviva, Mme Rossi Rosina, and Zuchelli the old guardian, roles not specified in *The London Stage*.

Three days later the paper reiterated the theme, saying that 'in the composition of his dances, [Le Picq] has proved incontrovertibly, that there could be grand ballets without the assistance of *all hell broke loose*, and divertissements in the demi-character without tinsel and frippery, yet by no means destitute of plot and intrigue; of the first, the Sabines, is an instance; as the *Tuteur trompé* is of the latter'.

These comments sought to make a virtue of necessity, since management must have known by this time that there would be no money for full-scale *ballets d'action* this season. *Les épouses persanes* attempted far too complex a story for dance; it disappeared after seven performances. So many substitutions were advertised during the nineteen nights of *Il riposo del campo* that it cannot be considered more than a *divertissement*. *Le tuteur* endured, and it was enlivened with Spanish dances on 10 April. Six other ballets were not reviewed, being *pièces d'occasion*. At least one of them was so sloppily got up that Mme Théodore, the beneficiary, apologized for it in her thanks to the public.[1]

Borghi's score for *Le tuteur trompé*,[2] like that of *Il ratto delle Sabine*, shows a carefully worked out, rounded key structure, with simple but lively pieces, some of whose titles may relate to the story: 'I Cacciatori' and 'Il Vecchio', for example. The final numbers, a 'Pas de Basque' and a 'Contradanza', are more generic but maintain the high spirits. The music of *Les épouses persanes* ('La sposa persiana') and *Il riposo del campo* (*The Celebrated Opera Dances*, Book [IV]) is fragmentary. Only six pieces of the former survive, and the latter includes the 'Seguedilla' and 'Fandango' that were added to *Le tuteur trompé*.

Taylor tried to set up a trust on 17 March 1783, but his first effort left his creditors unplacated. Seventeen of them banded together, obtained a writ of habeas corpus, and had Taylor arrested on 5 April. Though their debts ran from £12 to £1,400, the group included no performers, who as a rule did not want to pay steep legal fees or face the hassle of a foreign legal system. The second group that kept Taylor in gaol was thirteen strong. They materialized on 7 May, being owed between £14 and £920 (the latter to Hayling). The only performer was Mme Théodore: no wonder she was willing to

---

[1] In the *Morning Herald* of 10 May 1783 she regrets the disappointment of the second ballet, 'which was really owing to a violent ague fever, the which for want of her attendance at the theatre, retarded Mons. Lepic from commencing the composing the Ballet till the morning of the Benefit'. Such an apology was most unusual.

[2] *The Celebrated Opera Dances*, Book [III] (1783).

speak to the audience on 10 May, at the risk of sexist slurs and satiric debunking of her plea. The Sheriff's sale on 14 May was so obviously rigged that it discouraged a number of other people. Le Picq joined the lawsuits on 20 June, hoping for £867 in back pay; Slingsby joined on 10 July (though he later signed the deed of trust).

On the last night of the season, along with *Il riposo del campo* and *Le tuteur trompé*, Le Picq scheduled *The Four Nations*, the *pièce d'occasion* he had done at the 17 and 24 June Pantheon benefits for his beleaguered colleagues. This healing gesture, which presented Mme Simonet as the representative of France, Slingsby and Mme Théodore for England, Zuchelli and Signora Crespi for 'Africa', and himself and Mme Rossi for 'Poland', suggests that Le Picq had decided to remain. Gallini was nominally in charge from early in June, and his dance company was said to be set after a visit to Paris in July.[1] By 30 August Le Picq was 'fixing his residence' in London, ready to give dance lessons and live a less hectic professional life.[2]

## Ballet under the Trustees, 1783–1785

### Ballet Repertoire for 1783–84[3]

*Divertissement*, no choreographer credited, 29 November 1783 (2 performances)

*New Divertissement*, no choreographer credited, 29 November 1783 (8 performances)[4]

*The Pastimes of Terpsycore*, Dauberval, 6 December 1783, 'an Allegorical Ballet', music by Barthélemon (14 performances)

*Friendship Leads to Love, or L'amitié conduit à l'amour*, Dauberval, 6 December 1783, 'a new Anacreontic Ballet' (19 performances)[5]

*The Slaves of Conquering Bacchus*, Dauberval, 17 January 1784, 'an entirely new dance, connected with the Opera', music by Barthélemon (3 performances)

*Le réveil du bonheur*, Dauberval, 3 February 1784, 'an entirely new Anacreontic Ballet, first time', music by Barthélemon (15 performances)

*[Second] Divertissement*, Dauberval, 7 February 1784, music by Barthélemon (9 performances)

---

[1] *Morning Herald*, 19 and 22 July 1783.

[2] He advertised lessons in the *Morning Herald*, 30 Aug. 1783.

[3] The *London Stage* roster of ballets for 1783–84 is seriously defective: at least fifty-one performances of several dances are not included in the statistics. This problem arises in part because advertisements for *divertissements* are especially confusing this season, but also because the dances that were part of the opera *La regina di Golconda* were overlooked.

[4] Said to be 'part of the ballet of *Auld Robin Gray*, which for want of time could not be completed'; the *Morning Herald* review of 1 Dec. 1783 was highly complimentary of 'the manner in which [Mme Rossi] painted in her pantomime the distress of the poor forlorn *Jenny . . .* [she] *acted* feelingly *every word* of the song'. A ballet entitled *Robin Gray* was not done at the King's Theatre until 14 Apr. 1785.

[5] The review in the *Morning Herald* of 8 Dec. 1783 shows that this ballet had a Middle Eastern setting.

*Le cocq du village; ou, La lotterie ingénieuse*, Dauberval, 26 February 1784, 'an entirely new ballet in the Rural Stile' (12 performances)

*Orpheo*, Dauberval, 6 March 1784, 'new Grand Ballet', music by Barthélemon (3 performances)

*Le magnifique*, Dauberval, 11 March 1784 (1 performance)

*\*Ballet* (of warriors) in *La regina di Golconda*, Dauberval, 18 March 1784 (11 performances)

*\*Dance* (of shepherds) in *La regina di Golconda*, Dauberval, 18 March 1784 (11 performances)

*The Four Ages of Man* in *La regina di Golconda*, Dauberval, 18 March 1784 (4 performances)

*Pygmalion*, Dauberval, 25 March 1784, a 'new ballet, composed for the occasion' (1 performance)

*Le tuteur trompé*, Le Picq, 25 March 1784, revived from 1782–83 as a *pièce d'occasion* with new dances (7 performances)

*\*[Second] New Divertissement*, Dauberval, 24 April 1784, 'in the Serious and Demi Character' (12 performances)

**Le déserteur; ou La clémence royale**, Dauberval, 13 May 1784, 'an entirely new grand Ballet, or Tragi-Comic Dancing Pantomime', some of the music from Monsigny's opera (16 performances) (p. 490)

*Sémiramis*, Le Picq, 20 May 1784, 'a Grand Heroic Pantomime Ballet' (3 performances)

In Paris Gallini made final arrangements for Vestris jun. to be principal dancer and Dauberval to be ballet-master. Dauberval had been one of the major dancers of his generation and had spent a successful season in London in 1763–64. He was a thoroughly experienced ballet-master in the French tradition. Gallini and Dauberval assembled a balanced and varied company, the French component holding pride of place, with Vestris jun. and Mme Théodore Dauberval as the principals, but Le Picq and Mme Rossi provided a very strong Italian second couple. New Italian-trained dancers were Blake (a native of Ireland), Monetti (who disappeared after two months), and Pitrot (who arrived in May). Zuchelli and Henry remained and Slingsby deferred his retirement. Mme Simonet worked regularly, but retired at the end of the season; her family appeared only on occasion.[1] The company was much better provided with male than female dancers.

While Gallini jockeyed with the trustees for control of the company, there was not a great deal of money to spend on dance. Two factors make this season difficult to evaluate. Advertisements highlight a wider variety of featured dances within *divertissements* than usual, making the basic *divertissement* harder to identify. This change may represent a freer approach on Dauberval's part, or it may be a disclosure of standard policy with such

---

[1] Louis Simonet may not have participated in anything except his wife's benefit. Leonore and Rosine were dancing at the Royal Circus in January, but were advertised at the King's Theatre in March.

dances, as well as a means of promoting the dancers' specialities. Second, for unknown reasons dance received short shrift in reviews this season. The most important production from a historical point of view, *Le déserteur* (hereafter referred to as *The Deserter*), was not reviewed at all, because it came out at a benefit. One-line formulas praising dancers abound: 'nothing could be more pleasant than Vestris and Theodore', or 'we shall have said enough [about a *divertissement*] when we add that it concludes by a *pas de trois* between Le Picq, Slingsby, and Madame Rossi'.[1] Perhaps the most informative comment of the season says that the ballets integrated into *La regina di Golconda* 'could not have more conspicuous aid—Theodore, through a whole act, almost always on the stage. Le Picq, Vestris, never were seen more, or to more advantage. . . . The conclusion of the middle dance, where all the principal dancers are seen on a rising ground at the end of the stage, is, in respect to attitudes, a scene most exquisitely finished.'[2] Not everyone agreed. The *Morning Post*, hostile to the entire production, stated that the ballets 'by no means answer our expectation. Monsieur D'Auberval certainly is one of the most elegant dancers that ever appeared on any stage, but the dances exhibited last night seemed too full of grimaces, and conveyed very little meaning' (*Morning Post*, 19 March 1784). The *Morning Chronicle* of 23 April found the opera 'nothing very striking . . . What makes it bearable are the pageantry and the dances. These with the chorusses working at the same time, produce effects of the most agreeable kind.' Since lack of money had ruled out full-length *ballets d'action* this season, there was less in the way of stories for reviewers to discuss. The strength of the company was in its stars, and Dauberval put more effort into showing them off than into telling elaborate stories. That effort, of course, disappeared with the dances it produced.

A miscellany of dances issued by the violinist and répétiteur Felice Chabran with a title-page date of 1783 may contain some dances from the previous season, but was promoted using the names of dancers in the 1783–84 company. The first volume includes sixteen dances, only one of which, an *andantino* in A major (pp. 28–9) for Vestris and Mme Théodore, is attributable to a specific work: 'Pastorello', which either came from *The Pastimes of Terpsycore* or was the *pas de deux* added to the *New Divertissement* for the couple on 16 December.[3]

[1] See the *Morning Chronicle*, 6 Mar. 1784, and the *Morning Herald*, 17 Dec. 1783.
[2] *Morning Chronicle*, 19 Mar. 1784.
[3] *The Celebrated Dances Performed by Messrs. Le Picq, Vestris Junr. and Slingsby Mesds.*

The plethora of titles in the repertoire demonstrates that Dauberval kept his company busy. The pattern of offerings was affected by Le Picq's illness throughout January, by attempts to integrate ballet with operas, and by the trustees' regaining control of the company in mid-February. These factors resulted in a high proportion of benefit-related premières, which may be a sign of cash-flow problems. Most benefit productions this season were retained for multiple performances.

Building dances into an opera carried some risk: the more closely they were identified with an opera, the more difficult they might be to separate from it. In January 1784 Dauberval and the composer Barthélemon prepared *The Slaves of Conquering Bacchus* to complement *Il trionfo d'Arianna*, but when the opera disappeared after only three performances, the ballet disappeared with it, despite a positive review. The *Orpheo* in March (intended to go with *Demofoonte* for Pacchierotti's benefit, but delayed) was also seen only three times.[1] The story concerns 'the destruction of the infamous rites of Bacchus [called] . . . Orgies. This miracle was reserved to Orpheus, who by the power of harmony "soothed the savage breasts of the Bacchants", and forced them to confess that the only worship that can be acceptable to the Deity, is that which is founded on virtue and moral equity.' One of the attractions was the opportunity for Mme Rossi as the Priestess Evohe to show both 'her heaven inspired fury' and 'her melting to the soft, all subduing lyre of Orpheus', but Le Picq, whose return was welcomed, had visibly not yet recovered.[2]

For *La regina di Golconda* Dauberval made a much-publicized suite of three dances.[3] The *Dance of Warriors* and that of *Shepherds* continued to be used at subsequent performances, but *The Four Ages of Man* was offered only four times. Dauberval appeared among the shepherds and also as Mme Simonet's partner in the 'Old Age' *pas de deux* even though he was not being paid to dance: he chose to perform because the production was his benefit.[4] Small discrepancies between the libretto of *Alina: or, The Queen of*

*Theodore D'Auberval, Simonet and Sigra. Rossi at the King's Theatre Hay Market 1783 Adapted for the Harpsichord, Violin or German Flute. Composed by Mr. Barthelemon Sigr. Rauzzini, and others . . . Engrav'd Printed and Sold by F. Chabran* (London: James Freeman, n.d.).

[1] No scenario appears to survive for the London production, but the *Morning Herald* reported on the opera and the dance together, and the subjects are appropriately classical.

[2] See the pre-show notice in the *Morning Herald* of 6 Mar. 1784 and the review there on 8 Mar.

[3] See the *Morning Herald*, 2, 15, 16, and 18 Mar. 1784.

[4] On Dauberval's pay, see the *Morning Herald* of 22 May 1784.

*Golconda* (H. Reynell, 1784) and advertisements suggest that the ballet underwent some late changes. In the libretto the improbable 'Chinese' coda to the four 'ages of life' was a quartet, but only three men were advertised when the production opened. The omission of Monetti, who was not advertised after 3 February, is related to the trustees' dissatisfaction with his dancing. At an unstated date in the spring they actually bought out his contract (C31/233, no. 322).

If the campaign for *Golconda* featured ballet, so did the campaign against it. The *Morning Post* fiercely attacked the production; the *Morning Herald*, which covered the arts most systematically, tended to be hostile to Gallini and hence was pro-*Golconda*. A creditor signing himself 'J. S.' objected to the fact that the very first performance was to be a benefit night, the more so because Dauberval had been paid £150 beyond his salary for the dances in the opera.[1] A more plausible interpretation is suggested by a paragraph of estimates of benefit takings in the *Morning Chronicle* of 20 April, which reports that Dauberval's night brought in £700, but that he had sold it to the management for £150. If so, he essentially allowed them to use his name and the novelty of a new production in exchange for a flat fee.

The *Golconda* controversy provides another insight into the internal politics of the company. Dauberval had been Gallini's choice as ballet-master. Why was he then *persona grata* to the trustees, especially in view of the undistinguished reviews he garnered? A story with the earmarks of a publicity release that appeared in the *Morning Herald* of 15 March 1784 explains that when Simon Slingsby was dancing at the Opéra (1765–66), he had the good fortune to be chosen to serve as Dauberval's 'double', that is, to dance his roles in second casts. The energetic Slingsby, although popular, was not satisfied with his own dancing and sought further instruction. Dauberval 'no sooner heard of the laudable emulation of the little *Englishman*, as Slingsby was then called, than he returned on purpose from the country, took upon him to teach him those admirable steps in which he himself is inimitable'. The puff goes on to celebrate their friendship and their talents. The point here is that Dauberval had an ally who was a trustee, a fact that goes far to explain special arrangements made for him and Théodore.

### *Dauberval's* The Deserter

Whoever made the investment, the lasting glory of this season was *The Deserter*, which quickly became a classic. (Among its numerous revivals was

---

[1] *Morning Post*, 18 Mar. 1784. 'J. S.' might have been John Siscotti, Joseph Smith, or Joseph Saunders.

one by Dauberval at the Pantheon in the spring of 1791, which will be discussed in vol. 11.) In the *Morning Post* of 25 March 1784 Mme Théodore announced that in response to 'the desire which several of the Nobility and Gentry have expressed, of seeing a Grand Ballet d'Action', her benefit would include *The Deserter*. No scenario was published for this production, because the fairy-tale of a malicious truth-test of lovers was familiar to the London audience from Charles Dibdin's 1773 musical, likewise based on Sedaine's libretto for the Monsigny *opéra-comique*.[1]

A soldier (Le Picq), distracted by the false intelligence that his sweetheart (Mme Rossi) has married in his absence, tears off his accoutrements and runs away. He is arrested for desertion and condemned. Friends and colleagues try ineffectually to help, one (Dauberval) by attempting to get him drunk. His sweetheart ignores bureaucracy and contrives, by throwing herself on the King's mercy, to get him a pardon, which she delivers barely in time to save him from the firing-squad, and the lovers are united. The story allows for a peasant wedding procession, a royal review of troops, and the last-minute rescue, as well as many individual exchanges such as the drinking scene with Skirmish and the King's hearing of the plea.

The enthusiastic reviewer in the *Public Advertiser* of 15 May 1784 was able to evaluate what he saw, in part because he was reporting on the presentation of a story more than on the dance and mime conveying it. Thus he pointed out that 'D'Auberval's Drunkenness was well managed; Rossi's Fainting Fit, her Agitation preceding it, and her Revival from it: Le Picq's hovering over Rossi when in the Swoon, and in his Separation from her, were all told very expressively indeed.' Dauberval's 'Pas in a Style entirely new, and never before attempted in England', promised in advertisements, elicited no comment. About dance the reviewer could only resort to generalities: 'Le Picq is the most graceful Dancer in Europe, and excells every Competitor in the Narrative and Pathos of Gesticulation'; 'Vestris and Theodore were both inimitable; their Capriccios were more feathered than ever.' Vestris played the character known in England as Simkin, whom Dauberval later described as the 'Supposed Husband' (see below). Mme Théodore played the jealous friend who started the rumours of Louisa's

---

[1] Zuchelli had done a 'pantomime Dance' entitled *Il disertore* on 14 Dec. 1779. Lack of scenarios prevents direct comparison, but Dauberval's version must have been much more elaborate. The story was popular. The same newspaper that carried Mme Théodore's announcement also advertised a dramatization at the Academy and Military Room, Exeter-Change, Strand, by a 'Theatrical Comic Company of Dogs'. The more elaborate advertisement in the *Morning Herald* of 18 Sept. 1784 identifies the trainer as Signor Scaglioni and shows that his plot included no love interest.

marriage, not a very attractive character for her benefit night. However, music late in the score implies that she and Simkin were sorry for the trouble they caused and that by the end of the story she had turned her attentions to Skirmish. Mme Théodore's 'Capriccios' may have come in the dances at the end of the ballet, or perhaps the reviewer was referring to the evening's other ballet, *Le réveil du bonheur*.[1]

Dauberval tactfully acknowledged the contributions of Le Picq and Mme Rossi. The 15 May 1784 *Morning Herald* reported that

A circumstance happened on Thursday night last at the conclusion of that night's entertainment at the King's Theatre, which does great honor to the feelings of Mons. d'Auberval. When Mrs. Theodore came forwards to make the usual reverence, the plaudits she met with so far affected M. d'Auberval, that in a kind of extacy he closely embraced M. Lepicq and shewed him to the audience, as much as to say 'this is the man to whom I chiefly owe the success of this night.'—This is doing strict justice to merit, for in truth the amazing exertions of Mr. Lepicq and Mme Rossi in the acting part of the pantomime of the Deserteur, must certainly entitle them to the fullest gratitude of Mr and Mrs d'Auberval, who, without the assistance of two such admirable actors could not have got up the above drama in so complete a manner.

This vignette confirms the practice of star calls for dancers, at least at benefits.

Dauberval's *The Deserter* is the first *ballet d'action* produced by the King's Theatre during the period under consideration that owes a substantial debt to an opera: Pierre-Alexandre Monsigny's eponymous *opéra-comique*. More music survives for the ballet (and the 1785 revival) than for any other discussed in this book, though the dances and pantomime links are in some disarray and thus no easier to fit to the scenario than the music of other less well-preserved works. The score of the 1784 production exists in two versions: *The Deserter A new Grand Ballet by Mr. D'Aubervall Performed with great Applause at the Kings Theatre Hay Market 1784 Adapted for the Harpsichord Violin or Ger: Flute Compos'd by Mr. Monsigni*, Book IV (printed for F. Chabran by James Freeman); and *The Deserter . . . Revived by Mr. Le Picq . . . 1785. The Music by Mr. Monsigni with several new Airs Composed and the whole properly adapted for the Harpsichord, Violin, or German Flute By F. H. Barthelemon* (Longman and Broderip). Chabran also published a second volume of music for the 1785 revival, which is discussed

---

[1] For what little is known of this ballet, see the *Morning Herald* of 5 and 19 Feb. 1784. Vestris and Théodore shared a brilliant *pas de deux* in it.

below. Apart from two substitutions, the contents of the two productions are identical, though with quite different piano arrangements: Chabran's basses are often quite inept while Barthélemon's left-hand parts are generally more idiomatic and harder to play, but there is little to choose between them for ubiquitous crudity.[1] Although both title-pages proclaim that the music was 'composed by Mr. Monsigni', the ballet is in fact a pastiche with a clear musical connection to Monsigny's immensely successful *opéra-comique* of 1769. Anyone familiar with the original might have detected the following adaptations:

1. the brief C major overture to the ballet is the first section (allegretto soutenato [*sic*]) of Monsigny's overture;

2. no. 2,[2] an andante danced by Mme Rossi, is based on Louise's 'Peut on affliger ce qu'on aime?' in Act I, Scene i;

3. no. 3, a brief allegretto, is based on Jeanette's 'J'avois gar' in Act I, Scene iii;

4. no. 4, Le Picq's adagio–allegro, is based on Alexis's 'Ah! je respire' in Act I, Scene iv;

5. no. 10, a D minor andante, begins like Alexis's air 'Mourir n'est rien' in Act II, Scene ii;

6. no. 11, a grazioso with two adagio interpolations, and thus probably a section of pantomime, resembles Montauciel's 'Je ne déserterai jamais' in Act II, Scene iii;

7. no. 13, an andante, points to Louise's 'Dans quel trouble' in Act II, Scene vi;

8. no. 14, a gavotte-like dance in G minor, is very closely related to the duet for Bertrand and Montauciel, 'Vive le vin', in Act II, Scene xvii.[3]

The ballet also owes something to the English version of Monsigny's opera given in Drury Lane in 1773, from which Charles Dibdin had filtered out 'that sameness which so particularly characterizes the French music'. He

---

[1] John Ward has suggested to us that Chabran, a violinist, may have worked with a répétiteur, while Barthélemon, an experienced composer, based his more demanding left-hand parts on the full score. This would also explain why Longman and Broderip's title-page describes Barthélemon's version as 'properly adapted', implying that Chabran's was not.

[2] The numbers assigned to individual dances in this discussion are editorial.

[3] We are grateful to John Ward for pointing out that almost all the borrowings are from the vocal and not the instrumental parts of the opera and that they occur in their original order.

TABLE 13. *Comparison of the 1784 and 1785 productions of* The Deserter

| no. | title or tempo | dancers in 1784 | dancers in 1785 |
|---|---|---|---|
| — | Overture | | |
| (1) | Andantino | Mme Théodore, Mme Rossi | Sigra Zuchelli, Mlle Dorival, Mme Rossi |
| (2) | Andante | Mme Rossi | Mme Rossi |
| (3) | Allegretto | Mme Théodore | Mlle Dorival |
| (4) | Adagio–allegro | Le Picq | Le Picq |
| (5) | Poco lento | Le Picq | Le Picq |
| (6) | Allegretto | Vestris and Mme Rossi | Nivelon and Mme Rossi |
| (7*a*) | [untitled] | Mme Théodore | [not in 1785] |
| (7*b*) | Andantino | [not in 1784] | Mlle Dorival |
| (8) | Allegro spirituoso | Mme Théodore, Mme Rossi, Vestris | Mlle Dorival, Mme Rossi, Nivelon |
| (9) | Grazioso | Le Picq | Le Picq |
| (10) | Andante | Le Picq | Le Picq |
| (11) | Grazioso | Dauberval | Slingsby |
| (12) | Gavotta | Mme Rossi | Mme Rossi |
| (13) | Andante | Le Picq and Mme Rossi | Le Picq and Mme Rossi |
| (14) | untitled | Dauberval and Vestris | Nivelon and Slingsby |
| (15) | Allegretto | Vestris and Mme Théodore | Slingsby and Nivelon |
| (16) | Lento | Mme Rossi | Mme Rossi |
| (17) | Adagio | Le Picq | Le Picq (ending shortened) |
| (18) | Andantino | Mme Rossi | Mme Rossi |
| (19) | [untitled]*a* | Mme Rossi | Mme Rossi |
| (20) | March | no dancer named | no dancer named |
| (21*a*) | Allegro | Vestris and Mme Théodore | [not in 1785] |
| (21*b*) | The slow March | [not in 1784] | Nivelon and Mlle Dorival |
| (22) | Minuetto | Mme Rossi and Le Picq | Mme Rossi and Le Picq |
| (23) | Allegro | Mme Rossi and Le Picq | Mme Rossi and Le Picq |

| no. | title or tempo | dancers in 1784 | dancers in 1785 |
| --- | --- | --- | --- |
| (24) | Allegro | Dauberval and Mme Théodore | Slingsby and Mlle Dorival |
| (25) | Finale | tutti | tutti |

*a* John Ward suggests to us that nos. 18 and 19 form a single number: the first ends on the dominant and is marked 'volti'.

accordingly 'selected what I thought the beauties, and what I could not effect by having recourse to the original, I endeavoured to supply myself'.[1] Apart from the possible association of certain tunes with Sedaine's or Dibdin's words, the music of the ballet alone conveys little sense of the story; everything would have depended on the pantomime.

The surviving music for the 1784 production comprises an overture and twenty-five dances (an exceptionally large number for such printed collections), including a finale that gives the impression of completeness. But in 1785 Chabran brought out a second book, whose pagination is continuous with the first and which includes a further twenty-seven pieces. Unlike Book I, no dancers are named and the music is of a largely different character: short, sometimes inconclusive pieces, rarely with titles, and some with frequent shifts of metre and tempo. All this suggests that Book II is an appendix of music for the pantomimes, which, when taken out of context, makes very little sense, however essential to the narrative. The first book may also include music for pantomime. Suspicion falls particularly on no. 9 (see Table 13), which includes five changes of tempo, and no. 21*a*, which has six—typical of music designed to accompany action.[2]

In terms of number of performances, *The Deserter* was a great success. It was given sixteen times, that is, at all but four of the performances remaining in the season. However, its triumph was marred by an outburst of temperament from Vestris, who thought he should have had the title-role.[3] Rivalry between him and Le Picq had been crackling at least since Le Picq had recovered his health.[4] Vestris was so hissed in the theatre and berated in

[1] *The Deserter; a New Musical Drama* (London: T. Becket, 1773), p. v.

[2] We are grateful to John Ward for this observation.

[3] For hostile reactions to his swelled head, see the 19–22 May 1784 *Morning Post* and *Morning Herald* reports.

[4] See e.g. the *Morning Herald*, 26 Apr. 1784.

the press that the former idol saw the wisdom of a public apology. He had accepted a lesser role only because this was a *pièce d'occasion*, which he did not expect to be repeated.[1] This disingenuous excuse points up the success of the ballet, but also the potential landmines in company politics. For Dauberval the incident still rankled years later. In an 'Avertissement au Public Sur la reprise du Ballet du *Déserteur*', obviously after 1789, he recounts the creation for 'Citizen Vestris' of a 'character quite worthy of [him], that I called the Supposed Husband', which would show off the many talents he generously attributes to the young dancer.[2] That character seems to be closer to Simkin in the Dibdin version of the story than to Bertrand in Sedaine's 1769 original. Le Picq emerged from the production with great credit, Vestris jun. with a tarnished reputation.

Most of the rest of the ballet music in 1783–84 was composed or arranged by Barthélemon, who seems to have worked particularly well with Dauberval. Chabran's *Celebrated Dances . . . for 1784*, composed by Barthélemon and Rauzzini, includes an overture and thirteen numbers of an unnamed work. The individual titles ('Pastorello', 'Scotch Dance', 'Polonoise', 'Allemande', and so forth) might give a clue to its identity, but most ballets of the period, whether *divertissement* or *d'action*, include a similar miscellany. Two comments about the execution of dance music deserve attention. Noting the unusual integration of opera and ballet in *La regina di Golconda*, one reviewer pointed out that the first violin continued to lead for the dances. He considered that the usual procedure, of the first violin's 'sitting unoccupied during the dance, and deputing the conduct of it to inferior players', was a 'privilege' that should be withdrawn (*Morning Chronicle*, 23 April 1784). However, a such a change would not have improved the performance unless the first violin had rehearsed extensively with the dancers. Time constraints made that difficult or impossible. There was a separate 'leader of the dances' because he needed to practice with the dancers in order to learn what tempos they wanted. A further comment on this subject appeared in the review of *The Deserter* in the *Morning Post* of 15 May 1784: 'As to the Band of the Dances, Borghi, the best and only proper Leader, is driven from the Lead by the abominable Penury and Dullness of the present

---

[1] What is announced as a translation of his speech is printed in the *Morning Herald* of 22 May 1784, which goes on to comment that, having agreed to participate, Vestris did so wholeheartedly. However, a whiff of truth remains in the summary that appeared the previous day in the *Morning Post*, which says Vestris resented having to take a role 'greatly beneath his dignity and pre-eminence as *premier Danseur absolu*'.

[2] Undated flyer bound into a collection of scenarios at the University of California, Berkeley (Bancroft PQ1222.C2, vol. 33); our translation.

Managers, and some new Subaltern last Night was foisted into his Place.' Whether Borghi was asking for more money or was only ill, management could not do away with the 'leader of the dances'.

Reviewing the season of 1783–84, one finds that Dauberval kept the company functioning smoothly despite the administrative chaos caused by double management and the hazards of star egos. To the developing repertoire of the *ballet d'action* in London he was able to add only a single piece, but *The Deserter* proved that ballet could tell a full-length contemporary story. At the end of the year the Daubervals went off to Bordeaux, where they flourished.

## Ballet Repertoire for 1784–85

*Divertissement,* Le Picq, 18 December 1784, 'entirely new' (20 performances)

*Le parti de chasse d'Henry IV,* Le Picq, 18 December 1784, 'new Grand Ballet' (4 performances)

*Le tuteur trompé,* revival by Le Picq of his 1783 production, 1 January 1785, 'with several new Airs composed by Barthélemon' (6 performances)

*The Deserter,* revival by Le Picq of Dauberval's 1784 production, 11 January 1785, 'with several new Airs composed by Barthélemon' (21 performances)

*Il convito degli dei,* Le Picq, 5 February 1785, 'an entirely new Divertissement', music by Barthélemon (3 performances)

*Le jugement de Paris,* Le Picq, 12 February 1785, 'an entirely new Divertissement', music by Barthélemon (6 performances)

*\*New Divertissement,* no choreographer credited, but the *London Magazine* of March 1785 implies Nivelon, 3 March 1785, 'part of the Music composed by Barthélemon' (10 performances)

*A la plus sage, ou La vertu récompensée* (a version of Gardel sen.'s *La rosière de Salency*), no choreographer credited, but the *London Magazine* of March 1785 implies Nivelon, 3 March 1785 (6 performances)

**Il convitato di pietra**, also advertised as *Don Juan, or The Libertine Destroyed*, Le Picq, 12 March 1785, 'entirely new Ballet . . . music by Gluck', selected and arranged by Barthélemon (18 performances) (p. 499)

**Macbeth**, Le Picq, 17 March 1785, 'a new Heroic Ballet . . . the original Music by Matthew Locke [probably Richard Leveridge] is entirely preserved; the rest partly new [by Barthélemon], partly compiled from the most favourite Scotch Airs' (1 performance) (p. 501)

*L'amour soldat,* no choreographer credited, 7 April 1785, 'an entirely new Ballet' (1 performance)

*Les amours d'été,* Le Picq, 14 April 1785, 'an entire new Ballet, the subject taken from a much admired French Opera' of the same title (1 performance)

*Robin Gray,* no choreographer credited, 14 April 1785, music by Barthélemon (6 performances)[1]

---

[1] That this ballet was given its première at Le Picq's benefit almost certainly means he was the choreographer. Part of the ballet was done at the beginning of the previous season, to avoid delaying the season on account of Théodore's illness and Vestris's late arrival.

Dances incidental to Gluck's *Orfeo*, Le Picq, 12 May 1785, additional music by J. C. Bach
and Handel (10 performances)
*New Divertissement*, Simonet, 18 June 1785 (2 performances)

For 1784–85 Taylor's beleaguered trustees employed Le Picq as both ballet-
master and principal dancer. Along with Mme Rossi and the increasingly
fragile Slingsby, he had Nivelon, who had taken the place of Vestris jun. at
the Opéra the previous season.[1] Among the newcomers were Carolina Pitrot
Angiolini and her husband Pietro (who was basically a *figurant*); Mons.
Frédéric; and, to replace Mme Théodore, Mlle Dorival, in whom the Prince
of Wales developed a much-discussed interest.[2] In October the opera advertised a try-out for other dancers, the first during the period surveyed in this
book: 'Dancers of both Sexes, who may think themselves capable of dis-
charging the duty of Coryphees and Figure Dancers', were invited to a
meeting 'for the purpose of fixing upon the number of couples wanted for
the approaching Season'. Twenty such dancers are listed in the libretto for
Tenducci's adaptation of Gluck's *Orfeo*.[3] The Simonets are missing from
the regular roster. Rosine Simonet played Cupid in *Orfeo*, and her father
was responsible for a *New Divertissement* very late in the season, but those
are the only traces of the family.[4] The company's offerings show that the
production budget was severely restricted and, despite the enormous popularity of *The Deserter*, of which a burlesque version appeared, complaints

[1] Which Nivelon is a tricky question. The authors of the *Biographical Dictionary*, xi. 33
and 36, identify the Nivelon who came to London with Noverre in 1781–82 as Louis-Marie
(?), *b.* 1760 (?), and the Nivelon of 1783–84 as 'C. Nivelon' (*fl.* 1784–93), and speculate that
he was the son of Louis-Marie, though this is hardly possible if the latter was born about
1760. The *Morning Herald* of 21 Dec. 1784 comments on rivalry between [Louis-Marie?]
Nivelon and Vestris jun. and welcomes Nivelon's return to England. One cannot disentangle
all references to the Nivelons with confidence, but we have worked on the hypothesis that
the Nivelon of both 1781–82 and 1783–84 was Louis-Marie.

[2] See e.g. the *Morning Post* of 7 Feb. 1785, and 5 and 23 Mar. Keeping such company was
more than Mlle Dorival could afford on her £350 salary: several performances were disrupted
when she was arrested for debt near the end of the season. See LC 7/3, fo. 191 and the *Morning Herald* between 21 and 27 June 1785.

[3] See the notice in the *Morning Herald* of 23 Oct. 1785. The list sent to press with the
libretto of *Orfeo* (J. Jarvis, 1785; BL 162.g.17) was so badly written that some of the misinter-
preted names remain a mystery. No doubt some of these people had been hired abroad. *Figurants* included A. Henry, Counle [Coindé], Duguene [Duquesney], Sala jun., Kincen, Sala
sen., Terry, [Pietro] Vigano, Blurton, Menade [Menage]. *Figurantes* included Mesdames
Julian, Trenier, Daiguiville [D'Egville], Hervey [Harvey], Sala, Fusi [Fuozi], Woodcock,
Cooper, Parish, and Vidini. According to a partial list of salaries for this season in LC 7/3, fo.
191, imported *figurants* were paid £80–5.

[4] Louis Simonet was owed money and petitioned the Lord Chamberlain for employment
(LC 7/3, fo. 252ʳ). This undated request may explain his late addition to the company.

were printed in the newspapers to the effect that Le Picq was shirking his duty.[1] The revival of *The Deserter* was marked by Longman and Broderip's publication of Barthélemon's revision (but without the music for the pantomime). The dancers and musical contents of the two productions are compared in Table 13 on pages 494–5.

Le Picq tried his hand at making new ballets but did not have much success. Several pieces received no more than six performances. Even the local origins of *Robin Gray*, bolstered by new *Caledonian Reels*, could not sustain it. In the first of their series of *Opera Dances*, Longman and Broderip, the King's Theatre's contracted music publishers, issued a score of *Robin Gray*, an overture and nine short pieces, including 'The Scotch Reel' and a 'Contredance'. They also published three other ballets this season, which are discussed below. Dances integrated into *Orfeo* managed ten performances, but also demonstrated a risk: when Le Picq came down with a 'sudden and dangerous illness', and Mlle Dorival was 'still indisposed' (that is, in gaol), the 21 June performance of the opera had to be cancelled for lack of principal dancers.

A Don Juan ballet, *Il convitato di pietra*, enjoyed eighteen performances, many favourable comments, and even a burlesque at the Little Theatre in the Haymarket danced by a number of the opera *figurants*.[2] The subject was not new to ballet or opera, but this version comes before the flowering of 1787 that included *Don Giovanni*, so Le Picq was ahead of fashion.[3] The detailed report in the *London Magazine* for March 1785 downplays the sexual element of the story. The tryst between Don Juan and the *commandeur*'s daughter received no comment. Instead there was only admiration for Don Juan's outrage with the father for opposing her 'disgrace'. The fugitive Don Juan carried off a village bride, a sequence not in all versions; he then returned to town and challenged the statue. The highlight of the evening was apparently Le Picq's *pas de trois* with Mlle Dorival and Mme Rossi before the banquet was interrupted. Unlike operatic versions, the ballet ended in hell, with the cliché of furies tormenting Don Juan. Nivelon was the betrayed bridegroom, Mlle Dorival his wayward sweetheart, so Mme Rossi must have been the *commandeur*'s daughter. The Pietro Angiolinis

---

[1] See the *Morning Post*, 4 Feb. and 3 Mar. 1785, and the *Morning Herald*, 19 Mar. Delpini was responsible for the burlesque, which began as a special production at the Little Theatre in the Haymarket in February.

[2] The burlesque, advertised without title on 15 Apr. 1785, was reviewed negatively in the *Morning Post* the next day.

[3] John Platoff, *Opera Grove*, i. 936–7. See also Winter, 132–6.

performed an amusing lovers' quarrel, probably before the wedding; and Frédéric got warm notices for his valet 'Crispin', who performed a Spanish dance. The run of *Don Juan* shows that Le Picq's work could still please most of the audience.

Longman and Broderip published the overture and twelve pieces, a mixture of dances and music to accompany pantomime. The title-page of the *Convitato di pietra* score states: 'The Music by the celebrated Chevalier Gluck in which is introduced a favorite Pas de Trois[.] Part of the Music by the above Author, and the whole adapted for the Harpsichord, Piano Forte, Violin & Flute, by F. H. Barthelemon.' The score borrows four numbers from Gluck's music for the influential ballet-pantomime *Don Juan ou Le festin de pierre* (Vienna, 1761, choreography by Gasparo Angiolini): besides the overture, the London production used nos. 1, 2, and 18.[1] The first two are for pantomime: 'Don Juan (Mr Le Picq) at night near the Commandeur, tells Crispin (Mr Frederic) to prepare for a Serenade to Donna Elvira'; 'Crispin with the Musicians for the Serenade.' Since the Longman and Broderip score presents only a selection, one cannot tell whether Barthélemon's version retained the most famous and remarkable part of Gluck's original: no. 31, the immolation of Don Juan. The harmonic complexity and furiously repeated semiquavers of this piece, not to mention its great length, would probably have precluded inclusion in Longman and Broderip's easy piano arrangements, but Gluck's ballet now seems unthinkable without it. Whether Le Picq and Barthélemon shared our modern scruples is another question.

As a dancer Le Picq had long since lost the appeal of novelty, but as a choreographer he was trying to be adventurous despite the limitations imposed by management. Like Dauberval, he was willing to co-operate with the opera department on an integrated production, as *Orfeo* proves. In the course of the season he also attempted two experiments, one minor and one major. He began his own benefit with *Les amours d'été*, a *pièce d'occasion* that was placed, quite exceptionally, *before* the opera, and did two other short ballets during the evening. Part of the reason for the placement of *A Summer's Love Tale*, about a fisherman's daughter and a miller's son, may have been to allow children to attend. The *Morning Chronicle* of 16 April 1785 reported:

---

[1] Citing the numbers in Christoph Willibald Gluck, *Sämtliche Werke*, ed. Rudolf Gerber, II/1 (Kassel: Bärenreiter, 1966).

The dances being almost the only attraction of this season, the dancers at their benefits fare accordingly. Le Picq had as great a receipt as Rossi! The pit was so entirely crowded, that the Prince could scarcely find room, before the curtain drew: and on going out after the first dance, could not, on his return, find a second place. The House was not ordinarily full, but filled, in several parts, so as to be doubly profitable, with children. Thus boxes had six, in which there usually are three or four chairs, and so on.

The same paper described the piece as 'a hasty expletive for the evening', but added that although 'The business, in regard to the mechanical parts, was rough and incomplete, the dancing as good as the subject allowed'. A much more severe review commented, 'On machinery at this Theatre the less stress is laid the better. The boat, of which, had it been good, there was too much use, was very far from good. The representation of Le Picq swimming transgressed as little the commandment. And as to the ascent of Le Picq in the bucket, that was so badly managed as to put us in heart-felt trepidation' (*Public Advertiser*, 16 April 1785). In happier times ballet-masters had conjured good technical support out of the staff, but this effort was late and hasty, and he was not well served.

## Le Picq's Macbeth

The importance of this ambitious but ill-advised project is that it demonstrates Le Picq's vision of what the *ballet d'action* could be. For Mme Rossi's benefit on 17 March he mounted *Macbeth*, 'a new Heroic Ballet founded on Shakespeare's Historical Play'. The advertisement made plain that *Macbeth* would go outside the norms of ballet, for it specified 'Vocal Parts' taken by Tasca, Franchi, Bartolini, and Signora D'Orta—that is, the principal singers —as well as 'Grand Chorusses'. Stimulated by management's interest in integrating the arts, Le Picq set out to reverse the usual process. Instead of blending incidental ballet into an opera, he tried adding vocal music to a story most of which was conveyed by dance and mime. The vocal music was announced as being the 'original' composed by Matthew Locke from the 1673 'operatical' version of the play, but only fragments of that score survived into the eighteenth century; what is referred to here is almost certainly the so-called 'Famous Musick' composed in 1702 by Richard Leveridge and soon thereafter misattributed to Locke until the present century.[1] The vocal music was apparently not danced to, rather the ballet itself was composed and arranged from Scottish folk-songs by Barthélemon. A clear sign that the

[1] See Fiske, *English Theatre Music in the Eighteenth Century*, 26–8.

company hoped for great things from Le Picq's hybrid production is the publication, proudly announced in the 23 March 1785 *Morning Post*, of Barthélemon's music for Act I.[1] Although published in piano rather than in full score, this is extremely important, being the only substantial fragment of a *ballet d'action* to survive for a 1780s King's Theatre production in which the function and position of the various dances are given.

Le Picq's choice of subject might appear daring, even bizarre, but he was in fact riding the crest of a wave of interest in *Macbeth*. The most recent revamping of the music for the play had been Samuel Arnold's collection of 'Favourite Scotch Airs' arranged for the Little Haymarket production of 1778. In 1780 J. A. Fisher composed a long, elaborate score that included two scenes for the witches not previously set to music, but whether this was intended for stage or concert performance is unclear.[2] *Macbeth* was much discussed during the winter of 1785: at just the time Le Picq's ballet was announced, Sarah Siddons played her first Lady Macbeth in London. John Philip Kemble had not yet joined her in the production that proved definitive for the end of the century, but challenging the theatre on Shakespearean ground was a bold innovation.[3] Unfortunately, the ballet was not repeated, and the rest of the music was apparently never published. Most of the cast is not known with certainty. Le Picq himself was the title character and Mme Rossi was Lady Macbeth. From the order in which dancers were advertised and from the music Pietro Angiolini appears to have played Banquo while Nivelon took Duncan (a role to which his rank in the company entitled him). Frédéric and Signora Pietro Angiolini were probably the Macduffs, and Mlle Dorival was a ranking lady of the court in Act I. Slingsby headed the Scottish peasants.

The first act of Barthélemon's score seems to survive intact. It includes a *Sturm und Drang* overture in D minor with a contrasting *andante* middle section, followed by fourteen separate numbers, most with descriptive titles—for example, 'Macbeth (Mr Le Picq) consulting the Witches'; 'Macbeth telling Lady Macbeth of the intended Visit of Duncan'. Several of

---

[1] *Macbeth, a grand ballet* (London: Longman and Broderip, n.d.). Copy used: Folger M1526 B17 Cage.

[2] See Paul F. Rice, 'John Abraham Fisher's Music for the Opening of Macbeth', *College Music Society Symposium*, 26 (1986), 7–13. See also B. N. S. Gooch and D. Thatcher, *A Shakespeare Music Catalogue* (Oxford: Oxford University Press, 1991), ii. 722, no. 6839.

[3] Siddons was potent competition, and in a benefit-thanks notice Mme Rossi said tactfully that 'To reach perfection in so trying a character' as Lady Macbeth 'she ever deemed for herself impossible. One actress alone could and has done it' (*Morning Herald*, 19 Mar. 1785).

Ex. 7.1. François Hippolyte Barthélemon, from *Macbeth*, Act I

these pieces are elegant and characteristically harmonized arrangements of well-known Scottish folk-tunes, such as 'The Braes of Ballanden', used to announce 'the coming of Duncan and his Courtiers'. Other numbers are newly composed links or narrative passages, more akin to *mélodrame* than *ballet d'action*. No. 5, 'Lady Macbeth (Sigra. Rossi) reading the Letter' is a good instance (see Ex. 7.1). No. 13, an extended piece whose function is not specified, is constructed exactly like a chain finale in an *opera buffa*. The first act ends with 'Macbeth conducting Duncan to bed', mimed to a mock Scottish tune in which Barthélemon exploits the ambiguity between G major and E minor to portentous effect (see Ex. 7.2 on page 504). Perhaps

Ex. 7.2. Barthélemon, from *Macbeth*, Act I

Barthélemon was carrying local colour to ridiculous extremes, but at its best his *Macbeth* music is wistful without being sentimental.

As these music examples show, the audience needed no scenario and none was published. *Macbeth*, however, strained the limits of what *ballet d'action* could do. The scenes that would translate into dance are immediately apparent. Battlefield rewards, a welcoming procession, preparations for murder, discovery and feigned surprise, banquet, sleep-walking, and final battle can all be visualized in the dance idiom of the time. Viewers would not have needed to be told that the man with Macbeth during the first scene with the witches was Banquo, nor would they have required an explanation of Macduff's enmity. Le Picq chose to expand Duncan's arrival at

Inverness into an entire ceremony, with peasants bringing fruits and flowers, and with various formal dances by the king and principal courtiers, that is, much of the first-act finale discussed above. Le Picq also neatly avoided one potential problem. Macbeth's response to prophecies drives the narrative, but the future tense is difficult to convey in dance. Following local custom (established as early as Locke's 1673 version), the witches sang rather than danced. Unfortunately, the Neapolitan choreographer was deaf to the 'farcical effect' of an Italianate chorus foretelling disaster for 'Macka-bet', and so, apparently, was everyone else who might have advised him.[1]

The inevitable resistance from bardolators was stated both seriously —'But what action can convey the sublime ideas of *Shakespeare's* language! The attempt is *profanation!*'—and jokingly—'If the heroic Macbeth is to be compelled to *dance* in the Haymarket . . . he has sufficiently atoned for the *murder of the gracious Duncan!*'[2] Although the reviews contain unusually detailed suggestions for improvement, making a number of infelicities clear, critical reaction was more positive than one might expect. The critics were willing to tolerate contractions of the story and various adjustments to the medium of dance, such as the 'well designed Scotch reels' introduced 'after the death of *Macbeth*' in the traditional place of the grand ballet (*Morning Post*, 18 March 1785).

The critics, however, imply that the audience as a whole found the experiment difficult to take seriously. For example, Act II of the Garrick text familiar to the audience ends with the witches celebrating Duncan's murder. Le Picq eliminated that scene, which meant that 'Scarce was the spirit of *Duncan* . . . sent to visit the shades, when *Macbeth* came dancing on in his royal robes.' The unexpected cut 'occasioned one of the audience to observe, "the *ballet-master's* genius far exceeded the poet's, for Shakespeare's hero only *killed the King*, but our modern one had likewise *stolen his coat!*"' (*Morning Herald*, 19 March 1785). Yet most reviewers' comments on the performance of Le Picq in the title-role and particularly of Mme Rossi as Lady Macbeth were positive: '*Lepicq* in the *dagger scene* was very able; his

---

[1] See the *Morning Chronicle*, 21 Mar. 1785. We are reminded of Hester Thrale's anecdote of Millico's attempt to sing Handel's 'I come my Queen to chaste delights', which he pronounced 'I comb my Queen to catch the Lice'; *Thraliana*, ed. Katharine C. Balderston, 2 vols. (2nd edn.; Oxford: Clarendon Press, 1951), i. 533.

[2] Quotations from the *Morning Herald*, 19 Mar. 1785, and an advance comment in the *Morning Post*, 19 Feb. The satirical 'Diary' of the Prince of Wales, which appeared sporadically in the *Morning Post*, queried, 'Could *Shakespeare* have danced Macbeth?—No.—Then, I say, *Le Picq* is the greater man of the two' (16 Mar.).

horror at the sight of Banquo's apparition was well expressed'; Mme Rossi's 'first scene with Macbeth was significant; where she stimulates him to the murder, she had also great force', and her rendering of 'I have given suck, and know / How tender 'tis to love the babe that milks me' 'conveyed this passage very distinctly'. But elsewhere, as the same notice in the *Morning Herald* pointed out, there were signs of haste. In the banqueting scene, Lady Macbeth 'was deficient in her courtesy to the guests; and they seemed *sensible* of it, as not one of them made a *pretence* to eat!'—strange failures, both. Minimal rehearsal also shows in comments like, 'Some little mistake in respect to time, destroyed the effect of *Banquo's Ghost*. A like inattention, in *knocking* too soon, in the scene where Duncan's murder is depending, was equally out of season.' A scene shift was botched: 'The witches have clearly a new power assigned them; it is demonstrated in a *subterraneous wood*, which appears growing at the back of their cave.' The accumulated criticism and ridicule disheartened the dancers, and despite newspaper encouragement to try again, Le Picq abandoned the production and recycled some of the Scottish incidental dances into *Robin Gray*.[1] All these criticisms obscure the daring reach of Le Picq's project, which may not have been apparent to more than a few connoisseurs.[2]

The sudden interest in ballets *qua* music, as evinced in the publication of the complete first act of Barthélemon's *Macbeth*, is also reflected in Longman and Broderip's first book of *Opera Dances* for 1785, which included nine numbers of 'The Ballet in the Divertisement', probably the *New Divertissement* (première 3 March), and nine dances for the 1785 revival of *Le tuteur trompé*. The latter, which presumably comprises the 'several new airs composed by Barthélemon', but which must essentially have replaced Borghi's score of the 1783 original, is particularly interesting in that there is some evidence that the dances were meant to form continuous chains. For example, the opening A major *andante* (for Nivelon and Dorival) ends on the dominant, thereby leading to the following *allegretto* in E major, a *pas de deux* for the same dancers that includes a difficult solo violin part. And later on, an *adagio* in B flat major is joined to an F major *allegro*, both danced by the Pietro Angiolinis. A reviewer in the *Public Advertiser* of 10 January 1785 joked that Mme Rossi's '*Fandango* is undoubtedly powerful and grateful

---

[1] The *Morning Post* of 21 Apr. expressed regret that the ballet 'is not to be repeated' and mentioned the reused dances.

[2] Roland John Wiley informs us that after the turn of the century Didelot proposed *Macbeth* in St Petersburg but it was refused, probably on account of censorship.

electricity—but is it *quite safe?*—Mezzo putana!' The *Tuteur trompé* suite concludes with a long, exciting *Gavotta allegretto* for Signora Angiolini. In terms of the preserved music, Barthélemon's ballets for the 1784–85 season represent the high-water mark of dance at the King's Theatre this decade.

The trustees' second and final season limped to its conclusion on 2 July 1785. Given the chaotic state of the company, we may marvel that its dance offerings were as respectable as Le Picq managed to make them. He also appears to have maintained the dancers' morale under trying circumstances.[1] According to the newspapers, all performers were paid in full, but the Lord Chamberlain was not satisfied with the trustees, and hiring for the next season could not be concluded.[2] Le Picq and Mme Rossi accepted an invitation to dance for Catherine the Great, and in August they departed for St Petersburg, where they were to spend the rest of their lives.

## V. The Gallini Regime, 1785–1790

As far as dance is concerned, the Gallini management began in mediocrity and ended with riots and lawsuits. (The season of 1789–90 at the Little Haymarket was strictly a holding operation.) In fairness one should recall that Gallini was functioning merely as Taylor's trustee and was unquestionably hampered by the £18,000 per annum budget cap enforced by the Court of Chancery. But Gallini had danced as a principal at the opera in the 1760s. He knew the subject from the inside, and one might expect him to have made a special effort to enhance ballet. In the event, he did nothing of the sort. On the contrary, his emphasis (as reflected in the budget) was very much on opera and singers.

### The Disappointing Seasons of 1785–86 and 1786–87

### Ballet Repertoire for 1785–86

*Divertissement sérieux*, Giroux, 24 January 1786, music by Sacchini (7 performances)
*Divertissement villageois*, D'Egville, 24 January 1786 (22 performances)
*Acis and Galatea*, no choreographer credited, 18 February 1786, 'a new Ballet Historique' later entitled *Divertissement* (6 performances)
*New Divertissement*, Giroux, 11 March 1786 (13 performances)
*Dance incidental to *Perseo*, no choreographer credited, 21 March 1786 (5 [?] performances; only the first advertised)
*Le premier navigateur; ou, La force de l'amour*, Gardel sen., supervised in London by Vestris, 23 March 1786, music by Mazzinghi (7 performances)

---

[1] *Morning Post*, 4 Feb. and 9 Apr. 1785.
[2] See notices in the *Morning Herald*, 5, 16, and 20 Aug. 1785.

*L'amour jardinier*, D'Egville, 1 April 1786, music by Mazzinghi (20 performances)
*La fête marine*, D'Egville, 27 April 1786, 'an entirely new Ballet', part of the music by Grétry, arranged by Mazzinghi (17 performances)
*Les deux solitaires*, Giroux, 23 May 1786, music by Mazzinghi (9 performances)
*Les amans surpris*, production by Simonet (revived from June 1781), 1 June 1786 (5 performances)
*Ninette à la cour*, production by Vestris sen. (revived from July 1781), 1 June 1786, part of the music by Mortellari (8 performances)

Gallini had no doubt made some preliminary agreements but could not begin hiring officially until 16 September 1785, which meant that many of the best performers were already committed elsewhere. Problems getting a licence from the Lord Chamberlain delayed the start of the season until 24 January 1786, and Michele Fabiani, the ballet-master named in the company's season advertisement in the *Morning Herald* of 14 January, did not reach London until mid-March.[1] In the mean time his place was shared by Gabriel Giroux and Peter D'Egville. After the second performance an alert critic pointed out that, despite the name, the *Divertissement villageois* could 'claim . . . a full year's antiquity, the steps and the music having last season engaged our attention'.[2] Such recycling was a prominent feature of the season. No great perception was required to recognize that 'the more cooks the worse broth'—and Fabiani was not in fact credited with composing any of the six ballets that were mounted after he arrived.[3] Vestris jun. was probably responsible for staging or reviving three uncredited works, which, while first put forward as *pièces d'occasion*, saw a total of twenty-three performances. They would help explain his disproportionate salary of £1,200 (LC 7/3, fo. 208), but the work was apparently not original enough to put his name to. D'Egville's work was seen most often but got very mixed reviews.[4] Gallini testified in C107/201 that D'Egville received only £50 as ballet-master, plus the proceeds of a masquerade in February for which he had to put up £30.

[1] On 9 Nov. 1785 Gallini informed the Lord Chamberlain that he had sent a power of attorney to Italy to enable unnamed agents there to hire performers. He noted that Fabiani and a Signora Campioni were 'the best Dancer's now to be had in Italy', and that Lord Cowper strongly recommended them (LC 7/3, fos. 207ʳ–208ᵛ).
[2] *Morning Post*, 30 Jan. 1786. If this charge is true, it raises interesting, though unanswerable, questions about the preservation of dances at the King's Theatre. The steps were, of course, executed by different dancers, but somebody—Peter D'Egville is the most obvious candidate—must have had some notes and a good memory. The assertion also implies that some dances were repeated exactly enough that they might be recognizable.
[3] The *Morning Chronicle* of 26 Jan. 1786 reported the idea of three ballet-masters with great dubiety.
[4] For example, the *Morning Post* of 26 Jan. 1786, the *Morning Herald* of 30 Jan., and the *Public Advertiser* of 6 May.

Gallini had put his money into bringing Vestris jun. back, paying him £400 more than Madam Mara. Given that Vestris was the best dancer in Europe at the time, this choice cannot be said to signal neglect of the dance department. The rest of the company, however, was not in the same league. Vestris's half-sister, Mlle Mozon, met with some enthusiasm. Signora Crespi, who had been absent since 1782–83, was invited to rejoin the company; she was prosecuting Taylor for back pay even as she danced for Gallini.[1] Carolina Pitrot Angiolini continued through the season, though her husband was not advertised.[2] One-time *figurants* such as Duquesney and the Simonet sisters now found themselves regularly advertised.[3]

The 1785–86 season saw Barthélemon replaced by the factotum Mazzinghi as dance composer-*pasticheur*. Perhaps for this reason, the quality of the music published by Longman and Broderip drops off sharply, despite a change of policy to issuing complete works in separately numbered volumes: Book I, an unnamed work; Book II, *L'amour jardinier*; Book III, *La fête marine*; Book IV, *Les deux solitaires*. Mazzinghi's music is generally more sectionalized and choppy than Barthélemon's, apparently being closely tailored to D'Egville's choreography, though in *La fête marine*, for example, the long, discursive finale is constructed like a sonata movement.

In the few years since the arrival of *ballet d'action*, the quality of dance journalism in London had improved noticeably. Critics began to analyse, not just to describe or praise. The *Morning Herald* of 26 January 1786 suggested that Mlle Mozon 'is a charming performer, but more action in her arms, and the head to have a little motion, will be an improvement. . . . Of the music, it was very indifferent; it has little animation, and less passion.' Nor was the social dimension neglected: the *Morning Post* commented waspishly about the *figurantes* that 'The present untempting show of the female Phalanx keeps our Honourable and Right Honourable Butterflies at a distance', but also criticized the Prince of Wales for roaming through the

[1] Taylor counter-sued on 25 Feb. 1786 to block her King's Bench action (C12/1261/57).

[2] She is not noticed separately in the *Biographical Dictionary* and is confusingly listed as Signora Carolina in the season advertisement, Signora Angiolini on 23 Mar., and Signora Pitrot on 1 Apr.

[3] As we interpret the evidence, Lauchlin (rather than his father) was the Duquesney who danced at the King's Theatre, probably beginning in 1782–83 (cf. *Biographical Dictionary*, iv. 517–18). With the change of management, Slingsby finally retired. Henry was hired only after Taylor complained on his behalf (C31/239, no. 206). One of the men hired as a principal dancer, Spozzi, was demoted to *figurant*: he was dropped from the *Divertissement villageois* as of 18 Feb. and not listed in any other dance except *Le premier navigateur*. The *Morning Post* of 26 Jan. 1786 had singled him out for an unusually negative comment.

auditorium like a 'royal humblebee' (30 January and 15 February 1786). This season presented critics with the challenge of comparing Vestris with the newcomer Fabiani. Technical vocabulary was unavoidable; that it was comprehensible is a measure of how public appreciation of dance had developed. The *Daily Universal Register* opined on 16 February 1786 that '*Vestris* was as great as usual, or perhaps greater—his *peroettes* exhibited a degree of ease and stability which we never before saw equalled.' He remained the bench-mark of excellence, as accounts of Fabiani show. According to the *General Advertiser* of 13 March 1786, Fabiani, 'in point of vigour and activity, is superior to any dancer we can call to our recollection. He likewise moves with dignity, and possesses the *moelleux* in a superior degree; but seems rather deficient in the graces, at least inferior to Vestris and Le Picq; but, after them, we think that Signor Fabiani may, with justice, be considered as the best dancer that ever appeared in this country.' A week later the same paper found him

unrivalled in the following particulars—*Le Moelleux* and *L'Aplomb*;—but his figure seems rather unfavourable, or at least not so well calculated for the *grand serieux*— which we observed to proceed, in a great measure, from his want of taste in dressing for the Stage:—With regard to the graces, he is eclipsed by *Vestris*, and inferior to Le Picq—but being a very young man, and having now the finest pattern of the French school before his eyes, we think he may easily improve, so as to grace his vigour and nimbleness, with the elegance of those enchanting dancers.

Such commentary was unknown even two or three years earlier.

Not all critics were well informed or skilful in their use of technical terms or even clichés, but collectively they could help change meanings. The more knowledgeable were aware of Gaetan Vestris's sobriquet, but his possession of the title was under the assault of time. Searching for superlatives, the *Morning Herald* of 13 March 1786 declared, 'Vestris [jun.], as may naturally be supposed, feeling the spur of emulation, never was so justly admired, it was not the son of the God of Dancing, it was that deity itself.' The same paper reported on 8 May that 'The light-footed *Vestris* and *Fabiani*, in *La Fete Marine*, disputed for honors with uncommon emulation. It is to the praise of Fabiani, that he maintained a contention against *Le Dieu de Dance*. In the tip-toe pas, from its duration, he approved himself by no means a *falling Angel!*'

More important than their comparisons of individual skills, critics' attitudes show that the world had changed. In its very first review of the season the *Morning Chronicle* put the point:

Our wish is short, more matter and less method, Let us have *un Ballet d'Action*. For incomparable as Vestris is, there is no doing any thing in the way of strong captivation by mere dint of simple Chaconnes. *Himself a host*, may in some sort be true of an individual [of] superior talents in other departments; but at the Opera, we do not feel that a single dancer, though that dancer be the best in the world, the Vestris, is *himself a Ballet*. (26 January 1786)[1]

Critics' loss of patience with the dance department shows in responses to *Le premier navigateur*, the one new *ballet d'action* of the season, which Vestris, a member of Gardel's original cast in 1785, staged for his own benefit. Daphnis claims Melide as his 'prize' for winning a rural dance contest. When an earthquake and flood interrupt their wedding, he must overcome both physical and psychological hazards to rescue his bride, before Venus blesses their match.[2]

Despite elaborate technical support and lavish publicity, reviews of *Le premier navigateur* were so mixed that there was talk of abandoning the production.[3] The first reviewer, though acknowledging the 'scientific' prowess of Vestris and Mlle Baccelli, said the Paris production was better; the next two disagreed about the success of the earthquake, particularly its 'subterraneous fires'; another complained that Delpini could be seen and heard directing scene changes; all recommended cuts, though they agreed only in suggesting that three acts should be condensed to two.

The unusual range of disagreement reflects the fact that the ballet was underrehearsed. Vestris was simply not able both to star in and to supervise a production on this scale, however eager the audience was to appreciate his efforts. London welcomed Mlle Baccelli, his partner of choice, after an absence of four years, but she felt obliged to apologize in the newspapers for arriving only two days before the première. How could that have been enough time for even the most seasoned professional to fit smoothly into so complex a production? Perhaps the most wounding review was the one that compared the acting of Baccelli and Vestris unfavourably with that of Rossi and Le Picq, an unusually barbed comment on a benefit performance.[4] In

---

[1] See also the *Morning Herald* of 30 Jan., which calls for 'greater things' in the way of ballets, and the notice in the 21 Mar. *Morning Post*, anticipating the 'regular Ballet' in preparation.

[2] Plot summaries appeared in the *Morning Post*, the *Morning Herald*, and the *Public Advertiser* of 23 Mar. 1786.

[3] See the 24 Mar. 1786 *Morning Herald* and the 25 Mar. *Public Advertiser* and *Morning Chronicle* (which estimates the house at £600), and the *Morning Post* of 27 and 28 Mar., the latter wondering why the ballet was being withheld.

[4] The *Public Advertiser* of 25 Mar. went on to say 'Vestris is yet, with all the power of execution, perhaps not yet in the maturity of his profession.' The same paper lamented on 6

short, this imitation of a famous French production did not live up to expectations, however outstanding the lead dancers may have been as technicians.[1] Longman and Broderip published a substantial amount of the music for *Le premier navigateur* in two parts, an overture and twenty-six separate numbers 'Selected, and adapted . . . By Sigr. Mazzinghi'. Part II includes a high proportion of music evidently designed to accompany pantomime—hence frequent changes of tempo, starts and stops, and lots of fermatas. No doubt the restricted budget helped dictate the revivals of *Les amans surpris* and *Ninette à la cour* near the end of the season. The part of the audience interested in dance had reason to be unhappy. Most of the performers were mediocre, and the choreography was the least ambitious since 1779–80.

### Ballet Repertoire for 1786–87

*\*Divertissement*, no choreographer credited, 23 December 1786, music by Mazzinghi (46 performances)[2]

*La chercheuse d'esprit*, no choreographer credited, 23 December 1786, some music by Sacchini (?) (3 performances)

*Le berger inconstant*, no choreographer credited, 6 January 1787 (4 performances)

*L'heureux événement*, Hus, 20 January 1787, 'an allegorical Ballet . . . divided into 3 Quadrilles', music by Mazzinghi (9 performances)

**Zemira and Azor**, no choreographer credited, 13 February 1787, 'a new Pantomime Ballet', music by Grétry arranged by Mazzinghi (6 performances) (p. 514)

*The Muses on Mount Parnassus*, no choreographer credited, 1 March 1787 (part of *Giulio Cesare in Egitto*) (10 performances)

*The Triumph of Julius Caesar*, no choreographer credited, 1 March 1787 (part of *Giulio Cesare in Egitto*) (10 performances)

*La fête provençale*, Hus, 8 March 1787, music by Mazzinghi (13 performances)

*La bergère capricieuse*, Hus, 8 March 1787 (1 performance)

*La jardinière*, no choreographer credited, 22 March 1787, 'a new Divertissement in the Pastoral style' (7 performances)

*Sylvie*, Hus, 22 March 1787, 'an entirely new ballet' (2 performances)

May 1786, 'how bad are the present times—at any rate what good times were the past—when we had the Fandango by Le Picq and Rossi—how bad are the present times to give us the same Fandango with a couple of children' (Miss De Camp and Master D'Egville, according to the *Morning Herald*, 1 May 1786).

[1] Baccelli did not dance again in England after this season. A note in the *Diary* on 1 Jan. 1790 reports that she 'went, last year, from the Duke [of Dorset's] Hotel at Paris, for the purpose of fulfilling an engagement at Venice'; cf. *Biographical Dictionary*, i. 193.

[2] A writer in the *Morning Herald* of 25 Dec. 1786 assumed, conventionally, that balletmaster Hus was responsible for both initial dances. Hus does not seem to have sought credit for much of his work this season, so we have followed the advertisements in not crediting a choreographer.

*Le cossac jaloux*, Hus, 17 May 1787, 'an entirely new ballet' (2 performances)
*Le divertissement asiatique*, no choreographer credited, 14 June 1787 (7 performances)

For 1786–87 Gallini tried hard to improve the ballet but was hampered by a run of extremely bad luck. The season announcement in the *Morning Chronicle* of 28 November 1786 lists Pierre Gardel and Antoine Trancart as 'Composers of the Ballets' and Gardel and Michele Fabiani as principal male dancers—but none of them appeared. Trancart had been teaching in partnership with Simonet in 1783; there is no information about why he did not join the King's Theatre.[1] Fabiani had died in Paris 'shortly before 30 October';[2] if Gallini knew that, this season announcement is more cynical than optimistic. He had claimed earlier that he was negotiating with Gardel, and on 3 January 1787 the *Daily Universal Register* reported that 'Gardel and Vestris were to have contributed their light fantastic toes, in aid, or rather in support of the ballets—but as the French treaty was not ratified, the *Grand Monarque* refused them *passports*.'[3] While these might be diversionary press releases, they are not necessarily implausible. Such dancers as did come were delayed. A cancellation notice on 20 December 1786 explained that 'The Master of the Ballets, and some of the principal Dancers, not having arrived until Monday [18 December], obliged the Manager to postpone the Opera intended for yesterday evening.'

The substitute choreographer was Jean-Baptiste (?) Hus,[4] whose work found no favour with the audience. The best male principals who managed to get to England were one Goyon, who proved less than satisfactory, and the young Laborie. The fact that neither received a benefit is evidence of their status. Among the dancers only Hus and the two principal women, Mme Perignon (née Gervais) and the returning Mlle Mozon, received benefits this year, that of the latter reported as disappointing.[5] The rest of the company also came in for criticism, the *Daily Universal Register* referring to 'the *Lumber Troop* of *figurants* and *figurantes*'.[6]

---

[1] See the *Morning Herald* of 6 May 1783.

[2] The *Biographical Dictionary*, v. 134, specifies no cause of death.

[3] Gallini's travel bulletin is preserved in a cutting in Theatre Cuts 41, fo. [99ᵛ], dated in MS only '1786', with no paper identified. On 10 Jan. 1787 the *Morning Herald* reported an attempt to spring Gardel, working through the diplomatic channel of the Duc de Lazun, but the negotiations failed—Gardel became ballet-master at the Opéra after the death of his brother Maximilien in Mar. 1787. The Vestris in question would have been Auguste.

[4] On Hus, see Winter, *The Pre-Romantic Ballet*, 33.

[5] *Daily Universal Register*, 15 Mar. 1787.

[6] The reviewer could compliment them only for staying out of the way of the principals (17 Jan. 1787). In its initial review the *Morning Herald* advised management to provide a bet-

The offerings of 1786–87 were again decidedly old-fashioned, neglecting *ballets d'action* in favour of extended *divertissements.* Hus opted for variety, changing dances often. As if coaching, the *Morning Herald* observed on 8 January 1787, that Hus

is very open to conviction; this, together with a laudable ambition of pleasing the public has no doubt induced him to observe, that dumb show is not what the spectators in general look for in that species of entertainment over which he is appointed to preside. We also observe with pleasure, that he has taken *Variety* for his motto, and resolved to deviate from the beaten paths of his predecessors in office, who tired the town with a repetition of the same dances. Within a fortnight we have had three new dances, and we hear with satisfaction that his intention is to vary the dances every week in the season.

Yet the dance most often performed—an excessive forty-six times—was the year's *Divertissement.* However its components may have changed, the standard complaint about the repertoire was lack of stories. As early as 8 January 1787 the *Daily Universal Register* noted of *Le berger inconstant* that 'the applause at the *finale*—excepting from a *"few followers"*—was *hissing* hot— in short, a *divertissement* would have shewn off the abilities of [the dancers] to the full as well'. At the third performance of *L'heureux événement* the same paper reported that 'when the curtain dropt, not a single plaudit graced its *fall*' (29 January). For his benefit Hus made a *Cossac jaloux*, showing off the season's most popular dancer, Mme Perignon. However, at its second performance it was hissed—and it did not appear again.[1]

When Hus did attempt a *ballet d'action*, his discomfort with the genre showed. On 13 February he offered *Zemira and Azor*, but the ballet appeared only six times, even after a series of 'alterations and improvements'.[2] Nevertheless, it is a remarkable work and unique for the theatre and period under discussion for being based closely on an opera—Grétry's *Zémire et Azor*, already familiar to London audiences in the Italian translation discussed in Chapter 4 (see Table 14). Longman and Broderip's piano score names Mazzinghi as adapter, but he had to do less work for this ballet than for almost any other entrusted to him. The score is essentially a number-by-number abridgement of the opera minus the vocal parts. The King's

ter *corps de ballet* (25 Dec. 1786).

[1] See the *Daily Universal Register*, 21 May 1787. This paper, which was new, was unusually outspoken in its arts criticism.

[2] For comments, see the *Morning Herald*, 14 and 19 Feb. 1787, and the *Daily Universal Register*, 23 Feb. and 3 Mar.

TABLE 14. *Comparison of Hus's ballet with Grétry's* Zémire et Azor

| no. | 1787 ballet | Grétry | comment |
|---|---|---|---|
| **Book I** | | | |
| | Overture | Overture | storm music cut |
| (1) | Chase | — | not in opera |
| (2) | Allegro | *L'orage va cesser* (Ali), I.i | shortened; ends on dominant |
| (3) | Allegro | *Le malheur me rend* (Sander), I.i | instrumental introduction only |
| (4) | Allegretto | *Les esprits, dont on* (Ali), I.i | much cut; ends on dominant |
| (5) | Andante | *Le tems est beau* (duet), I.i | loose rendition, but retaining essentials |
| (6) | Larghetto non troppo | *La pauvre enfant* (Sander), I.ii | instrumental introduction only |
| (7) | Maestoso | *Ne vas pas me tromper* (Azor), I.ii | drastically shortened; ends on dominant |
| (8) | Larghetto | — | new, poss. replaces 'Symphonie qui exprime le vol du nuage' |
| (9) | Andante | *Veillons mes sœurs* (trio), II.i | instrumental introduction only |
| (10) | Allegro | — | through-composed dance, not in opera |
| (11) | [untitled] | — | pantomime, not in opera |
| (12) | Allegro assai | *Je veux le voir* (duet), II.viii | shortened |
| (13) | Larghetto | *Ah! quel tourment* (Azor), III.i | instrumental introduction only |
| (14) | Tempo giusto | *Rassure mon père* (duet), III.ii | somewhat shortened |
| **Book II** | | | |
| (15) | Largo | *Entrée des Génies,* III.iv | slightly shortened and joined to continuation after dialogue |
| (16) | Andante grazioso | — | not in opera |

TABLE 14 *continued*

| no. | 1787 ballet | Grétry | comment |
|-----|-------------|--------|---------|
| (17) | Grazioso | Pantomime, III.iv | virtually identical |
| (18) | Antantino | — | not in opera |
| (19) | Andante | *Ah! laissez-moi* (ensemble), III.vi | based on this piece |
| (20) | Grazioso gavotta | — | not in opera |
| (21) | Allegretto | *J'en suis encore* (Azor), IV.i | instrumental introduction only |
| (22) | Andantino | — | not in opera |
| (23) | Andante | echo scene, IV.iv | complete |
| (24) | Allegro | — | not in opera |
| (25) | Allegro | — | not in opera |
| (26) | Andante | — | not in opera; for pantomime |
| (27) | Andantino | — | not in opera |
| (28) | [untitled] | — | not in opera |
| (29) | [untitled] | — | not in opera |
| (30) | Contra Dance | — | not in opera |

Theatre orchestra could simply have played from marked-up opera parts, except for a few insertions and a group of final dances not found in the Grétry. A curious feature of Mazzinghi's method of abridgement, which might at first glance appear ham-fisted, is that several pieces are cut or altered to end on or in the dominant, but not necessarily the dominant of the next number. These half-cadences were probably designed, however, to link up with pantomimes (not printed by Longman and Broderip), which took the place of the spoken dialogue. We are not surprised that *Zemira and Azor* was coolly received, because it was boldly experimental.

For the most part dances this year were independent; the only ones designed specifically to fit into an opera were part of Arnold's version of Handel's *Giulio Cesare*. These served for ten performances of the opera, but no more. While *The Triumph of Julius Caesar* might not have been readily movable, *The Muses on Mount Parnassus*, if it had proved popular, should have been. At the last performance of the opera, on 16 June, the standard

*Divertissement* and the just-presented *Divertissement asiatique* were substituted for the purpose-made dances. The change may reflect the fact that the opera dropped out of the repertoire between mid-April and early June, but it gives the impression that the dance department was taking the easy course.

The Hus season cannot be counted a success, and Gallini was lucky to get through the spring without a riot. London audiences were no longer satisfied with second-rank dancers or with an unvarying diet of *divertissements*. Critics pointed out relentlessly that Mme Perignon had no adequate partner and that dance after dance had little or no story. Gallini acknowledged the complaints, despite his own preferences in dance. He scraped together enough money the following year to bring Noverre back, and with him a number of French stars. Sorely needed improvements were forthcoming.

## The Return of Noverre, 1787–88

### Ballet Repertoire

*Divertissement, Chevalier, 8 December 1787 (14 performances)
Les offrandes à l'amour, Noverre, 8 December 1787, music by Mazzinghi (23 performances)
The Military Dance, Chevalier, 12 January 1788 (12 performances)
L'Amour et Psiché, Noverre, 29 January 1788, music by Mazzinghi (19 performances) (p. 521)
*New Dance, no choreographer credited, 21 February 1788 (10 performances)[1]
Les fêtes de Tempé, Noverre, 28 February 1788, 'an entire new ballet', music by Mazzinghi (15 performances)
Euthyme et Eucharis, Noverre, 13 March 1788, 'a new grand Tragic Ballet, never performed' (5 performances)[2]
*New Ballet, Noverre, 3 April 1788, 'serious and demi-charactere' (20 performances)
Adela of Ponthieu, Noverre, 17 April 1788 (4 performances)
La bonté du seigneur, Didelot, 22 May 1788, 'an entire new ballet' (2 performances)
Richard Cœur de Lion, (Didelot—London Stage), 22 May 1788, 'an entire new ballet in 5 acts' (1 performance)
The Deserter, Dauberval, revived anonymously, 29 May 1788 (6 performances)

This season ended two years of decline and drift in the ballet department. It could not be so prodigal a season as 1781–82, with Gallini hampered by

---

[1] *The London Stage* regards the *Divertissement* advertised without cast on 29 May 1788 as the one that was first given on 8 Dec. 1787. However, the standard dance practice was to discard such dances in the course of the season, and that one had not been done since 11 Mar. We have therefore counted the 29 May *Divertissement* under the *New Dance*, which was in the current repertoire.

[2] Moore notes, however, that Noverre had created a ballet under this title in Vienna in 1773 ('Unlisted Ballets', 17).

financial restrictions and Noverre by increasingly poor health.[1] Still, he brought with him excellent principal dancers, and given the level of performance he was able to draw from the whole company, a vast improvement in dance offerings must have been apparent. The audience responded accordingly: when they called for Noverre at the première of *L'Amour et Psiché* on 29 January, he appeared and accepted their tribute. But the season did not flower. Gallini hired the father of the *ballet d'action* not to develop the genre but to mark time.

As had been the case in 1781–82, Noverre had someone else compose *divertissements*. Unsurprisingly, reviewers wanted more Noverre and less Pierre Chevalier. One reporter refused to credit Chevalier at all, commenting on the amended *Military Dance* that 'The capital dancers have hitherto danced to their own compilings, and what they have danced abroad'; he then looked forward to the Noverre production in rehearsal.[2] When Gardel made a guest appearance between 21 February and 10 April (perhaps fulfilling the previous year's contract), he contributed special numbers of his own to *Euthyme et Eucharis* and the *New Ballet*, though he is advertised for so little dancing that his departure had no effect on the repertoire.[3] Didelot was allowed to compose both dances got up for his benefit, among his first major efforts at choreography.[4] No one is credited with the revival of *The Deserter*, but the person likeliest to have been in charge of it was Vestris jun., since he had been in the original cast and took the opportunity to play the leading role this year.

Vestris continued to defy description. When the season began the *Daily Universal Register* conceded that 'every thing under the superlative, must be eclipsed by the giant power of Vestris' (17 December 1787). An intrepid pamphlet-writer, attempting to put into words the impression Vestris made, said that he 'has this privilege above the lot of other men, that he seems, like a real divinity, to touch the ground by choice only, not by necessity; the grace and lightness of his motions conveying the idea that the air, if he

---

[1] See Lynham, *Chevalier Noverre*, 105. Noverre was unable to provide dances for a masquerade, for example: see the *Public Advertiser* of 4 Feb. 1788.

[2] For resistance to Chevalier, see the *Public Advertiser* of 17 Jan. 1788 and *The Times* of the same date and 7 Apr.

[3] Gardel was last advertised on 10 Apr. and had surely left before Noverre's benefit on the 17th, at which he would have had some professional obligation to appear. On 12 Apr. the dances were disrupted because people had been expecting Gardel, despite the fact that his name was not in the advertisement for that performance (Theatre Cuts 42, no. 233, fo. [8ʳ], misdated in manuscript 13 [for 14] Apr. 1788).

[4] See Mary Grace Swift, *A Loftier Flight: The Life and Accomplishments of Charles-Louis Didelot, Balletmaster* (Middletown, Conn.: Wesleyan University Press, 1974), 18, 194.

pleased to tread it, were quite sufficient to support him'.[1] However extravagant, this praise suggests the unity of Vestris's strength, musicality, and acting abilities. Perhaps the clearest hierarchical statement about the season comes from the 10 December review in the *Morning Herald*, which as usual did not comment on Vestris, but compared Chevalier to Fabiani and Didelot to Nivelon.[2] The only person Vestris could be said to have competed with this season was Gardel, and that was a game, not really a serious contest. A report of the première of the *New Ballet* on 8 April 1788 said, 'Last night Monsieur Vestris and Monsieur Gardel exhibited a kind of *cockfighting*. . . . They strained every nerve in order to outvie each other in the various accomplishments of the capering art.'[3] But this critic resented the display of technique. He asserted that

the art of dancing degenerates apace into downright tumbling: the chief merit of a modern dancer, consisting in various turnings and windings in imitation of the whirligig, which windings must abruptly end in the attitude of *Mercury*. This posture being evidently painful, becomes rather a tumbler than a dancer, who is ever supposed to move with ease; besides that it is so often repeated, that every dance offers a dull and tedious uniformity.

Ballet was moving further and further away from its connections with social dancing.

Even Vestris could not assure the success of everything in which he danced. The elaborate production of *Euthyme et Eucharis* for his benefit night suggests that management hoped to move that ballet into the repertoire, but it lasted only five performances. Perhaps classical characters like Mars and Bellona were losing their fascination for the audience. A more interesting case is the late revival of *The Deserter*, probably chosen because the deputy manager, Carnevale, expected it to be the 'chief attraction'.[4] He did not reckon on a logical comparison, however:

those who have beheld *Le Picque* and *Rossi*, were cruelly disappointed in their substitutes: Nature has denied to the *Henry* [Vestris] and *Luisa* [Mlle Hilligsberg] of

[1] [Robert Nares], *Remarks on the Favourite Ballet of Cupid and Psyche* (London: J. Stockdale, 1788), 29.

[2] On 10 Dec. 1787 the *World* called Chevalier and Didelot 'very successful scholars of Gardel and Noverre', which also suggests that even if Chevalier was helping with choreography, he was by no means on a level with Vestris as a performer.

[3] Theatre Cuts 42, fo. [8ʳ], no. 231. A similar comment, also undated, says that Vestris 'has adopted a new stile of dancing, the principal object of which seems to be a display of muscular vigour and Herculean activity' (no. 253), fo. [10ʳ].

[4] This phrase and the following quotation come from Theatre Cuts 42, no. 248, fo. [10ʳ] (dated 30 May [1788] in manuscript).

the night, many advantages; and a want of judgment made further abatements. . . . *Hilligsberg*, in her efforts to please, over-acted the part;—and *Vestris* possesses not powers of expression to place him on a footing with his predecessor. . . . Miss *Simonet* supported little *Skirmish* with great merit;—she adhered to *Dauberval* as much as possible.—*Didelot* supplied the part originally given to Vestris, with considerable success.

The ballet was done at half the performances remaining in the season, but Le Picq and Rossi had made it their own; consequently it was no longer the sure draw it had been in 1784–85. London audiences were beginning to be able to compare productions of canonical ballets.

Mlle Coulon, who was hired to be the principal woman dancer, was acceptable but did not attract much critical attention. She may, however, have been part of the reason Gardel made his visit, since at some unknown date they married.[1] The shadowy Signora Bedini, who may or may not have been related to Badini, although advertised as a principal dancer, was largely ignored by critics and did not receive a benefit. The real discovery of the season was Mlle Hilligsberg. Trained abroad, she was hailed in the newspapers as a native of England, though this may have been a publicity ploy.[2] She got less rapturous attention from the papers than their initial notices might have predicted, but not because her dancing was at fault. She was Vestris's partner in the 'favourite' *pas de Russe*, the Psyche to his Cupid, the Eucharis to his Euthyme. Gossip said she was having an affair with Vestris, which was construed as making her unacceptably cold to patrons' attentions.[3] In a Noverre company not only the Simonet girls but their father were welcome.[4] A notice in December said that 'The *Corps de Ballet* seems

---

[1] See the *Biographical Dictionary*, iv. 7, which reports gossip that she was the object of Lord Brudenell's attentions. According to the *World*, 10 Dec. 1787, the Coulon who came with her was her brother. She and Gardel had parted by 1795, when he married Marie Elizabeth Millard (or Miller). Ivor Guest informs us that Mlle Coulon was still alive in 1814 (private letter, 10 Mar. 1994).

[2] See the *Daily Universal Register* of 10 and 17 Dec. 1787. Capon identifies her as a pupil of Vestris sen. See Gaston Capon, *Les Vestris: Le 'diou' de la danse et sa famille (1730–1808)* (Paris: Société du Mercure de France, 1908), 263–5.

[3] For example, 'Mad. *Hillisberg* is under the tuition and *immediate inspection* of Vestris, who takes a world of pains for her improvement. He regularly gives her a *private lesson* every day, and often practices with her at nights: and if the common report may be credited, she is at present almost *twice* as clever, as she was before she received her instructions!' (Theatre Cuts 42, no. 251, n.d.). See also no. 253, n.d. (but after 13 Mar. 1788), fo. [10$^r$]. Capon confirms that she returned to France with Vestris, much to his father's displeasure.

[4] Simonet was not named in an advertisement until 29 May 1788, but a review in *The Times* of 17 Jan. documents his presence earlier with a negative comment.

altogether more complete than it was last season'—and for this reason, among others, spectators returned to the stage.[1]

Of this year's new productions, only *L'Amour et Psiché* was commemorated in a scenario and is undeniably a *ballet d'action*.[2] Several minor works were shrugged off, and in April the critic for *The Times* declined to report on dance until 'something better' came along.[3] Noverre's return does not seem to have been aided by Mazzinghi's music, as represented by the *Favourite Opera Dances* brought out by Longman and Broderip this season. Some of the numbers for *L'Amour et Psiché*, including the *chaconne*, are long and tedious; the substantial score titled *La fête Tempé* (that is, *Les fêtes de Tempé*) is frankly dull from beginning to end. There is one hint that another large project was scheduled but then scrapped: 'A Ballet by *Mons. Noverre*, on a magnificent plan, like his *Medée et Jason*, was intended to have been brought forward on Saturday next:—The *Death of Hercules* furnishes the story; but the want of a *Le Picque* will prevent its being represented this season.'[4] The late notice of cancellation is odd, as is the excuse of personnel, when Vestris, Didelot, and for a few weeks Gardel were on hand, albeit slightly young for the role.[5] That Gallini was reluctant to underwrite the costs of a second major production is a more plausible explanation, given that he had to keep the season total under the budget cap. Whatever their origins, the limitations on the season of 1787–88 differentiate it sharply from the glorious one of 1781–82.

Noverre's dancers were certainly enthusiastic. The papers reported that at the end of the dress rehearsal for *L'Amour et Psiché*, Noverre 'was lifted in *triumph* on the shoulders of the dancers, and received very great praise for the composition'.[6] An unusually thoughtful review in the *Public Advertiser* of 7 February 1788 recognized that Noverre had chosen 'a subject of no great extent on account of the small number of Actors', yet had contrived to make 'the utmost of the few good Dancers, by giving them a proper employ'. Noverre's preface to the scenario says that Cupid has laid aside his

---

[1] On the *corps de ballet*, see the *Morning Herald*, 10 Dec. 1787. On spectators, see *The Times*, 21 Jan. and 5 Apr. 1788, and the *Morning Post*, 6 Feb. 1788.

[2] Theatre Cuts 42, fo. [7$^r$], no. 223 (dated 4 Mar. 1788) says, 'after the representation of *Cupid* and *Psyche*, it is hardly possible for any ballet to succeed, or at least to excite any idea of wonder'.

[3] See *The Times*, 7 Apr. 1788, rejecting the *Military Dance* and *Les fêtes*.

[4] Theatre Cuts 42, fo. [9$^r$], no. 220, dated *c.* Mar. 1788 from context.

[5] The cancellation cost Vestris the chance to play the title-role in *La mort d'Hercule*, which his father claimed in the 1791 production.

[6] Theatre Cuts 42, unnumbered clipping on fo. [5$^v$] (dated in manuscript Jan. 29).

childishness, inconstancy, and infidelity, along with his wings—though Act I belies this premiss.[1] Cupid, who has had Psyche abducted, courts her teasingly until she is on the verge of identifying him, then abandons her to furies. Pursued through the underworld and variously tortured, she finally appeals to love, whereupon Cupid appears on a cloud to rescue her. The third act is devoted to reconciling Venus to her son's choice, crowning Psyche an immortal at Jupiter's command, and celebrating the marriage of Cupid and Psyche.

The *Public Advertiser*'s critic thought the music was 'not very striking in general', but it had 'many pleasing passages, and upon the whole it [was] well adapted' for the ballet. He felt that the scenery, 'no doubt . . . directed by' Noverre, had been skimped on by management. He liked the palaces of Cupid and Venus and the air-borne Jupiter. He also noted that 'The representation of Phlegethon, the mountains to cover the Titans, and the entrance of Tartarus, in the second Act, were also well presented; but the exit of Psiche from Tartarus, and her departure with Cupid, were bare of scenery.' In his view the second act was 'rather too long', since 'a Dance of Furies can please but a little while'. His only comment on performers concerned Mlle Hilligsberg, who, though almost overparted, tried hard and in the end did well. The pamphlet *Remarks on Cupid and Psyche* is strongly positive, though point by point the two reviewers often disagree.[2] The pamphleteer praised both Vestris and Hilligsberg, but criticized the execution of some effects quite acutely. He was not entirely satisfied with the sea of fire through which Psyche fled to a rock, and he also had a practical suggestion about the next sequence.

After the tremendous leap of Psyche into the flaming gulph, she is forcibly brought up by the Demons, through a chasm in the infernal soil, which is in fact a trapdoor. This we know it must be; but alas, to all who sit in a situation more elevated than the pit, the work of the carpenter is perfectly conspicuous; and the bursting flames, which ought to fill the soul with horror, are seen to issue through a regularly square opening of planed wood. A piece of false floor with edges irregularly broken, and properly coloured, would remove the defect entirely. (34–5)

---

[1] *Cupid and Psyche* (London: Reynell, 1788), 6. Copy used: New York Public Library, Lincoln Center Dance Collection MGTZ-Res. A hostile paragraph about the production included in Theatre Cuts 42, fo. [6ʳ] (dated in manuscript only Jan. 1788) suggests that Vestris wore wings.

[2] Published anonymously. The catalogue in the Dance Collection at Lincoln Center, New York, credits it to 'Robert Nares, 1753–1829', on the basis of an attribution in Robert Watt's *Bibliotheca Britannica*, 2 vols. in 4 (Edinburgh: Archibald Constable; London: Longman *et al.*, 1824), 695j.

He was even willing to suggest an improvement in Noverre's plot: in Act I 'sleep falls on Cupid ridiculously', brought by Morpheus on behalf of Venus. Why not just have the couple dance until exhausted, he asked. The pamphlet ends with a rather heady interpretation of the ballet as moral allegory, a notion which the author recognized many audience members would not share. Nevertheless, the attempt to assert a larger purpose for ballet is a measure of how far the dance had come.

The dancers' enthusiasm for *L'Amour et Psiché* carried over to at least part of the audience. Noverre took a curtain call, for which he was roundly criticized in the press. The dancers were apparently in a mood to honour Noverre, and if they had a laurel wreath handy—well, Noverre was at least as important to the ballet as Voltaire had been to the theatre when he was honoured by the Comédie-Française in 1778. Nor was this the first time the London audience had been prepared to join the dancers in paying homage to Noverre.[1] One of the more rampantly chauvinistic accounts of this episode objected that 'So prepared was the pantomimic trick of bringing *Noverre* before the audience at Tuesday's Opera, that one of the *Figurants* had a *Laurel Chaplet* ready to place over his head:—The fellow who thus presumed, deserved an *oak stick* laid over his shoulders.'[2] The commentator found this a foreign custom to be resisted because, he grumbled, 'it seems to imply, that we never beheld a Theatric spectacle of greater merit.—Were *Shakespear*, or *Congreve*, of less consequence than a French adventurer?—Was the Author of the *School for Scandal* called upon to receive a public tribute for his matchless wit?—No—then fie upon such *parade!*—it is an innovation to which *Folly* only can give countenance!' A more sober objection came from the *Public Advertiser* of 7 February 1788, which 'supposed Mr. Noverre is now sensible of the error he has been led into, by suffering himself to be presented to the audience, in order to be complimented. The Public's applause was enough, without his coming forward, as his name and person are so well known in this country.' This critic went on to say that the practice occurs not across the Continent but 'at Paris, and a few capital French towns only', where it is pursued by the parterre, not by the better people, who laugh at it. But, said the critic, Noverre should understand that the London opera 'is quite different'.

---

[1] See above, sect. III. *Remarks upon Cupid and Psyche*, 28, celebrates the recognition of Noverre.

[2] This and the following quotation are from Theatre Cuts 42, fo. [6r], no. 210. Cutting no. 211 denies that Badini was the author of this denunciation.

Noverre had organized a highly efficient, if not an innovative, season. However, the over-reaction of dancers and aficionados alike to even so small-scale a *ballet d'action* as *L'Amour et Psiché* should have been a warning signal. Gallini's economies were to cause major problems the next year.

## The Tumultuous Season of 1788–89

### Ballet Repertoire

*New Divertissement*, no choreographer credited, 10 January 1789 (34 performances)
*L'embarquement pour Cythère* (Didelot—*London Stage*), 10 January 1789 (7 performances)
*Les fêtes provençales*, Noverre, 31 January 1789, 'an entire new ballet' (13 performances)
*La nymphe et le chasseur*, Coindé, 3 March 1789, 'a new Anacreontic Ballet' (13 performances)
**Les jalousies du sérail**, Noverre, 17 March 1789, 'a new Grand Ballet' (15 performances) (p. 527)
*Admète*, Noverre, 31 March 1789, 'a new Allegorical Ballet', music by Mazzinghi (15 performances)
*Annette et Lubin*, Noverre, 28 April 1789, 'a new Pantomine Ballet', music by Federici (3 performances)
*Les caprices de Galatée*, Noverre, 7 May 1789, 'an entire new Ballet' (7 performances)
*Ninette à la cour*, Gardel sen., revived by Mlle Guimard, 14 May 1789, 'a new Ballet' (2 performances)
*Le tuteur trompé*, Le Picq, revived anonymously from 1783–84, 15 June 1789 (2 performances)

This season did not begin until 10 January 1789, and as has been explained in Chapter 2, there were tensions in management. Another contributing factor to the late start was the uncertainties of government during George III's first bout with porphyria.[1] By 7 November 1788 the possibility of a regency was being discussed by those closest to the King. At a time when some thought the theatres should be closed, the Lord Chamberlain might well have been reluctant to approve opening the opera-house. Whatever the causes of delay, the dance company was of astonishingly poor quality. The only dancer potentially of international reputation was Didelot, and this season he had no partner worthy of him. Nor were there many promising youngsters in evidence.

The blandly positive initial comment in the *Morning Post* contains no hint of trouble, but the more plain-spoken critic for the *World* parodied opening reviews at the expense of the second male dancer, Beaupré—'The man turns quite round, with a neatness beyond all we ever saw'—and goes on to remark that 'The Lobbies had good fires, which is well for the Female

---

[1] Ida Macalpine and Richard Hunter, *George III and the Mad-Business* (London: Allen Lane the Penguin Press, 1969), chs. 2 and 3.

Dancers; for they do not bribe by their Beauty'.[1] On 19 January 1789 *The Times* suggested that 'As nothing better . . . [was] to be had—we must make the best of a bad bargain—depending on the genius of *Noverre* for something beyond the insipidity of a *divertissement*—something where the *interest* of the *Ballet* may render the dancers interesting.' But even Noverre could not disguise the weakness of this company. Reporting on *Les fêtes provençales*, the *World* of 2 February 1789 opined that 'The Dance, if such it can be called, was like the movements of *heavy Cavalry*. It was hissed very abundantly.' On the same day the *Morning Post* noted that the ballet was 'not well received, as it exhibited nothing of that grand style to which the audience are now accustomed'. Moreover, the paper reported that Noverre 'repines that the terms of his articles should preclude him from exerting the whole of his genius'. Perhaps symptomatically, all dancers' names were omitted from Longman and Broderip's *Favorite Opera Dances* this season. Gallini was also suffering from the bad publicity (not to mention the practical difficulties) associated with a raid by customs agents that found contraband trim for costumes, both in the tailor's shop in the theatre and at his house. Harassed by officialdom, Gallini was dangerously vulnerable on this point: the bail and possible fines projected in the newspapers ran from £25,000 to £126,000, though all agreed that the merchandise itself was not particularly valuable.[2] *The Times* pursued the matter so relentlessly that for a few weeks the opera-house ceased to send in advertisements.[3]

Real trouble was brewing. At the next performance the dancers 'tried, by kicking their shoes off, to excite some laughter', while backstage 'one of the gentlemen most heroically wanted to fight the Manager', but Gallini retreated.[4] A column appeared in the *Morning Post* on 6 February 1789, explaining that Gallini had done what he could, but not everybody wanted to come to England, and not all rulers would let those who wanted to come do so: 'The King of France wrote himself a letter of interdict, as to those he wished to retain.' The column emphasized the quality of the singers and the band, and promised that better dancers were to come. 'Under these circumstances, is not complaint rather unreasonable', it asked, but audience

[1] Both reviews appeared on 12 Jan. 1789.

[2] The bail figure comes from the *Morning Post*, 17 Mar. 1789, the fine from *The Times*, 27 Jan., 14 and 17 Feb. 'Veritas', *Opera House*, 3, reports the actual fine as only £10,000.

[3] See coverage on 27 and 31 Jan. and 2, 6, and 11–13 Feb. 1789. The *Morning Post* carried a series of letters from a disgruntled 'Subscriber', but balanced them with others such as that from 'An Impartial Observer', 14 Mar. 1789.

[4] *Morning Post*, 4 Feb. 1789.

patience was about to snap.[1] At the performance on Saturday, 7 February, the second ballet was interrupted by demands 'why had we not better entertainments?' from Mr. C. Greville, the brother of Mrs Crewe, among others.[2] Gallini had fled. When Carnevale dodged the question, a group of 'young men . . . evidently in liquor' attacked the scenery and were restrained from damaging musical instruments only by the plea that they were private property. 'The whole of what was destroyed can, it is said, be repaired at a very small expence. The ladies, far from being intimidated by the probable consequences of this tumult, seemed highly to enjoy the *fun*, and did not retreat till the glasses appeared to be in danger.' Meanwhile, 'the Coffee-Room was as gay and peaceable as if nothing had happened'.[3]

At the end of the opera on the following Tuesday Gallini appeared, 'evidently under considerable embarrassment' and, after some noise, was allowed to apologize, which the house seemed to take well. On 11 February 1789 the *Morning Post* reported distribution of a handbill before the performance 'in which the Manager stated *seven* reasons in justification of his conduct'. They were:

First, That he had offered Le Picq and Rossi their own terms, without success. Secondly, That in the midst of his treaty with [Mlle] L'Anglois she died. Thirdly, That finding the Subscribers wished Coulon to be re-engaged, he had revived her salary; but after receiving the contract she had declined. Fourthly, That all his endeavours to retain several foreign performers had been unsuccessful, but that he had engaged Noverre on his own terms, and the best dancers that could be obtained. Fifthly, That he had engaged Signor Bennucci, universally allowed the first comic singer that ever graced the Italian stage, and Signora Storace. Sixthly, That as the Public was not satisfied Ravelli was dispatched for the best dancers that could be procured; and Seventhly, That Noverre is to prepare a grand ballet on a subject extremely interesting on their arrival.

Gallini was clearly humiliated by having to make a public apology; putting out a handbill was a means of overcoming the handicap of his Italian

---

[1] The opera riots may have been fuelled by tensions concerning the King: at precisely this time his recovery denied power to those who had been hoping for government positions under a regency. Some of them may have vented their frustrations on the opera.

[2] C. Greville, Esq.—perhaps the Hon. Charles Francis (1749–1809)—is listed in Box 58 of the 1789 subscribers' list bound into British Library 163.g.66, *La villana riconosciuta*. For accounts of this riot, see the *Morning Post*, *The Times*, and the *World* of 9 Feb. 1789, with further stories in the *Morning Post* and the *Public Advertiser* on 10 Feb. Accounts of the two 1789 riots are quoted at length in Ch. 2; see also Swift, *A Loftier Flight*, 19–21.

[3] A follow-up in the *Morning Post* of 10 Feb. 1789 joked about different people's reactions, saying that 'Lord Edgecumbe went among the soldiers, whose protection he anxiously solicited. Lord Brudenell was afraid of a broken head, and therefore prudently retired.'

accent. Much of the press continued overtly hostile to him, though the *World* admitted that 'the Ladies seemed much struck with the force of the Chevalier's argument' (11 February 1789).

More than the ballet itself was probably at issue. Women subscribers might be appeased by the promise of 'better entertainments', but the men had additional concerns. Dancers were sexual objects subject to male scrutiny and exploitation—and Gallini had provided a very unexciting set of specimens. The newspapers harped on the scandal of allowing an accused smuggler to run the opera. Privately, consumers of luxury goods might sympathize with Gallini's attempt to evade customs duties, a game in which many people participated. Women could choose to shrug off the charges, but after the raid men had officially to take a more serious view of the matter. One commentator noted that some tradesmen and local manufacturers were 'determined to carry the business to the last extremity, for the sake of public example'.[1] Had Gallini not been rich, with social connections and a papal knighthood, he might simply have been hounded out of the opera-house as Taylor had been before him. He had the resources to ride out the storm, but did so with difficulty.

In early February Gallini had problems more immediate than the delay in obtaining new dancers. The *Morning Post* reported on 10 February that Mlle Normand had gone missing,[2] but, far worse, Didelot 'had nearly broke his leg in dancing on Saturday night' and was out until 3 March. Although Noverre's part of *Les jalousies du sérail* was well advanced, Gallini appears to have given priority to a new opera production, and, as a letter to the *Morning Post* on 2 March asserted, 'it was not in the power of the painter to paint at the same time the decorations for the new opera, and the new ballet'. Relations between the manager and his ballet-master cannot have been helped by reports of hostilities between them in the press, such as the *Morning Post*'s story on 6 March that Gallini had refused to honour passes signed by Noverre. A month to the day after the first riot, Gallini tried to address the audience, but instead they demanded Noverre, whose appearance had been promised in the press. Noverre

---

[1] According to an extremely hostile 'Subscriber' in the *Morning Post* of 17 Mar. 1789.

[2] She was not advertised after 9 Feb., and the *Morning Post* implies she had run away. Like the Duke of Queensberry, thought to have 'retired with some tender female', 'Mademoiselle Normand, the beautiful little dancer of the Opera House, is also missing. This is the charming damsel who occasioned such *tender struggles* in the heart of Lord Brudenell, and produced the late emulative gallantry between him and Sir Richard Symonds.' This incident was memorable enough to be referred to in 1794 by Peter Pindar when he called Mlle Normand 'A pretty black-eyed Figurante at the Opera' (*Biographical Dictionary*, xi. 46).

nimbly stepped forward, and after much clamour, and twenty very low bows, was permitted to proceed to the following effect: "Messieur et Mesdames, J'espere que vous etes persuadé de mon profonde respect, et de mon activité de vous plaire; mais point d'argent, point de Ballet. La troupe de la danse n'est pas assez suffisante pour vous donner une spectacle tres brillante. J'ai prepare une ballet—*les Jalousies du Serail*, mais on ne peut pas le representer mardi prochain,[1] comme ni le tailleur, ni le machiniste son prets. Aussi la faute n'est pas a moi."[2]

Five young men in what *The Times* describes as 'a fashionable mob' proceeded to threaten Gallini with violence, but friends spirited him away. The rioters 'then came forward on the stage, and with great *sang froid* broke every lamp in the orchestra, and would have proceeded to other violence, but the audience feeling the impropriety of their conduct, gave a general hiss, desiring them to quit the stage'. Lord Barrymore is named as among those who pulled down some scenery. *The Times* concluded its account with a strong expression of editorial disapproval: 'What passed on Saturday, was not the mode to correct [management deficiencies], nor would such conduct have been tamely permitted at any other than the Italian theatre. It was an insult to the audience, in stopping their entertainment. The breaking the lamps was still worse, and should have met with chastisement, as several pieces of the glass flew into the Pitt, and struck some ladies.' The *Morning Post* and the *World* were equally censorious.

A trio of reinforcements—Nivelon, Mlle Dorival,[3] and Mlle Saulnier—arrived just in time to witness this riot from an upper box, and 'such was [Saulnier's] horror at the proceedings of those who called themselves "Gentlemen", that she declared the next day, she would never appear on the English stage'.[4] Preparations for *Les jalousies du sérail* went ahead, but on 13

---

[1] The 19 Feb. 1789 *Morning Post* reported a rehearsal at which '*Noverre*, and a set of voluptuous *figurantes* . . . engrossed the stage, and the gallant *ballet-master* seemed to be so delighted with many of their *movements*, that he had them repeated before him till he seemed to be entranced into a state of Asiatic luxuriousness. The dance which these nymphs, most of whom were in a state of enticing *dishabille*, were thus rehearsing, is to be something about the jealousie of the Sultan.'

[2] This and the following quotations (in faulty French) come from *The Times* of 9 Mar. 1789. For other accounts, see the undated cutting preserved in the Huntington Library and quoted in the *Biographical Dictionary*, v. 448, and Theatre Cuts 42, fo. [40ʳ], headed 'Opera Fracas' (manuscript date only '1789') quoted in Ch. 2. This disturbance is not noted in *The London Stage*.

[3] The favourite of 1784–85 had died in 1788. The newcomer is identified in the *Biographical Dictionary*, iv. 455, as Dorival à Corifet, stage name of Marie Catherine Brida. The opera bill in the *World* of 9 Mar. 1789 gives her name as 'Dorival à Ceriffee', but in the librettos for *La villana riconosciuta* and *La vendemmia* she is listed merely as Dorival.

[4] Theatre Cuts 42, fo. [14ᵛ] (dated 11 Mar. [1789] in manuscript). The *Morning Post* of 21 Feb. credited Lord Brudenell with persuading her to relent. The same issue of that paper

March, three days before the scheduled opening, customs agents again raided the theatre.

Opera Seizure!!! Yesterday about eleven o'clock Mr. Tankard and six of his *myrmidons* paid a visit to the opera and entered the taylor's rooms, where they made a seizure of a large quantity of contraband gold and silver lace, spangles, foils, &c. provided for the decorations of the opera dresses.—They next entered the wardrobe, on the story beneath, where they seized about twenty dresses, which had been made up for the dancers in the new *Turkish Ballet* now getting up. . . . Some lacemen and silk weavers were present, who united in declaring the property in question to be of French manufacture.[1]

One paper editorialized, 'That the manager of a theatre, the support of which depends upon the public liberality, should so far forget the duties he owes the country, as to enter into illicit practices against its manufactures, betrays an ingratitude, which places [him] in the most shocking and despicable light.'[2] This can hardly have been the first occasion on which contraband had been used to make or trim theatre costumes, and the timing of the two raids, interspersed with the riots, suggests that a concerted attempt was being made to harry Gallini into retirement. However, he was not fazed. Although 'the loss of so many dresses threatened an interruption to the new dance, a reinforcement of hands was immediately called in', and the ballet opened on schedule.[3]

*Les jalousies* was the first ballet of the season that appears to have given even limited satisfaction. It achieved fourteen performances, the last at Noverre's benefit on 21 May. Reviews noted 'scenes, decorations and dresses being very brilliant, and of course very expensive', but questioned whether 'the Ballet itself . . . [was] worthy the great reputation of Noverre, from whom, indeed, something better was certainly expected'.[4] There was some

reported Nivelon's salary as £800, Saulnier's as £1,000, plus clear benefits. Both seem excessive for a partial season, compared with La Guimard's (see below).

[1] Theatre Cuts 42, fo. [14ʳ], dated '15' (for 14) Mar. in manuscript. More restrained accounts appear in the *Morning Post* and *The Times* of 14 and 16 Mar.

[2] This and the following quotation come from Theatre Cuts 42, fo. [40ʳ], dated in manuscript 10 Apr. 1789.

[3] On 11 Dec. 1789 *The Times* reported that the verdict in both actions had gone against Gallini, but gave no details of the fines.

[4] These quotations are from the *Morning Post*, 18 Mar. 1789. The idea of the ballet—'the rivalry of the women for the honour of the Sultan's preference, and their anxiety after he had selected the favourite of the night, who is, however, neglected when a more beautiful female appears'—was a cliché by 1789. Lynham lists *Les jalousies* as a revival of a ballet first created at Lyons in 1758, but then comments ambivalently, 'Relationship of this revival to two previous productions unknown' (*Chevalier Noverre*, 165).

carping over the new dancers, but Didelot seemed to stand up well to the challenge of Nivelon.

The flurry of riots and raids subsided, and on 31 March Noverre brought out *Admète*, a 'new Allegorical Ballet'.[1] Since he himself had produced *Le triomphe de l'amour conjugal* in 1782, the London audience was familiar with his earlier version of the Alcestis story, but there is no evidence on which to distinguish the two. Although Longman and Broderip omitted to name any of the dancers in the published score, Nivelon probably danced the title-role and perhaps Mlle Saulnier took Alcestis.[2] Mazzinghi's music, whatever unknown sources it may have been 'selected and adapted' from, is a marked improvement on his previous efforts. Instead of the expected boisterous D major overture, there is a plaintive E flat major *largo* leading directly to an *allegro* in the all-too-rare key of C minor. Other pieces, some of them very long by King's Theatre standards, are also linked together. Unfortunately, since no scenario was published, there is no way of knowing what Noverre meant by describing this treatment of the story as 'allegorical'.

The most expensive of the reinforcements to the dance company was the great Mlle Guimard, who had been a key performer in the Opéra ballet for twenty-five years. According to *The Times* of 30 April, she came as a guest on a lavish expense account, with a clear benefit performance her only direct compensation. The Duchess of Devonshire, a close acquaintance, no doubt helped rally support for her, and Guimard wrote back to Paris that she had made 950 guineas and been offered an engagement for the rest of the season at 650 guineas.[3] London responses to her were sharply divided. The opera press was mostly grudging and sometimes overtly hostile, complaining about how little she danced and calling her 'the grandmother of the Graces',

[1] Celebrations for King George's recovery were in progress, and *The Times* reported that 'the most heartfelt delight was manifested at the transparencies in *Admete*, of "Vive le roi!"' (13 May 1789).

[2] Mlle Saulnier used *Admète* for her 14 May benefit, which seems more plausible for Alcestis than for Hebe or Iris, assuming they were in this version of the story.

[3] Details of the two contracts differ slightly from one account to another, but contemporary sources make clear that Guimard came for a very brief guest stint to be compensated by a benefit and that Gallini then hired her to dance for the rest of the season. Her second contract was terminated by the fire, after which Gallini attempted unsuccessfully to renegotiate with her. He had already paid her 325 guineas. On the two contracts, see Guimard's 'Address' and the response to it by 'Pas de Deux' in Theatre Cuts 42, fos. [16ʳ] and [15ᵛ], dated in manuscript 29 and 30 June 1789; and her letters of 26 May and 20 June 1789 printed by Edmond de Goncourt in *La Guimard* (Paris: Bibliothèque-Charpentier, 1893), 240–51. Goncourt misdates these letters 1784 and 1787: Guimard danced in England only in 1789.

but part of the audience seems to have appreciated her.[1] *The Times* reported receipts of 448 guineas (plus subscribers' tickets) at her second performance, 'the largest [receipt] ever known' (7 May 1789)—if true, the receipts were close to those documented for Marchesi's début (see above, Ch. 6).

Even a Guimard could not expect to take roles in existing ballets away from their current holders. She had to be grafted into existing dances, at least to begin with. Hence we find Didelot squiring her in 'the celebrated *Minuet* of Iphigenia, performed with universal applause in Paris' and in a 'new *Pas de deux anacréontique*, composed by Noverre', for her first appearance on 28 April in *Admète*.[2] The full-length ballets worked up for her, *Annette et Lubin*, *Ninette à la cour*, and *Les caprices de Galatée*, were not often scheduled, and it is easy to conclude that Guimard was not working very hard. At half her eighteen performances she appeared in only one ballet, not both, but most of those were complete, not just interpolated dances. Criticism arose because London audiences expected stars to appear in both ballets every night, unless they were injured. Questionable insertions of her *pas de deux russe* with Nivelon into *Admète* (7 May) or of the *Minuet* from *Iphigénie* into *La nymphe et le chasseur* (6 June) also made a travesty of the repertoire. Little wonder that the anti-Guimard faction played on age differences. The report of the command performance before the Queen and royal family on 12 May noted of *Admète* that 'Guimard displayed her usual grace; but Mad. Saulnier possesses such inflexion [that is, flexibility] of limb, and always meets the eye in such elegant disposition, that there were numbers who last night subscribed to the quivering foot of *youth*, against the Dancer who charmed *thirty years* ago'.[3] Yet after the fire Guimard's absence was regretted by some. On 29 June the *Oracle* noted,

Of the Dancing, we can only say that Madem. Guimard was not there. The other Dancers endeavoured by efforts the most strenuous and pleasing to compensate for her absence; but still the general cry was Guimard! Guimard! The Ladies *pirouetted* in the most fascinating manner to no purpose. Mme Saulnier showed a very handsome leg, so did Madem. Adelaide.—Rosine Simonet showed—something more [that is, part of her thigh]: but in spite of all this *Jambage* and *Cuissage*, the cry was still *Guimard! Guimard!*—the ancle of Guimard was worth *it all!*—Guimard, however, had put, it seems, in the opinion of Sir John Gallini, too high a price upon her

---

[1] See the 13 May 1789 *Morning Post*. She was not 60, as one newspaper reported, but 46. See the *Biographical Dictionary*, vi. 447–9.

[2] Guimard had appeared in the première of Gluck's *Iphigénie en Aulide* (1774), so the *Minuet* would have been a famous excerpt.

[3] Theatre Cuts 42, fo. [39$^r$], dated 14 May in manuscript.

ancle:—but in this, as in many other points, the *Public* and *Sir John* were not agreed.

Whether her accomplishments were evident or public response was merely to her stardom, she was by no means so universally scorned as some of the newspapers imply.

After the fire, however, there was considerable agitation over the terms of her engagement. Gallini had paid her half the 650 guineas she was owed, but tried to appeal to her charity to help him out at a lower rate for the rest of the season. She describes their negotiations in her tart letter to Perregaux of 20 June, culminating in her uninvited appearance with witnesses at a rehearsal, whereupon 'Ravelli went all red, and Gallini was stupified; they both thought had seen the head of Medusa' (our translation), and the rehearsal was dismissed. The 'Address' she published 'to the Nobility and the Public' on 29 June to explain her disagreements with Gallini is undeniably a selfish document, abrasive in tone, and it provoked a mock defence attacking the accuracy of her account.[1] Although Guimard remained in England until at least the end of June, she did not dance again in public. She sued Gallini for the rest of her salary, but the judgment went against her because, however sloppily the contract had been handled, she had not fulfilled her side of the bargain.[2] For once the press preferred Gallini to his antagonist, no doubt in part because she was French and a woman.

The destruction of the King's Theatre by fire in June has naturally tended to distract historians, but Noverre's statement of 7 March sums up this and the previous season: 'point d'argent, point de Ballet'. Audiences learnt that regardless of the imagination of the ballet-master, he had to have both dancers and a budget before he could function. The emergency dance recruits pacified the audience sufficiently to get Gallini through the spring of 1789 without further riots, but Guimard cost him a lot of money and was hardly an unqualified success. Noverre apparently left the country before his own benefit, so he was not around to help with negotiations or restaging after the fire. A hostile newspaper commentary on the state of the ballet in mid-May reported that

Noverre has received 700 Guineas as Ballet Master, and in addition to this, he proposed to himself a benefit. The Ballet of Dido was advertised as a *novelty*, to make his night *prosperous*.—And although he was aware how *ill* the Subscribers had been

---

[1] Theatre Cuts 42, fos. [16ʳ] and [15ᵛ]; de Goncourt, *La Guimard*, 240–44.

[2] On the lawsuit, see Theatre Cuts 42, fo. [28ᵛ], dated 28 June [1791] in manuscript, and *The Times*, 21 July 1791.

treated through the season, he declined producing Dido, till he connected it with his *own interest*. The expence of the ballet was the next object; but this was in Mr. Gallini's province, and if report be correct, Noverre has relinquished his right to Mr. Gallini for £460 and thus we suspect Didone has been got rid of.[1]

In other words, rather than pay the production expenses for *Énée et Didon*, Gallini bought out Noverre's benefit. Gallini was clearly trying to get by on makeshifts. Another example is *Il sogno di Rinaldo*, an entertainment that mixed singing and dancing under the joint direction of Marchesi and Guimard planned for 18 June but abandoned in the wake of the fire.[2] Each compromise had its reason, but they added up to a very patchy set of offerings for the last season of the old theatre.

### The Little Haymarket Season of 1789–90

Ballet Repertoire:

*Divertissement*, no choreographer credited, 7 January 1790 (27 performances)
*La bergère des Alpes*, Blake, music adapted by Chabran, 7 January 1790 (31 performances)
*Les mariages flamands*, Blake, music adapted by Chabran, 13 February 1790, 'an entire new ballet' (26 performances)
*Les caprices*, no choreographer credited, 25 March 1790 (6 performances)
*La jalousie sans raison*, no choreographer credited, music adapted by Chabran, 25 March 1790 (15 performances)
*New Ballet* (*Lauretta*), no choreographer credited, 22 April 1790, 'an entire New Ballet' (7 performances)[3]
*The Generous Slave*, no choreographer credited [by Blake for his benefit?], music adapted by Chabran, 13 May 1790, 'an entire new pantomimical Dance' (12 performances)

Why Gallini soldiered on after the fire is discussed in Chapter 6. He economized on his ballet-master and instead spent relatively freely on principal dancers and, tellingly, on sixteen *figurants*.[4] The people who squeezed into the Little Theatre in the Haymarket seem to have taken the crowded stage as an attempt to please them. For instance, on 7 April 1790 the *Public Advertiser* reported that the dance 'had as much merit as the size of the Theatre would permit'. If not satisfied, at least the audience did not riot.

---

[1] Theatre Cuts 42, fo. [16ᵛ], dated 18 May [1789] in manuscript. The *World* says as early as 20 Feb. that Mazzinghi had been composing music for the ballet, and an advertisement in *The Times* shows that the project was still on as late as 20 Apr. On 23 Feb. *The Times* had carried an accusation that Gallini habitually 'saved' débuts of productions and performers until his own benefit night.

[2] See Smith, *Italian Opera*, 9, and *The Times* of 10 and 11 June 1789.

[3] Title deduced by Smith, *Italian Opera*, 15, from *The Favourite Opera Dances for the year 1790 . . . selected by F. Chabran*.

[4] See the *World*, 8 Jan. 1790.

The ballet-master was the Mr Blake who had been in the company in 1783–84; his credentials are unknown other than his Italian training.[1] The titles of his ballets imply a regressive repertoire policy. The season comprised only five dances, plus two *pièces d'occasion* that quickly got pulled into the repertoire, but notices were mostly dismissive. Critics who bothered to mention dance concentrated on performers. Laborie at about 19 and Mlle Hilligsberg at not much over 20 were well matched, and she was warmly welcomed home. She was called 'too exquisite a dancer to waste her talents on such trumpery as the Divertissement and *Bergere des Alpes*' (*The Times*, 25 January 1790) and on 9 January 1790 the *Public Advertiser* praised her 'improved beauty and fascination—All that the mind can picture of aerial vision, of fairy lightness, and of polished grace, are to be found in this charming little creature.' By contrast Mlle Del Caro 'was treated unhandsomely by the French faction, merely because she was an Italian; she found, however, in the justice of England, fair protection', according to the papers.[2] This is the most direct statement to be found of the tensions between the French and Italian schools of dance. Newspaper critics were either unaware of such subtleties or lacked the room or inclination to spell them out. A sign of priorities is the initial review of the returning Mlle Dorival, which found her 'more lovely than ever', but added, 'we sincerely wish that her talents may equal her beauty'. Gallini thought it worth while to note in the bill for the opening night that Mlle Coulon had 'refused to come, though engaged'. As his musical *pasticheur* and répétiteur, Gallini employed Felice Chabran, who selected and adapted the four books of *Favorite Opera Dances* published this season by Birchall. The scores of *La bergère des Alpes* and *La fête flamand* (*Les mariages flamands*) are substantial works, the former especially designed to exploit the extraordinary talent of Mlle Hilligsberg. Her music is uniformly of a soft character, marked *amoroso, patetico e dolente, espressivo, pastorale, grazioso*, and so forth. The music of *La jalousie sans raison* is much slighter, and in that for *The Generous Slave* Chabran seems to have lost heart, except for the last piece, a raw and primitive Celtic hornpipe that makes one regret that no scenario was published for this ballet (see Ex. 7.3).

In addition to the advertised dancers in the *London Stage* season roster, lists printed in the librettos of *Ninetta* at the beginning of the season and in *L'usurpator innocente* and *Andromaca* at the end document the following

---

[1] The few instances in which his name is recorded in London playbills are listed in the *Biographical Dictionary*, ii. 147.
[2] *The Times* reported on 8 Jan. 1790 that Del Caro was hissed.

Ex. 7.3. Felice Chabran, from *The Generous Slave*

partners: Sala and Mlle Dorival; Ferreri (Ferrère) and Mlle De La Croix; Ross or Roff (Rossi? Roffey?) and Mlle Laborie. These unadvertised dancers were part of the large *corps de ballet*. Simonet was listed in the season announcement but cannot otherwise be traced, and his daughters were at Covent Garden for much of the season. Some evidence of a squabble within the company has survived. A week before the season began, a gossip columnist noted, 'A quarrel has already arisen between *Duquesnay*, and a dancer of more eminence [Laborie?]. The particulars, which are curious, we shall give in a future paper.'[1] Nothing further is known of this incident.

[1] Theatre Cuts 42, fo. [16ʳ], dated 30 Dec. [1789] in manuscript.

This season showed that the London audience could tolerate journeyman choreography if the principal dancers were sufficiently flashy—but perhaps only if a new theatre and a new administration were in prospect.

## VI. The State of Ballet in London in 1790

Two points stand out in this long survey. First and most important, the innovations in dance introduced by the Sheridan and Taylor managements permanently altered expectations and demands. An audience that had seen major works of Noverre and become accustomed to virtuosity at the level of the best dancers hired by the King's Theatre during the 1780s was prepared to riot when not provided some reasonable facsimile of these entertainments. Looking back over the whole history of the opera-house, John Feltham noted in his *Picture of London for 1802* that 'Latterly . . . dancing has so greatly prevailed as to have threatened to triumph over the more refined and noble art of music. To allow time for the performance of ballets, operas, which originally consisted of three acts, have been reduced to two; and a ballet is now often extended to a greater length than an act of an opera.'[1] As Chapters 4, 5, and 6 have shown, dance was not the only factor that contributed to the changing shape of operas, but the two-act format could more easily accommodate *ballet d'action*. Dance gradually claimed more time and prominence in the evening's programme.

A second and unexpected point is that Gallini's accession to power failed to benefit the ballet in London. He was 57 years old when he finally gained control of the King's Theatre and had been over 30 when Noverre made his first great experiments in the *ballet d'action* back in the 1760s and 1770s. As a principal Gallini had practiced an earlier mode of dance. In his 1762 *Treatise on the Art of Dancing* (however derivative), he had expressed a commitment to what may be called a more purely aesthetic and formal theory of dance. In the 1772 edition he endorsed the concept of *ballet d'action*, but the 'poetic dances' he 'furnished as hints' (*Venus and Adonis* and *The Coquette Punished*) are fairly rudimentary. Gallini was indeed a ballet-master, but not of a generation and outlook wholeheartedly to embrace the new wave in ballet.

When Gallini hired Dauberval for 1783–84 he assumed that as owner of the King's Theatre he could operate it as he pleased. When he got in the door to stay in 1785 he was merely Taylor's trustee, and subject to a budget

---

[1] (London: Lewis and Co. for R. Phillips *et al.*, n.d.), 199. Preface dated 10 Aug. 1802.

cap imposed by the Court of Chancery. He quickly discovered that he would also suffer vicious and unceasing legal harassment from Taylor and others. No doubt he believed in 1785 that he would soon gain full control of the theatre. By 1787–88 Gallini's temper was obviously fraying as he began to realize that he would *never* be able to run the opera company the way he wanted to, or without constant interference. In these circumstances he might well have been doubly reluctant to spend his own money on an entertainment for which he had no great personal sympathy. The result, however, was a regression in the nature of the dance offered, and a serious decline in performance standards.

In a larger European context, ballet may be said to have benefited from what happened in London over the decade. Le Picq ran the company for two of those years, working for Dauberval and dancing with Vestris in the year between. His experience of a foreign habitat in England stood him in good stead when he went to St Petersburg, though he remained unwilling to return to London. Didelot had a whole year to consult with Noverre, who gave him two of his first opportunities to make ballets. Vestris learnt, with some difficulty, the advantages and disadvantages of being out from under his father's thumb. Women dancers had less power in the company and were more expendable, yet during the time Mme Théodore Dauberval spent in England she expanded her range considerably, as did Mme Rossi. Younger dancers must also have benefited. Although models were available to the whole *corps de ballet*, journalistic attention was apt to focus on the development of native dancers. The Simonet girls were well taught at home but needed to see dancers more recently trained than their parents. Mlle Hilligsberg was good enough not to need to trade on the English origins claimed for her, but chauvinistic journalists eventually led Duquesney to overestimate his accomplishments.[1] For example, as early as 27 June 1785 the *Morning Herald* had praised him and Miss Harvey, in defiance of the opinion of unnamed French dancers that the couple, 'having had the misfortune of being born in England', could not hope to achieve 'grace and elegance'. Nevertheless, the fact that there are a number of 'English' dancers in the generation following Slingsby (an isolated phenomenon in the 1770s) is a sign of overall improvement. The King's Theatre had its own intrigues and hazards, but London provided a pleasant haven to a fair number of dancers, especially the French.

[1] For discussion, see vol. II.

The degree to which Gallini had altered the balance of the company's offerings is obvious from some salary figures. In 1784–85 (the season before he took over) the company had spent £3,900 on salaries of principal singers and £4,365 on salaries of principal dancers, with an additional £975 on *figurants*.[1] The trustees' second season was a decidedly shabby one for dance, but even then the principals' salaries totalled roughly 112 per cent of the principal singers' salaries. A comparison with figures for 1789–90 yields surprising differences of emphasis. The source is 'An authentic LIST of the principal performers engaged at the Opera House for the year 1789, with their salaries'.[2] The excerpts that follow omit both singers and dancers who arrived in mid-season or later, and also some relatively minor performers (for example, two of the Simonet girls). It does, however, give quite a good sense of what Gallini intended to spend on dance in 1788–89 and of company hierarchy.

| | |
|---|---|
| Didelot | £600 and a benefit |
| Mlle Adelaide | £400 and a benefit plus travel |
| Mlle Colombe | £300 and a benefit plus travel |
| Beaupré | £270 and a benefit |
| Duquesney | £250 and a benefit |
| Coindé | £165 and a benefit |
| Mlle Normand | £100 and a benefit |

To the subtotal of £2,085 must be added 700 guineas and a benefit for Noverre, making a total of £2,820.[3] The total for the singers listed comes to £5,607 (plus at least eight benefits). Thus in 1789–90 the budget for principal dancers is almost exactly 50 per cent of the budget for principal singers. Four years earlier the dance budget had actually exceeded the opera budget. These figures confirm that Gallini had chosen to emphasize opera and drastically economized on dance. He did, strictly under duress, add something

---

[1] Bedford Opera Papers, 2.A.29. In the comparison that follows *figurants'* salaries are ignored because there are no comparable figures for 1789–90.

[2] The 'List' is found in Anthony Pasquin (i.e., John Williams), *Poems* (London: J. Strahan *et al.*, [1789]), ii. 268. This appendix (not present in all copies) is a more complete form of a letter to the editor printed in the *Morning Post* on 26 Feb. 1789. Williams gives no clue as to his source of information. We have used the British Library copy.

[3] Noverre's salary is stated as £735 in the Pasquin 'List' and as 700 guineas in a newspaper report in Theatre Cuts 42, fo. [16ᵛ], dated 18 May [1789] in manuscript. For the singers' salaries in the 'Pasquin' list, see 'Opera Salaries', 51–2.

to the dance budget when emergency replacements were rushed in from Paris. And though Mlle Guimard was expensive at more than £680 for only part of a season, no dance salary amounted to even half the £1,500 (plus benefit and free housing) given to Marchesi as *primo uomo.* Gallini hired singers late in the season as well. Whatever might have been expected of him as impresario, what he chose to do was to de-emphasize dance.

Clearly this was not what the audience wanted. International stars, elaborate and elegant staging, and a choreographer able to devise impressive *ballets d'action* were not only desired but positively demanded by the audience, some of whose members were prepared to tear the theatre apart if disappointed. By 1786 an opera company in London needed to invest heavily in ballet—and to provide the kind of dance and dancers the opera-house audience had come to expect. *Divertissements* and happy peasant frolics were acceptable in moderation (especially in the first dance), but a reasonable proportion of stronger meat had become obligatory. An audience that had seen the best of Noverre was not to be fobbed off with the shabby wares Gallini had provided. This was a lesson that both William Taylor and the Pantheon proprietors were to take to heart.

CHAPTER 8

# Fire and Rebuilding, 1789–1791

THE Gallini regime was rudely interrupted on 17 June 1789 when the King's Theatre, Haymarket, burned to the ground. The company's debts were upwards of £100,000, and unpaid interest was spiralling them ever higher. The budget cap of £18,000 per annum necessitated economies that made the audience restive, and Gallini himself was personally unpopular. Management by trustee was unsatisfactory, but what would replace it was unclear. The fire precipitated a mad scramble between those who wanted to rebuild and those who wanted to start over from scratch, thereby jettisoning the millstone of the old company's debts. We have told this story elsewhere:[1] the concern of this chapter is how the King's Theatre came to be rebuilt and why it was constructed on so gigantic a scale. The fact that the King's Theatre, Haymarket, *was* rebuilt after the fire has occasioned virtually no surprise or analysis. Vanbrugh's theatre had been London's principal Italian opera-house for nearly a century, and Michael Novosielski's new theatre of 1791 was to remain so until the late 1840s. The emergence of the new Haymarket from the ashes of the old has seemed natural, and scholars have accepted it as a matter of course. In fact, it was nothing of the sort. William Taylor (the proprietor) was discredited and penniless and held a ground lease of only fourteen years on the site of the old theatre. Powerful and well-to-do members of the nobility were eager to erect a new opera-house on a different site and to rid opera of Taylor in the process. The King agreed to grant a patent to a rival venture. None the less Taylor persevered and somehow contrived, against all expectations, to arrange financing and get his theatre rebuilt.

---

[1] See 'A Royal Opera House in Leicester Square' and vol. II, Ch. 1.

# I. The Destruction of the Old Theatre

The fire of 17 June 1789 was extensively reported in the newspapers, most clearly in the *London Chronicle* of 16–18 June.

Last night, at five minutes before ten o'clock, a most dreadful fire broke out at the King's Theatre, at the time the performers were practicing a repetition of the dances which were to be performed this evening. The fire burst out instantaneously at the top of the Theatre, and the whole roof was in a moment in a blaze. It burnt with so much rapidity, that while the people were running from the stage, a beam fell in from the ceiling. The fire soon communicated to all parts of the house, and from the nature of the articles with which it was filled, the blaze soon became the most tremendous we ever witnessed. The whole of the structure in a very short time was rendered an entire shell, and its progress was so rapid that it was impossible to save any material part of its contents. The flames extended to Market-lane, and nearly consumed Union-court. Notwithstanding a great number of engines were in readiness, it was with extreme difficulty they could be supplied with water. There perhaps never was, upon any occasion of similar distress, so large a concourse of spectators as were collected on the spot and the neighbourhood; it is generally understood, however, that no lives are lost. Fortunately five very large barrels of oil were got out from the store-rooms under the Opera House before the flames reached them. From the manner of the flames first appearing, there is strong reason to believe the building was set on fire maliciously, as no person had been employed with any light where it broke out since Tuesday morning.

The *Oracle* of 18 June states that 'at the time this alarming accident commenced, a Rehearsal was performing, preparatory to the intended spectacle of today, in which was to be introduced a novel firework; the combustibles prepared for which, having anticipated the intention of the Proprietors, unhappily realized the scene, and rendered it in every sense most truly tragical'. The *World* of 19 June says the cause was 'Turpentine varnish boiling over'; like the 'fireworks' report this seems implausible. Small quantities of turpentine may have been on hand for use in making models and painting properties, but scene paint was water-based.[1] The *Oracle* of 19 June says that 'The fire began in that part of the House above the stage which is called the *Fly*. They were rehearsing a Ballet below; and the first notice they had of the mischief was sparks falling upon their heads. No persons were above at the time. These circumstances necessarily give rise to suspicions of a premeditated design on the part of some incendiary.' A rumour attributed the fire to a drunken carpenter carrying a candle into the scene loft, which might

---

[1] For an account of a misguided attempt to use oils to paint scenery for a private theatre, see Patrick Conner, *Michael Angelo Rooker* (London: Batsford, 1984), 136n.

account for the facts if the fire were indeed accidental (*Morning Post*, 19 June 1789).

As early as 19 June *The Times* was hinting that Gallini was responsible for the fire.

Our conjectures upon the great probability that this theatre was set fire to intentionally, is [are] confirmed by every inquiry, and some persons are strongly suspected. . . . Gallini and Novosielski had agreed only the beginning of this week, to share the management of the Theatre next season [not otherwise known, if true]. The former will be perhaps a gainer by the accident, as independent of his wish to get rid of the concern, the property was insured at the Hand in Hand, Royal Exchange; and Sun Fire Offices.

This charge seems highly improbable. Gallini's insurance totalled only £8,000, and the fire ended any reasonable hope of his recovering some £25,000 he was owed by the venture, as well as depriving him of a position he apparently continued to covet.[1] The total insurance on the property may have been as much as £18,000. The *Public Advertiser* of 20 June says that 'the whole sum of the insurance . . . amounts only to 14 or £15,000'; the *Oracle* of the same date reports the sum of £18,000, 'five thousand of which was encreased within the last three months'. In *A Plan* Taylor lays claim to £4,500 'applicable to the Rebuilding of the Theatre', and in his later pamphlet he complains that Edward Vanbrugh withheld £3,500 he had received.[2] Gallini was paid in full;[3] whether Vanbrugh was paid is not known. However, neither Gallini nor Vanbrugh had anything to gain from burning the theatre and collecting the insurance. On 22 June Gallini published an advertisement: 'Whereas there is great Reason to believe that the Opera House was maliciously set on fire, I hereby offer a reward of £300 to any one who will give information of the person or persons who set the same on fire, so that he or they may be convicted thereof.'[4]

---

[1] Nalbach (68–70) concludes that Gallini held £18,000 in insurance, though Taylor (*A Plan . . . for Rebuilding the King's Theatre* [see below], 2) and O'Reilly (*An Authentic Narrative*, 54) agree on £8,000. Taylor's 1799 memorial gives the figure £8,500 and complains bitterly that Gallini 'detained it for himself' rather than contributing it towards the rebuilding of the theatre (PRO CRES 6/121, p. 329). Nalbach's account of Gallini's position vis-à-vis the opera-house is marred by serious errors and misunderstandings. He imagines, for example, that after the fire Gallini 'would still have to pay off the mortgage of £18,000, return the £12,000 to the stockholders, and pay the "Simple Contract Debts" of £31,000' (69). In fact, Gallini owned the mortgage (he did not owe it), and the other debts were Taylor's.

[2] *A Concise Statement*, 36.

[3] C31/255, no. 393 (sworn testimony by George Merrifield that he saw Gallini receive £8,000 insurance money at the Royal Exchange Assurance Office on 5 Mar. 1790).

[4] *Morning Post*. There is no recorded response.

The person usually charged with responsibility for the alleged arson is Carnevale, who had been Gallini's assistant manager from 1785 to 1788 and was replaced in 1788–89 by Ravelli.[1] Such a rumour may have been current at the time, but the charge was first publicly brought by 'Veritas' *c.*1818.[2] This tale was embroidered upon without acknowledgement by Edward Wedlake Brayley, writing more than thirty-five years after the fire. Brayley says that on his deathbed Carnevale confessed to a priest, adducing jealousy of Ravelli as his motive.[3] The authors of the *Biographical Dictionary* challenge Brayley on several points in their account of Carnevale. Writing in the same year as Brayley, Michael Kelly (an eyewitness of the fire) says, 'I knew the person suspected. He was an Italian, who had been in the employ of Gallini, but having disagreed with him, it was reported that he set fire to his theatre; for my own part, I never believed it; but such was the report, certain it is, at all events, that the suspected incendiary was coolly supping at the Orange Coffee House, watching the progress of the flames.'[4]

Another candidate with a very doubtful motive is Taylor. He certainly wanted to displace Gallini and regain control of his theatre, but destroying the premises was not the best way of doing so. Taylor's only known income was a £200 annuity from Gallini; the King's Theatre and its ground lease were all the property Taylor had in the world; and the fire did not in fact dispossess Gallini, who retained first claim on the ruins. All one can really conclude is that the causes of the fire are unknown.

## II. Competing Plans, Summer–Autumn 1789

Would the King's Theatre be rebuilt or replaced, and by whom? The Gordian knot of the opera company's legal snarls certainly needed to be cut, but the fire complicated matters more than it clarified them. The *Public Advertiser* of 20 June 1789 mockingly suggested that the fire would put an end to '30 suits in Chancery. 22 actions in the King's-Bench. 18 ditto in the Common Pleas. 13 ditto on the case in the Exchequer. Besides 18 cross bills filed, 16 drawing out, 74 common writs not executed, 12 petitions for rehearings

[1] On Carnevale, see *Biographical Dictionary*, iii. 76–7.

[2] *Opera House*, 3. Veritas's lurid hints are difficult to interpret in the absence of other evidence. He charges Carnevale not only with 'putting the torch to the original embarrassed theatre' but with 'the impoisoning of the poor tool Gallino [otherwise unknown] lest he should divulge the secret'.

[3] Edward Wedlake Brayley, *Historical and Descriptive Account of the London Theatres* (London: J. Taylor, 1826), 26.

[4] Kelly, *Reminiscences*, i. 320–1.

at Lincoln's-inn-hall, 93 complicated accounts referred to the Masters in Chancery, and four appeals to the House of Lords'. All comic exaggeration aside, the fire settled virtually nothing.

Writing six days after the fire to Mary and Agnes Berry, Horace Walpole asked 'Have you shed a tear over the Opera House? or do you agree with me, that there is no occasion to rebuild it? The nation has long been tired of operas, and has now a good opportunity of dropping them. Dancing protracted their existence for some time—but *the room after* [the supper room] was the real support of both.'[1] To judge from the enormous increase in subscribers in the 1780s and 1790s, however, Walpole's views were not those of most of the opera-going nobility and gentry. Social display may have outweighed love of Italian opera and ballet, but London society wanted an opera-house.

Any attempt to rebuild the old theatre would be complicated by ownership disputes. Taylor remained technically the proprietor of the theatre building ruins and the company but was insolvent. His arch-enemy Gallini (acting as Taylor's trustee) would retain legal possession of both ruins and company until he was paid the very large sums owed him or until the Court of Chancery turned him out—unless some kind of bargain could be struck. There was an additional complication: the old theatre did not occupy a freehold; rather, it was built on land held under a Crown lease by Edward Vanbrugh. In 1777 he had granted a 21-year lease on the theatre site to James Brooke (commencing in 1782), who later sublet to Taylor (without consulting Vanbrugh). So after a fashion Taylor owned the remains of the theatre and rights to its site up to 1803; Gallini held immediate control of the ruins as mortgagee; and Vanbrugh would again control the site after 1803. But even if they could somehow agree to rebuild and could find the necessary capital, the occupants of the new building would inevitably be sued for the accumulated debts of the previous venture.

Yet a further problem—one whose implications dawned slowly on those warring over the remains of the Haymarket—was the lack of a licence or a patent.[2] By the terms of the Licensing Act of 1737 only two theatres and one opera-house were to be tolerated in London, and each of those venues required either a royal patent or a licence from the Lord Chamberlain.[3]

[1] Letter of 23 June 1789; Walpole, *Correspondence*, xi. 14–15.
[2] See above, Ch. 1, sect. 1.
[3] The Little Haymarket was a special case, Samuel Foote having received a 'summer' patent for it in 1766.

After the expiration of the Royal Academy patent in 1740, the King's Theatre, Haymarket, received annual licences, though the rights of the opera-house were sufficiently established by custom that the authorities did not always bother with the formalities. But if the Lord Chamberlain refused his licence, any performer who defied the ban was subject to arrest under the vagrancy act—a non-bailable offence. Anyone could build a theatre, but using it was something else. Nor was this a matter of theory or olden times: John Palmer had built the Royalty Theatre in 1787, defied the law, and duly been prosecuted and his theatre shut down.[1] To build a theatre without assurance of the right to perform would be folly. No one connected with the King's Theatre, Haymarket, seems to have thought about this in July 1789; more immediate problems claimed everyone's attention.

In the days after the fire contradictory rumours surfaced in the newspapers. As early as 20 June the *Oracle* said that '*Leicester House* has been named as the situation best adapted for a *New Opera House*', adding that others 'recommend the *scite* of the *King's Mews* in preference'. On the 29th the same paper said that 'Speculation is allotting various places for the erecting of the *New Opera House*', and on 1 July it reported (prematurely) that 'It is now determined that the New Opera-House is to be erected on the *old scite.*' The *Public Advertiser* noted that 'Several schemes are already proposed for the rebuilding of the Opera House, or erecting a new one' on 22 June, and a day later that 'several builders are already in treaty for restoring the Opera-house to its late condition, and that without enlargements, or even much change'.

In view of the entangled condition and insolvency of the old enterprise, many onlookers doubted the feasibility of rebuilding on the old site. A group of noblemen headed by Lord Cholmondeley and the Duke of Bedford got up a scheme described in the *Public Advertiser* of 30 June 1789:

The Nobility are determined to have an Opera on a grand scale, and worthy the opulence of the nation. It is not fixed whether it is to be on the old scite or not. The Prince of Wales, the Duke of Bedford, and the other movers of the subscription, are anxious to give the mortgagees and creditors of the late property a fair preference. If they will come to an amicable agreement, and will offer a good plan, it is to be adopted; if not, Leicester-house is to be the scite.

On 3 July Cholmondeley wrote a letter to the Lord Chamberlain describing

---

[1] See *The London Stage*, Part 5, ii. 911–12. For a view of this imbroglio as it pertained to the King's Theatre, Haymarket, see *The Times* of 26 Mar. 1791.

the venture, enclosing a copy of his letter to Troward (solicitor for the old theatre), and assuring him that 'we are engaged therein upon the presumption of the very great improbability (as it appears to us from every thing we can learn) of the present building being re-established'.[1]

Complications and competition notwithstanding, both Gallini and Taylor were determined to 're-establish' the old theatre. According to a letter of 7 July from the Lord Chamberlain to Cholmondeley, Salisbury had 'already received proposals from Mr. Gallini, for reinstating the old building for the benefit of the Proprietors and Claimants'.[2] At about the same time, despite their long-standing animosities, Taylor approached Gallini and proposed that they join forces or that Gallini sell out to him. In August 1789 Gallini agreed to do the latter—but then stalled endlessly over completing the paperwork.[3]

Although Gallini agreed to clear the way for Taylor, he secretly engaged in a counter-scheme, for he wished to run the opera—without Taylor. In conjunction with a young man about town named Robert Bray O'Reilly, he sought legal advice about attempting to rebuild on the old site.[4] The replies were discouraging. 'The opinions of the most eminent Counsel were taken . . . who were unanimous, that it would be impracticable to build upon the old scite, without the interference of Parliament, on account of the numerous suits that did then, and still do affect that concern.' A petition to the House of Lords was drawn up, but refused.[5] Gallini and O'Reilly then proceeded to join forces with the nobles who had proposed a new building in Leicester Square. The Prince of Wales promised his support, and in September 1789 O'Reilly went off to the Continent to recruit performers and refine his architectural plans. Gallini busied himself with arrangements for a stopgap season at the Little Theatre in the Haymarket for spring 1790, and continued to stonewall Taylor. But Taylor thought he was going to buy Gallini out with an IOU, rebuild the theatre, and reclaim direction of the company he had been forced to yield control of in April 1783.

---

[1] Printed in Taylor, *A Concise Statement*, 13–16.

[2] Ibid. 17.

[3] See Taylor's public notice (dated 31 Oct.) in the *Oracle* of 3 Nov. 1789 and a subsequent item in the same paper on 7 Dec.

[4] O'Reilly, *An Authentic Narrative*, 49–50, 52.

[5] 'A Bill was brought into the House of Lords, a few days since, by Lord Bathurst, to oblige the proprietors of the Opera House to dispose of their respective shares, in order to vest the whole in the hands of Gallini. The [Lord] Chancellor saw the drift immediately, and frowned it into *nothing!*' Theatre Cuts 42, fo. [39$^r$], manuscript date 30 July [1789].

## III. Financing the New Theatre, January–April 1790

At the end of November 1789 Taylor first caught wind of the Leicester Square project. He thereupon wrote a series of furious letters of protest to the Lord Chamberlain, who ignored the first, scorned the second, and merely reported that he had presented the third to His Majesty—who had, it would seem, been carefully schooled to approve the Leicester Square proposal.[1] By early January the news was public. Detailed plans for Leicester Square were announced in the *London Chronicle* of 9–12 January 1790, and by the 13th the *World* was trumpeting the news of the King's promise of a royal patent for the enterprise.[2] By all logic, Taylor was defeated and the Haymarket opera was dead. According to a detailed and persuasive list of debts assembled by his enemy O'Reilly, Taylor was personally liable for £90,000 of unpaid opera debts;[3] he was penniless; his competition was supported by the Prince of Wales, the Duke of Bedford, and secretly by the Marquis of Salisbury (who just happened to be Lord Chamberlain); and the King had tentatively approved a 31-year patent to O'Reilly. But Taylor had only begun to fight.

The claimants warring over the remains of the Haymarket had not been able to agree on anything. Faced with the loss of all prospect of payment, they were more amenable to compromise. Taylor needed the co-operation of his innumerable creditors before he could even begin to try to raise construction money. He held meetings with them on 21 January and 15 February 1790.[4] From the first meeting he got agreement to present a memorial to the King, protesting against a patent grant that would remove all possibility of rebuilding the Haymarket and paying off its creditors. From the second he got agreement to accept a plan for payment of old debts after a new theatre had been built. Persuading the old creditors to be patient might, however, be easier than finding enough capital to build a new theatre.

Neither the *Survey of London* nor Nalbach's history of the theatre comments on the appalling difficulties in Taylor's way, nor do they explain how he went about acquiring the necessary capital. The generally reliable 'Veritas' quotes Taylor as saying 'When I stood upon the reeking ruins, and laid the foundation stone [on 3 April 1790], I had nothing in my pockets but

---

[1] Printed in *A Concise Statement*, 20–9, letters of 8 and 18 Dec. 1789 and 1 Jan. 1790.
[2] We have traced the history of this abortive plan in 'A Royal Opera House in Leicester Square'.
[3] *An Authentic Narrative*, 42–5.
[4] *A Concise Statement*, 30.

both my hands, and I would have given the world for one guinea.'[1] We do not know how much money he actually managed to raise, how he spent it, or what construction debts may have remained. In the Harvard Theatre Collection, however, there is a unique copy of Taylor's financial proposals, printed for distribution to potential investors and dated 10 March 1790: *A Plan, Proposed by the Proprietor, and Approved of by the Different Classes of Claimants for Rebuilding the King's Theatre.*[2]

Taylor needed cash for construction costs and to pay off Gallini's old mortage; he needed the promise of future cash to appease past creditors; and he needed enough annual income to keep the opera afloat. These needs were contradictory. Taylor's proposals fall into two essentially separate parts—a stock offering and a set of rental deals on boxes, designed to raise immediate capital at the cost of future income. The stock offering was extremely simple: Taylor proposed to define 'The *New* Undertaking' in terms of twenty-five shares of £750 each. Five would come to him ('in Consideration of my Money embarked, and Interests in the Old Theatre') and twenty would be sold, raising £15,000. No one other than Taylor could hold more than three shares. Investors would get a share of the (entirely hypothetical) profits, plus the right of free admission for themselves and one other person.

The box-rental proposals are far more complicated. Boxes could be rented by the season or taken on long leases. Taylor evidently felt he needed a minimum of £44,000 in addition to what he might get from new stock-holders (plus insurance money, and so forth). Roughly a third of it was to come from thirteen-year leases on fifteen boxes (confusingly described as 'sold out-right for the Term of Thirteen Years'). The rest would come from similar thirteen-year rental of single places in various categories of boxes. In essence, Taylor was offering single places for £16 per annum instead of the usual £21, with the price guaranteed over thirteen years. That limit, of course, was determined by the expiration of his lease on the ground on which the new theatre was to be built—a point he took care not to emphasize in the prospectus.

From sale of stock and long-term rental of boxes and individual places in boxes, Taylor projected collection of £43,785 in capital. A figure he does not

---

[1] 'Veritas', *Opera House*, title-page epigraph.

[2] HTC bTS 318.84. A complete transcription is printed in Curtis Price, Judith Milhous, and Robert D. Hume, 'The Rebuilding of the King's Theatre, Haymarket, 1789–1791', *Theatre Journal*, 43 (1991), 421–44, Appendix.

give, but which can be calculated from this document, is the total annual loss of potential income from boxes to be sold to raise construction money and to discharge obligations carrying over from the old theatre—the startling and depressing sum of £7,007. In other words, Taylor projected that the operating budget would be some £22,000 per annum, but the *de facto* payment on principal and interest would be about £7,000 of money that would otherwise have been available for singers, dancers, costumes, and scenery. In the September 1790 box-plan discussed below Taylor stated that 'Forty of the principal Boxes are appropriated for the purpose of compleating the Building of the Theatre, paying the Mortgagees, &c. After which there will remain a clear Annual Subscription of £13,700 at least for the Establishment of the Theatre.'[1] This assumes 100 per cent occupancy of the boxes, and payment in full. Even with those assumptions, by our calculations Taylor was overstating the annual income available for theatrical operations by some £1,700 in this document.

Whether Edward Vanbrugh would contribute *his* insurance money was much to be doubted (in fact, he did not),[2] and the £1,500 allowance for 'Lead, Iron, &c.' to be salvaged from the old theatre seems high. But *if* Taylor could sell stock and rent boxes as projected, he could probably raise a total of about £70,000. He guaranteed a maximum expenditure of £22,000 after the first year, to be paid from £11,739 in remaining box income plus £12,241 in estimated 'Receipts at the Doors' plus 'Rents, Coffee-Rooms, &c'. This looks all right in principle, but the extant totals for 1786–87 and 1787–88 suggest that the stated figure for daily receipts was high by £3,000 or £4,000. And Taylor's figures for box income presume that *all* seats would be paid for every night.

Taylor did not, to be sure, state a total debt to be paid off, and one might quarrel with some of his figures and assumptions (whether honest or otherwise). For our present purposes, the point is that Taylor had put forward a proposal that seemed to offer the possibility of satisfying past creditors while still providing enough capital to build a new theatre. In fact, he did not allow nearly enough capital for construction and was mortgaging future receipts to a degree that was to prove ruinous in the course of the 1790s. Why anyone should invest money in a theatre that had no guarantee of the right to perform is a mystery, but perhaps the public assumed that tradition would be upheld. At all events, the old creditors agreed, and the

---

[1] British Museum, Burney Collection of Theatrical Portraits, vol. ix, p. 66 (no. 102).
[2] Taylor, *A Concise Statement*, 36.

venture appears to have been set in motion on the terms proposed. On 18 March 1790 the *Public Advertiser* reported 'general satisfaction' with the 'arrangement respecting the Opera House', which it praised for 'justice' and 'responsibility', and described as consisting 'of twenty-five Proprietors' along the lines proposed by Taylor.

On 17 March Taylor 'took possession' of the ruins of the old opera-house (yielded by Gallini), and 'Upwards of an hundred men were set to work in order to clear away the old timbers, and other useless sacrifices of the late fire' (*London Chronicle*, 16–18 March 1790). The same source reports 'that £16,000 have been already subscribed' for the project. However speculative the financing, Taylor was plunging ahead, probably on the principle 'nothing ventured, nothing gained'. On Saturday 3 April 1790 he conducted an elaborate public ceremony in which a corner-stone for the new theatre was laid by the Earl of Buckinghamshire—an occasion that attracted some 4,000 or more spectators (*London Chronicle*, 3–6 April). This event was reported in *The Times* of 5 April as follows.

Last Saturday being fixed for laying the first stone of the new Opera House in the Haymarket, upwards of 5000 persons were assembled by one o'clock, of whom at least five or six hundred were men of fashion and gentlemen; but, alarmed at the ruinous state of the premises, very few ladies were present upon the ground, the adjoining houses, however, particularly Market-lane, exhibited a most splendid assemblage of female beauty and fashion. The band belonging to the Coldstream Regiment of Guards, attended and played the whole time. The walls of the old theatre were covered with the workmen employed in the building. About a quarter before two o'clock, the Earl of Buckingham, attended by his two daughters, the Ladies Caroline and Amelia Hobart, whose beauty and elegance added lustre to the solemnity of the occasion, arrived at the theatre, and being met at the bottom of the stairs by Mr Taylor, his Lordship proceeded, though with great difficulty, from the pressure of the immense crowd of people, to the spot on which the foundation was to be laid. When Lord Buckingham approached the stone, Mr Taylor presented him with a variety of the latest coin of the present reign, which his Lordship placed in a hole, purposely cut in it, and then the workmen suspending the stone by pul-lies, Lord Buckingham, spread the morter underneath with a silver trowel, of the most elegant workmanship, with which he was presented by Mr Novosielski: on one side of which, was engraven his Lordship's full arms, on the other '*This is the trowel with which the Earl of Buckingham laid the foundation stone of the New Opera House, in the Haymarket, on the 3d of April, 1790, in the 30th year of the reign of King George the Third.*' During the whole of this ceremony; the band of music played *God save the King*, and as soon as it was over, the workmen rent the air with shouting for several minutes.

Upon the top of the stone were engraven these words: —*The first stone of this New Theatre, was laid on the 3d of April, 1790, in the 30th year of the reign of King George the Third, by the Right Hon. John Hobart, Earl of Buckingham*; at the bottom of which was his Lordship's motto, *Auctor pretiosa facit; the Founder makes it more valuable*, which was very applicable to the occasion; upon one of the squares of the stone was, *The King's Theatre in the Haymarket, first built in the year 1703*; on another, *But unfortunately burnt down on the 17th of June, 1789*; and on another *Prevalebit Justitiae*.—Lord Buckingham gave a purse of ten guineas for the workmen to drink.—The ceremony being over, the bricklayers begun immediately the building of the foundation wall, which is 12 feet thick, and during the remainder of the day, the theatre was crowded with men of fashion, to see the progress of it.

Whether this was a triumphant new beginning or sheer folly remained to be seen. Taylor held only short-term rights to much of his theatre site and must have been desperately short of the money needed to finance construction. All this might be moot: if O'Reilly received the patent of which he was in imminent expectation, then Taylor's theatre was probably going to remain a hole in the ground.

## IV. The Leicester Square Theatre Patent Hearings, April 1790

O'Reilly hit on a brilliant way to scupper his rival. On 1 February 1790 he signed an agreement for a reversionary lease on the plot of ground on which the old theatre had been built.[1] As early as 24 July 1789 Vanbrugh had refused point-blank to lease the site to Taylor.[2] With his whole scheme in dire jeopardy, Taylor battled on. He could erect anything he liked on the site until 1803, but at that point the ground—and whatever might happen to stand on it—would fall into the hands of Robert Bray O'Reilly. The stratagem is obvious enough: investors would be reluctant to risk money on a costly building with a projected life-span of thirteen years. When Taylor issued his financial prospectus and started to clear the ground for construction, O'Reilly published a warning to potential investors that he had bought rights to the ground and advised them not to invest in Taylor's scheme.

For the information of those, who through ignorance of the real state of the ground and premises in the Haymarket (lately the old Opera House), may be prevailed

---

[1] C12/958/64 (*Vanbrugh and O'Reilly* v. *Taylor*, bill of complaint). Confirmed in PRO LC 7/88, p. 73.

[2] 'I do not know that you are the Assignee of the lease of the premises of the Opera-House, granted by me, in 1777, to Mr. Brooke. I have never acknowledged any other tenant of that property than Mr. James Brooke. . . . I do not conceive that it will be for my advantage to renew the above lease.' O'Reilly, *An Authentic Narrative*, 50–1.

upon to lend Money on the Security of the Building, which, by Advertisement in several Morning Papers, it is announced is about to be erected there:—it is deemed necessary to state that Mr. O'Reilley has actually purchased from Mr. Vanbrugh all his interest in those premises. The persons adventuring therefore in the proposed building, are invited to risque their money on the security of a lease for twenty-one years, of which twelve years and a half only are unexpired, during which time Mr. O'Reilley will be intitled to Mr. Vanbrugh's rent, and at the expiration of the lease, will become sole proprietor of the whole property.[1]

Taylor replied angrily in a long statement printed in *The Times* on 26 March in which he denied (quite untruthfully) the pending expiration of his lease, and insisted that the ground at issue would not 'be much more than a third of the space upon which the new Theatre and the necessary adjoining buildings will be erected'. O'Reilly was slow to pick up the hint: Taylor intended to create legal confusion by erecting a larger building on a site that comprised Crown land leased to persons other than Vanbrugh.

O'Reilly's immediate concern was to discourage investment in the proposed theatre, and he replied to Taylor in a long and windy notice dated 27 March. After denouncing 'the deception which lurked in some recent Advertisements, inviting Subscribers to risque their Money' on the new King's Theatre, Haymarket, he flaunted his (unnamed) patrons and the presumption that his patent grant for Leicester Square would soon pass the Great Seal, 'gross falsehoods which have been propagated on this subject' notwithstanding.

It is become incumbent on me, therefore, to state, that the Patent, for which his Majesty has been graciously pleased, some time since, to issue his warrant, has already passed through the following Offices, viz. Those of the Lord Chamberlain, the Attorney General, the Secretary of State for the King's Sign Manual, and the Signet and Privy Seal. It lies at present at the Great Seal Office, where, in the usual course of business, it must remain for a very short period.

To this statement of facts it may be necessary to add, for the general information, that there is no other Patent in existence for the performance of Italian Operas in the Haymarket or elsewhere, and that no such Opera can in fact be represented without the especial Licence of his Majesty. . . .

The Subscribers are, in the mean time, respectfully cautioned against the delusions which are held forth at the present moment. I shall not, however, presume to urge farther, what is, on the first view, so obvious, that they should not advance their money on the faith of the Haymarket. . . . (*World*, 29 March 1790)

---

[1] *World*, 22 Mar. 1790. Cf. Taylor, *A Concise Statement*, 35–6.

O'Reilly was trying to winkle the theatre site out from under Taylor, while scaring off any investors. At the same time Taylor was trying to block a patent grant that had (as O'Reilly accurately said) sailed through the cumbersome government bureaucracy and now needed only the application of the Great Seal to become final. Taylor's lawyers had opposed the grant, but the newspapers treated prompt approval as a foregone conclusion; probably everyone was surprised when the Lord Chancellor jibbed.

The issue came formally before Lord Chancellor Thurlow on 14 April 1790, and was reported briefly in *The Times* on the 15th.

An application was made yesterday morning by Mr Mansfield, on the part of Mr O'Reilly, for the Seal to be affixed to his Patent, for the Opera House in *Leicester Fields*. The Lord Chancellor with that attention to strict justice, which has always distinguished his conduct, and with becoming adherence to the forms of the Court, desired to have before him a full statement of the claims and interests of Mr O'Reilly, before the business was brought to a final decision. This statement not being attended by any possible difficulty or delay, and his Lordship not wishing farther to impede the proceedings the hearing was adjourned to Tuesday next.

A virtually identical account appeared in the *World* on the same day: this was, in essence, a press-release issued by O'Reilly. The report in the *London Chronicle* of 13–15 April was far more extensive; it also contained some details ominous to the hopes of those who were trying to extricate opera from the morass of the old theatre's debts.

Yesterday morning came on before the Lord Chancellor, in Lincoln's-inn-hall, by special appointment, the discussion of the Patent for building an Opera-house on the ground of Leicester-house, a matter which has so long engaged the public attention, and agitated, if not materially injured, the parties interested in the established Theatre in the Hay-market. His Lordship appeared to be wholly uninformed of the particulars of this extraordinary transaction; for the first question he asked, was, By what authority the Opera house had been hitherto carried on, whether it was not under an annual license; and if so, why was a Patent now required?[1] And it being explained, that this grant was for a term of years to a new Patentee, to build upon new ground, his Lordship desired the grounds to be stated to him upon which this Patent was founded, together with the pretensions of the petitioner to such a grant, which, the Counsel for Mr O'Reilly not being ready to state, they desired time to possess themselves of the information required by the Lord Chancellor. His Lordship then said, that a very strong case indeed must be made out, to induce him to put the Great Seal to the present Patent; namely the pretensions and qualifications

---

[1] Thurlow was probably not so uninformed as he affected to be.

of the person proposed, his ability to carry it into effect, and above all, that those persons, who were the proprietors of the present Opera-house, could not reinstate their Theatre and carry it on, as usual, in the hope at least of recovering the large sums of money which very probably they had embarked upon the faith of an establishment of many years existence, and which undoubtedly they must have, in a great measure, lost by the calamity that had lately happened to that undertaking. His Lordship added, that, unquestionably, the King had a right to grant a patent for a new playhouse in Covent-garden, and another in Drury-lane; but the obvious consequence would be, that those new grants must ruin the already-established Theatres; which would be so manifest an injustice to those persons who had advanced large sums of money, perhaps £100,000 of the property of the subject, that it could never be in the royal disposition to sanction such a measure. He stated the present attempt to be a similar case to that of erecting a new market in the neighbourhood of one long established, which was a matter that had been lately determined in favour of the latter. In that view the present Proprietors of the Old Opera-house had unquestionably the tenant-right of carrying on the usual entertainments of their Theatre, without any competition whatever. His Lordship declared, that if they were able and ready to give a proper entertainment to the Public, such as they had been used to do, the feelings of every man must shudder and revolt at the idea of depriving them of the right of doing it. The Counsel for Mr O'Reilly prayed time till Tuesday to make out their case, which the Lord Chancellor granted, upon condition that they should file the affidavits in support of their pretensions on Saturday next, in order that the parties upon the other side might have an opportunity of answering them.

Lord Thurlow was notoriously incorruptible and independent-minded. He was concerned here with justice to the creditors, procedure, and precedent. The old theatre's numerous creditors were being ignored, and O'Reilly was not, in fact, a proper person to receive a patent for a new opera-house—he lacked the necessary financial resources, for a start. The legality of the grant was not in question: the King had a right to make it. Whether the grant was one a just king should make was another question.

Round two was fought on 20 April and was reported in *The Times* of the 21st as follows:

The affidavits made by Messrs Taylor, &c. in Opposition to the Patent granted by his Majesty to Mr O'Reilly for an Opera House in Leicester Square, came on yesterday to be heard before the Lord Chancellor, as did likewise the affidavits of Mr O'Reilly, in respect to the connections he had with Gallini, from his first acquaintance with that person to the present time.

The Lord Chancellor deferred the final decision to Friday. But he made some observations which did honour to his judgment—to his justice—and to his thorough knowledge of the business—he said that Mr Taylor's interest in the Opera, properly, might be compared to the *wreck of a passing cloud.*—His Lordship also observed, that he had been told of the first stone being laid, and of some proceedings in rebuilding the Opera House in the Haymarket. This he said was raising a pile to serve as materials for numberless *Law Suits*—and not for a House of public amusement. His Lordship, no doubt, here alluded to the ground on which Mr Taylor was building, being the property of Mr O'Reilly.

Upon the whole of this business, it is now clearly evident that there will be but one Italian Opera House, and that the building will be according to his *Majesty's Patent*, and the wishes of all the fashionable circle, in *Leicester Square*, as formally [formerly?] mentioned in this paper.

A report in the *World* on the same day covers some of the same ground and quotes Lord Thurlow's witticisms about a foundation for lawsuits and Taylor's claims being 'merely *"as the rack of a passing cloud"* '. The *World* also, however, adds some interesting details.

Mr Mansfield stated, in a very forcible narrative, the claims of Mr O'Reilly to the Patent . . . and the situation of those persons who brought forward the present opposition, and who, in fact, were more hostile to each other than they were to his client.

Mr Gallini wished (as it appeared) that the Patent should issue; whilst Mr Taylor, with only a remote equity of redemption, and with a legal interest so distinct, that it could not come in for *three hundred years*, if the Haymarket Opera-House were so long to exist, had stept forth in decided hostility to the present Patent.

Mr Mansfield stated, also, the purchase of Mr Vanburgh's property in the Haymarket Theatre, by Mr O'Reilly, and his expenditure of £38,000 on the concern in Leicester-square, after he had been convinced that a Theatre could not be erected on the old scite with a probable hope of success. . . .

The Lord Chancellor objected, that the restrictions on the management (of which he much approved) were not inserted in the Patent, but were distinctly agreed and bound to the Lord Chamberlain. . . .

By this point in the proceedings Taylor's claims and objections counted for little: Lord Chancellor Thurlow was far more concerned with the rights of the creditors and the nature of the proposed grant to O'Reilly. When the hearing resumed on 23 April the issues crystallized: the argument had become the propriety of a patent grant in principle, and the Lord Chancellor was questioning whether such a grant was required at all.

The matter of Mr O'Reilly's Patent was further argued at Lincoln's Inn Hall yesterday. . . . Mr *Gallini* claimed that right which Mr Taylor insisted was his, and that both these rights militated against the *right of his Majesty* to grant a Patent, and in this Opposition they were joined by the Proprietors of Drury Lane and Covent Garden Theatres, who thought that every additional House of Entertainment would be injurious to their property.

The Chancellor after hearing Counsel on both sides, did not think the case fully explained, and Counsel are to be further heard on Monday. His Lordship, in the course of the arguments observed, that if his Majesty sent down his warrant to the Chamberlain commanding him to grant a Licence to an Opera House in Leicester Fields, that was equally valid in point of law as a Patent—his Majesty having an undoubted right to do so, either in that mode or by Patent. (*The Times*, 24 April 1790)

The last hearing occurred on 26 April, and was reported in some detail in *The Times* on the 27th.

Yesterday Mr Mansfield made a short reply to the Counsel who argued on Friday against Mr O'Reilly's Patent, after which the Lord Chancellor said, that he should read over the affidavits made by the different parties, the substance of which, as well as of what Counsel had advanced on each side, he should, as it was the duty of his office so to do, *lay before the King*. The noble Lord took occasion to observe, that so far as he might venture to give an opinion on the subject, he thought that the patent to Mr O'Reilly should be worded in a different manner. That it should derive its authority from the Sovereign, and not from the Lord Chamberlain—that the business and the property should not be divided—and that every precaution should be taken to prevent the transfer of the patent by mortgage, sale &c. so as to avoid as much as possible those intricate debts and multiplicity of lawsuits which ruined the property in the Haymarket. The facts, as far as they were proved to him, he was bound by his situation to report to the Crown, and if either from the very ill conduct of those concerned in the long litigated affair of the old Opera House, or if from an act of benevolence to Mr O'Reilly, or from any other cause, *his Majesty* ordered him to put the Great Seal to the patent, it was his business to obey, and he should do it accordingly.

He said that Mr. O'Reilly's being bred to the law was no objection to his having an Opera House; but he thought that Mr Gallini and Mr O'Reilly were rather harsh to the creditors, for whom some little provision should be made.

The result of all this will be just as we at first announced. Mr O'Reilly will have a patent for building his Opera House in Leicester-square; some provision will be made for the *real* creditors of the late House, and the patent, according to the Chancellor's idea, will be so worded as to prevent its going to 'Change-alley.

The Chancellor sat in Westminster Hall, not in Lincoln's Inn, as on Friday, and the Court was very much crowded.

*The Times* was clearly assuming that the patent grant for Leicester Square was a *fait accompli*, and that it would go through with a few technical adjustments. The brief summation of the final hearing in the *London Chronicle* of 24–27 April appears more accurately to reflect the severity of the Lord Chancellor's reservations.

After Mr Mansfield had replied to the arguments of the Counsel on the other side, the Lord Chancellor said, the principal question for his consideration was—what representation he ought to make under all the circumstances of the case to his Majesty? His Lordship said, he was totally careless whether an Opera House was built in Leicester-Square or not; he was not personally interested in it; but it was his province and duty to take care that the object of the Crown in granting the patent in question was not defeated, and that his Majesty should not be imposed on by false representations. . . . The business, therefore, stands over till his Lordship has made the proper representations to his Majesty upon the subject.

'False representations' seems like an accurate description of anything that could be said in favour of O'Reilly as opera patentee.

Exactly what happened next will probably never be known. No public announcement was ever made, and no documentation appears to survive. O'Reilly continued to believe that the patent would be granted, but it never was. Lord Thurlow must have communicated grave doubts to the King and, notwithstanding the support of the Prince of Wales and the Lord Chamberlain for the grant, George III accepted the Lord Chancellor's advice and stopped the patent. Thurlow clearly felt that the creditors of the old theatre deserved consideration. He objected to a patent grant that would convey saleable property to the recipient, or would leave the theatre insufficiently regulated. Qualms about O'Reilly's qualifications and financial resources are evident. Thurlow's scepticism about O'Reilly as patentee was not allayed by the hearings. His suggestion that a licence would be as good as a patent may have been disingenuous: sane investors would not pour a fortune into a venture whose right to perform rested year-to-year on the whim of the Lord Chamberlain. Thurlow may well have used the possibility of a licence as a smokescreen for his determination to scuttle the patent grant. O'Reilly was in fact merely a cat's-paw; Salisbury was grossly abusing his position as Lord Chamberlain to favour a venture in which he was secretly involved; the claims of the creditors of the old theatre were being ignored—the whole business was malodorous, and Thurlow had reasonable grounds for cautioning the King not to let the venture proceed. The irony is that the effect of his prudence and honour was to create ruinous competition between two opera-houses and ultimately to return control of opera in London to the hands of the egregious Taylor.

The immediate result of the stoppage of the patent was to give Taylor hope while leaving O'Reilly and his backers scurrying to find an alternative venue—one that would require a more modest investment than the £150,000 projected for Leicester Square. They wound up renting the Pantheon in Oxford Street for a term of twelve years, and James Wyatt was engaged to convert his fancy exhibition hall into an opera-house at top speed.[1] On 30 June 1790 Salisbury granted a four-year licence for the Pantheon.[2] Taylor, meanwhile, pushed his building along as fast as he could, hoping to complete the new King's Theatre by January 1791 and to open at the beginning of the opera season in direct competition with O'Reilly. Taylor had won a crucial round, but the battle was far from over. By early July, O'Reilly had begun to realize that Taylor was erecting a theatre that far exceeded the dimensions of the old site, and that this was both a terrible threat to him and a legal opening that he might be able to exploit.

## V. The Battle over the Site, July–December 1790

Taylor's counter to O'Reilly's signing a reversionary lease on the King's Theatre site was to build the new theatre so as to comprise additional ground for which Taylor had acquired long leases. Come 1803 O'Reilly could exercise his right to the old site, and much good it would do him. Under those circumstances O'Reilly would be legally entitled (perhaps) to demolish part of the new theatre, but not to use the whole of it. Confusion and leverage were ever Taylor's tools, and in this case he used them to great effect.

Most of what is known about this battle comes from Vanbrugh and O'Reilly's bill of complaint filed in the Court of Chancery on 29 November 1790 (C12/958/64). In more than 16,000 words they recite the history of Vanbrugh's claim to the ground (and his transfer of that right to O'Reilly) and then report on recent events. Knowing that Taylor had started to rebuild the Haymarket Opera House, on 2 July 1790 they

gave written directions to John Soane of Albion Place Esquire a Surveyor of Great Eminence to survey the said intended New Building on your Orators behalf and to

---

[1] On which see Curtis Price, Judith Milhous, and Robert D. Hume, 'A Plan of the Pantheon Opera House (1790–92)', *Cambridge Opera Journal,* 3 (1991), 213–46, and vol. II, Chs. 2 and 5.

[2] So O'Reilly states in *An Authentic Narrative,* 64. We have not found the licence in the Lord Chamberlain's records. The first public announcement appeared in *The Times* on 10 July 1790; not until 9 Aug. did the Lord Chamberlain's office put out a public notice (*London Gazette,* 7–10 Aug.).

Observe in what respects the same differed or was likely to differ from the plan of the late Opera House. And the said John Soane being previously furnished with a plan of the late Opera House . . . accordingly on the third day of July last went to the said premises . . . but the said William Taylor or some or one of his Agents or Servants refused to admit the said John Soane to the Premises.

Taylor succeeded in stalling until 21 July, and then the next day had Soane and his employees ejected from the ground, with the result that 'the said John Soane was prevented from taking an Accurate or proper Survey of the Scite'.[1] Not until 'the latter End of the Month of September last when the Foundation of the New Opera House had been laid and the Walls thereof raised to some height' did Vanbrugh and O'Reilly succeed in obtaining definitive evidence that Taylor 'was building the New Opera House in such a Manner that the Scite of the New Opera House is not the same with the Old Scite'.

This they report as being 132 feet long and 60 feet wide, whereas the new site is some 168 feet by 92 feet 4 inches. The net result was, of course, that 'the New Opera House will be useless to your Orator Robert Bray O'Reilly at the End of the Term which was demised' to Taylor, when O'Reilly takes possession in 1803. Vanbrugh and O'Reilly regarded this as 'Committing Waste on the said Premises', and as a clear violation of 'the true . . . intent and meaning of the Indenture of Lease of the late Opera House dated the 4th of July 1777' under which Taylor was operating as a sub-tenant. Consequently on 13 and 14 October they served formal notice on Taylor 'to desist from proceeding in such Building', but he ignored the order, made specious excuses, and continued construction.

The history of this ruckus is likewise traceable in the notebooks of Sir John Soane.[2] On 6 May 1790 Soane recorded that he 'talked over Old Opera House' with O'Reilly. On 3 July the notebook entry says 'Called at the old Opera house refused by Mr. Taylor admittance without an order from Mr. Vanbrugh.' The abortive survey of 21–2 July is recorded, as is the one in September. In their Chancery bill Vanbrugh and O'Reilly requested

---

[1] The passage continues, 'before they had nearly finished they were interrupted by Signor Carnivale who was an agent of or employed by the said William Taylor'. In other words, Soane was turned off by Carnevale, who was later rumoured to have set the fire that destroyed the old theatre. To find him working for Taylor is surprising, for they had been bitter enemies five years earlier. On 19 Nov. 1785 Taylor sent Gallini a vehement objection to the employment of Carnevale (C12/2012/54).

[2] Preserved in Sir John Soane's Museum, Lincoln's Inn Fields, London. The rough entries are in his *Journal N: 1*, fos. 42ᵛ, 53, and 77ᵛ; a fair copy (marked 'Opera, &c') is in *Ledger B*, fos. 242ᵛ–246ᵛ.

permission to annex 'a true and correct Plan', obtained from Soane. He prepared at least three, possibly four versions. On 13 October he records his having left with O'Reilly's solicitor 'a drawing of Old Opera House with the outline of the new one shown upon it'. On 1 November he 'deliv'd a plan of old opera house & a plan of new ditto with the old one shewn in dotted lines'. On 27 November he paid £5. 5s. 'for an attested plan of the old Opera house', evidently needed for court purposes.[1]

On 30 November 1790 the court duly 'ordered that ye Plaintiffs be at Liberty to amend their Bill by annexing a plan Drawn on parchment'.[2] (See Pl. 14.) The plan shows the old site with the former coffee-room and some small rooms on the west side of the original theatre covered by the enormous horseshoe of the new auditorium, and the new stage extending south of the old property on to land obtained by Taylor from a Mr Darrell. This is, in essence, a simplified and site-oriented version of the 'superimposed plans' of the two opera-houses first published (so far as we are aware) by Leacroft in 1973 and implicitly attributed by him to the architect Michael Novosielski.[3] That plan comes from the Soane Museum; given what is now known from Soane's notebooks, plus his address ('Albion Place') on the plan annexed to the lawsuit, we have no hesitation in attributing the plan to Soane. Novosielski designed the new theatre, but the superimposed plans were done by Soane.

The lawsuit describes the 'annexed plan' as follows:

the Premises of the Old Opera House are described by the Black Lines on the said Plan and the New Buildings by the red Lines thereon and the interior Black Lines in an Oblong Square denote Accurately so much of the Premises belonging to the Old Opera House as was or ever had been used for the purpose of the Old Opera House. . . . And the Space on the Outside of the Western part of the four interior Black Lines was occupied by the Coffee House Dressing Rooms and other Conveniencies belonging to the Old Opera House. . . . And your Orators charge that the Red Lines on the said Plan denote the New Building as the Defendants are proceeding to Erect the Same . . . that part of the said Plan which is marked with a Blue Shade[4] denotes correctly the Premises purchased by the said Defendants or

---

[1] The day before, on 26 Nov., O'Reilly wrote to William Sheldon (front man for the Duke of Bedford): 'Mr Soane has got at a Copy of the original Plan of the Hay Markett which he says is every thing we require—he is to have it from the Surveyor Generals Office tomorrow.' Bedford Opera Papers, 5.D.11.

[2] C33/476, Decrees 1790B, fo. 26ᵛ.

[3] Leacroft, *Development of the English Playhouse*, fig. 87.

[4] The blue has faded badly, but is still distinguishable from other colours in the Soane Museum copy, which is not true of the lawsuit version.

one of them from the said Mr Darell And it appears Evidently by the said Plan as your Orators charge the truth to be that a great Part of the Body of the New Opera House is intended to Stand on those Premises late belonging to Mr Darrell and that the beginning of the Stage is intended to be at that Part of the said Plan where the red Lines are turned inwards So that so much of the Stage as is intended to be on the premises demised by your Orator Edward Vanbrugh is to be only the Space of Thirteen feet or thereabouts behind the Orchestra. . . .

Vanbrugh and O'Reilly go on to complain that

it will be impossible to make any Use of the said New Building as an Opera House unless your Orators have both the said premises granted by the said Crown and those purchased by the said Defendants. And the said Defendants as Proprietors of the Premises purchased of the said Mr Darrell as aforesaid may Eject your Orators from the Premises if your Orators should take possession thereof. And it therefore evidently Appears that the said new Building will be useless to your Orator Robert Bray O'Reilly at the End of the said Term [in 1803] unless the Defendants consent to sell him the said Premises and unless he submits to whatever Conditions they chuse to impose upon him.

To possess a theatre in which you hold rights to only part of the stage is a limited blessing. And if O'Reilly wanted the use of the stage, he would have to pay whatever price Taylor demanded. If he cared to wait until 1803, he indubitably had the right to eject Taylor from the auditorium, but Taylor could keep him from taking possession or making use of the stage. This state of affairs would have appealed to W. S. Gilbert.

Vanbrugh and O'Reilly asked the court for an injunction against further construction and an order limiting any new theatre to the old site. As usual, Taylor stalled; he put in no answer to the bill of complaint. On 8 December 1790 (building frantically the while) he sent his counsel to court to say that the bill of complaint was 'impertinent', and hence that no answer should be required.[1] The court duly referred the matter to a Master in Chancery and on 8 January 1791 John Wilmot reported to the court 'that the said Bill is not impertinent'.[2] And this, unfortunately, is the end of court records in the case. Taylor was by then only about six weeks away from being able to open the rebuilt theatre, but O'Reilly's failure to pursue the case is surprising. Perhaps his counsel got adverse opinions (especially since the new building was so far advanced). Possibly O'Reilly was distracted by his efforts to finish

[1] C33/476, fo. 38ʳ.
[2] C38/768 (unpaginated), Master's report in *Vanbrugh* v. *Taylor* (Michaelmas Term, 1790).

and open the Pantheon. Conceivably someone bought off Edward Van-brugh. Possibly the suit was not pressed while high-level negotiations to unite the two ventures were conducted in January under the aegis of the Prince of Wales.[1] But whatever happened, the case was allowed to die.[2]

The importance of the wrangle over the site should not be overlooked amidst its comic aspects. Taylor clearly realized that only a *much* bigger theatre—one that positively had to occupy an enlarged site—would suit his purposes. As far as we are aware, no theatre historian has expressed any sur-prise at the massiveness of the new opera-house, perhaps because the new versions of Covent Garden and Drury Lane put up shortly thereafter in 1792 and 1794 are similar examples of theatrical elephantiasis. But an opera-house is a rather different case. Comparison of capacity has been rendered difficult by lack of precise figures for either the 1782 or the 1791 Haymarket, but in crude terms the square footage of stage and auditorium doubled—and the cubic footage went up proportionally. Whether this expansion was natural evolution or a dreadful mistake may be debated. The new theatre was the subject of much admiring commentary in contemporaneous news-papers, but it hardly conduced to effective opera performance. At any rate, as the lawsuit demonstrates, Taylor's motive in making the theatre so big was at least in part legal rather than purely artistic or financial.

## VI. The New King's Theatre, Haymarket

The theatre that Novosielski erected for Taylor was to be London's princi-pal opera-house for more than half a century. At the time it was built it was hailed as an architectural marvel of a size and magnificence to rival Pierma-rini's La Scala in Milan. It was one of the venues of the famous concerts directed by Haydn during his first visit to England in 1791 and 1792, and later in the decade the theatre produced operas by Martín y Soler and Lor-enzo Da Ponte. Many great singers made their London débuts there—for

---

[1] On these negotiations, see Ch. 9, sect. I.

[2] Taylor eventually obtained long-term rights to his site. Shortly before O'Reilly fled to Paris 'to avoid his Creditors', he 'did by Deed Poll of 30th July 1791 Assign . . . [to trustees] all his reversionary Interest in said Theatre in the Haymarket' (General Opera Trust Deed, LC 7/88, p. 75). According to a legal opinion written by J. Mansfield on 11 Dec. 1797, the trustees never accepted the assignment (Bedford Opera Papers, 6.F.13). But this was a moot point, because on 2 Feb. 1792 Edward Vanbrugh acquiesced in a lease of the ground to R. B. Sheridan and Thomas Holloway (LC 7/88, p. 81), and on 1 Aug. 1792 they signed it over to Taylor (lease from Sheridan and Holloway to Taylor, LC 7/88, pp. 1–63).

example, Giacomo Davide, Brigida Banti, Angelica Catalani, and Giuditta Pasta (who brought Bellini's *Norma* to London in 1833). This is not the place for a detailed architectural analysis of the theatre—virtually impossible in any case, owing to lack of evidence—but some attention to the impression the building made at the time it was opened is in order. Several particular points also need to be addressed: the haste with which the theatre was constructed; stage machinery, acoustics, and lighting; capacity; and cost.

## Construction

The theatre had to be built in a desperate hurry, and scraping together the cash to keep construction going must have been a constant problem. How successfully Taylor had peddled his stock and box leases is unknown. On 7 June 1790 he advertised in *The Times* that 'the pressing demand for Boxes beyond the number actually contained in the New Theatre' would not allow him to reserve places for former box-holders any longer—but this was evidently a sales stratagem; the September 1790 box-plan discussed below shows fifty of 179 boxes unspoken for at that time—most of them, to be sure, on the fourth and fifth tiers. By 5 July Taylor was promising performances by Christmas and boasting of the engagement of 'Several of the most capital performers both of France and of Italy' (*The Times*). On 12 August *The Times* implies that the Lord Chancellor had released various escrowed funds in Chancery that could be applied to construction costs, and the building proceeded apace without any reports of unpaid workmen. Puffs appeared from time to time. For example, the *London Chronicle* of 5–7 October 1790 reported that 'This stupendous fabric . . . will rank among the finest pieces of architecture in Europe', boasting that 'the span of the roof is 25 feet wider than that of Westminster Hall, supposed to be the largest in England'. More helpfully it adds

The audience part of the theatre in formation gives the idea of a Lyre. The boxes consist of four complete tiers, besides an additional tier on each side. The whole, as they rise, are thrown back, by which means every person in the boxes will be visible from any part of the house. The boxes in number exceed those in the former theatre, [by] sixty. There are no pilasters.

The *Morning Chronicle* of 5 January 1791 says that 'In the body of the house but very little remains to be done, besides papering and painting. The several parts of the Stage are all prepared and adapted to each other, so that it may be erected in a very short time.' But on the same day *The Times*—a less partisan source—says 'Whether the House can be ready by the end of the present month, time will shew; but we consider it impossible. The roofing is not yet covered in, nor is the inside of the theatre near in a finished state. Every exertion is making however to fulfil the terms of the engagement with the Subscribers.'

By early January 1791 Taylor was inserting paragraphs in the papers announcing that his theatre was virtually ready to open. He had a particular motive for wanting to stage a performance in January: his agreements with subscribers for boxes guaranteed that the bankers who had received the money (Messrs Hammersley & Co., Pall Mall) would refund it in full 'if an Opera is not performed in the Theatre now erecting on the old scite in the Haymarket, on or before the month of January, 1791'.[1]

An alarming set-back occurred on 15 January, when 'the principal stone staircase', not yet completed, collapsed under the weight of a crowd of workmen, injuring several and killing one (*The Times*, 17 January). Public alarm was such that both opera-houses were challenged to demonstrate their safety, and a formal investigation was carried out and the reassuring results published later in the month.[2] The full extent of the sloppy workmanship was not to be publicly revealed until some thirty-five years later.

The speed with which this large and well-equipped theatre was erected in brick and timber is astonishing by any standards. While the remaining walls were surveyed within a few days of the fire of 17 June 1789 and pronounced to be 'as good as ever',[3] the site was not properly prepared for construction until late March 1790. Despite a period of inactivity in May and June 1790,[4] the new Haymarket was opened to the public on 23 February 1791 (at least for a rehearsal), a mere eleven months later. The full consequences of Taylor's haste and Novosielski's faulty engineering were uncovered by a survey of the fabric undertaken in 1825. Acting on the then Lord Chamberlain's genuine concern for public safety, the Surveyor General ordered a preliminary investigation. On 29 January 1825 his surveyors reported 'that the North and South walls are in a very defective state from their original bad construction, both as to Materials and workmanship'.[5]

---

[1] *The Times*, 20 Aug. 1790 and 5 Jan. 1791.

[2] *Morning Chronicle*, 26 and 27 Jan. 1791.

[3] See e.g. the *Oracle*, 1 July 1789.

[4] 'The reconstruction of the old *Opera House* is at a stand still; but whether from a want of common *mortar*, or any other cementing ingredient, we do not presume to determine' (*The Times*, 29 May 1790).

[5] Sir John Soane's Museum, Corresp. Cupboard 2, Division 12, C(5), item 4. Copies of these 1820s surveyors' reports are preserved in PRO LC 7/4 (Box 2).

The report was sufficiently alarming for the Surveyor General to commission Robert Smirke and (ironically) Sir John Soane to make a thorough structural survey. They uncovered a catalogue of horrors. Novosielski's new north wall of 1790 was found to bow outward an indeterminable number of inches and needed immediate shoring up. The south wall was also bulging in several places, it being merely the old wall of Darrell's property carelessly encased in new brick and far too flimsy to support so large a structure safely. Even more seriously, the floor joists of the gallery were made of small scantling rather than the necessary heavy timbers, 'and when it is considered that they have no solid bearing for many feet within the north wall, it is evident that when the Gallery is full, the upper part of it must cause a great pressure on the North wall already so defective'. Other problems, for which Novosielski was perhaps not directly responsible, included rotted or spliced joists under the floors of the boxes, decayed timbers beneath the stage, and 'One of the tie Beams under the Loft, & near to the place where they stow away scenery over the Stage opening, is not less than 5 or 6 inches below the horizontal line, in the middle'. Smirk and Soane recommended extensive repairs (which kept the theatre closed until April 1825) and concluded that 'the whole of the Structure appears to have been originally executed in a very improper and unworkmanlike manner'.[1] Novosielski's speed was achieved at the cost of some serious corner-cutting.

## The Nature of the New Theatre

Shoddy construction notwithstanding, the new theatre was immensely impressive to the audience of 1791. Newspaper commentators were awed by its size and all agog over Novosielski's gaudy decoration. Quotations would provide a long string of adjectives ('spacious', 'commodious', 'grand', 'splendid', 'superb'), but little idea of what the building was actually like. Unfortunately, no detailed plan of the theatre as originally rebuilt survives. Two pieces of visual evidence are known: a mid-construction box-plan and a tantalizing sketch of the floor plan in Angelica Kauffmann's 1791 portrait of Novosielski. 'A Plan of the Boxes of the King's Theatre September 1790' is preserved in a unique exemplar in the Burney Collection of Theatrical Portraits in the British Museum.[2] (See Pl. 15.) It is a printed diagram, evidently produced for sales and promotion purposes, showing 163 numbered boxes in five tiers, plus sixteen lettered pit boxes (eight on each side). The fourth

---

[1] The full survey is preserved in the Soane Museum, Corresp. Cupboard 2, Division 12, C(5), items 6–22, and is briefly mentioned in *Survey of London*, xxix. 243.
[2] Vol. ix, p. 66 (no. 102).

and fifth tiers are at the gallery level, comprising twenty-six boxes (thirteen on each side) rather than thirty-seven boxes as on the first three tiers. If average capacity were five, the total would be 895 places in the boxes. The Kauffmann portrait shows a rounded horseshoe auditorium with slightly angled straight benches on either side of the pit, divided by a central aisle. (See Pl. 16.) The forestage is minimal, and nothing much can be learnt about the rest of the stage, conventionally supplied with five wing and shutter positions. The plan shows that the concert room on the east side of the theatre was part of the original design, though not built until 1793–94, when money could be found for it. Novosielski took advantage of the expansion to improve public space and traffic patterns. A trio of public rooms is shown across the northern end of the building. The principal (carriage) entrance continued to be through a relatively narrow vestibule from the Haymarket at the north-east corner of the building, but Novosielski appears to have provided much-improved corridors and staircases for access to various parts of the building, particularly a pair of major staircases at the north-east and north-west corners of the auditorium.

The most helpful description of the theatre appeared in the *Oracle* of 10 January 1791 while construction was in its late stages. A slightly mangled version of the same description (evidently a press release) appeared in the *St James's Chronicle* of 8–11 January and the *Star* of 11 January.

S'il y a proportion, variété, unité, c'est pour le rendre plus aisé, plus solide, plus commode. Batteux.

Such ought to be the principle invariably pervading works of this nature. —Magnificence must be commensurate with the dignity of the purpose; that magnificence must be subjected to the demands of utility.

A building devoted to the reception of the Majesty of this great Nation, must naturally excite in the mind of the architect, plans of grandeur of comprehensiveness.—Ornament will be in his idea secondary; *space* conduces more to the excitement of the sublime than the labour of *decoration.*

So fully did M. Le Texier enter into this position, that it was his wish to have completely taken down the house to the corner of Pall-Mall—His idea has however been complied with in part—as far as *Union-Court,* all now standing will be pulled down, and laid open for the erection of a noble front. Let us however approach the building—

What, *pro tempore,* is the front, will be shortly, what in the design of the Architect it *is,* merely the corner of the front.—Upon your entrance, a spacious vestibule discovers at the further end a double semi-circular staircase, which by flights, leads you on the right, and on the left, to all parts of the building.—The corridores communicating with the boxes, wind elliptically from one corner of the Stage to that opposite—a more extensive range cannot easily be imagined. Of these corridores, there are three complete stages; and so entirely removed is every idea of damp, that there is nothing like plaister about them—Wall is covered by wood, wood by canvas, canvas by paper.

Immediately over the third stage of boxes, rises a magnificent Gallery, calculated to contain *one thousand* persons. To this gallery there are five entrances—at the four corners one in each, and a *central* door; by which it will be easy to fill the place completely, and prevent the cluster of the audience towards the top, when there may be room sufficient for accommodating them by compressing those below, who are apt to sit extremely wide.

There is but this one gallery, meant to be the *Crown Gallery,* as it has been termed.—From the top of this, the Stage is completely visible every part of it; no descending bulk, no cross-looking ceiling intercepts the sight. A semi-circular arch is thrown across, much higher than the summit of the gallery, to be painted *cerulean* blue.—From the gallery the eye surveys with awe, on account of the height, a very capacious Pitt of an elliptic form, with in like manner entrances at the corners.

Mr Novosielski is entitled to universal admiration for the complete beauty of this noble structure.

Immediately over the Vestibule is the temporary Coffee Room, at present nearly square, but which, upon the erection of the remaining parts of the Front, is to be extended to the length of 102 feet, forming one of the most beautiful Rooms in the Kingdom; the ceiling is lofty, and the whole will be simply magnificent.

Close to the different stages of the boxes are several commodious Retiring Rooms, convenient, and all spacious.—There is no *littleness* any where discernible.

### The Stage

We were favoured with a sight of, at the place where it was constructed, *Lambeth*; and here the ingenious skill of M. Le Texier has discovered itself in mechanism of the most astonishing power. The Stage is the amazing width of 84 feet, constructed too without a Nail—all mortised together. Its depth near 80 feet. It is moreover a *three decked* vessel, for there are two floorings underneath for the working of the machinery, which occupy in depth 22 feet. The men hereon can work without the smallest inclination of the body.

Of contrivance perfectly original, is to be named the mode in which the Stage lights are intended to be managed—These upon our Theatres are generally affixed to the Wings, and darkened by folding blinds; but here the lamps are suspended before the wings upon Posts, which by one mechanic power are moved together—gradually receding for the coming on of Night—gradually approaching with the increasing blushes of Aurora.

This week the Stage will be fixed; every thing is completely cleared from the foundation. (*Oracle*, 10 January 1791)

The authors of the *Survey of London* comment, justly, that 'In general, Novosielski appears to have taken Piermarini's La Scala, Milan, for his model' (xxix. 238). This is manifestly true of the horseshoe auditorium, with its five tiers of boxes: the 1791 King's Theatre marks a major step towards the Italian style that was then all the rage on the Continent, and can be seen today in Covent Garden. Izenour comments that La Scala represents the culmination of all that is good and all that is bad about eighteenth-century Italian horseshoe opera-houses: 'gloriously festive'; splendid for viewing the audience; full of seats with terrible sight-lines; acoustically unsatisfactory.[1] In all probability, however, Taylor got what he wanted.

The expanded site still imposed some limitations. There was no way Novosielski could provide the free-standing temple advocated by all the best Continental theorists: the exteriors and 'vues en perspective' of which Victor Louis made so much in his *Salle de Spectacle de Bordeaux* (1782) were out of the question in a site still hemmed in among shops and houses. Financial considerations delayed completion of the concert room for three years,[2] and such plans as Novosielski drew for the Haymarket façade were not only pedestrian but left incomplete until after his death in 1795.[3] Novosielski provided a huge and elegant auditorium, surrounded by enough public space to reduce the crush in getting in and out of the theatre, and to allow for cards and refreshments. Since only the roughest ground-plan of the theatre survives for the period prior to Marinari's substantial alterations of 1796, any attempt at detailed analysis would be rash. There can be no doubt, however, of the essential nature of the building as Novosielski conceived it, or of the contrast the new building offered to earlier versions of the King's Theatre.

The crux of the comparison is the proportion of the theatre's length devoted to the auditorium versus the stage. One can measure in a variety of ways, but the details are not the point. Omitting the vista stage, the Dumont plan of the pre-1778 King's Theatre shows a building in which only about one-third of the length is devoted to the auditorium (Pl. 2). The

---

[1] George Izenour, *Theater Design* (New York: McGraw-Hill, 1977), 274–5.

[2] The concert hall proved expensive: £19,900 exclusive of 'Decorations in painting' (£1,460), furniture and furnishings (£10,600), an organ (£580), chandeliers (£1,400), and smith's work (£1,083). See PRO CRES 6/121, p. 337.

[3] For the design and its execution, see *Survey of London*, xxx, pl. 29*b* and *c*.

Soane and Saunders plans suggest that the 1782 theatre increased the proportion of space occupied by the auditorium to roughly half the total (Pls. 3
and 5). Working from the superimposed plan of the new theatre on the old
site (Pl. 14), the stage can be calculated as occupying just 37 per cent of the
length, leaving 63 per cent to the auditorium. Indeed, not only did the proportion of length devoted to the stage diminish drastically, but despite the
enlargement of the theatre the actual depth of the stage (ignoring the old
vista stage) appears to have dropped from about 60 feet (Dumont) to about
50 (1782) to what we estimate as no more than 48 feet in the 1791 theatre.[1]
The proscenium opening does, however, appear to have increased noticeably: about 42 feet in the 1791 theatre, in contrast to what was probably no
more than 38 feet in 1782. Feltham confirms this analysis: 'The scenery is, in
general, rich and brilliant; but the space behind the curtain is by no means
equal to that which the Opera machinists enjoyed before the conflagration.
The audience part of the house is, however, built on a scale of great magnitude.'[2]

Emphasis on the auditorium notwithstanding, the opportunity to create
a modern, more mechanized stage was not missed. Technical details are
lacking, but from newspaper commentary one may deduce that Novosielski's stage was designed to accommodate elaborate machine spectacle, and
that in some respects it represented a considerable technical advance for
England. A puff in the *Morning Chronicle* of 29 January 1791 says

The Stage . . . is perfectly new in principle, for though of an extent so greatly
beyond every stage of this Country, it has not a single nail in it.—The whole is an
elastic frame running in grooves, by which it may be either partially or wholly
removed; and by mechanick powers attached to it, the stage, sidewings, scenes, and
all, may in one instant be lowered, so as to exhibit a perfect void. The scenes and
sidewings, move up and down as well as inwards and outwards; and they all move
by the mechanic principle at the same instant, so that for both grandeur and illusion, it must be superior in its effects on the mind, to any spectacle in the universe.

On 23 March the same paper reported the success of the new stage lift system: 'The whole is on a new principle: and instead of the small traps used in
other theatres, enables the machinist to throw the whole stage into a yawning gulph.—Nothing could be more grand and striking than the *illusion* in
the Infernal Regions. They threw up at times torrents of fire; and the

---

[1] Langhans, 'The Theatres', 64, calculates the stage depth as only 45 feet, but the sources
are so rough as to make precision misleading.
[2] *The Picture of London in 1802*, 200.

rapidity of the transitions heightened the astonishment.' The stage was reported to be well suited for dancing: 'To the elasticity of the Haymarket boards, Vestris and Hilligsberg are not a little indebted for their airy flights, and for this evident improvement in the dance, the public are to thank Mons. Le Texier' (*The Times*, 29 March 1791).

Grandiose and elegant as the theatre indubitably was, reports on acoustics and lighting were mixed. The favourably inclined *Morning Chronicle* said after the first public rehearsal, 'Spacious as the theatre is, the sound spreads with the most perfect volume, and the finest Piano movement touches and vibrates on the ear in every part of the House with equal harmony' (21 February 1791). On 23 March it added: 'though the area is so immense, every accent is as audible, and the volume of sound propagates as truly as even at the Hanover-Square Concert [Room], though that house has been esteemed the first musical room in town'. *The Times* was far less rapturous about the acoustics: 'Much alteration is wanting in order to have the sound conveyed to the back part of the Pitt, and to the inside of the Boxes; for at present not a note can be distinctly heard in those places. Indeed the Boxes are formed in such a manner at present, as if they were meant to oppose the entrance of what passed in the Orchestra and on the Stage' (14 March 1791).

Lighting too was subject to criticism. Oil lamps had provided the principal part of the illumination at the old theatre for many years, but candles were evidently used for the new auditorium.

It was tried whether one very large branch, consisting of about an hundred wax candles, would be sufficient to illuminate the audience part of the Theatre, and by those who desire to see the scenery and performance in its true relief, this mode of lighting the place would be preferred, all chandeliers attached to the boxes dazzling the eye and interrupting the view; but perhaps there are many who think a clear sight of the boxes an essential part of the entertainment—and to gratify all parties a middle line should be drawn. Perhaps two or four smaller lustres, also pendant from the cieling would be the best contrivance. (*Morning Chronicle*, 24 February 1791)

On 28 March *The Times* commented snidely that 'Some alteration must be made in lighting the Theatre—particularly so far as respects the centrical chandelier from the cieling—for as it was—the *Sparks in Fops alley* had the *nouvelle* effect of putting the *Ladies to Flight.*' On 30 March the same paper said more sedately, 'An improvement in the illumination of this House must take place, ere it can bear the slightest degree of comparison, in point of brilliancy with the Pantheon Theatre.'

From the point of view of the theatre's finances, the capacity of the auditorium is of special concern, though detailed plans or firm figures are lacking. Huge as the building was, one piece of evidence of crowding in audience accommodations appears in a complaint in *The Times* of 8 February 1791 that 'The Builder of the Haymarket Opera House has committed an egregious blunder in making a superfluous tier of boxes—neither Beau or Belle of any decent heighth can at present be on their legs in the boxes with any convenience.' Crowding would indeed appear to have been the principle on which the auditorium worked.

Two contemporary sources give very different figures for capacity, though the second dates from after the alterations of 1796. What appears to be an undated newspaper cutting quoted by the generally reliable William C. Smith states that the new theatre was 'capable of holding nearly 3,300 persons'.[1] However, a capacity closer to 2,500 is implied by a much more detailed description written after 1800.

The stage is sixty feet in length, from the wall to the orchestra, and eighty feet in breadth from wall to wall, and forty-six feet across from box to box. From the orchestra to the centre of the front boxes, the pit is sixty-six feet in length and sixty-five in breadth, and contains twenty-one benches, besides passage rooms of about three feet wide, which goes [*sic*] round the seats, and down the centre of the pit to the orchestra. The pit will hold eight hundred persons; price of admission half-a-guinea. In altitude, the internal part of the house is fifty-five feet from the floor of the pit to the dome. There are five tiers of boxes, and each box is about seven feet in depth, and four feet in breadth, and is so constructed as to hold six persons with ease, all of whom command a full view of the stage. Each box has its curtains to enclose it according to the fashion of the Neapolitan theatres, and is furnished with six chairs; but [they] are not raised above each other as the seats of our English Theatres. The boxes hold near nine hundred persons, and price of admission to them is half-a-guinea. The gallery is forty-two feet in depth sixty-two in breadth, and contains seventeen benches, and holds eight hundred persons, price of admission five shillings.[2]

The 900 total for boxes corresponds to known box-plans. Likewise the total obtained by dividing the number of feet of benches by 18 inches per

[1] Smith, *Italian Opera*, 12.

[2] John Feltham, *The Picture of London for 1806* (London: W. Lewis for R. Phillips, [1806]), 260–1. Nalbach, 82, argues that this passage was written in 1802 or 1803, but it does not appear in earlier editions of Feltham.

occupant yields a capacity of roughly 800 in the pit and another 800 in the gallery. This description is, however, for an altered state of the theatre, and one must note that the space allowed per bench, especially in the pit, is relatively large—more than 3 feet, as opposed to the traditional 9-inch bench plus 15 inches between benches. We calculate that if as many benches as possible were squeezed in, the total seating capacity of the auditorium would indeed approach 3,300—albeit with great discomfort to the patrons.

One piece of evidence for the higher potential capacity being exploited soon after the theatre was built is a notice in *The Times* of 17 February 1791, commenting on plans to rent the building to the Drury Lane performers while that theatre was being rebuilt: 'the House is sufficiently large to repay the additional expence. It will hold near £600.' The prices charged by the Drury Lane forces in exile were 6s. for boxes, 3s. 6d. for the pit, and 2s. for the gallery. Multiplying by the Feltham figures yields a total take per night of only £490, but if one assumes 900 in the boxes, 1,200 in the pit, and 1,200 in the gallery, that would generate exactly £600 from 3,300 seats. The comfortable capacity was clearly substantially lower, and from the Feltham figures one can deduce that Taylor had found either that people would not tolerate such discomfort at opera prices or that no more than about 2,500 normally came in any case. The *Morning Chronicle* of 8 March 1791 states that 'near 4000 Tickets are to be issued' for the dress rehearsal of the 10th, and reports on the 11th that 'There certainly were not fewer than 5000 persons assembled in the Theatre.' This could be dismissed as newspaper puffery save for a comment in the same paper on 16 March: 'the strength and security of the Theatre having been most abundantly proved, by the admission last Thursday into the Building of above 2000 persons more than could be conveniently accommodated, no more Tickets will be issued for Saturday [19 March] than the number of persons which the Theatre is calculated with ease to contain.' The *Morning Chronicle's* report on the rehearsal of the 10th states that scenery could not be employed because of 'The multitude that crowded on the stage' (11 March), and whatever the overage may have been, it was probably accommodated in stage and backstage space. By implication, however, the auditorium seating capacity was at least 3,000.

Against all logic and financial probability, William Taylor had managed to get his theatre rebuilt. More than that, he had constructed an edifice whose size and decorative elegance gave it a glamour that the rival Pantheon could not match. Exactly what it had cost, and how Taylor raised the money, is difficult to say. In a plea for a licence published in the *Morning Chronicle* on 16 March 1791 Taylor states that 'this Theatre has been rebuilt, at an expence approaching to £40,000', which is very much in line with the estimate in his prospectus of a year earlier. One might think that Taylor would wish to exaggerate the cost rather than minimize it, though he could have been hiding cost overruns from his investors, or trying to conceal the actual amounts of money he had raised by sale of rights to boxes. Eight years later, however, in his 1799 memorial, he supplied some figures that are consistent with this total.[1]

| | | |
|---|---:|---:|
| The Principal Bill of the Architect for building the Theatre including the Machinery of the Stage | | 31,600 |
| Besides Smith's Work | 433 | |
| Plumbers Ditto | 1,170 | |
| Furniture | 4,200 | |
| Tin and Iron Work | 2,300 | |
| Chandeliers and other Glass work | 1,200 | |
| Surveyors | 530 | |
| | 9,833 | |

The implied total of £41,133 seems startlingly low, especially when one recalls that Le Texier estimated £60,000 for a much smaller and less elegant theatre.[2] *The Times* of 5 January 1791 stated that 'The New Theatre will cost £60,000 before it is completed.' By the issue of 18 February the figure had grown considerably: 'The New Haymarket Opera House has cost £70,000 in the building—to which may be added about £20,000 more in the fitting of it up.' In lawsuit testimony delivered in November 1794 Taylor himself remarked in passing that 'the rebuilding and reinstating of the said Theatre . . . Cost upwards of Sixty thousand pounds'.[3] No doubt different figures reflect varying assumptions about what was included, but how the building itself could have cost less than this sum is difficult to imagine. Whatever the total was, Taylor had to mortgage the theatre's future to raise the requisite construction money.

[1] PRO CRES 6/121, p. 336. Although the authors of *Survey of London*, xxix and xxx, cite the costs of the concert room from this source, they passed over these figures in silence, perhaps because they found the total too low to believe.

[2] *Ideas on the Opera*, 52.

[3] C12/195/32 (answer).

Considering the financial, legal, and political obstacles, the rebuilding of the King's Theatre, Haymarket, must be regarded as a minor miracle, albeit a mixed blessing for the future of opera in London. Despite the raptures of the *Morning Chronicle* over the new theatre, *The Times* sounded a cautionary note when it reported that 'at present the voices cannot be distinctly heard even in the boxes nearest the stage', and observed that 'The House is by much too large' (23 March 1791). Taylor had built a *very* large and expensive opera-house, and one whose future insolvency was virtually guaranteed. In the spring of 1791, however, he had a more pressing problem, for the Lord Chamberlain flatly refused to license the theatre, and whether the building could ever be used was anything but clear.

# CHAPTER 9

# *Haydn and the Opening of the New Theatre, Spring 1791*

═══════════

IN January 1791 the state of Italian opera in London could fairly be described as muddled. William Taylor was working frantically to complete his theatre but had little prospect of obtaining legal authority to open it. A company had been hired for both opera and ballet, but how could it be paid unless it could perform? And how could the company perform without the manager landing in gaol? The Pantheon backers had nearly completed their own building; Salisbury had provided them with a licence; and within weeks Taylor would be engaged in hot competition with a formidable rival. No London opera company had ever done much better than break even, so how could two of them achieve any semblance of solvency? Neither side wanted a financial blood-bath and, though Taylor had no licence, the Lord Chancellor's refusal of a patent to the new company gave him some leverage. Complex, high-level negotiations for a merger dragged on for weeks before they ended in failure, leaving Taylor to go broke or break the law. How he succeeded in opening his theatre in defiance of the Lord Chamberlain is an important part of the story that follows.

Apart from Haydn's letters there are few records of Gallini's part in the management this spring; nor is there evidence as to what legal advice Taylor received. Reviews are few and scanty. A newly discovered concert programme is a great help in reconstructing the dance company, and some of the ballet offerings can be assessed with reasonable confidence. The musical entertainments are a far murkier matter. The organization's great competitive advantage was of course having Haydn as composer in residence. But, ironically, the season is most noteworthy for the company's inability to produce his last opera, *L'anima del filosofo*. The circumstances in which this unfinished and now neglected work was suppressed have been seriously misunderstood by historians. Artistically, Haydn made the season a success; finances were another matter. The company lost nearly £10,000 this spring.

## I. The Failure of Merger Negotiations

The lunacy of having two opera companies had always been obvious, but not until 31 December 1790 did representatives from both sides sit down to discuss a settlement. The sensible time to conduct negotiations would have been the previous May or June: by the end of December tens of thousands of pounds had been invested in two buildings, and two companies had been engaged, making any compromise infinitely more difficult. Between 31 December and 19 January four formal meetings were held under the auspices of the Prince of Wales, and they were reported in the press in considerable detail.

On 31 December the Prince of Wales, his brother the Duke of York, the Duke of Bedford, the Marquis of Salisbury, the Earls of Cholmondeley and Buckinghamshire, Sheridan, Harris, Hammersley (the banker), O'Reilly, Troward, Sheldon, and three lawyers met at Carlton House, the Prince's London residence. According to *The Times* of 4 January 1791, the meeting was called by the Prince at the request of 'the friends of the Old Opera House' to put a proposal to the Pantheon group.[1] As the writer notes, expenses had been heavy, no licence had been granted, and the Pantheon was more nearly ready to open. The 'proposal was made to Mr. O'Reilly, that if he would relinquish his concern at the Pantheon, his expences should be indemnified, the Lease to the Proprietors made good, and all his engagements with performers taken off his hands; and further, that he should have the general management of the New Opera House'. The proposal foundered on the issue 'of who was to be the security for these engagements'. Taylor is curiously absent from all accounts of this meeting, but one can hardly imagine that he would willingly have resigned management of his new theatre to a man he loathed and despised—and a rank amateur, at that. The only result of the first meeting was the establishment of a 'Committee of Gentlemen' comprising the Duke of York, the Duke of Bedford, and the Marquis of Salisbury ('On the part of Mr O'Reilly'), Sheridan and the Earls

[1] Both the *London Chronicle* of 6–8 Jan. and the *Morning Chronicle* of the 7th suggest that the impetus came from the Earl of Cholmondeley, who proposed that both sides submit to arbitration, the losing party to be duly compensated 'on a fair valuation'.

of Buckinghamshire and Cholmondeley ('On the part of the Old House'), with 'the Prince of Wales to be umpire between both parties'. At this first meeting Troward reportedly agreed to Cholmondeley's proposition for Taylor and the Haymarket creditors; Sheldon, acting for O'Reilly, declined to submit to binding arbitration, on the grounds that 'O'Reilly had no impediment whatever to the progress of his Theatre, having the King's Licence' (*Morning Chronicle*, 7 January 1791). The second meeting occurred on Thursday, 6 January and produced claims and counter-claims, but no agreement except that the dispute 'should be referred to the men of business then present, to meet together and devise a plan for the settlement of the several claims' (ibid.).

According to *The Times* of 3 January the Prince of Wales was 'much disposed to patronise the New Opera house erecting in the Haymarket, although he and his friends have each taken a Box at the Pantheon; but as Mr O'Reilly and those concerned with him, have expended a very considerable sum of money, it is but fair they should be reimbursed'. The unrealistic nature of the proposed compromise is made clearer in a report in the *Star* of 4 January, the gist of which is that the creditors should be satisfied by 'a public Subscription for the National Theatre of £100,000', with opera then to be given at the King's Theatre, Haymarket, while the Pantheon could be used 'for *light* and *select* entertainments of Music and Dancing'. Whether £100,000 could indeed be raised 'in a few days' (as the *London Chronicle* of 6–8 January claims) seems questionable. As the committee was soon to learn, that sum would not have been more than a start towards covering operatic debts.

The third meeting was held on Sunday, 16 January. Somewhat contradictory reports appeared in the *Morning Chronicle* of the 17th, *The Times* of the 18th and the *London Chronicle* of the 15th–18th, but the essentials seem clear: (1) opera should be given by a consolidated company at the Haymarket, 'as the only place where Operas could be performed with grandeur as a national spectacle, and with the means of prosperity as a private speculation'; (2) after payment of both companies' debts, future profits would be divided between the two groups of proprietors; (3) £40,000 should be raised immediately by extending box leases; (4) both Taylor and O'Reilly should be excluded from management, and control given to 'a Committee of Noblemen'. No mention is made of the future of the Pantheon. *The Times* said that O'Reilly's friends objected to his exclusion, but all parties agreed that 'it was advisable . . . to consolidate their Interests, and to have but one

Opera' (*Morning Chronicle*). Consequently 'The Gentlemen of the Law were directed to prepare and digest a detailed plan for this consolidation'.

The fourth meeting took place on Wednesday 19 January and was reported in similar terms in the *Morning Chronicle* of the 20th and *The Times* of the 21st. In essence, the King's Theatre, Haymarket, was to acquire a monopoly at the cost of becoming responsible for all debts contracted in connection with the Pantheon. Specifically, £20,000 was to be paid immediately to creditors—£10,000 to those of each theatre. Renters' arrears on the King's Theatre were to be dealt with by extending their terms of years. Beyond this, £1,000 per annum would be 'taken from the receipts for the Creditors', and the remainder of the (presumptive) profits would 'be divided equally between the Proprietors of both Theatres'. This improbable solution was met with what amounted to point-blank refusal by Salisbury's solicitor, who demanded immediate payment of the whole of the £20,000 to the Pantheon's creditors, plus £3,500 owed to the King's Theatre, Haymarket, by an insurance company.

At this point, the first sign of a split appeared among the Pantheon's backers, for the Duke of Bedford 'seemed by no means to adopt the Answer as the sense of the Pantheon Referees', and said that within two days, 'at farthest . . . a Proposition should be made by the Pantheon to the Haymarket Party'. The stiff-necked Salisbury was apparently not in favour of yielding an inch, and Bedford's efforts to find a middle ground came to naught. On 24 January the *Morning Chronicle* states that Bedford had 'sent a message . . . stating that he finds the differences between the two parties so wide, that he cannot suggest any plan likely to produce a compromise, at least for the present season'. The negotiations probably came too late to allow any real possibility of compromise, and they had in any case failed. A private rehearsal had taken place at the Pantheon as early as 10 January (*Star*, 11 January) and a private dance rehearsal on the 19th (*Gazetteer*, 20 January): O'Reilly believed he was only a fortnight away from being ready to open. He had a licence and hence the whip hand. Bedford had qualms, but Salisbury was taking a hard line. Taylor, meanwhile, was presumably resisting amalgamation with any means at his disposal, and the King's Theatre's creditors were not going to agree to any peace treaty that further compromised their already slim hopes of recovering what was owed them.

Two factors made compromise impossible: pride and money. Salisbury and O'Reilly had no desire to yield up power. Perhaps even more crucially, the financial arrangements for a joint company made sense neither in the short term nor the long, though how well the participants understood this is not clear. As part of the preparations for the meeting of 16 January both sides were to state their financial obligations. What figures the King's Theatre offered is unknown, but probably cloudy ones, as the Pantheon backers objected to a joint company's accepting responsibility for Taylor's 'unknown and uninvestigated' debts (*The Times*, 18 January). We now know that pre-1789 debts amounted to upwards of £100,000; the rebuilding cost some £60,000; fitting up the theatre was probably another £20,000; and the company hired for spring 1791 was said to cost £18,000 for the season (*Morning Chronicle*, 16 March)—a startlingly high figure, if true. Thus the old company's debts and current obligations probably amounted to upwards of £200,000, less whatever cash had actually been paid towards the new building and £15,000 in subscriptions reportedly in hand (*St James's Chronicle*, 8–11 January). The list of 'Pantheon' debts and obligations presented by O'Reilly is preserved in the Bedford Opera Papers (5.K.7), and a nearly identical version was published in the *Morning Chronicle* of 19 March 1791, to which total liability for rent and taxes is added. It includes £11,400 for the Leicester Square venture (part of which should have been recoverable by selling the site), some £14,000 in Pantheon construction and start-up costs, upwards of £17,000 in salaries owed for spring 1791, and £44,500 owed in rent on the Pantheon and an adjacent house—a total of some £86,500. The stalemate is hardly surprising, given the unmanageable magnitude of the debts on both sides. A compromise just might have been worked out in the spring of 1790 before two opera-houses had been built, but once the two ventures had got themselves into this ludicrous predicament, there was no tidy way out. However dubious the financial prospects, the Pantheon proprietors were plunging ahead; Taylor was left to decide whether he preferred the prospect of bankruptcy or gaol.

## II. Salisbury and the Licensing Dispute

For several months after the fire of June 1789 those connected with the King's Theatre seem not to have realized that even if they managed to rebuild the theatre they would need a licence to operate it. This blindness is not altogether surprising: the King's Theatre had been in business since 1705 and the licence had long been treated as a matter of custom and practice. The imbroglio over a 31-year patent to O'Reilly that culminated in the Lord Chancellor's hearings of April 1790 and the refusal of a patent brought the issue to everyone's consciousness, but what might come of it was entirely unclear. Since 8 April 1790 O'Reilly and his backers had been taunting Taylor in print: 'Have you either a PATENT or LICENCE for performing, supposing the building is ever made complete? Or have you so much as a promise of either?' (*The Times*). When Taylor discovered that Salisbury was one of the secret backers of the Pantheon is not known, but quite possibly not until the summer of 1791. And if Salisbury was prepared ruthlessly to abuse his position as Lord Chamberlain, Taylor's rival venture was catastrophically vulnerable to refusal of a licence—or so Salisbury seems to have presumed. Throughout the summer and autumn of 1790 Taylor's opponents hammered on the licensing theme in a press campaign, warning that the theatre would not be permitted to open and that any performer who flouted the law would certainly be arrested under the Vagrancy Act.[1]

Taylor made one serious attempt to reply, arguing that the old theatre had 'been established now upwards of 87 years; that it stands upon ground leased from the Crown, for the express purposes of a Theatre; and it has been excepted and recognized, as an established undertaking, in all Acts of Parliament' (*The Times*, 13 August 1790). 'His Majesty's known justice', Taylor maintains, would not allow him to shut down a venture on which large sums of money had been embarked in confidence of continued royal sanction. But this argument was questionable: in the hearings of April 1790 the Lord Chancellor had sided with the old theatre's creditors, but at the same time had pointed out that the king could do as he pleased.

No one seriously contemplated the possibility that the rebuilt King's Theatre could function without a licence. The issue was merely whether Salisbury could be shamed or pressured into granting one. No record survives of early requests or negotiations, but on 11 February 1791 Salisbury 'formally signified to the Proprietors of the King's Theatre in the Haymarket, that "he has granted a licence for operas to be performed in the Pantheon, and that His Majesty did not think any other Italian theatre necessary"' (*Morning Chronicle*, 14 February). On the 19th *The Times* said, 'We are authorized to assure the public that the Lord Chamberlain has signifyed to the undertakers of the Haymarket Theatre, that no licence will be given to them.' If true, this was presumably fatal. The recent precedent of John Palmer's Royalty Theatre was discouraging.[2] On 26 March 1791 *The*

---

[1] See, for example, *The Times* of 12, 13, and 20 Aug., and 15 Oct. 1790.
[2] See *The London Stage*, Part 5, ii. 911–12. For contemporary pamphlets on the Royalty case, see Arnott and Robinson, nos. 177–89.

*Times* printed a long piece rehearsing the story of the Royalty and pointing out its direct applicability to the King's Theatre, Haymarket. Most observers in February 1791 probably assumed that Taylor was stymied. On 16 February *The Times* said 'We believe that all thoughts of performing at this new Theatre in the Haymarket are given over, unless indeed it is for one night, to try whether the performers will be taken up, as not acting under any legal authority, which is a thing expected, and will certainly happen.'

What were Taylor's options? One might be to rent out his theatre to Sheridan for use while Drury Lane was torn down and rebuilt on a grander scale. The possibility is reported in *The Times* of 17 and 21 February, and this did happen, though not until the end of the following summer. Sheridan had a good deal of trouble arranging financing, in part because investors wanted assurance that Drury Lane's 21-year patent would be renewed. But renting to Sheridan was at best a temporary expedient. A permanent solution might be to purchase the 'dormant patent' attached to the Covent Garden theatre, but whether this manœuvre was legal was unclear, and there were other difficulties. Thomas Harris apparently could not produce the original Killigrew patent itself; Taylor had no cash with which to make the purchase—and Harris knew from experience how bad Taylor was about paying his bills. Exactly why the negotiations reported in the *Morning Chronicle* of 7 and 14 March came to nothing is unknown. (Harris's extra patent was ultimately sold to Drury Lane, and continued to be the subject of legal dispute.) But in any case the dormant patent proved no magical solution to Taylor's problems.

Taylor sought legal opinions, apparently with mixed results. 'The Lawyers who have made a present of their advice to the Haymarket Theatre, inform them that they may perform Operas in spite of the Law—while those Gentlemen, who have been paid for their consultation, are of a different opinion' (*The Times*, 26 February). On 24 February Taylor held a meeting of his mortgagees and other creditors, which resulted in the appointment of 'a Committee personally to wait on the Right Honourable the Lord Chamberlain' to make representations on behalf of the theatre and its creditors. The members were the Earls of Cholmondeley and Buckinghamshire, Sir John Lade, George Hobart, Stephen Lushington, Thomas Hammersley, Albany Wallis, Robert Burton, and William Brummell (*Morning Chronicle*, 26 February). Two days later the same paper reported that 'The Lord Chamberlain does not think proper to give the Committee appointed by the Mortgagees and Creditors of the Haymarket Theatre a meeting; but he tells them, that his Office is open for any further representation they may chuse to make to the King.' Salisbury continued to stonewall.

The problem did not become dire until the middle of March, because only then was the new theatre in a condition to make regular performances feasible. Public rehearsals of Paisiello's *Pirro* were given on 23 February and 10 March, and a third on 22 March. Between the second and third of these free performances Taylor mounted an aggressive press campaign designed to bring pressure on Salisbury. A series of items friendly to Taylor in the *Morning Chronicle* indicates that pressure. On 8 March the paper reports that 'Mr Erskine, and several other of the most eminent Counsel at the Bar, have given an opinion, that the Lord Chamberlain is amenable in a Court of Law, if, under his auspices, expence has been incurred in an undertaking, which afterwards, without an avowed cause of complaint, he has prevented from proceeding.' On the 10th Troward is reported to have been asked 'to prepare a case for the opinion of Counsel, Messrs Erskine, Pigot, and Bearcroft, whether a prosecution, by indictment, would not lie against the persons for a conspiracy [that is, including the Lord Chamberlain]'. A rave notice of the second rehearsal appeared on 11 March, followed on the 14th by a long list of the 'most distinguished people of fashion' who had attended 'in their several boxes', among them the Prince of Wales. On 16 March Taylor ran a long plaint attached to his advertisement on page 1, decrying the Lord Chamberlain's refusal of a licence. 'The hardship of the case is without example: a property that had cost £60,000 and on which only £8,000 was insured . . . was in one night entirely consumed, after an establishment of 87 years.' Taylor points out that the Lord Chamberlain had encouraged them to rebuild if they could,[1] and that the Lord Chancellor had confirmed the strength of the creditors' claims in advising rejection of O'Reilly's patent. 'On the faith of this sanction and encouragement, this Theatre has been rebuilt, at an expence approaching to £40,000 and a Company of Performers have been engaged and brought over at a still

---

[1] Although this was true, the Lord Chamberlain's office published a vehement denial, stating that 'the Lord Chamberlain never did directly or indirectly give any Encouragement to Mr *Taylor*, or any other Person concerned or interested in the Haymarket Property' (*Morning Chronicle*, 17 Mar.). Taylor riposted by publishing Salisbury's letters to Cholmondeley of 7 July and 17 Aug. 1789, stating that 'preference' must be given to 'reinstating the old building for the benefit of the Proprietors and Claimants' (ibid., 18 Mar.). Salisbury angrily denounced this unseemly publication of a gentleman's private correspondence (Theatre Cuts 42, fo. [16<sup>r</sup>]), but he was hoist by his own petard.

further expence of nearly £18,000.'[1] None the less, 'the usual Licence is to be withheld, because one has already been given to another person'.

What to do? Whether by luck or good judgement, Taylor steered a middle course. In the same public plaint he announced that he was 'determined to give no offence either to his Majesty or to the Law', that 'it remains only to shut up the Theatre, until the hardship of the case shall be made known to His Majesty', and that 'in the mean time' to help defray the salaries of the performers, concert entertainments would be given at Gallini's own concert rooms in Hanover Square. Some time in the following week Taylor decided on a bolder and riskier course of action: he would give his 'Entertainments' in the King's Theatre itself. The logic may have been largely financial: the audience capacity of the Hanover Square rooms is not known, but it was surely far less than what the grand new theatre could hold.[2] On 26 March 1791 the King's Theatre formally opened, advertising 'Collections' of serious and comic music, interspersed with the ballet entertainments customary at the opera. The theatre's advertisements claimed that it had opened because the proprietors had 'found that, without offence to law, the entertainments advertised for the Hanover-square Rooms may be given at this Place'. At best, this was a questionable claim, but popular sentiment and some influential members of the nobility were on Taylor's side.

Reference to the licensing records of the 1780s leaves little doubt that in purely legal terms Taylor did not have a leg to stand on. The standard form of licence issued to the King's Theatre in the 1780s ran as follows:

I [the Lord Chamberlain] do hereby give Leave and Licence unto Richard Brindley [*sic*] Sheridan Esq To have Italian Operas performed at The King's Theatre in St. James's Haymarket, within the liberties of Westminster between Michaelmas 1780 and Michaelmas 1781, and do not allow that any other species of Entertainment, whatever, shall be Exhibited there, without application specifying the Nature of such Entertainment, being previously made to and Permission obtained from me for that purpose. Given this 26th Day of September 1780. . . . Hertford. (PRO LC 5/162, p. 251)

[1] The figure for 'performers' seems inflated. £18,000 was the entire annual budget under Gallini from 1785 to 1789, and the Pantheon's actual performer total for a flashy and expensive company in 1790–91 was under £14,000. Judging from figures from the later 1790s (and allowing for high salaries and an extraordinary contract for Haydn) the total for performers is unlikely to have been more than about £12,500. See 'Opera Salaries'. Taylor may, of course, have been including funds budgeted for scenery, costumes, and start-up expenses.

[2] Simon McVeigh reports figures as high as 900, with 500 closer to normal. See *Concert Life in London from Mozart to Haydn* (Cambridge: Cambridge University Press, 1993), 20 and 168.

Taylor received an identical licence for 1782–83 (LC 5/162, p. 282). The argument that non-theatrical entertainments lay outside the Lord Chamberlain's power does not hold up. Anyone who cares to skim through the licensing books (LC 5/162 and 5/163) will find an enormous number of licences for concerts, masquerades, and other forms of entertainment, many of them valid for only a single night. The Lord Chamberlain's record-keeping became more rigorous and systematic during the 1790s, but on any appeal to precedent, Taylor's case was hopeless.[1]

Had Taylor mounted an opera with scenery and costumes for paying customers he would probably have been arrested. Many onlookers clearly expected this to happen forthwith. Commenting on the third and final 'rehearsal', *The Times* (23 March) expressed its regret that 'so elegant a theatre' must 'remain useless'. A long piece signed 'Lex Talionis' in the same paper on the 26th rehearsed the history of the Royalty Theatre and the recent prosecution of the Royal Circus, and concluded that 'there is very little doubt but the dancers who may venture to exhibit at the Theatre in the Haymarket, will be committed to Bridewell, and prosecuted'. Another long letter (signed 'Truth') appeared on 1 April, pointing out 'the illegality as well as the unblushing arrogance of the proceedings now carrying on in the Haymarket, sanctioned by no authority' and predicting the prompt 'committal of the offenders to Bridewell'. A notice on 4 April says that performances go 'on as merrily as if every thing was fair and above board; probably the *change* of the *scene* to *Bridewell,* so often advertised, may prove only a "weak *invention* of the *enemy*"'. And on 8 April *The Times* observed flippantly that rumours of both prosecution and structural deficiency have proved unfounded: 'neither *constables* nor *cracks* have appeared'.

Lack of arrests was not the result of any magnanimity on the part of O'Reilly. On the very first night of 'public' performance, he laid an official complaint against the performers at the Haymarket.

---

[1] In a directly related case heard on 4 May 1793 the Court of King's Bench dismissed a breach of contract suit by Gallini against the dancer Laborie on the ground that the King's Theatre, Haymarket, had held no licence at the time of the offence, and hence that a performer could not be required to commit an illegal act. Lord Kenyon held that 'the intent' of the Licensing Act was 'to put all places of public diversion' under regulation, that dancing fell within the meaning of the act, and that the King's Theatre, Haymarket, had no right to exhibit any *entertainment of the stage* . . . without the Lord Chamberlain's license'. Charles Durnford and Edward Hyde East, *Reports of Cases Argued and Determined in the Court of King's Bench* (London: A. Strahan and W. Woodfall for J. Butterworth, 1794), v. 242–4.

On Saturday evening, Mr O'Reilly lodged an information at the Public Office in Bow-street, against the Exhibitions given that evening at the King's Theatre, in the Haymarket; but the Bench of Justices have declined interfering, on account of the recognition of that Theatre in the Acts of Parliament, which, in the opinion of some of the first lawyers in the kingdom, amounts to a legal authority, at least for the present Entertainments given there, if not even for Italian Operas themselves; and because the consequences of enforcing a penal statute in a doubtful case, and where so much property is at stake, were of too great and too serious a nature for the Justices to encounter, before the opinions of the Courts of Judicature are taken upon the point of law. (*Morning Chronicle*, 31 March 1791)

The refusal of the local magistrates to interfere in what had become a *cause célèbre* is not altogether surprising. The King's Theatre, Haymarket, had long been licensed under the 1737 act; it had a history of royal support; a great deal of property was at stake; and the gentry were supporting the place. The Prince of Wales had attended the initial rehearsal and been loud in his praise of the theatre, and he had occupied his double box on 10 March.[1] He also attended the first public performance, mingling with the crowd in the pit during the last act (*The Times*, 28 March). On 5 April he 'gave a grand dinner to several friends at Carlton-House; after which he went to the Haymarket Opera-House' (*The Times*, 6 April). The list of those attending the second rehearsal (published in the *Morning Chronicle* of 14 March) included 'all the most distinguished people of fashion', and the roster of box-holders published with a concert programme on 11 April (discussed below) is even more impressive. By no means all the boxes were rented as of that date, but the box-holders were, collectively, a noble, rich, and powerful group. To shut down a theatre that enjoyed such patronage and newspaper support would be politically dangerous, even for the government.

In theory, Salisbury could himself have issued an order of silence, but he chose not to do so. Two scraps of evidence preserved among the Pantheon papers suggest both confusion and panic on the part of the anti-Haymarket forces. In a letter evidently written about 27 March 1791, O'Reilly assured Sheldon 'I did not order the people to go to Bow Street they went of themselves—Mr Maddox was the cause of it who foolishly imagined he & the Rest of the Evidence were to attend there.'[2] Below this Sheldon wrote 'Mr Madox at my request came to my Chambers and assured me that the last words Mr O'Reilly said to him in Lord Salisburys house was to be sure and

---

[1] *Morning Chronicle*, 24 Feb. and 14 Mar. 1791.     [2] Bedford Opera Papers, 5.D.14.

be at Bow Street Next morning at 8 O'clock & that he went accordingly.' The laying of information at Bow Street was clearly planned from Salisbury's house, though O'Reilly managed to bungle it. Why did Salisbury not then take matters into his own hands? The answer is probably simple: fear of successful legal action against the Pantheon proprietors, the Lord Chamberlain included. Taylor had leaked legal opinions to the press about the feasibility of suing the Lord Chamberlain earlier in the month (quoted above), and the second bit of manuscript evidence suggests that the threat alarmed the Pantheon proprietors. A letter from O'Reilly to Sheldon refers to one of these newspaper paragraphs and says if it 'is not answered it will add many obstacles that oppose the Pantheon—You will perceive it is aimed as well against the Duke of Bedford as me—from the threat of *an action of Conspiracy*'.[1]

Whether Taylor could have sued successfully for damages is anyone's guess, but he could probably have proved in court that Salisbury had licensed an opera company of which he was co-proprietor while refusing to license the rival whose claims had been endorsed by the Lord Chancellor. This would have been extremely embarrassing, for Salisbury had definitely abused the powers of his office. In the event, he did not have the nerve to move against Taylor. No previous scholar seems to have realized that this was the case. The editor of Part 5 of *The London Stage* states that 'at long last the Lord Chamberlain saw fit to extend to Taylor a license . . . which would permit him to open the theatre as a kind of concert hall', but cites no evidence.[2] We have found no such licence in the Lord Chamberlain's records, and no announcement of a licence appeared in the newspapers. Astonishingly, the Lord Chamberlain continued to refuse to license the Haymarket but did not dare to close it down.

Apparently the only formal recognition of the King's Theatre's defiance of the law was *Maddox* v. *Vestris*, a 'penal action' brought as a test case in King's Bench against one of the most prominent (and presumably solvent) of the performers. An account in *The Times* of 29 June 1791 reports counsel for the plaintiff as saying that 'this was the gentlest way that could be thought of to try a question; it was much better than imprisoning the performers, as had been done in a similar case: it was very material to the managers of both the Opera Houses that this question should be decided. This was the best and easiest way of trying it.' So far as we are aware, no

---

[1] Bedford Opera Papers, 5.D.16.    [2] *The London Stage*, Part 5, ii. 1,277.

conclusion was reached: the lawyers got bogged down on technicalities, and competition came to an end before they were resolved.

## III. 'Rehearsals' and 'Entertainments' at the New Theatre

Against long odds—and indeed against the law—William Taylor managed to get his new theatre opened but only under circumstances both parlous and unsatisfactory. The dance company could perform more or less what it had been hired to do, but the opera company would have to get by with makeshift entertainments, and the theatre could not compete for long against its better financed rival, which was able to offer fully staged operas.

### Management

Who was responsible for the artistic direction of the new King's Theatre? Taylor remained in overall control of the building, though his name appears only in newspaper controversy concerning the licensing dispute. He evidently took little or no part in the artistic decisions concerning music and dance. Dance was of course the province of the ballet-master, Vestris sen., who was one of the company's prime attractions. The bitter complaint he published in the *Morning Chronicle* on 15 April 1791 that *La mort d'Hercule* was ruined by Gallini's failure to support it 'according to his promises'—that is, to provide the necessary scenes and machines—confirms that Gallini was financially responsible. Likewise Gallini's letter to Perregaux in Paris of 24 December 1790 (discussed in sect. v) implies that he was administering the company and in a position to authorize salary advances.

Managerial responsibility for the musical establishment is better documented. *The Times* of 18 February 1791 reported:

Gallini, whose life for some years past has been a scene of strife, misery, and unhappiness to himself, will, if he lives but a few years longer, probably die a beggar. By the performances at the new Haymarket Opera House, he loses the penalty of all the musical engagements made at that theatre, which amount to many thousand pounds. He forfeits to Haydn £1000 and to David and Capelletti £500 each.

The next day it printed a clarification: 'In the paragraph in our paper of yesterday, respecting Mr Gallini—it should have been stated that he will forfeit £2000 to three of the performers as the penalty, if the new Opera House is not licensed.' This probably means that Gallini had recruited Haydn and the singers, and that three of the principals had received contracts with penalty clauses, in case the new theatre was unable to open. If *The Times* is correct, Gallini had made himself personally liable for salaries and penalties—as presumably he had done the previous season when he ran the company at the Little Haymarket. This interpretation is confirmed by two passages in Taylor's memorial of 1799. Having described his struggle to rebuild the theatre after the fire, Taylor complains that 'he engaged a Company of the most eminent Artists and Performers in Europe; but the usual Licence having been refused, your Memorialist in consequence suffered a loss during that season alone of no less than £9700'.[1] How the company came up with the cash to keep going is succinctly explained in Taylor's 'Schedule' of debts, one item in which is £31,400 owed to Gallini, 'including 9,700 of a Loss incurred in 1791 when the usual Licence for the Opera was refused'.

The nature of Gallini's agreement with his enemy Taylor is not known with certainty. Taylor had to obtain Gallini's co-operation in order to rebuild. According to the General Opera Trust Deed of August 1792 Taylor paid Gallini £11,000 of the £19,500 principal then directly owed to him on 24 September 1790,[2] and in return Gallini probably signed a release allowing Taylor to repossess the theatre site. O'Reilly states that late in 1790 or early in 1791 Gallini and Taylor 'entered into an agreement' by which Gallini 'was permitted to receive the £8,000 insurance money . . . for his own benefit, and was put into full possession of the new Opera-House, without any check or controul whatsoever in his accounts, either as to his receipts or disbursements', the understanding being that Gallini 'is to hold that possession quietly, till he shall have repaid himself a further sum of £8,500'.[3] If true, this helps explain the anomaly of Gallini's participation in the management of a theatre owned by Taylor. In the public view, the two men were jointly responsible for what went on at the King's Theatre. On 4 April *The Times* published an unpleasant letter addressed 'To Messrs. Taylor and Gallini', denouncing their 'setting the law at defiance, and insulting the authority of the Crown' (and also failing to play 'God Save the King'); on 6 April the paper ran a follow-up, commencing, 'We have authority from Messrs. Taylor and Gallini, to contradict the Letter in our Paper of Monday last.' As of April 1791 Gallini was obviously an active member of the King's Theatre management.

[1] PRO CRES 6/121, p. 331. Following quotation from p. 337.
[2] Bedford Opera Papers, Box 6, vol. Ia, item 3. Another copy is in PRO LC 7/88, pp. 63–135.
[3] O'Reilly, *An Authentic Narrative*, 64–5.

Gallini served as artistic director for the theatre, evidently holding that position by virtue of his ability and willingness to accept financial responsibility for performer salaries. The *Oracle* of 16 February 1791 states that Gallini is 'under Operatic Engagements to the tune of £12,000 for this Season', and asks, 'if he cannot *dance*, who is to *pay the piper?*' A further complication, however, is the shadowy presence of Antoine Le Texier at the theatre this spring. Several references to the stage and machinery in 1791 credit Le Texier with their design. For example, the *Morning Chronicle* of 29 January 1791 says, 'The Stage of the Hay-Market Opera will be equal in wonder to all the other parts of that magnificent Theatre; and it does the utmost honour to the invention of M. le Tessier.' This has the ring of a puff, but the credit to Le Texier (whose name is often spelled phonetically in the papers) can probably be accepted. On 28 March, praising the effect of the ballet *Orpheus and Eurydice*, the same paper calls the stage 'highly creditable to the inventive powers of M. le Tessier', and the next day *The Times* credits his design for the 'elasticity' of the stage that assisted the 'airy flights' of the dancers. Le Texier had been out of management since 1779 and unemployed by the opera-house since he guest-directed *La regina di Golconda* in 1784, but evidently Novosielski had drawn on his expertise in designing the stage. Le Texier was actively involved in the King's Theatre management in spring 1791. A reference in *The Times* of 3 January 1791 implies that he was to superintend the opera department—a non-position, as events fell out, but Le Texier seems to have made himself useful as best he could. On 19 May, seeking to vary its 'Entertainments', the company gave 'A New Kind of Concert' mingling music and dance, advertised as a 'Benefit for the Author'— meaning the designer of the entertainments, identified in the *Oracle* of 21 May as Le Texier.

Taylor served as proprietor of the building; Gallini was financially responsible for the company and co-ordinated music and dance; Le Texier was intended to function as artistic director for operas; Vestris sen. handled day-to-day dance matters (but had no budgetary authority). The secondary staff was extremely strong. William Jewell was a vastly experienced (and trusted) treasurer. Badini was 'poet' (and received a benefit on 17 June, despite limited need for librettos). Salomon served as 'leader'.[1] Federici was

---

[1] The only other identifiable member of the orchestra this season was Franz (or František) Kočžwara, the Czech double-bass player. When he died of autoerotic asphyxia *The Times* (5 Sept. 1791) was quick to say that Gallini had brought him to London, though in fact he had arrived *c.*1775. See the *Biographical Dictionary*, ix. 76–7.

'Director of Music' (he was an experienced adapter of operas and provider of ballet music). And the crowning glory was Haydn himself as 'Composer'.

Earlier in the 1780s Haydn had received several invitations to travel to England, the most notable being those from the publisher Bland and the organizers of the Professional Concerts.[1] Gallini may have first approached him to become house composer at the King's Theatre in 1783. Burney wrote to his friend Thomas Twining on 6 September 1783, 'I have stimulated a wish to get Haydn over as opera Composer—but mum mum—yet—a correspondence is opened, & there is a great likelihood of it, if these Cabals, & litigations ruin not the opera entirely.'[2] Haydn was said to have asked for £600. On 10 October 1786 the *Morning Chronicle* reported that Gallini was in Vienna 'for the express purpose of engaging the celebrated Haydn as composer to the Opera House for the ensuing season'. Gallini tried again less than a year later, and Haydn responded in a letter of 19 July 1787, demanding £500, a free benefit, and the right to perform at the Hanover Square concerts.[3] His duties at Eszterháza of course prevented him from accepting offers to travel such a great distance, but the death of Prince Nicolaus on 28 September 1790 and the almost immediate disbanding of the court orchestra freed the 58-year-old composer from all official musical responsibilities. Johann Peter Salomon arrived opportunely at Vienna in autumn 1790 with an offer of a contract for London, which Haydn quickly accepted upon learning that he would be paid in advance. An event of immense importance, the signing of the contract is poorly documented, as is Salomon's role in the negotiations.

Salomon had resided in London since 1781 and was identified almost exclusively with the concert world, at first with the Professional Concerts and then as a freelance leader and violin soloist. He was not at this time as highly regarded as Wilhelm Cramer or even old Felice Giardini and did not play in the Italian opera orchestra, which was generally regarded as the premier ensemble in London. He became acquainted with Gallini mainly through the Hanover Square concert room, which Gallini rented to various performers and impresarios. For instance, in his letter inviting Mozart to

[1] See Jens Peter Larsen, in *New Grove*, viii. 343; see also Cecil B. Oldman, 'Haydn's Quarrel with the "Professionals" in 1788', *Musik und Verlag: Karl Vötterle zum 65. Geburtstag* (Kassel: Bärenreiter, 1968), 459; and Christopher Roscoe, 'Haydn and London in the 1780s', *Music & Letters*, 49 (1968), 203–12.

[2] *The Letters of Dr Charles Burney*, i. 382. For Haydn's demands, see 401.

[3] H. C. Robbins Landon, *Haydn at Eszterháza 1766–1790* (London: Thames and Hudson, 1978), 696.

London, O'Reilly offered the composer 'l'avantage d'écrire pour le concert de la profession'.[1]

No formal agreement between Gallini and Salomon, or indeed between Salomon and Haydn, survives, though all Haydn's early biographers refer to such a contract, supposedly signed on 8 December 1790. For example, G. A. Griesinger (1810) reported that the agreement included 3,000 gulden for a new opera, besides concert fees, the total sum to be deposited by Gallini in a Vienna bank in advance. C. F. Pohl gave different details of the contract but mentions no opera;[2] neither did the earliest announcements in the London press of Haydn's imminent arrival:

To the Musical World.

By a Letter just received on my arrival in Town, from Mr Salomon, I am authorised to lay before the Public an Advertisement, written by Mr. Salomon at Vienna, which he desires may be immediately inserted in the English Newspapers.

John Baptista Mara.

'Mr. Salomon having taken a journey to Vienna, purposely to engage the celebrated HAYDN, Chapel Master to his present Highness Prince Esterhazy, to come to England, most respectfully acquaints the Nobility and Gentry, that he has actually signed an Agreement with Mr. Haydn; in consequence, they are to set out together from Vienna in a few days, and hope to be in London before the end of December, when Mr. Salomon will have the honour of submitting to the Public a Plan of a Subscription Concert, which he flatters himself will meet with its approbation and encouragement.' Vienna, December the 8th, 1790. (*The Times*, 28 December 1790)

Gallini's name is conspicuously absent from this announcement. In his letters, Haydn implies that an opera commission from Gallini was part of the original package, and Salomon, with Gallini's money behind him, was more emissary than originator of the successful bid to bring Haydn to London. Given the uncertainty of Taylor and Gallini's enterprise at the new King's Theatre and the doubts they must have harboured about receiving a licence for Italian opera from the Lord Chamberlain, the terms of Haydn's opera commission may deliberately have been kept vague. The composer was paid in advance (see his letter of 14 March 1791, quoted below), but whether the lump sum that was deposited in his bank at Vienna included a separate fee

---

[1] Printed in Gustav Nottebohm, *Mozartiana* (Leipzig: Breitkopf & Härtel, 1880), 67–8. For discussion, see 'Opera and Arson', 69.

[2] Pohl lists six symphonies, personally directed, for £300, a further £200 for the copyright, and a benefit guaranteed at £200. *Mozart und Haydn in London* (1867; repr. New York: Da Capo, 1970), 102–3. See also H. C. Robbins Landon, *Haydn in England 1791–1795* (London: Thames and Hudson, 1976), 30.

for an opera is still unknown. Once he arrived in London at the beginning of January 1791, Haydn dealt directly with Gallini (not Taylor) on all matters concerning his opera.

## Singers and Repertoire

With the future of Italian opera at the new King's Theatre hanging in the balance, Gallini nevertheless began to assemble a company of singers and dancers that would have to compete with Pacchierotti, Madam Mara, Didelot, and Mme Théodore Dauberval at the Pantheon. He trumped O'Reilly by engaging Vestris jun. and sen., two of the most famous dancers of the age and, eventually, Marie Louise Hilligsberg, a local favourite.[1] Gallini could risk heavy investment in this side of the company, since ballet was unlikely to be prohibited at the King's Theatre even if the Lord Chamberlain refused to issue a licence for Italian opera. The singers were much more of a gamble, not just because of the licence dispute: even if Taylor and Gallini were brave enough to defy the Lord Chamberlain and offer Italian opera this season, it would be in direct competition with the Pantheon, which was basically a replica of the old King's Theatre establishment, set up to produce both serious and comic works and employing many of the same staff. Most impressively, the rival company would be headed by Pacchierotti, who had last sung on stage in London in 1784 and who was by now a legend, and Madam Mara, held over from the Little Haymarket season. The two had never sung together in Italian opera in London and promised to be extremely popular, though Haydn, after attending performances at the Pantheon,[2] thought the new opera-house would fail 'because the castrato and the *prima donna* are too old'.[3]

Gallini shrewdly decided not to attempt head-to-head competition with O'Reilly's opera department, engaging an entirely different kind of company. He planned to concentrate on serious and semi-serious opera, thereby capitalizing on the experience of his two house composers, Haydn and Federici, yet he would dispense with the hitherto obligatory *primo uomo*. Instead, he hired the great Italian tenor Giacomo Davide as his star attraction. This was a daring move. Only once before had an *opera seria* been attempted in London without a castrato in the leading role: Cherubini's *Giulio Sabino* in 1786, which may have failed for precisely this reason. For

---

[1] For discussion of these negotiations, see 'Opera and Arson', 66.
[2] Bedford Opera Papers, 3.C2.4.a.
[3] Letter of 14 Mar. 1791, quoted in Landon, *Haydn in England*, 59.

Gallini to have contemplated a whole season of opera without a male soprano or contralto of at least the quality of Rubinelli must have seemed rash indeed, especially when Marchesi's extraordinary singing had helped save the stopgap season at the Little Haymarket. In retrospect, of course, Gallini was only acknowledging the incipient demise of the operatic castrato: Pacchierotti at the Pantheon in 1791 was to be the last world-class male soprano to hold the rank of *primo uomo* in London. Even Haydn slipped in calling Davide 'primo uomo', a term that had always been reserved for a castrato.

Davide, who had first been sought for the King's Theatre in 1779 by Le Texier,[1] did not disappoint during his one season in London: his glorious voice reportedly filled the huge new King's Theatre with thrilling effect.[2] The rest of Gallini's company was much less distinguished. Only the *basso* Francesco Albertarelli is noteworthy; he had sung the title-role in the 1788 production of *Don Giovanni* in Vienna. The *prima donna* was Rosa Lops from Munich, whom Haydn did not like, though she had been a pupil of Regina Mingotti. Her initial appearances were politely if ironically received in the papers ('every accomplishment but youth and beauty');[3] she left the company for reasons unknown and was replaced on 16 April by Signora Maffei, of whom Haydn pithily said, 'bella, ma poco musica'.[4] Giovanna Sestini was a competent second woman who had performed at the King's Theatre on and off since 1775 and was near the end of her career. In 1788–89 she had been engaged for '£200 or a benefit'.[5] Giuseppe and Teresa Cappelletti were nonentities, and Giovanni Tajana is otherwise unknown.

The erratic recruiting pattern this season clearly reflects the uncertainty over the licence but also the absence of advice from Lord Cowper, who had died in 1789. Davide came from Naples, but the others were engaged from far and wide; lack of an informed foreign agent may account for this imbalanced cast. Albertarelli, Signora Sestini, and the Cappellettis were probably intended to form the nucleus of a comic troupe. And Nancy Storace, who had been auditioned for the position of *prima buffa* at the Pantheon, would probably have been available for opera at the King's Theatre, since she sang frequently in Haydn and Salomon's concerts this season. But Gallini clearly signalled his intention to produce a new kind of repertoire with the only opera he was able to present this season: Paisiello's *Pirro*. The composer

---

[1] See Gibson, 'Earl Cowper', 239.  [2] *Morning Chronicle*, 24 Feb. and 11 Mar. 1791.
[3] *Morning Chronicle*, 24 Feb. 1791.  [4] Landon, *Haydn in England*, 39.
[5] See 'Opera Salaries', 52.

himself claimed it was (for him) a new style of serious opera, with concerted ensembles, including *introduzioni* and action finales usually reserved for *dramma giocoso*. Above all, it required a tenor in the demanding title-role.[1] None of this would have been new to Italian opera in London, even though the tenor lead was strongly identified with Davide, who had sung this part at the première at Naples in 1787.[2] But *Pirro* reflects Gallini's continuing interest in exploring new kinds of repertoire, both serious and comic. And by all accounts Davide triumphed as formerly only a castrato could have done.

*Pirro* needed to be given quickly: Taylor had guaranteed his subscribers performance of an opera by the end of January 1791, a deadline he missed by more than three weeks. But Taylor and Gallini decided they could not risk a fully staged Italian opera without a licence from the Lord Chamberlain. Their compromise was to offer a public rehearsal of *Pirro* on 23 February, but only with singers in street clothes.[3] On that day the *Morning Chronicle* (a paper friendly to the King's Theatre) commented: 'It is a curious fact that of all the Subscribers to the Haymarket Opera, but *one person* has withdrawn his subscription in consequence of their not procuring a licence to play in January. Since the failure of the Pantheon, he has returned with an humble entreaty to *replace* his money and *recover* his box—But the Box was *let*, and he and his company are completely *ousted.*' *Pirro* was performed twice more, on 10 and 22 March 1791. Haydn says that for the 10th Gallini distributed 4,000 free tickets, but that 'more than five thousand came'.[4] Gallini and Taylor shied away from selling tickets for the opera and money was not taken until 26 March, when fully staged ballets were performed after each half of a concert of miscellaneous vocal music.[5] The managers had another shoal to negotiate in late March when they had to ask subscribers formally to accept a change from opera with ballet to concerts with ballet. The advertisement for the first 'public' performance (that is, one counted towards the fulfilment of the subscription, and at which money was

[1] See Gordana Lazarevich, 'Pirro', *Opera Grove*, iii. 1020.

[2] See Sartori, no. 18767; also in this production were Franziska Lebrun and Francesco Roncaglia, both of whom had sung at the King's Theatre in the seasons around 1780.

[3] Horace Walpole wrote on 31 Mar., 'They have opened twice, taking money, in an evasive manner, pretending themselves concerts; the singers are in their own clothes, the dancers dressed, and no recitative—a sort of opera in dishabille' (*Correspondence*, xi. 232).

[4] Landon, *Haydn in England*, 59. Haydn may have been echoing the *Morning Chronicle* of 8 and 11 Mar. The *Oracle* of 11 Mar. estimated attendance of 'Four Thousand Persons'.

[5] See *The London Stage*, Part 5, ii. 1335.

taken) contains a special note to subscribers, both those 'who have already offered to retain their Boxes' and those now requested to confirm their subscriptions despite 'the change of Entertainments' (*Diary*, 26 March 1791).

## IV. Haydn's *L'anima del filosofo*

Haydn first mentioned his commission for the King's Theatre in a letter to Maria Anna von Genzinger of 8 January 1791, in which he described the last stages of his journey from Vienna and initial reception in London: 'At present I am working on symphonies, because the libretto of the opera is not yet decided on.'[1] In an undated letter, perhaps written a day or two later to Prince Anton Esterházy, Haydn gave more details, showing that plans had quickly advanced: 'The new opera libretto which I am to compose is entitled *Orfeo*, in 5 acts, but I shall not receive it for a few days. It is supposed to be entirely different from that of Gluck. . . . The opera contains only 3 persons, *viz.* Madam Lops, Davide, and a castrato, who is not supposed to be very special. Incidentally, the opera is supposed to contain many choruses, ballets and a lot of big changes of scenery.'

Haydn's last opera has been the source of considerable misunderstanding and controversy. Scholars have speculated about the meaning of the title, *L'anima del filosofo*, and debated whether the work as it stands in the Henle edition is virtually complete or whether Haydn never got round to composing a fifth act with a *lieto fine*. The violent ending of this version of the Orpheus and Eurydice myth, the closest libretto yet to Virgil and Ovid, is certainly perplexing, even disturbing. The coolness of some of the music and Haydn's apparent lack of engagement with highly dramatic scenes are also puzzling, as is the style of the opera itself, which veers between classical *opera seria* and oratorio, while approaching *dramma giocoso* and even *ballet d'action* in places. Landon's summation of the work as 'basically a magnificent failure—despite unforgettable moments and points of real dramatic interest'[2] reinforces a widespread critical belief that *L'anima del filosofo* is anomalous to all the main forms of late eighteenth-century opera.

To make sense of this strange work one must start with the libretto. In his *Entwurf-Katalog* Haydn names the author as Badini; the text was not printed and therefore has to be extracted from the various scores.[3] The

---

[1] Landon, *Haydn in England*, 37. Following quotation from 38.
[2] Ibid. 351.
[3] For a discussion of the sources, see *Joseph Haydn Werke*, xxv/13, *L'Anima del Filosofo*, ed.

composer already knew Badini's work: his libretto *Le pazzie di Orlando* had been adapted by Nunziato Porta for Haydn as *Orlando paladino* (Eszterháza 1782). As the most experienced poet employed at the King's Theatre and a long-time associate of Gallini, Badini was the obvious choice. Haydn reported (before he received the libretto) that the opera was to be in five acts, but in the *Entwurf-Katalog* he recorded that the opera was in four acts. Either number seems strange: since the early 1780s all London Italian operas had been in two acts. Even Paisiello's *Il barbiere di Siviglia*, originally in four acts, was reconfigured in two, as were all three-act *opere serie*. Why Badini should have departed from this well-established format is unclear. In almost all other respects the libretto is perfectly in line with both general developments in the London Italian opera since the early 1780s and Badini's own rather eccentric and experimental style.

Leaving aside Haydn's music for the moment, the salient 'oddities' of the libretto are: (1) warped treatment of a familiar opera *topos* (warped, that is, in comparison to Metastasian and Gluckian aesthetics; Badini was unusually faithful to his classical sources); (2) the inclusion of a chorus that is both an active participant in the drama (as courtiers, shepherds, savages, cupids, lost souls, frenzied Bacchantes) and a rational observer of the action; (3) the tragic climax and violent coda, which would have needed elaborate stagecraft for proper effect. After Euridice's 'second death', the Bacchantes, offended by Orfeo's defaming of womankind ('Io rinunzio all'amore e ai piacer de' mortali, al vostro sesso imbelle'—I renounce love and all mortal pleasures of your frail sex), give him poison, and he dies in agony; as they are about to dismember the body, a storm arises and the opera ends with the Bacchantes on the point of being drowned ('Siam vicine a naufragar'—we are nearly shipwrecked).

To deal with the least problematic of these features first: the chorus was a fairly regular feature of both comic and serious Italian operas in London throughout the 1780s. The King's Theatre does not seem to have retained a regular group of singers, but hired them in as needed (there are no records of payments to choristers). Only in *La regina di Golconda*, Tenducci's *Orfeo*, and *La cosa rara* did the chorus play a prominent *musical* part; judging from the rudimentary surviving music for earlier productions, Haydn's score would not have especially taxed the London choristers had the opera been produced.

Helmut Wirth (Munich: Henle Verlag, 1974), pp. vii–ix.

Much more troublesome are the related questions of the apparent tragic ending and the degree of completeness of Haydn's score. Although the composer stated in his letters that the opera was to be in five acts, the last two very short, in the *Entwurf-Katalog* he described it as 'Orfeo for England in 4 Acts'. Haydn did not have the *Katalog* with him in London in 1791, and the entry was probably made no earlier than August 1795. Also relevant to the following discussion is the fact that Haydn did not, with a single exception, include unfinished works in the *Entwurf-Katalog*.[1] The most logical arrangement of the surviving music is in four acts, as presented in *Joseph Haydn Werke*. The editor, Helmut Wirth, assumed that the last scene constitutes the fifth act, while other scholars have suggested that Haydn and Badini compressed the last three acts into two during composition.[2] Landon has asked, 'What can the fifth act have possibly included? Until fresh evidence comes to light—and it is unlikely that it will—we are safe in asserting that Haydn's last opera has come down to us complete and in four sources the combination of which provides us with a textually reliable score.' Recently, however, an opposing view has gained favour: that Haydn abandoned the opera before composing an apotheosis for Orfeo and Euridice. Silke Leopold has noted:

Der vorhandene Schluß ist zudem so merkwürdig, daß die Frage naheliegt, wieweit die Komposition als vollständig anzusehen ist. . . . Daß aber das Finale des IV. Aktes ein mehr als eigenartiger Opernschluß wäre, blieb bei diesen Überlegungen entweder unberücksichtigt oder wurde mit der Bemerkung erklärt, ein tragisches Ende sei, wenn auch für Haydns Zeit ungewöhnlich, so doch ästhetisch (für uns) allemal befriedigender als ein angeklebtes Happy end.[3]

(Moreover, the ending as we have it is so remarkable as to raise the question to what extent the composition can be regarded as complete. . . . However, the fact that the finale of Act IV would be a more than peculiar ending for an opera was either ignored in these discussions or explained away with the comment that a tragic ending, even if unusual for Haydn's time, is (for us) always aesthetically more satisfactory than a tacked-on happy ending.)

F. W. Sternfeld generally supports this view: 'such a *fine tragico* both for Orpheus and the Bacchic women runs counter to what we know about librettos of the eighteenth century in general, and Haydn's late operas in

---

[1] We should like to thank David Wyn Jones for this information.
[2] See Landon, *Haydn in England*, 328. Next quotation from 324.
[3] 'Haydn und die Tradition der Orpheus-Opern', *Musica*, 36 (1982), 131–5.

particular'.[1] But he is reluctant to accept Leopold's speculation that Genio was to have reappeared to preside over a Tamino/Pamina-style reunion of Orfeo and Euridice.

Both the assertion that the *fine tragico* was inimical to late eighteenth-century operatic convention and the theory that *L'anima del filosofo* is lacking a final act need to be examined in light of Badini's career and the artistic policy that Gallini had developed at the old King's Theatre. The last extant scene of Haydn's opera is what has been identified and defined in Chapters 5 and 6 of this volume as a chaos finale. This phenomenon first appeared in the finale of Jommelli's *Fetonte* (Ludwigsburg, 1768, libretto by Verazi),[2] and later emerged in *dramma giocoso* in the mid-1780s, first in adaptations, such as Anfossi's *L'avaro* of 1783, when the third (and final) act was cut, allowing the opera to end with the turmoil and chaos of the second-act finale. Soon, some works were expressly designed to end in disarray, dramatically if not musically. The best example is Sarti's *Le gelosie villane* of 1784. In Badini's own libretto *Il trionfo della costanza*, which was set by Anfossi in 1783, the second finale leaves the drama effectively unresolved. This device later reappeared in serious opera, most spectacularly Tarchi's *Virginia*, which ends in mid-rape. Unvarnished operatic tragedies, though rare, were certainly not unknown in London.

A few years before, Badini had derided the 'operatical rhapsodies commonly imported from Italy', and at least three of his earlier librettos included elements of parody: *Il bacio*, a satire on composers and singers with small voices; *L'inglese in Italia*, a burlesque of pastiche composition and foreign recruiting practices; and *La vestale*, a more subtle satire on *opera seria* with a feminist slant. The last was not so much a send-up as an attempt to create a drama that is both moving and compelling in its own right but also a witty critique of the Metastasian aesthetic it sought to replace. In this context one should recall practically the first thing Haydn said about his Orpheus opera: 'It is supposed to be entirely different from that of Gluck.' Someone, presumably Gallini, had already informed him that the idea was to move as far as possible away from Gluck's *Orfeo* or at least from the version with which Gallini and Badini were familiar:

---

[1] *The Birth of Opera* (Oxford: Clarendon Press, 1993), 133.

[2] See Marita P. McClymonds, 'Crosscurrents and the Mainstream of Italian Serious Opera 1730–1790', *Studies in Music from the University of Western Ontario*, 7 (1982), 99–136; ead., 'Haydn and his Contemporaries: *Armida abbandonata*', in *Proceedings of the International Joseph Haydn Congress* (Munich: Henle, 1986), 325–32.

Tenducci's attempted reconstruction of the original, which Antonio Andrei had helped adapt in 1785. With what Wirth calls its 'chilly rationalism' (rationalistische Kühle) and nihilistic ending replacing Gluck's humanized ritual and sentimental finale, *L'anima del filosofo* is an anti-*Orfeo*. But, like *La vestale*, it is reflective and analytical of its antithesis rather than being merely satirical. Winton Dean has written less charitably that Badini 'had been imbibing some of the more half-baked ideas of the Enlightenment', but notes that he 'was challenging history, and in particular the already classical treatment of Calzabigi and Gluck'.[1] The libretto displays a conscious, even ostentatious, awareness of its Ovidian roots, most notably in resurrecting the prurient side of the Orpheus myth: Aristaeus' attempted rape of Eurydice is the catalyst of her first death. In Haydn's opera she is bitten by a snake while trying to flee from an emissary of Aristaeus (here called 'Arideo'), who wishes to abduct her. The libretto also flaunts a knowledge of the early history of opera itself by quoting lines from Rinuccini's *Euridice* (1600).[2]

Haydn's reaction to this bastardized and inchoate libretto is (not surprisingly) inconsistent. For nearly three acts the score is a throw-back to conventional, mid-century *opera seria*. Most of the action is concentrated in simple recitative or happens off-stage, while large, virtuoso arias of stock emotional content carry most of the musical interest. Haydn was largely unable to overcome this compartmentalized design and even seems at a distance from the main events of the drama. Only once does he enter into Badini's spirit of parody and allusion. In Act IV, just before Orfeo's fatal glance at his wife, Haydn quotes the beginning of Gluck's 'Che farò' in the recitative 'Dov'è 'l dolce amato sposo'. Though brief, the quotation—in the original key of E flat major—is unmistakable (see Ex. 9.1 on page 600). This occurs at a crucial point in the drama: Haydn was hardly being ironic, even though Euridice sings the tune Gluck wrote for Orfeo. What is surprising is that Badini and Haydn should have retreated into *opera seria* here, of all places: Euridice's definitive death happens within the space of a bar and a half and is followed by Orfeo's extended reaction in *recitativo accompagnato* and the beautiful aria 'Mi sento languire', which in Landon's view is 'musically speaking out of place. . . . The words, too, are at painful variance with the lilting tune.'[3]

---

[1] 'Haydn's *Orfeo*', in *Essays on Opera* (Oxford: Clarendon Press, 1990), 99.
[2] Leopold, 'Haydn und die Tradition der Orpheus-Opern', 132.
[3] Landon, *Haydn in England*, 339.

Ex. 9.1. Joseph Haydn's parody of Gluck's 'Che farò', from *L'anima del filosofo*, Act IV

This and many other inconsistencies and apparent lapses are doubtless owing in part to the fact that the opera was never put into rehearsal.[1] When Haydn later authorized Breitkopf & Härtel to publish extracts in 1806, the *Allgemeine musikalische Zeitung* noted that *L'anima del filosofo* was 'not mounted on the stage and also not quite completed'.[2] The latter remark may have been an exaggeration. On 14 March 1791, Haydn wrote 'My opera . . . will be staged at the end of May; I have already completed the Second Act, but there are five acts, of which the last are very short.' But had Badini even finished the libretto? Study of the Larpent copies of his earlier operas, starting with *La governante* (admittedly an extreme example of writing on the trot) shows that even up to a few days before a première Badini could still be making extensive changes. In *Virginia*, too, several arias were added at the last minute and the entire first-act finale was replaced. The uncertainty hanging over the production of *L'anima del filosofo* would only have exacerbated Badini's usual bad habits, whether they stemmed from ineptitude or procrastination.

In the letter of 14 March 1791 quoted above, Haydn wrote that after hearing 'our *prima donna*' (presumably Rosa Lops) in Paisiello's *Pirro*, he decided not to use her in his opera. A hint of her intended replacement is provided by the inclusion of an unnamed cantata by Haydn in Salomon's

---

[1] Haydn's biographer Albert Christian Dies reported a conversation of 1806 in which the composer claimed that officials entered the theatre and stopped a rehearsal after only forty bars, and the whole opera was 'declared contraband'. See Vernon Gotwals, *Joseph Haydn: Eighteenth-Century Gentleman and Genius* (Madison, Wis.: University of Wisconsin Press, 1963), 132. There is nothing to corroborate this obviously embroidered and sensationalized account. Had such a rehearsal been planned and then interrupted, it would surely have been reported in the newspapers.

[2] Quoted in Landon, *Haydn in England*, 351.

concert at Hanover Square, 27 May 1791, sung by Nancy Storace. Landon points to a note in the Budapest score of the opera next to Euridice's aria 'Del mio core' in Act II: 'Cavatina—May 27. in the Opera of Orfeo.'[1]

Is *L'anima del filosofo* complete? This is quite a different question from whether Haydn finished it, which he clearly did not: the score would naturally have been altered and polished during rehearsals. Whether the violent and negative ending would have survived revision is undeterminable, since Badini was wont to make radical and unpredictable changes at the eleventh hour. Yet there were several precedents for such an ending in London Italian opera productions. 'Oh, che orrore!', the chorus of Bacchantes, does not, however, *feel* like a finale. It is paradoxically neither chaotic nor resolute enough; that is, in a chaos finale one would expect a stepped increase in tempo, perhaps some close imitation or other contrapuntal treatment, with the grim D minor eventually giving way to D major. The chorus begins darkly, is chromatically portentous and agitated, but simply peters out. This is dramatically very daring, but not musically satisfying. Even the immolation scene in Mozart's *Don Giovanni*, which is perhaps not coincidentally in the same key, shifts to the parallel major near the end. Haydn's opera also needs an 'Ah dove è il perfido', that is, a denouement, not necessarily a *lieto fine*, but some resolution of the musical tension similar to that provided by Mozart's sextet.

Haydn continued to work on *L'anima del filosofo* for some considerable time after he realized a stage performance would be impossible this season. He was probably encouraged by the example of Paisiello's *Pirro*, which was a great critical success. Why then did Taylor and Gallini not offer Haydn's opera in one of the King's Theatre concerts, without scenery and with the singers in their own clothes? For all its gaps, flaws, and inconsistencies, it is still far better than Paisiello's *Pirro*. The reasons for this seemingly odd failure to capitalize fully on Haydn's music are easily guessed: *L'anima del filosofo*, especially the final scene, would have depended to a far greater extent on scenic spectacle than *Pirro*; and perhaps in the circumstances Haydn lost interest in the project. The company's cancellation of this puzzling opera should not, however, prevent us from viewing it as the culmination of Gallini's managerial career and a legitimate embodiment of his enlightened artistic policy.

[1] Ibid. 81.

The abandonment of opera at the King's Theatre, Haymarket, this season was a late and unexpected development, and it forced the company into expedients. The musical repertoire from 26 March was a mixed bag. Each night the company performed a mini-concert in place of an opera act, followed by the sort of ballet that usually accompanied Italian opera. Thus on 26 March Part I was 'A Collection of Serious Music by different composers, but particularly by Paisiello', featuring Davide, Tajana, and Lops. This was followed by Vestris sen.'s *Divertissement* for the season. Part II was 'A Collection of Comic Music by different composers, but principally by Paisiello', featuring Albertarelli, Davide, Signora Cappelletti, and Signora Sestini. The performance concluded with a full-length *ballet d'action*, a new production of *Orpheus and Eurydice* featuring Vestris jun. and Mlle Hilligsberg, perhaps by way of compensation for the cancellation of Haydn's Orpheus opera. The programme was repeated on 29 March, and again on the 31st—in the latter case with a new *Overture* by Haydn added to Part II.

Because the theatre opened towards the end of March instead of in December, Taylor had to cram in as many performances as possible. Consequently the company performed on Tuesdays and Saturdays in head-on opposition to the Pantheon opera, but also on Thursdays, and sometimes Mondays as well. Some variety was offered by the ballet repertoire, but the degree of repetition from night to night was alarmingly high, despite various shifts and dodges designed to provide a semblance of change. On 26 April the programme was substantially revamped 'under the direction of Haydn', and on 12 May the company tried 'A Selection of New Music', including a song composed specially by Haydn for the occasion (Davide's benefit). On 24 May the songs were said to be 'all changed for this Evening'; on 2 June the programme was altered again, with songs 'entirely new' and 'an *Italian Catch* composed by Haydn'. When the programme was offered on 4 June a 'new Sextette composed by Federici' was added. The Haydn catch proved popular and was advertised regularly, but by 17 June the company was resorting to gimmicks. On that occasion comic songs were sung 'by two Magic Flowers, a real Tulip and a real Rose'—that is, singers were concealed in pedestals, upon which pots of flowers were placed.

## V. Ballet at the New Theatre

When Taylor and Gallini recruited their company for 1790–91, they naturally expected to offer the usual fare: an opera each night with a ballet after each act. In this arrangement dancers and singers were of virtually equal importance, but under the restrictions described above greater weight had to be given to dance. Among the singers, only Davide was truly a front-line performer, while three of the dancers were names to conjure with. At the age of 63 Vestris sen. was primarily a choreographer, but Vestris jun. was Europe's foremost performer and Mlle Hilligsberg was a proven partner for him. When, after three opera 'rehearsals' and a month of sparring, Taylor and Gallini decided that they could not risk staging opera, they were probably glad to have a company tilted in favour of dance, which would leave the audience with the image of a production, not just a concert. The results, however, were evidently disappointing: the ballet repertoire was old-fashioned, the dancers were uneven, and the theatre was unable to provide the technical support Vestris sen. wanted.

Evidence about the King's Theatre's ballet offerings this year is woefully sparse. The company advertised few dancers, and only one ballet scenario survives. Reviews are occasional and scanty. The inadequacy of information is particularly galling because so much is known about the Pantheon for the same season, and the imbalance makes comparison difficult. Yet even granting the lack of evidence, there can be no doubt that the artistic policy of the King's Theatre dance department was conservative in comparison with the Pantheon's—indeed, almost reactionary. The company staged too many flimsy pieces and too many based on Noverre's lesser creations, relying heavily on nostalgia. The newspapers were kind but evidently more out of reverence for the Vestris family and love of Mlle Hilligsberg than out of respect for the company's artistic achievement.

## The Dance Company
### Ballet Repertoire Spring 1791[1]

*Divertissement*, [Vestris sen.], 10 March 1791 (19 performances)
*Orpheus and Eurydice*, [Vestris sen.], 10 March 1791 (17 performances)
**La mort d'Hercule**, [originally by Noverre; staged by Vestris sen.], 'a new Historical Dance', music by Van Esch, 11 April 1791 (6 performances) (p. 612)
*La fête des matelots et des provençaux* [also advertised as *La fête provençale*], [Vestris sen.], 14 April 1791 (14 performances)
*L'amadriade*, [Vestris sen.], 'a new Historical Dance', 5 May 1791 (15 performances)
*New Divertissement*, [Vestris sen.], 19 May 1791 (1 performance)
*Les folies d'Espagne*, [Vestris sen.], 26 May 1791 (6 performances)
*La capricieuse*, Vestris jun., 2 June 1791 (3 performances)
*Ninette à la cour*, [originally by Gardel sen.; rev. Vestris sen.], 6 June 1791 (1 performance)
*La fête du seigneur*, [Vestris sen.], 25 June 1791 (4 performances)

[1] No choreographer is credited for most of the ballets this season. Vestris sen. was presumably responsible for the dances.

The dance troupe at the King's Theatre cannot be reconstructed from advertisements. Not even all the principal dancers were regularly named and, with two exceptions, *figurants* were altogether ignored in the company's publicity. No salaries are known, and there is no way to estimate what part of the alleged £18,000 performer budget was invested in dancers.[1] The company's full roster of dancers is given in a pamphlet that has apparently not been known to previous scholars: *Music and Dancing. New Songs, by the Most Eminent Composers As Performed at the King's Theatre Haymarket, with an Explanation of the Dances, Composed by Sig. Vestris, Sen. To which is added, a List of the Subscribers to the Boxes*.[2] This pamphlet seems to have been published for the night of 11 April, when *La mort d'Hercule* received its première: it contains a scenario for this new ballet. The company had not performed publicly until 26 March, and this was the first addition to the opening repertoire. Probably the subscription list was only starting to settle down, and any earlier publication would have been premature. The New York Public Library copy of the pamphlet includes an extra single sheet of 'New additional songs for this evening' that correspond to the advertised offerings for 2 June. *Music and Dancing* is of interest for its identification of subscribers and its concert programme. It is also a godsend to the ballet historian, because a full list of the dancers precedes the scenario. As of 11 April the dance company, including no fewer than 28 *figurants*, was as follows:[3]

Ballet-Master: Sig. Vestris sen.
Principal Dancers: Vestris jun., Vermeilly [Vermigli], Victor; Mlle Hilligsberg, Mlle Prevot [Prost], Mlle Mozon, Mlle Amant [St Amand], Mlle Augustine, Mlle Dorival.
Figure Dancers: Mr Hus, Mr Rogat, Sig. Gianni, Sig. Sala, Mr Gaurier [Gouriet], Mr Bourgeois, Mr Ferrers, Mr Puns, Sig. Giorgi sen., Mr Giorgi jun., Mr Arnoire, Sig. Casali, Mr Biache (?), Mr Roffe; Mlle De la Crois [Croix], Mme Dupin, Mlle Dromat [Droma], Mlle Prault, Mlle Fusi [Fuozi], Madam Ferrers, Mlle Peullié, Mlle Gabanel sen., Mlle Gabanel jun., Mlle Matthieux, Mlle Puns, Mlle Rivard, Mlle B. Giorgi, Mlle P. Giorgi.

*Music and Dancing* includes most of the principals advertised this season and shows that some of those not advertised until May and June were on

---

[1] This figure is claimed in advertisements such as that in the *Diary* of 5 Apr. 1791.
[2] London: J. Hammond, 1791. A copy is preserved in the Music Division of the New York Public Library at Lincoln Center, shelf-mark Drexel 5715.4.
[3] The list deflates the claim printed in the *Diary* of 11 Mar. 1791 that the King's Theatre had sixty *figurants* this season.

hand earlier.[1] Sixteen of the dancers named in the pamphlet are not otherwise known to have been in England at this date. Some were probably new to the London theatre; others may just not have been important enough to be advertised or otherwise noticed. These lesser lights include Arnoire, Biache, Bourgeois, Hus, Puns, and Rogat; Mlles Augustine, Droma, Dupin, B. and P. Giorgi, Mattieux, Peullié, Prault, Puns, and Rivard.[2] Many of these names are French, so Vestris had probably imported a number of them, but there are no hidden stars in this lot. That leaves eleven dancers with some known career in London who were not advertised for the 1790–91 season and have not been associated with the company at the King's Theatre until now. Eight of these dancers come from dancing families well established in London, though one Sala or Giorgi or Giani cannot always be distinguished from another.[3] Dauberval employed a Roffey, a Giani, and a Giorgi at the Pantheon in 1792 as his lowest-paid male dancers, and members of the latter two families danced in the opera ballet for at least the next ten years; the Cabanel sisters and Gouriet also continued to dance for some years after this. None of these dancers was ever to amount to much; at the Pantheon, by contrast, such *figurants* as Aumer, Fialon, and Boisgirard were to go on to long and in some cases distinguished international careers.

Most of the King's Theatre's *figurants* had not been advertised in London before. At the Pantheon salaries for imported *figurants* were quite decent (£70–80), but those for local talent much less so (£30–45). After seeing what London had to offer, Dauberval chose to send to Paris for Mlle Puisieux to complete his ranks of *figurantes* for the Pantheon—and that was in early December 1790, long before the first public rehearsals at the King's

[1] The publicized dancers are Casali, Vermigli ('Vermeilly'), the two Vestris, and Victor; and Mlles De la Croix, Dorival, Hilligsberg, Mozon, Prost ('Prevot', 'Provert'), and St Amand. Joubert and Mlle Aimé will be discussed separately.

[2] There is a musical family of Bianchis, one of whose offspring might be hiding under the deformation 'Biache'. The *Biographical Dictionary*, iv. 455, has a [Marianne?] Dromat, *fl.* 1792–95, but that is Marie Magdeleine Droma, who danced at the Pantheon the following season. She is the first of several King's Theatre employees documented at the rival theatre the next year. The Giorgi girls, otherwise unknown, are surely related to the male Giorgis, but how is not clear: the Signor and Ann who brought the name to England danced in the late 1750s and are not known to have performed after 1787. These may be their grandchildren. This Mons. Hus is surely not the choreographer from the 1780s, unless he had come down in the world.

[3] The families include Cabanel, Ferrers, Fuozi, Giani, Giorgi, Roffey, and Sala. For details, see the relevant volumes of the *Biographical Dictionary*.

Theatre.[1] Comparison suggests that the King's Theatre troupe was uneven: some major stars, and probably a few good *figurants*, but a steep falling off in quality after that. Any junior dancer with a choice would have been wise to opt for the Pantheon—a licensed and seemingly well-funded theatre. A letter to O'Reilly on behalf of Catherine Sala (a *figurante* at the King's Theatre from 1782) says that she would prefer to dance at the Pantheon rather than at the King's.[2] But she was employed at neither theatre, probably being considered too old.

As one might expect from the disparity between famous and virtually unknown dancers, the company promoted Vestris jun. and Mlle Hilligsberg heavily, and others almost not at all. Among the alleged principals, Mlles Dorival and Mozon were advertised for name roles, but Vermigli and Baptiste Victor were so rarely mentioned that their place in the company is difficult to assess. Mlle Augustine was never advertised, Mlle Prost only once,[3] and Mlle St Amand chiefly when she replaced Mlle Dorival for a few days at the end of March on account of injury or illness. Thus three of the women listed above as 'principal' dancers would be virtually unknown except for the roster in *Music and Dancing*.

Much of the dance publicity was devoted to Vestris sen. The company made few claims of novelty: the ballet-master's job was to stage ballets, not necessarily to invent them, and Vestris is rarely advertised as having 'composed' particular pieces. He was content to recycle ballets created by Noverre and Gardel. At the Pantheon, by contrast, Dauberval was at least restaging some of his own pieces. But Vestris sen. had been a celebrity when he visited London the previous decade, and now his own stage appearances were trumpeted in the papers to the exclusion of most other names. Despite his age, he danced the title-roles in *La mort d'Hercule* and *La fête du seigneur* and was featured in a *Minuet de la cour* and in the *Devonshire Minuet*, both of which were regularly transposed into several of the season's ballets. Vestris sen. appeared many more times this year at the King's Theatre than Dauberval did at the Pantheon, though generally in undemanding roles. The repeated use of the *Devonshire Minuet* as a special attraction is a measure of the conservatism of Vestris's offerings: he had introduced it a full ten years earlier (27 March 1781).

---

[1] See vol. II, Ch. 9.

[2] Bedford Opera Papers, 2.A.57.

[3] For deformations of this dancer's name, see the *Biographical Dictionary*, xii. 155. We prefer to use Anne Marie Prost, the form on her contract as a *figurante* at the Pantheon (Bedford Opera Papers, 2.M.16). If this identification is correct, the change in her status is telling.

As the season wore on, a few dancers from the *corps de ballet* were given a chance at identified roles—perhaps because the company was feeling the strain of thrice-weekly performances. Mlle De la Croix got a named role in *La fête du seigneur* on 25 June. Luigi Casali made a 'first appearance' on 2 June, danced a named role in *La fête*, was added to publicity for *Les folies d'Espagne*, and replaced Vestris jun. in the *Divertissement* on the last night of the season. An anomalous case is Mlle Aimé, whose 'first appearance' was advertised on 2 June. She does not appear in the *Music and Dancing* list, but perhaps she was a student of Vestris. Anne-Catherine Augier made her début at the Paris Opéra in 1793 as 'Mlle Aimée', and in 1795 she married Auguste Vestris.[1] Another anomalous person in King's Theatre advertisements is Joubert ('Juber'), who evidently appeared at Mlle Mozon's benefit as a guest, dancing a *pas de deux* with her as well as his own *pas seul*.[2] The fact that Mozon would reach outside the company suggests that she was not happy with the partners available inside.

The King's Theatre was competing against the Pantheon for its performers and, considering the circumstances, Taylor's makeshift company was at least respectable. However mediocre the rest of the company, Vestris sen., Vestris jun., and Mlle Hilligsberg were names sufficient to bedazzle the public. Unfortunately, the repertoire was stodgy, the new theatre not yet fully rigged, and money for lavish productions in short supply.

## Repertoire and Production

One of the traces of Gallini as manager at the King's Theatre in 1790–91 is a letter to J. F. Perregaux, the banker in Paris who was also employed for liaison and salary guarantees by the Pantheon. It is dated 24 December 1790.[3]

I beg the favor of You to send for Mr Vestris [jun.] & to inform him his father has begun to make new Ballets which makes it necessary to have all his Company here therefore pray request the son & Miss Hillisberg to set off certainly before the 5th January—if in the mean time they have occasion for some money pray advance it on account of their salary & charge it to me.

---

[1] Mlle Aimé was also advertised on 6 June for 'one principal Character' in *La capricieuse*, though since the ballet evidently did not succeed, it did not do her much good. For Anne-Catherine Augier, see Capon, *Les Vestris*, 268.

[2] Smith, *Italian Opera*, 21, either lists him as 'Mons. Mojon' or lists Mlle Mozon incorrectly as a male. Joubert was advertised as a 'principal dancer from France', but is not otherwise known in England unless he was the dancer named as a *figurant* in company rosters for 1803–04 and 1805–06.

[3] Printed here from a facsimile in Golden Legends catalogue no. 29 (Nov. 1988), where it is misdated '1729'.

My son will remit you some titles which concern Maddle Rose[1] —pray make her sensible of the necessity of her setting off at the same time or before if pleases—You will find in these letters that we want other Dancers—as to the figurants, if they cannot get two Couples they must get one at least good.

Since Vestris sen. was ballet-master hiring decisions would have been his, but Gallini had to authorize the spending of money.

The first ballets were not mounted until the 'rehearsal' of 10 March, when Vestris sen. produced *Orpheus and Eurydice* along with the usual *Divertissement* for the season. The latter proved durable, chalking up nineteen performances during the spring, but the newspapers provide no specific commentary on it. The *Orpheus and Eurydice* was presumably based on the 1763 Noverre creation at Stuttgart, in which Vestris had alternated with Lépy as Orpheus.[2] It seems to have been liked, managing seventeen performances, but reviews are almost entirely lacking. The *Diary* of 28 March 1791 commented that 'The grace, activity, and neatness of the motions of Vestris and Madam Hillisbergh beggar description, nor were Victor, Vermilly, Mozon and Dorival unmeriting of most commendatory notice', but offered no details.

Most early reviews say as much about the new theatre and the audience as about performances. For example, the *Diary* of 11 March, responding to the first 'rehearsal', found room only to mention applause for Davide and Vestris jun. Along with general praise for the building and enthusiastic notice of the higher-ranking members of the audience, the report describes 'a grand and regular Rehearsal' in which 'the Performers and Dancers were all in their proper Dresses, and the Stage was decorated with the Scenery meant to be displayed on that occasion'. One suspects an optimistic press release, because other accounts contradict this one. A diarist notes that, at least on 26 March, the singers, 'to avoid the [Licensing] Act', wore their own clothes and merely sang the arias, omitting the recitative.[3] This was

[1] Identity uncertain. On 4 Oct. 1790 Charles-Louis Didelot signed a contract for himself and his wife Rose with the Pantheon (Bedford Opera Papers, 4.A.24), though a notice in the *World* of 25 Sept. suggests that they had been negotiating with both companies. Why Gallini should be concerned with Rose Didelot late in December is unclear, unless she meant to break her Pantheon contract or he was serving as Perregaux's London contact for both opera companies. This seems unlikely because of his bitter break with O'Reilly the previous spring.

[2] Lynham, *Chevalier Noverre*, 167. Dauberval's *Orpheus* at the King's Theatre, Haymarket, in Mar. 1784 presented another story. There is no reason to think that the dances integrated into Tenducci's reconstruction of Gluck's *Orfeo* in 1784–85 had any connection with this ballet.

[3] Windham, reported in *The London Stage* under 26 Mar.

clearly an attempt to avoid prosecution, to which dance might be less liable because it was not spoken. In all probability the early ballet performances were costumed but without full scenic effects.[1] The *Diary* also says that 'the new invented stage of Le Tessier [Le Texier] contributes to the whole, 'for the Infernal Regions *will be* displayed by a perfect gulph of fire'.[2] This hint fits with later reports that the scenery 'could not be . . . sufficiently displayed' at early performances on account of the crush of spectators on stage.[3] Other reviewers commented on the Elysian Fields, which involved 'lights placed behind gauze', casting 'a filmy hue' and causing 'the figures [to] assume the appearance of aerial beings'.[4] Apart from general praise ('The Scenes and Machinery were grand and beautiful'—*Diary*, 28 March 1791), one learns little about the theatre's equipment, except that at Vestris sen.'s benefit it was either inadequate or not functioning.

By April, when Taylor felt confident that the venture would escape suppression, the dance company could expand their repertoire. *La mort d'Hercule* was mounted for Vestris sen.'s benefit on 11 April and should have given them an alternative *ballet d'action*. Despite minimal discussion of ballet by reviewers, the surviving scenario makes this much the best-documented dance of the season—ironically, since it achieved only six performances. To what extent technical and budget limitations proved fatal is hard to say, but the disappointment must have been considerable: this production was evidently meant to be the major effort of the season.

Just three days later, on 14 April, Vestris provided *La fête des matelots et des provençaux* for his former pupil Mlle Hilligsberg's benefit.[5] It proved popular, running up fourteen nights under various titles. This was probably a variant of ballets staged at the King's Theatre as *La fête provençale* by Hus in 1787 and Noverre in 1789. Indeed, one may wonder whether costumes had been stored outside the main theatre building and hence escaped the fire—in which case there is a strong possibility that this ballet was restaged in part because costumes for it were available. The only other production this season that was successful, at least in number of performances, was *L'amadriade; ou, la nimphe des bois* (5 May; fifteen nights), staged for Vestris

---

[1] See Walpole, *Correspondence*, xi. 232, quoted above. In fact, the eventual court case named Vestris jun.—a dancer—as defendant (discussed above, sect. II).

[2] Quotation from the second of two reviews in the *Diary* of 11 Mar. 1791 (emphasis added).

[3] *Diary*, 11 Mar. 1791; and see comments in the 28 Mar. *Gazetteer*.

[4] *Gazetteer*, 28 Mar. 1791.

[5] For Hilligsberg as Vestris sen.'s pupil, see Capon, *Les Vestris*, 264–6.

jun.'s benefit. Newspaper reports are unhelpful. The *Diary*, for example, says merely that the ballet 'does great credit to the taste and invention of the elder Vestris, the Composer', and that 'young Vestris, in the part of Hylas, performed with wonderful grace, spirit, and agility' (18 June 1791). However, *The Times* printed two negative opinions, couched in paragraphs, not formal reviews (23 May 1791). One asserted that 'The new Ballet of L'Amadriade—has not any pretension to the appellation of "Historical"—and is in every respect much beneath the attention of such dancers as Vestris and Hilligsberg.' The other grumbler made an invidious comparison with a *pièce d'occasion* discussed below: 'With all the applause which attended the entertainments of Monsieur Le Texier,—why were they not repeated? Sure the Animated Pictures would have been infinitely preferable to the still life exhibition on Saturday evening [21 May].'

The remaining five dances for this season were either strictly *pièces d'occasion* or failures. Lack of information makes evaluation difficult. A *New Divertissement* 'by Mlles Dorival, St. Amand, Provert and other Dancers, to introduce the Animated Pictures' at Le Texier's benefit on 19 May was probably never intended as anything but a *jeu d'esprit*, since it involved personnel ordinarily not considered worth naming. It was offered only the one night.[1] *Les folies d'Espagne* was produced for Mlle Mozon's benefit on 26 May, grandiosely described in the advertisements as 'an entire new Ballet' composed by Vestris jun. Over the course of six performances it accommodated several changes in cast and probably of component parts: it was basically a *divertissement* with an exotic setting, not a *ballet d'action*.[2] *La capricieuse* (2 June), by Vestris sen., is another nondescript dance with flexible components. It was offered only three times in the fourteen nights left in the season and cannot be accounted a success.

On 6 June the company mounted an unusual benefit for 'such of the Principal Dancers as have not distinct Nights, and all the Figurants'. The

---

[1] On 19 May 1791 *The Times* carried a paragraph that reads very much like a puff for Le Texier's benefit: 'The new dances at the Haymarket Opera-House have been so uncommonly attractive, and very deservedly so, for there never was any thing equal to them seen in this country. This evening they will be seen in their utmost perfection, and several novelties will be added to the general entertainments, particularly some Catches and Glees, by the best English singers. The House is expected to be very crouded.' The singers were probably borrowed from Covent Garden (see the 17 May advertisement), but the 'Animated Pictures' could presumably have been recycled.

[2] If the King's Theatre, Haymarket, did indeed have a costume storage depot out of range of the 1789 fire, it might have contained costumes for two 'Spanish' ballets from 1782–83, Le Picq's *Le tuteur trompé* and Simonet's *Le déjeuner espagnol.*

performance included three segments of dancing, the last of which was *Ninette à la cour*, in which Vestris sen. had made his English début as the Prince ten years earlier. In 1781, *Ninette* had been a major production. To attempt it as a one-off seems peculiar, even assuming that the two Vestris and a number of other members of the company more or less knew the ballet, and that ten-year-old costumes could be pulled from storage. It was publicized to promote Vestris sen. as the Prince: he was described as the 'principal Character' and his *minuet de la cour* with Mlle Dorival (presumably the Countess) noted. Ninette went unnamed. Mlle Hilligsberg (aged no more than 24) was the most logical person to dance the title-role, which would make the 39-year disparity between the Prince and the country girl rather glaring. Though the story of his unsuccessful efforts to exploit Ninette could have been played for revolutionary implications, Vestris sen. seems unlikely to have emphasized that aspect, unless his considerable vanity had mellowed with age. The advertising suggests that the company was hoping to capitalize on nostalgia, but, if so, the lure did not work: *Ninette* was not repeated. Finally, on 25 June, with only four more performances in the season, Vestris sen. presented 'an entire new dance', *La fête du seigneur*, in which he played the title-role. The list of characters—Colin; Tomas, père de Colin; Paysiens; La Dame and Le Seigneur; Colette; Cateau, mère de Colette; paysiennes—makes clear that this is basically a love-story ending in a 'happy peasants' dance. The seigneur and his wife presumably worked out some difficulty between the parents of Colin and Colette, and a wedding festival followed. But even if this thin and traditional piece was effective, it came too late to be of much use to the company.

The whole season feels old-fashioned. Too many of the ballets were so malleable as to have no definite form. The attitude towards dancers was that only the three stars deserved publicity, the ballet-master chief among them. While some choices may have been forced on Vestris sen. by the existence of costumes, and while analysis is limited by lack of information, comparison with what Dauberval was offering at the Pantheon makes clear that dance at the King's Theatre this season was backward-looking and no more than competently presented. Some of the conservatism may have derived from Gallini, and budget constraints probably did not help. The dance troupe was predicated on virtuosity and demonstration of the familiar, rather than the risk of experiment.

La mort d'Hercule

The four-page scenario printed in *Music and Dancing* and a complaint by Vestris sen. after the première make possible evaluation of the aims and execution of the company's principal *ballet d'action* for the season. Under Noverre's direction, Vestris sen. had created the title-role in *La mort d'Hercule* in Stuttgart in 1762 and in the Vienna revival the next year. The ballet had never become one of Noverre's hallmark productions: he proposed it for the Opéra in 1777, but without success.[1] Whatever the virtues of its dance, the story was handled awkwardly in places and the moral, at least in the English context, not very clear. *La mort d'Hercule* had the virtue of novelty, but for a variety of reasons it was a bad choice.

Vestris sen. kept the role of Hercules. His son was the age he had been when he created the role; but it had been conceived for a *danseur noble*, not one *demi-caractère comique*.[2] These categories were not mutually exclusive, but bending them required a kind of imagination Vestris sen. does not seem to have had. He did not take the opportunity to expand his son's range and pass Noverre's ballet on to another generation. Instead, he preferred to display his own virtuosity. Only the death scene demands much physical exertion from Hercules, so in that regard it was a good choice for the aging *maître*. Vestris jun. played Hilus, the son of Hercules and Dejanira; Mlle Dorival took the role of the wife who inadvertently causes her husband's death. Mlle Hilligsberg was Iolé, the princess who sparks the father–son rivalry and causes the wife's jealousy. The only other dancers named in advertisements are Mlles St Amand and Mozon and Mons. Victor, all of whom portrayed captives in the first act. The scenario calls for several crowd scenes, so other 'principal' dancers and *figurants* must have been employed in filling the large stage of the new King's Theatre.

In Act I, Dejanira welcomes home the conquering hero. Among Hercules' trophies is the 'captive Princess' Iolé. Hilus, 'struck with the claims of Iolé, solicits her liberty', and after a little prodding from Dejanira, Hercules sets free all the prisoners. Celebrations follow. In the privacy of the palace in Act II, the young people promptly fall in love, and Dejanira encourages them to think of marriage. However, Hercules, joining the family group, in turn

---

[1] Lynham, *Chevalier Noverre*, 91 and 167.
[2] This description of Vestris jun. comes from Capon, *Les Vestris*, 220.

falls in love with Iolé, and perceiving an amorous correspondence between Iolé and his son, excites his resentment against the latter, who seeks refuge in the arms of Dejanira his mother. By this circumstance, Dejanira, convinced of the infidelity of her husband, feels the serpent of Jealousy preying upon her heart, and Philoctetes tries in vain to sooth the distraction of her mind.

Angry and distressed, Dejanira leaves, and hence is unaware that her husband, 'brought to a sense of his duty' by Philoctetes, has agreed to the match. Later in Act II Dejanira suffers nightmares when she tries to rest: Juno appears and directs the 'green-eyed monster Jealousy' to disturb her sleep. When Dejanira wakes, she recalls the magic 'tunic dipped in the blood of the Centaur Nestor', and believing it will 'have the effect of preventing her husband from loving other women', dispatches it to Hercules.

Act III takes place at a shrine on a promontory. Vestris described it as 'a great place, at the bottom of which we see the sea, the pile of wood for the sacrifice Hercules intends to make to the Gods'.[1] Hercules 'no sooner puts on the vestment than he falls into a most desperate distemper, feeling within himself a devouring fire that circulates in all his veins. In the height of his fury, he falls on Lycas [the servant who delivered the tunic] and slays him, then sinks into the arms of Hilus and Philoctetes, who grieve at the unaccountable accident and the unfortunate hero'. Dejanira arrives to find that she is 'the innocent cause of his misery'. Hercules mounts a funeral pyre, which Hilus cannot bring himself to light; however, Jupiter sets it afire with a thunderbolt. Dejanira stabs herself, while Philoctetes prevents Hilus from immolating himself with his father. The story ends with a transformation from hell-on-earth to heaven, where 'Jupiter appears in all his glory surrounded by Deities. Hercules rises from his ashes, his pile half-consumed, changes to a pompous car, which carries him to Olympus. While he is ascending the spheres, he consigns his arms to Philoctetes. Jupiter receives him in heaven, and places him among the Demigods, which concludes the Apotheosis of Hercules.'

The scenario provides a number of opportunities for colourful dances by warriors, Asian slaves, and furies. Depending on how skilful the *corps de ballet* was, it could noticeably enhance the presentation, or throw the weight largely on to the principal dancers. All five principals have serious acting to do, multiple moods to convey. The women's roles seem slighter than the men's in the scenario, though they may still have had equal dance time.

[1] *Morning Chronicle*, 15 Apr. 1791.

Hercules unquestionably has the most difficult role, though more in terms of acting than of dancing. What one sees of Hercules, until he mounts the funeral pyre, is singularly unheroic, unless conquering his yen for Iolé is meant to be an accomplishment.[1] None the less, Hercules' magnanimity in Act I and the process of his death are imagined in the sort of detail typical of Noverre at his best. To have Jupiter, rather than Philoctetes, light the funeral pyre demonstrates that Hercules is special and prepares for the apotheosis—which, properly handled, ought to conclude the piece with the sort of *coup de théâtre* that sends an audience off too dazzled to worry about gaps and loose ends. There are, however, rather a lot of these.

The guiltless wife, manipulated by a hostile fate, ought to be sympathetic. But Hercules' straying, as Noverre chose to present it, is so brief and inconclusive a domestic drama that it is hard to understand why Dejanira should be prostrated by it. A more serious difficulty is the introduction of the poisoned tunic. How can Dejanira tell that story? She can show that the garment is special by approaching the trunk carefully and handling the tunic cautiously or reverently. The tunic itself might be sinister: black or too rigid. But she could hardly mime 'this tunic will have the effect of preventing Hercules from loving other women'. When Dejanira arrives at the scene of the tragedy, she must admit to being the innocent accomplice of a villain who is not present in the ballet. Her suicide is predictable, but the fact remains that an audience member who did not know the history of the poisoned tunic could not deduce it from the dance. Too much in the scenario requires the audience to remember its classical education, and some crucial bits of the story have to be entirely omitted from the ballet.

The failure of *La mort d'Hercule* was probably less a matter of casting or the narrative flaws in the scenario than severe deficiencies in 'spectacle'. Four days after the première, Vestris sen. aired a long and indignant complaint in the *Morning Chronicle* (15 April 1791). His making such a document public implies acute tensions backstage.

King's Theatre, Haymarket.

Mr Vestris begs leave to thank the Public for the favour they shewed him on the night of his Benefit. His intention was to give them on that night a spectacle with

---

[1] Noverre rewrote Ovid on this point, since the classical Iolé had suffered the usual fate of captive princesses before arriving in Thessaly and would have been of no interest to Hilus as a marriage partner. See Robert Graves, *The Greek Myths*, 2 vols. (Harmondsworth: Penguin, 1955), ii. 200–6. The death and apotheosis come from Ovid, *Metamorphoses*; earlier parts of the story seem to come from the *Trachinian Women*.

all its pomp, and worthy of this metropolis, if he had been supported by Mr GAL-
LINI according to his promises. Mr Vestris had then the flattering hope to give a
Ballet in its full splendor, and worthy to be admired by a tasteful and enlightened
Public.

Mr Vestris takes therefore leave to represent respectfully all that was necessary to
perform his Grand Ballet.

First Scene—A public place representing the heroic actions of Hercules, with a
Triumphal Arch.

Second Scene—The apartments of Dejanira.

Third Scene—Dejanira's Garden, and an agreeable Grotto where she falls
asleep.

Fourth Scene—A great place, at the bottom of which she sees the sea, the pile of
wood for the sacrifice Hercules intends to make to the Gods.

Fifth Scene—From which depends the whole success of the 3d and last act, the
Olympus descending, which shall fill the whole stage with clouds, and a Glory in
which one shall see Jupiter with his whole Celestial Court; Hercules shall appear
there mounting in the Olympus to receive his Apotheosis; the Ballet shall be concluded by a general acclamation of joy and admiration of all the people assembled
in the place.

Mr Vestris leaves an impartial Public now to judge if the Ballet was provided
with all the above necessary things—hopes from the same kind impartiality, that on
his side, such as dancing, music, ordinance of the Ballet, and in general all that was
in his department, nothing was wanting. There might have been some Scenes perhaps a little too long, which he proposed to shorten.

This was fancy, expensive, and impressive, but not in any way extraordinary, especially for a new theatre. Gallini had not made rash promises, but
in the event he and Taylor proved unable to deliver. What Vestris describes
as the key to the success of the finale is simply a *gloire*. Astonishing as it may
seem, the King's Theatre did not manage to come up with so vital a
machine for one of its keystone productions. Vestris would never have
embarked on *La mort d'Hercule* had he supposed that it would have to be
staged without the usual scenes and machines. A few years earlier such a
deficiency would probably have incited riots. Lack of audience uproar and
newspaper ridicule is testimony to the popular support for Taylor's embattled theatre. By the standards of the better seasons of the 1780s, however,
the King's Theatre's dance offerings of 1791 were decidedly a let-down. Perhaps the theatre could provide better technical support by late spring, but
subsequent productions featured happy peasants; the company did not
attempt another new *ballet d'action*.

## VI. The New Theatre in Limbo

The season concluded on 9 July 1791 after just forty-one official performances. A public announcement on the 11th noted that the subscription could not be completed but promised that the deficiency would be made good with extra tickets the next season, 'to Entertainments which, it is hoped, that they [the subscribers] will find more worthy of their liberality than those performances which, under the circumstances of the present season, have been permitted at this Theatre'.[1] This is a discreetly phrased admission that the King's Theatre could not survive as an 'opera-house' unless it could perform opera. The key to the peculiar and long misunderstood season of 1790–91 was Lord Salisbury's inability to suppress the Pantheon's unlicensed competition. Taylor had acted strictly on the counsel of despair but had managed to open and stay open—and between Haydn, Davide, and the principal dancers, his theatre had put up creditable competition against overwhelming odds.

During the season there were two attempts to negotiate a compromise. One of these was minimally publicized; the other appears to have been carried out entirely behind the scenes. At the end of February and the beginning of March, the failure of the January negotiations notwithstanding, the Pantheon party made a proposal to their rivals. It is spelt out at length in *The Times* of 17 March, and the chief points are merely summarized here: (1) All mortgagees and creditors with 'claims upon the Haymarket Theatre and property' (old and new) must sign an agreement 'not to commence any legal proceeding against that property; nor the person in possession thereof'. (2) All sales and leases of boxes in the new King's Theatre, Haymarket, are to be cancelled, and money returned. All goods and materials and labour supplied and paid for with box obligations are to be paid for 'upon a fair estimate'. All creditors who have been given box rights must surrender them; their debts will be paid 'in a rateable proportion with other creditors'. (3) 'Such annuity to be secured to Mr Taylor, as shall be judged reasonable.' (4) 'The whole plan to be submitted to his Majesty', with a request for a patent grant 'for such term of years as shall enable the trustees to raise . . . such sums of money as shall be necessary' to discharge immediate claims (that is, for labour and materials on the new theatre).

---

[1] Theatre Cuts 42, fo. [55ʸ].

Lord Cholmondeley appears to have been the intermediary. A letter dated 5 March 1791 from Taylor is appended, stating his 'total refusal' in case 'it is intended that Mr O'Reilly shall take any part, either directly or indirectly' in the management, though Taylor states disingenuously that he does 'not desire to be concerned in the future management' himself. By this time the Pantheon backers may have been prepared to throw O'Reilly out on his ear, but the creditors of the old theatre would surely not unanimously have agreed to waive all right to sue for their money. The plan presented by Cholmondeley represented the only reasonable way to re-establish opera on a financially stable basis in London: old debts needed to be shed; money needed to be raised to pay the costs of the new theatre without enormous inroads on its receipts for the next twenty years; and removing Taylor from management would have spared the venture much agony and embarrassment. But this desirable plan could not be implemented.

Probably no one really believed that Taylor would manage to open his theatre without his performers being arrested. As late as 18 March *The Times* reported that 'Vestris and Hilligsberg . . . have wisely offered their services to Mr O'Reilly' (for the Pantheon). But once the King's Theatre *did* open, it drained off a substantial portion of the potential audience at the Pantheon. The shockingly poor receipts at the latter in March and early April nearly drove O'Reilly frantic and, as will be seen in due course, by the middle of April William Sheldon had a shrewd idea of future prospects. Only a merger could save the Pantheon from appalling losses—but no plausible terms of accommodation could be found.[1] On 18 August 1791 *The Times* printed an unsigned notice intended to refute 'Reports of a discreditable nature' about the Taylor–Gallini management. It stated that 'not only the Building of the Theatre itself has been compleatly paid for . . . but that the Performers, Tradesmen, Servants, and other Persons employed here last season, have likewise been fully paid and satisfied'. There is some doubt that the building debts had been discharged, but there is no evidence of unpaid salaries this spring—because Gallini had paid them. At this point, he disappears from the King's Theatre: perhaps this further set of losses and the prospect of having to deal with Taylor was finally enough to cure him of his long infatuation with opera management.

After nearly a decade of bitter legal and financial battles, the temporary alliance between Taylor and Gallini at the new theatre must have been

---

[1] See vol. II, Ch. 2.

strained. We have sung Gallini's praises as opera impresario throughout this volume. He was undoubtedly aided by Lord Cowper and usefully advised by Cherubini, Storace, Tarchi, and the other well-travelled composers he engaged. How much he depended on deputy managers (particularly Ravelli, with his experience at Naples) is impossible to say. In any case, Gallini's achievements were considerable. Most important among them were the close links he established with Vienna and the introduction to London of the sophisticated *dramma giocoso* of Casti, Da Ponte, Paisiello, and Martín y Soler; the encouragement of post-Metastasian tragic opera; the appointment of Cherubini and Davide, which helped to precipitate the end of the soprano *primo uomo* in London; and above all the engagement of Haydn, who could not have arrived in England at a more opportune moment for his development as a symphonist nor at a worse one for opera. Haydn was not a great opera composer, and it would be pointless to weigh the London symphonies against an unperformed *L'anima del filosofo*. There can be no doubt that the history of dramatic music in England was determined to a far greater extent by the opposition of commercial interests and fickle noble patronage than by the pursuit of an enlightened artistic policy or the presence of a composer of Haydn's immense stature.

More than anyone else, Gallini, during the years 1785–90, attempted to harness patronage and commercial necessity for the greater benefit of Italian opera itself, and for a while he succeeded. Beyond constant bureaucratic and legal harassment, his ambition sustained three crippling blows. The first was the Haymarket fire of June 1789, the second was the reappearance of Taylor as proprietor of the new opera-house, and the third was competition from the Pantheon in 1791. If Gallini's view of the future of ballet was less than innovative, he none the less understood the necessity of hiring fine performers and might have been cajoled into financing *ballet d'action*. As we have demonstrated, the King's Theatre was able to function at a minimal level without anyone being in overall charge, with decisions about performers and repertoire being taken collectively by minor figures within the company. But Italian opera, even after eighty-five years of nearly continuous production in London, was still alien to English culture and could produce worthy results only under a controlling hand which, if not musical, was at least Italian. The problem with Sheridan and Taylor was that they were neither.

\*

What did the future hold for Taylor and his glamorous new theatre? The immediate prospects must have seemed precarious in the extreme. Taylor had no licence and no cash to cover another season of competition at a disadvantage. As will be seen in Volume II, he rented the theatre to Sheridan to serve as a temporary home for the Drury Lane company while Henry Holland built their vast new theatre of 1794. Stalling was, in fact, an effective strategy. By May 1791 rumours of cash-flow problems at the Pantheon were all over operatic London, and word of O'Reilly's flight to Paris that summer must have been music to Taylor's ears. Whatever discussions were held about possible accommodation in July and August clearly came to naught, but Taylor had secured himself at least a season's respite and could afford to wait and see how the competition fared. If the Pantheon flourished—or if its backers were willing to accept reasonable losses indefinitely, then Taylor was in a tough spot. If not, then the opera licence could probably be regained. To return opera to a concern so ruinously encumbered with debts was lunacy, but one must remember that the impossibility of the venture's ever paying its debts was not fully understood at the time. The other factor in Taylor's favour was the sheer size of his new theatre: it held a lot more people than the Pantheon, and so its potential gross was far larger. If London's opera company was to run without subsidy, then logically it ought to inhabit the largest building available—and that happened to be, after a fashion, the property of Mr William Taylor. Against reason, logic, and immense odds, Taylor had managed to rebuild his theatre and to open it in defiance of the law. If the Pantheon survived and flourished, Taylor's goose was cooked. If not, then with a bit of luck his eight years in the wilderness would soon be at an end. The great question for the future of opera in London was whether the Pantheon experiment was a splendid new beginning or a temporary aberration.

# Chancery Materials on Opera, 1778–1790

Bills of Complaint are listed here in chronological order with their Answers. Town Depositions, Affidavits, and Masters' Reports connected with these suits are listed below. Chancery Masters' exhibits are given separately at the end. We have included only substantive items, omitting most technical and procedural material.

## C12 (BILLS OF COMPLAINT AND ANSWERS)

(1) C12/578/30 (*Gallini* v. *Brooke, Yates, Brooke, Harris, Sheridan, and Hoare*). Bill filed 26 May 1780. Answers by James Brooke (8 November 1780), Richard and Mary Ann Yates and John and Frances Brooke (8 November 1780), Henry Hoare (11 November 1780), Harris and Sheridan (2 December 1780). Concerns Gallini's mortgage and his claim for possession of the opera-house.

(2) C12/947/18 (*Gallini* v. *Sheridan, Harris, Taylor, Hoare, Brooke, and Yates*). Bill filed 21 July 1781. Answers by Sheridan (17 January 1782), Harris (17 May 1782), Taylor (24 May 1782), and Henry Hoare jun. (12 November 1782). See also C12/584/35 (25 November 1782), an answer by James Brooke *et al.* filed under a separate number. Concerned with Gallini's mortgage and his claim for possession of the opera-house.

(3) C12/133/13 (*Smith* v. *Taylor and Rowntree*). Bill by Joseph Smith filed 22 October 1783. Answer by Thomas Rowntree (16 February 1784). Concerns opera-related loans taken out by William Taylor.

(4) C12/592/17 (*Gallini* v. *Crawford, De Michele, Grant, Sutton, Novosielski, Slingsby, Siscotti, Burton, Bromwell, and Stone*). Bill filed 3 March 1784. Answers by Peter Crawford (19 April 1784), Siscotti, George Grant, Sutton, Novosielski, and Slingsby (19 April 1784), De Michele (22 May 1784), Robert Burton, William Bromwell, and Richard Stone (16 August 1784). Concerns an effort by Gallini to oust Crawford, who was refusing to deposit profits in a joint bank account. Gallini requests that the court appoint a receiver.

(5) C12/947/23 (*Gallini* v. *Harris*). Bill filed 29 March 1784. Answer by Harris (10 June 1784). Concerns the sale to Gallini in June 1783 of Harris's interest in the opera.

(6) C12/602/50 (*De Michele v. Taylor, Siscotti, Grant, Sutton, Slingsby, and Novosielski*). Bill filed 17 December 1784; amended 11 May 1786. Answers by Siscotti (6 November 1786), George Grant, Sutton, Slingsby, and Novosielski (23 December 1786, 3 and 12 January 1787). See also C12/615/9 (12 November 1787), an answer by Taylor in this case filed under a separate number. Concerns money that De Michele, a former trustee, claims Taylor's other trustees owe him for a trip to Italy and for music-copying.

(7) C12/1546/73 (*Taylor v. George Grant, Sutton, Slingsby, Novosielski, De Michele, and Siscotti*). Bill filed 5 March 1785. No answers. Concerns the amounts of money Taylor's trustees were supposed to pay him and the accounts he was supposed to be able to inspect.

(8) C12/2012/53 (*Taylor v. Gallini*). Bill filed 22 April 1785. No answers. Taylor charges that Gallini conspired with Harris, Sheridan, and others to get possession of the opera-house, defrauding him of money in the process. Dropped by mutual agreement, 19 December 1785 (C33/466, Decrees 1785B, fo. 326ᵛ).

(9) C12/1989/86 (*Taylor v. Hayling*). Bill filed 18 February 1786. No answers. Case dropped on advice of Taylor's attorney. Concerns alleged overcharges for theatre lighting in 1780–81 and 1781–82.

(10) C12/1261/57 (*Taylor v. Crespi and Cole*). Bill filed 25 February 1786. Said to be 'amended by order dated 15 March 1786', but no amended bill or answers have been found. A countersuit to block a King's Bench action by Rosalinda Crespi to recover her salary as a dancer on a note of hand Taylor gave to her and to Nicola Cole, a hairdresser.

(11) C12/2012/54 (*Taylor v. Gallini, Harris, Richard Troward, and Taylor's trustees*). Bill filed 13 April 1786. No answers. Concerns charges by Taylor that Gallini, in his capacity as Taylor's trustee, has mismanaged the opera.

(12) C12/2171/23 (*Taylor v. Luppino*). Bill filed 22 January 1787. Answer by Thomas Luppino (14 November 1793). A countersuit to block a King's Bench action by Luppino for payment as theatre tailor.

(13) C12/2147/14 (*Taylor v. Hayling*). Bill filed 15 March 1787. Answer by Hayling (4 September 1787). Concerns alleged overcharges for theatre lighting in 1780–81 and 1781–82. Dismissed with costs to the defendant (C33/470, Decrees, fo. 259).

(14) C12/618/12 (*Storace v. Longman and Broderip*). Bill filed on 25 January 1788 for an injunction to stop sales and a claim for damage for publication of an aria by

Storace. Answers by Longman and Broderip (4 February and 4 April 1788).

(15) C12/1703/11 (*Longman and Broderip* v. *Storace*). Countersuit to the preceding item. Bill filed 12 February 1788. Answer by Storace (17 April 1788).

(16) C12/624/2 (*Taylor* v. *Hayling*). Bill filed 29 April 1788. No answers. A repetition of the previous suit, likewise dismissed with costs awarded to the defendant (C33/476, Decrees 1790B, fo. 441).

(17) C12/623/35 (*Storace* v. *Longman and Broderip*). Claim for damages, following a verdict in King's Bench. Bill filed 14 February 1789. Answer by Longman and Broderip (18 April 1789).

(18) C12/958/64 (*Vanbrugh and O'Reilly* v. *Taylor and Charles Frederick Brooke*). Bill filed 29 November 1790. No answers. Attempts to block Taylor's construction of the new King's Theatre on a site larger than the old one.

(19) C12/195/32 (*Theodore Henry Broadhead* v. *Taylor*). Bill filed 16 June 1794. Answer by Taylor (13 November 1794). Concerned in part with renters' shares and box rental from 1782 to 1789. Mrs Broadhead's dispute with Lady Jersey was recorded in *The Opera Rumpus, or The Ladies in the Wrong Box!*

(20) C12/661/3 (*Taylor* v. *Broadhead*). Bill filed 12 February 1795. A counter to the preceding suit. No answers.

## C24 (TOWN DEPOSITIONS)

1. C24/1883, *Gallini* v. *Sheridan et al.* Interrogatories for Sheridan and Taylor: 9 November 1782. Depositions: 9 November 1782, John Watson Reed, Thomas Lloyd, James Taylor.

2. C24/1884, *Gallini* v. *Sheridan et al.* Interrogatories: 28 November 1782. Depositions: 28 November 1782, William Cholwich; 4 December 1782, John Robert; 5 December 1782, Henry Hoare jun.

3. C24/1929, *De Michele* v. *Grant et al.* Interrogatories: 20 October 1788. Depositions: 21 October 1788, Thomas Walker, John Wiber; 22 October 1788, Peter Crawford; 24 October 1788, George Parkhurst; 29 October 1788, Felice Chabran, Joseph Mazzinghi; 24 November 1788, Charles Francis Badini.

4. C24/1936, *Longman and Broderip* v. *Storace.* Interrogatories: 9 June 1789. Depositions: 12 June 1789, Crawford; 13 June 1789, De Michele, Mazzinghi; 17 June 1789, Badini, Gallini; 26 June 1789, William Dixon (clerk).

5. C24/1939, *Taylor* v. *Hayling.* Interrogatories: 16 January 1790. Depositions: 18

January 1790, Henry Johnson, Peter Crawford.

6. C24/1940, *Taylor* v. *Hayling.* Interrogatories: 11 November 1789. Depositions: 11 November 1789, Harriott MacMahon; 19 November 1789, Badini; 26 November 1789, Slingsby; 27 November 1789, John Lowe.

7. C24/1964, *Skillern and Goulding* v. *Longman and Broderip* (C12/185/34, 24 November 1792). Interrogatories: 26 November 1792 and 6 December 1792 (two sets, with additions dated 6 February 1793). Depositions: 26 November 1792, Mazzinghi; 27 November 1792, John Wolcot, John Baptist Mara, Lewis Borghi; 28 November 1792, Gertrude Elizabeth Mara, Barrington Wood; 4 December 1792, Gregorio Patria; 5 December 1792, John Wall Callcott; 11 December 1792, J. B. Mara; 18 December 1792, G. E. Mara; 19 December 1792, Phillip Jacques Meyer; 9 January 179[3], Anthony Ravelli; 16 January 1793, William Winter.

8. C24/1982, *Theodore Henry Broadhead* v. *Taylor.* Interrogatories: 31 January 1795. Depositions: 5 February 1795, Howell William Grose; 12 February 1795, Abraham Holden Turner.

## C31 (AFFIDAVITS)

C31/230, no. 232: acceptance of Master's Report in *Gallini* v. *Sheridan* (4 December 1783).

C31/231, no. 74: Edward Day (4 February 1784); no. 76: clerk to Wallis and Troward (5 February 1784); no. 78: Parkyns MacMahon (5 February 1784); no. 322: Gallini (11 March 1784); no. 372: Henry Johnson and Thomas Quayle (13 March 1784); no. 670: Thomas Quayle (27 April 1784).

C31/232, no. 196: Henry Johnson and Edward Watson (24 May 1784); no. 210: Johnson and Watson (26 May 1784); no. 211: Thomas Quayle (26 May 1784); no. 251: Novosielski and MacMahon (28 May 1784).

C31/233, nos. 314 and 315: Gallini (15 July 1784); no. 322: MacMahon and Slingsby (16 July 1784); no. 348: Novosielski (20 July 1784); no. 395: clerk to Gallini's solicitor (26 July 1784); no. 489: Novosielski (29 July 1784); no. 490: Slingsby (29 July 1784); no. 678: Siscotti (27 October 1784); no. 689: clerk to solicitor for Taylor and others (29 October 1784); no. 690: Slingsby and Novosielski (29 October 1784); no. 691: MacMahon (29 October 1784); no. 717: clerk to Gallini's solicitor (2 November 1784); no. 718: Taylor (2 November 1784).

C31/234, no. 13: Siscotti (5 November 1784); no. 106: copy of the motion presented to the court (and approved on 19 November) that the trustees be allowed to repay

Gallini £2,849. 18s. he advanced for contracts and that the receivers appointed the previous May be discharged (17 November 1784); no. 567: detailed legal history of the King's Theatre from 1778 sworn by Gallini and Harris (18 January 1785).

C31/235, no. 29: James Seton (27 January 1785); no. 30: Taylor (27 January 1785); no. 44: George Grant, reporting the appointment of Robert Mawley as receiver for the opera-house under bond (1 February 1785); no. 74: clerk to Wallis and Troward (3 February 1785).

C31/238, no. 326: Taylor's solicitor (16 December 1785); no. 328: Taylor's solicitor (16 December 1785).

C31/239, no. 205: MacMahon (13 February 1786); no. 206: Taylor (13 February 1786); no. 233: Taylor's solicitor (18 February 1786); no. 286: clerk to Taylor's solicitor (20 February 1786); no. 387: Gallini (2 March 1786).

C31/243, no. 97: Taylor (3 February 1787).

C31/247, no. 38: Richard Long's evidence in *Storace* v. *Longman and Broderip* (28 January 1788); no. 39: Storace (28 January 1788); no. 81: De Michele (31 January 1788); no. 82: application for injunction (31 January 1788).

C31/248, no. 122: clerk to James Longman's solicitor (24 April 1788); no. 285: Taylor (20 May 1788); no. 286: clerk to Taylor's solicitor (20 May 1788).

C31/249, no. 45: Gallini (28 May 1788); no. 46: Crawford (28 May 1788); no. 71: Taylor (31 May 1788); no. 135: clerk to Taylor's solicitor (5 June 1788); no. 303: George Grant and Novosielski (27 June 1788); no. 316: clerk to the solicitor for George Grant, Slingsby, and Novosielski (28 June 1788); no. 355: Novosielski (1 July 1788).

C31/250, no. 211: solicitor for mortgagees (4 December 1788).

C31/251, no. 207: Taylor (23 February 1789); no. 251: clerk to Gallini's solicitor (27 February 1789); no. 255: Taylor (28 February 1789); no. 296: Taylor's solicitor (4 March 1789); no. 301: Gallini (5 March 1789); no. 372: Taylor (10 March 1789); no. 373: clerk to Thomas Holloway (10 March 1789); no. 425: Hayling's solicitor (13 March 1789); no. 534: clerk to Thomas Holloway (24 April 1789).

C31/252, no. 54: George Grant (5 May 1789); no. 70: clerk to Thomas Holloway (6 May 1789); no. 295: clerk to Longman and Broderip's solicitor (11 June 1789).

C31/253, no. 36: subpoena notice in *Storace* v. *Longman and Broderip* (16 June 1789); no. 212: George Grant (4 July 1789); no. 213: Longman's solicitor (4 July 1789); no.

215: Taylor (4 July 1789); no. 217: clerk to Thomas Holloway (6 July 1789); no. 228: William Dixon (6 July 1789); no. 233: Storace's solicitor (7 July 1789); no. 249: Taylor (11 July 1789); no. 258: Novosielski (11 July 1789); no. 269: clerk to Thomas Holloway (13 July 1789); no. 325: Taylor (18 July 1789); no. 384: Gallini (21 July 1789); no. 387: Clerk to Thomas Holloway (21 July 1789); no. 549: clerk to Thomas Holloway (29 July 1789).

C31/254, no. 249: clerk to Wallis and Troward (5 December 1789).

C31/255, no. 393: George Merrifield (22 March 1790).

C31/257, no. 360: clerk to Thomas Holloway (16 July 1790); no. 479: clerk to Harris and Gallini's solicitor (27 July 1790).

## C38 (CHANCERY MASTERS' REPORTS)

C38/708: Master P. Holford's report of 6 August 1783 in *Gallini* v. *Sheridan et al.* (C12/947/18).

C38/715: Master John Hett's three-part report of 21 and 22 May and 11 June 1784, and Master W. Graves's report of 12 November 1784, in *Gallini* v. *Crawford* (C12/592/17). For Exceptions, see C40/4 (12 November 1784).

C38/722: Master William Weller Pepys's report of 16 July 1785 in *Gallini* v. *Harris* (C12/947/23).

C38/745: Master Pepys's report of 7 May 1788, and Master Thomas Walker's report of 19 November 1788 in *Gallini and Harris* v. *Crawford et al.* (C12/592/17). These reports indicate that Harris had joined the suit and even put his name first.

C38/754: Master Pepys's reports of [no date] March, [21] July, [25] and 28 November, and [no date] December 1789 in *Gallini and Harris* v. *Crawford et al.* (C12/592/17).

C38/763: The Accountant General, Thomas Walker, certifies that on 4 August 1790 he drew up cheques totalling £4,597. 12s. 3d., payable to Gallini, in connection with C12/592/17.

C38/768: Master John Wilmot's report of 8 January 1791, in *Vanbrugh and O'Reilly* v. *Taylor and Brooke* (C12/958/64).

## C107 (CHANCERY MASTERS' EXHIBITS)

We have ordered this list chronologically, but the numbers are editorial, since Masters' Exhibits bear no piece numbers.

C107/64

1. 21 JUNE 1770: Thomas Vincent to John Gowland, assignment in trust of one-third part of the opera-house as a security for debt.

2. 11 JANUARY 1773: tripartite indenture among George Hobart, James Brooke, and Elbro Woodcock.

3. 17 FEBRUARY 1773: John Gowland to James Brooke, assignment of one-third part of the opera-house. Two copies.

4. 4 FEBRUARY 1774: James Brooke to Henry Hoare, mortgage of his share of the opera-house for security on £4,500.

5. 24 MARCH 1775: Henry St George Darell Trelawny to James Brooke *et al.*, 21-year lease of grounds and houses in the Haymarket.

6. 4 JULY 1777: Edward Vanbrugh to James Brooke, lease of the opera-house and other tenements.

7. 24 JUNE 1778: Henry Hoare of the Adelphi to James Brooke, Richard and Mary Ann Yates, Thomas Harris, R. B. Sheridan, and Henry Hoare of Fleet Street: assignment of the opera-house in trust as security for a mortgage.

8. 23 AUGUST 1781: Sheridan to Harris, assignment of the opera-house as indemnity against debts due.

9. 20 MARCH 1783: James Grant to Taylor, opera-house release.

10. 5 AUGUST 1784: Gallini to Harris, assignment of £4,282 secured upon the opera-house.

C107/65

1. 1 SEPTEMBER 1761: Edward Vanbrugh to Peter Denis, seven-year lease.

2. 25 NOVEMBER 1765: Peter Denis to Peter Crawford and others, assignment of the opera-house.

3. 1 APRIL 1767: Peter Crawford, Thomas Vincent, and John Gordon, agreement to prevent survivorship.

4. 24 OCTOBER 1767: John Gordon to Jonathan Baker, assignment of moiety of a one-third share in the opera-house.

5. 6 JULY 1768: Thomas Vincent and Adam Frederick Hesse to William Boulton, mortgage of a one-third share in the opera-house for £2,560.

6. 30 JUNE 1769: John Gordon and Jonathan Baker to George Hobart, assignment of two undivided moieties of a one-third share in the opera-house.

7. 1 JULY 1769: George Hobart to John Gordon and Jonathan Baker, guarantee of

fulfilment of share transfer conditions.

8. 1 JULY 1769: George Hobart to Jonathan Baker, mortgage for security, £2,300.

9. 17 DECEMBER 1772: John Gordon to James Brooke and Oliver Farrer, transfer of interest in the opera-house.

10. 5 FEBRUARY 1774: declaration of trust concerning rights of survivorship by James Brooke, Richard and Mary Ann Yates, John and Frances Brooke.

11. 25 SEPTEMBER 1775: Edward Vanbrugh to Sir Peter Denis, lease of the opera-house.

12. 19 JUNE 1779: Harris and Sheridan to Robert Drummond and Henry Drummond, collateral security for £2,000, part of £8,000 due on bond.

13. 17 FEBRUARY 1781: Sheridan and Gallini, articles of agreement.

14. 21 AUGUST 1781: Harris to Sheridan, assignment.

15. 7 NOVEMBER 1781: Taylor to Sheridan, bond of indemnity against rent on the opera-house.

16. 20 FEBRUARY 1782: Taylor's agreement with Domenico Angelo, to be manager.

17. 17 MARCH 1783: Taylor to Albany Wallis and Richard Troward, deed of trust.

18. 20 MARCH 1783: Taylor to George Grant, bond as security for £2,000.

19. 20 MARCH 1783: George Grant to Taylor, release; with explanation of how Taylor proposed to meet his debts.

20. 16 APRIL 1783: proposals, Taylor to his creditors (multiple copies).

21. 22 MAY 1783: Sir Robert Taylor and Benjamin Cole, Sheriff of London, to Harris, bill of sale on the opera-house, including property and stage inventory.

22. 28 MAY 1783: Sir Robert Taylor and Benjamin Cole's notice of selling Taylor's goods.

23. 19 NOVEMBER 1783: heads of an agreement between Gallini and Taylor's trustees.

24. 7 AUGUST 1784: Harris to Gallini, declaration of trust.

C107/66

1. 6 JULY 1768: transfer of interest in the opera-house from John Adam Frederick Hesse to William Boulton. Verso: transfer from Boulton to John Gowland, 22 March 1771.

2. 30 SEPTEMBER 1769: Peter Crawford to George Hobart, assignment of moiety of a one-third share in the opera-house.

3. 6 MARCH 1770: declaration by the Archbishop of Canterbury to Oliver Farrer

about trust arrangements concerning the opera-house with George Pitt and Jonathan Baker (deceased).

4. 1 AUGUST 1770: George Pitt and Oliver Farrer, assignment of a one-third share in the opera-house.

5. 11 JANUARY 1773: George Hobart, James Brooke, and Elbro Woodcock: declaration of trust concerning the opera-house.

6. 11 JANUARY 1773: George Hobart to James Brooke, assignment of shares in the opera-house.

7. 30 SEPTEMBER 1773: Sir Peter Denis to James Brooke and Peter Crawford, assignment of the lease of the opera-house.

8. 25 AUGUST 1781: Sheridan to Taylor, assignment of a one-third share in the opera-house for £3,333. 6s. 8d. paid, £4,000 more to be paid.

9. 10 MAY 1782: Taylor to Robert Burton and Albany Wallis, grant of a rent charge of £800 and theatre privileges for fifteen years.

10. 29 MAY 1782: Taylor to Maurice Lloyd, agreement for granting forty renters' shares of £20 each charged on the opera-house with privileges for fifteen years as a collateral security for £6,000.

11. 8 APRIL 1783: Taylor to Albany Wallis and Richard Troward, assignment in trust concerning Taylor's settlement.

12. 5 JUNE 1783: agreement between Harris and Gallini, with receipt for notes totalling £1,490, for which Harris resigns his rights in the opera-house to Gallini.

13. 1 JULY 1783: Sir Robert Taylor and Benjamin Cole, Sheriff of London: notice of sale of goods from a house in Market Lane to Harris; with inventory.

14. 17 JULY 1783: Taylor to George Grant, James Sutton, and others, deed of trust with signatures of creditors. (For details, see App. II.)

15. 25 JUNE 1785: *Harris and Gallini* v. *Crawford et al.*: Richard Troward's affidavit and a long schedule of papers submitted in the case.

C107/201 (non-theatrical items are omitted)

1. 5 AUGUST 1784: Gallini to Harris, assignment of £4,282. 4s. 5d. secured upon the opera-house and due to be paid on 6 August 1784. (Not found in the box in January 1994.)

2. 2 JULY 1785: *Harris and Gallini* v. *Crawford et al.*: Taylor's interrogatories for Harris *et al.*, allowed by Pepys, 2 July 1785.

3. 5 JULY 1785: *Harris and Gallini* v. *Crawford et al.*: Harris's answers to Taylor's interrogatories.

4. 7 MAY 1788: *Harris and Gallini* v. *Crawford et al.*: Taylor's interrogatories (allowed by Pepys on this date).

5. 24 APRIL 1789: *Harris and Gallini* v. *Crawford et al.*: Gallini's answers to Taylor's interrogatories (undated; made in response to a court order of 24 April 1789).

6. 27 MAY 1789: *Harris and Gallini* v. *Crawford et al.*: Taylor's interrogatories for Gallini (allowed by Pepys in his report of 27 May 1789).

7. 21 JULY 1789: *Harris and Gallini* v. *Crawford et al.*: Gallini's answers to Taylor's interrogatories (incomplete).

8. 8 DECEMBER 1789: *Harris and Gallini* v. *Crawford et al.*: Gallini's answers to Taylor's further interrogatories.

# APPENDIX II

## William Taylor's Creditors

Five sources contribute to this list of people who made legal claims for money against William Taylor: a notice in the *Morning Herald* of 6 June 1783, the deed of trust in C107/66, commitment warrant no. 4778 in PRO PRIS 2/48, the Discharge Book of the Fleet Prison, PRIS 10/51, p. 64, and Taylor's 1799 'memorial' (copy in PRO CRES 6/121, pp. 338–9). None of these sources contains information about whether individual claims were met. Obviously the list includes only people who tried to collect by means of legal action, and it probably represents only a part of those to whom Taylor actually owed money. The memorial reports many of the same names, sometimes with different sums. The following names appear only in the memorial: Mr Richard, £600; Mr Luppino, £320; Mr J. Grant, £236; Mr Dudley, £247. 10s.; Messrs Wallis and Troward, £560; Mr Bottarelli, £78. 18s.; Mr G. Thompson, £250. They are not included in the list below because these may be later debts.

Taylor's own version of the incidents that produced these documents says 'your Orator some time in or about the Month of March [*recte* 5 April] 1783 was Arrested by several of his Creditors for large sums of Money which he was not able to pay And was therefore afterwards removed to his Majesty's Prison of the Fleet where he remained until the month of July following during which time several Meetings and Consultations were held between many of your Orators friends and Creditors . . . to consider on the most eligible and effectual means of securing your Orators Property in the said Theatre and secure the payment of your Orator's debts' (C12/1546/73).

Throughout the winter of 1783, major creditors had been pressing their claims. For example, at the end of January Taylor had agreed to an instalment plan to pay Joseph Hayling (C12/624/2). In March Taylor signed deeds that directed his trustees to pay his creditors at the rate of 5s. to the pound over the course of the next four years (C12/2012/53). However, some theatre employees and a number of tradespeople who dealt with the theatre, lacking confidence in the trustees, chose to sue Taylor. According to commitment warrant no. 4778, on 7 May 1783 Taylor 'was Committed unto the said Marshal's Custody for want of Bail upon a Writ of Habeas Corpus directed to the Sheriff of Middlesex . . . at the suit of' the longest list of creditors of anyone that year. These were necessarily people who could afford to prosecute lawsuits. Some of their actual claims are not large, but most also sought damages. Because they appear to vary according to lawyers' advice, they are not reported here. More than one figure is reported for some people, presumably as part but not all of their debts were paid off. Since the Discharge Book largely duplicates the commitment warrant, it is not separately noticed here. A few people joined lawsuits but were later persuaded to sign the deed of trust. Even Taylor's trustees were divided. For example, Simon Slingsby joined the lawsuit on 10 July, but he was the twenty-first person to sign the deed of trust.

These lawsuits and Taylor's arrest in April 1783 put pressure on the trustees. They needed to demonstrate their good intentions towards the creditors and to convince as many as possible not to join the lawsuits. Beginning on 17 July, the trustees accepted signatures from claimants who were willing to settle out of court. The majority of those who signed the deed of trust were theatre employees of all ranks. They expected to continue to work for the King's Theatre, and many of them did not have the money to participate in lawsuits. Their best hope of collecting what was owed them and of retaining their jobs was to sign the deed of trust.

This list is incomplete. Among those agreeing to Taylor's discharge appears the name of Auguste Vestris, via an agent, which implies that he had a claim (Discharge Book, PRIS 10/51, p. 64). Claims for the singers Viganoni, Scovelli, Morigi, Nonini, and Signora Morigi appear only in the *Morning Herald* of 6 June 1783, but some are so large that they were probably turned over to agents, to be pursued after these Italians left England. Other names may be similarly hidden, since by no means every employee of the theatre either signed the deed of trust or sued.

This list precedes and is more complete than lists of employees protected by the deed of trust in LC 7/3, fos. 248 and 320. Identifications come from those documents; from the *Biographical Dictionary*; from vol. II, App. I, and from the *London Directory* (1780) and *Wakefield's Directory* (1790). Spellings and abbreviations of names follow the source documents. When first names are known, initials have been expanded. Debts over £50 have been rounded to the nearest pound.

1. Ackrey, Joseph. Deed of trust: £15. 15s. House servant. Pantheon lampman.
2. Adems, Abram. Deed of trust: £79 (by M. Novosielski). Memorial: £80. Painter?
3. Andreas, [blank]. Deed of trust: £20. Dancer?
4. Anfossi, Pasquale. Deed of trust: £370. Commitment warrant: £200. Composer.
5. Angelo, Dominico. Deed of trust: £614. Memorial: £300. The riding- and fencing-master whom Taylor hired to manage for him (see Ch. 3).
6. Armstrong, Miss [Elizabeth]. Deed of trust: £110 (by J[ohn] Moody, who later married her). Dancer?
7. Ayre, Joseph. Commitment warrant: £60.
8. Ayre, Ralph. Commitment warrant: £50; £40.
9. Badioli, J[ohn]. Deed of trust: no sum. Coal merchant. Pantheon tradesman. *London Directory*: Italian merchant; *Wakefield's*: John Badioli, Italian warehouse, 3 Haymarket, St James's.

10. Barthélemon, F[rançois] H[ippolyte]. Deed of trust: £118. Memorial: £114. Band leader and composer-arranger of ballet scores.

11. Bartolini, Vincenzio. Deed of trust: £200. Commitment warrant: £100. Singer.

12. Bennett, W. Deed of trust: £595. Memorial: £595. *Wakefield's*: William Bennett, coal merchant, Bankside, Southwark.

13. Bernardi, Angelo. Deed of trust: £15. Butta-fuori, or call-boy.

14. Bianchi, Gio[vanni] Battista. Deed of trust: £110. Commitment warrant: £107. House composer.

15. Blake, B[enjamin]. Deed of trust: £3. 15s. Violinist.

16. Blissatt, Edward. Deed of trust: £12. 12s. Engraver of ivory tickets. Pantheon tradesman. *Wakefield's*: turner and toyman, 209, Piccadilly.

17. Blunt, Robert. Commitment warrant: £28. 14s. 6d.; £23. 14s. 6d.

18. Books or Brooks, Mary, Executrix of Robt Robinson. Commitment warrant: £14.

19. Brady, Chas. Deed of trust: £40. Stage door-keeper.

20. Browne, William, Michael Raynes, & Joseph Langhorne. Commitment warrant: £65.

21. Bullock, Edwd. Deed of trust: no sum.

22. Buttall, J[onathan] and T[homas]. Deed of trust: £369. Commitment warrant: £120; £100. Memorial: £488. 15s. *London Directory*: ironmongers, Greek Street, Soho. *Wakefield's*: as Jonathan & Son at the same address.

23. Byrne, Thos. Deed of trust: £19. 9s. 6d. Box- and lobby-keeper.

24. Cameron, Richard. Deed of trust: £13. 5s. 6d. House servant?

25. Cannon, Richd. Deed of trust: £17. 2s.

26. Carnevale, Andrea. Deed of trust: £100. Commitment warrant: with wife, £51. Deputy manager.

27. Cervetto, James. Deed of trust: £23. 12s. 6d. Violoncellist.

28. Collins, Ann. Deed of trust: £37. 16s. (by her son William).

29. Combes, Anne. Deed of trust: no sum.

30. Cooper, Elis: (?). Deed of trust: £25. 12s. 8d.

31. Cooper, S. Deed of trust: £17. 11s. 9d.

32. Cotes, Nathaniel & John Compton (or Crompton?). Commitment warrant: £20. Pantheon tradesman: Nathaniel Cotes, mercer.

33. Crawford, Peter. Deed of trust: £125. Memorial: £125. Assistant manager and treasurer.

34. Crespi, Rosalinda. Deed of trust: £139 (by Siscotti) and £159. Dancer. According to C12/1261/57, she held two notes of Taylor's; hence the double entry.

35. Dale, William. Deed of trust: £13. 5s. 6d. House servant?

36. Dall, Ann, widow. Commitment warrant: £293. Memorial: £290 (as 'Ann Dolt'). Purveyor of scene cloth and canvas. Pantheon tradeswoman.

37. Dalmeine, G. C. Deed of trust: no sum. *Wakefield's*: embroiderer to his Majesty, 7, Bow Street.
38. Dance, William. Deed of trust: £5. 5s. Violinist.
39. Dauberval, John Bercher [on behalf of] Magdalena his wife. Commitment warrant: £373; £300. Mme Théodore Dauberval danced both at the King's Theatre and the Pantheon.
40. Davis, Rd. Deed of trust: £16. 2s. 6d.
41. De Baulieux, François. Deed of trust: £17. 10s. 6d. Dancer.
42. Degville, Sophie. Deed of trust: £57. Dancer.
43. Demaria, John. Deed of trust: no sum. Scene painter?
44. De Michele, Leopoldo. Deed of trust: £414. Memorial: £514. Music-copyist at the King's Theatre and the Pantheon; Taylor trustee.
45. Den, Francis. Commitment warrant: £77.
46. Dickinson, Saml. Deed of trust: no sum. *Wakefield's*: linen warehouse, 171, Fenchurch Street.
47. Dixon, [Cornelius]. Deed of trust: no sum. Scene painter for both the King's Theatre and the Pantheon.
48. Dowley, Ann. Deed of trust: no sum.
49. Duffield, Henry. Commitment warrant: £400.
50. Dunn, Elizabeth. Deed of trust: £20. Renter.
51. Duquesney, Lauts. [i.e. Lauchlin]. Deed of trust: £16. 13s. 4d. Dancer at the King's Theatre and the Pantheon.
52. Durbridge, Stephen. Deed of trust: £8. 17s. Box- and lobby-keeper.
53. Egerton, John. Commitment warrant: £100.
54. Evans, Thomas. Deed of trust: £10. Chorus member?
55. Fisher, James, and Peter Fisher. Deed of trust: £390. Memorial: £390.
56. Fox, Benjamin. Commitment warrant: £109.
57. Gaskin [or Gosken], Fredrick. Deed of trust: £12. 19s. 6d. Dresser.
58. Gerardi [i.e., Gherardi], Teresa. Deed of trust: £170 (by Pasquale Anfossi). Singer. Commitment warrant: £90 (also by Anfossi). Singer.
59. Giardini, Felice. Commitment warrant: £385. Band leader.
60. Giorgi, Gius[eppe]. Deed of trust: £77. Commitment warrant: £50. Harpsichordist.
61. Gough, Peter. Deed of trust: £12. 15s.
62. Gow, A[ndrew]. Deed of trust: £3. 12s. Violinist.
63. Gow, J[ohn]. Deed of trust: £5. 14s. 3d. Violist.
64. Grant, George. Deed of trust: £950. Taylor trustee. *London Directory* and *Wakefield's*: merchant, 1, America Square.
65. Grant, Isabella. Deed of trust: £11. 12s. 8d. Box- and lobby-keeper, or perhaps the widow of one.
66. Grant, Wm. Deed of trust: £200. Commitment warrant: £200. Memorial: £200.

67. Green, Charles. Deed of trust: £9. 16s. Box- and lobby-keeper.
68. Greenwood, Peter. Deed of trust: £22. 7s.
69. Guinand, [blank]. Deed of trust: no sum (by C. Dixon, so perhaps a scene painter).
70. Hart, T. [or J.?] Deed of trust: £2. 17s. 6d.
71. Harvey, D. Deed of trust: £43. 3s. Dancer (female).
72. Hatton, Wm. Deed of trust: £13. 9s.
73. Hayling, Joseph. Commitment warrant: £800; £120. Tinman and lighting contractor. *London Directory*: brazier, St James's Market. *Wakefield's*: lamp contractor and oil merchant. Pantheon tradesman.
74. Henry, Antoine. Deed of trust: £65. Dancer.
75. Holloway, Thomas. Deed of trust: £52. 10s. Memorial: £52. 10s. *London Directory*: attorney, Bream's buildings, Chancery Lane.
76. Jarvis, Stephen. Commitment warrant: £99; £96. 18s. 11d. Tallow chandler?
77. Keen, Wm. Deed of trust: £16. 13s. 4d. Dancer?
78. Kirkman [i.e. Kirckman], J[acob?]. Deed of trust: £47. 7s. 6d. (by J. Kirkman, jun. for his uncle). A member of the family of harpsichord-makers, perhaps the one who served as tuner for Drury Lane. *Wakefield's* lists Abraham Kirkman [Kirckman] as harpsichord-maker to her Majesty, 19, Broad Street, Carnaby Market.
79. Klose, F. [Francis]. Deed of trust: £3. 13s. 6d. Violist.
80. Köhler, Friedrich. Deed of trust: £6. 5s.
81. Lanz or Lance, T. (?) Deed of trust: £14 (by F. Gosken). Dresser.
82. Lee, William. Deed of trust: £6. 6s. Under-treasurer. Pantheon box superintendant and coffee-room concessionaire.
83. Le Picq, Charles, Esqr. Commitment warrant: £867. 6s. 8d. (claimed jointly with Richard Brinsley Sheridan, who may have been acting as Le Picq's agent). Dancer and choreographer.
84. Long, John. Deed of trust: £15. 5s. Box- and lobby-keeper.
85. MacMahon, Parkyns. Deed of trust: £150. Memorial: £150. LC 7/3, no. 187: 'for the business of the bills of the theatre; in the newspapers & otherwise, also for regulating the boxes & acting under the manager'.
86. Maddock, William. Deed of trust: £13. 10s. Box- and lobby-keeper.
87. Martin, Michael. Deed of trust: £9. 9s. 6d. Dresser.
88. Meyer, Philip. Deed of trust: £16. 12s. 6d. Harpist for both the King's Theatre and the Pantheon.
89. Miles, David. Deed of trust: £16. 12s. 6d. Constable.
90. Moore, James. Deed of trust: £18. 5s. 6d. Chorus singer?
91. Morigi, Andrea. *Morning Herald*, 6 June 1783: £275. Singer.
92. Morigi, Margherita. *Morning Herald*, 6 June 1783: £433. Singer.
93. Mountford, John. Commitment warrant: £500 and jointly with Richard Brinsley Sheridan £1,000. Memorial: £1,100. Master carpenter and scenery

supervisor at the King's Theatre and for the Pantheon company at the Little Theatre in the Haymarket.

94. Nonini, Signor. *Morning Herald*, 6 June 1783: £75. Singer (not advertised this season, but evidently a member of the company).

95. Novosielski, Michael. Deed of trust: £1,500. Memorial: £450. Scene designer; Taylor trustee.

96. Oliver, Jas. Aldwell. Deed of trust: £8. 1s. 6d. Clarinettist for both the King's Theatre and the Pantheon.

97. Parish, Charlotte. Deed of trust: £20. 17s. 8d. Dancer.

98. Parkinson, Wm. Deed of trust: £2. 12s. 6d. Violinist.

99. Patrick, Thos. Deed of trust: no sum. Lamp and tinman. *London Directory*: tin-plate worker, 94 Newgate Street; *Wakefield's*: pin maker to her Majesty, 27, Holborn & 43 Cornhill.

100. Patton, Robert. Commitment warrant: £130. Attorney?

101. Pollone, Clara. Deed of trust: £154. Commitment warrant: £100. Singer.

102. Price, John. Deed of trust: £17. 8s. Dresser?

103. Rauzzini, Venanzio. Deed of trust: £100. Composer and singer.

104. Rebecca, Biagio. Deed of trust: £21. Scene decorator.

105. Rennett, Charles. Commitment warrant: £400.

106. Reynell, Henry. Deed of trust: no sum. Printer and bookseller.

107. Reynolds, Saml. Deed of trust: £190. Memorial: £190. Money-taker, King's Door.

108. Rice, William. Deed of trust: £12. 10s. Box-keeper or under-treasurer. Treasurer and office-keeper for the Pantheon company at the Little Theatre in the Haymarket.

109. Rogers, George. Deed of trust: £40. Renter; perhaps the man who was proprietor of Vauxhall Gardens.

110. Rolt, Mary. Deed of trust: £6. 1s. Dresser.

111. Rossi, Geltruda. Deed of trust: £390. Commitment warrant: Dominic Rossi [her husband], £233. Dancer.

112. Rowntree, Thomas. Deed of trust: no sum. Moneylender employed by both Sheridan and Taylor: C12/133/13. *London Directory* and *Wakefield's*: agent, Essex Street, Strand.

113. Sala, Antonio, and Caterina Sala. Deed of trust: £46. Dancers.

114. Saunders, Joseph, and Edward Gray Saunders. Commitment warrant: £300; £105. Memorial: £698. 10s.

115. Sawer, Roger. Commitment warrant: £12. 17s. 4d.

116. Schinotti, Giambat[tis]ta. Deed of trust: £80. Singer.

117. Scott, Charles. Commitment warrant: £120.

118. Scott, Sarah. Deed of trust: £18. 5s. Dresser.

119. Scovelli, Gaetano. *Morning Herald*, 6 June 1783: £350. Singer.

120. Serafini, Joseph. Deed of trust: £23. 2s. Perhaps the prompter whose death

was reported in *The Times*, 8 May 1789.

121. Sharpnell, James. Commitment warrant: £364.

122. Sherlock, Samuel. Deed of trust: £22. 19s. Commitment warrant: £22.

123. Silvester, Edwd. Deed of trust: £40. Property man, a position he also held at the Pantheon.

124. Simonet, 'Cesare' [Ciriac?] (by Slingsby). Deed of trust: together with Zuchelli, £386. Commitment warrant: Ciriac Simonet, £386. A dancer by this name had been injured and demoted to *figurant,* according to the *Public Advertiser* of 12 December 1782. The sum and the entry on the deed of trust suggest that he and Zuchelli were acting as agents for Louis and Adelaide Simonet, who were owed that amount according to a notice in the *Morning Herald* of 6 June 1783. C. Simonet is not noticed in the *Biographical Dictionary.* Although Slingsby signed Zuchelli's name as Thomas, we have assumed that the man in question was Alessandro. See *Biographical Dictionary,* xvi. 373–4.

125. Siscotti, John. Deed of trust: £640. Commitment warrant: £280. Memorial: £640. Taylor trustee.

126. Slingsby, Simon. Deed of trust: £680. Commitment warrant: £680. Dancer; Taylor trustee.

127. Smith, Jos. Deed of trust: £600. Coach-master (C12/133/13).

128. Smith, Sarah. Deed of trust: £53, and £6. 1s. 5½d. for books. Commitment warrant: Sarah Smith, widow: £50. Stationer.

129. Stacie, John. Commitment warrant: £1,400. Memorial: £1,690.

130. Stevenson, Theo. Deed of trust: £14. 5s.

131. Stone, Marie. Deed of trust: £15. 4s. 4d.

132. Strang, William. Deed of trust: £7. 7s. 6d. Constable.

133. Sutton, James, & Co. Deed of trust: no sum. James Sutton, one of Taylor's trustees, was described as a silversmith in C12/2012/53. *London Directory* and *Wakefield's*: merchant, 1, Dyer's Court, Aldermanbury.

134. Tattersall, James, and Solomon Davis. Commitment warrant: £130.

135. Thomas, Wm. Deed of trust: £6. 16s. 6d.

136. Thompson, Hugh. Deed of trust: £17. Commitment warrant: [probably represented by] Judith Thompson, widow, £20. 4s. 6d.; £24. 4s. 6d. Box- and lobby-keeper.

137. Tomlo, S Phil (?). Deed of trust: £30. 18s.

138. Tonioli, G[irolamo]. Deed of trust: £34. 5s. Cellist.

139. Toosey, G. P. Deed of trust: £50. Money-taker, pit front-door. Pantheon box-keeper.

140. Trussler, Reverend John, DD. Commitment warrant: £30.

141. Turby, Geo. Deed of trust: £5. 4s. 6d.

142. Turner, Edwd. Deed of trust: £112. Memorial: £111. 7s.

143. Turpin & Kelk. Deed of trust: £54.

144. Varley, Anna Maria. Deed of trust: £8. Dresser.
145. Vidini, Vitoria. Deed of trust: £20. Dancer.
146. Viganoni, Giuseppe. *Morning Herald,* 6 June 1783: £403. Singer.
147. Ward, William. Commitment warrant: £171. Memorial: £160. Colour-man.
148. Warriner, Rich., for Geo Hesse. Deed of trust: £60 (renter).
149. Weltje, Tonir. Deed of trust: £73. Memorial: £73. Presumably related to the caterer Louis Weltje, who helped provide food for the coffee-room and for masquerades. See also C12/1989/86.
150. White, John. Deed of trust: no sum. Box- and lobby-keeper.
151. Whittey, William. Deed of trust: £13. 5s. 6d.
152. Willcox, Michl. Deed of trust: £14. Dresser.
153. Woodcock, Catherine. Deed of trust: £11. 18s. Dancer.
154. Wyatt, Edward. Commitment warrant: £153; £150. Carver and gilder. Pantheon tradesman.
155. Wyatt, P. Deed of trust: £160. Memorial: £160 (as E. Wyatt).
156. Yarrell, Francis. Deed of trust: £22. 14s. Commitment warrant: £20; £12. 17s.
157. 'Zuchelli, Thomas' (by Slingsby). Deed of trust: together with Simonet, £386. Dancer. See above, no. 124.

# Joseph Hayling's Lighting and Tinkering Accounts

As part of his defence in C12/2147/14, Joseph Hayling included his day-by-day accounts related to the King's Theatre for the seasons of 1780–81 and 1781–82. This unique record of lighting practice in an eighteenth-century English theatre comes in three parts. The first concerns performances, the second masquerades, and the third materials and services. Rehearsals for the first season are listed in the perform-ance account, but for the second season Hayling was directed to enter them under materials and services. In this transcription we have condensed repetitive entries that differ only by date, omitted most of the masquerade material, regularized the expression of pounds, shillings, and pence, and expanded abbreviations.

*

The Schedule . . . Containing . . . First, An Account of the Monies which became due to the said Defendant during the said two Seasons of 1780/1 and 1781/2 for Lamps furnished and Lighted &c Vizt

## Opera Nights

**1780 NOVEMBER**

25th, Stage Lamps, 214, 2 lights each: 428; Front Lights three Rows, 150 each: 450; Passage Lamps and all over the House as per List [not in Schedule]: 494. [Total number of lights:] 1,372. £3. 18s. Extra Lamps to move about instead of Candles Vizt On Blinds, 61, 2 [lights] each: 122; Fills, 110, 2 [lights] each: 220 Ground Blinds: 130 [additional lights:] 472 [additional cost:] £1. 12s. 6d. [Total cost for the night:] £5. 10s. 6d.

28th, The like this Opera Night: £5. 10s. 6d.

29th Lamps for Practice of Opera: Stage Lamps, 70; Fills Ditto, 40; Ground Blinds, 40. Five Gallons Oil used to Ditto: £1. 10s.

**DECEMBER**

1 [rehearsal] The like Four Gallons and half oil used: £1. 7s.

2, The like Lamps this Opera Night as 25th November except 48 Stage Lamps which did not burn all the Opera: £5. 7s. Added 50 Fills Lamps two lights each, 100: 6s. 6d.

4th Lamps for practice of Opera: Stage Lamps, 60 burning five Hours 7*s*. 6*d*.; A Ladder 20 feet furnish'd 10*s*. 6*d*.

5th, The like Lamps this Opera Night as the second instant the whole burning all the Opera £5. 17*s*.

9th, 12th, 16th, 19th, The like this Opera Night £5. 17*s*.

22nd, Lamps for Practice Scenes &c. 2 Gallons Oil 12*s*.

23rd, 30th, The like this Opera Night as 2nd instant £5. 17*s*.

## 1781 JANUARY

1st [*recte* 2nd], 6th, The like this Opera Night £5. 17*s*.

9th, The like this Opera Night £5. 17*s*.; 4 Back Blinds 96 Lights not lighted - 5*s*. 6*d*. [=] £5. 11*s*. 6*d*.

13th, The like this Opera Night £5. 11*s*. 6*d*.

16th, The like this Opera Night £5. 17*s*.

20th, The like this Opera Night £5. 11*s*. 6*d*.; 2 Ground Blinds 20 Lights each added + 3*s*. 6*d*. [=] £5. 15*s*.

23rd, The like this Opera Night £5. 15*s*.

27th, The like this Opera Night £5. 15*s*.; Lamps for practice the 21st instant the Opera Methridates four Gallons of Oil and attendance £1. 6*s*. 6*d*.

29th, The like this Opera Night as 20th instant £5. 15*s*.

## FEBRUARY

3rd, 6th, 8th, The like this Opera Night £5. 15*s*.

9th 50 Stage Lamps for Practice 6 Quarts Oil 9*s*.

10th, The like this Opera Night as last £5. 15*s*.

12th 40 Fills Lamps for Practice 5 Quarts Oil to ditto 7*s*. 6*d*.

13th, The like this Opera Night as last £5. 15*s*.

14th Lamps for Practicing Scenes &c 50 Stage Lamps, 60 Fills and top of House 11 Quarts Oil 16*s*. 6*d*.

15th The like this Opera Night as last £5. 15*s*. [Performance accidentally omitted in *The London Stage*. Newspaper advertisements list *Rinaldo* with *The Fortunate Escape, Grand Serious Ballet*, and *Les amans surpris*.]

16th Lamps for Practice Stage Lamps 50; Fills Ditto 50; 6 Ditto every day this Week 19*s*. 6*d*.

17th, The like this Opera Night as last £5. 15*s*.

19th Lamps for Practice &c Stage Lamps 40; Fills Ditto 20; and Ditto top of the House; Ten Quarts of Oil 15*s*.

20th, The like this Opera Night as last £5. 15*s*.

21st Lamps for Practice Scenes and Opera Stage Lamps, 80, 2 lights each 160; Front Lights two Rows, 150 Ditto, 300; Fills, 100, 2 Ditto 200; Twenty Lanthorns, 2 Ditto 40; 1 ten Ground Blind 10; Lamps lighted top of the House [total:] £2. 14*s*. 6*d*.

22nd, The like Opera this Night, Benefit Monsr Vestris [jun.], as 20th instant £5. 15*s*. 6*d*.; 1 Row more front Lights added and Lamps burning longer than usual: £1. 6*s*. 6*d*.: [total:] £7. 1*s*. 6*d*.

24th, The like this Opera Night as 20th instant £5. 15*s*. 6*d*.; One Row front Lights more, 150: 8*s*. 6*d*. [total:] £6. 3*s*. 6*d*.

27th, The like this Opera Night as last £6. 3*s*. 6*d*.

**MARCH**

1st, 3rd, 6th, The like this Opera Night £6. 3*s*. 6*d*.

8th, Benefit of Roncalio [Roncaglia]; The like this Opera Night £ 6. 3*s*. 6*d*.; Fills, 50, 2 each left off - 6*s*. [ = ] £5. 17*s*. 6*d*.

10th, 13th, 15th, 17th, 20th, 24th, 27th, The like this Opera Night as last £5. 17*s*. 6*d*.

28th Lamps for Practice &c.; Stage Lamps, 100, 2 lights each 200; Fills Ditto, 120, Ditto 240; Front Lights one Row 150; Top of the House 1 each 70; Ten Lanthorns, 2 each 20; [total number of lights:] 680; Ditto ditto lighted again 680 [total cost:] £4. 9*s*.

29th, [benefit for] Monsr Vestris Senior; The like Lamps this opera Night as 27th instant £5. 17*s*. 6*d*.

31st, The like this Opera Night £5. 17*s*. 6*d*.

**APRIL**

3d, 5th, 7th, The like this Opera Night £5. 17*s*. 6*d*.

[9–14 Passion Week]

17th, The like this Opera Night £5. 17*s*. 6*d*.

19th, Lamps lighted as usual for Benefit of Decayed Musicians [concert not in *The London Stage*]: £3. 0*s*.

21st, 24th, The like this Opera Night as 17th instant £5. 17*s*. 6*d*.

26th, The like this Opera Night Benefit Miss [*recte* Adelaide] Simonet £5. 17*s*. 6*d*.

28th, The like this Opera Night £5. 17*s*. 6*d*.

MAY

1st, The like this Opera Night £5. 17s. 6d.; To an extra Man to attend the Lamps as Till refused to attend as usual 1s. 6d.; [total:] £5. 19s.

4th [i.e., 5th], 8th, 10th, 12th, 15th, 19th, 22nd, 26th, The like this Opera Night £5. 19s.

27th Lighting Lamps Practising, two Gallons Oil &c 13s. 6d.

29th, 31st, The like this Opera Night as 26th instant £5. 19s.

JUNE

[5 June. Hayling treated *L'omaggio* as a masquerade and listed all four performances, untitled, in his masquerade account. Scores of small lamps were lighted each night, but because some of the decorations had to be altered or replaced and the socializing lasted different lengths of time, he charged very different rates. Preparations and the cost of lighting the first night came to £69. 14s. (5 June 1781). A domed framework such as he describes is illustrated in *Survey of London*, xxx, plate 25b. Itemization the first night was as follows: Lighting and Furnishing 2707 Illuminating Lamps: £38. 3s. 0d.; 8 Festunes Altering and fixing with New Hooks Tea Room: 9s. 0d.; 12 Ribbs for a Doom [dome] 19 Hooks each for Lamps and Nailing on at 3s.: £1. 16s. 0d.; a Tin Ornament for Top with 72 Hooks: 18s. 0d.; A Circle for Doom and fixing: 7s. 0d.; two Arches for 50 Lamps each: 15s. 0d.; 9 Diamonds on Arches for 15 Lamps and fixing: £1. 7s. 0d.; 19 Pyramids 27 Hooks and fixing at 9s. each: £8. 11s. 0d.; 62 Rounds, 9 [lamps] each at 1s. 6d. each: £4. 13s. 0d. 61 Diamonds at 1s. each: £3. 1s. 0d.; 2 large Sprays and fixing at 6s. 6d. each: 13s. 0d.; 12 Festunes altered in the Gallery at 1s. 6d. each: 18s. 0d.; 32 Pyramids at 1s. 6d. each: £2. 8s. 0d.; 32 Small Festunes to Ditto at 6d. each: 16s. 0d.; Altering Festunes and fixing 12 Ovals Staples I: 11s. 0d.; 17 Benacled Lamps fixed Top Pedaments two lights each: 17s. 0d.; Lighting Lamps to work by on the Stage: 7s. 6d.; Sending to Carlisle House for Lamps three times and to Drury Lane Theatre per the Order of Mr Sheridan: 6s. 0d.; Lighting the Lamps in the Passages: £2. 12s. 6d. The cost of the 8 June performance was £51. 4s. 6d., with the basic lighting charge at £47. 2s. because Hayling added 660 lamps. Despite many repairs, the last two performances were less expensive. Hayling lit only 1835 lamps and he deducted £4 on each of those nights 'as an Allowance for Lights not burning so long as usual'. Consequently he charged only £27. 0s. 4d. (14 June) and £40. 2s. 4d. (16 June).]

9th, 12th, 19th, 21st, 23rd, 26th, 30th, The like this Opera Night £5. 19s.

JULY

3, The like this Opera Night £5. 19s.

## 1781 Opera Nights this Season

**NOVEMBER**

17th, Stage Lamps, 214, 2 lights each 428; Fronts Lights three Rows, 150 each 450; Passage Lamps & all about the House as per List [not in Schedule] 494; [total lights:] 1372 [total cost:] £3. 18*s.*; Extra Lamps behind the Scenes to move about instead of Candles Vizt Ground Blinds, 4, ten each 40; Ditto, 6, fifteen each 90; One Row more front Lights 150; Stage Lamps added, 40, 2 lights each 128; 24 Lanthorns about the House; Fills Lamps, 120 each 240 [additional cost] £2. 2*s.* 6*d.* 648 [additional lights]. [Grand total:] £6. 0*s.* 6*d.*

20th, The like Lamps this Opera Night £6. 0*s.* 6*d.*; Fills Lamps above 60, 2 lights, 120 7*s.* [total:] £6. 7*s.* 6*d.*

24th, The like this Opera Night £6. 7*s.* 6*d.*; Except one Row front Lights left off, 150 - 8*s.* 6*d.* [ = ] £5. 19*s.*

28th, The like Opera this Night £5. 19*s.*

**DECEMBER**

1, The like Opera this Night £5. 19*s.*

4th, The like Opera this Night £5. 19*s.*; Fills, 40, 2 lights each 80 3*s.* 6*d.* [total:] £6. 2*s.* 6*d.*

8th, 11th, The like this Opera Night £6. 2*s.* 6*d.*

13th, The like this Opera Night £6. 2*s.* 6*d.* [Dismissed? See ' Oil . . . furnished', below.]

15th, 20th, 22nd, 27th, 29th, The like this Opera Night £6. 2*s.* 6*d.*

**1782 JANUARY**

1st, 5th, 8th, 10th, 12th, 15th, 17th, 19th, 22nd, The like this Opera Night £6. 2*s.* 6*d.*

25th Lighting Lamps this Night; Benefit decayed Musicians [concert not in *The London Stage*]: £3. 0*s.* 0*d.*

26th, 29th, 31st, The like Lamps this Opera Night as 22nd instant £6. 2*s.* 6*d.*

**FEBRUARY**

2nd, 5th, 7th, 9th, 12th, 14th, 16th, 19th, 21st, 23rd, 26th, 28th, The like this Opera Night £6. 2*s.* 6*d.*

**MARCH**

2nd, 5th, The like this Opera Night £6. 2*s.* 6*d.*

7th, Extra Oil Benefit Paccheroti £6. 11*s.*

9th, 12th, 14th, 16th, The like this Opera Night as 5th instant £6. 2*s.* 6*d.*

19th, Extra Oil, Benefit [Mlle] Theodore £6. 11*s.*

21st, The like this Opera Night as 16th instant £6. 2*s.*

23rd, The like this Opera Night £6. 2*s.* 6*d.*

[25–30 Passion Week]

**APRIL**

2nd, 4th, 6th, 9th, The like this Opera Night £6. 2*s.* 6*d.* [See below: Three Gallons of oil for practice 2 April.]

11th, The like this Opera Night £6. 2*s.* 6*d.*; Extra Oil, Benefit Monsr Novere £7. 12*s.*

13th, The like this Opera Night as 9th instant £6. 2*s.* 6*d.*; Fills 10 Lamps, 2 lights each 20 added: 1*s.* 6*d.*: £6. 4*s.*

16th, The like this Opera Night £6. 4*s.*

[18th] Extra Oil, Benefit [Signora] Allegrante £6. 11*s.*

20th, 23rd, 25th, 27th, The like this Opera Night as 16th instant £6. 4*s.*

30th Extra Oil, Benefit [Mme] Simonett £6. 11*s.*

**MAY**

4th, 7th, The like this Opera Night as 27th [April] £6. 4*s.*

9th Extra Oil, Benefit Monsr Gardell £7. 12*s.*

11th, 14th, The like this Opera Night as 7th instant £6. 4*s.*

16th Extra Oil, Benefit Nevelon £6. 17*s.*

17 The like Lamps this opera Night as 14th instant £6. 4*s.*

21st The like this Opera Night £6. 4*s.*

23rd Extra Oil benefit Sestini £6. 11*s.*

25th The like this Opera Night as the 21st instant £6. 4*s.*

27th Extra Oil Benefit Mrs [J. C.] Bach £6. 11*s.*

**JUNE**

1st The like this Opera Night as the 25th [May] £6. 4*s.*

5th Extra Oil Benefit Le Picq £6. 11*s.*

6th, 8th, 11th, 15th, 18th, 22nd, The like this Opera Night as 1st instant £6. 4*s.*

26th [*recte* 25th] The like this Opera Night £6. 4*s.*

29th The like this Opera Night £6. 4*s.*

[Hayling's masquerade accounts are omitted here.]

An Account of all the Oil and other Materials and Necessarys by the said Defendant furnished to and for the use of the said Theatre during the said two Seasons (Except as above said) together with the times the materials were so furnished and also the just and fair prices of all such Oil and other Materials Vizt

1780 SEPTEMBER

19th To a Tinder Box and Steel 8*d.*

22nd A Glue Pot Carpenters 2*s.* 6*d.*

26 two Quarts of Oil for Lamps for House 3*s.*

NOVEMBER

10th 1 Gallon of Ditto 6*s.*

14th 1 Gallon of Ditto 6*s.*

18th a pound of Tow 4*d.*

20th 1 Gallon of Oil 6*s.*

23rd One Gallon of Ditto 6*s.*

24 200 Tin Sockets for Transparencies and Nailing on One hundred 10*s.* 5*d.*; two Lanthorns mended 4*d.*

25th 12 two light Glass Lamps with Tops 8*s.*; a Fork for Neptune 1*s.* 6*d.*; One Gallon of Oil Mrs Doyles Lamps 6*s.*

27 Six Dozen of Lamp Pipes Ground Lights 3*s.*; A Tin for a Wood Pine Apple 1*s.*; Six Candlesticks Musick Porter 1*s.* 6*d.*; One hundred and forty Straps for Fills Lamps 3*s.*

29th One Gallon Oil 6*s.*; Twenty Six New Tops to stage Lamps 3*s.*; Fifty Ground Light Pipes 6*s.* 4*d.*

30 a Gallon Oil House Lamps 6*s.* 4*d.*

DECEMBER

1 A Gallon Ditto Practice 6*s.*; a Water Pot 2*s.* 6*d.*; a Gallon Oil Practice 6*s.*

2d A Gallon Ditto 6*s.*; Thirteen Tins mending Caps 2*s.* 2*d.*; Fifty pipes Ground Lights, Sixty Six Ditto Fills Lamps 12*s.* 8*d.*; Thirty Six Tops for Stage Lamps 100 Lamps 100 backs, New Fills Lamps £5. 0*s.*; 114 Sockets to Nail on for Candles 9*s.* 6*d.*; 100 Straps and Nailing up for Fills Lamps 4*s.* 2*d.*; A Man repairing the Wings three Days &c Nails 10*s.* 6*d.*

5th Mending a Brass Sconce 1*s.*

6th two Gallons Oil Practice 12*s.*

7th One Gallon Ditto 6s.; Lighting a Lamp from 26th November 1779 to 26th November 1780 £1. 16s.

11th A Gallon of Oil 6s.

12 A Glass Lamp fitted to a Rim 5s.; a Burner to Ditto 6d. [total:] 5s. 6d.

13th A Gallon Oil 6s.

14th a Jappaned Candlestick and extra Snuffers, Painter 2s. 6d.

15th A Gallon of Oil 6s.

16th two pair Snuffers 1s.

18th a Gallon of Oil 6s.; three pair of Snuffers 1s. 6d.

19th Eight Candlesticks to order 12s.; Mending a Gun Lock 9d.

20th A Gallon of Oil 6s.; A Tin Kettle 1s. 3d.

22nd A Gallon Oil 6s.

23d Six Tins for Caps 5s.; a pound of Tow 4d.; two pound Ground Rossin Sifted 6s. 4d.

25th A Gallon of Oil 6s.

28th A Gallon of Ditto 6s.

1781 JANUARY

1st To a Fender 3s. 6d.; A Lamp and Head put up at the Kings Door 5s. 6d.; Two large Glass lanthorns and Lamps 10s.; Two pair of Snuffers 1s.

2d A Gallon of Oil 6s.

9th A Gallon of Ditto 6s.

11th A pint pot 5d.; Four large spread Eagle Lanthorns &c at 5s. 6d.: £1. 2s.; Two less Ditto at 3s. 6d.: 7s.; Six, two light Glass Lamps to Ditto 4s.

12th Ten Chains, one yard each at 1s.: 10s.; Six pair of Snuffers at 6d.: 3s.

15th A Gallon of Oil 6s.

17th A Gallon of Ditto 6s.

18th Illuminating the front of Opera House £4. 11s. 11d. for the Queen's Birthday

22d four pound of Tow 1s. 4d.; a Gallon of Sperm Oil 6s.

23d Three 3 spout Lamps to Vauses fitted up with Chains 10s. 6d.; Fifty Straps to Fills Lamps 2s. 1d.; Twenty four Tin Sockets 4s.; 25th a Gallon of Oil 6s.; 26th a Gallon of Ditto 6s.; Mending two Candlesticks 4d.

27th Fifty Wires to hang on the Canvas 4s. 2d.; two pound of Tow 8d.

29th a Gallon of Oil 6s.; Altering a Blower 3s.

30th A Gallon of Oil 6s.

**FEBRUARY**

1st a Gallon of Ditto 6s.

3d two pound of Rossin Sifted 1s. 4d.; two pound of Tow 8d.; a Gallon of Oil 6s.

8th two Bottoms to French Horns and Lackering 5s.

9th a Gallon of Oil 6s.

10th Nine Covers for Lamps 3s.

14th a Gallon of Oil 6s.; Three Dozen of Broad Straps Fills Lamps 1s. 6d.

15th Three mouth pieces for French Horns 9d.; Three pound Wire and a Quarter pound Neal'd Ditto 2s. 6d.

16th four pound of Tow 1s. 4d.

19th three Flambeaus for Furies finished 10s. 6d.; three Ditto unfinished 6s.; Two dozen Sockets for Fills Lamps as before 4s.; a Gallon of Oil 6s.

20th a Block [black?] Tin Vause or urn to Silver pattern 9s. 6d.; a Large raised Bason 4s. 6d.; two pair of Tin Garden Sheers 9s.; Mending a Branch 6d.; a Gallon of Oil 6s.

22d Tining two Axes 3s. 6d.; a Piece of Oval Tin for a Bracelett 6d.; Four dozen Broad Straps Fills Lamps 2s.; Fifty pipes front Lights 6s. 3d.; Thirty Six Ditto Fills Lamps 4s. 6d.

24th Twelve large knitting needles 9d.

26th a Gallon of Oil 6s.

28th To one Stone fine Wire 7s. 6d.; One Stone next Size 7s.; One Stone next Size 6s. 6d.

**MARCH**

1st A Candlestick 6d.; a Pair of Snuffers 8d.

2d a Gallon of Oil 6s.

3d a Chamber Furnace 3s. 6d.

6th a Lamp (broke at) Kings Door 5s.; Mending a Fender 6d.

7th a Gallon of Oil 6s.

12th a Gallon of Ditto 6s.; a Stone of fine Wire 7s. 6d.

13th four Dozen broad Straps for Fills Lamps 2s.

15th two Socketts for Sconces 6d.; A large Square planish'd Box & altering several times 15s.

15th a Tinder Box and Steel 8d.; Two pair of Snuffers 1s. 4d.

16th A Gallon of Oil 6s.

17th Twelve Sockets 2s.; Twenty five Machines for Lightning £3. 15s.

20th Mending a Scene 6d.

22d Four Daggers with Springs 10s.; A Gallon of Oil 6s.

23d A Gallon of Ditto 6s.

24th A Gallon of Ditto 6s.

26th A Goblett Lackered 3s. 6d.; Cottoning twenty Seven Furies Trunchions or Machines for the Lightning 13s. 6d.

27th Ten Lightning Flashers three Foot long Tubes £1. 5s.

28th Two Tin Daggers 3s.

29th Two Ditto 3s. 6d.; Three pieces of Tin 6d.; Opening Holes in Furies Trunchions 2s. 6d.; a New Fury's Trunchion 3s.; a Globe Lamp fitted to a Rim 5s.

31st Wire and attendance 3s. 6d.; A Gallon of Oil 6s.

**APRIL**

2d a Man half a day repairing Furies Trunchions 2s. 6d.

3d three Sheets of Tin 1s.; Nailing Eighteen Sheets of Tin for Fire Works 2s.

4th Mending three Candlesticks 9d.; a Gallon of Oil 6s.

7th a pound of Ground Rossin 8d.; Twelve Plates wired at bottom 6s.; Stays for ditto and fixing to Wood for fire Works 2s.; Twenty four plates nailed on Wood 12s.; A Man for two days Work 6s.

11th Mending a Chimney Hood 6d.

13th A Gallon of Oil 6s.

14th repairing and revitting [riveting] the Tin for the Lightning, two men a day each and twelve Sheets of new Tin: 18s.

17th Mending two furies Trunchions 3d.

21st Mending Six Ditto 1s.

27th a Gallon of Oil 6s.

**MAY**

1st Twenty five Hasps to Furies Trunchions 6s. 3d.

3d a Gallon of Oil 6s.

11th A Gallon of Sperm Oil 6s.

17th a Gallon of Ditto 6s.; a Glass Lamp with a Foot 1s.; half a Stone of Wire 3s. 6d.

24th A Gallon of Oil 6s.

28th A Gallon Ditto 6s.

30th A Gallon Ditto *6s.*

**JUNE**

2d A Gallon Ditto *6s.*

4th Furnishing and Lighting Lamps Kings Birthday £4. 11s. 11d.

11th A Gallon Oil *6s.*

12th Mending two Daggers *1s.*; Ditto One Furies Trunchion *4d.*

21st Ditto Same *2d.*

26th Ditto same two *6d.*

**JULY**

3d Ditto same ten *2s. 6d.*

4th A Gallon Oil *6s.*

7th A Gallon Ditto *6s.* [tinkering total for the 1780–81 season:] £61. 19s. 6d.

Tin Work Oil &c for the Season 1782

**OCTOBER**

18th To a pint best Oil *9d.*

20th A Chamber Furnace *3s. 6d.*; A pint of Oil *9d.*

**NOVEMBER**

3d Two Gallon of Oil Practicing *12s.*; Attendance *3s.* [total:] *15s.*

7 A pint and one half Oil *1s. 1½d.*; Mending a Candlestick *2d.*; Two Extinguishers *4d.*

8th A Gallon of Oil Practicing *6s.*; A Gallon of Ditto House Lamps *6s.*

10th Sixteen Spears to order £1. 12s.; two Quarts of best Oil *3s.*

12th One Ditto Ditto *1s. 3d.*; Repairing five Lanthorns *2s. 8d.*; A Gallon of Oil *6s.*

15th A Gallon of Ditto *6s.*; two Single Casements 22¼" by 16" at *3s. 6d.*; two Ditto Ditto 19½" by 16⅜": *5s.*; One Ditto Ditto 20¼" by 13⅜": *2s. 9d.*

16th Eight Dozen pipes front Lights at *1s. 6d.*: *12s.*; four Ditto Ground Blinds Ditto at *1s. 6d.*: *6s.*; Six Ditto Ditto Fills Ditto at *1s. 6d.*: *9s.*; Repairing a Square pan *1s.*; two dozen new Stage Lamps at *8d.*: *16s.*; Twelve Glass Lamps to Lanthorns, two spouts *8d.*: *8s.*; Three Spears *3s.*; Seven Dozen Straps to hang Lamps on *3s. 6d.*; Six dozen spring Cases for Candles at *10s.*: £3. 0s.; Punching holes in pans and fitting Ditto 72: *3s.*; Twenty four new Lanthorns and Glazing Ditto *4s.*: £4. 16s.; Three pound Ground Rossin *1s. 6d.*; One pound of Tow *3d.*; Repairing the Lamps and mending Lanthorns three men four Days Tow and Sand &c £2. 12s. 6d.; A pan for

Spirits 3 feet 8 inches long 6s.; Four Tins for Tamborines Lackered 5s.; Four pieces of Tin 3d.; Nine Chamber Lamps and Tops two lights and long Stalks 9s.; Eighteen Common Ditto two lights 12s.; One pound Tow 3d. one pair Snuffers 8d. one Extinguisher 2d.: 1s. 1d.; Fourteen Wings Seven Lamps on each practising 196 Lights, One Row of the Front Lights 150, Twelve Lanthorns Passages lighted from 6 to 11, 24 [lights]. [Total:] £2. 8s.; Some burnt all the time Carpenters; Eight Gallons of Oil used; A Man attending 2s. 6d.

17th A Gallon of Oil House Lamps 6s.

19th three Dozen of Straps 1s. 6d.; One Gallon of Oil Practising 6s.; Lighting Lamps Practising three Gallons of Oil &c 19s. 2d.

20th Three Dozen of two Stage Lamps at 8s.: £1. 4s.; Three large Glass Lamps & tops long stalks 3s.; One Extinguisher to fix on a Stick 4d.; Two pans to burn Spirits and altering the other 9s.

22nd One Gallon Oil 6s.

24th Four Tin Urns with Socketts and hung with three Yards of Iron Chain to each at 7s. 6d.: £1. 10s.

27th a Gallon of Oil 6s.

28 Three Dozen of Straps Fills 1s. 6d.

29th a Gallon of Oil Practising 6s.

**DECEMBER**

4th Two pound of Ground Rossin 1s. 4d.

5th Lighting Lamps Practising Fifty Stage Lamps; two Gallons and half Oil used and attendance 16s. 6d.

6th One Gallon of Oil Practising 6s.; One Quart of Ditto 1s. 6d.

7th a Tin Kettle no Cover 2s. 6d.

8th a Ditto Ditto 2s. 3d.

9th Lighting 60 Stage Lamps practising 2 lights 120; Ditto Fills Ditto Ditto 120; One Dozen Lanthorns 24: 14s.; Two Gallons Oil Extra 12s.

10th Lighting 84 Stage Lamps practising; Ditto 80 Fills Ditto 2 Hours; Lanthorns & two Rows front Lights: £2. 0s.; Five pound twelve ounces wire 6s. 6d.; Six Dozen and half Straps 3s. 6d.; Four pair of Spectacles 4s.; Four Dozen and half Backs for Fills Lamps 8d.: £1. 16s.; Nine Dozen of pipes for Ditto at 1s. 6d.: 13s. 6d.; four Ditto & half Lamps and tops to them 9s.; Three Ditto of Lamps and Backs compleat 16s.: £2. 8s.; Two Lackered Ink Horns 2s.; Two Ditto Sand Dishes 2s.

11th One pound twelve Ounces Nealed Wire 2s. ½d.

12th two Gallons Oil 12s.; Wire 2d.

13th A Glass to spying Glass *6d.*; two Ditto to Spectacles *1s.*; a Spring Barrell Mumford [Mountford] *10s. 6d.*; Six Dozen of Socketts to order at *1s. 6d.*: *9s.*; three Ditto of Straps *1s. 6d.*; Six pair of Common Snuffers *3s.*: *4s. 6d.*

14th Cleaning and preparing three thousand Lamps Cottoning &c fit for use for the 13th instant £4. *10s.* but not used [masquerade cancelled]; Getting ready the Tin work and repairing old and new work forwarded 1,500 Hooks per order Novosielski £2. *10s.*

15th Six Dressing Room Candlesticks *7s. 6d.*; two Dozen Candlesticks with springs at *10s.*: £1. *0s.*

17th two Gallons of Oil Practising *12s.*

18th One Dozen of Buckles, *6d.*: *6s.*

20th three brass Candlesticks per Mr Crawford *9s. 6d.*

24th One Gallon and one pint and half of Oil *7s. ½d.*

28th One Gallon of Oil *6s.* Two Cups *4d.*: *6s. 4d.*

31st One Gallon of Ditto *6s.*; two Glass Lamps and Tops *1s. 4d.*

1782 JANUARY

2nd One Gallon of Oil House Lamps *6s.*; One Gallon Ditto Porter Brady his Lamps *6s.*

4th One Gallon Ditto *6s.*; A Flat Candlestick *8d.*; a pair of Snuffers *8d.*: *1s. 4d.*; A Chimney Hood 18 Plates to Ditto *14s.*

7 One Gallon Oil *6s.*

8th A Quart best Oil *1s. 6d.*; One Gallon Ditto *6s.*; Sixty four Oval pieces of Tin hollowed *9d.* dozen: *4s.*; Sixty four Tin Diamonds Ditto *9d.* Dozen: *4s.*; Thirty two Small oval pieces hollowed *9d.*: *2s.*; Fourteen Dozen pieces of Tin turned *9d.*: *10s. 6d.*

10th two Tin Flambeaus to order Lackered *4s. 6d.*: *9s.*; Six neat Chandeliers Six Branches each to order *27s.* each: £8. *2s.*; two pound and half Ground Rossin *1s. 3d.*; Sixty four Diamonds hollowed &c *9d.* dozen *4s.* Eight Dozen & four small Ovals *9d.* dozen: *6s. 3d.*; Two Square Pans 4 inches by 3 and 2 Deep *7s.*

11th a Gallon of Oil Practising *6s.*; Lighting Lamps for the Carpenters at different times this two Months past at bottom of the Blinds sometimes twelve and more lighted Eight Gallons Oil used to the above: £2. *8s.*; Lighting a Lamp Union Court from the 26th November 1780 to 26th November 1781 £1. *16s.*

12th Two neat Chandeliers as before at *27s.*: £2. *14s.*; Mending a Brass Sconce *2d.*; a Planish'd spring Dagger *3s. 6d.*; Six Dozen of Straps for Fill *6d.*: *3s.*; Eight Ditto and four Tin Diamonds 9*d.*: 6*s.* 3*d.*; Twelve Ditto and Six large Ovals 1*s.*: 12*s.* 6*d.*; fforty four Ditto and Eight small 9*d.*: £1. 13*s.* 6*d.*; Twelve Square pieces 1*s.* 3*d.*

14 a Gallon of Oil Practice 6*s.*; Six Dozen of Tin Leaves 9*d.*: 4*s.* 6*d.*; Four Ditto of Tin Studs hollowed 3*s.*

15th Four Dozen of Slips of Tin with Six Studs Solder'd on each and hollowed at 6*d.* each: £1. 4*s.*; A Spring Dagger 3*s.* 6*d.*; A Gallon of Oil 6*s.*; Mending two Candlesticks 3*d.*

17th Thirty seven dozen and Six small Ovals 6*d.*: 18*s.* 9*d.*; Eight ditto and four large Ditto 9*d.*: 6*s.* 3*d.*; Twelve Square Diamonds 1*s.* 3*d.*; a Spring Dagger 3*s.* 6*d.*

18th Queen's Birthday. Furnishing Lighting Lanthorns 15: 5*s.*; Lighting 126: £2. 7*s.* 3*d.*; Transparencies 160: £1. 16*s.* 8*d.*; [lighting subtotal:] £4. 11*s.* 11*d.*; Furnishing Burners 72: 3*s.*; Furnishing five Dozen Lanthorns 10*s.*; Six Dozen round Studs at 6*d.*: 3*s.*; four Dozen and two Diamonds at 9*d.*: 3*s.* ½*d.*; Twelve Ditto and Six large Ovals at 9*d.*: 9*s.* ½*d.*; Five Ditto Leaves at 9*d.*: 3*s.* 9*d.*; Twelve Squares 1*s.* 3*d.*

21st Fifty large Ovals at 1*s.*: 4*s.* 2*d.*

22d a Gallon and half best Oil for Lamps 9*s.*; A Gallon Ditto Carpenters use 6*s.*

24th A Glew Pot Mr Coombes 3*s.* 6*d.*

26th Six Quarts Oil Carpenters to light Lamps at the top of the House 9*s.*; One Gallon of Oil House Lamps 6*s.*

28th A pint Oil Mrs Rogers 9*d.*; A Gallon Ditto Brady Porter's Use 6*s.*

30 Twenty four Slips of Tin Six Studs solder'd on each at 6*d.*: 12*s.*; A Gallon of Oil House Lamps 6*s.*

**FEBRUARY**

2d A Casement 2*s.* 6*d.*

4th A Gallon of Oil Practice 6*s.*; Six Dozen of Ovals pieces Tin cut small 4*d.*: 2*s.*; Three Ditto round Ditto 4*d.*: 1*s.*; One Ditto Squares 4*d.*; two Ditto Diamonds 8*d.*

5th Two Chimney Funnels with Hoods and Painting at 14*s.*: £1. 8*s.*

7th Three Dozen of Oval pieces of Tin hollowed 9*d.*: 2*s.* 3*d.*; One Ditto Squares 9*d.*; One Ditto Diamonds 9*d.*; Three Ditto Pieces of Tin Cut small at 4*d.*: 1*s.*

8th A Gallon Oil Practice  House Lamps 6*s.*

11th A Gallon Ditto Ditto Ditto 6*s.*; A Gallon  Ditto Carpenters Lamps 6*s.*

12th Quiver Case to take off in half and Lackering 5*s.* 6*d.*

13th Six Dozen Fills Straps at 6*d.*: 3*s.*; One pound of fine Neal'd Wire Combes 1*s.* 6*d.*; A Gallon of Oil Practice &c 6*s.*

15th Two pieces of hollow'd Tin 6*d.*: 1*s.*; two Ditto Ditto 8*d.*: 1*s.* 4*d.*; Thirteen Fluted Furies Truncheons each 3*s.* 6*d.*: £2. 5*s.* 6*d.*; Painting Ditto Red 6*d.*: 6*s.* 6*d.*; Repairing twenty four Old ones 8*s.*; Painting twenty four Ditto and Cleaning 6*d.*: 12*s.*; Cottoning thirteen new and fitting on 6*d.*: 6*s.* 6*d.*; A Planish'd Shield with Looking Glass and Foil &c 10*s.* 6*d.*

16th One Gallon of Oil, Porter 6*s.*; Two Dozen Tin Sockets at 1*s.*: 6*s.*

18th One Gallon of Oil House Lamps 6*s.*; Six pound Ground Rossin Sifted fine 4*s.*; A Quart Boyler for Spirits 1*s.* 2*d.*; Five Slaves Chains at 4*s.* 6*d.*: £1. 2*s.* 6*d.* Two Quarts best Oil 3*s.*; Seventeen Dozen of Ovals and Diamonds at 9*d.*: 12*s.* 9*d.*; Five Ditto of Sockets 1*s.*: 5*s.*; Mending two Lightning Blowers 4*d.*

19th A Pair of large Vause Lamps and Heads Fifteen Inches over compleat and painting £3. 0*s.*; A pair of neat Scrowl Lamp Irons for Ditto and Fixing at Kings Door Market Lane £1. 16*s.*; Two, three Spout Burners to Ditto 1*s.* 4*d.*; Twelve pieces of Tin at 2*d.*: 2*s.*; Four Dozen of Sockets 4*s.*; Six Lightening Blowers at 2*s.* 6*d.*: 15*s.*; Practising the 17th instant Vizt Stage Lamps 192, Lights 384; Top House 120; Fills Lamps 200 [total number of lights:] 704; [total cost:] £2. 5*s.*; A Man Attending Ditto 2*s.* 6*d.*; Practising the 18th instant Vizt Stage Lamps 96, 192 [lights]; Top House 120; Fills Lamps 200 [total number of lights:] 512; [total cost:] £1. 7*s.* 6*d.*; A Man attending Ditto 2*s.* 6*d.*

20th Practising Wednesday Vizt 96 Stage Lamps four Hours and Half the whole Stage Lamps, three Hours Fronts [*sic*] Lights and 300 Fills the same time, Sixteen Ground Lights, Lighting top of the House the same as an Opera £6. 1*s.* 6*d.*; Sixty pipes for Fills Lamps at 1*s.* 6*d.*: 7*s.* 6*d.*; Four Chamber Lamps with Tops at 9*d.*: 3*s.*; Putting together Eighteen Strong Tin plates and fitting to Figure Head to fire works 13*s.* 6*d.*; Altering the above two men to Ditto and refix it 5*s.*; Fourteen Plates to Ditto fixed for Fire Works two men Nails &c to ditto 10*s.* 6*d.*; Altering Five Chains 10*d.*

21st Mending two Shade Candlesticks 4*d.*

22d Five Quiver Cases to take off in half and Lack[er]ing at 7*s.* 6*d.*: £1. 7*s.* 6*d.*; A planished Shield 7*s.* 6*d.*; Twelve Dozen Wire Hooks at 4*d.*: 4*s.*; Six pieces of looking Glass soldered on a Shield 1*s.* 6*d.*; Practising Vizt all the Stage Lamps, Front Lights Ditto Three hundred Fills, twelve Ground Lights £5. 10*s.*

23rd Some pieces of Tin for a Shield 4*s.*; Two Lightning Machines at 3*s.* 6*d.*: 7*s.*; Painting five Chains red Vermillion 2*s.*: 10*s.*; Eight Dozen Tin Sockets 4*s.*; A Tin pipe to order Mr Novosielski 5*s.* 6*d.*; Mending a Quiver Case 4*d.*

25th A Gallon of Oil Practice and House Lamps 6*s.*

26th Mending four Tin Locks to Wood Guns 1s. 6d.: 6s.; Ditto three Furies Truncheons 9d.; Four Dozen of Tin Sockets 4s.; A Gallon of Oil Practice 6s.; Four Dozen and two spring Candlesticks at 10s.: £2. 1s. 8d.

27th Four Ditto of Straps at 6d.: 2s.; One Ditto of Sockets 1s.

28th Eight New Tops to Furies Truncheons at 9d.: 6s.; Cottoning Ditto at 6d.: 4s. fifty Spring Candlesticks at 10s.: £2. 1s. 8d.

**MARCH**

1st To a Gallon of Oil 6s.; Two Chandeliers as before at 27s.: £2. 14s. 6d.; One Ditto with Diamonds and Drops £2. 2s.

2d Four Dozen and two Pans to hold spring Candlesticks at 4s.: 16s. 8d.

4th Mending a Shield and a Chain 6d.; Ditto a Fury's Truncheon 2d.; Six Dozen of Fills Straps 3s.; Repairing two Flambeaux's 1s.

5th One Dozen of Pans to hold spring Candlesticks 4s.

6th Mending a Glue Pot 2d.; One Gallon Oil 6s.; [total:] 6s. 2d.

7th One Gallon of Oil Porter 6s.; A Quart Oil pot 1s.; [for] Luppino: Fourteen Front Pieces for Caps 14s.; Fourteen Tops for Ditto 1s. 6d.; One Ditto Ditto 6s.

8th A Gallon of Oil 6s.

9th Six Dozen Spring Candlesticks for Chandeliers £3. 0s.

11th A Gallon of Oil 6s.; Four Gallons Ditto Carpenters Lamps four Weeks £1. 4s.

12th Mending a Chandelier 6d.

14th Seventy one Spring Candlesticks painted White 12s.; One pound twelve Ounces Neal'd Wire 2s. 7½d.

15th a Gallon of Oil House Lamps &c 6s.; Seven front Pieces for Caps 7s.

16th Eight Dozen Straps Fills Lamps 4s.; One Quart of Oil Mrs Rogers 1s. 6d.

20th One Gallon of Oil House Lamps &c 6s.; One Ditto Ditto Porters Use 6s.; Mending four Tin Candlesticks 3s.

23rd Thirteen Tin hunting Spears at 3s.: £1. 19s.; One Double Ditto 4s.; A Top to a Furies Truncheon 9d.; Repairing two Shields and two Axes 9d.

26th Four pounds of Neal'd Wire 5s.; A Gallon of Oil 6s.

27th Six Lamp Candlesticks 6s.

28th Twelve Wire Hoops Solder'd and Altering 10s.

**APRIL**

2nd Mending two Candlesticks 3d.; Three Gallons of Oil for Practice 18s.; Mending a Furies Truncheon 4d.

3d One Dozen of Tin Spear Tops 18*s*. 6*d*.; Twelve Shields at 3*s*. 6*d*.: £2. 2*s*.; A Chimney Funnell and Painting Ditto 18*s*.; A Gallon of Oil the Porter 6*s*.

4th Nine New tops to Furies Truncheons 6*s*.; Cottening Ditto again 1*s*. 6*d*.

5th Eight plates rivited together for Fire Works and repairing fifteen old ones 8*s*.

6th Four new tops to Furies Truncheons 2*s*. 8*d*.; A New Body and top to a Ditto 1*s*.; A Gallon of Oil 6*s*.

8th Altering a Box holes punched in the top and a hole in the Bottom 2*s*. 6*d*.; Finishing two Iron Shields 3*s*.

9th Repairing three Furies Trunchions 1*s*.; Mending a Chandelier and spring Socket 6*d*.

9th a Pint and a half best Oil Mrs Rogers 1*s*. ½*d*.

10th A Gallon of Oil practice &c 6*s*.; Fifty seven Plates wired and rivited together to fix across the stage for Fire Works £1. 18*s*.; Tinning two Axes 3*s*. 6*d*.

11th A Tin Kettle 2*s*. 6*d*.; a pound of Tow 6*d*.: 3*s*.; a Tin Goblet 3*s*. 6*d*.; a Lightning Blower 3*s*. 6*d*.; Two Tin Daggers lackered 4*s*.; Three spring Ditto 6*s*.; Repairing two Axes 8*d*.

13th Repairing Eleven Furies Truncheons 4*s*.; Three new Top[s] to three Ditto 2*s*.; Cottoning four Ditto 8*d*.

15th a Gallon of Oil Practice &c 6*s*.

18th One Gallon of Ditto Porter 6*s*.

22nd One Quart of best Oil Mrs Rogers 1*s*. 6*d*.

23rd Mending five Furies Truncheons 1*s*. 8*d*.; Two new Top[s] to two new Ditto and repairing Ditto 1*s*. 6*d*.; Cottoning two Ditto 4*d*.; Mending a Chain 6*d*.; Ditto a Chandelier 1*s*.

24th a Gallon of Oil 6*s*.

25th a New Spring Dagger 2*s*.

26th A Gallon of Oil Practice 6*s*.

29th a Gallon of Ditto 6*s*.; Bottoming a Glue pot 3*d*.

30th Mending a Furies Truncheon 3*d*.; Two new Top[s] to two Ditto 1*s*. 4*d*.

**MAY**

1st 1 Gallon of Oil 6*s*.

4th One Ditto of Ditto 6*s*.

6th a Sheet of Tin 6*d*.

7th a new Rose to a Water pot and Handle 1*s*.

9th Two Glass Lamps and Tops 1s. *6d.*

10th a Gallon of Oil Practice *6s.*

11th Mending a Tin Shade *4d.*

15th Ditto Eleven Furies Truncheons 2s. *9d.*

16th a Gallon of Oil *6s.*

20th a Gallon of Ditto *6s.*

21st Mending two Furies Truncheons *4d.*; new Dagger 2s.: 2s. *4d.*

22nd a Gallon of Oil *6s.*

23rd Mending three Furies Chains 2s. *6d.*

27th Ditto three Ditto Truncheons 1s.; A Gallon of Oil  Porter *6s.*

29th a pint and an half of Oil  Mrs Rogers 1s. 1½*d.*

JUNE

3rd a Large Shield Planished *6s.*; a small Ditto 3s. *6d.*

4th Lighting Lamps front Opera House Kings Birth Day see the 18th of January as before £5. 1s. 11*d.*

5th half pound Tow, Combes *3d.*; a Tin Trumpet Lackered 2s. *6d.*; Two Tin Vauses Lackered to Patterns 13s.; a Tin Cup planished 3s. *6d.*

10th Mending twenty two Tulips 3s. *8d.*; ditto 4 Chandeliers *5s.*

14th a Gallon of Oil *6s.*

15th a Quart Ditto Mrs Rogers 1s. *6d.*

22nd Mending a Furies Truncheon *4d.*

28th A Gallon of Oil *6s.*

[Total for tinwork and oil:] £175. 18s.

[less] February 20th  By 14 New Plates - 3s. *6d.* [ = ] £175. 14s. *6d.*

# APPENDIX IV

## *Noverre's Scenario for* RINALDO AND ARMIDA *(1782)*

Gauged by the number of ballet scenarios advertised in London during the 1780s, few have survived. As an example of a relatively full and helpful text, we reproduce here Noverre's *Rinaldo and Armida*. Like the much-published *Medea and Jason*, this ballet constitutes his engagement with a great text, one familiar to his audience from operatic versions if not directly from Tasso. Although the story begins *in medias res*, the scenario develops Rinaldo's conflicts clearly and allows Armida to display an even wider range of emotions. Unlike some operatic versions, which graft on a happy ending, Noverre's ballet closes with a vision of destruction. Hence *Rinaldo and Armida* again demonstrates his great ambition for his art-form, the controversial idea that ballet could tell serious stories. On a practical level, the production of 1782 was done by a talented troupe of dancers and with no restraints on costs, such as Noverre was to labour under during his return visits to London. It therefore seems a better illustrative choice than, say, *L'Amour et Psiché* (1788).

Lynham believes that *Renaud et Armide* was 'created before 1760, probably [at the] Opéra, Lyons', but he does not document this statement (*Chevalier Noverre*, 166). The first production of which we have record is that for the Duke of Württemberg's birthday celebration in Stuttgart in 1761: this and other ballets are listed in the French and Italian libretto for Jommelli's *L'Olimpiade* (Sartori, no. 16978). The production was revived in Stuttgart in 1763. Lillian Moore notes a production in Vienna in 1768 ('Unlisted Ballets by Jean George Noverre', *Theatre Notebook*, 15 [1960], 15–20). Lynham lists a production in Milan in 1775, for which Sartori, no. 16860 is the Italian libretto and a copy in the British Library appears to be the French text.[1]

Our copy-text is Cambridge University Hib.7.782.11. A purchase date of 14 March 1782, destroyed in binding, suggests that this is the second issue of the scenario (see the *Morning Herald* of 4 March 1782). With minor changes the same text is printed in volume iii of Noverre's *Works* (1783).

*

*Historical Account of Rinaldo and Armida, A Ballet d'Action, or Dramatic Representation*; Composed by Monsieur Noverre, and Translated from the Original French by Parkyns Mac Mahon. (London: Printed for the Author, by H. Reynell, [1782]). Price Six-Pence.

---

[1] British Library 906.e.3 (2): Jean Georges Noverre, *Renaud et Armide, Ballet Heroique* (Milan: Jean Montani, 1775).

To the *Ladies of Great-Britain*: the dramatic representation of RINALDO AND ARMIDA, is, most humbly inscribed, by the author and translator.

## Preliminary Discourse.

The subject of the following Ballet, or rather dramatic representation, is taken from Tasso's *Jerusalem*, a poem which reflects immortal honor on the author, and on Italy that gave him birth. By taking my subject from so plentiful a source, I have the advantage of laying before the public, an event which is perfectly known, and to the truth of history joins the illusion of magic charms. I readily acknowledge that my model is above imitation. How can the mute expression of pantomime, do justice to that beautiful style, those noble comparisons, that sublime eloquence which are the exclusive privilege of poetry alone? it would be unjust to look for perfection in an art, which is as it were, hardly out of its cradle, and speaks as yet in broken accents. Let the indulgence of the Public, the enlightened Encourager of all the arts, supply the defect. If my plan be injudiciously chosen, if my endeavours prove fruitless, and cannot meet with their approbation, I shall comfort myself with the consciousness of having done the best I could. It requires some time to study the taste of the Public; that time, which I would esteem the happiest part of my life, has been but short: three months are not sufficient to please at once sensations diametrically opposite; it is impossible within that space to tune to the unison, so many jarring strings wound up by different passions. In order to reach that almost unattainable harmony, the artist should be acquainted with the various inclinations of individuals, he must crowd in the same picture all the different compositions, and employ all the variegated tints which diversify the taste and inclinations of each spectator: In short, he must have the extraordinary talent of reconciling extremes, and chaining together, as it were, tastes in many respects contradictory to each other. Such a work has no bounds, nor can it be performed by man.

Thus situated, and finding it impossible to assume so many different forms, and go through all kinds of imitations, I shall confine myself to assure the nation at large, that I have no other wish than that of pleasing them, and that if I should fail, it is not to be imputed to a want of application, care, or zeal, on my part.

## *Rinaldo and Armida,*
### A Dramatic Representation.

Men: Rinaldo—Mons. Gardel; Danish Knight—Mons. Nivelon; Ubaldo, another Knight—Mr Simonet; Hatred—Mons. Leger; Jealousy—Mons. Bournonville; Revenge—Mons. Henry. Women: Armida, Princess of Damascus—Madame Simonet; A Spirit representing Lucinda, a lady beloved by the Danish Knight—

## Scenario for Rinaldo and Armida

Mademoiselle Baccelli; Another Spirit personating Clorinda, beloved by Ubaldo—Madamoiselle Theodore; The three Graces—Signora Crespi, Mademoiselle Dumont, and Miss Andreas; Spirits and Demons under the most pleasing forms, Cupids, &c.

The Scene at Damascus, in and about the Palace of Armida. The Magnificent Scenes and Decorations, devised and executed by and under the Direction of Signor Novosielski.

### SCENE I
*An island on the* Oronte, *a river of* Syria.

Rinaldo, by delivering the Knights whom Armida detained in captivity, had brought upon him the hatred of that revengeful Princess. By means of her enchantments, the young Warrior is led to the banks of the *Oronte.* An inscription[1] engraved on a marble pillar excites his curiosity, he steps into a boat, which carries him down the stream, and he lands on the island, to enjoy the sight of those prodigies hinted at in the inscription. Finding his curiosity disappointed, Rinaldo resolves to return to the boat, but is stopped in his way by Spirits, who under the lovely forms of Nymphs, &c. employ all their allurements to stay him; a somniferous vapour seizes on all his senses, and he falls asleep on the grass. Armida, who had concealed herself behind a thick grove, comes forward, her whole deportment is expressive of the barbarous joy she feels at having her enemy in her power. She flies towards Rinaldo, ready to sheathe a dagger in his breast—a power superior even to her incantations, stays her arm, Yet! as if ashamed to relent, she a second time raises the murdering steel over her defenceless victim: But casting her eyes on Rinaldo's features, animated by that bewitching smile which love and pleasure alone can imprint, she relents, the fatal weapon drops from her hand, tender feelings melt her down to soft pity: Her throbbing heart which breathed nought but revenge, now beats to love alone. With garlands of flowers she encircles Rinaldo, and carries him off to her palace!

### SCENE II
*The magnificent gardens in* Armida's *palace.*

The Princess and Rinaldo are discovered surrounded by the most ravishing objects, the Pleasures, Graces, Cupid, and a crowd of fortunate lovers compose their train,

---

[1] 'Whoever thou art, O traveller! whom fortune or choice has brought to this shore, know, that the sun in his career, never beheld a spot so full of wonders as yon island: If thou wouldst know more, hie thyself there.'

659

and by their attitudes and actions express their felicity. This enchanting spectacle makes the deepest impression on the heart of our young warrior, the love of glory vanishes, he now prefers the roses of Venus to the laurels of Pallas; the Nymphs adorn him with flowers, and crown him with myrtle. Rinaldo falls at Armida's feet, and the two lovers, after having expressed by their action, their mutual happiness, retire with their train, to enjoy the sport of the fields.

Ubaldo and the *Danish* Knight, having, by means of a golden wand, surmounted all the obstacles that the magic art had raised in their way, enter the garden. Beautiful Nymphs, headed by Clorinda, prevent their going further, bid them forego all thoughts of glory, and give themselves up to the pleasures of love. Cupid and the Graces surround Ubaldo, who opposing but a weak resistance, seems inclined to follow the seducing objects: He is almost overpowered, when the *Danish* Knight wresting the wand from the feeble hands of his yielding companion, waves it in the air, and the enchantment disappears.

The two Knights pursue their search, but are once more caught in Armida's snare; a Nymph under the form of Lucinda, the mistress of the *Danish* Knight, accosts him with all the seducing wantonness of love and desire. It is now his turn to waver and delay. The feint [feigned] Lucinda recalls to his mind his former vows, and blushingly confesses her impassionate regard for him. The Knight sees, hears, and thinks of nothing but his beloved Lucinda. In vain does Ubaldo expostulate, and endeavours to bring him away; the *Danish* Knight is deaf to his remonstrances. Lucinda bids him follow her; but at this critical instant Ubaldo, in his turn, waves the wand, and the false Lucinda disappears; the illusion is no more, and the *Danish* Knight ashamed of his weakness, retires with Ubaldo, blaming himself for his foolish credulity, when they are once more delayed by a troop of Demons, whose efforts however to stop the Knights, are effectually defeated.

### SCENE III
*An Apartment sumptuously decorated within* Armida's *palace.*

Armida and her lover are seated on a rich sopha, their brilliant and lovely train vie with each other in sportive dances, and in various attitudes form themselves into different groups round Rinaldo and Armida. This Princess holds in her hand a looking-glass, a gift of the God of love, she admires the graceful and manly features of Rinaldo, reflected on the polished glass. The young warrior contemplates in his turn, Armida's irresistable charms, their eyes meet and confess the approaching bliss. The Princess of *Damascus* has exhausted all that art and coquetry can devise to set off her natural charms, and Rinaldo by his action, expresses his heart-felt satisfaction.

But now the hour is come when Armida must attend to finish those spells, which are intended to secure Rinaldo's affection; she leaves him—yet, tho' only for a moment, can either bear the idea of being asunder, her absence gives to Rinaldo the deepest concern; grief and melancholy o'erclouds his manly brow.

Ubaldo and the *Danish* Knight, who have been at a distance, eye-witnesses of what has pass'd, make up to Rinaldo. At this unexpected sight, he looks confused and abashed. Ubaldo holds up to him the enchanted shield. No sooner does the young hero cast his eyes on this faithful mirror, whose peculiar use is to show vice and weakness in their natural deformity, than he starts back with shame and horror, the sight of his effeminate accoutrement inflames him with wrath, he tears his apparel, stamps on his crown, plucks off the garlands of flowers, and divests himself of those childish ornaments and inglorious garments.

The *Danish* Knight improving the opportunity, brandishes before him the arms which he has brought, Rinaldo seizes on them in a kind of extatic transport, he deeply regrets the time he has stolen from glory, honour, and duty, to bestow it on idleness and effeminacy. He embraces the two Knights, entreating them to tear him from a spot where his virtue might encounter new dangers.

They all three prepare to set out, when Armida, who by her art had forseen her impending misfortune, enters with the greatest precipitancy. Rinaldo dreading the powerful charms of the Magician, dares not lift up his eyes. She loads him with reproaches, then has recourse to entreaties, and at last embraces the knees of her stern conqueror. Rinaldo wavering between love and glory, opposes but a weak resistance to this last attack. But his friends ashamed at his want of courage, endeavour to inspire him with thoughts more worthy of a hero. They force him from the arms of Armida, of whom he takes the most affectionate farewell. The love-sick Princess unable to support the torturing idea of parting for ever with the man whom she holds most dear, falls senseless in the arms of her women. Rinaldo wounded to the heart, cannot resist the impulse of his love, disengaged from his friends, he flies towards Armida, in an instant is at her feet, lays hold of her hands; bedews them with his fast flowing tears, and endeavours in vain to recall her to life. The two Knights offended at Rinaldo's returning weakness, present before him once more, the truth-disclosing mirror, and force him away. Rinaldo's departure is marked with all the impassionate regrets of an heart deeply affected, of a lover who sacrifices inclination to obey the calls of glory. The hero retires with slow steps, his eyes constantly fixed upon Armida, and expressing the excess of grief and despair, which tears his inmost soul.

Armida at last opens her beauteous eyes, but alas, how hateful that light which confirms her misfortune, and discloses to her the flight of the inconstant Rinaldo;

in vain she calls to him, in vain she breaks out in the most passionate yet tender reproaches, her lover can hear her no more: provoked at the irreparable loss, she gives way to those sentiments which despairing love alone inspires. She calls to her assistance the hell-born Deities of Hate, Fury, and Revenge; submissive and obedient, the infernal powers obey her summons. The Princess breaks to pieces the quiver and arrows of the God of love, tears off his bandage, and wresting from the Goddess of Revenge, her flaming torch, sets fire to her own palace; the thunder roars, swift lightning flashes through the clouds, a river of fire issuing from the mouths of two frightful dragons, rolls along with the utmost impetuosity, some of the Demons precipitate themselves into the burning fluid, others sink into the fiery abyss, and that spot which was before, the abode of enchanged Beings under the most pleasing forms, now becomes the dreary mansion of wild beasts and shapeless monsters.

*Finis.*

# INDEX

Rowntree, Thomas 69, 71, 621, 636
Royal Academy of Music 4, 7, 9–10, 113, 367
Royalty Theatre 545, 580
Rubinelli, Giovanni Maria ix, 230, 336, 338, 341–2, 346, 353, 358, 360, 366, 369, 372, 376, 401, 593
   approved by Lady Mary Coke 180, 369
   hired by Gallini 106
   influence on repertoire choice 27
   London début 351
   loses novelty appeal 123, 384
   range 371
   salary 127–8, 339, 341
   talents wasted on 1787 repertoire 375
Ruf, Wolfgang 385
Rumbold, Valerie 206
*Rural Sports, The* (ballet) 146, 450–2
*Ruses de l'amour, Les* (ballet) 480
Rutini, Giovanni Marco 378
Rutland, Duchess of 99

Sacchini, Antonio ix, 1–2, 19, 188, 194, 260, 335, 358, 398, 405, 434
   affected by illness 267
   Bertoni's debt to 232
   commissions 27, 358
   compared with J. C. Bach 196, with Rauzzini 277
   dispute with Ansani 250, 252–3, with Rauzzini 264, 266
   faculties impaired by age 254
   harmonic sophistication 38
   house composer: advertised in 1779 187; expected to contribute to pasticcios 27; given choice in librettos 118, 262; musical responsibilities 30; paid 40 guineas for revival 267; as star in 1770s 52; writes for Pacchierotti 241
   music used: in ballet 507, 512; in *Didone abbandonata* 340, 357; in *Ezio* 262; in *La frascatana* 384; in *L'Olimpiade* 247
   renowned as vocal coach 210
   resists new simplicity 261
   satirized 25
*L'amore soldato* 247; analysis of 199–200; full score published 195; scenery 147–8; in 1777–78 repertoire 193; in 1779–80 repertoire 221
*L'avaro deluso* 202, 220; dances in 448; scenery 146–7, 151, 153

*Cimene* 294
*La contadina in corte* 185, 222, 267, 280, 453; analysis of 227–30; costumes 162; dances in 450; drastically revised 227; properties for 158; rights to 267–8; take-offs in revival 273; in 1779–80 repertoire 221; in 1781–82 repertoire 263
*Creso* 193, 195
*Enea e Lavinia* 202; analysis of 207, 209–10, 212; costumes 160; dances in 445, 447, 449; *Favourite Songs* 209; lavish production of 182; scenery 149, 151, 154
*Erifile* 193; analysis of 197, 199; costumes 159; exceeds norms of genre 202; properties for 159; scenery 146, 148–9
*Euriso* 249, 461
*Mitridate* 249, 259, 435; analysis of 250–4; *Favourite Songs* 254; music used in *Medonte* 290; newly commissioned 249; properties for 158–9; row with Ansani over 115; scenery 146, 148; translation of 35–6
*Perseo* 340; dances in 507; vehicle for Mara 357
*Rinaldo* 177, 190, 221; analysis of 237–40, 243; comparison of versions 241; delayed by composer's illness 238; dispute over added scene 186–7; *Favourite Songs* 240; lavish production of 182; lighting for 169; performance discussed by Susan Burney 240; performance omitted from *The London Stage* 640; rehearsed in coffee-room 190; revived 249; Sacchini unable to conduct première 192; scenery 150, 154, 240; storm scene 170; in 1779–80 repertoire 221; in 1780–81 repertoire 249
Sackville, Lady 179
Sadie, Stanley xxiv, 266
St Amand, Mlle 604, 606, 610, 612
Saint-Aubin, Jeanne Charlotte 366
Sala, Agostino (?) 498
Sala, Antonio 82, 498, 535, 604, 636
Sala, Caterina 484, 498, 606, 636
salaries 85–6, 93, 106, 127–32, 187, 248, 259, 263, 285–6, 299, 304, 311, 321, 339, 341–2, 345, 360–1, 367, 385, 432, 440, 480, 483, 498, 508, 528, 530, 532, 538–9
   secret abatements of 128, 134